Preserving the Desert

FIG A. In 1936, most of the roads in Joshua Tree National Monument consisted of dusty wheel ruts such as these in Lost Horse Valley. Superintendent Cole chose which of the scores of such rudimentary "roads" would form the transportation infrastructure of Joshua Tree. Photograph by George A. Grant, a photographer for the National Park Service, 1936. Harpers Ferry Center, Grant Collection, JOTR #45, National Park Service.

Preserving
the Desert

A HISTORY OF
JOSHUA TREE
NATIONAL PARK

Lary M. Dilsaver

GEORGE F. THOMPSON PUBLISHING
in association with the
Joshua Tree National Park Foundation
and American Land Publishing Project

FIG. B. Movie producers found the scenery of Joshua Tree National Monument perfect for film-making, especially Westerns. One of the better-known movies filmed in the monument was "Buck Benny Rides Again," starring Jack Benny, Eddie "Rochester" Anderson, and Ellen Drew. Released by Paramount Pictures in 1940, the site was supposed to be a Nevada ranch. Photograph by Ralph Anderson taken near Lost Horse Well on December 17, 1939. Harpers Ferry Center, JOTR Collection, National Park Service.

The deserts are not worthless wastes. You cannot stop all creation with wheat and alfalfa. Some sections must lie fallow that other sections may produce. Who shall say that the preternatural productiveness of California is not due to the warm air of its surrounding deserts? Does anyone doubt that the healthfulness of the countries lying west from the Mississippi may be traced directly to the dry air and heat of the deserts? They furnish health to the human; why not strength to the plant? The deserts should never be reclaimed. They are the breathing-spaces of the west and should be preserved forever.

—John C. Van Dyke,
The Desert: Further Studies in Natural Appearances (1901)

FIG. C. Exploring Joshua Tree National Monument during 1939 meant finding one's way through scores of rough dirt tracks. Here, deep ruts show the immediate popularity of Cap Rock as a destination. Photograph by Ralph Anderson, December 1939. Harpers Ferry Center, Anderson Collection, JOTR #53, National Park Service.

CONTENTS

FIG. D. Chemehuevi basket makers at the Oasis of Mara in 1897. A decade later,
Americans began forcing the Chemehuevi tribe to move to other reservations, although
they maintained a dry parcel of land adjacent to the park, upon which they recently
opened a casino. Photographer unknown. Joshua Tree National Park Photo Archives,
General Collection.

LIST OF FIGURES, PLATES, AND MAPS

Note: All figures and plates are photographs, except Fig. 1.1, which is a diagram. Also, "n.d." means "no date" or "date unknown."

Color Maps

Text Maps

FIG. E. Camping in Joshua Tree National Monument was haphazard before the National Park Service paved the roads and organized a pattern of campground loops. This bird's eye image of Hidden Valley was taken during the late 1930s. Photographer unknown. Joshua Tree National Park Photo Archives, Cat. 20575, Image 2176.

PREFACE AND ACKNOWLEDGMENTS

MY FIRST EXPERIENCE WITH NATIONAL PARKS came when I accompanied high school friends on trips to the Sierra Nevada. From San Francisco, we drove the half-day drive to Yosemite National Park on weekends and usually found an available campsite, something not remotely possible today. Hiking in the valley, attending ranger campfire talks, and pondering the magnificence around me, I heard the message of the national park system. Later, we explored Point Reyes National Seashore, Pinnacles National Park, and Death Valley National Park, my first experience with southern California's Mojave Desert. Eventually, I visited Sequoia and Kings Canyon National Parks and began a long relationship with the giant sequoias and deep canyons of the southern Sierra.

After gaining my doctorate degree in geography and a job at the distant University of South Alabama, I continued to camp in Kings Canyon whenever possible. At a campfire there in September 1985, I told my sister and her husband, "I ought to find a way to work in the national parks." A week later, at my university office, I read an appeal in a national geography bulletin for scholars to research and write administrative histories of national parks. I called Bureau Historian Barry Mackintosh, who had issued the appeal and had recently completed the model history for Assateague National Seashore. He assured me that Sequoia and Kings Canyon needed a history as did all the units of the system that now numbers more than 412 parks and other places. My research career took a new and fascinating course.

In January 1986, I camped in Joshua Tree National Monument for the first time. My perception of the desert was not a positive one. During the earlier trip to Death Valley, we had been trapped there by a sandstorm for more than two days. The gritty material clogged meals, cameras, and eventually our vehicle. But the trip to Joshua Tree was idyllic. The desert offers a straightforward view of both geologic processes and the forces that determine biogeography. And few places can match the night sky. These experiences introduced me to the dichotomy of cultural attitudes that Americans have for the desert. Later, National Park Service (NPS) historian David Louter offered me the opportunity to research and write the administrative history of Joshua Tree. An administrative history of a national park explains the natural and cultural resources of the place, the campaign and legislation that established the unit, the resource-management history, and visitor actions and policies that shape its use. It primarily serves as a historic document that informs a park's management staff on how the unit evolved and offers data and perspective on the issues they face.

Many conundrums affect what is, in the end, a political creation of the U.S. Congress that can be eliminated by a simple majority vote on a bill to delist it. How does the NPS provide use and recreation for today's public while preserving the resources "unimpaired" for future generations? How does it deal with private property and previous land-use rights in a new park? A web of laws and policies exist that order the NPS to let natural/ecological processes shape the habitat, preserve the historic imprint of earlier generations, provide for current recreation and education, and enforce stringent wilderness regulation. Which takes precedence when they all apply to the same place? At what point do visitors, their vehicles, and their recreational activities endanger a park that is being 'loved to death?' How does the undersized and underfunded agency keep up with scientific advances, adapt to new constituencies, maintain the tourism infrastructure, and cope with threats and demands from politicians, businesses, and the public? Each park unit is a laboratory of ecological, legal, political, and cultural processes, and no two are managed exactly the same way. Each is the product of compromises made during both its creation and the reaction to the environment and human designs that surround it.

In writing this history, I have done my best to research all aspects of the park's development and to present the material in a thorough and, hopefully, engaging way. The result is the first comprehensive history of Joshua Tree National Park (JTNP), but much can be learned about how conservation works in the United States, how the NPS operates under its legal and organizational constraints, and how American culture shapes every action and process. In the case of JTNP, a legacy of disinterest in arid lands has shaped its history, but recollection of the educational, recreational, and spiritual benefits of the desert has grown to challenge that negative perception.

Many people and organizations helped with my research and production of this book. First and foremost, the NPS covered my travel and research expenses for the project. I carried out the research inductively, relying on extensive field work, lessons learned from previous park history projects, and the reports, plans, interviews, and correspondence found in the park and in archives from California to Maryland. The staffs at the National Archives and Records Center in Maryland; its regional branch in San Bruno, California; the Huntington Archives in San Marino, California; and the Denver Service Center of the NPS were very helpful. Chief Historian Robert Sutton at the NPS's headquarters in Washington, D.C.; Timothy Babalis, Vida Germano, and Greg Gress, of the Pacific West Regional Office in San Francisco; and Robert Bryson at Mojave National Preserve also lent their expertise and encouragement. I thank the University of South Alabama, particularly Charlene Lamonte, who coordinated the distribution of the agency's funds for my project expenses, and Sam Stutsman, whose consulting firm, Delta Cartography, drafted the maps used in the book.

Critical to the success of this park history were staff members of JTNP, both past and present. Former superintendents Mark Butler, David Moore, Ernest Quintana, and Curt Sauer contributed interview time and data resources as well as enthusiastic support. Melanie Spoo, the librarian/archivist/museum curator of the park, had the task of supervising my research and reading the first draft of the manuscript. Resource management staff, including Andrea Compton, Jerry Freilich, Josh Hoines, Robert Moon, Luke Sabala, and Michael Vamstad, helped me overcome a dearth of natural resource files in the park's archives. Management Assistant Karin Messaros; maintenance officers Kirk Diamond and Scott Tremblay; interpretation rangers David Denslow, William Truesdell, and Joe Zarki; and GIS specialist Sean Murphy also provided welcome information. Members of the local communities provided maps, data, and interviews, including Donna and Larry Charpied, Paul F. Smith, and Elizabeth Meyer.

Professional support came from George F. Thompson Publishing, in the persons of George himself, who personally oversaw the final editorial development of the book and sequencing of the photographs and maps; Mikki Soroczak, editorial and research assistant; Sherri Byrand and Purna Makaram, the copyeditors; and David Skolkin, the book's designer. The Joshua Tree National Park Association, particularly Meg Foley and its publication committee consisting of the aforementioned Messrs. Smith and Truesdell, provided substantial financial support as well as another review of the manuscript. Thanks, also, go to the anonymous academic peer reviewers who made worthy suggestions for the final draft.

Finally, one person stands out for the hard work and generous advice he provided throughout all phases of the project: Chief Ranger Jeff Ohlfs, an excellent local historian in his own right, provided field trips, reviewed each chapter as I wrote it, and made suggestions and corrections where needed. This was not part of his job description, but his help is much appreciated.

Preserving the Desert

FIG. I.1. Many tall Joshua trees such as this one in Queen Valley greeted National Park Service (NPS) inspectors as they visited the new monument in 1936. Neither the tree nor any record of its fate exists today. Photograph by George A. Grant, a photographer for the NPS. Harpers Ferry Center, Grant Collection, JOTR #32, National Park Service.

INTRODUCTION:

Coping with the Desert

THE NATIONAL PARKS CONSERVATION ASSOCIATION repeatedly lists Joshua Tree National Park (JTNP) as one of the ten most-threatened units in the entire national park system. The dangers include industrialization at a defunct mine less than one mile from the park's boundary, the worst ozone pollution in the national park system, energy developments planned around the park, subdivisions under construction near its northern and southern boundaries, plus all the issues that come from overcrowding and crime in popular destinations. Damage from vandalism and the ominous reality of climate change add to worries for the future of the park. Yet Joshua Tree is hardly new to problems and controversy. Even before its proclamation as a national monument by President Franklin D. Roosevelt in 1936, many people opposed the idea of an environmental preserve in California's deserts. Fourteen years after the monument's inception, the National Park Service (NPS) sacrificed a third of the unit's territory to prevent new mining claims throughout the remaining land. The public disinterest and active opposition faced from 1936 through the 1950s, although muted today, are but one aspect of the difficulty Joshua Tree has faced throughout its existence. Much of its trouble stems from a longstanding negative perception of deserts held by Americans and derived, in turn, from European and Middle Eastern civilizations.

The most widely read book during nineteenth-century America was *The Holy Bible*. Indeed, for most households it was the only reading material available. In Isaiah, 30: 6, God refers to the Egyptian desert as a land of "trouble and distress" where fierce animals and other dangers abide. Other passages refer to the deserts of Israel as "wilderness," a pejorative term until the late nineteenth century, when the modern conservation movement took hold. To be "cast into the wilderness" was virtually a death sentence. Geographer Yi-Fu Tuan has noted that some Europeans went so far as to deny that God had deliberately designed such places. Perhaps stemming from the human destruction of forests in the Mediterranean region during the classical Greek and Roman eras, they believed that deserts are now ruined landscapes. Although deserts had been useful, even kind, to people, after gross misuse they remained forlorn, disfigured, and debilitated. Hence, desert people were regarded as descendants of an abusive culture that had destroyed its own habitat. Later, Europeans carried these ideas to the New World. No Native American tribes received the level of contempt shown by white Americans as did those of the Great Basin and deserts of the American Southwest.[1]

The initial failure of Americans to cope with arid areas added anger to the pessimism and fear spurred by their apparent hopelessness. Historian Patricia Nelson Limerick has described the attitude:

> Faced with aridity, the problem of mastering the continent seemed to have reached a non-negotiable limit. By all conventional standards for value and habitability, the desert was an irrational environment, a betrayal of the promise of abundance fulfilled elsewhere in North America.[2]

Thus, when Major Stephen Long encountered the southern Great Plains in 1820, he called it "an insufferable obstacle to settlement." John C. Frémont's description of his exploration of the American Southwest during the mid-1840s featured adjectives such as "inhospitable," "desolate," "dismal," and "revolting" for the desert. Both Long and Frémont saw the desert as an area of hardship to be crossed at considerable risk.[3]

The reaction to California's two deserts, the Mojave and the Colorado, was no different. In November 1853, Lieutenant J. G. Parke, a topographical engineer scouting for a railroad route from the Mississippi River to the Pacific Ocean, left the tiny Mormon settlement of San Bernardino and crossed San Gorgonio Pass (elevation 1,591 feet) into the Colorado Desert. He noted the declining elevation to the south toward the Salton Basin and continued east for some days before turning back to rejoin his main survey party. He reported his findings to trip leader Lieutenant R. S. Williamson, who dutifully recorded them in his report:

> A mountain range extends from San Bernardino Mountain in a southeasterly direction nearly, if not quite, to the Colorado [River]. Between these mountains and the mountains of the Mohave nothing is known of the country. I have never heard of a white man who had penetrated it. I am inclined to the belief that it is barren, mountainous desert composed of a system of basins and mountain ranges. It would be an exceedingly difficult country to explore on account of the absence of water and there is no rainy season of any consequence.[4]

Williamson's report reinforced the worry that the desert would be difficult for a railroad to cross and useless for anything else.

After initial shock and hesitation, some optimistic and pragmatic Americans adopted the idea that deserts might be reclaimed through scientific research and transformation. Major John Wesley Powell proposed in 1878 a comprehensive irrigation plan "by which these lands may be rescued from their present worthless state." Much later, that hopeful attitude spawned a large-scale drive by the United Nations, at the urging of the United States, to bring "development" to the world's arid zones. Irrigation schemes of sometimes dubious benefit followed during the decades after World War II. Concomitant with this approach was the idea that humans are at war with the environment. The desert became a villain as well as a forbidding place.[5]

Ultimately, Americans found two uses for the desert. First, after the discovery of minerals during the 1860s, the desert suddenly became a place to extract wealth rather than simply struggle through. Gold and silver drew the earliest miners, but other metals eventually commanded attention. People went into the "forbidden land" hoping to find a fortune and quickly move on. Their presence drew transport in proportion to the richness of the discoveries. The desert still threatened, but the lure of wealth conquered cultural resistance. Later, American deserts drew another aspect of intermittent human activity, becoming sacrifice zones where unwanted people and materials could be dumped. Doctors told people who were suffering from tuberculosis to move to the arid zones not only to improve their chances of survival, but also to get them away from others whom they might infect. As towns and cities grew, the desert became a place for dumping trash and unwanted, even dangerous, materials. And why not? Few people lived or even visited such places. In a society where economic value superseded all other considerations, any use of the desert became a justifiable option.[6]

The Holy Bible nevertheless described another aspect of the desert: as a retreat for various prophets seeking prayer, meditation, and renewal away from the confusion and temptations of civilization. This planted the seed of an idea that the desert could serve as a place to embrace solitude and purification. That seed bore fruit by the end of the nineteenth century, assisted by how desert land owned by the federal government remained available there decades longer than it did in the hospitable agrarian parts of the nation. Some miners grew to appreciate the desert and stayed after abandoning their hunt for minerals. Other people moved into the desert to escape convention, crowding, or, in some cases, prosecution. By the 1890s, tourists such as John C. Van Dyke, Edna Brush Perkins, and George Wharton James felt the lure of simplicity, solitude, and a different kind of beauty, as did the ascetics and prophets millennia earlier.[7] A trickle of visitors became a modest stream with the invention of the automobile. The Colorado and Mojave Deserts in California enabled middle-class weekenders to explore the interior desert land in mini-adventures that exhilarated and refreshed. As the sprawl of the urban littoral breached the Coast Range, settlers moved into the edges of the desert, and it became ever less threatening. More and more people found recreation in rugged areas previously inhabited only by Native American hunter–gatherers and traversed by itinerant prospectors.

As this most recent perception of the desert evolved, American attitudes toward the natural world also changed. The twin movements of conservation and preservation began in earnest in the United States during the last quarter of the nineteenth century. Conservation, the careful use of resources in a sustainable fashion, became the mantra of the U.S. Forest Service and later the Bureau of Land Management (formerly the General Land Office). But, in the desert, conservation had little resonance until the 1930s, because no sustainable resources, except for water, were recognized. The preservation movement, which sought to preserve unimpaired scenes of stunning sublimity and grandeur, arose largely from artists such as Thomas Moran and writers such as John Muir. Yellowstone's thermal features, Yosemite Valley, the Mariposa Grove of giant sequoias, and the Grand Canyon's gaping chasm became showpieces of natural America, an answer to the historic legacy of a "grand nature" (such as the Alps) in Europe. For the first half-century after Yellowstone's establishment as the first national park in the U.S. and the world in 1872, preservationists promoted magnificent places with epic or highly unusual features. Prior to the 1930s, the young NPS, founded in 1916, only preserved historic or archaeological sites or examples of profoundly unusual geologic activity in the desert. Then, the federal agency began hunting for representative examples of all the nation's natural regions and resources. From this new concept came the agency's attention to desert environments, although cultural tradition and environmental perception persisted, and some within the NPS dismissed the idea of a desert national park. Nevertheless, the confluence of the preservation movement with a growing familiarity and appreciation of arid lands led to the establishment of Joshua Tree National Monument in 1936. Yet, after the proclamation of Joshua Tree became a reality, irate miners refused to accept that any use of the desert other than their own was justified.[8]

In 2016, as the United States and the world celebrated the centennial anniversary of the NPS, has the American perception of the desert changed? Recently, a Chevrolet commercial showed a pickup truck sitting on a dirt road amid a scattering of Joshua trees and other desert vegetation, as the narrator warns that drivers need a reliable vehicle when they have to get through such a "no man's land."[9] And there it is. Abandoned by God, useless for humanity except as a source of removable minerals and a place to dump garbage, populated by a higher than average percentage of eccentrics, and still called a wasteland by those speeding through on the interstates, the desert remains an uncertain and potentially dangerous place. The rush to place solar and wind energy farms in California's deserts is not just a function of sunshine days per year. Why not put them in the desert? After all, there's nothing there! A battle is just beginning over the propriety of sacrificing fragile desert habitats for their use when urban roofs can supply energy without hundreds of miles of transmission lines.

The history of JTNP must be seen in the context of cultural attitudes, in particular for how American culture traditionally has disdained the desert, affecting the way both the general public and the NPS have viewed the park for most of its existence. This historic contempt has made every aspect of Joshua Tree's management difficult since its proclamation as a monument, so much so that NPS employees in Joshua Tree have had to fight those who would take its land to dig for minerals, create sacrifice zones, and carve out personal retreats. The general belief that the desert is a ruined or empty place has made it hard for many in the public to accept that it is unavailable for consumptive use or worthy of preservation.

Nonetheless, the qualities of arid land that drew ancient prophets seeking isolation, serenity, and freedom from convention arose to counteract that tradition of disdain. Some miners, as noted, chose to stay in the desert after their prospecting days ended, and then adventurous tourists challenged the harsh lands and came to appreciate the desert's allure and stark beauty. One wealthy widow, Minerva Hamilton Hoyt, became so entranced that she generated and financed a campaign that led to Joshua Tree's proclamation as a national monument. Facilitated by the automobile, today more than 2,000,000 visitors annually now seek the scenery, solitude, and adventure offered by the national park. Indeed, problems of overcrowding plague its most popular areas. A common solution to many spatial problems at JTNP is to divide the land into zones of useful habitat and unworthy emptiness. In Southern California, the tug of war between these positive and negative perceptions continues to evolve, as society subdivides its arid space into "crown jewels" surrounded by "wasteland."

Joshua Tree:

A VISUAL JOURNEY, 1936–2015

PLATE 1. The San Jacinto, Santa Rosa, San Bernardino, and San Gabriel Mountains west of Joshua Tree National Park intercept moist, westerly winds and create a rain-shadow effect that reinforces the park's desert climate. The high snow-covered peak is 10,834-foot Mount San Jacinto. Photograph by the author, January 2013.

PLATE 2. Skull Rock and most other exposed boulders in Joshua Tree National Park have undergone a process called exfoliation that causes onion-like layers of rock to peel away from the surface after the overburden has been removed. Here, erosion at the level of the former soil surface has formed small, cave-like indentations called *tafoni*, which give the boulder its striking appearance. Photograph by the author, January 2009.

PLATE 3. Rock climbers have located and scaled more than 8,000 separate routes in the boulders of Joshua Tree National Park, especially in Lost Horse and Queen Valleys. Climbing bolts are heavily controlled in the wilderness portions of the park but are allowed in non-wilderness areas such as this mass of boulders near Split Rock. Photograph by the author, January 2013.

PLATE 4. A classic alluvial fan on the southern base of the Coxcomb Mountains (highest elevation 4,416 feet) shows the spreading array of sediment that continues to wash from the canyon at its apex. The Coxcomb Mountains are among the most rugged, remote, and lightly traversed places in Joshua Tree National Park. Photograph by the author, January 2013.

PLATE 5. The creosote bush (*Larrea tridentata*) dominates the Colorado Desert portion of Joshua Tree National Park as well as other deserts in the American Southwest. Photograph by Pat Flanagan, March 2015, and used with her permission.

PLATE 6. A winding dirt track to Pushawalla Canyon crosses an alluvial fan in Pleasant Valley and approaches the "Blue Cut," one of a number of earthquake faults found in the park. The crest of the Blue Cut forms a de facto pass between the park and the lower desert to the south. Thus, residents of the Coachella Valley south of the park favored this route as a shortcut to Twentynine Palms and eventually to Las Vegas, Nevada. Photograph by the author, January 2013.

PLATE 7. In the center of the picture is the northern entrance to the "Blue Cut" from Pleasant Valley. It was one of several routes proposed by Coachella Valley residents for a north-south route through the monument west of the existing one that passes by Cottonwood Springs. Photograph by the author, January 2013.

PLATE 8. In this view of the Pinto Basin looking east from the Cholla Cactus Garden, one sees a rich display of silver cholla cactus (genus *Opuntia*) and, in the distance, the surrounding mountain ranges that were removed from the monument in 1950 to placate miners. They were returned to the park in 1994 with few new mining claims. Photograph by the author, January 2013.

PLATE 9. This panoramic view of the Pinto Basin was taken in 1936. Inclusion of the basin in the monument was controversial both before and after President Franklin D. Roosevelt's proclamation earlier that year. Photograph by George A. Grant. Harpers Ferry Center, Grant Collection, JOTR #19, National Park Service.

PLATE 10. In this panorama of the Coachella Valley from Keys View in the Little San Bernardino Mountains, looking southwest, one sees a dark line of low hills (in the center) that marks the path of the San Andreas Fault. Photograph by the author, January 2014.

PLATE 11. An unidentified National Park Service employee surveys the Coachella Valley and Salton Sea from Keys View (elevation 5,185 feet) in 1957. Unfortunately, air pollution from the Coachella Valley and the huge cities west of it make this level of visual clarity increasingly rare. Photograph by Donald Black, Joshua Tree National Park Photo Archives, Cat. 20575, Image 277, National Park Service.

PLATE 12. This road serves as the western entrance to Joshua Tree National Park from the village of Joshua Tree. It cuts through a rugged and rocky terrain that characterizes much of the park's landscape. Most visitors still enter the park by this scenic route, despite the location of the main visitor center and park headquarters at the northeastern end of the road in Twentynine Palms. Photograph by the author, January 2013.

PLATE 13. Rattlesnake Canyon near Indian Cove provides easy access to the Wonderland of Rocks from the towns on the northern border, including Twentynine Palms, site
of the park's headquarters and visitor center. Photograph by George A. Grant, 1936.
Harpers Ferry Center, Grant Collection, JOTR #67, National Park Service.

PLATE 14. Jointing, fracturing, and exposure to weathering have shaped the popular climbing landscape of Joshua Tree National Park. Here, the Wonderland of Rocks separates the main state access road to the park's northern entrances from principal park attractions such as Lost Horse Valley and Keys Ranch. Photograph by the author, January 2013.

PLATE 15. Many tall Joshua trees such as these in Queen Valley greeted inspectors who arrived at the new national monument in 1936. Today, the tallest Joshua trees persist mainly in and around Covington Flat in the northwestern part of the park. Photograph by George A. Grant. Harpers Ferry Center, Grant Collection, JOTR #32, National Park Service.

PLATE 16. A lone National Park Service inspector sits beneath a huge Joshua tree (*Yucca brevifolia*) in Hidden Valley. Challenges from miners to allow new claims plus one-third of the monument's land in private hands gave pause to even the most-confident agency official. Photograph by Ralph Anderson, December 1939. Harpers Ferry Center, Anderson Collection, JOTR #52A, National Park Service.

PLATE 17. Joshua trees dominate the vegetation in the higher-elevation Mojave Desert along the road from Hidden Valley to Keys View. A few other places in California boast similar stands of the iconic species, but none can match the surrounding sculpture of the rocky mountains and outcrops. Photograph by the author, January 2014.

PLATE 18. Early campers used the Split Rock site before the establishment of the national monument in 1936. Today, the parking area gives easy access to those who wish to go "bouldering" or picnicking in the rugged topography. Photograph by the author, January 2013.

PLATE 19. Today, Cap Rock is the site of a .4-mile nature trail and is popular for informal instruction in basic rock climbing. Here, a climbing instructor demonstrates technique. Photograph by the author, January 2013.

PLATE 20. National Park Service (NPS) planners proposed popular Cap Rock as a site for a second visitor center in 1971. Two years later, friends and fans of influential singer/songwriter Gram Parsons spirited his body away from Los Angeles International Airport (LAX) and tried to cremate him at the site, as he had wished. NPS rangers discovered the burning body and coffin before the cremation was complete. Parsons was eventually interred at Memorial Lawn Cemetery in New Orleans, Louisiana. Photograph by the author, January 2013.

PLATE 21. The jumbled rock formations plus the botanical diversity of California's two deserts—the Colorado and Mojave—attracted hikers and campers long before President Franklin D. Roosevelt proclaimed the monument on August 10, 1936. Today, as a national park, it hosts more than 2,000,000 visitors per year. Photograph by Ralph Anderson, December 1939. Harpers Ferry Center, Anderson Collection, JOTR #92A, National Park Service.

PLATE 22. The stabilized ruins of the Ryan Ranch Homestead blend in with the natural terrain near Hidden Valley, one of the premier settlement sites with both scenery and a water source. The Ryans were among the earliest permanent settlers and pursued both mining and stock raising. Photograph by the author, December 2009.

PLATE 23. White Tank is one of the natural depressions in the rocky terrain near Arch Rock that occasionally held water before and during the early days of Joshua Tree National Monument. In this photo, an inspector ponders the water storage that has been augmented by previous ranchers. These water sources were critical for grazing cattle but are of no use now. A combination of decreasing precipitation and depletion of ground-water by communities north of the park have made the collection of water in almost all similar sites in the park infrequent and short-lived. Photograph by George A. Grant, 1941. Harpers Ferry Center, Grant Collection JOTR #367, National Park Service.

PLATE 24. Barker Dam (opened in 1900) still retains the original portion built by cattleman C. O. Barker and the upper portion added in 1949 by rancher William F. ("Bill") Keys. Although the government correctly held that the water is a public water reserve, Keys continued to insist that he owned it. Photograph by the author, January 2013.

PLATE 25. This reservoir, impounded by Barker Dam on November 2, 1936, is a gathering place for picnickers, anglers, and a plethora of desert birds and wildlife, including desert bighorn sheep. In 2014 and 2015, it was empty due to drought. Photograph by George A. Grant. Harpers Ferry Center, Grant Collection, JOTR #56, National Park Service.

PLATE 26. Between 200 and 300 desert bighorn sheep (*Ovis Canadensis nelsoni*) reside in Joshua Tree National Park. They are often seen near Barker Dam, as pictured here. Photograph by Michael Vamstad, date unknown but after 2000. Joshua Tree National Park Natural Resource Division files.

PLATE 27. The desert tortoise (*Gopherus agassizii*), California's official state reptile, was placed on the California and U.S. Threatened Species Lists, respectively, in 1989 and 1990. Loss of habitat, roadkill, and urbanization have contributed to their threatened status. Their preservation has become rationale for environmental policy throughout the California deserts. Photographer and date unknown but after 2000. Joshua Tree National Park Natural Resource Division files.

PLATE 28. The Gold Crown Mine in 1936, at a time when mining still employed scores of men in the new national monument during the Great Depression. This major mine produced more than $1,000,000 in gold during its lifetime, but it quietly closed in 1938 when auriferous ore declined. Photograph by George A. Grant. Harpers Ferry Center, Grant Collection, JOTR#16, National Park Service.

PLATE 29. Mining has left its legacy on the landscape of Joshua Tree National Park. The Desert Queen Mine had several different shafts and left tailings scattered around the northern Queen Valley site. Note the dark rectangular grate (center-right) placed over the shaft to prevent visitors from entering its unsafe passages. The historic mine was mired in financial controversy, frequent changes in ownership, and occasional violence during the time between its discovery in 1892 (or 1893) and its takeover by William F. ("Bill") Keys in 1917. Thereafter, Keys sporadically worked the mine or leased it to other miners until the General Land Office challenged the legality of his claim during the early 1940s. The mine produced more than $2,000,000 in gold in its lifetime. Photograph by the author, December 2010.

PLATE 30. William F. ("Bill") Keys erected the Wall Street Mill to process ore from his own myriad claims as well as material from neighbors' mines for a fee. The National Park Service's plans to develop the mill as an interpretive site had to be dropped due to vandalism and theft of the equipment. Photograph by the author, May 2010.

PLATE 31. The William F. and Frances Keys Ranch in 1969. The remote 160-acre homestead was listed on the National Register of Historic Places in 1975. Today, the ranch serves as the primary interpretive feature in the park. The ranch house, schoolhouse, store, and workshop still stand and the orchard replanted. The land, of course, is also littered with rusting cars, trucks, and mining equipment. Photograph by F. Ross Holland. Joshua Tree National Park Photo Archives, Cat. 20575, Image 2237.

PLATE 32. Charles Stokes built his getaway home on land he purchased from the Southern Pacific Railroad Company near Hidden Valley. He vigorously opposed any effort to remove landowners from Joshua Tree National Monument. Eventually, the National Park Service acquired the land and structures in January 1958 and later added to the house and converted it into a ranger station. Photograph by the author, December 2013.

PLATE 33. The first headquarters for Joshua Tree National Monument at the Oasis of Mara was dedicated on April 3, 1954, and is shown here at the time of its completion in November 1954. The National Park Service dropped plans to build employee housing at the site at that time. More recently, the agency has added six other buildings, a mobile structure, and a nursery around it. Photographer unknown. Joshua Tree National Park Photo Archive Files, Accession No. 651, Cat. 19430, Image D3423, Folder 61.

PLATE 34. Cecil Doty, one of the National Park Service's most influential architects, designed the Joshua Tree National Park (JTNP) Visitor Center, a classic example of *Mission 66* architecture that was completed in 1963. The new building gave JTNP's staff additional space, but the fact that it sat upon the Pinto Mountain Fault led the agency to study a new location outside the original Oasis of Mara tract. The author took this photograph from the nature trail through the Oasis of Mara, January 2014.

PLATE 35. California fan palms (*Washingtonia filifera*), as seen here at the Oasis of Mara in Twentynine Palms, can rise to seventy-five feet, making them among the tallest of North America's palms. Roger Toll, then Superintendent of Yellowstone National Park, took this picture of the palms at the oasis on March 10, 1934, during his inspection for proposed additions, including desert lands, to the national park system. He did not find the area worthy of national monument or park status. Harpers Ferry Center, JOTR Collection, Negative #WASO-H-707, National Park Service.

PLATE 36. The Oasis of Mara, as viewed from the northwest on October 5, 1941. After the Chemehuevi tribe and miners moved out of the national monument, much of the lower-elevation vegetation reappeared. Photograph by George A. Grant. Harpers Ferry Center, Grant Collection, JOTR #306, National Park Service.

PLATE 37. The vegetation at the Oasis of Mara has changed greatly during the park's history. Today, mesquite (*Prosopis juliflora*) clogs the grove of California fan palms, and the dark areas in the understory vegetation are mistletoe (*Santa lales*). All three species are native to the region, but creeping mesquite (*Prosopis reptans*) is not. Photograph by the author, January 2014.

PLATE 38. An isolated California fan palm (*Washingtonia filifera*) at the Oasis of Mara shows the characteristic foliage cloaking the trunk below the living fronds. The surface around the tree's base periodically has been deliberately cleared to stop growth of mesquite and mistletoe from increasing the risk of fire damage. A single mature tree may drop as many as 350,000 palm seeds to germinate. Photograph by the author, January 2014.

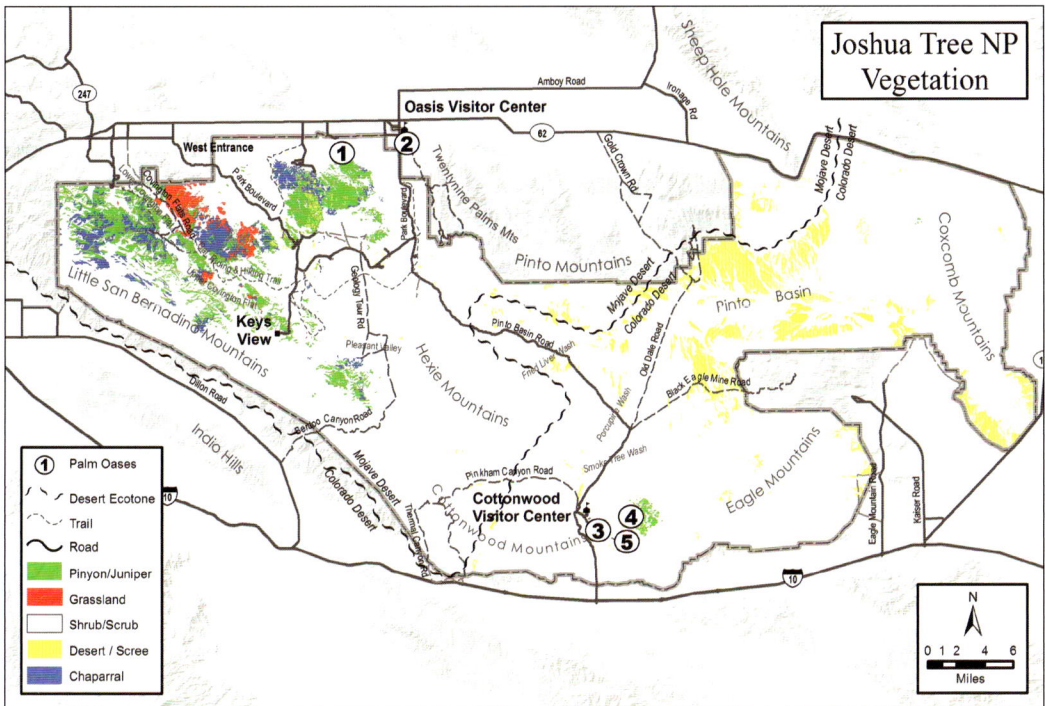

MAP A. Vegetation of Joshua Tree National Park. A distinct ecotone winds through the middle of the park, separating the higher-elevation Mojave Desert in the west, which supports Joshua trees, grasslands, and a pinyon-juniper forest, from the lower-elevation Colorado Desert, with its creosote bush-dominated shrub/scrubland and exposed rock. The numbers identify the sites of the five palm oases in the park: (1) Fortynine Palms Oasis; (2) Oasis of Mara; (3) Cottonwood Spring; (4) Munsen Oasis; and (5) Lost Palms Oasis. Data source: Joshua Tree National Park GIS files. Delta Cartography.

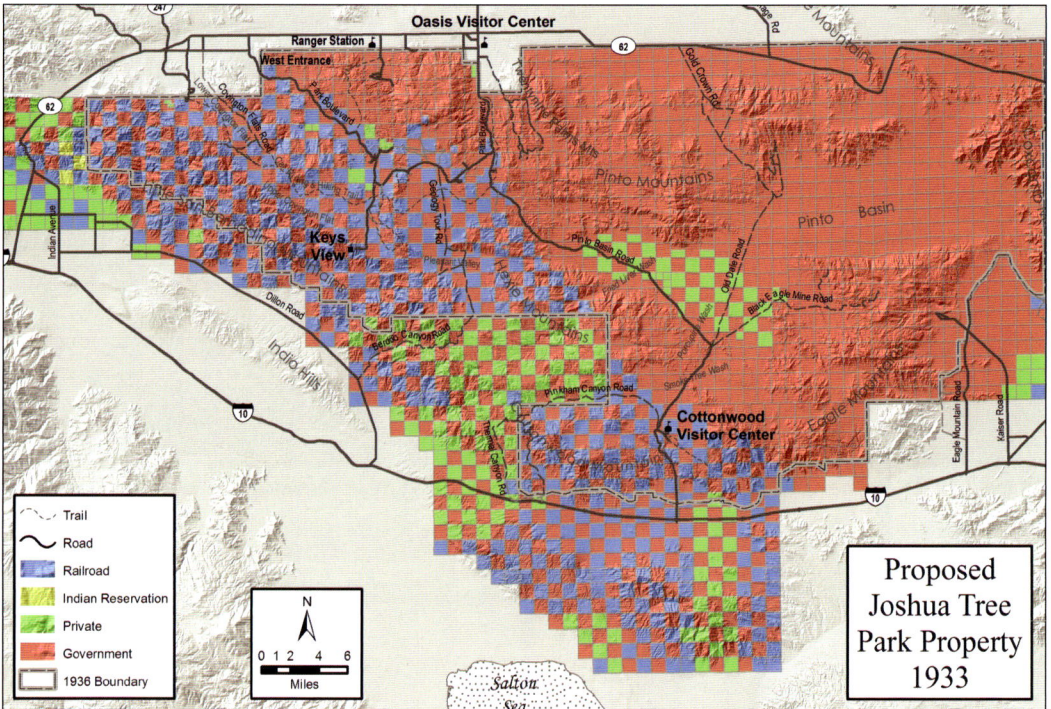

**Proposed
Joshua Tree
Park Property
1933**

MAP B. With key encouragement from Minerva Hamilton Hoyt, President Franklin
D. Roosevelt withdrew more than 1,100,000 acres of land from the public domain in
1933. As this map shows, however, the Southern Pacific Railroad Company and scores
of private citizens owned a huge percentage of the land in the proposed park. Land-
acquisition problems would force the National Park Service to relinquish much of the
western and southern portions and accept a smaller national monument of around
800,000 acres. Data source: "Proposed Joshua Tree National Monument" (April 6, 1936),
Joshua Tree National Park Map Archives, No. 20130116-014845. Delta Cartography.

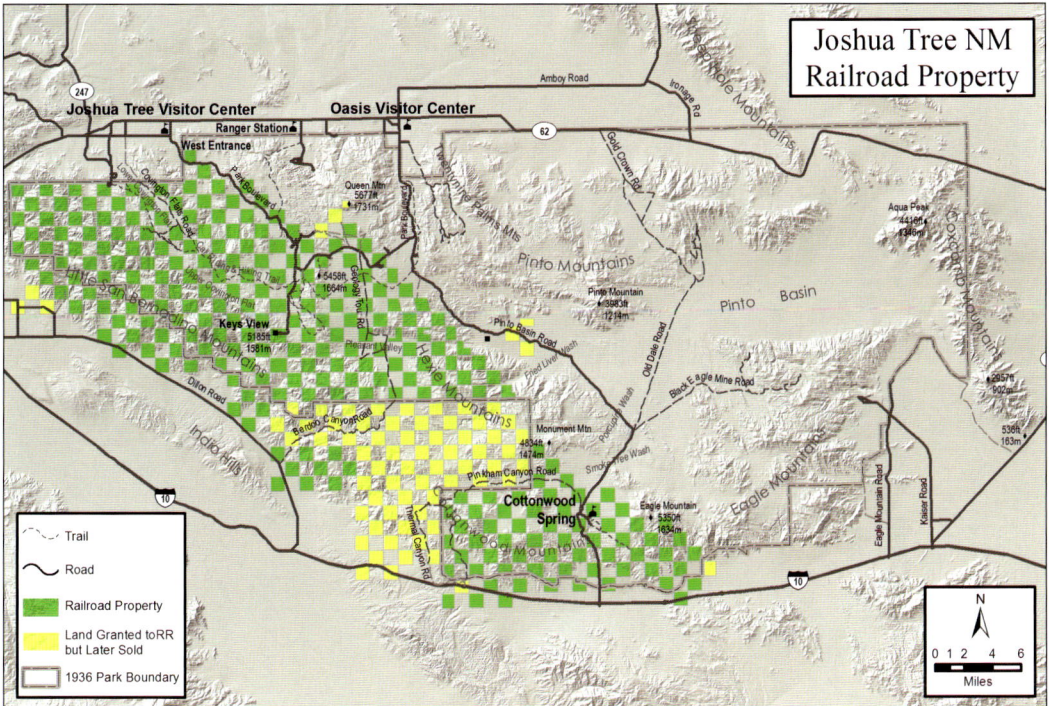

MAP C. The Southern Pacific Railroad Company owned numerous surveyed sections of land throughout the scenic western part of the proposed national park. The company quietly sold most of its land in the Cottonwood Mountains to private individuals, forcing the National Park Service to exclude the area from Joshua Tree National Monument as established in 1936. Data source: Joshua Tree National Park Archives, Map Drawer 5, No. 20100806-0002. Delta Cartography.

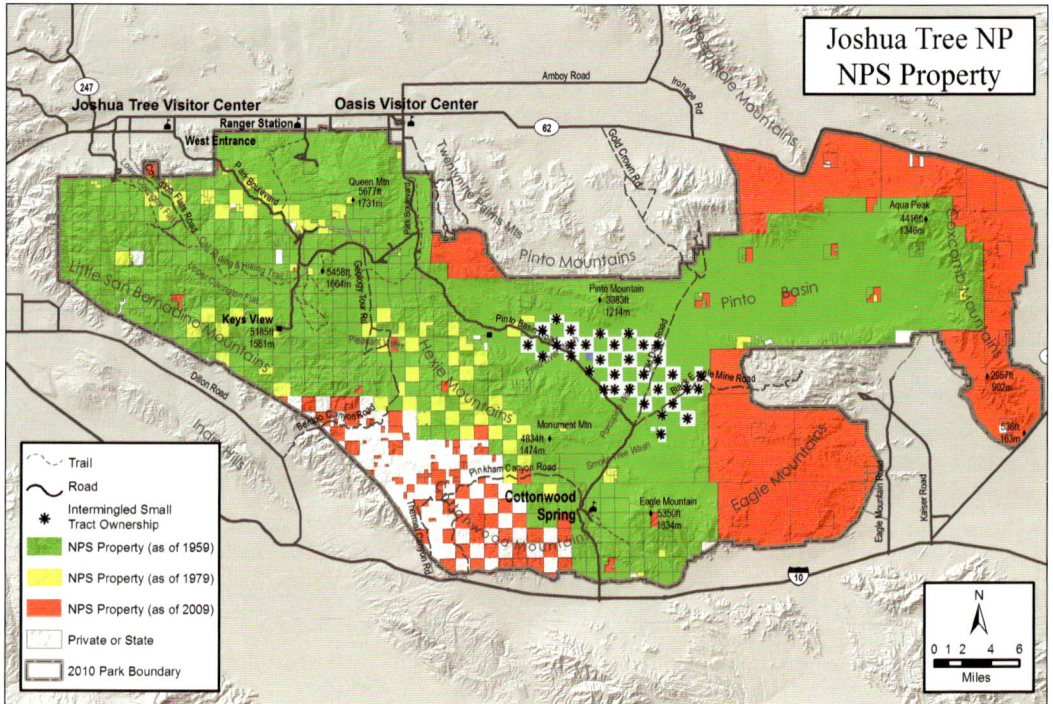

MAP D. Land acquisition by the National Park Service (NPS) between 1936 and 2009. Most of the land acquired by 1959 came from purchases of the Southern Pacific Railroad Company's land or tripartite exchanges involving other public lands. During the next two decades, the NPS sought parcels in and around the most-popular visitor areas. Most of the red areas were former Bureau of Land Management (formerly the General Land Office) land added by the 1994 California Desert Protection Act, including a segment with many private parcels west of the Cottonwood Spring that had never before been in the park. Data source: Joshua Tree National Park GIS files. Delta Cartography.

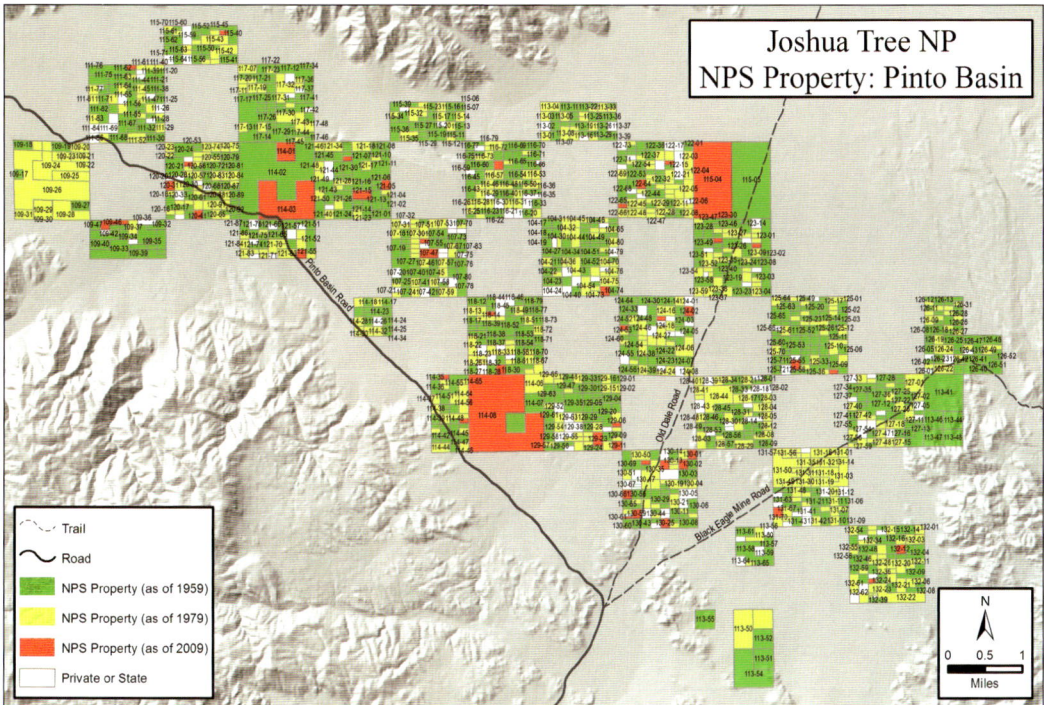

MAP E. Sales of Pinto Basin land by the Security Land Corporation during the late 1920s left alternating sections with hundreds of five- to twenty-acre parcels for the National Park Service to acquire. The small plots lacked a water source, and owners soon found that the taxes they owed amounted to more than their land was worth. Nevertheless, many of these tiny parcels are still privately owned. Data source: Joshua Tree National Park GIS files. Delta Cartography.

MAP F. External threats to Joshua Tree National Park after 1989. A surge in renewable-energy schemes has almost surrounded the park, with the major ones focused on areas immediately to the east and southeast. In particular, the tongue of non-park land from Desert Center to the Eagle Mountain Mine is part of the Riverside East Solar Energy Zone. The gigantic complex of pits of the former iron mine is itself the focus of competing development projects. See, also, Maps G.1 and G.2. Data source: Joshua Tree National Park GIS files. Delta Cartography.

Eagle Mountain Land Exchange and Landfill

Landfill Phases
Landfill Facility
Kaiser Patented
NPS Wilderness
BLM Exchanged Land
2010 Park Boundary

Eagle Crest Pumped Storage

Storage Facility
Water
NPS Wilderness
2010 Park Boundary

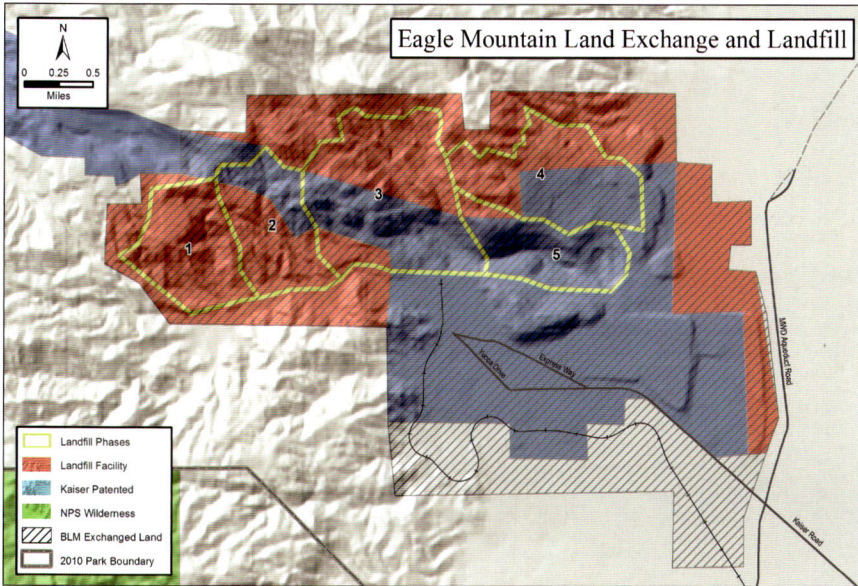

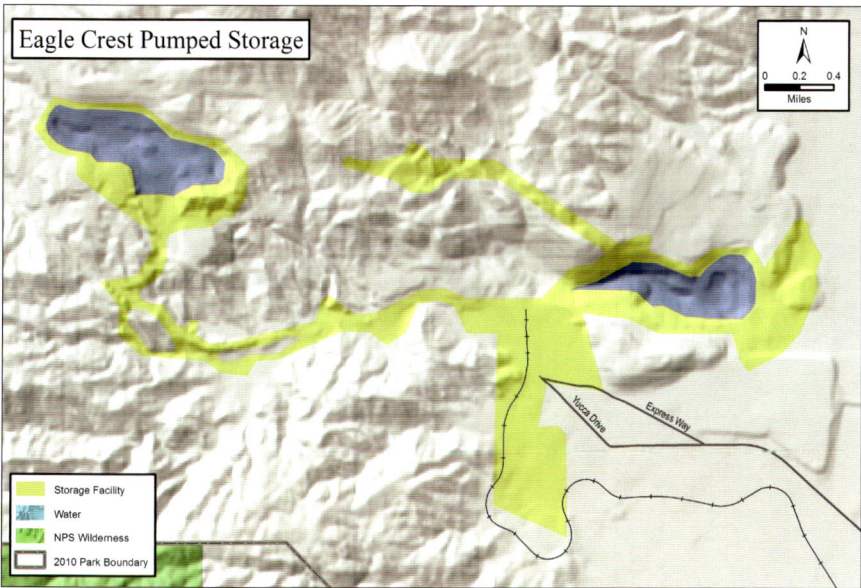

MAP G.1 (above). The plan for the Kaiser's Eagle Mountain Landfill Project. At a cost of multiple millions of dollars, the company fought to develop the mining pits for 117 years of waste disposal at a rate of 20,000 tons per day. Begun in 1989, its campaign finally died when the U.S. Supreme Court refused to hear its last appeal in 2013.

Map G.2. (below). The Eagle Crest Company's plan to pump water back and forth to generate electricity during periods of high demand. In August 2016, the project was close to approval. The National Park Service opposes both projects. Data source: Joshua Tree National Park GIS files. Delta Cartography.

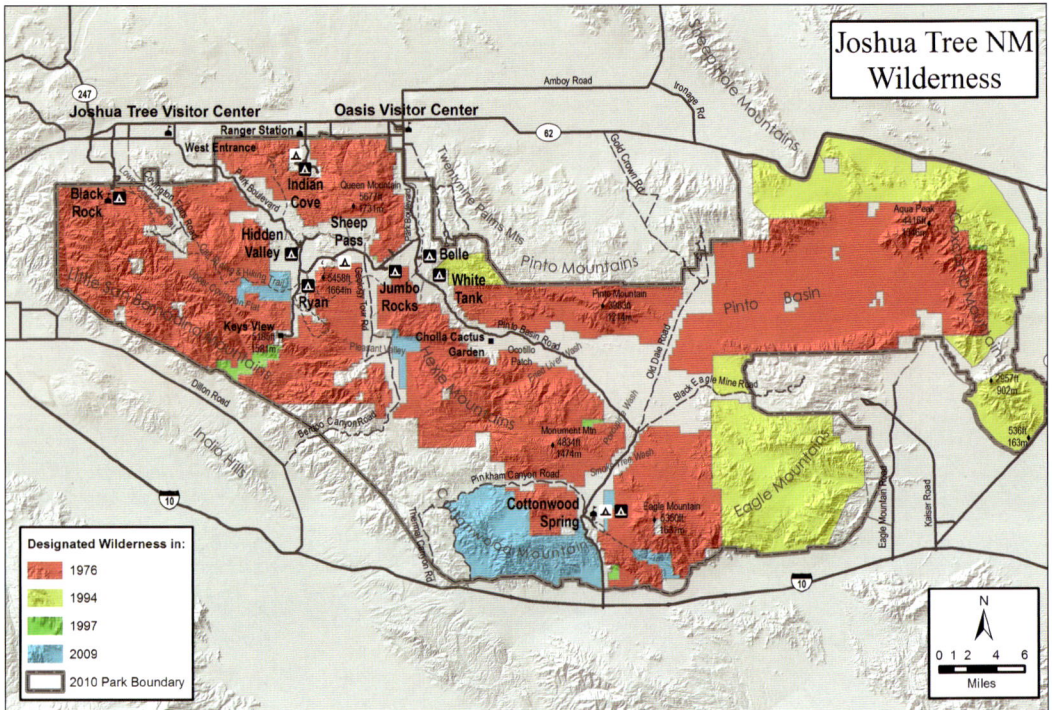

MAP H. Designated wilderness additions from 1976 through 2009. The 1976 designation came after virulent debate and criticism of the National Park Service by an emboldened environmental constituency. A road connecting Hidden Valley and Covington Flat, a favored project of Superintendent Homer Rouse, was one casualty of the push for more wilderness. Most of the rest of the designated wilderness accompanied land added by the 1994 California Desert Protection Act. Data source: Joshua Tree National Park GIS files. Delta Cartography.

PART I

SAVING A DESERT GARDEN

THE STORY OF A NATIONAL PARK begins with the idea that a particular place is worth saving. In other words, it contains natural or cultural resources of compelling value to the entire nation. Some person or group then proposes that the National Park Service (NPS) should protect the place in perpetuity. The agency evaluates the place and gives a recommendation to the U.S. Congress and the President. Thereafter, people, organizations, and other government agencies, both near and far, argue for and against the idea. Finally, the proposal either passes or fails.

In this section, I relate these processes for the establishment of Joshua Tree National Monument. In Chapter One, I present the geographical, geological, biological, and historical components, including patterns of human use and settlement, that led people and organizations to propose Joshua Tree as a desert landscape worthy of designation as a unit of the national park system. In doing so, I explain the tasks the NPS faces as it applies laws and policies to protect the resources while eliminating human activities that challenge that mission. In Chapter Two, I show how a dedicated group of people and the NPS overcame substantial opposition and serious doubts about the propriety of a park unit in the desert to get Joshua Tree National Monument established. Key individuals, particularly society matron Minerva Hamilton Hoyt, showed what determination and political influence can accomplish in such a campaign for the public good.

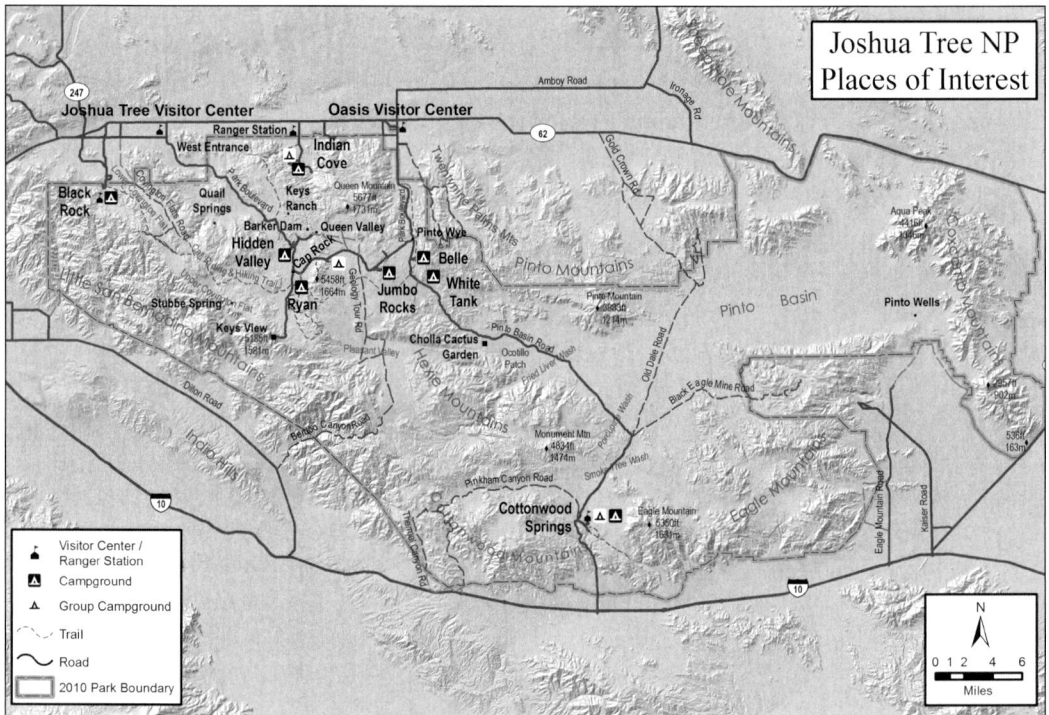

Joshua Tree NP
Places of Interest

Legend:
- Visitor Center / Ranger Station
- Campground
- Group Campground
- Trail
- Road
- 2010 Park Boundary

N

0 1 2 4 6
Miles

MAP 1.1. The major natural and human features of Joshua Tree National Park are shown on this map derived from the National Park Service's official map. Paved roads, trails, two visitor centers, and nine campgrounds are concentrated in the western portion of the 792,510-acre park, showing the influence of higher elevations and cooler summer temperatures. Data source: Joshua Tree National Park GIS files. Delta Cartography.

CHAPTER ONE:

The Nature of Joshua Tree's Land and People

THE AREA THAT IS TODAY'S Joshua Tree National Park (JTNP) is a stark and unforgiving place. Yet it is also a wondrous landscape that draws nearly a million and a half visitors per year. Sprawled across the ecotone between the Mojave and Colorado Deserts of Southern California, it has witnessed a variety of people adapting to its harsh habitat and pursuing its varied forms of wealth. Throughout its history as a national monument and, later, as a national park, people have contested its purpose and use. Millennia of occupancy and decades of mineral and grazing exploitation shaped a landscape that was both damaged and of intense historical interest. In 1936, the federal government elected to protect the land and its resources to inspire, educate, and provide recreation for the benefit of future generations. It has not been an easy task. To understand the story of JTNP, one must begin by surveying the origins and development of the resources it is designated to protect.

The Land

The most striking thing about the landforms of Joshua Tree is the fact that, in a state, region, and nation dominated by mountain ranges running north to south, most features in the park are oriented east to west. Five of the six mountain systems in the park are part of the Transverse Ranges that seal off Southern California from the longitudinal-trending Coast Range, Central Valley, and Sierra Nevada. The Little San Bernardino, Hexie, Pinto, Cottonwood, and Eagle Mountains all stretch along lines of latitude (Maps 1.1 and 1.2). Only the easternmost Coxcomb Mountains, an extension of the Basin and Range topography, follow the north-to-south pattern that dominates the entire American West. In between lie canyons and basins that reflect differential tectonic uplift or other faulting processes. Eroded material from the highlands blankets the lowlands, reaching a depth of thousands of feet in the Pinto Basin. The tectonic forces and erosion continue to shape the mountains and basins that form the park's landscape.

The story of Joshua Tree's formation began at least 1,700,000,000 years ago, when a mix of igneous and metamorphic rocks, including Pinto gneiss, developed deep under a massive mountain system that geologists call Rodinia. It stretched across a supercontinent from what is now Scandinavia through North America to Australia and Antarctica. That type of metamorphic rock is extremely resistant to erosion, and a combination of faulting, volcanic intrusions, and erosion of softer material above it has exposed pockets of it in the Cottonwood, Pinto, and Eagle Mountains. During the Mesozoic era from 250,000,000 to 75,000,000 years ago, there was active subduction of the Pacific Plate under the North American Plate, leading to more upwelling of intrusive volcanic material that formed several types of granite. One of the most common is Monzogranite, a fractured and jointed type that weathered into the extraordinary climbing formations of the park. It composes the Wonderland of Rocks area as well as large portions of the Pinto, Eagle, and Coxcomb Mountains.[1]

The modern uplands of the Transverse Ranges result from tectonic forces along the San Andreas Fault system, which runs from the Gulf of California to a point off the Pacific Coast at Cape Mendocino. The 800-mile fault first formed along California's coast, as the plates shifted from a direct collision to a pattern where the Pacific Plate moves in a northwesterly direction while the North American Plate moves west. The crust atop the Pacific Plate south of the park consists of material that was originally part of the North American Plate, but it was separated from the rest of the continent with the rifting of the Gulf of California. As the plates ground against each other, that separated portion of the crust, thick and dense, compressed and lifted the Transverse Ranges from the Eagle Mountains to the northern Channel Islands west of Santa Barbara.[2]

The San Andreas Fault is actually a system of roughly parallel faults that appear around and in Joshua Tree National Park. The actual San Andreas Fault lies just southwest of the park and can be seen from Keys View as a line of hills at the northern end of the Coachella Valley (Plate 10; Map 1.2). The San Andreas Fault and the parallel Dillon Fault formed the Little San Bernardino Mountains. North of them lies the Blue Cut Fault that boosted the ranges south of Pinto Basin. Along the northern boundary of the park lies the Pinto Fault, which formed the mountains of the same name, sealed the northern edge of the Pinto Basin, and now lies directly beneath the park's headquarters in Twentynine Palms. Other smaller fractures, including a few that trend north–south have also helped shape the jumbled landscape of JTNP. When crustal material shifts along the major faults of the park's area, significant earthquakes occur. They are unpredictable but certain to occur in the future. Several recent tremors have taken place on the Pinto Fault, leading to worries about the future of the park headquarters complex.

The six mountain ranges in JTNP surround several valleys and basins that have received the weathered material from the uplifting terrain adjacent to them. As that sedimentary material eroded away, several processes contributed to the popular geomorphic features of today. First, isostatic uplift occurred. Earth's crust rests on a liquid layer of subsurface rock that is weighed down by the burden. Like a memory foam mattress rebounding after a person leaves, the land rises as erosion reduces the weight of the crustal material above it. This is what is partly responsible for bringing deep, intrusive rocks such as Pinto gneiss and monzogranite up from miles below the surface. Eventually, the erosion exposes these rocks, which are far harder than the material that covered them.

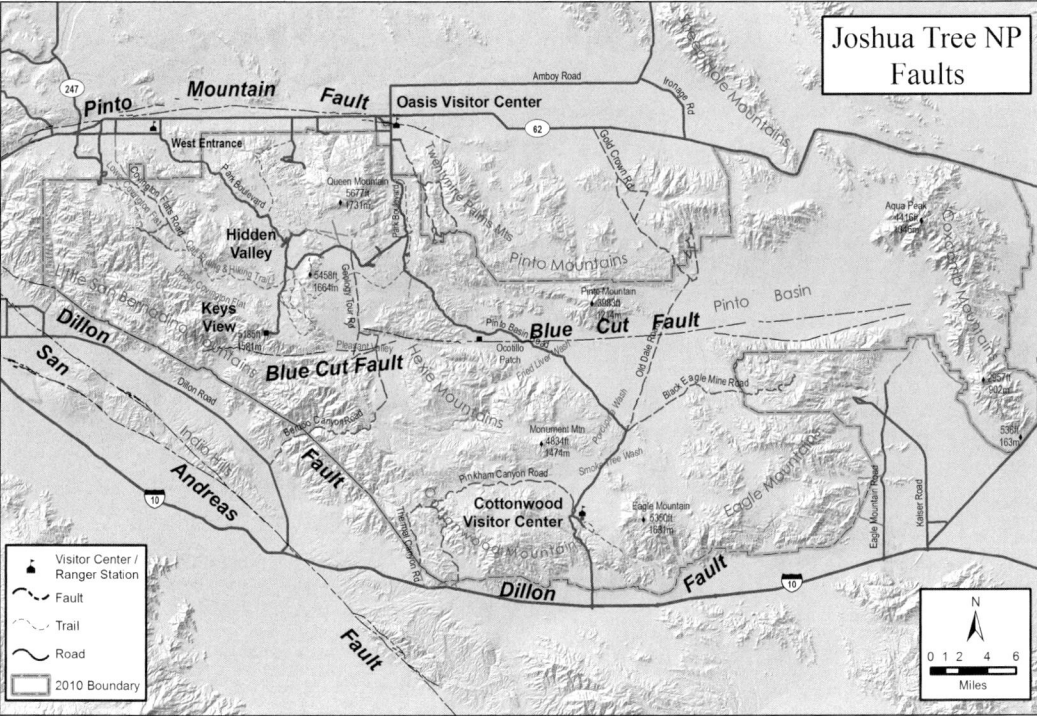

MAP 1.2. Four faults, including the San Andreas, have formed six distinct mountain systems in Joshua Tree National Park. The Little San Bernardino, Hexie, Pinto, Cottonwood, and Eagle Mountains are components of the east-west trending Transverse Ranges that extend to the Channel Islands off the coast of Santa Barbara. The rugged Coxcomb Mountains run parallel to the northwest-southeast axis of most of the other mountain systems in California. In between them are valleys and basins that have seen millennia of human activity. Data source: Joshua Tree National Park GIS files. Delta Cartography.

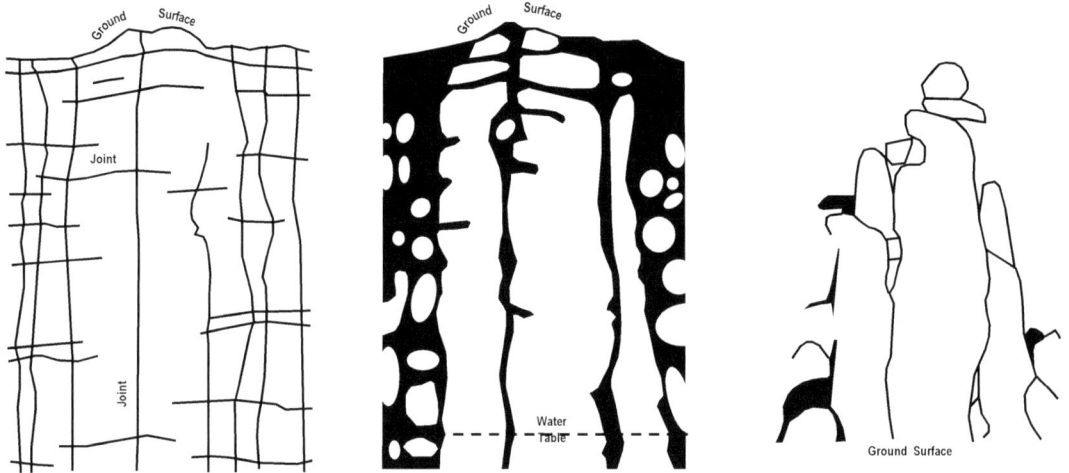

FIG 1.1. Intrusive igneous rock makes up most of Joshua Tree National Park's uplands. The rock develops fissures when cooling that are then exposed when the overlying material erodes away. The remaining blocks then undergo further weathering and erosion, resulting in the "boulder-pile" appearance of much of the park's landscape. Source: Joshua Tree National Park, "Geologic Formations"; http://www.nps.gov/jotr/naturescience/geologicformations.htm.

The monzogranite, in particular, undergoes a second process of jointing or cracking along vertical and horizontal fissures while still under the surface. When exposed to the atmosphere, the fissures widen and create blocks of rock. Physical weathering then erodes the fractured blocks into rounded boulder-like pieces that make up the distinctive piles of stone so popular with rock climbers (Fig. 1.1 and Plate 14). Another process that happens is called exfoliation. When erosion removes the heavy overburden, intrusive igneous rock like granite can actually swell slightly, causing outer layers to peel away like the layers of an onion. These sheets of weathered rock can range from fingernail-thin pieces on a small boulder to several feet thick as occurs in the domes of the Sierra Nevada. Finally, a third process sculpts exposed rock at the surface of the surrounding soil. Acid and water collect against the rock base and erode pockets into it. Later, erosion may leave these features, called tafoni, above the ground level like indents in the rock face. Skull Rock is one example of this curious modifying process (Plate 2).[3]

The massive amount of rock and soil eroded over millions of years from the rising mountains has filled the basins of Joshua Tree to great depths. Along the edges of the uplands, erosion creates another type of distinctive desert landform: the alluvial fan. Water coursing through a narrow canyon moves quickly and can carry a significant amount of eroded debris. Once the water exits a stone-walled canyon, it spreads out and immediately slows down. Without the speed caused by the narrow defile, much of the load of alluvium drops, beginning with the heavier pieces. What results is a fan-shaped slope of debris, with the finest material near the bottom (Plates 6 and 38). Along a mountain front, one can see these fans formed at the mouth of each outlet between individual peaks. In many areas, the fans will coalesce over time at the foot of the mountains into a broad apron of material, .called a "bajada." These long, steady slopes, such as the one leading from the park to the Oasis of Mara, make for interesting driving and enjoyable views.

The Desert Climates

Three factors dominate Joshua Tree's weather and climate. First, the southwestern portion of the contiguous United States falls under the Hawaiian High Pressure Cell. Air that lost its moisture as it rose at the equatorial and subpolar low-pressure latitudes flows toward this area in the upper atmosphere and warms as it descends toward the surface. It arrives parched of moisture and inhibits surface air from rising to elevations sufficient for condensation and precipitation. Although the cell moves north and south with the seasons, it extends over Southern California for much of the year. Along the Pacific Coast, the cell is the major factor in creating a Mediterranean-like climate that features dry summers and winter cyclonic storms carried on westerly winds. In Joshua Tree during the late summer and early fall, the cell weakens enough to allow a "monsoon" effect of moist air flowing from the Gulf of Mexico and bringing much of the region's rainfall. Forty-one percent of the park's precipitation falls between July and September.

The San Jacinto, Santa Rosa, San Bernardino, and San Gabriel mountain ranges to the west and southwest of the park form a second factor that determines the park's climate. While winter winds bring some rain to the coast, the mountains create a rainshadow effect by leaching the eastward moving air of moisture as it rises over them. Once across the mountains, much of the air descends, drying out and bringing further aridity to the park.

A third climate factor is elevation, which influences both temperature and precipitation. The eastern, lower portion of the park below 2,000 feet is known as the Colorado Desert, a subregion of the Sonoran Desert that also dominates Arizona and adjacent portions of northwestern Mexico. It is warmer and drier than the Mojave Desert in the western part of the park. This 'high' desert extends north and east into Nevada and Utah. The higher elevation of the mountains in the Mojave portion of the park, especially the area around Covington Flat, has a better chance to intercept what moisture does get by the wall of mountains to the west.[4]

The combination of these factors results in a climate that averages forty-nine degrees Fahrenheit in January and nearly eighty-nine degrees in July. Twentynine Palms receives 4.33 inches of precipitation per year, while the southeastern part of the park gets considerably less.[5] The limiting impact of descending high-pressure air means that most moisture comes in convection storms riding powerful updrafts and accompanied by lightning and thunder. These bursts of rain can quickly deposit a lot of water in a very short time, leading to flash floods that can destroy roads and other infrastructure. One dangerous characteristic of desert thunderstorms is that a mass of water can rush through canyons and gullies, carrying tons of sediment and debris. The flood may flow through washes miles away from the area where the rain fell and threaten anyone camping or wandering along a normally dry pathway. Cold temperatures in the winter can result in snow on the upland of the park, but it usually does not stay on the ground very long. By contrast, the much higher peaks to the west, such as Mount San Jacinto (elevation 10,833 feet) and Mt. San Gorgonio (elevation 11,503 feet), may have a snowcap for six or more months of the year, providing a scenic backdrop to the desert foreground of the park (Plate 1).

The stark, sometimes dangerous climate of JTNP has not always dominated the area. Throughout the Pleistocene era (2,588,000 to 11,700 years ago), the area was dry but not as arid as it is today. During the time of the Pinto culture, some 5,000 years ago, more moisture fell in the region and probably supported a larger biomass of vegetation. For several decades, archaeologists and other scientists speculated that the Pinto Basin was the site of a Pleistocene-era lake or major river. Recent investigations suggest that the area might have been an ephemeral or permanent wetland with higher rainfall that contributed to the large aquifer under the basin today.[6]

Flora and Fauna

Two important characteristics of the vegetation in Joshua Tree led to its establishment as a national monument and its continued protection. First, the aridity of the area means that most of the species are xerophytes, plants with adaptations to low-precipitation and high-evaporation rates. Among the adaptations are the ability to store water, woody stems and leathery or waxy leaves to minimize water loss, and either deep tap roots or roots radiating widely from the plant to capture water quickly in a rare precipitation event. Increasing distance from one plant to another is often a sign of decreasing rainfall, although other factors can contribute to this spatial pattern. Generally, trees are scarce, except in higher elevations and cooler, wetter sites. Thus, viewing the desert landscape ecologically, the xerophytic plants and trees one sees scattered about actually represent a "climax" ecology, not a scene of barrenness.

The second characteristic of the park is that it is the meeting ground for the Colorado and Sonoran Deserts. The ecotone between the two deserts winds through JTNP, marking the increase in elevation toward the northwest (Map A). It includes the southern extent of the Joshua tree (*Yucca brevifolia*), the indicator species for the Mojave Desert, and the northern extent of ocotillo (*Fouquieria splendens*). The indicator species for the Colorado Desert, the creosote bush (*Larrea tridentata*), occurs in both parts of the park. In a region that many travelers—especially those living in forested landscapes east of the 100th Meridian—regard as desolate, the mixing of these two groups of species and the substantial variation in elevation mean that nearly 800 species of plants grow in the park. A recent study suggests that, despite climate change during the Holocene (the last 10,000 years), the assemblage of species in the park has remained relatively stable, although certain species have expanded or contracted their distribution.[7]

With so many species present in the park, a wide variety of vegetation associations exist. For ease of understanding, park interpreters have divided the plants into tree-dominated, shrub-dominated, herbaceous-dominated, and sparse/non-vegetated associations, the first three named after the most conspicuous type of plant. Tree-dominated plant associations in Joshua Tree include the Joshua tree, California juniper (*Juniperus californica*), singleleaf pinyon pine (*Pinus monophylla*), desert willow (*Chilopsis linearis*), ironwood (*Olneya tesota*), California fan palm (*Washingtonia filifera*), blue palo verde (*Parkinsonia florida*), smoketree (*Psorothamnus spinosus*), Frémont cottonwood (*Populus fremontii*), and mesquite (*Prosopis juliflora*). Forty-nine shrub-dominated associations exist, demonstrating their spatial prevalence. They include the creosote bush, ocotillo, blackbrush (*Coleogyne ramosissima*), brittlebush (*Encelia farinosa*), Mojave yucca (*Yucca schidigera*), and teddy-bear cholla (*Cylindropuntia bigelovii*). Herbaceous-dominated associations (grasslands) include two primary associations: big galleta grass (*Pleuraphis rigida*) and the exotic European cheatgrass

(*Bromus tectorum*). The non-vegetated association is characterized by desert pavement, rocky outcrops, dunes, playas, washes, and areas with vegetative cover of less than two percent. Patrick Leary, in his 1977 survey of Joshua Tree's vegetation, claimed that no true chaparral existed in the monument, but several notable species from that community can be found in the northwestern part of the park, including Sonoran scrub oak (*Quercus turbinella*), manzanita (*Arctostaphylos glauca*), and desert ceanothus (*Ceanothus greggii*).[8]

The distribution of major vegetation communities in Joshua Tree appears in Map A. Due to its greater elevation, the western part of JTNP includes most of the tree and herbaceous associations, divided into the pinyon–juniper woodland, the Mojave's mid-elevation scrubland, the chaparral-scrubland, and the annual–perennial grassland. The remainder of the park consists primarily of the creosote bush–mixed scrub association. Finally, most of the exposed rock and scree occur in aprons around the Pinto and Coxcomb Mountains. It is important to remember that a particular vegetation community represents an overlapping of the ranges of all its species. Hence, borders between them are rarely as clear as delineated on a map. In addition to these 'higher' plants, dozens of species of mosses and lichens thrive on the park's rock and soil surfaces.

Three species of plants are worthy of closer attention because of their dominance in several communities and their importance to humans ranging from Paleo-Indians to today's sightseers: the Joshua tree, creosote bush, and California fan palm. The Joshua tree is a member of the agave family (Plates 14–16). Older books and pamphlets describe it as a member of the lily family, but recent studies have divided that group into forty separate plant families. It is related to the Mojave yucca (*Yucca schidigera*), which can be distinguished by its longer and wider leaves and hair-like filaments. Both types of yuccas often grow together in the park. Legend has it that Mormon pioneers named the tree after Joshua, the biblical figure, seeing the branches of the tree as reaching up in prayer. Settlers and ranchers used the Joshua tree's limbs and trunks for fencing and corrals, while miners burned them to power steam engines for processing ore. Botanists remain uncertain about what exact conditions lead to flowering on the Joshua tree, but reproduction usually depends on the yucca moth. In a textbook example of symbiosis, the moth collects pollen while laying eggs inside the flower's ovary. The tree relies on the moth for pollination, and the moth's larvae rely on the tree's seeds for food. The Joshua tree is also capable of sprouting from roots and branches.[9]

The creosote bush has the largest range of any species in the park (Plate 5). A pungent smell and small, yellow flowers in spring and summer are notable features of this plant, which dominates arid lands all the way east to central Texas. Genetic and fossil evidence indicate that the creosote bush is a relative newcomer to California's deserts, arriving some 12,000 years ago, near the end of the most recent Ice Age. Formerly, a juniper woodland and grasses dominated the area, but these plant communities retreated to the western mountains as the climate warmed. The creosote bush successfully competed for scarce water and now dominates two thirds of the park. Although the plant produces seeds at each flowering, most of its slow growth and persistence in a location comes from a cloning process, whereby new branches from the original seed replace the earlier and older ones above ground. Hence, the modern plant may be the end result of generations of branches growing and dying only to be replaced by genetic copies. One study has shown that the original of a creosote bush known as King Clone, located near Lucerne Valley, California, may have sprouted more than 11,000 years ago.[10]

The third noteworthy species, the California fan palm, grows in oases created in an otherwise hot and dry environment by water seeping to the surface through faults. The park contains five of the 158 palm oases located in North America. The desert fan palm is native to the low, hot deserts of Southern California, where it can live for up to eighty years. A mature desert fan palm may reach seventy-five feet in height and three tons in weight (Plates 35 and 38). It has fan-shaped leaves that continue to cling to the bottom of the trunk after dying, until fire clears them away. Fire kills young palms but removes competitors and opens up space for as many as 350,000 palm seeds from one mature tree to germinate. A number of other species crowd into the relatively moist micro-environment of the palm oasis, including mesquite, the non-native tamarisk (*Tamarix ramosissima*, *Tamarix chinensis*, or *Tamarix aphylla*), and various grasses (Plate 37). The five palm oases in the park include the Oasis of Mara and Fortynine Palms Oasis along the northern edge of JTNP and the Cottonwood, Lost Palms, and Munsen Oases near the park's southern boundary.[11]

The surprising richness of floral species in Joshua Tree is matched by its fauna. The environment is demanding, but the park's animals have adapted to its constraints by coping with great heat, a high diurnal temperature range, a lack of water, and a scarcity of food. To combat high temperature, many species are active only at night and retreat to burrows or other protected places during the day. Primarily nocturnal animals include mammals such as kangaroo rats (*Dipodomys deserti*), coyotes (*Canis latrans mearnsi*), and black-tailed jack rabbits (*Lepus californicus deserticola*). Water is a necessity for mammals, but many of the smaller species of rodents gain moisture from the food they eat. Reptiles need little water and also gain some from what they eat. The low biomass of vegetation means the carrying capacity for animals is lower than in wetter habitats, but nearly every species of plant serves some of the desert's wildlife.

Joshua Tree National Park is home to fifty-two species of mammals, including twenty-four small rodents. A few desert mammals such as the round-tailed ground squirrel (*Spermophilus tereticaudus tereticaudus*), a diurnal rodent, enter a state of aestivation when the days become too hot and the vegetation too dry. They sleep during the hottest part of the summer and also hibernate in winter to avoid the cold. Unlike the rodents, larger mammals, such as desert bighorn sheep (*Ovis canadensis nelsoni*) (Plate 26) and mule deer (*Odocoileus hemionus fuliginatus*), must drink water during the hot summer days from the springs and seeps in the park. Joshua Tree is home to many reptiles, including eighteen species of lizards, twenty-five species of snakes, and the desert tortoise (*Gopherus agassizii agassizii*) (Plate 27). The latter has become the most important species in the park from a political standpoint due to its listing in 1989–1990 as a threatened species on state and federal endangered species lists. The California treefrog (*Pseudacris cadaverina*) and the red-spotted toad (*Bufo punctatus*) are amphibians that inhabit the park. Other than myriad types of insects and arthropods, the most numerous set of species in JTNP are birds. Their high metabolism and need for a lot of food and water would be a hindrance to survival in the desert, but their mobility means they can access resources over larger areas than other types of animals. Ornithologists have recorded more than 250 species of birds in JTNP, but only seventy-eight nest in the park. Most of the rest are migratory species traveling the Pacific Flyway from Alaska to South America, especially during the winter. They appear at the reservoir behind Barker Dam when it has water, and many stop at the Salton Sea after passing through the park.[12]

The First Peoples

Scholars from archaeology, linguistics, and genetics argue continually about the origin of the first people to occupy the Western Hemisphere, in general, and California, specifically. For several decades, most scholars accepted the comfortable "Clovis Theory," which posited that big-game hunters entered the hemisphere between 11,000 and 12,000 years ago over a land bridge from Asia to North America by way of present-day Alaska. That they were first has been challenged by linguistic theory on the rate of divergence of languages, by recent archaeological finds, such as the 13,000-year-old Arlington Man site on the Channel Islands, and by evidence that suggests a coastal route in addition to the mainland one. This period coincided with the last glacial stage of the Pleistocene epoch. An increasing number of scholars accept the idea that California was inhabited by people at least 15,000 years ago. Archaeological evidence in and around the region of Joshua Tree National Park confirms that people lived and hunted in a cooler and more-moist grassland environment between 10,000 and 4,000 years ago. Archaeologists Elizabeth and William Campbell studied transitory campsites in the Pinto Basin during the 1920s and 1930s and described a culture of adept hunter-gatherers called the Pinto Culture. Although their hypothesis that a lake or permanent stream existed in the basin has proven incorrect, their work on reconstructing the human ecology of these semi-nomadic people was groundbreaking. The Campbells collected relatively large, triangular spear points that Pinto hunters attached to a wooden shaft and propelled with an atlatl. Archaeologists believe the early Pinto Culture was a mobile population dependent upon hunting large-game and gathering seasonal plants. Eventually, moisture decreases during the period of Pinto Culture led to a climate similar to the present one. People gradually adapted by hunting smaller game and processing small seeds.[13]

When European settlers entered California during the late-eighteenth century, three groups of Native Americans occupied the Joshua Tree area: the Cahuilla, Chemehuevi, and Serrano tribes. All three groups spoke Uto-Aztecan languages, parts of a language family that included Paiute, Comanche, Hopi, and Aztec. The Mojave Indians, a family tribe from the Colorado River area that spoke the Hokan language, also regularly used the resources as they traveled through on long trading and social visits to the Pacific Coast. The Chemehuevi were the most recent arrivals, having moved southwest from the Great Basin of Nevada by 1500. All four groups interacted through shared resource extraction, ceremonial activities, and intermarriage. The Serrano inhabited the San Bernardino Mountains and the desert eastward to the Oasis of Mara. They practiced a hunting-and-gathering regime that exploited different elevations, depending on the availability of seasonal resources. As the closest group to the Spanish settlements along the California coast, they became targets for capture and conversion by Franciscan missionaries. Forced removal, disease, and persecution by Euro-Americans impacted their population to the degree that they abandoned their semi-permanent camp at the Oasis of Mara by the mid-nineteenth century.[14]

Most of the Chemehuevi lived along the Colorado River in close association with the much larger Mojave Indian tribe. The agricultural Mojave people tolerated the Chemehuevi, because they exploited different resources. The latter group used the resources of the Mojave Desert more extensively, including the area now included within the national park. After decades of living in proximity to each other, pressure from white settlers led to a war between the Chemehuevi and the Mojave from 1864 to 1867. At that time, the outnumbered Chemehuevi temporarily retreated into the desert, and some moved to the abandoned Oasis of Mara. Later, after peace returned, many moved back to the Colorado River, but some families stayed at the oasis. The descendents of those who remained form the Twentynine Palms Band of Mission Indians. They own a reservation in the city close to the park's headquarters as well as in other lands.[15]

The Cahuilla are closely related to the Serrano and lived south of them from the San Jacinto Mountains eastward to the Coachella Valley and beyond. Like the Serrano, they followed a seasonal pattern of resource exploitation that utilized different altitudinal zones. In many cases, both the Cahuilla and the Serrano gathered food in the mountains and transported it to semi-permanent camps at oases in the desert. The Cahuilla occupied semi-permanent camps at different elevations and differentiated themselves into mountain, Morongo Pass, and desert subgroups. The desert Cahuilla used Cottonwood Spring in the southern part of the park as well as Palm Springs and Thousand Palms further west. The latter was a major ceremonial site that drew participants from all four tribes at different times. Today, the descendents of the Cahuilla occupy a number of the tiny reservations scattered across the section of Southern California south of the park.[16]

The only truly agricultural people prior to European contact were the Mojave, who had permanent settlements and a sizeable population, but they traveled more widely than the others. Several routes, both north and south of Joshua Tree, became 'salt trails': regular pathways to the coast that utilized water and food resources along the way. Later, these trails served Spanish and American travelers. The Mojave claimed much of California's desert land as part of their traditional territory, but they did not begrudge the other tribes. Thus, the Serrano, Cahuilla, and Chemehuevi not only accepted their passage and transitory use of food resources, but usually welcomed them as purveyors of information, trade goods, and social interchange. The Mojave even established food caches along their paths near sources of water, which the other groups apparently respected. One of their salt trails passed through the Oasis of Mara, and, later, a few Mojave Indians moved into the area with the Chemehuevi.

This pattern of residence and resource use illustrates important characteristics of the Native American experience in Southern California. First, each group had traditional areas they occupied and exploited, but they also shared abundant resources. Boundaries were approximate and changed through time. In some cases, a subsequent group might replace the pictographs of an earlier one by scouring petroglyphs over them to identify their claim. Much of the Joshua Tree area served all four groups, occasionally two or more at the same time in the same place. No band of any tribe would wipe out a source of food. Instead, they would leave enough for others and for future natural production. Second, tribal groups interacted regularly for social and ceremonial purposes. The population density was low, and the onslaught of Euro-American activities forced them to rely on each other. After the latter, pressure limited them to the small reservations, and many individuals from different tribes chose to live together. Though their numbers are small and their languages are deeply threatened, the Cahuilla, Chemehuevi, Mojave, and Serrano people still live around Joshua Tree National Park.[17]

The Native Americans who lived around the park found plenty of food in the environment, belying the initial European belief that the place was uninhabitable. An intimate knowledge of the plant resources and their seasonal patterns of growth and reproduction afforded a varied diet, medicinal remedies, and materials for clothing, tools, and shelter (Fig. D). Particularly important were nuts from pinyon pines, acorns, and mesquite pods as well as fruit from cactus and palms. Joshua trees provided flower buds, raw or roasted seeds, and leaves that could be worked into baskets and sandals. Creosote bushes provided leaves for medicinal or honey-sweetened tea and for remedies for bruises, wounds, and illnesses. Fan palms supplied fronds, used for making huts, as well as food. The Cahuilla burned the palm groves to increase the yield of fruit and moved palm seeds to auspicious locations, suggesting that California's Indians who lived away from the Colorado River had a pre-agricultural adaptation. Many animals provided protein, including bighorn sheep, deer, lizards, rabbits, and even insects and their larvae.[18]

The environment also supplied material for weapons, tools, and cooking implements. Hunters used arrows, sinew-backed bows, nets, and wooden traps to procure animals. The skins of rabbits and other wildlife could then be used for clothing and blankets. Craftsmen modified horns and bones for spoons and stirring utensils, and they used the copious monzogranite for manos and metates (grinding stones and bowls). Because of their composition, these are the most widely found relics in the park's archaeological sites. Some metates are actually ground into rock faces and can be seen by the discerning visitor. Natives also used stone from the area's formations to flake or carve arrowheads, knives, scrapers, and other tools. Fibers from the agave, yucca, and other plants supplied material for bags, cording, and mats.[19]

After Anglo-Americans moved into the region for good during the late nineteenth century, the Native American population quickly dwindled. The U.S. government established "trust areas" in the vicinity of the future national park, beginning with the Cabazon, Morongo, and Torres-Martinez Reservations during the mid-1870s. All were designated for the Cahuilla, although Serrano people also moved to the Morongo Reservation. During the 1890s, the government established another clutch of reservations, including the Augustine and Agua Caliente sites for the Cahuilla, the Twentynine Palms unit for the Chemehuevi, and, well to the west, the San Manuel Reservation for the Serrano. Most of the Mojave stayed on reservations along the Colorado River, although a few moved in with the Chemehuevi and the Cahuilla. By 1913, the Chemehuevi abandoned the Oasis of Mara, ending centuries of intermittent use and occupancy. By that time, Anglo-Americans had usurped the native descendants' opportunities to live at the oasis and hunt and gather in the surrounding desert. This new culture had different ideas about the desert and what livelihood and wealth it could provide.[20]

Arrival of the Europeans and Americans

The first Europeans to explore any part of California's deserts came from Spain. Alta California did not particularly appeal to the Spanish, but religious and political considerations drew them to the region. The missionaries' desire to "save Indian souls" led them to urge expansion of Spain's colonial empire. The subsequent Russian, British, or American incursions into the area galvanized the Spanish government to protect its claim by the 1770s. The most successful and famous of these moves brought Franciscan friars, led by Father Junipero Serra, up the Pacific Coast to the future San Francisco in 1769. Ultimately, the Spanish established twenty-one missions in California, from San Diego to Sonoma. Their efforts to find an overland route from Sonora to the southern coastal missions, however, did not enter the area known today as Joshua Tree National Park.

Supplying the missions by ship was expensive and difficult, so from the beginning, the Spanish sought a land route from its northwestern base in Sonora via the Colorado River area to the coastal missions. Unfortunately for them, harsh desert conditions and the hostility of the Yuma Indians rendered the trip dangerous and costly. In 1772, Pedro Fages, the future governor of Alta California, led an expedition from the coast eastward into the San Bernardino area hunting for escapees from the mission at San Diego. This episode did not establish a route but did introduce the Europeans to the Joshua tree, which they called a date palm. From 1774 to 1776, Juan Bautista de Anza led two expeditions specifically to open a route from Sonora to the southern coastal missions. The route he chose passed through the Imperial Valley but did not approach the modern Joshua Tree area. On one of his expeditions, Father Francisco Garces followed the Colorado River north and crossed the desert along the Mojave Trail, a popular Native American trade route that passes through Mojave National Preserve. Neither of these routes proved easy or safe, and the Spanish authorities essentially abandoned them.[21]

The principal problem the Spanish missions had was holding onto its "neophytes," as they called the baptized Indians. Runaways established contacts with interior groups, including the Cahuilla, and encouraged them to raid the sheep and cattle of the missions, but they also inadvertently spread European diseases. Meanwhile, Spanish officials planned to build another north–south axis of missions in the interior to protect the coastal ones while expanding their programs of settlement and proselytism. They could not, however, find the funds or personnel to carry this plan forward. In 1823, Mexico gained its independence from Spain and revived the effort to find a land route from the southern California coast to Sonora. That same year Captain Jose Romero traveled from the San Gabriel Mission in Los Angeles to find a Native American path called the Cocomaricopa Trail. The two-year expedition failed, but its sojourners probably reached the Eagle Mountains.[22]

Not long after the Romero expedition, to the consternation of the new republic's political authorities, American fur trappers appeared in Southern California, having come overland from the east. Jedediah Smith, of the Rocky Mountain Fur Company, led the first group along the Mojave Trail in November 1826. Soon, other trappers and guides, including Ewing Young and Christopher "Kit" Carson, followed. By the 1830s, some Americans stayed in California, usually with the encouragement of the local Mexican settlers. Although the Mexican government opposed this practice, skilled sailors from the American whaling ships would abandon their harsh, shipboard life to practice blacksmithing and other trades, which the far-flung Alta California province needed. Marriage to local senoritas contributed to the appeal of this practice by sailors who, if caught by their captains, were subject to severe punishment or even execution. Communications from these 'new' Mexican citizens and reports from traders and whalers returning to the East Coast ignited a strong desire by the American government and people to acquire California. After Mexico rebuffed

American efforts to buy the future state, a short and one-sided war (1846–1848) resulted in the militaristic acquisition by the U.S. of nearly half of Mexico's land, including California.[23]

The U.S. and Mexico signed the Treaty of Guadalupe Hidalgo on February 2, 1848. Nine days earlier, a work crew building a sawmill on California's American River far to the north found gold. Over the next five years, nearly a half-million people made their way to the state in search of instant wealth. Most failed. Many retreated from the Sierra Nevada to look for other goldfields, take up farming or ranching, or find jobs in coastal cities like Los Angeles. Compared to San Francisco, the southern metropolis grew slowly during the middle of the nineteenth century, but, later in the century, it began its meteoric rise to become, in 1984, the second-largest urban area in the nation. Many of the people drawn to Southern California began exploring the adjacent deserts. Others deliberately sought the 'frontier' qualities of the desert, including its possible mineral resources, its meager but untapped grazing potential, and a lifestyle removed from the conventions and legalities of the city.[24]

Economic Exploitation

For Euro-Americans, the two initial means of making a living in California's deserts were ranching and mining. Both were hardscrabble occupations that supported a relatively dispersed population and made nobody truly wealthy. The first Americans to use the Joshua Tree area consistently were cattlemen during the 1870s. At the time, the western, higher-elevation part of the future park received more rainfall than it presently does and supported a variety of native grasses, cactus, and other desert vegetation suitable for cattle. One of the earliest was William "Bill" McHaney, who drove Texas longhorns into the Lost Horse, Queen, and Pleasant Valleys in 1879. His brother, Jim McHaney, soon established an operation that brought cattle his gang rustled from Mexico and Arizona and returned stolen horses to those areas. They headquartered in an area called Cow Camp on the western end of the Wonderland of Rocks and kept their herds penned in Hidden Valley. The gang operated successfully for more than a decade. The attraction of this desert locale was its isolation. The nearest law enforcement officials were based in Banning, nearly fifty miles to the west. The establishment of Riverside County in 1893, immigration by miners into the area, and better law enforcement curtailed the illegal cattle operation during the last years of the nineteenth century.[25]

Legitimate cattle businesses moved into lands of the future park from the Morongo Basin (and Devil's Garden) and took advantage of the infrastructure developed by McHaney and others. One of the key figures was part-time miner C. O. Barker. A resident of Banning, he and his partner Will Shay, who served many years as sheriff of San Bernardino County, ran both cattle and horses in the higher-elevation valleys near modern Yucca Valley and Joshua Tree village. Barker began a dam that bears his name and which William F. ("Bill") Keys (Fig. 5.2) later improved. Barker and Shay ran the cattle operation until 1923, after which several short-term operators took over. In 1929, Katherine Barry and Harry Stacey acquired the interests but sold off their cattle upon establishment of the national monument in 1936. Nevertheless, grazing continued beyond the proclamation of Joshua Tree National Monument and did not officially end until the conclusion of World War II. South of the future park, a pair of brothers named Cram used Cottonwood Spring to water their herds. In addition to these professional ranchers, three of the miners who lived in the monument—Bill Keys, who moved to the area in 1910, and Tom and Jepp Ryan, who arrived shortly thereafter— began running cattle. Bill Keys clashed with the Barker–Shay operation when he filed homestead claims that eventually blocked the cowboys and their herds from the reservoir behind Barker Dam. The ensuing struggle resulted in at least one episode of non-fatal gunplay and a bristling enmity between Keys and Sheriff Shay. It set the stage for a major altercation three decades later that sent Keys to prison for manslaughter.[26]

The impact of the grazing business on the future park primarily affected the water resources. Ranchers and settlers built small dams to amass water in low places among the many rocks and boulders. These 'tanks' added to springs that the cattlemen adapted and to natural catchment sites available after precipitation. Most of the structures associated with the cattle business are gone, but remnants exist, particularly at Cow Camp where water troughs and the foundation and chimney of a cabin remain. The impact of the cattle on Joshua Tree's vegetation and on animals such as the bighorn sheep that depended on it is uncertain. If the number of cattle reached nearly 900, as some old-timers suggested, it surely diminished the vegetation and water at the time. Grazing may have hurt bighorns in the long run by decimating the forage, or it may have helped by providing water sources that would not otherwise exist.[27]

The discovery of gold in the Sierra Nevada foothills made mining the leading economic function in California for several decades after 1848. Although it came much later to the deserts, it dominated the region prior to World War I. Gold and silver attracted miners initially, but other minerals, including lead, zinc, and iron, also proved worthy of attention. Mining for gold began during the late 1860s in the Twentynine Palms area. The presence of water at the Oasis of Mara made it a natural headquarters for the brief flurry of mining that ensued. The town would come later, but the oasis immediately established its importance.[28]

When gold mining came to a new area, several needs had to be met. First, the infrastructure for mining had to be assembled. In many parts of the West, the initial technique was placer mining. This involved using a pan, rocker, or sluice to separate alluvial gold from a slurry of water and sedimentary material. Running water was scarce in the desert and had been for a long time. In the Joshua Tree area, "dry placering," a technique that used gravity and the wind to separate heavy gold particles from lighter material, did not produce much gold because its alluvial form was scarce. Commercial concentrations of minerals developed when they precipitated out of liquid magma, solidifying into igneous or metamorphic rock. When gold separated from the other material, it tended to collect together. Virtually all the gold and other minerals in Joshua Tree lay unexposed in solid rock. Thus, the miner needed tools and machines to dig out the rock, crush it into a fine powder, and separate the gold from the rest of the "tailings." Initially, digging was by hand but later was done with the use of power drills and earth-moving machines. All the precious metal mining in Joshua Tree was pit mining, where the workers dug vertical shafts and horizontal tunnels called "stopes" to access the gold-bearing ores. This required plenty of wood from surrounding higher-elevation forests to brace the tunnels and provide shelter on the surface for miners and their machinery (Plate 28).[29]

After removing ore by tram or conveyor belt, a miner had to pulverize it. The earliest miners used a device called an arrastra, which was nothing more than heavy stones attached to a turnstile pulled by horse, oxen, or people. The stones dragged over and crushed the ore. If the mine promised a good return, the claimants could use a California stamp mill, which raised and smashed down a series of heavy, iron "stamps" or drums attached to a camshaft. These machines required power by steam engine or electricity. They made a dreadful racket, as the stamps pounded down on the iron base and the partially broken ore. After reduction by the stamp mill to a powder, the gold in it could be separated by two processes.

The first, dating back centuries, was called amalgamation, and it required 'quicksilver' (mercury). Millworkers washed the ore across a mercury-covered plate, and the gold adhered to the mercury, forming an alloy. The rest of the material washed away. In Joshua Tree, mining companies located mills near a water source or piped water to the mine from a well or spring. Once the mercury/gold amalgam was separated, it could be heated to burn off the mercury. Amalgamation was also used for silver ore. The second dates to the late 1880s, when three Scots in Glasgow invented a more efficient method of separating the gold in a process known as cyanidation. Gold had an affinity for cyanide, as did silver, lead, and zinc, and it dissolved into a solution with the poisonous chemical. Millworkers mixed low-grade ore with the cyanide and water and stored it in large vats beside the mine or mill. The auriferous fluid could then be tapped and further treated to secure the gold.

Cyanidation extracted a much higher percentage of the gold from the ore than did amalgamation. Hence, when the process came to the mines of Joshua Tree, it allowed miners to re-work tailings from the earlier amalgamation. This process became important with the renewal of mining during the 1930s. In some cases, miners only partially processed their ore before shipping it to another millsite, where the gold could be better refined for a fee. One such location was the Wall Street Mill operated sporadically by Bill Keys from 1932 through the early 1950s (Plate 30). Keys made most of his money during the Great Depression by processing ore brought by other miners.[30]

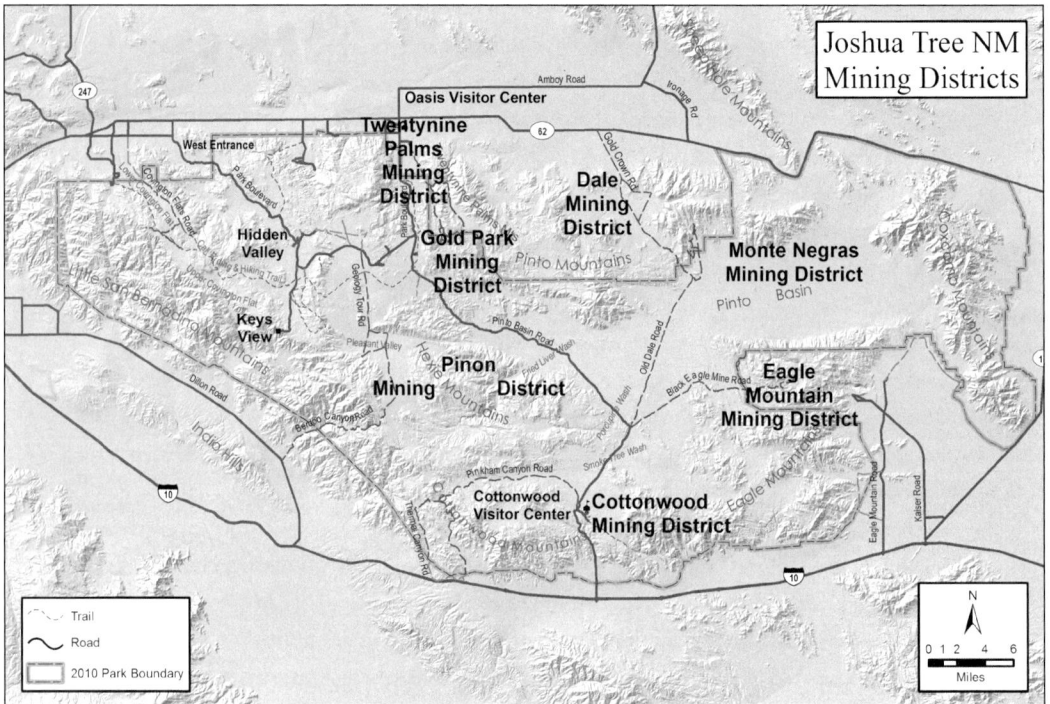

Joshua Tree NM
Mining Districts

247

Amboy Road

Oasis Visitor Center

Twentynine
Palms
Mining
District

West Entrance

62

Ironsite Rd

Gold Crown Rd

Dale
Mining
District

Monte Negras
Mining District

Hidden
Valley

Gold Park
Mining
District

Pinto Mountains

Pinto   Basin

Keys
View

Pleasant Valley

Pinto Basin Road

Pinon
Mining   District

Hexie Mountains

Old Dale Road

Dillon Road

Berdoo Canyon Road

Pinkham Canyon Road

Black Eagle Mine Road

Eagle
Mountain
Mining District

Smoke Tree Wash

Cottonwood
Visitor Center

Cottonwood
Mining District

Eagle Mountains

Eagle Mountain Road

Kaiser Road

Little San Bernardino Mountains

Coxcomb Mountains

Indio Hills

10

10

1

Trail
Road
2010 Park Boundary

N

0 1 2   4   6
Miles

MAP 1.3. Following procedures honed in the California Gold Rush of the mid-nineteenth century, miners established various districts to organize claims by individuals and small companies. Later, the General Land Office and, after 1946, the Bureau of Land Management assumed control of the claims process. Most of the successful gold mining took place from 1890 to 1910, with a brief revival during the 1930s. By the time the U.S. Congress established Joshua Tree National Monument most of the mines in the western and central areas had played out. Data source: Joshua Tree National Park GIS files. Delta Cartography.

The distance of the Joshua Tree mines from major settlements and suppliers of industrial machinery and tools required transportation over land that only a few Native American trails crossed.
Thus, miners had to scrape out wagon roads to and from every mine and mill to connect with the
railroads and rudimentary highways that passed by to the north and southwest. Miners in the
rugged slopes and canyons between the Little San Bernardino, Pinto, and Eagle Mountains also
demanded food, clothing, and daily necessities. A rudimentary supply system created nodes of
commercial activity, especially around Twentynine Palms. As occurred all over the western United
States, when miners flocked to an area, transportation and service workers followed. In this case,
people intimately explored and established settlements of varying duration in a region previously
regarded as largely useless and even threatening.

In the early California gold camps, miners invented a legal system whereby an individual or
group could lay claim to an area for mining purposes. The land technically was federal property, but
a miner could hold his claim as long as he (or she) continued working it. Mining districts formed
to hammer out the rules and enforce them. This home-grown system became law with the federal
Mining Acts of 1866 and 1872. Mining districts continued to be established, but registering a claim
became a function of the General Land Office (later the Bureau of Land Management). In the
mountains of Joshua Tree, the sparse population and distance from law enforcement meant that
holding a claim for the first several decades was by no means assured. Individuals who found likely
sources of gold or silver usually had to sell the claim or take on partners to defend the mine against
outlaws and claim jumpers. When production and work crews increased and settlements grew
larger, the danger from outlaws waned, as did rustling and horse thievery in the grazing business.
Eventually, seven major mining districts formed within or adjacent to the area now encompassed by
the national park (Map 1.3). The small strikes around Twentynine Palms led to formation of the
first district with the same name during the early 1880s. The Gold Park District just to the south
soon followed. During the 1890s, miners organized the Dale District around much richer ground
to the east of Twentynine Palms. During the same period, they explored the ranges to the south
and east in the Hexie, Cottonwood, and Eagle Mountains and organized four more districts called
Piñon, Cottonwood, Eagle Mountain, and Monte Negras.[31]

The most productive period for mining gold lasted from the 1890s until just before World
War I. Prospectors sank hundreds of exploratory shafts, frequently finding nothing of value. They
filed scores of claims and set up dozens of mines, most of which returned meager to modest profits.
Several, however, handsomely repaid their investors. The most successful was the Lost Horse Mine
on the mountain of the same name, approximately one mile east of the road to Keys View (Fig.
5.1). Frank Diebold discovered the promising quartz vein but, fearing the McHaney gang, sold it in
1893 to Johnny Lang, another recent arrival to the area. Lang understood Diebold's concern, for he,

too, had met Jim McHaney. Earlier, he had lost a horse and, while searching for it, wandered into the McHaney camp. He was fortunate to escape with a warning. After this episode, he supposedly named the area Lost Horse Valley. Lang took on three partners for protection, filed the claim in December 1893, and began working the new mine to which he gave the same name. Despite their success, Lang's partners sold their rights to the mine in 1895 to Thomas and Jepp Ryan. In a later interview, Bill Keys insisted that Lang retained an interest in the mine but was forced to give it up when he was caught stealing some of the gold. The Ryan group, including wealthy Montana rancher Matthew Ryan Jr., and several others, patented the mine two years later. Financial backing from Matthew allowed them to replace Lang and company's old two-stamp mill with a ten-stamp one. They also ran a water pipeline three miles from the Lost Horse Spring to facilitate the milling. Ultimately, the Ryans encountered a fault running through the mine and lost the ore-bearing seam of quartz. By 1907, the mine played out, although it continued to receive periodic investigation and reworking of its tailings as late as the 1930s. In 1982, geologists E. J. and D. L. Fife estimated that the mine ultimately produced 10,500 ounces of gold and 16,000 ounces of silver, which would be worth around $4,300,000 today.[32]

The Desert Queen Mine was another early, successful venture, although it reinforced the fears of early miners about holding their claims. Frank L. James, an employee at the Lost Horse Mine, discovered the rich vein in 1894 while prospecting on his day off in the northern Queen Valley east of the McHaney homestead. Jim McHaney and his gang learned of the discovery, and one gang member, Charles Martin, subsequently shot and killed James. Somehow he was acquitted on a self-defense plea, and McHaney took over the mine. Since the McHaneys were cattlemen and lacked the experience and finances to fully develop the mine, they brought in outside investors, who ultimately extracted more than 3,700 ounces of gold during the next five years. After the turn of the twentieth century, however, the yield steeply declined. Bill Keys bought an interest in the mine in 1911 and, not long after, took over Bill McHaney's old homestead, which he renamed the Desert Queen Ranch. Keys worked the mine himself and also leased it to other miners on a yearly basis. Work continued well beyond the establishment of Joshua Tree National Monument, although it only produced 144 ounces of gold during the twentieth century.[33]

Mining for precious metals lagged in the region after World War I, but the Great Depression and adoption of cyanidation brought desperate people back either to prospect for new mines or scour the old pits and tailings for anything they could find. Many came from Los Angeles, forging a relationship between the city and Joshua Tree's mines that would later bedevil the early managers of the national monument. With improved technology, a number of new operations began, including the Gold Crown, Mastodon, and Silver Bell mines. Most of these latter-day miners struggled to eke out a living while trying to supplement their incomes with other jobs. Many dispirited mine owners eventually quit, at which point the always opportunistic Bill Keys purchased or simply took over their abandoned claims.

By 1936, miners paid more attention to the less-precious minerals in the area. One of the most significant finds was a substantial body of iron ore in the Eagle Mountains. Initially, miners looked for gold and silver, but, later, they excavated some copper and zinc. Iron was not as valuable, but it was present in large quantity. William Stevens and Thomas Doffelmeyer located the Iron Chief Mine around 1892, sold it in 1897, but quickly reacquired and operated it until 1902. During that decade, the mine produced approximately $150,000 in gold at the prices of the time. They piped water eighteen miles from Cottonwood Spring for milling the ore. They continued to file claims on parcels adjacent to their original mine, until they controlled a strip of land eight miles long and up to two miles wide. The gold-mining operation was essentially moribund in 1909, when L. S. Barnes purchased it and other nearby claims. He sold them to the Southern Pacific Railroad for $300,000. Everyone knew about the iron ore, but the mine remained underdeveloped until decades later, when the nation needed iron and steel to wage World War II in the Pacific.[34]

The impacts of mining and milling on the landscape and resources of Joshua Tree National Park are both obvious and potentially dangerous. Recent studies have located more than 300 abandoned mines within the park's current boundary. Many have multiple adits, airshafts, and other openings. Abandoned infrastructure lies rusting in many parts of the park. Hazard investigators have identified tailings laced with mercury or cyanide. During the boom era and again during the Great Depression, miners cut much of the arboreal vegetation for fuel, mine timbers, and building construction. The NPS has attempted to rehabilitate much of the dense network of wagon roads and trails, but many routes remain visible, especially in the backcountry. Nevertheless, the history and artifacts of mining attract visitors and serve as a primary historic fabric for park interpreters. The chief cultural resource sites that draw tourists include the Lost Horse and Desert Queen Mines and the Wall Street Mill. Indeed, the Desert Queen Ranch of Bill Keys is the primary interpretive site in the park, including its mining story, for that was his primary activity during his productive years in the deserts of Joshua Tree.[35]

The Desert for Tourism, Health, and Escape

Miners and ranchers sought to exploit the deserts of the future Joshua Tree National Park for financial benefit. Other Americans came to the deserts for land, health, and recreation. Available land always generated enthusiasm for a new region, even one as seemingly forbidding as the deserts of California. Two laws passed by the U.S. Congress in 1862 dramatically facilitated land acquisition in the western United States and encouraged people to move to the deserts east of San Bernardino and Riverside. The first, the Homestead Act, was enacted after frontier settlement bogged down in the Great Plains. It gave 160 acres for only a ten-dollar filing fee to any head of household who would settle there for five years.[36] The second law was the Pacific Railroad Act, which awarded land to railroad companies to encourage construction of the transcontinental railroad through the empty Western states and territories.

The Central Pacific Railroad was one of the companies that built the first transcontinental railroad, and it subsequently became the Southern Pacific Railroad (SPRR). In 1873, the SPRR began constructing a line through the Colorado Desert. By May 1877, it connected Los Angeles with the western bank of the Colorado River opposite Yuma, Arizona. Not only did it provide easy transportation into the desert, but it caused the Government Land Office to survey much of the land surrounding the rail line. The Pacific Railroad Act promised the company alternate sections of land totaling ten square miles for every mile of track that it built. These lands were to be located within a strip of territory ten miles wide on each side of the tracks. If such land was already settled or allocated for another purpose, then the railroad would receive "in-lieu" or "indemnity" lands somewhere else. These lands could then be sold to settlers, reimbursing the railroad for its construction costs and providing future clientele for its trains. The Homestead Act plus cheap railroad property provided ample opportunities for people wishing to acquire desert land well into the twentieth century.[37]

Miners and cattlemen such as Bill Keys used the Homestead Act and mining laws to develop homes and bases for their economic activities. Others settled to work for the railroad or to serve travelers on the evolving transportation system. These service activities boosted the populations of the settlements around the future national park. The city of Indio began when the Southern Pacific Company opened a depot and hotel at the halfway point between Yuma and Los Angeles in order to supply well water to passing trains. The company worked hard to develop a town that would satisfy its employees and railroad tourists in such a hot and desolate area. Those efforts soon drew other people to the town. Among the travelers riding those trains at the turn of the twentieth century were men and women seeking adventure and excitement in the exotic environment of the desert. Some wrote newspaper articles, books, or guides, highlighting their experiences and explaining the attractions and perils of the area. John C. Van Dyke, in particular, caught the attention of readers in both California and the eastern states. Born in New Jersey, he became an art historian and critic. His urge to study and describe California's deserts stemmed from his aesthetic appreciation of the landscape and its natural history. Scientists, too, came to explore the region's geology, botany, and archaeology.[38]

Sites with adequate water became early favorites among the explorers and new residents of the deserts. One was Palm Springs, an oasis lying at the base of Mount San Jacinto. Another was the site of a well dug by cattleman Chuck Warren and his sons. Known as Warren's Well or Lone Star (after the local Lone Star Ranch), it is now within the town of Yucca Valley. A third location was the Oasis of Mara, site of the city of Twentynine Palms. All three benefitted from the realization by late-nineteenth-century doctors that dry desert air could help patients with respiratory problems. Judge John Guthrie McCallum, of San Francisco, came to Palm Springs in 1884 seeking health for his son who suffered from tuberculosis. He was the first permanent non-Indian settler. He purchased land from the Southern Pacific and built an aqueduct to supply water. It was the first step in the irrigation that would make the town and Coachella Valley into a rich agricultural center producing crops such as alfalfa, apricots, dates, figs, grapefruit, grapes, and oranges. Two years later, the tiny community had its first hotel. In 1887, the town became official with platted lots and an expanding irrigation network. Shortly after the turn of the twentieth century, hotels and other tourism businesses proliferated, convincing the owners of some sanitariums to convert them into tourist inns. By the late 1920s, the town had become famous as a winter resort for movie stars and other wealthy patrons.[39]

Warren's Well was an important stop for ranchers, miners, and horse-drawn supply trains traveling to Twentynine Palms and the Coachella Valley. Several wet years, beginning in 1912, drew some homesteaders to the area, hoping to develop farms and ranches. Many failed when dry years returned. During the 1920s, however, veterans of World War I who were suffering from the effects of mustard gas sought the hot, dry desert climate for its healing properties. The dawn of automobile travel also brought residents and roadside businesses that formed the town of Yucca Valley during the years from 1923 through the 1940s.[40]

Dr. James B. Luckie, of Pasadena, California, treated many war veterans who had suffered inhalation of toxic gases and other people afflicted with respiratory or heart ailments. During the 1920s, many doctors still sent people with breathing problems to Santa Monica. According to Frank Bagley, a veteran who suffered from asthma, Luckie began exploring the desert in search of a place with clean, dry air plus an elevation of at least 2,000 feet, making it cooler than Palm Springs. He settled in Twentynine Palms and began attracting veterans and other health seekers to his clinic. Bagley was one of the first veterans to relocate to the town and acquire land. He opened one of the first stores in the new town, which became a center for the growing but dispersed population. By the mid-1920s, Twentynine Palms widely advertised its salubrious climate and available land in regional newspapers. Although Yucca Valley and Twentynine Palms did not achieve the success of Palm Springs as resort destinations, both drew permanent residents and seasonal visitors seeking their own desert properties and experiences. Many maintained primary residences in the coastal cities but enjoyed the contrast offered by vacation properties in the desert.[41]

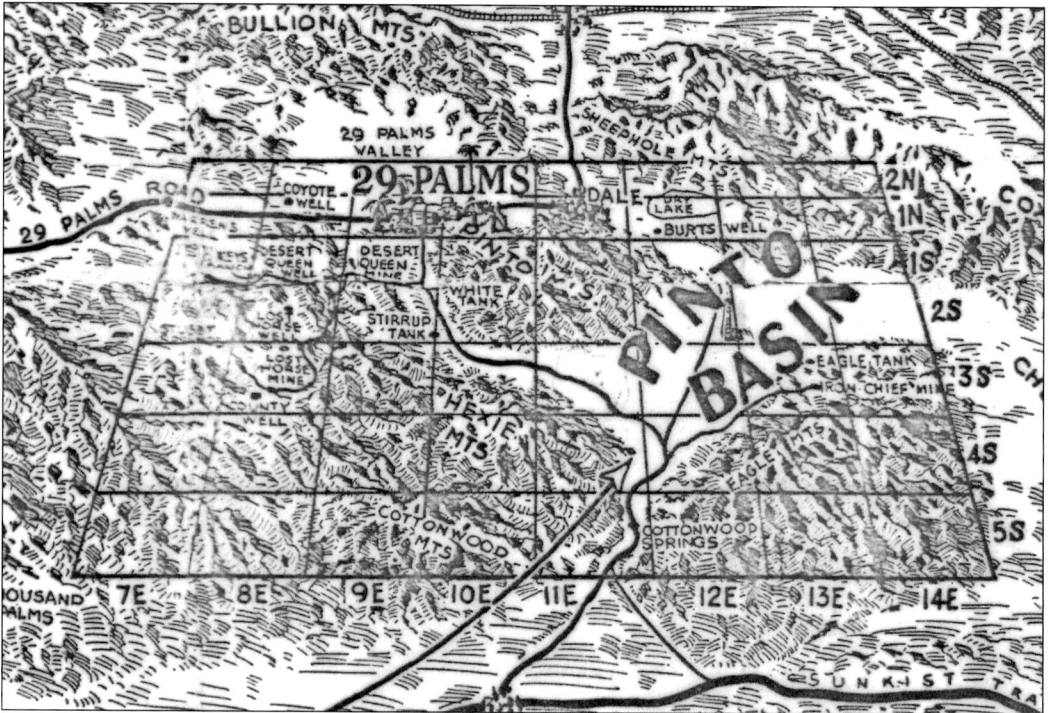

MAP 1.4. Beginning in the 1920s, real-estate agents widely advertised property and subdivision opportunities in the Joshua Tree area. This promotional map shows a proposed grid for land division in the region. From 1928 to 1931, the Security Land Corporation sold hundreds of former Southern Pacific Railroad Company plots in the Pinto Basin before going bankrupt. Source: Huntington Archives, HM 68366. Huntington Library, San Marino, California.

It did not take long for real-estate dealers and assorted speculators to move in and take advantage of the emerging positive image of the desert and its financial promise (Map 1.4). As interest in the Morongo Valley and Twentynine Palms areas grew, developers from Los Angeles saw opportunities for quick profits. They promoted a number of exurban subdivision schemes with ads and short articles in local newspapers and produced flyers and mailers, urging people to buy property not only for a residence or vacation home, but also as an investment. Every ad promised that land prices would soar in the future. so those who bought lots for speculation would reap great rewards. One ad, promoting a subdivision near Twentynine Palms, featured blurbs about the rich mines and booming tourism of the area plus a "report" about the huge profits made by an investor wise enough to buy desert land near Tucson, Arizona, before the town expanded in that direction. All the promotional literature assured potential buyers that development of water systems and transportation was imminent. Most of the settlement focused on the dirt track that would become CA 62 from Yucca Valley to Twentynine Palms, but, by the mid-1920s, speculators turned their attention to several valleys and basins that would become parts of JTNP.[42]

The principal areas that developers coveted were the Hidden, Lost Horse, and Pleasant Valleys and Pinto Basin. Half of the land belonged to the SPRR and the rest to the federal government in a checkerboard pattern. Real-estate companies purchased land from the railroad, because federal laws made acquisition of government tracts by a commercial entity problematic. The price for SPRR lands in the Hidden and Lost Horse Valleys was comparatively high, so most sales there went to individuals. One development company investigated Pleasant Valley but did not carry out its plan. The Pinto Basin, however, by far the largest area between the Coachella Valley and CA 62, seemed ripe for development. Speculator LeRoy Harrod, of Los Angeles, purchased land in the basin as well as in Twentynine Palms. When Lake County Development Syndicate, Inc., bought large tracts there in 1928, Harrod urged it to raise lot prices, which he called "ridiculously small," hoping to see his own property rise in value. The company soon changed its name to the Security Land Corporation, hired an engineer to determine the status of water in the basin, and began advertising its lots with an order form that urged urban customers to "Speculate! This is Your Chance at California Real Estate Profits."[43]

The ads worked, and scores of people bought more than 300 lots, most of them ranging in size from five to twenty acres. But problems soon surfaced. Security Land Corporation fired its president, Jay J. MacSweeney, in October 1931, alleging misappropriation of funds. A company called Pinto Basin Mutual Water Company that formed to find and deliver water to the new landholders had to sue Security Land to secure payment for work already accomplished. Meanwhile, land purchasers did not receive deeds for their property and land taxes were not paid in 1931 and 1932. Soon, the California Supreme Court appointed a receiver, who then had to contact all the landholders and

FIG. 1.2. The Colorado River Aqueduct, one of the primary sources of drinking water in Southern California, runs through the park near the Coxcomb Mountains. The Metropolitan Water District of Southern California (based in Los Angeles) conceived of and built the aqueduct from 1933 to its opening on January 7, 1939. It conveys water some 242 miles from Lake Havasu in San Bernadino County to Lake Mathews in Riverside County. Photograph by the author (original in color), January 2013.

straighten out the financial mess. It took until December 1932 for many property owners to receive official deeds. In the interim, they found out that water in the Pinto Basin was too deep to be economically accessible. Thousands of acres of land were now in private hands with no prospect of development or resale. Most were also tax delinquent.[44]

One other development project significantly affected the Joshua Tree area during the campaign to establish the unit and throughout its subsequent history. The City of Los Angeles had secured water from the Owens River east of the Sierra Nevada in 1913, but many local officials and leading citizens worried that it might prove inadequate for the population growth they foresaw. One likely source for more water was the Colorado River. Already the Imperial Irrigation District, which formed in 1911 and received approval for an All-American Canal seven years later, had a major diversion of water from the river. In 1923, Chief Engineer William Mulholland, of the Los Angeles Bureau of Water Works, began surveying a possible route for an aqueduct from the distant river to the rising metropolitan area. The price tag for such a project would be so large that the city organized a consortium of regional towns to justify it. After receiving approval from the state legislature and Governor Clement C. Young, the Metropolitan Water District of Southern California (MWD) officially incorporated on December 6, 1928 (Fig. 1.2).

For the next several years, the MWD pursued legal and financial support for the enormous project. Two key events occurred in June 1932 that enabled the project to go forward. First, on June 6, the California Supreme Court confirmed the legality of a $220,000,000 bond issue to finance the aqueduct. Twelve days later, on June 18, Congress granted a right-of-way through federal land to construct it. The aqueduct was an enormous project that would take almost seven years to complete. Its route began at Lake Havasu behind the Bureau of Reclamation's Parker Dam, tunneled under portions of the Coxcomb, Eagle, and Cottonwood Mountains, and then hugged the base of the Little San Bernardino Mountains. The right-of-way included not only the actual aqueduct path, but also parcels of nearby land for work camps, borrow pits, and areas to hold spoils from digging the waterway. Many of the parcels would later be included in the national monument.[45]

The Joshua Tree Area in 1936

The natural environment of Joshua Tree is a complex and difficult one. Six mountain ranges surround dry, desert basins and valleys with limited water and sparse vegetation. Yet people have lived in the area for millennia. The Native American imprint was light and has been all but eliminated by subsequent Euro-American activities. Spanish exploration and American surveys left equally shallow footprints. Only during the late 1860s did people begin to alter the environment and landscape in noticeable ways. Grazing and mining seriously impacted the natural vegetation, generated infrastructure, and left waste. Later, the automobile opened the area to exploration and adventure, and people from Los Angeles and other towns in Southern California began to see the place as something other than a wasteland with only mineral resources. Among them were early asthma and gas-warfare victims of World War I who moved in, seeking health and comfort in the arid atmosphere. Recreationalists came, too, and some filed for homesteads. Eventually, tendrils of semi-urban development stretched along highways, ranches, and water projects north and south of the future park. Real-estate speculators followed with schemes of variable merit. This last wave brought more people than all the previous activities combined. By early 1936, Twentynine Palms was a booming health resort, while Palm Springs and the Coachella Valley were on their way to world fame. Then came the National Park Service.

CHAPTER TWO

A Monument at Any Price

ON AUGUST 10, 1936, President Franklin D. Roosevelt signed Proclamation 2193, establishing Joshua Tree National Monument on 825,340 acres of land east of Riverside and north of Palm Springs, California. It capped a complex and problem-riddled campaign to protect a broad swath of desert flora, including the Mojave Desert's signature species, the Joshua tree. The proclamation, however, ignored problems that would plague the unit's managers for decades to come. For example, tens of thousands of acres of railroad lands, state school lands, private holdings, and mining claims lay widely-scattered throughout the monument. In an effort to minimize these problems, the acreage of the proposed monument was reduced by twenty-seven percent, omitting a variety of recommended resource sites and angering its most enthusiastic proponents. The story of Joshua Tree National Park's initial establishment as a national monument is thus one of ambition, idealism, reality checks, and compromise brought through negotiations and political maneuvering.[1]

Three factors led to the establishment of Joshua Tree National Monument despite significant local problems and the previous establishment of a much-larger national monument in California's Death Valley. First, scientists, conservationists, gardening enthusiasts, and desert aficionados sought protection for the fragile flora of the desert, especially the iconic Joshua tree. Second, officials and residents of Los Angeles craved a major recreation area to cope with the demands of the city's rapidly growing automotive public. Third, the National Park Service (NPS) and the occasionally competing California State Park (CSP) system looked for ways to fill out their systems with quality examples of the natural and cultural heritage of the region as well as geographical representation within the state.

Minerva Hamilton Hoyt and Protecting Desert Flora

In 1926, O. W. Howard, a wealthy resident of South Pasadena, staged an exhibition of desert plants in Los Angeles to a curious and appreciative public. Among those in attendance was his friend and neighbor, Minerva Hamilton Hoyt, another ardent supporter of protecting and displaying the desert's extraordinary flora (Fig. 2.1). Born on a cotton plantation in Mississippi, she married a wealthy surgeon from New York City, Dr. Albert Sherman Hoyt, and the couple moved to California during the late 1890s. While traveling westward, she was captivated by the desert vegetation, as the

FIG. 2.1. Minerva Hamilton Hoyt, from Holmes County, Mississippi, became a leading socialite in Pasadena, California, and a self-trained expert on desert botany. Her floral displays in New York City, Boston, and London won awards. She founded the International Desert Conservation League in 1930, received worldwide recognition and honors for her work, and almost single-handedly drove the government to establish what today is Joshua Tree National Park. She is an example of a woman in the conservation movement who used her keen mind, indefatigable energy, and considerable fortune to build the national park system at a time when men dominated the National Park Service and the rest of the national business/government scene. Photographer unknown, early 1920s. Photograph donated to the park by the Hoyt family. Joshua Tree National Park Photo Archives, Cat. 20575, Image 065.

train carrying her to Los Angeles passed through the unfamiliar and often desolate territory she would later work so hard to protect. She settled in South Pasadena and quickly became a leader in Southern California's artistic, social service, and gardening organizations. After the death of her husband in 1918, she increasingly turned to the desert for exploration, peace, and solace. She later wrote, "the desert with its elusive beauty . . . possessed me, and I constantly wished that I might find some way to preserve its natural beauty."[2]

In 1927, when Howard again arranged a desert display, this time for the Pasadena Horticultural Association, Hoyt convinced him to help her develop a desert conservation exhibit for the Garden Club of America show in New York City the following spring. During the next two years, she created elaborate displays using live flora and fauna in New York City, Boston, and, finally, London, England. She had multiple railroad cars and a ship loaded with plants and animals for ever-larger display areas, plus up to eight airplanes to provide fresh blossoms each day. She stressed the fragility and eerie beauty of the scenes and emphasized the dangers faced by this and other desert biomes. Her magnificent exhibits easily won top honors at all three shows as well as personal awards and recognition from scientists and political figures around the world. Based on this platform of renown and internationally recognized authority, she turned her attention to her adopted desert with the idea of permanently protecting it.[3]

In California's deserts, things were not going well for the biotic resources. Ironically, encouraged by Howard's and Hoyt's lavish exhibits, Southern Californians enjoyed surrounding their urban and suburban homes with transplanted desert vegetation, especially cactus. Particularly alarming was the fate of a broad alluvial fan near Morongo Pass called the Devil's Garden. Desert traveler and author George Wharton James described it in his 1906 book, *The Wonders of the Colorado Desert*:

> It is simply a vast native, forcing ground for a thousand varieties of cactus. They thrive here as if specially guarded. . . . Delightfully interspersed with these various cactuses are flowering creosote bushes, the whole forming a singularly strange and grotesque piece of landscape gardening. As far as I know it is unique in the United States.[4]

Unfortunately, its proximity to the road from Los Angeles to Palm Springs, as well as the ease of removing mature desert plants like the barrel cacti, led to its denudation and destruction by commercial florists and amateur gardeners.

As the Colorado Desert gave up its cacti and native palms, the Mojave Desert's most-famous species also suffered destruction. While smaller Joshua trees were uprooted to adorn urban lots, larger specimens also attracted unwanted attention due to the qualities of their wood. Reporter Harry Carr explained:

Nobody paid much attention to the Joshua until lately. As soon as they began to realize its beauty and unique character there began the wholesale foray into the desert to dig them up. A Joshua tree means absolutely nothing except in the desert. What gives it interest and charm is the setting. . . . There is no use kidding ourselves about it. At the present rate of destruction the cactus of the desert and the Joshua trees will be gone within two years. That is the opinion of experts; not my opinion. There are also the manufacturers. Yuccas and Joshua trees are used in various manufacturing businesses. They are made into artificial limbs; into shields for young, growing trees and into furniture for the movies. The chairs that comedians slam each other over the head with are usually made of yucca or Joshua trees. The third marauder is the idiot child who goes out with his girl on an automobile ride and sets Joshua trees on fire to see them blaze. They have a habit of signaling to each other—auto parties—with these blazing torches.[5]

Botanists and conservationists throughout the region and the nation decried the wanton burning of Joshua trees by motor-tourists, who they called ignorant and short-sighted. The mindless destruction reached a crisis point in June 1930, when someone set fire to the largest and possibly oldest of the Joshua trees eighteen miles east of Lancaster. Many estimated the tree, eighty feet high and nine feet in diameter, to be more than 1,000 years old.[6]

Flushed with success from her popular desert exhibits, Hoyt was enraged by rampant destruction of desert environments nearby and throughout the world. On March 15, 1930, she announced the formation of the International Desert Conservation League (IDCL). As its founder and president, she immediately began a campaign to protect California's deserts in some type of government reserve, preferably as a unit of the national park system. Ironically, her initial success at convincing a government to save a plot of desert flora took place in Mexico. With her vigorous encouragement, the Mexican government established a 10,000-acre cactus forest reserve near La Paz, Baja California, in May 1931. At the same time, the National University of Mexico conferred on her the honorary title of Professor Extraordinary of Botany, the fourth person and first woman in the world to receive the award.[7]

The IDCL quickly established a large board of honorary vice presidents, including a cross-section of the world's famous and expert botanists as well as important university presidents, museum directors, and a few significant government figures such as Gifford Pinchot, founder of the U.S. Forest Service (USFS), and Horace Albright, the second director of the NPS. Dr. N. L. Britton, of the New York Botanical Garden, explained the league and its purposes: "the necessity for withdrawing from private ownership, selected desert areas, with characteristic, often endemic plants and animals and prohibiting the removal of floral and faunal elements, has become apparent, and this is given emphasis as a major purpose of the League."[8] Soon, Minerva Hoyt would use the prestige of her honorary vice presidents, and her own personal funds, to direct the local campaign for a national park or monument for her beloved desert. She also offered a $100 reward for the apprehension of the vandals who had destroyed the huge Joshua tree near Lancaster.[9]

The Recreation Imperative

While conservation-minded Southern Californians fretted about the destruction of desert flora, the protection of other striking desert wonders and provision of a large, nearby recreation area consumed many government and civic leaders. As early as 1927, a group of scientists, conservationists, and educators from Los Angeles, calling itself the "Joint Parks Committee," wrote to the commissioner of the General Land Office (GLO) requesting that he withdraw from the public domain specific sections of land containing important attractions in the deserts of California. Included among them were Red Rock Canyon, Morongo Pass (and Devil's Garden), Painted Canyon near Mecca, and Thousand Palm Canyon near Edom.[10]

Once Minerva Hoyt's campaign for a desert national park became known, letters of support poured in to NPS officials. According to a state-funded study, Californians owned eight percent of the nation's automobiles, well above the per capita rate for the nation as a whole.[11] Organizations such as the Automobile Club of Southern California urged the government to recognize the need for a large, protected recreation area for its growing membership. Yet Stephen Mather, the enthusiastic first director of the NPS, believed national parks should foster inspiration, the study of nature, and passive enjoyment of America's heritage and natural wonders. Many forms of outdoor recreation were not appropriate in the national parks as Mather envisioned them.[12]

Nevertheless, many Southern Californians preferred the mantle of national park status due to the financial benefits of having a park supported by federal taxes as well as the prestige it brought to the region and, presumably, its inhabitants. W. H. Anderson, a leading attorney and businessman from Los Angeles, wrote to Secretary of the Interior Harold Ickes:

> Southern California feels that it has not been duly recognized in the matter of our great national monuments. None such, unless I am very much mistaken, has been created in our part of the State. Northern California has its many National Parks and monuments, which have been recognized and are under the fostering care of the nation. Central California has its wonderful Yosemite Park and Death Valley. There are other like preserves scattered through other parts of California. Southern California alone is without any such. Therefore, all of us feel that the time is ripe for recognizing our section of the state in this behalf, and there could be no more distinctive recognition than the selection of her rarely beautiful and unique desert to that end.[13]

Eventually, the NPS had to warn locals about this provincial approach, explaining it was an unacceptable rationale to justify a new park. Assistant Director Harold C. Bryant responded to another urging from C. K. Edmunds, President of Pomona College, that "no emphasis [should] be placed on the fact that there is no national park in southern California. If it is a purely southern California matter it must eventually become a state park rather than a national one."[14]

Designing Two Park Systems

Another motivation for founding a desert park stemmed from the desire by both state and national park agencies to expand their systems, somewhat belying Bryant's comment above. Both the NPS and California State Parks (CSP) were shaped by a progressive philosophy that government should engage in conservation and provide recreation opportunities for the public, and they cooperated to an extent in assuring protection for quality sites in California.[15]

The U.S. Congress had established the NPS on August 25, 1916, to manage the collection of parks and monuments haphazardly run by a few officials at the U.S. Department of the Interior. Stephen Mather and his assistant and ultimate successor, Horace Albright, came to their tasks with missionary zeal. They had good reason to pursue their tasks with vigor. The USFS, a part of the U.S. Department of Agriculture (USDA), loudly argued that it should run the parks and that this division of land management between multiple agencies was unnecessary and improper. Hence, the very survival of the new NPS was at stake.[16]

Mather and Albright sought to popularize the national park system by expanding its distribution to all parts of the nation and establishing their agency as chief protector of important natural and historical sites. In response, a variety of public officials, academics, and ordinary citizens nominated hundreds of sites. Provincial pride and economic hopes led many to propose any and all areas in their regions, but many of them were either too small, inaccessible, or of dubious quality. The NPS wanted only the very best examples of ecosystems and historic places, yet it was loath to dismiss any proposal outright. Director Mather proposed one solution in 1921 by co-hosting a meeting of state officials aimed at fostering park systems in each state to absorb less-significant sites and provide for more common recreational pursuits.[17]

The NPS's drive to expand a representative system and the public's enthusiasm for nominating potential parks brought the agency to the deserts of Southern California. NPS leaders came with specific rules and 'traditions' in their hunt for new parks. In 1929, the Camp Fire Club of America, with editorial approval from NPS Director Horace Albright, published a small brochure entitled "National Park Standards," which described what steps should be taken to identify, evaluate, nominate, and eventually manage a proposed site. First, it explained two considerations to guide park proposals: (1) The park areas must be of national significance to warrant their commitment to national care, and (2) the area of each unit should be large enough to ensure proper management of its resources. After a discussion of correct management guidelines, the brochure's author elaborated specific NPS and legislative steps necessary to ensure adherence to the above standards. Chief among them was complete control of the assessment of proposed areas by the NPS. The brochure warned that "Congress should not empower individuals, committees, or commissions to choose new National Parks or to determine their contents and boundaries, but it should depend on the government's one permanent expert park organization, the National Park Service, which alone possesses the requisite knowledge, tradition, and experience, united with responsibility to the people."[18] The NPS would seek input from experts and be cognizant of local support or opposition, but it would make the final decision on whether to recommend a new proposal to Congress. This would become a significant factor in the campaign to establish Joshua Tree National Monument, as agency personnel could not agree on the worthiness of the area for national park system status.

During the 1920s and early 1930s, a curious assortment of Southern California places, ranging from the pristine and beautiful to the bizarre and unexpected, was brought to the attention of the NPS. Among them were Borrego Palm Canyon, Giant Pictograph, Inscription Canyon, Kokoweef (as well as several other caves near Valley Wells), Morongo Pass (and Devil's Garden), Mystic Maze, Painted Canyon, Red Rock Canyon, Salton Basin (and Sea), and Thousand Palms. Congress authorized a national monument for Indian Palm Canyon adjacent to Palm Springs in 1922, but the Agua Caliente Band of Cahuilla Indians refused to give up the land, which the act required. Despite its legislative mandate, the proposed national monument never became a reality. Today, the Agua Caliente Band still manages and protects the canyons for both tourism and its own non-consumptive uses. Eventually, on February 11, 1933, President Herbert Hoover proclaimed Death Valley National Monument. It was clearly a worthy scenic and scientific addition to the park system, but it lay far east of the main population center in Los Angeles. To the weekend tourists of the nearer desert realms, it was welcome but still inadequate for their needs. In addition, many maintained that its vegetation poorly represented the ecological variety of California's deserts.[19]

Meanwhile, the state also pursued a vigorous search for new sites to add to its park system. The earliest state park in California was Yosemite Valley and the Mariposa Grove of Giant Sequoias granted by Congress in 1864. Poorly managed by the state, it reverted to the federal government in 1906 to add to the rest of what today is Yosemite National Park. Despite this embarrassing setback, the state had established another park, Big Basin Redwoods, in 1902. By the 1920s, however, California's leading citizens strongly pushed for a full-fledged state park system. The California legislature passed, and Governor Clement C. Young signed, a bill for that purpose in 1927. They followed a year later with an act that promised $6,000,000 from the state if the public passed a bond initiative for an equal amount. The combined funds were to acquire lands that represented the richness of California's natural and historical heritage and met the recreational needs of its widely distributed population.[20]

With money in hand, the new CSP Commission hired eminent landscape architect Frederick Law Olmsted, Jr., to study the state's resources and to identify and prioritize specific areas for acquisition. The resulting study set goals for the state that still resonate today. With $15,000 in funding from the state legislature, Olmsted relied on a primarily volunteer staff to gather an immense amount of data on more than 330 areas in the state. He and his core staff of professional landscape architects, including former NPS employee Daniel Hull, divided the state into twelve districts, one of which included Riverside and San Bernardino Counties. Three other districts included the remaining parts of California's desert in Imperial, Inyo, Los Angeles, Mono, and San Diego Counties. Each district had one or more advisory councils as well as volunteer field inspectors. Unsurprisingly, Minerva Hoyt was heavily involved in the Riverside and San Bernardino part of the study and assisted in the Inyo and Mono Counties' district.[21]

Olmsted submitted his report to the California legislature during the final days of 1928, and the state published it the following year. The survey team recommended 125 areas to be considered seriously for state park status. In the desert region, it proposed Indian Palm Canyon, which the NPS had failed to secure; Painted Canyon; Red Rock Canyon; Borrego Palm Canyon in San Diego County; the Santa Rosa Mountains; and the Salton Sea region. It also included the Joshua trees at Victorville, the Morongo Pass (and Devil's Garden) area, and two parcels that would eventually be proposed as Joshua Tree National Monument: the Lost Horse Valley and a broad stretch from Edom Palm Canyon near Mecca up to Twentynine Palms. Olmsted admitted that funding limitations would preclude immediate acquisition of many of the 125 areas, but he strongly recommended an even geographic distribution of what could be acquired over time.[22]

When discussing California's desert, Olmsted eloquently highlighted the reasons why the state should establish parks in the region:

> Certain desert areas have distinctive and subtle charm, in part dependent on spaciousness, solitude, and escape from the evidence of human control and manipulation of the earth, a charm of constantly growing value as the rest of the earth becomes more completely dominated by man's activities. This quality is a very vulnerable one. Its bloom is easily destroyed by comparatively slight changes made by man. The very conditions which make a desert what it is leave every man-made scar upon its surface so completely unsoftened by natural processes as to produce a rapidly cumulative deterioration of its precious wildness.

The desert is in general worth so little for any other purpose than occasional enjoyment of its untamed character, and so much of it in southeastern California is within easy reach by automobile of so large a population, that it seems a clear duty of the state to acquire and preserve inviolate several desert areas large enough for future generations to enjoy in perfection the essential desert qualities. As in the case of the ancient redwood forests, only such public action by the present generation on an adequate scale can preserve this heritage for the people of centuries to come. Nowhere else are casual thoughtless human changes in the landscape so irreparable, and nowhere else is it so important to control and completely protect wide areas.[23]

The report came six weeks after California voters approved the $6,000,000 bond issue that matched the state's appropriation. The Olmsted report not only gave direction to the state, but also simplified the NPS's mission to find quality parks in California, especially in the desert. The extraordinary abilities and fame of both Olmsted and Newton Drury, a member of the California State Park Commission and a future director of the NPS and CSP, were more than enough to qualify them as experts whom the federal agency should consult.[24]

In the meantime, the NPS was developing a master plan with a classification system for future parks to direct the system's expansion. New NPS Director Albright wanted representative examples of geological and biological diversity of the nation as well as historic sites in order to create parks in the East. As the NPS investigated these various potential parks and monuments, its planners and leaders came to recognize four distinctive plants in the deserts of the American Southwest that deserved protection in the national park system. The first of these was the saguaro cactus (*Carnegiea gigantea*), a signature species of the Sonoran Desert found in Arizona, primarily between Tucson and Phoenix. On March 1, 1933, two days before he left office, President Hoover proclaimed Saguaro National Monument (now a national park). The second was the organ pipe cactus (*Stenocereus thurberi*), also in the Sonoran Desert but near the Arizona–Mexico border. President Franklin Roosevelt assured its protection when he proclaimed a monument with that name on April 13, 1937. The third species was the California fan palm that occurred in washes throughout much of the Colorado Desert and south into Baja California. Aside from the unsuccessful Indian Palm Canyon preserve, small groves of these trees were subsequently protected in both federal and state parks.[25] The fourth unique and impressive desert species was the Joshua tree.

Finding the Best Joshua Trees

Since both the CSP and the NPS sought to protect the Joshua tree as an indicator species of the Mojave Desert, various scientists, local citizens, and government officials offered a variety of locations.

Rimo Bacigalupi, of the USFS Experiment Station at Berkeley, California, sent a map to the NPS that showed the distribution of the species across the Mojave Desert (Map 2.1). Based largely on herbaria specimens and research by C. Hart Merriam, an eminent desert botanist, it identified sixty-seven groves, including thirty-eight in California, twenty-five in Nevada, and four in Arizona.[26] Walter P. Taylor, a senior biologist for the USDA's Biological Survey, informed the NPS that the Joshua trees in Nevada were probably a different species, simplifying the search. In California, the largest area stretched some 150 miles from Lost Horse Valley to west of the Antelope Valley and included major groves at Victorville, Palmdale, and Lancaster. From the beginning of the serious search for a national park or monument in Southern California, the NPS focused on protecting biotic resources. Other resources were important and could help distinguish between similar stands of Joshua trees, but they were absolutely secondary.[27]

The man charged with surveying the various Joshua tree sites and evaluating their qualifications for inclusion in the national park system was Roger Toll, the superintendent of Yellowstone National Park (Fig. 2.2). He occupied the position that Horace Albright formerly held before his promotion to director in 1929. As such, Toll was the agency's senior field man and the recognized expert in evaluating proposed park sites. When presented with the task of identifying an area for a desert vegetation park or monument, he relied on his biologist at Yellowstone, W. B. McDougall, who was the author of a series of botanical circulars about that park. During the ensuing inspections and political campaign, these two men would play important roles.[28]

Although the NPS considered many Joshua tree locations, the choices basically came down to five areas. Frederick Law Olmsted, Jr., favored a large grove south of Victorville. Newton Drury, however, wrote to Toll that he had personally inspected the site as well as one at Palmdale and found that the state park system faced "insurmountable obstacles to the acquisition of a consolidated block of land, because of intervening private holdings and because of mining claims that had been filed.[29] A second area of interest was the nearby Antelope Valley. At Toll's suggestion, McDougall wrote to Philip A. Munz, a botanist at Pomona College, asking for his advice on choosing the best Joshua tree site. Munz, who would later write a massive and definitive volume entitled *A California Flora* (1959), responded that the country west of Palmdale and Lancaster have "veritable forests of Joshua trees" but are located in "rather flat open country." He preferred the "Keyes Ranch" [sic] area that "has a good development of Joshua trees and other interesting plants, with a striking rock formation of red granite."[30]

Willis Jepson, a prominent botanist at the University of California, Berkeley, recommended to the Save-the-Redwoods-League and later to Newton Drury a site twenty-seven miles north of Barstow known as Coolgardie Yucca Mesa. Munz also mentioned the area and even offered to accompany Toll there to survey it. Once again, Drury had already checked the site and, in a letter to McDougall,

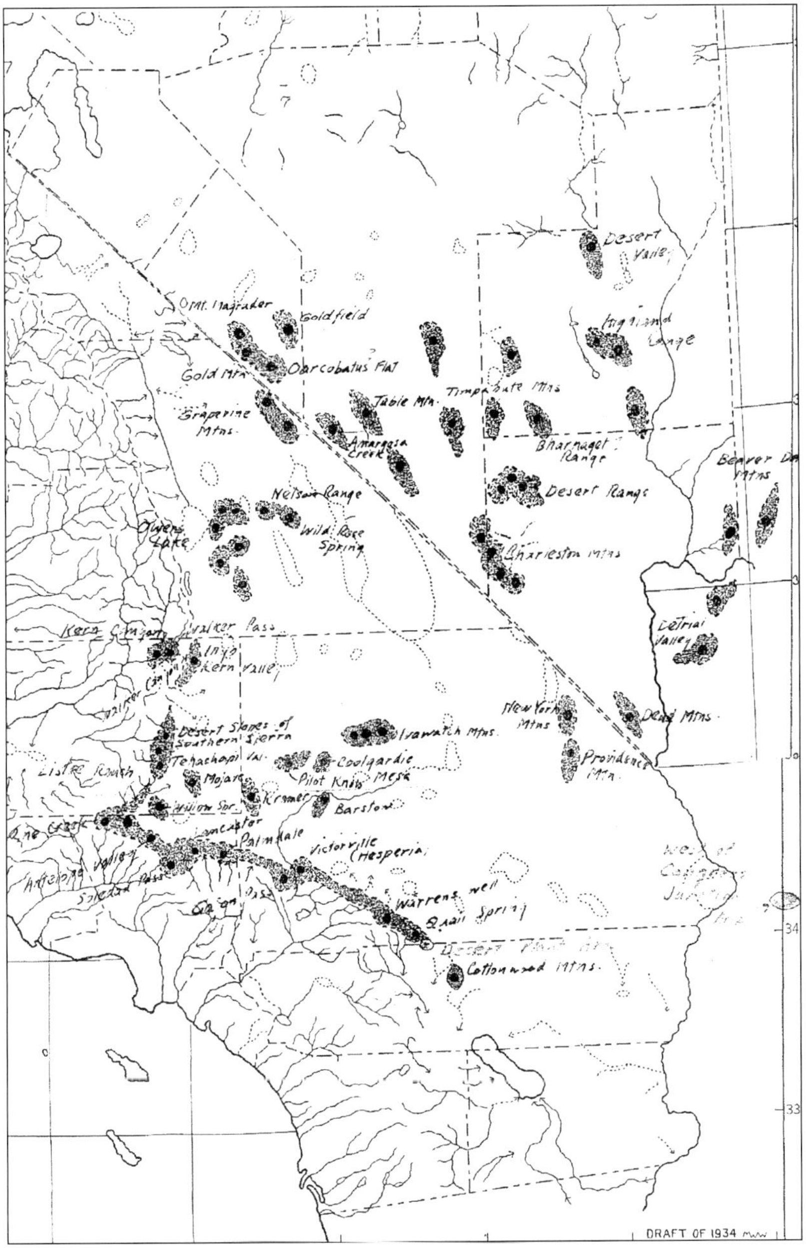

MAP 2.1. Scientist Rimo Bacigalupi mapped the distribution of sixty-seven groves of Joshua trees across the Mojave Desert. The National Park Service focused on the Joshua Tree, Palmdale-Lancaster, Cima Dome (now Mojave National Preserve), and the Coolgardie Mesa areas of California in its search for a national monument to protect and display the species. Source: Roger Toll, "Report on the Proposed Desert Plant National Park" (1934), Joshua Tree National Park Archives, Acc. 752, Cat. 25175, Folder 13.

FIG. 2.2. Roger Toll served as both Superintendent of Yellowstone National Park and the primary inspector of proposed additions to the national park system. Somehow, Toll set up this self-portrait while holding a bobcat at Carlsbad Caverns in southern New Mexico on November 18, 1931. Toll would probably have been the next director of the National Park Service had he not been killed in an automobile accident near Deming, New Mexico, that also took the life of George M. Wright, the agency's most important scientist. The two were returning from an inspection of the proposed Big Bend National Park in Texas in February 1936. Harpers Ferry Center, JOTR Collection, Negative WASO-H-165, National Park Service.

explained that the area, while interesting, was "pretty well riddled with mining claims, the working of which involves the destruction of the flora on the surface." It was for this reason and because of inadequate funding, he added, that the CSP abandoned the site as a potential state park.[31]

The most serious contender for a national monument to protect Joshua trees was the Cima Dome area in what is now Mojave National Preserve. This was recognized as one of the largest stands of the species, although opinions differed on its quality compared to the groves south of Twentynine Palms. Thomas Vint, NPS's Chief Landscape Architect, reported a conversation with engineer T. R. Goodwin, who had studied Joshua tree stands for the state and would later become Superintendent of Death Valley National Monument. Goodwin told Vint that, in his opinion, the Cima Dome group was the most impressive stand. Vint immediately wrote to Toll, indicating that Goodwin was "well informed on this particular section of the State" and should be contacted for further information. Later, a number of people in the eastern Mojave enthusiastically sought protection for the Cima Dome grove, even offering to drive Toll around the area during his inspection trip.[32]

The fifth area was the Lost Horse Valley region southwest of Twentynine Palms. In January 1932, Clinton G. Abbott, Director of the Natural History Museum in San Diego, wrote to Drury in favor of this area that he had also inspected. Although locals were already talking about a planned state park in the area, he saw "few persons with energy enough to push it" and noted that "it provides an unparalleled combination of fantastic rock formations, primitive Joshua forest, Indian pictographs, natural water 'tanks,' etc." But he warned that, with miners already in the area, it would be ruined within five years.[33]

Minerva Hoyt's work for the Olmsted Report had convinced her of the superiority of a huge area lying east of Palm Springs from Twentynine Palms to the Salton Sea. Others on the state survey favored the area west of the Salton Sea (today's Anza-Borrego Desert State Park), but those tracts had no Joshua trees. The area Hoyt proposed had four advantages. First, it spanned both the Colorado and Mojave Deserts, promising a wide variety of floral species in addition to the Joshua trees. In this idea she was ably supported by Phillip Munz, desert expert and author Dr. Edmund C. Jaeger, and other academic and scientific authorities. Second, the area contained five of the nine desert sites recommended in the Olmsted study, specifically Lost Horse Valley, Morongo Pass (and Devil's Garden), Painted Canyon, the Edom Palm Canyon area, and the northern tip of the Salton Sea region. Third, it lay close to Los Angeles and its nearly 2,000,000 inhabitants, which meant it was readily accessible to seekers of recreation and deeply threatened by vandals and cactus thieves. Finally, it boasted relatively undamaged biotic resources unlike the areas near Victorville and Lancaster. The area Hoyt proposed contained more than 1,100,000 acres, admittedly well interspersed with private land, mining claims, roads, and a utility corridor, but she believed it offered the best chance for a monument to protect biological resources (Map B).[34]

Ironically, in April 1935, more than two years after Hoyt's proposal became the focus of NPS's attention, another recommendation for a park or monument to protect and display Joshua trees

surfaced in western Arizona. Charles Vorhies, an entomologist at the University of Arizona, be-
latedly urged the agency to reconsider an unidentified site, where he reported that "sahuaros [sic],
junipers, and Joshua trees are growing all together and in profusion." Assistant Director Bryant
responded that the plans for a monument at the site proposed by Hoyt were too advanced to consider any other candidate.[35]

The Campaign Begins

As Minerva Hoyt and her widely publicized IDCL pushed for a park to protect desert flora and as
Southern Californians clamored for a reserve to enjoy on day and weekend excursions, the complicated process of creating a monument or park began. Three considerations had to be taken into
account. First, everyone wanted a unit that would protect the very best array of vegetation, especially the Joshua trees. Second, the government should seek the largest area possible in order to
encompass the diversity of flora, fauna, and landscapes offered by the more than 25,000,000 acres
of California's desert lands. Finally, past land alienation and consumptive land uses had impacted
resources in ways that, eventually, would have to be solved.

Hoyt and her IDCL allies clearly felt that the NPS would provide the best protection at the
least cost to Californians. Stephen Mather's original message that his agency should preserve the
finest sites with the greatest degree of legal and managerial protection had resonated with Californians as well as other Americans. As early as 1930, Hoyt wrote to NPS Director Albright to offer
her proposal. Unfortunately, the agency was embroiled in complicated negotiations to create Death
Valley and Saguaro National Monuments, two areas that were troubled by private land ownership
and mining claims. These presaged the issues that would also complicate Joshua Tree's establishment and shape its management for decades thereafter.[36]

For a time, Hoyt occupied herself with other desert-protection activities, including the cactus
park in Mexico. When her attention returned to the California desert campaign, she was shocked to
find that a Twentynine Palms faction had convinced State Assemblyman John Phillips to introduce
Assembly Bill 1292 for a much smaller "California Desert Park" in the Lost Horse Valley area, which
he did on January 26, 1933, while the NPS was busy fielding recommendations for the best stands
of Joshua trees. The bill focused primarily on the iconic trees as justification for its proposed reserve,
but Hoyt and others suspected that real-estate speculators were behind the effort to highlight the
region in order to inflate land prices. Furthermore, a disheartening letter came from Albright
suggesting that a large national park in the area she wanted would be difficult to justify after the
recent establishment of Death Valley National Monument in California's eastern Mojave Desert.[37]

Hoyt now faced two challenges. First, she had to find a way to block the state's proposal that
would cut the heart out of her more-ambitious plan. Second, she would have to convince NPS

leaders of the worthiness of her project. She acted immediately to forestall state action. Rather than trying to combat Assembly Bill 1292 in the state legislature, she went directly to Governor James Rolph, Jr., and asked him to veto it, so that the campaign for a national unit could proceed. After the state legislature passed the bill on May 12, 1933, Governor Rolph acceded to her request by returning it unsigned with an explanation of his pocket veto. As it turned out, there were procedural and legal problems with the bill as well, because the CSP Commission had not approved it and the state owned only a fraction of the land in the proposed area.[38]

Governor Rolph's veto sent proponents of a California Desert State Park into confused reevaluation. Most members of the CSP Commission had favored a desert park in the Anza-Borrego area of eastern San Diego County. On March 3, 1933, the Congress passed Public Law 72-425, which transferred to the state much of the land that now forms the state's principal desert park. Nevertheless, upon hearing of the proposed withdrawal of federal land, Assemblyman Phillips hurriedly contacted Harold Ickes on July 18, 1933, asking whether the area had already been declared a national monument. Apparently, the state legislature was still considering the area, despite Governor Rolph's veto. Public Law 72-425 had the desired effect, however, since it allowed the establishment of Anza Desert State Park that year, temporarily derailing the state's pursuit of a park specifically for Joshua trees. Ultimately, California did create a Joshua Tree State Park in Antelope Valley on land acquired in 1957. Six years later, it officially opened, and, in 1972, the name was changed to Saddleback Butte State Park. In 1998, the state added another unit with Joshua trees called Arthur B. Ripley Desert Woodland State Park, west of Saddleback Butte.[39]

Minerva Hoyt Visits Washington, D.C.

In spite of Albright's discouraging response, the NPS continued to evaluate California's deserts. Roger Toll visited the region from December 1932 through January 1933 in order to inspect a number of sites suggested either by the Olmsted Report or local citizens and officials. Among the sites he viewed were Indian Palm Canyon, Thousand Palms, the Morongo Pass (and Devil's Garden) area, and Joshua tree stands near Palmdale and Lancaster. With the exception of Indian Palm Canyon, Toll was uniformly unimpressed. He found the palm groves in private ownership and, in some cases, burned by movie studios to make them look more appropriate for films about Arabia. Although he did not visit Cima Dome or the Lost Horse Valley areas, he was disappointed with the Joshua trees he did see, writing in his later report, "I have not as yet seen any area of Joshua trees that seems desirable for a national monument. In some cases private holdings interfere and in other cases the stand of Joshua trees is not exceptionally heavy and would not be of outstanding public interest."[40]

His evaluation of Morongo Pass (and Devil's Garden) was similarly negative. In his report, he noted that the area was reputed to have a larger number of desert plants than any other, but it did

FIG. 2.3. U.S. Secretary of the Interior Harold Ickes addresses a crowd in Chicago and a CBS radio audience in October 1937. Sitting behind him and wearing a top hat is President Franklin D. Roosevelt. Photographer unknown. This is a still picture from a film held by the Library of Congress. The picture is at the Harpers Ferry Center, Franklin Delano Roosevelt Collection, Negative Number LC-USZ62-96485.

not contain any of the four desirable desert species that the NPS was seeking. After adding that Death Valley and Borrego Palm Canyon in the proposed state park also had extensive vegetation, Toll delivered a negative verdict: "It does not seem that this area has outstanding interest of a national character to justify its consideration as a national monument." Although Toll did not visit the area that would become Joshua Tree National Park, he reported that D. F. Geil, of the Morongo Valley Inn, described the Lost Horse and Queen Valleys as filled with many Joshua trees as well as huge granite boulders. Toll did find out that "the area is about half Southern Pacific land and about half Government land, with some homesteaders now making entries."[41]

With the immediate threat of a smaller state park removed, Hoyt decided it was time to tackle the NPS and the new administration of President Franklin D. Roosevelt head-on. First, she secured a letter from Governor Rolph to Roosevelt introducing her and explaining the worth of her project. Critical to success was getting new Secretary of the Interior Harold Ickes on board (Figure 2.3). Fortunately, Ickes, a famously irascible but progressive-minded conservationist, was well disposed to the project. Furthermore, he was a determined individual untroubled by such difficulties as extensive private lands and mining claims. The primary purpose of Hoyt's visit in June 1933 was to convince the President to withdraw the area in her proposal from the public domain in order to halt any further alienation of land to private interests. She convinced Ickes that it was necessary to allow the NPS to study the region properly and make a decision based on the expertise of its inspectors. While in Washington, D.C., she met with a number of NPS officials, including future director Conrad Wirth, who was heavily involved in the identification of potential new parks. During the meetings, the proposed unit took on the working title of "Desert Plant National Park."[42]

As the summer of 1933 wore on, concern mounted over the fate of the proposed withdrawal of land. An impatient Hoyt chafed at the delays, and she wrote to Conrad Wirth, reminding him that Ickes had told her that, in the case of the withdrawal, "the President is for it, and I am for it." She pleaded with Wirth, "Don't fail us." She wrote a similar letter to Assistant Director Arthur Demaray mistakenly addressing him as "Mr. A. E. Dunaray," which may not have helped her cause. When NPS Director Arno Cammerer planned a trip to California, she wrote to encourage him to inspect the proposed park. Finally, Ickes responded with a telegram explaining that the executive order was in the process of execution. He also reminded her that, even with the temporary withdrawal, the area would still have to undergo a rigorous examination by the NPS to determine if it qualified as a park of national interest.[43]

One of the factors delaying the President's executive action was the bureaucratic necessity of checking with the GLO, which actually administered the federal lands in question. In response to a request from outgoing Director Albright, GLO Commissioner Fred W. Johnson provided a series of maps showing all or parts of sixty-two townships to be included in the withdrawal and indicating which parcels belonged to the Southern Pacific Railroad, the state, the Bureau of Reclamation, and private individuals. On July 28, 1933, the commissioner sent another letter suggesting text for the president's executive order that assured that existing rights and the provisions of existing withdrawals for the Metropolitan Water District of Los Angeles and several other water projects would be protected.[44]

Finally, on October 25, 1933, President Roosevelt signed Executive Order 6361 temporarily removing "approximately 1,136,000 acres" from the public domain (Map B). Significantly, it included most of the language suggested by Commissioner Johnson. Also of interest was the fact that, although Hoyt's proposal included the northeastern shoreline of the Salton Sea, the land legally described in the proclamation ended more than a mile short of it. But with most of the land she had recommended now unavailable for alienation to private interests, Hoyt and her allies in the IDCL felt that the primary hurdle had been crossed. They settled down to await the inspection trip by Roger Toll, scheduled for March 1934.[45]

Choosing a Name

In the months leading up to Roger Toll's inspection, correspondence supporting the proposal for the park increased and took two forms. First came letters and resolutions supporting the establishment of a national park or monument. In late November 1933, both the mayor and the Los Angeles Area Chamber of Commerce (LAACC) appealed to Secretary Ickes to save the area for its extraordinary vegetation, unusual rock formations, striking Indian "hieroglyphics," and proximity to the big metropolis. A few weeks later, Congressman John Dockweiler and the U.S. Chamber of Commerce also urged the secretary to preserve the area.[46]

At the same time, a more complicated issue arose, as many of the letters suggested that the eventual monument or park should be named for Minerva Hoyt. One of the earliest was a letter to Harold Ickes from William Simpson, President of the LAACC, who reasoned, "Mrs. Hoyt is internationally known as an authority upon desert life, and no more fitting name could be chosen for the great monument, the establishment of which is respectfully urged."[47] For the rest of the campaign to establish the national monument, a steady drumbeat of letters, telegrams, and resolutions followed from increasingly wide-ranging groups of scientists, conservationists, and supporters of Hoyt and her work. The respectful but official response from Secretary Ickes disappointed Simpson, but it did nothing to slow the groundswell of support for the Hoyt name:

> I agree with you that Mrs. Minerva Hoyt is entitled to much credit for her conservation
> work, but it is established policy of the Department to refrain from naming national parks

and monuments after individuals. Our leading conservationists are of the opinion that it is far more fitting to choose a name that bears a direct relation to the area's natural features or early history. However, if the monument is established, it might be possible to acknowledge Mrs. Hoyt's work by placing a plaque in the area. In none but exceptional cases does the Department permit even this memorialization [sic] of individuals, but it would seem that Mrs. Hoyt has earned such consideration."[48]

Even as Ickes mailed this response, more correspondence arrived backing the initiative. In early March 1934, Governor Rolfe wrote directly to President Roosevelt to thank him for withdrawing the land in Southern California from the public domain and to support Californians who wanted the reserve to be named for Hoyt. Meanwhile, a host of women's clubs, civic organizations, and local officials continued to exhort Secretary Ickes and Director Cammerer. Cammerer, like Ickes, finally responded that the NPS never names parks or monuments after living persons and that only four of the sixty-seven existing national monuments were named for any persons at all. In his words, "these are named for long dead historic characters who have been intimately involved in the historic background of the area." He listed George Washington Birthplace National Monument and Cabrillo National Monument as appropriate examples and added that naming the proposed monument after Minerva Hoyt "would establish an undesirable precedent."[49]

This explanation had no effect. Letters to Roosevelt, Ickes, Cammerer, and various members of Congress continued to arrive from around the nation. Joshua Green, a native of Mississippi who lived at the time in Seattle, wrote to Mississippi's state senators, urging them to back the Hoyt name in order to honor one of their own. Senator Pat Harrison, of Mississippi, forwarded the letter to Cammerer with his full support. Mrs. Edwin S. Fuller, noting that Hoyt herself favored the name "Joshua Tree Reservation," nevertheless called for the Hoyt name as a well-deserved honor for her great work.[50]

On June 16, 1934, Benjamin Fenton, of Pasadena, wrote to Cammerer, reminding him that Muir Woods National Monument, established in 1908, was named for John Muir, the famous conservationist and founder of the Sierra Club, while he was still alive. An embarrassed Cammerer responded to this "delightful note" by acknowledging the Muir exception but reiterating his unwillingness to establish such a precedent. "If such a policy were not followed we might have had a George Stewart National Park instead of a Sequoia National Park, a Steel National Park instead of Crater Lake National Park, and going farther back a Vest-Pettengill or Cornelius Hedge National Park instead of Yellowstone National Park."[51]

Through the rest of 1934 and 1935, correspondence favoring Minerva Hoyt National Monument continued to come in, some from as far away as London, England. As these broadened into organizational resolutions, the NPS developed a form letter to respond. It blithely ignored the case of Muir Woods and continued to refuse, citing its fear of setting a bad precedent. The public correspondence was not entirely one-sided. Former miner Chester A. Pinkham wrote, "I am interceding for all the old prospectors who wish the desert kept perfectly natural in both structure and name... it is their policy to give a name suitable to the natural grandeur alone, one suitable to the makeup of the territory." This would be the last time mining interests agreed with a policy of the future Joshua Tree National Monument.[52]

Finally, Hoyt herself weighed in on the name issue. In September 1935, she informed the Altadena Historical and Beautification Society that she preferred the name "Joshua Tree National Monument." The society immediately passed a resolution of support and its secretary, Rachel Vordermark, notified Ickes. Hoyt's decision and its communication to the Secretary of the Interior seemed to calm the frenzy surrounding the name, even as the overall campaign to establish a monument, including all the lands withdrawn by President Roosevelt in 1933, intensified. In March 1936, Southern California Congressman John McGroarty again suggested the Joshua Tree National Monument name to Harold Ickes, no doubt at the behest of Hoyt. This spurred a flurry of correspondence between the secretary and senior NPS officials that led to a general agreement that this was an appropriate replacement for the working title of Desert Plant National Monument. Ickes allowed that this name seemed a good one, even though he disliked Congressman McGroarty. A month later, a pleased Minerva Hoyt telegraphed her congratulations to Ickes and predicted that the new name would help the campaign to create the monument.[53]

The Roger Toll Inspection and Report

As news reports circulated about the withdrawn acreage and proposed national monument, Minerva Hoyt and her allies prepared for Roger Toll's all-important visit. Senator Hiram Johnson, of California, wrote to Ickes, urging him to have Toll meet Hoyt and be led by her during his inspection. Meanwhile Toll, as the NPS's senior judge of proposed additions to the national park system, planned an elaborate winter inspection tour of thirteen areas, including several in Southern California. One of the latter was the Cima Dome area, which he felt still deserved an inspection, in spite of its location well outside President Roosevelt's withdrawal of land. As for the inspections, Toll would use the three criteria he largely had developed and which are still used today to evaluate proposed areas. The first is national significance. Although he admitted, in a 1930 letter, that its quantification was impossible, it has always been the first and foremost filter through which any proposed unit must pass.[54] Is the resource important to the entire nation? This includes both its level of magnificence and whether it is the best representation of an historic or natural resource theme.[55] A second criterion is feasibility. Regardless of its significance, a proposed park that would cost too much for land acquisition or meet intense local opposition is not considered feasible. This would ultimately become the primary obstacle to the creation of Joshua Tree National Monument. The third criterion is suitability. The agency does not want areas that duplicate resources already in the national park system. This is what motivated Director Albright to suggest earlier that the existence of Death Valley National Monument might preclude the establishment of a Joshua tree unit.[56]

On March 8, 1934, Roger Toll arrived in Southern California for a four-day inspection to evaluate the withdrawn area's worth as a national park. The first three days consisted of an automobile tour of the region with Minerva Hoyt, her chauffer, and botanist Philip Munz from Pomona College. Toll kept a detailed, minute-to-minute log of the tour, identifying every stop, every road traveled, every site surveyed, and everyone with whom he spoke. The quartet left San Bernardino on Friday, March 9, and journeyed through Morongo Pass (and Devil's Garden) before inspecting the Coyote Holes, Quail Springs, Inspiration Point (Keys View), and the Lost Horse Well areas, ending the day at Twentynine Palms. Day two began with a visit to the palm grove after which the town was named and then meetings with Frank Bagley, a store owner and representative of the local American Legion chapter, Hesmel Earenfight of the town's chamber of commerce (and future national monument employee), and archaeologists Elizabeth and William Campbell. Thereafter, the group visited the White Tank area (Plate 23), some prominent mines, Cottonwood Spring, and the Lost Palms Canyon in the Eagle Mountains. On the third day, the travelers left their hotel in Blythe and visited the Chuckwalla Mountains, Hidden Springs, and Painted Canyon before returning to San Bernardino. On Monday, March 12, Hoyt brought Toll to visit supporters of the monument in the Los Angeles area, including some who had previously supplied data to Toll as he prepared for the inspection tour. He left the following day to begin compiling his reports on all the inspections he had conducted during the winter.[57]

The inspection tour was hurried, and it must have frustrated Hoyt to have so little time to show an area of more than 1,000,000 acres. The schedule was also tight, and nowhere in his detailed log of the visit did Toll mention lunch. At least one result of this harried itinerary was a very negative reaction by some people in Twentynine Palms, especially the Campbells, who had been proponents of the state park bill that Hoyt convinced Governor Rolfe to veto. Later, Mrs. Campbell wrote to NPS archaeologist Jesse Nusbaum:

By the time your good letter had reached us Mr. Toll had been here and gone. We found him a perfectly delightful person and wished with all our hearts that we could have sneaked him into a corner and had a good talk with him and said all that we would have liked to. Unfortunately Mrs. Minerva Sherman-Hoyt had him in tow (she is the one who is

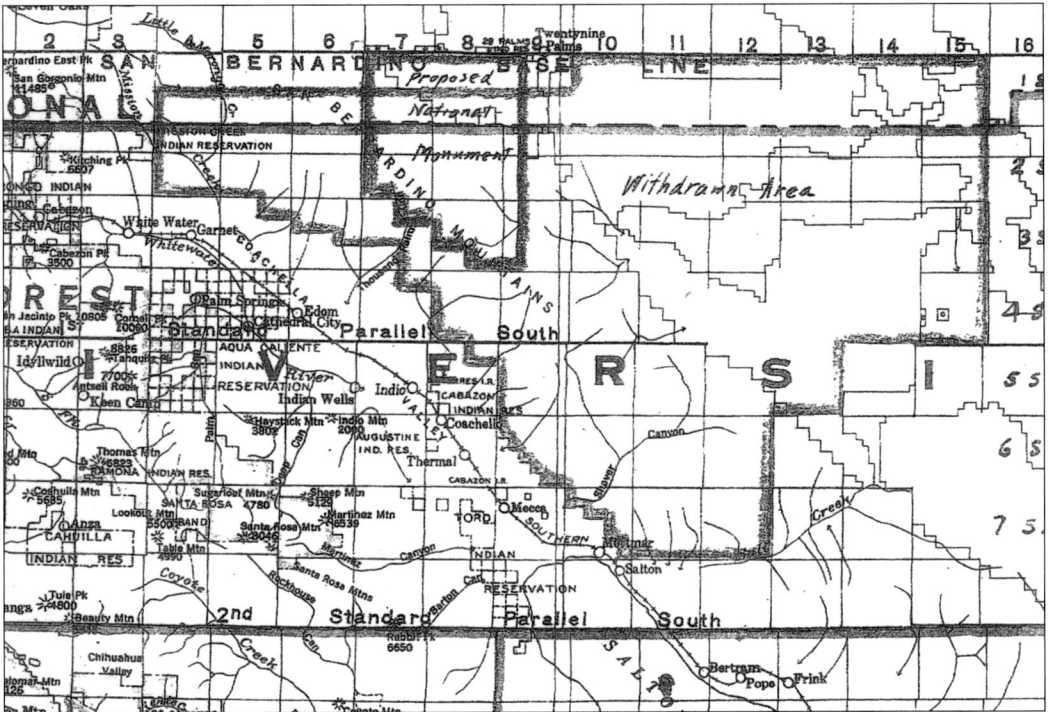

MAP 2.2. President Franklin D. Roosevelt withdrew 1,000,000 acres from the public domain so the National Park Service could evaluate the area for a national park. After his 1934 inspection, Roger Toll recommended only 138,240 acres in the Lost Horse and Hidden Valleys for a national monument. Source: Roger Toll, "Report on the Proposed Desert Plant National Park" (1934), Joshua Tree National Park Archives, Acc. 752, Cat. 25175, Folder 13.

sponsoring this Park idea on condition that it be dubbed 'The Minerva Sherman-Hoyt Memorial Desert National Park') and she wouldn't let us get a word in edgewise with Mr. Toll for fear we would say something about the name! She dragged him off by the elbow just when he and Bill were having a lovely time talking about all the things that are of interest in this district so our very few minutes with him were sort of sad! and he was such a lovely person and we so wanted to talk to him that day. You see our park was to be a state park and this woman went to Gov. Rolph and begged him not to sign the bill as it was not named for her in the state idea. People are already calling the proposed park 'the nerva-hoyt park' and really such a name is enough to blast all the desert growth and I don't suppose that there is much that we can do about it. Isn't it a mess? but funny![58]

It is uncertain where Mrs. Campbell got the idea that Hoyt's opposition to the state park stemmed from a preference for a unit in her own name. California's park agency has always been far likelier to name its units after people, living or dead. In all likelihood, this spiteful conclusion resulted from the earlier foiled plans for the state park as well as Hoyt's frenzied schedule and single-minded drive to convince Toll of the worthiness of a much larger, federally protected park.

With a mass of data and a personal inspection behind him, Toll began compiling his report to NPS Director Cammerer. Due to the high-profile campaign and the President's withdrawal of land for the potential monument, it needed to be as complete and detailed as possible. The final report ultimately contained more than 170 pages of site descriptions, analysis, correspondence, news reports, maps, photographs, and other explanatory data. It began with a cover letter, in which Toll dropped the bombshell:

It is believed that the area is not suitable for a national park, for the following reasons: [1] It is not the outstanding desert area of the United States. Death Valley National Monument is far superior to it in scenic quality and has many important features of interest not possessed by the area under consideration. [2] The area is interesting and of great value for local and state use, but is lacking in any distinctive, superlative, outstanding feature that would give it sufficient importance to justify its establishment as a national park.[59]

Instead, Toll suggested that the Lost Horse Valley area might be appropriate for a much-smaller national monument of some 138,240 acres that would feature a lesser quality group of Joshua trees but one surrounded by interesting geological formations (Map 2.2). He then proceeded to justify his recommendation with a series of photographs and a discussion of his proposed boundaries. He explained that Hoyt's proposed area contained the Metropolitan Water District of Southern

California (MWD) aqueduct, that the state park system wanted the Salton Sea area, and that numerous mining claims existed in the larger region. He reported that, although there were few grazing or other non-mining uses in the area, much of the land was not in federal ownership. Citing county assessors for Riverside and San Bernardino Counties, Toll claimed that Hoyt's preferred area included 227,130 acres owned by the Southern Pacific Railroad Company (SPRR), 22,275 held by the state, and 95,319 in other private hands, for a total of 344,724 acres the government would have to acquire (Map C). On the other hand, in the area that he recommended for the monument, SPRR would have only 48,960 acres, the state 4,800 acres, and private interests 4,548 acres, for a total of 53,016. Although Toll admitted that, in his proposed area, the status of another 26,880 acres was unknown, this presented a more-realistic goal of land acquisition for the NPS. As a postscript, he attached a letter from the city engineer of San Bernardino, who requested that, if the monument were to be proclaimed, it should remain open to new mining claims.[60]

Toll bolstered his argument for a smaller monument on April 16, 1934, by forwarding a letter and data from the MWD, citing the city's 250-foot right-of-way along its aqueduct as further evidence that the larger proposed area was not feasible. This seemed to resonate with Conrad Wirth, the NPS's Chief of Lands, who supported Toll's position.[61] Director Cammerer agreed and sent a letter to Minerva Hoyt on July 2, asking for her response to the idea of a smaller unit. The long delay between Toll's report and follow-up and Cammerer's letter stemmed from the delicacy of the situation. Hoyt was an internationally-respected expert on the desert, and she had spent great effort and considerable money pursuing her dream of a large desert preserve in California. The first draft of the director's letter to her, written by NPS employee Donald Alexander, flatly stated that the only plant of concern in the area was the Joshua tree and then cited land acquisition concerns, the water district's aqueduct, poor road conditions, and uncertainty that the Antiquities Act of 1906, the principle mechanism for establishing national monuments, could be used for such a large area as reasons to support a smaller unit. Evidently, the director decided that this was too insensitive, because the letter he finally sent only mentioned the concerns about the land and aqueduct and simply asked Hoyt to study the map and information about Toll's smaller proposal. At the same time, he ordered Toll to begin studying the road approaches to the smaller area.[62]

Roger Toll apparently foresaw the reaction his report would cause among the backers of the Hoyt proposal, or perhaps his colleagues suggested that he strengthen his argument with some scientific support. On April 10, just three days after sending his initial report to Cammerer, Toll wrote to Forrest Shreve, an eminent desert ecologist and Director of the Carnegie Institution's desert laboratory in Tuscon (founded in 1903), asking him to evaluate the botanical merits of Hoyt's proposal. Shreve responded, on April 19, that the area north of Indio was certainly worthy of preservation, although he feared that the public attention it would draw could be detrimental to the vegetation. He ridiculed the notion publicized by the IDCL that the Joshua tree was the oldest type of plant in the desert but supported the idea of a national monument in the area, because it held species from both the Mojave and Colorado Deserts. He concluded that the Joshua tree area was equal in value to the proposed Big Bend National Park in Texas. Toll's appeal to an eminent scientist had backfired.[63]

Hoyt Fights Back

During the delay between Toll's report and Cammerer's letter to her, Minerva Hoyt had been busy. Letters from her friends and supporters of the project continued to pour in to Secretary Ickes and the NPS. On June 5, 1934, Congressman J. H. Hoeppel sent a letter signed by fifteen of the twenty California members of the U.S. House of Representatives to Ickes, endorsing her proposal. The next day, Henry I. Harriman, President of the U.S. Chamber of Commerce, presented President Roosevelt with two books Hoyt had designed, containing pictures and information about her proposed monument. Harriman reported that the President was both delighted and deeply interested.[64]

The letter and reduced proposal from Cammerer shocked Hoyt. In response, she turned to her vast network of scientists, friends, and politicians. And, soon, the NPS began to receive letters from scientists, educators, civic officials, and leading local citizens decrying the proposal for a smaller monument and seeking to justify the larger one. Typical was one from Dr. Frederick A. Speik, of Los Angeles, ridiculing Toll's proposal as too small for the recreational needs of Southern California, lacking in the diversity of the larger proposal by eliminating Painted Canyon, Hidden Springs, and "open, more desolate places," and ignoring the ocotillos, smoke trees, and native palms that also deserved protection. It turns out that the letter was based on a draft prepared by Philip Munz.[65]

Faced with this aggressive reaction, the NPS scheduled a second inspection, this time by Assistant Director Dr. Harold C. Bryant, a trained zoologist who had earned degrees at Pomona College and the University of California, Berkeley (Fig. 2.4). As a scientist and a native of Pasadena, he knew many of the people who had been writing to the agency. It was hoped that his biological training and senior position in the agency's main office in Washington, D.C., would provide a more definitive evaluation that would placate the locals. When Hoyt learned that Bryant would be coming in late August 1934, she immediately organized another inspection tour and an extravagant series of events and meetings. She knew that the success of her proposal hinged on this highly unusual second inspection.[66]

Bryant arrived at Hoyt's home on the evening of August 10, where he was welcomed by more than 100 eager supporters of the desert monument, including state legislators, local businessmen, and the social elite of the area. After a buffet supper, Bryant addressed the crowd, noting that, as a biologist, he was interested in "seeing such monuments well-rounded and of larger areas so as to

FIG. 2.4. Dr. Harold C. Bryant (1886–1968), a native of Pasadena, California, received degrees in zoology from Pomona College and the University of California, Berkeley. At Yosemite National Park during the 1920s, he was instrumental in establishing an interpretation program for educating visitors. Later, he became Assistant Director of the Branch of Research and Education, serving under Directors Albright and Cammerer until 1938 and then Superintendent of Grand Canyon National Park. In August 1934, he carried out the highly unusual second evaluation of the Joshua Tree area and disagreed with Roger Toll's pessimistic conclusion. Photographer, site, and date unknown. National Park Service Historic Photograph Collection.

give full protection to the fauna and flora that desert lovers seek to perpetuate and protect." The next morning, he left with Hoyt, desert authority Edmund Jaeger, and a group of supporters. They breakfasted at Inspiration Point overlooking the Salton Sea (Keys View) and then proceeded with an inspection tour that emphasized many of the areas Roger Toll sought to omit.[67]

The entire inspection tour went well, and Bryant seemed impressed with the larger area, even as he warned Hoyt that the presence of so much private land and the intersection of the MWDs aqueduct, various roads, and other infrastructure still made it difficult to foresee a monument of the size she desired. He suggested that she again gather data, especially scientific justification, for including the Pinto Basin and areas south of the aqueduct with which he could bolster his recommendation to Director Cammerer.[68]

Meanwhile, the newspaper notoriety accompanying Bryant's visit and the sheer size of the proposed monument drew the attention of many who lived in and around the region. Some landowners and homesteaders were simply curious about what would happen to them and their land if the monument were to be established. Others were afraid of losing their homes and wondered what compensation, if any, they might receive. Still others were anxious to sell and wanted some assurance that the money would be forthcoming soon. Miners, too, worried about their claims, both patented and unpatented. Even before the two independent inspections by Toll and Bryant, Gordon Stewart, the city engineer of San Bernardino and a U.S. mineral surveyor, implored the U.S. Department of the Interior (USDI) to protect the rights to claim and mine this "richly mineralized" area. The NPS responded to landowners that the boundaries of the monument were uncertain, but that if it were to include their land they would be fairly compensated.[69]

At the same time, self-proclaimed "old desert prospector" Chester Pinkham, of Eagle Rock, California, wrote to W. C. Mendenhall, Director of the U.S. Geological Survey, to comment on what should and should not be included in the proposed monument and to complain about the idea of naming it after Minerva Hoyt. Mendenhall forwarded the letter to Arno Cammerer, and soon a correspondence developed between the NPS and the former prospector. Pinkham, in his initial letter, gave a brief history of mining in the area and explained that his fellow miners wanted to name Painted Canyon after him, but he rejected the idea as inappropriate. He added that he personally knew "Bill Keyes [sic], Shorty Harris[,] and that blowhard Scotty [of Death Valley fame] who never really was a genuine prospector." He recommended the Cottonwood area for preservation, but claimed it was too far from the Keys Ranch area to be included in the same unit. He commended Hoyt for trying to protect the desert scenery but absolutely opposed naming a park after her. Perhaps, he mused, the park should be named "Desert Wonderland." Cammerer responded that the area had just been inspected by Bryant, that his information was welcome, and that he should contact Hoyt in order to help the campaign.[70]

Three weeks later, Pinkham wrote to Cammerer, stating he had been unsuccessful in getting a response from Hoyt but he would accept the director's invitation to offer his views on the proposal. He thus recommended a park that would include Fortynine Palms, White Tank, Keys Ranch, and Pinon Mountain. He added that Cottonwood Spring should be a secondary unit, while Hidden Springs and Painted Canyon should be preserved as completely separate attractions, due to their distance from the main area. Harold Bryant then wrote to Hoyt to recommend that she contact Pinkham because of his familiarity with the region. The two advocates of the desert unit discussed their proposals over the phone and immediately disagreed. Pinkham later wrote, "I am thoroughly convinced she does not care to work with anyone who will not readily agree with her ideas."[71]

Minerva Hoyt, on the other hand, began gathering information about Pinkham. She later informed Bryant that he was listed as private secretary to capitalist F. F. Stetson and had spent many years in the U.S. Secret Service. She wondered if he might be a part of the "selfish interests set" that opposes any national park or monument in Southern California's deserts. Pinkham then decided that he would not participate in the movement for fear that his efforts might be perceived as an obstacle to a successful campaign for the monument. As a parting shot, he strongly recommended that any thoughts of including the northeastern waterfront of the Salton Sea be abandoned because of extensive private landholdings and the fact that the area was "one of the most uninviting sites of the entire Salton Sea."[72]

Hoyt and the IDCL steadfastly continued to urge its members and others to write to the NPS and oppose any reduction in the size of the monument. Following Bryant's recommendation, she sought letters from botanists and other scientists to justify preserving all the area in her proposal. Among the first to respond were the two desert scientists most closely associated with Hoyt's proposal—Edmund Jaeger and Philip Munz—who composed a lengthy memorandum to the NPS by way of the IDCL that listed a variety of reasons to oppose any diminution of Hoyt's suggested area. Jaeger pointed out that inclusion of the full area would allow adequate protection for desert bighorn sheep and provide an opportunity to reintroduce antelope, which had been eradicated from the region. The lower elevations, he continued, had most of the reptiles and many birds adapted to the vegetation of those niches. He added that a large monument would offer recreational space for many people during the winter when other popular areas were inaccessible. Munz insisted that floral species from both the Mojave and Colorado Deserts be included as well as the array of geological and anthropological features scattered throughout the proposed monument.

Soon, other letters to the NPS followed. Loye Miller, a biologist at the University of California, Los Angeles, wrote to Bryant to urge the preservation of ironwood trees in the southern part of Hoyt's proposed area, which locals were cutting for firewood. Munz penned another letter to Bryant, in which he admitted that the flora south of the aqueduct was relatively sparse but argued that the southern area contained species not found further north and stressed that the areas around Painted Canyon and Hidden Springs included scenic features that were "utterly different" from anything north of the aqueduct. Finally, he added, the southern area also held interesting spots, such as the old Butterfield stage station and Monson Canyon, suggesting that the monument be enlarged even further to include the Chuckwalla Mountains.[73]

Unexpectedly, letters of support also appeared from sources more likely to oppose the entire monument concept. Hoyt forwarded a letter she had received from E. Avery McCarthy, whom she identified as "the head of Real Estate matters in Los Angeles," enthusiastically suggesting that the monument would be one of the world's greatest nature preserves in another sixty years. James H. Howard, a general counsel for the MWD, also backed the larger area that would include the aqueduct. He noted that "while the proposed monument includes several highly interesting but widely scattered points, and it may be suggested that there are extensive areas of no particular interest, I am told that these intervening areas support many rare desert plants which should be preserved."[74]

Harold Bryant already favored a much-larger area than that proposed by Roger Toll when, on February 8, 1935, Minerva Hoyt again appeared at the headquarters of the NPS in Washington, D.C. A bill had recently been introduced to transfer more federal land to the California park system and she was terrified that it was the portent of another attempt to create a small state park in the heart of the area she wanted for the national monument. She met with Bryant, Arthur Demaray, and other senior officials who assured her that the bill referred to land west of the Salton Sea, land that would ultimately expand Anza Desert State Park. After this reassurance, the group discussed the problems inherent in trying to create and manage a monument of the size Hoyt wanted.

One significant outcome was an agreement by everyone that the northern boundary should be moved to the road leading to Twentynine Palms (modern-day CA 62). The southern boundary, however, was a different matter. Hoyt vehemently defended her plan's inclusion of the southern slope of the Little San Bernardino Mountains south of the aqueduct. She flatly refused to consider excluding the vegetation there, which, she claimed, was so different from that north of the mountains. She insisted that the presence of the MWD's aqueduct within the boundaries of the monument would have no significant impact on the unit's purpose or character. At the conclusion of the meeting, NPS official J. Lee Brown noted in a memo to Conrad Wirth, "I believe Mr. Demaray and Dr. Bryant were practically persuaded to overlook the presence of the aqueduct and to include all of the withdrawn area."[75] A few days later, Bryant informed Director Cammerer that Hoyt and Harriman were assiduously working to solve the most-pressing problem: acquisition of the vast tracts of private and state land within the area withdrawn by President Roosevelt two and one-half years earlier.[76]

Problems with Land Acquisition

In spite of Minerva Hoyt's persuasive skills and the barrage of correspondence and scientific testimony in support of her plan, huge obstacles faced the NPS as it studied the large area she proposed. Most of the problems arose from the clash of the NPS's policy of fee-simple land ownership with the reality that an appalling amount of the land was in private or state hands. The agency faced three types of land owners. The biggest, in terms of acreage, was the SPRR, which owned alternate sections of land through the heart of the proposed monument (Map B). Second was the State of California, which also had many sections scattered widely throughout the region. Finally, there were so many small parcels held by private individuals that neither of the counties could provide accurate data on the total acreage or its distribution. The SPRR's lands had always presented a foreboding picture to the NPS, but Hoyt and her allies did not hesitate to plunge ahead, trying to convince the company to donate its acreage and, if not, to exchange it for other government lands.[77]

Henry Harriman, President of the U.S. Chamber of Commerce and a member of the IDCL, opened the negotiations with the company on March 26, 1935. He approached New York–based business acquaintance Paul Shoup, Vice President of the SPRR, and asked if the railroad would donate its desert acreage. Shoup replied that he and the rest of the management of the public corporation could not justify such a giveaway to their stockholders. He added that he was familiar with the area from childhood and thought that a much smaller monument, perhaps ten percent of the Hoyt proposal, might satisfy the conservation purpose. If not, he recommended that the NPS contact SPRR's land agent in San Francisco, a Mr. C. F. Impey, to try to effect an exchange of some sort.[78]

Before Director Cammerer could contact Impey, another complication arose. On June 28, 1934, Congress passed the Taylor Grazing Act in order to control widespread overgrazing on public lands. President Roosevelt then issued Executive Order 6910 on November 25, 1934, banning homestead claims and grazing applications on more than 12,000,000 acres in California and many more in other Western states. This temporary withdrawal was designed to allow the formation of grazing districts based on sound studies of the carrying capacity of the forage. A report issued in early summer 1935 specified that 1,043,205 acres in Riverside County and 4,222,528 in San Bernardino County were among the affected areas. The upshot of this was that it would take an act of Congress to allow an exchange of these lands for the railroad's parcels. The NPS was not particularly bothered by this extra requirement, but it did further complicate an already difficult process. Cammerer wrote to Impey, arguing that the biological and recreational benefits of the proposed monument far outweighed any other type of land use. He acknowledged that special legislation or a presidential revocation of part of Executive Order 6910 would be required for an exchange, but he suggested that an arrangement might be possible based on the land values of the respective parcels rather than an acre-for-acre swap.[79]

Impey cautiously answered by inquiring as to what lands the government planned to offer for exchange and expressing doubt that the company would agree. Cammerer then sent a package of materials, including copies of President Roosevelt's land-withdrawal order, a draft of a bill to allow the exchange based on a successful one used at Petrified Forest National Monument (now Park) in Arizona, and an explanation of how the President could revoke Executive Order 6910 for the areas chosen by SPRR. Meanwhile, Minerva Hoyt promised that she would travel to San Francisco to see President McDonald, of SPRR, as well as Impey. She urged the NPS to redouble its efforts, telegraphing, "We are working everywhere and every way we can, but need you. Won't you splendid Park men put your shoulder to the wheel with us and let's go over the top with [a] million-acre reservation?"[80]

Soon, the NPS did just that, sending Harold Bryant to San Francisco to negotiate with Impey and the SPRR. What company officials told Bryant, however, was disheartening. Its preliminary survey of President Roosevelt's 1,136,000-acre withdrawal showed only 836,000 acres still in the public domain. The SPRR held approximately 148,000 acres, many within the heart of the most desirable part of the proposed monument. Furthermore, the company held rights to choose at least 72,000 indemnity acres from the remaining government land. Even more distressing was that the railroad recently had sold many acres, increasing the total of land owned by private individuals to 92,000 acres (Map C). The railroad's survey also confirmed that the state controlled at least 42,000 acres. Impey told Bryant that the lands desired by the NPS were the best-selling parcels that the company had in the entire desert region and were going for as much as $1.80 per acre. Nevertheless, he offered to "cut the price to the bone" if the government would make a block purchase. In his summary to Director Cammerer, Bryant wrote that the company wanted to be helpful and the NPS probably could buy the land for one dollar per acre. Unfortunately, the agency had neither the funds nor the legal ability to purchase land.[81]

After Bryant's trip to California, direct negotiations with the railroad bogged down as the NPS doggedly sought government land in California of sufficient value to exchange. In October 1935, a frustrated Bryant penned a letter to Minerva Hoyt, with copies to Philip Munz, Edmund Jaeger, and Loye Miller, starkly presenting the options: "We are now faced with the decision as to whether to attempt an almost impossible thing or to compromise on size sufficiently to make a trade and thus consolidate a part of the area hoping that the years will bring eventually the opportunity to enlarge it." He explained that the NPS could probably trade for land the railroad had just sold or still owned around the Lost Horse Valley but would have to leave out Cottonwood Springs and other areas south and east of it. This left a park or monument that almost matched the area originally proposed by Roger Toll. Bryant suggested that Hoyt and her friends "decide whether you wish to push the matter along rapidly by urging [this] initial area or whether you prefer to take the time to work out so major a land problem as is involved with the present boundaries." He concluded with an apology for even suggesting a change in the original plan for a larger monument.[82]

By December 1935, Minerva Hoyt and Philip Munz had opened a new front in the battle to secure the railroad's lands. It involved a series of letters between elite members of the New York and Boston social sets and was a roundabout way to seek influence on the SPRR. Both Munz and Hoyt decided to contact Boston socialite and fellow desert botanist Susan Delano McKelvey, an important figure at Harvard University's Arnold Arboretum. She had come to Boston and the arboretum years earlier, fleeing a broken marriage, and soon published a large volume on lilacs as well as a number of works on vegetation of the American Southwest. She was a cousin of President Roosevelt, the sister of famous architect William Delano, and a wealthy woman in her own right. Her circle of acquaintances included Henry W. de Forest, a member of the board of the SPRR. Frederic Delano, another relative, was another railroad owner as well as a member of the National Capital Park and Planning Commission and the uncle of President Roosevelt. She had spent many months in Indio and La Quinta during the 1930s and was soon enmeshed in a campaign to influence de Forest and, through him, the rest of the SPRR's board.

More than three months passed before de Forest responded to McKelvey's initial letter. He apologized for the delay and explained that he had suffered from an illness and temporarily misplaced her letter. He had discussed the matter with the "proper Southern Pacific people" and felt that some misunderstanding was interfering with the exchange. He reiterated that the railroad could not donate the land but hoped that "our people" would find a way to effect an exchange. It is hard to tell what influence this flanking movement had on the managers of the SPRR, but certainly it added to the chorus of encouragement they received to find a way to get their land to the NPS. A little over three weeks before President Roosevelt signed the proclamation establishing Joshua Tree National Monument, NPS's Acting Director Demaray wrote to the agency's chief engineer, Frank Kittredge, reporting that William Delano and Henry de Forest were still trying to work out a last-minute exchange.[83]

As the pro-monument movement drew in ever more advocates, the NPS continued to search for lands to exchange. In answer to a request from Cammerer, Fred W. Johnson, Commissioner of the General Land Office (GLO), reported that 9,599,616 acres of public domain lands were available in Imperial, Riverside, San Diego, and San Bernardino Counties, with more than seventy-eight percent of it in the latter. Demaray sent these figures to Impey, asking if the railroad would be interested in exchanging its holdings. Impey answered simply that the offered lands were of inferior quality, that the SPRR already had 3,000,000 acres of that type, and that company officials were quite satisfied with its current holdings in the proposed monument area, which were selling very well. With this response, senior NPS officials sensed the inevitability of sacrificing part of the land proposed for the monument in order to have quality lands withdrawn to exchange for the railroad's holdings within the final boundaries of the future unit.[84]

Although the negotiations with the railroad were agonizingly slow and disheartening, the situation with the state lands appeared much easier. The Land Ordinance of 1785 had directed the federal government to allocate section sixteen of each township in a newly surveyed area to its state to support education. In 1848, the federal government doubled that by adding section thirty-six to the lands available to each state upon admission to the Union for a total of 1,280 acres per township. If those specific sections were unavailable due to physical conditions or previous settlement, then the state could choose an equivalent amount of land in the same township. The latter were called indemnity lands. In March 1853, three years after statehood, California received almost 5,500,000 acres of land spread throughout the state. Unfortunately, notoriously incompetent or dishonest agents managed those lands to profit from their inside knowledge and control of land sales. By the 1930s, most of the land was gone, except the less desirable desert sections. The California State Lands Commission (CSLC), founded in 1938, today controls approximately 469,000 acres outright and the mineral rights of another 790,000. Much of this land is granted to oil and mining companies to generate money for California's teachers' retirement system.[85]

Minerva Hoyt took the lead in negotiating with the state for its 42,000 acres in the withdrawn area. On June 5, 1935, she excitedly reported that the state was willing to donate 22,000 acres of its school lands to the NPS for the national monument. Bogged down with the railroad negotiations, it took several weeks for Secretary Ickes to respond with a brief congratulatory note. Meanwhile, on June 11, the state legislature took up Assembly Bill 1344 to transfer the lands legally to the federal government. It passed immediately and, two days later, the director of the California Division of State Lands (CDSL) mailed copies of the new act to the NPS.[86]

For once it seemed that a land-acquisition problem could be solved without the turmoil and difficulty typically faced by the federal agency. However, it was not to be. A concerted effort in California to overcome its sordid history of misuse and squandering of its school lands was underway, a movement that led to the formation of the CSLC three years later. The act donating the acreage to the NPS specifically excluded the mineral rights, which were withheld for future revenue. It did not take long for NPS solicitors to spot that and block the donation. Cammerer wrote to Carl Sturzenacker, Chief of the CDSL, explaining that the federal government could not accept lands that it did not control in fee simple. The reason, he stated, was "the possibility of mining and oil drilling operations [that] would be incompatible with the administration of the area as a national monument, inasmuch as it is desirable to eliminate all commercial developments in the area."[87] A few weeks later, Sturzenacker acknowledged the position of the NPS and offered to exchange California's land in the monument area for other federal lands in the state. This was acceptable to NPS officials, who managed to get an amendment allowing such an exchange inserted in a bill to provide federal land to California for the expansion of Anza Desert State Park. When it passed, Public Law 74-838 enabled the eventual exchange of the state's 42,000 acres in the monument area for other federal land. What it did not do is provide the agency with fee-simple lands immediately as Joshua Tree National Monument moved closer to reality. Hence, the method was approved, but its execution was delayed.[88]

The situation with lands owned by private individuals or entities was dramatically complicated by the SPRR's sale of 89,600 acres. Some of the land was located in the defunct subdivision in Pinto Basin, but more lay in the area south of the MWD's aqueduct. The presence of CA 60 made these lands very attractive, especially for residents of Los Angeles. A popular movement to secure plots for recreation cabins was well underway and would lead eventually to the Small Tract Act of 1938, which provided five-acre parcels for recreation homes by lease or free of charge. Thereafter, these "jackrabbit homesteads" would crowd the monument's northern boundary. In 1936, however, the total acreage of the land owned by private individuals in Roosevelt's withdrawn area was uncertain and both Riverside and San Bernardino Counties maintained that they could not spare employees to assess the records and come up with reliable figures. The probability that many of the lands were tax delinquent somewhat alleviated the situation, because they might be obtainable later, perhaps through county donations. Nevertheless, as NPS officials pondered the cumulative total of lands held by the SPRR, the state of California and an indeterminate number of others, they knew they would have to disappoint Minerva Hoyt, in spite of all she had done to save California's desert flora.[89]

Threats to the Monument Continue

As that unhappy realization dawned on senior NPS officials, threats to the viability of a monument of any size appeared. The long delay had left the land in limbo while development pressures built up, especially along the southern flank of the Little San Bernardino Mountains and southward. The most significant issue by far was the MWD's aqueduct still under construction through the middle of Roosevelt's withdrawn area. In early 1935, the aqueduct's builders officially applied to the GLO for permission to build a camp and aggregate deposit sites along its right-of-way northeast of Chiriaco Summit. Initially, the NPS cited President Roosevelt's withdrawal order and balked, but an investigation by NPS Regional Inspector P. T. Primm in May and correspondence with the MWD and the GLO soon established that the district's rights preceded Roosevelt's withdrawal and, hence, were immune to its stipulations. Primm visited the camp, which had already been built, and found that "the only significant damage which has been done has been the denuding of the area from all plant life." Two months later, the MWD notified Primm that it would require four additional aggregate-deposit sites, amounting to 182 total acres in the proposed monument area, but they would not be operated by contractors on whom it blamed the destruction.[90]

In August, NPS officials sent Yellowstone biologist W. B. McDougall to assess the aqueduct's impact on the vegetation and wildlife. He found that one of the camps in Wide Canyon was much larger than it needed to be, but the others were of reasonable size. The principal damage came from the dumping of excavated material on the existing plant cover. With the on-site reports of Primm and McDougall in hand, NPS officials pondered the potential destruction of resources that might continue from ongoing construction and the long-term maintenance of the aqueduct. Again, Hoyt's plan for a huge monument, stretching nearly to the Salton Sea, faced a disturbing land-use problem.[91]

As the NPS grappled with the aqueduct issue, two more requests came for infrastructural improvements in the withdrawn area. In April 1935, the Southern California Telephone Company applied to the GLO to alter its rights-of-way in two areas south of the aqueduct and near CA 60. Because the two sites were so near an existing highway, the NPS did not contest this application. The other request concerned the road itself, or rather a cutoff from it at Indio stretching across the desert to Blythe. In February 1935, the GLO sent a letter with maps to the NPS, disclosing an application by the California Department of Public Works to build such a road. In a memorandum to Conrad Wirth, NPS official J. Lee Brown explained that the road would ascend the southern slope of the Little San Bernardino Mountains, "invading a portion of the desert which Mrs. Hoyt seems particularly desirous of preserving." The NPS did not approve the project and suggested that the state engineers should continue to follow the route of CA 60 further south before turning eastward. Then came surprising news that the state had been building the road for nearly a year, and it was nearly finished. It seems that the state forwarded to the GLO a map of the proposed road on March 2, 1934, and that an unnamed official there certified that only unpatented lands were involved. With this assurance and an act passed by the California legislature in 1931 to support the project, the state commenced construction. State highway Engineer C. H. Purcell reasoned that it was the fault of the GLO that they had proceeded without realizing that President Roosevelt had withdrawn the lands in question. He added that the state law to build the highway had preceded the federal withdrawal by two years and that the road was nearly done anyway. The NPS had no choice but to withdraw its disapproval. Somehow, in the midst of all the controversy over the monument's boundary, nobody seemed to notice state highway crews building a road through the middle of the proposed monument.[92]

The NPS faced increasing pressure as these land negotiations and threats unfolded. Proponents of the monument grew frustrated, and private landowners clamored for information about the future of their holdings. As early as February 14, 1934, California Assemblyman John Phillips demanded to know what was happening with the monument project after President Roosevelt's land withdrawal. A year later, Arno Cammerer ordered Harold Bryant to "put on some speed on the Joshua Tree National Monument . . . we are losing friends by not putting it across swifter." More and more landowners wrote, concerned that they might lose their land or simply anxious to know what was happening. Miners and their lawyers also wondered if they could keep their claims and whether mining would continue in the monument. Even ranchers sought assurance that they would be allowed to graze their cattle in the monument.[93]

As the drama of the campaign for the monument unfolded, ever greater numbers of settlers, tourists, and thieves visited the area with predictably unfortunate effects. By January 1935, Minerva Hoyt had watched her beloved desert suffer from inaction and a lack of protection. She fired a letter to Cammerer, asking:

> Why not declare this a Monument and put to work these unemployed men and boys for whom the Government is earnestly seeking *valuable* work such as road and trail building? A recent "show" and *sale* of cacti and succulents, staged in Los Angeles, sold truck loads of valuable plants from this area. Those who disposed of this immense collection said 'all raised in Gardens.' Desert League informed plants over a hundred years old were represented to an ignorant public as four or five years of age.[94]

The following September, Hoyt appeared at the Los Angeles branch of the GLO and pleaded with its agents to erect signs warning the public not to remove desert plants and to guard the area against any further depredations. She had previously asked the NPS to take action only to be told that it was not that agency's responsibility. The special agent in charge of investigating the situation did agree to erect signs but admitted it was far beyond the capability of his small force to patrol such a huge region. Apparently, the signs did little to stop the removal or destruction of vegetation. William F. ("Bill") Keys (Fig. 5.2) sent a letter, in March 1936, complaining that residents of Twentynine Palms, fence-building neighbors, and vandalizing picnickers were all ruining what had been a wonderland of desert flora. He suggested that, perhaps, the government should pay him to "look after things" until someone else could be appointed to protect the area.[95]

A Grudging Compromise and the Final Proclamation

By the early days of 1936, the NPS finally accepted that it would have to settle for a smaller monument than the one Minerva Hoyt desired. The cumulative problems of acquiring the checkerboard array of railroad lands, as well as those in state and private lands, and the broad swath of infrastructure containing the MWD's aqueduct, the Indio to Blythe Highway, and various transmission lines forced the agency to compromise. The immense amount of correspondence backing a monument covering the entire withdrawn area was difficult to ignore. The testimony of scientists and experts in the region who hailed the biotic resources south of the Little San Bernardino Mountains meant that a monument established specifically to protect flora for study and enjoyment would be incomplete. NPS officials dreaded telling Hoyt, who would be grievously disappointed after so much hard work and expense.

On February 5, 1936, Arno Cammerer wrote to Hoyt with the bad news. The NPS leadership had met to consider how to make Joshua Tree National Monument a reality as soon as possible. Everyone agreed that the aqueduct should be the southern boundary, primarily because this removed much of the land owned by the SPRR. Furthermore, approximately three townships north of the aqueduct in and around the Cottonwood Mountains were also dropped, because half the land had been sold by the railroad to private individuals. The director expressed his sorrow that the areas to the south were so hard to acquire and hoped that the land could be obtained in the future. He reasoned that getting some land into the system was better than continuing to negotiate, which would risk losing the entire area to development.[96]

Minerva Hoyt's response was quick and predictable. She had earlier explained her desert park project to her friend William McAdoo, Secretary of the U.S. Department of the Treasury under Woodrow Wilson and one of California's two U.S. senators from 1933 to 1938. Upon receiving Director Cammerer's letter, she wired McAdoo to express her outrage and claimed that the new boundary "withdraws all scenic beauty and our most valuable plants . . . [this] means absolute defeat." She added that this solution would cut out most of the land in Riverside County and leave a monument mostly in San Bernardino County, which was an "undesirable land of no beauty and little scientific value." She concluded by asking McAdoo to ignore the NPS and introduce a bill in Congress for the full acreage that the President had withdrawn.[97]

Senator McAdoo contacted Cammerer, which led to a flurry of correspondence and a hurried meeting between the senator and Harold Bryant on February 12. After the meeting, Bryant reported to the director that Senator McAdoo was very cooperative and readily understood the problems of acquiring land. The senator offered to introduce a bill to get funds from Congress for the purchase of the railroad's lands at one dollar per acre. Strangely, Bryant quashed the idea, explaining that Congress had always opposed such a solution and that it somehow would establish a bad precedent. McAdoo also asked about securing tax-delinquent private land, and Bryant told him that a Riverside County official thought the matter "could be worked out, but just at present all counties are avoiding the forcing of tax sales." The meeting concluded with McAdoo promising to explain the difficulties to Hoyt and hopefully secure her support.[98]

A few days later, Senator McAdoo wrote to Hoyt, urging her to be satisfied with the new boundary lines. At the same time, a hopeful Harold Bryant also wrote to her, cautiously asking if she had had a chance to study the new proposal and repeating the rationale that the railroad's lands made a bigger unit impossible. He thought it would be better to create the smaller area, giving the vegetation immediate protection, and try to add other lands in the future. The combination of Senator McAdoo's persuasion and the very real threat to the entire project from vandalism and commercial raiding of the desert flora finally convinced Hoyt. On March 9, Senator McAdoo phoned Bryant to report that she was satisfied with the new boundary but only if a later attempt would be made to enlarge the area by exchanging privately owned sections. The most delicate of the agency's responsibilities finally could be laid to rest.[99]

As spring 1936 wore on, the NPS continued to negotiate with the SPRR, still hopeful a solution could be found to enlarge the monument. But it was not to be. By late March, pressure from McAdoo and Secretary Ickes forced the agency's planners to come up with a definitive proposal that would include the final boundary. A few weeks later, Cammerer wrote to Ickes that the NPS proposed a unit of 843,690 acres. He suggested that the remainder of the land withdrawn by President Roosevelt in 1933 be retained in that status for possible exchange with the railroad as well as potential expansion of the monument. He promised that a draft proclamation for the President's signature would be forthcoming shortly.[100]

In order to compose the proclamation, NPS officials needed to consult the GLO. They sent a draft to Commissioner Fred W. Johnson, who replied in early June. He corrected some legal and textual inconsistencies and then got to the heart of the proposal. The area would consist of 825,340 acres, nearly half of which had not been surveyed. Within the new boundary, the federal government controlled approximately 650,000 acres. Meanwhile the SPRR held some 149,300 acres, the state 21,650 acres, and 3,420 acres had been patented under various agricultural and mineral land laws. Another 3,878 acres of the public domain were under pending homestead entries and 1,200 acres in public water reserves. Furthermore, some lands might require approval from the Bureau of Reclamation before they could be completely reserved for monument purposes. He added that the final southern boundary would be the northern boundary of the right-of-way for the MWD's aqueduct. His report provided the legal description of the lands that would be part of the final proclamation. The statistics supplied by Fred W. Johnson apparently did not count more than 100,000 acres of indemnity lands that the SPRR held in the unsurveyed portion of the proposed monument, which accounts for the difference between this report and the figure calculated by investigators after the monument's proclamation.[101]

Finally, it appeared that the proclamation would go forward and a smaller Joshua Tree National Monument would exist. Yet one last procedural snag remained. Prior to the President's issuance of the proclamation, it had to be reviewed by the Bureau of the Budget and the U.S. Department of Justice. Representatives of both offices questioned the legality of using the Antiquities Act in this particular case, just as the NPS's Donald Alexander had earlier. Congress had passed the "Act for the Preservation of American Antiquities" on June 8, 1906. One of the most important building blocks of the national park system, it gave unilateral power to the President to proclaim monuments on federal lands to protect not only archaeological remains, but also "objects of historic or scientific interest." Reflecting legislators' response to vandalism and theft at Native American archaeological sites, it stipulated that these reserves should be "confined to the smallest area compatible with the proper care and management of the objects to be protected." A lawyer named Carr, from the Bureau of the Budget, phoned J. Lee Brown, of the NPS, and suggested that a monument of 825,340 acres might not fit that prescription. Brown explained that his agency needed to protect a large area of vegetation to satisfy the purpose of this monument and that the agency already had monuments created with the Antiquities Act that were much larger. Thereupon Carr wondered if the existing rights of landowners could be protected in such an expansive unit. Brown re-stated that the language in the draft proclamation had been used in previous cases and no problems had surfaced. A doubtful Carr rang off, saying he would discuss the matter with his supervisor.[102]

In early July, M. O. Burtner, an attorney in the U.S. Department of Justice, questioned the use of the Antiquities Act, because he doubted that trees could be considered objects of scientific interest. He recommended a smaller unit to be named "Mohave Desert National Monument" in order to better fit the location of the monument. Cammerer explained to Ickes that Burtner was holding a new proclamation he had composed for secretarial approval. The director argued that this new name ignored the fact that the monument would encompass both of California's deserts. Ickes did nothing to change the original proclamation, and on August 7, 1936, just three days before President Roosevelt proclaimed Joshua Tree National Monument, NPS Assistant Director G. A. Moskey put this challenge to rest. He reminded the director that they had faced this problem before and that following Burtner's advice would cripple the agency's plans for future monuments. Moskey had located a Dr. T. S. Palmer, who had known Congressman John F. Lacey, the chairman of the committee that wrote the Antiquities Act. Palmer stated that the committee had in mind a broad act that would not warrant the narrow interpretation of the Department of Justice. Palmer was willing to work with a historian to prove this was the case. With such assurance, the agency ignored the Justice Department's lawyer.[103]

With this last pernicious hurdle out of the way, President Franklin D. Roosevelt issued Proclamation 2193 on August 10, 1936, establishing Joshua Tree National Monument with 825,340 acres of land, a third of it in private or state hands (Map 2.3). It was the end of a tortured process and, to stalwart supporters such as Minerva Hoyt, a bitter compromise. It is uncertain whether

JOSHUA TREE NATIONAL MONUMENT

CALIFORNIA

Note. All distances are from Park Headquarters.

DISTANCES FROM HEADQUARTERS

INDIAN COVE	9 MI.
SPLIT ROCK AREA	13 "
SALTON VIEW	26 "
HIDDEN VALLEY	22 "
CHOLLA CACTUS GARDEN	19 "
COTTONWOOD SPRING	42 "
HIGHWAY 60-70 (THRU MON.)	46 "

VICINITY MAP

LEGEND
- Park Boundary
- Paved roads
- Improved roads
- Secondary roads
- Unimproved roads

0   3   6 MILES
SCALE

Drawn by H. L. Golder July   NM-JT 7021

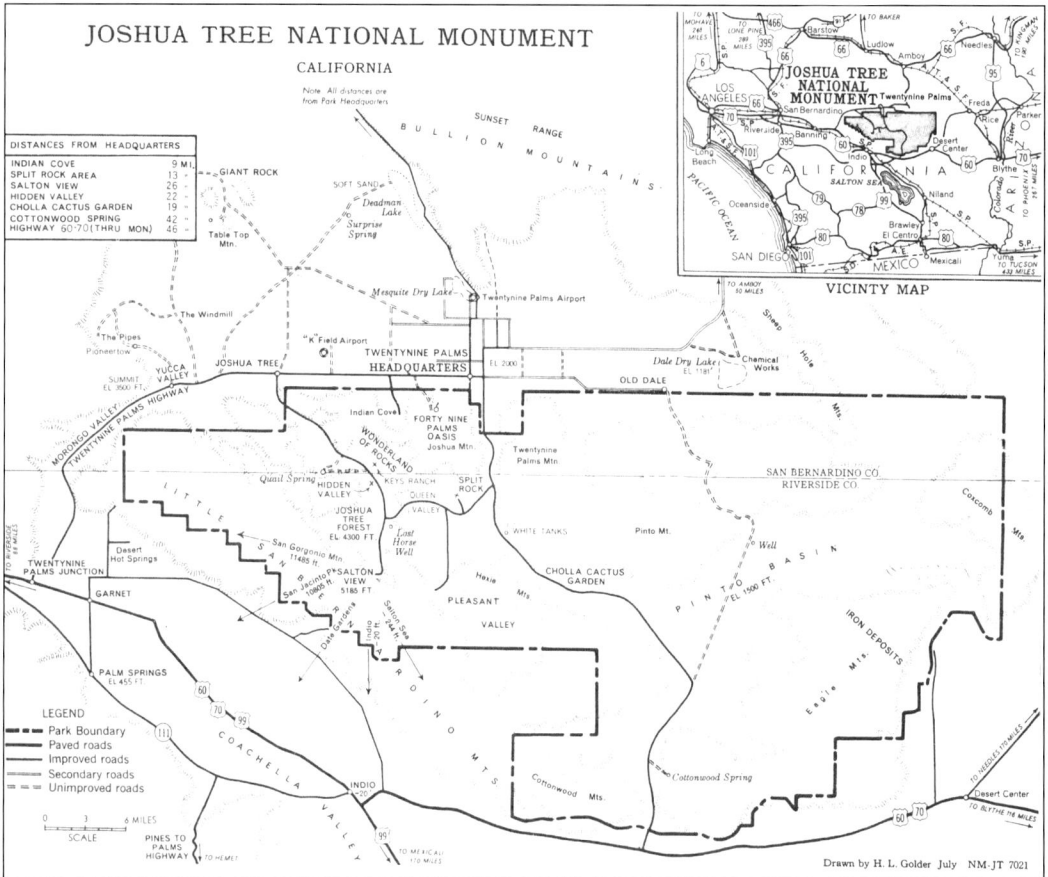

MAP 2.3. The final boundary of Joshua Tree National Monument as established on August 10, 1936. Among the areas excluded were all proposed lands south of the Colorado River Aqueduct and most of the Cottonwood Mountains, where the Southern Pacific Railroad Company had sold its lands to private settlers and investors. Drawn by H. L. Golder and printed in July 1947. Data source: Joshua Tree National Park Archives, Acc. 752, Cat. 25175, Folder 040. Delta Cartography.

Hoyt believed that the NPS would really try to add the lands south of the aqueduct at a later time. Nevertheless, she sent an effusive telegram to the President, thanking him for saving a large part of the desert she so loved. As the NPS prepared to inspect fully the lands it had been given and organize their management, Minerva Hoyt could at least be satisfied that she, almost single-handedly, had driven a campaign that resulted in a monument almost six times the size of the one recommended by Roger Toll.[104]

PART II

MANAGING A DESERT NATIONAL MONUMENT

THE SUCCESSFUL legislative establishment of a national park unit tends to make its backers sit back and celebrate, but the fight is rarely over. In the case of Joshua Tree National Monument, threats to overturn the legislation or suspend the laws that protect its vegetation continued from 1936 to 1956.

The National Park Service (NPS) faced three types of problems here. First, miners held thousands of claims and wanted the opportunity to establish new ones. Second, private companies and individuals as well as the State of California owned nearly a third of the monument's land, including the heart of the area most prized by visitors. Finally, the development of the new unit for visitors and the protection of its resources required personnel, careful planning, and funding for construction of infrastructure. All three were in short supply.

In this section, I not only relate these issues to the evolution of Joshua Tree as a national monument, but also explain the complexity and controversies of Joshua Tree's first two formative decades. In Chapter Three, I explain the difficult and sometimes vicious battle with miners that ultimately cost the monument one-third of its territory. In Chapter Four, I show how the NPS, forbidden at the time to buy property outright, used every legal means at its disposal to acquire two-thirds of the private land in the monument. In Chapter Five, I present the tasks undertaken to make the new unit viable, accessible, and safe from incompatible land uses by people who had moved earlier to the desert for its freedom and its extractive economy.

FIG. 3.1. Early pioneer William ("Bill") McHaney (1859–1937) was born in Missouri and came to Twentynine Palms to run cattle in 1879. His brother, Jim, was a notorious rustler with a dangerous gang, but Bill remained aloof from those activities and worked as a prospector in and around the future monument for the rest of his life. As the first-known white settler at the Oasis of Mara, Bill became an important source of information for the National Park Service and General Land Office about the Chemehuevi people and other Native Americans who befriended him. McHaney also located several of the important early mines in the area. Later, William F. ("Bill") Keys supported and protected him as the old-timer aged. He died shortly after Joshua Tree National Monument was established in 1936 and before the mining community realized what that meant for their way of life. Photographer and date unknown. Joshua Tree National Park Photo Archives, reference files.

CHAPTER THREE

Can This Monument Survive?

PEOPLE REACTED to the proclamation establishing Joshua Tree National Monument in a variety of ways depending on their personal beliefs and interests. Scientists, environmentalists, and urban public officials celebrated the success of their campaign and the protection of such a huge swath of desert ecology and scenery. Citizens in Twentynine Palms and the village of Joshua Tree happily envisioned a boom in tourism that would bolster their communities and economies. William F. ("Bill") Keys (Fig. 5.2) and others who lived inside the new monument warily wondered what it would mean for their traditional livelihoods and ways of life. Miners angrily protested the prohibition on future mining claims and plotted to overturn that standard national park policy as they had in Death Valley National Monument. Finally, National Park Service (NPS) officials faced the daunting task of determining what resources the nearly 1,300-square-mile preserve contained and how to protect and develop its harsh environment amid more than 280,000 acres of non-federal land and untold thousands of mining claims.

For the first twenty years of Joshua Tree National Monument, many of the controversies and difficulties that had characterized the political campaign to create it continued, in part because people held widely different attitudes toward the desert environment. Monument proponents saw the desert as a welcome retreat from urban modernity, a place where people celebrated individualism and self-reliance. Miners saw it as a bizarre and alien landscape to be explored or plundered. Many others saw it as a fearful wasteland and a place to be avoided into which unwelcome people and materials could be dumped. NPS officials were just as divided in their opinions, as shown by the contrasting reports of Roger Toll and Harold Bryant. The early years of Joshua Tree were marked by investigations of the unit to determine what was worthwhile and what was expendable, a glacially slow pace of development, exacerbated by World War II, a protracted and highly complex progress of acquiring private lands and validating mining claims, and a bitter excision of a third of the unit. Through these years, agency planners struggled to adapt NPS policy and infrastructure to an unfamiliar habitat and interpret enigmatic resources.

Rarely had the NPS received a new unit with so many basic land problems. Indeed, the very existence of the monument was still challenged. In a little over five years between the establishment of the monument and the start of World War II, the NPS carried out or commissioned nearly thirty separate inspections of its new unit. Senior regional office administrators, service-wide specialists, and General Land Office (GLO) investigators studied the area and recommended policies and actions that would shape the future of the new monument (Fig. 3.1). Each inspection resulted in a report that ultimately came before the NPS's director.[1]

Typically, officials at the NPS's headquarters in Washington, D. C., appointed a superintendent of a nearby large park to manage the infant unit. Colonel Charles G. Thomson, of Yosemite National Park, assumed the responsibility and conducted the first fact-finding inspection. Thomson waited two months after the monument was established to visit in late October 1936, when the temperature had cooled. He first interviewed many of the supporters who had fought to save the area, including Minerva Hoyt, Dr. Philip Munz, and groups from Palm Springs, Indio, and Twentynine Palms. He was pleasantly surprised by the landscape and the rich desert flora. He reported that building roads would be easy and passed along a local recommendation that one be constructed from Twentynine Palms through the Little San Bernardino Mountains to the towns and cities in the Coachella Valley. He did not expect fire to be much of an issue but warned that the water supply was scant and might seriously hinder development for visitors. The Yosemite superintendent also recommended that no visitor facilities be constructed in the monument because Twentynine Palms and other nearby communities could provide necessary tourist services. Thomson urged his bosses to develop the monument soon, because developers of subdivisions and individuals attracted to the desert lifestyle were rapidly moving into the region:

> No longer is the desert there a waste; it is a resource into which men and money are going with an amazing speed. The use and development of the monument are going to be colored by this extraordinary thing that is happening southwest, west, and north of it.[2]

He recommended intensive study of natural and archaeological resources, the survey and mapping of the monument, and preparation of interpretive materials for future visitors. Unfortunately, Thomson did not live to see his prescience confirmed because he died on April 6, 1937, leaving Joshua Tree temporarily leaderless. Officially, his task fell to his replacement at Yosemite, Lawrence Merriam, who later would become the director of NPS's western regional office in San Francisco.[3]

In addition to his initial inspection of the new unit, Thomson accomplished another important task during his brief tenure as superintendent of Joshua Tree. He appointed a Yosemite park naturalist, James E. Cole, to oversee the new monument (Fig. 3.2). Cole was born to American parents in Alberta, Canada, on September 10, 1902, and later moved with his family to Spokane, Washington. He studied natural history at the University of California, Los Angeles, and began working at Yosemite as a seasonal employee in 1933 and, two years later, as a full-time ranger–naturalist. Cole's initial involvement with Joshua Tree required him to handle specific monument issues for Thomson and

FIG. 3.2. Superintendent James E. Cole, who shaped the boundaries and layout of Joshua Tree National Monument, became its de facto manager while still serving as a ranger-naturalist at Yosemite National Park. Although World War II interrupted his leadership, he served at the monument until he was promoted to Regional Biologist at the NPS office in Omaha, Nebraska. Chief of Planning Thomas Vint wrote: "Superintendent Cole is doing a fine job. He knows the area, gets out and around it, explains the desert flora and fauna with ease and simplicity. He can roll a rock out of the road in the desert sun and peck at a typewriter by lamplight. He has what the National Park Service grew up on." Photographer and date unknown. Joshua Tree National Park Photo Archives, reference files.

Merriam, but he soon became the de facto manager of the unit. His official title changed during this time from a junior park naturalist to a custodian and, when the NPS opened an office in Twentynine Palms on September 19, 1940, to a superintendent. Although World War II interrupted his management of Joshua Tree, Cole spent more than five years at the monument, where he found himself in charge of a highly controversial unit and under personal attack by enemies of the NPS.[4]

Cole advised or participated in most of the inspections during these critical early years and initiated or contributed to complex debates about what the monument should be and how it should be managed. The inspections focused on five types of issues: (1) mining, both extant claims and heavy pressure from miners to reopen the monument to new claims; (2) land acquisition, especially the tracts belonging to the Southern Pacific Railroad Company (SPRR); (3) development, including a road system and a headquarters facility; (4) resource management, particularly the all-important location of water supplies, as well as baseline studies of flora and fauna; and (5) public use, both coping with traditional uses by residents in the monument and planning for visitation and interpretation. The decisions made and actions taken during the first two decades would shape much of Joshua Tree's history and administration. In this chapter, I focus on continuing threats first to the primary values of the monument and to its very survival.

Mining and the Boundary Question

During the campaign to establish Joshua Tree National Monument, miners wondered and worried whether their business could continue as usual in the unit. A few years earlier, President Herbert Hoover had proclaimed Death Valley National Monument with the normal stipulation against new claims. However, a few months later the U.S. Congress passed legislation that restored the right to explore and claim new mining sites in the huge monument. The NPS and Secretary of the Interior Harold Ickes did not dispute this action, admitting that mining was an integral part of Death Valley's heritage. The proclamation establishing Joshua Tree held that existing mines and claims could continue, as long as miners actively worked them; it also adhered to NPS's policy by banning any new claims. Once this became known, the miners erupted into a shocked rage and attacked not only the ban on new mining claims, but the existence of the monument itself.[5]

The opening shot came in December 1936, when California State Mineralogist Walter W. Bradley wrote to local congressman Harry Sheppard, decrying the prohibition and insisting that the legislator introduce a bill similar to the pro-mining act at Death Valley. The Mining Association of the Southwest (MAS) immediately organized "an advisory committee of eighty" to challenge the mining ban. Most of the agitation came from mining enthusiasts living in the Los Angeles area rather than within or near the monument. In their eagerness to overturn the ban in Joshua Tree, however, they discussed widening the organization to include miners throughout Southern California.[6]

After *The Los Angeles Times* printed a story about miners' opposition, monument allies tried to rebut it, arguing that the economic future of the desert area lay in recreation and tourism, not in the haphazard mining that had always characterized the region (Plates 28 and 29). One correspondent supported the ban on mining:

> The Joshua Tree National Monument is to become either a haven for tourists and lovers of the desert and the out-of-doors, or a mecca for prospectors, who if the regulations are amended, may under the mining laws go to Inspiration Point [Keys View], stake out a claim, blast a hole in the ground and exclude the public from the premises within the confines of the claim. He might even build a shack there, and charge admission to take a look at the Coachella Valley. Likewise a prospector could stake a claim to include Split Rock, put some powder under it, touch it off, scrape around in the gravel, and finding no gold could say; "Excuse me, I thought that would make a good mine."[7]

During Colonel Thomson's inspection, he placed the mining issue at the top of his agenda. His quiet discussions with locals led him to believe that most of the twenty-three mines he identified in his subsequent letter to NPS Director Arno Cammerer were either abandoned or producing very little ore. After describing local support for recreation and for the monument, Thomson offered a possible solution:

> This mining situation revives the question of final boundaries for this monument. It may well be that a practical solution rests in removing from the monument the northeast area which contains the Dale, Gold Crown, and possibly some other mining areas which are reported to be the good properties . . . My recommendation would be that you ask Congressmen Sheppard and Scrugham to go along patiently with us for a few months until the real facts concerning mining can be secured; that we then move energetically to secure the facts; and that in the meantime we encourage other interests in Congressman Sheppard's district to make themselves heard in behalf of the development of the Joshua area as a tourist asset to the surrounding communities.[8]

Together with the dire land acquisition problem, this mining issue led the NPS to organize several inspections, including one by investigators from the GLO. In March 1937, Samuel E. Guthrey

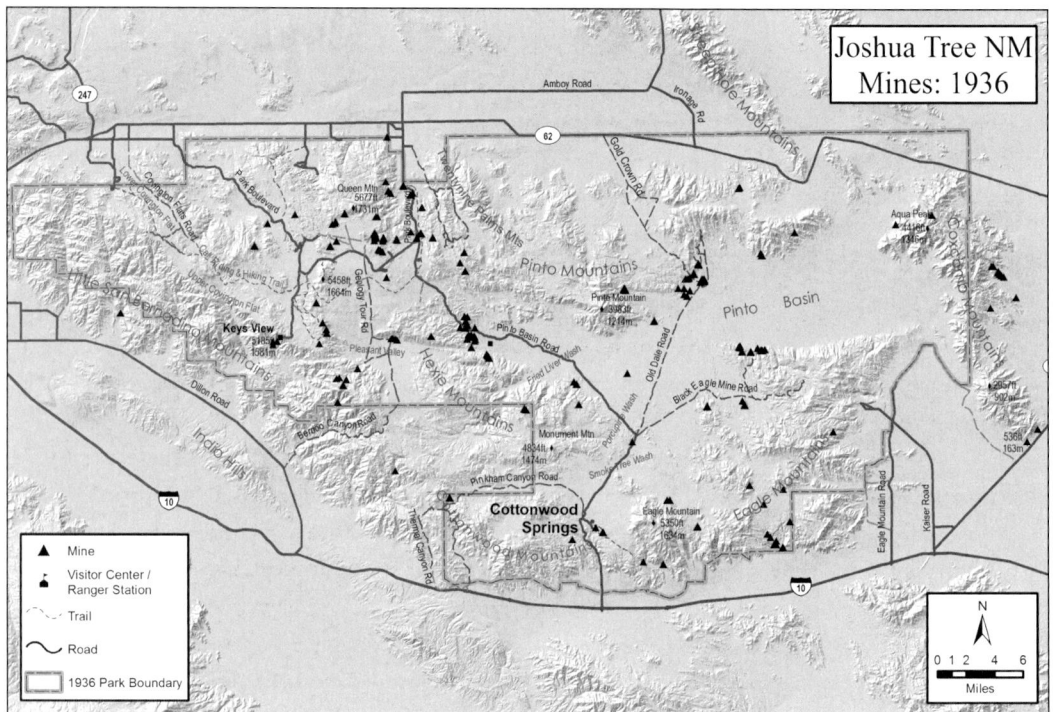

MAP 3.1. Major mines in and around Joshua Tree after the boundary change of 1950. Except for Bill (William F.) Keys, most miners had ceased active operations in the mines along the monument's paved roads. Those along the unpaved Old Dale Road and in the Eagle Mountains remained active and employed several hundred men. Data source: Joshua Tree National Park GIS files. Delta Cartography.

from that office conducted a lengthy survey of the mines in the young monument and reported that minerals with economic potential existed over most of the monument, but the only ones producing were in the eastern two-thirds of its area. He then described mines actively operating in more than thirty locations and estimated that they employed 250 men, with a payroll of $40,000 per month. Guthrey concluded that, since all of the mines were of the deep or lode type, they would not detract from such a "distinctly desert area, with no particular scenic features."[9]

At the same time, NPS engineer Frank Kittredge and landscape architect Ernest Davidson also inspected the monument, and each submitted a report in April 1937. Davidson suggested that mining was so dispersed that the idea of eliminating it was out of the question. He added that, in desert country, it should be part of the "local color." Kittredge bluntly stated that the closure of mining would throw 200 men out of work and cause much resentment. He reiterated that mining would not seriously affect the park's values and that it should be allowed under the same rules as those applying in Death Valley (Map 3.1).[10]

On June 17, 1937, Congressman Sheppard introduced H.R. 7558 to the U.S. House of Representatives, where it was referred to the Committee on the Public Lands. The short, eight-line paragraph simply extended the mining laws to the entire monument. A month later, Director Cammerer wrote to Sheppard, reminding him of the agency's request that he not submit legislation until the facts were known about the state of mining. He explained to the congressman that the first superintendent, Colonel Thomson, had unexpectedly died and that was why the NPS had not been in contact for some weeks. He restated why the agency opposed new mining and noted that, rather than allow it, park leaders would "recommend that approximately the eastern two-thirds of the monument, which contains the larger portion of the mineral deposits, be eliminated and that no prospecting or mining, except upon valid existing claims, or grazing, be permitted within the smaller remaining area."[11] Cammerer added that this would certainly be opposed by the people in California who had worked so hard to convince President Roosevelt to proclaim the unit a national monument.

Sheppard responded that he had asked to be kept informed about the NPS's study of the mining issue but that, whenever he inquired, agency officials would only tell him that Colonel Thomson was heading the investigation. The last time he received this response was three days after the superintendent had died. Clearly affronted, Shepherd introduced the bill and added that his own knowledge of the mining business, particularly in light of the ongoing economic depression, did not persuade him to change it. This, in turn, spurred the NPS to organize and conduct quickly another investigation. In August, Cammerer met with Frank Kittredge, now regional director, and assigned Ben Thompson and Merel Sager from the Washington, D.C., office to gather information that would undermine the bill. Apparently, Kittredge, always the good soldier, followed orders regardless of his personal opinion. Cammerer also contacted Senator McAdoo, who reassured him that he opposed opening the monument to new mining. H.R. 7558 died in committee later that year.[12]

In September, Sager submitted a report on his inspection of the monument that covered many planning and development issues but highlighted mining. He suggested that Guthrey had painted a rosy picture of mining based on a few mines that had produced well in the past. He quoted Sam Ryan, owner of the Lost Horse Mine, as saying, "the area might as well be a national monument as it is no good for anything else." Sager added that both he and Ryan believed that a major investment might produce worthwhile mines but that it would be risky, because lode mining is unpredictable. Sager added:

> The eastern segment of the monument, being lower in elevation than the central part, is decidedly lacking in recreational value, and undoubtedly is more valuable for mining. Therefore the writer heartedly concurs with the decision of the staff that should pressure be sufficient to pass the Sheppard bill, the eastern two-thirds of the monument [should] be eliminated. Indeed there is much to be said for eliminating the eastern section whether the Sheppard bill passes or not.[13]

Sager's report showed clearly that some in the NPS still regarded most of the desert as unworthy of inclusion in the system. Soon, people in Twentynine Palms and Joshua Tree village started criticizing the agency for its unwillingness to establish a local office or develop the infrastructure for tourism it had promised. NPS officials answered that they could do nothing until they solved the monument's twin problems of determining a final boundary and acquiring non-federal land. Over the next year, the NPS discussed the idea of cutting out part of the monument with local supporters. In September 1938, business leaders from Twentynine Palms met independently with the MAS to seek a compromise. After the meeting, *The Los Angeles Times* reported that a deal was close; it would eliminate three-fifths of the monument, a total of 500,000 acres, so that mining could return there. The article implied that the miners hoped that prospecting would surge and force the agency to open the remaining land to new claims. Meanwhile, Congressman Sheppard reintroduced a second bill, H.R. 3827, which again proposed opening the entire monument to mining. Subsequently, the NPS and local allies convinced Sheppard that opening the core area of the monument, in and around Lost Horse Valley, would destroy the entire purpose of the unit. Sheppard grudgingly agreed to reverse his position, and the second bill died in committee.[14]

By 1939, the NPS decided that the only way to prevent mining throughout the monument was to eliminate most of its eastern part. At the same time, land problems both within the unit and along its boundaries suggested that a complete reevaluation of the boundaries should occur. After another inspection in December 1938, agency officials P. T. Primm and James Cole recommended

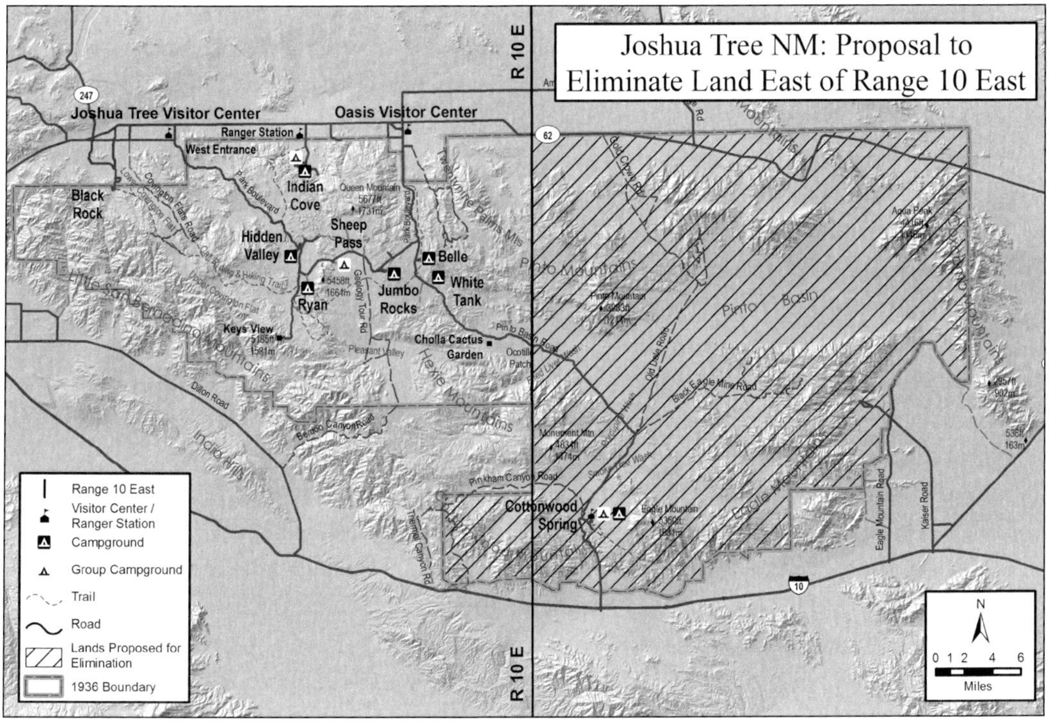

Joshua Tree NM: Proposal to
Eliminate Land East of Range 10 East

Legend:
- | Range 10 East
- Visitor Center / Ranger Station
- Campground
- Group Campground
- Trail
- Road
- Lands Proposed for Elimination
- 1936 Boundary

0 1 2 4 6 Miles

MAP 3.2. The initial Park Service proposal to eliminate the eastern two-thirds of Joshua Tree National Monument stemmed from beliefs that most of the potential mineral wealth in the area could be found there and that as a scenic and recreational resource the Pinto Basin was not worth much anyway. However, some in the agency argued that such a large exclusion of territory would establish a bad precedent for the rest of the park system. Data source: Joshua Tree National Park GIS files. Delta Cartography.

that all land east of Range 10 East of the land system grid be eliminated (Map 3.2). Yet some senior agency officials worried that eliminating a large part of the monument might harm wildlife and set a bad precedent for the future of the entire national park system. They determined to investigate all the ramifications of such an action. Victor Cahalane, acting chief of the wildlife division, consulted biologist Loye Miller, and the two agreed that the loss of the Pinto Basin and its surrounding mountains would not detract from the monument. In early April 1939, Regional Director Kittredge agreed but suggested that the southwestern boundary should be extended to the Metropolitan Water District's (MWD) aqueduct. During the campaign to establish the monument, a boundary was chosen that lay along the right-of-way for the aqueduct. After the proclamation, workers built the aqueduct south of its originally planned location. The resulting gap opened the area between the aqueduct and the monument boundary to settlement, enabled poachers to enter the canyons easily within the monument, and cut off part of the slope of the Little San Bernardino Mountains. The wildlife experts who agreed to shrink the monument worried about the survival of bighorn sheep, especially with the loss of all mountain areas in its eastern section.[15]

While the NPS struggled to defend its botanical unit against new claims, the GLO gathered data about the mines that already existed. Its records showed 3,782 claims in the western section and 5,000 in the eastern section. For a claim to be considered valid, it had to have evidence of ore and of active production. Most of the claims had been abandoned, some since the late nineteenth century. In 1941, Superintendent Cole reported that the GLO considered twenty-eight mines in the western section and 405 in the eastern section to be valid. Miners actually worked only a fraction of those claims. This strongly supported the agency's position that mining, in addition to being destructive, was fading as an economic function.[16]

In the spring of 1940, the NPS sent yet another senior official to study the proposed "boundary change." This time it was C. Marshall Finnan, Superintendent of the National Capital Parks. Minerva Hoyt had heard about the efforts to identify parts of the monument to eliminate, and she was extremely upset. Soon, letters began pouring in from botanists, community organizations, and her other allies. She demanded that Finnan consult with her while in California, which he did. Nevertheless, Finnan also agreed that the eastern section would have to go. This prompted new NPS Director Newton Drury to call for a special meeting at Yosemite National Park, where he and other senior officials would be attending a conference of the agency's advisory board. Joining Drury at the July 21, 1941, evening meeting were Regional Director Owen Tomlinson, Assistant Regional Director Herbert Maier, Superintendent Lawrence Merriam of Yosemite, and James Cole. Drury brought up the intense opposition to a boundary change by Hoyt and her allies. He urged Tomlinson to communicate to her that the alternative might be the elimination of the entire unit. He added that the NPS did not want a repetition of what had happened at Organ Pipe Cactus National Monument in Arizona. At that unit, proclaimed a year after Joshua Tree, miners drew national attention to their efforts to overturn a ban on new mining claims, embarrassing the NPS and ultimately succeeding.[17]

In fact, Director Drury had decided already to have a special committee of agency specialists make a final determination of whether the boundary should be changed and, if so, exactly where. Four days before the meeting at Yosemite, Tomlinson suggested a committee consisting of Maier as chairman, biologist Lowell Sumner, geologist J. Volney Lewis, planning chief Ernest Davidson, and James Cole. Later, the committee would also include Assistant Director Ben Thompson and Guy Flemming, of California's state park system. Before their serious work even began, Congressman Sheppard told Cole that recent evaluation of the old Iron Chief Mine in the Eagle Mountains had revealed a substantial amount of ore worthy of large-scale exploitation. He did not mince words, telling the superintendent that he would make sure that area was deleted from the monument. With this warning in mind, the committee conducted its inspection during September 1941. On the last day of the month, Maier wrote Tomlinson to say the final report would be forthcoming but that the committee agreed that the area east of Range 10 East should be deleted. On the bottom of the memorandum he penned that it was unfortunate that this would remove the Cottonwood Springs area as the southern entrance and could force the agency to build a more-difficult and expensive north-to-south road through the Little San Bernardino Mountains as suggested by people in the Coachella Valley.[18]

While Maier prepared the official report, each of the committee's members sent individual opinions to Tomlinson. The comments by biologist Sumner were particularly important. At the time, many in the NPS as well as in the public believed that bighorn sheep were close to extinction in the monument. Cutting out all the mountains in the eastern section would open them to exploitation and probable elimination in those areas. Sumner warned that this was a potential catastrophe. He alone among the committee members felt that the eastern section was worthy of retention for its botanical diversity. He admitted, however, that biological concerns were only part of the evaluation and that other management considerations might warrant the exclusion of the Pinto Basin and its surrounding mountains (Plates 8 and 9). Landscape architect Davidson regretted losing the great vistas available in the east, but admitted that the Dale Mining District probably should be removed and that cutting out all of the eastern section would simplify administration. State park superintendent Flemming agreed that the eastern area should be cut, the southwestern boundary should be moved to the aqueduct, and that the Indian Cove area in the north should be eliminated because of the presence of private lands. James Cole favored the elimination of the Dale Mining District, the Eagle Mountains, and two small pieces of land on the western side of the road from Twentynine Palms to the monument. Private lands dominated the two small tracts, and Cole recommended their deletion to simplify administration. This proposal, like Flemming's, showed how desperate the NPS was to solve disputes with private landholders and threats of incompatible development in the monument.[19]

Finally on October 13, 1941, Maier submitted his official report for the committee. He began with a clear statement regarding the relative values of different parts of the monument:

> In general I feel very strongly that every unit in the National Park System should be able to justify itself and should be in a position to defend its boundaries on the basis of the intrinsic and superlative values contained therein. It does not follow, however, that all portions of land within a unit must necessarily possess superlative scenery or outstanding natural phenomena. Frequently quite "ordinary" land is included in order to encompass or complete a wildlife range or a watershed, or to serve as a buffer strip along a boundary to facilitate protection and simplify administration. Such portions of land serve to round out the unit and their inclusion can easily be justified along with the whole.[20]

Having established that he did not favor elimination of any part of the monument unless there were compelling reasons to do so, Maier suggested that one option might be to remove the mountains in the eastern section but not the Pinto Basin itself. He admitted that this could force the NPS to maintain expensive roads in the area but argued that mining would not severely impact the visual appearance of the mountains and the basin itself would remain protected. In his conclusion, Maier stated that he agreed with the rest of the committee that, if necessary, the eastern edge of Range 10 East should be the boundary.[21]

Director Drury and other NPS leaders decided to forego changing the eastern boundary until pressure forced some action, but the idea of extending the boundary south to the aqueduct was sufficiently appealing that most wanted to pursue it independently. In November, Tomlinson ordered engineering draftsman G. E. Lavezzola and Cole to inspect the land between the current boundary and the aqueduct. The basic question was whether the benefits to wildlife from including the base of the mountains offset the fact that much of the land was in private hands. Lavezzola and Cole found that most of the land was tax delinquent and might be available for a low price set by Riverside County. They recommended that the agency go ahead and ask for a presidential proclamation to change the boundary. Meanwhile, Superintendent Cole learned from a state fish and game warden that a species of burro deer used the eastern part of Pinto Basin as part of its range. Cole suggested that Sumner return to study the situation and its implications for changing the eastern boundary. These questions and many more became moot with the onset of World War II a few weeks later. The War Production Board issued Limitation Order L-208 in October 1942, which suspended gold mining for the duration of the war. The purpose of the order was to focus on basic and strategic mineral production. The Eagle Mountain iron mine was insufficiently developed to become an integral part of that effort. For a time, Joshua Tree was safe from mining and any thoughts of diminishing its size.[22]

The Battle over Mining Resumes

On May 6, 1944, James Cole returned from military service to his position as Superintendent of Joshua Tree National Monument. He immediately raised the issue of adjusting the boundary and spent much of the summer studying maps and aerial photos in an effort to fine tune his recommendations. Perhaps spurred by Cole's renewed interest, Director Drury urged all the units in the national park system to evaluate their boundaries to make sure that they were defensible against criticism and potential invasion. In September, Cole submitted a 'preliminary' report with his new proposals. He called for elimination of the Gold Park and Old Dale mining districts, the Iron Chief Mine area, 480 privately owned acres just inside the boundary near Twentynine Palms, most of the Cottonwood Mountains, and a small area near the head of Berdoo Canyon that had been subdivided. He recommended that a corridor, including Cottonwood Spring and the road to it from the north, be retained and an area south of the Hexie Mountains be added. The latter had been dropped from the original monument proposal due to the sale of alternate sections of land by the SPRR. Cole determined that all but 200 acres in that area were tax delinquent and under the control of the state.[23]

Superintendent Cole clearly wanted the boundary question solved as soon as possible, but it was not to be. The agency was still understaffed, and nobody but the superintendent wanted to draw attention to the problem. And while the miners remained quiet for the rest of the war, others did not. Paul Witmer, of the GLO, wrote in early 1945 to inquire whether the NPS would give up a tract of 162 acres immediately south of Twentynine Palms and west of the Chemehuevi reservation for small-tract homesteads. Cole passed along the request, but Regional Director Tomlinson refused, because it would draw attention to possible boundary revisions. In mid-February, Witmer visited the monument and proposed that the NPS exclude five sections of land along the northern border, including a portion of Indian Cove and a block of territory adjacent to the western access road, from Joshua Tree village. A portion of the latter was already in private hands and promised to pose a difficult management situation. This time Herbert Maier answered that bringing up the subject would expose the agency to criticism for having "over-reached" itself during the campaign to establish the monument.[24]

On June 30, 1945, the government revoked Limitation Order L-208, and it did not take long for the mining lobby to restart their campaign to overturn the ban on new claims in the monument. Superintendent Cole pleaded with the regional office to speed up action on setting a final boundary, while Congressman Sheppard pondered introducing a new bill to quiet the controversy. On November 15, 1945, Sheppard introduced H.R. 4703 to Congress, which proposed the boundary changes Cole suggested and included an authorization of $215,000 to acquire the remaining private

FIG. 3.3. In 1934, when Roger Toll, then Superintendent of Yellowstone National Park in Wyoming, inspected the Joshua Tree area for the National Park Service, he was impressed by a relatively dense cover of desert biota in the higher-elevation Mojave Desert section of the future national monument. Despite Joshua Tree's rich variety of xerophytic vegetation, most later inspectors dismissed fire as a potential danger. They were proven wrong in 1949 and with increasing frequency in recent decades. Photograph by Roger Toll, March 9, 1934. Harpers Ferry Center, Joshua Tree National Park Collection, WASO-H-703.

land in the rump monument. The congressman hoped that cutting more than 310,000 acres from the eastern part of the monument might satisfy the mining faction.[25]

Unfortunately for Sheppard, the miners refused to accept anything less than complete access to the entire monument. They were joined in opposing his bill by hunters who rejected the NPS's prohibition on their activities, and by landholders in the monument, who feared expulsion if Congress approved the land-acquisition fund. An inholder named Charles L. Stokes spearheaded the resistance by landowners and soon proved to be extremely active and aggressive. Late in 1945, Stokes and several others had purchased a section of former railroad land in Hidden Valley, the heart of the monument's most scenic area (Fig. 3.3). Later, James Cole speculated that Stokes knew the land was in the monument and hoped to benefit financially from the deal. In opposing H.R. 4703, Stokes lost no opportunity to accuse monument personnel of duplicity, corruption, and intimidation. He challenged every aspect of NPS's management, especially anything having to do with the boundary change and efforts to acquire non-federal land. He accused Superintendent Cole of personally designing the new boundaries to enrich himself. He attempted to disrupt an exchange between SPRR, the NPS, and a company interested in obtaining government land north of the monument. He complained about the agency at every conference and hearing and finally sent a letter accusing Cole of exceeding his authority for "political" reasons by getting SPRR to halt sales to private individuals. He directed the letter to the Secretary of the Interior but also sent copies to every member of the congressional committee reviewing Sheppard's bill.[26]

After consultation up and down the hierarchy of the NPS, from Cole to the director, Secretary of the Interior Julius Krug answered Stokes. He explained the policies of the agency regarding land acquisition and then dismissed the accusation against the superintendent:

> Your criticisms of Custodian Cole are believed to be without basis. I am informed by Director Drury of the National Park Service that Mr. Cole at all times has acted in compliance with official instructions and that he has not exceeded his authority or taken any action that might be construed as being in his personal interest. It is true that Mr. Cole, pursuant to instructions, followed up with the Southern Pacific Railroad Company a request previously made by Director Drury that the Company suspend further sales of its properties within Joshua Tree National Monument pending the possible appropriation of Federal funds to acquire them. This request was reasonable and, I believe, in the public interest since it conceivably could prevent unwarranted development and exploitation of the properties by third parties in contemplation of their sale to the Government.[27]

Even this response to Stokes, with its final statement aimed directly at him, did not stop him, but it frustrated his attempt to get Cole and other monument employees fired.

Meanwhile, miners in the region, now organized as the Mining Congress of Southern California (MCSC), assessed H.R. 4703. Several sections of the bill troubled the miners. First, they opposed the prohibition against mining in the remaining monument. Second, the bill did not explicitly restore the mining laws to the areas removed from the monument; it merely said that the land would return to the public domain. Third, it stipulated that the President could unilaterally add lands to the monument in the future. The mining lobby and its allies, including the Southern California Council of the State Chamber of Commerce, saw the latter as an additional threat that could expand the monument and its restrictive policies. Arrayed against these forces were conservationists, local town councils, especially in San Bernardino County, most newspapers, and the NPS. Unfortunately for the anti-mining contingent, Minerva Hoyt passed away on December 15, 1945, removing the most-powerful organizer for protecting the monument. Yet her death simplified the solution the NPS had chosen, because, to the end of her life, Hoyt furiously opposed diminution of her prized achievement.[28]

In March 1946, the Southern California Council announced it would hold a forum at its next meeting to discuss Sheppard's bill and the future of mining in the region. During the previous several months, the NPS had worked hard to explain why the bill that cut more than a third of the unit was the best solution. Many in the environmental community were disturbed at this compromise but understood that the alternative might be elimination of the monument. An increasingly stressed James Cole sent dozens of long letters to conservation, recreation, tourism, and academic organizations, begging them to attend and speak on behalf of the monument. He also tried to communicate with the miners, finally expressing his frustration to Victor Hayek, Secretary of the MAS:

> It is obvious from your map that the bill proposes to give to the mining interests the mining districts they want and anyone would naturally think the miners and mining groups would not only be satisfied but would actively support the bill...The mining interests have not been able to obtain passage of a bill to open the monument to mining and now they are opposing a bill which without question gives them the only areas where there is any mining activity. Frankly, I cannot understand the psychology of miners and the groups you represent.[29]

In spite of or, perhaps, because of his efforts, pro-mining forces sought to discredit Cole by insisting that he had told them 115,000 acres were sufficient for the monument. Acting Director Hillory Tolson responded that it was "inconceivable" that Cole would say such a thing, because he had proposed the boundaries that were in H.R. 4703.[30]

A Forum on Mining and the Monument

The meeting took place on April 17, 1946, at the San Bernardino County Courthouse. The audience of approximately 100 consisted primarily of miners, land developers, and others who opposed the bill. James Cole, Herbert Maier, and several others from the NPS attended. The format was scheduled to allow Cole to speak for the agency, a limited number of others to speak for and against the bill, and then a period in which the NPS could answer questions and rebut any false claims. The first speaker was Frank Bagley, President of the Twentynine Palms Chamber of Commerce, who spoke in favor of the bill, noting that recreation and resorts seemed to be immune to economic downturns and should be the economic focus rather than mining. Next to speak was Congressman Sheppard, who carefully explained how he supported miners and why his bill would help them. Then Cole took the podium and explained how the bill would return 310,000 acres to the public domain while providing funds to acquire 30,000 acres of private inholdings. He argued that the compromise bill was a logical solution, even if it diminished the national monument. He particularly stressed the rapid settlement of the desert by the five-acre "jackrabbit homesteads" as well as larger and more permanent settlements and the need for a large protected area to cope with future demands for recreation.[31]

Next on the agenda came opponents of Sheppard's bill. First, Charles Stokes leveled numerous charges against the agency and Superintendent Cole. Then, G. A. Joslin, a miner and chair of the Los Angeles Area Chamber of Commerce, compared federal land agencies to Adolf Hitler and Benito Mussolini, insisting they had become lawmakers themselves. He complained about the tight regulations on government reserves and argued that "the state is becoming more important than the individual." Several more mining enthusiasts expressed shock that Joshua Tree was not open to new claims like Death Valley. These arguments against federal regulation, prohibition of economic exploitation, and loss of traditional livelihoods had been encountered many times by the NPS, and they continue to be emotional responses to land preservation today.[32]

Edmund Yeager followed and defended the purpose of the monument. He explained the scientific and educational benefits of a unit devoted to saving not just Joshua trees, but entire ecosystems. Several of the opposition had ridiculed Minerva Hoyt and the concept of protecting areas for future generations. He lashed out at them:

> I noticed that some have been filled with snickers and laughter when five hundred years is mentioned. Gentlemen, it is time this community in Southern California and the people of the United States look a little bit to the future and not simply down the end of our noses and

our own immediate living. The people of other countries have found that time does pass and that things they did not preserve are gone forever. We must preserve some areas or samples of wilderness, if you please, and when I say wilderness I do not merely mean barren places, but samples of unspoiled places for the men and women who must come in the future.[33]

Will Held, of the Sierra Club, stressed that Southern California would benefit economically far more if Joshua Tree became a world-class attraction rather than another unknown province of mining. He stated that the reason why the monument was not developed for tourism was that NPS was afraid to invest there with a threat of losing the unit to mining. Then, a Riverside County resident, Randall Henderson, attacked one of the points made earlier by the pro-mining faction about personal freedom. He explained that he enjoyed camping in Joshua Tree, but miners had put up "no trespassing" signs, curbing his right to explore the desert and camp where he wanted. This, he warned, was an abridgement of freedom.[34]

Undaunted, the miners and their allies fought back. W. B. Clemenger offered one of the leading arguments of the mining faction:

> There has been a lot said about our posterity—what they are going to enjoy, and our immediate future, and the millions that are going to enjoy the desert, and the rest of that. We have just got through one war and almost got caught short, and now the Federal Government has grabbed off millions of other acres of land and tells us that we can't prospect on it. Who found all these areas? Was it the wealthy companies? No! It was the little prospectors, like those who are here today. Who is taking the land? The Federal Government. If we can't prospect and we are caught in another war, where are we going to get our strategic minerals?[35]

Thereafter, Hal Boyce, representing the Sportsmen's Club in Banning, reasoned that his group was interested in conservation, especially of quail, and that the dearth of water in the monument was forcing the birds to congregate in large numbers near the few available springs. This exposed them to predators that the hunters could help control. He added that his group wanted to enjoy the monument "to the fullest."[36]

The hours passed as a few more miners spoke, and Maier began to wonder if the NPS would have the promised time to answer its opponents. When the rebuttal time did come, the first speaker again was Frank Bagley. He first expressed surprise that the NPS was so widely hated in the region. He sarcastically speculated on whether the parks at Yosemite and the Grand Canyon were mistakes and whether it might be dangerous to visit them. Then, he challenged the miners to show any year since the Civil War when mining made more money than tourism. At this point, Stokes began shouting at Bagley and had to be silenced by moderator Henry Mulryan.[37] With only minutes left, Maier took the podium to try, once more, to answer critics of the NPS. He explained that Death Valley was set aside for its landscapes and its historical uses, which included mining. Joshua Tree, on the other hand, was established as a botanical preserve. He stated:

> You cannot have a biological preserve, and I'm speaking now from an ecological standpoint which involves all biology—that is, animal life, plant life, insect life, bird life: the entire habitat— you simply can't have an ecological area and preserve of that kind and still have hunting and mining in it. There is no such thing in the world as a biological or ecological preserve in which mining and hunting and killing of wildlife is permitted... So I don't think—and I don't mean this is [in] an unkind spirit at all [—] I don't think this compromise which has been offered that we could settle this thing by opening up the area to mining and everything would be all right. I am sure it can't be done.[38]

Maier's impassioned defense received an immediate response as S. T. Schrieber, of the MCSC, blurted out that the only solution then was to abolish the monument entirely. The moderator then thanked everyone for attending and helping to "get all these facts down." Nobody's position had budged. If anything, the debate had become even more acrimonious. In his report to the regional director, Maier lamented that he and Cole had not been allowed time to fully rebut the many errors and misstatements they had heard. He pessimistically added that "speculation in desert land is the spirit of the day and every owner has several nibbles."[39]

After the April 17 forum, attention turned to the Committee on Public Lands, which would decide whether to recommend passage of H.R. 4703 to the full House of Representatives. On May 22, NPS Director Drury appeared before the committee to defend the bill. After he outlined its purpose, several congressmen grilled him about two points that disturbed them. They focused, first, on the provision that the President could unilaterally add lands in the future. Although the Antiquities Act of 1906 gave the President the right to proclaim a monument on federal land, several thought it was unclear about his authority to add to it. The committee decided to address that question later in executive session. Then, they took up the appropriation of $215,000 for land acquisition. Here, matters got difficult, as Drury tried to explain the difficulties in working out exchanges and the imminent threats of railroad lands being sold to private developers. The entire exchange took only a few minutes, but the outlook for the bill darkened.[40]

In the meantime, members of the MAS evaluated their position and offered a compromise amendment for Sheppard's bill to the committee. First, they recommended that the area to be deleted from Joshua Tree in the bill remain the same, but they also proposed that the remaining

monument be divided into a core area of no more than 50,000 acres surrounding the Lost Horse
Valley, where all commercial activities would be banned, and a buffer zone where mining could take
place. The miners offered to back this type of bill to the fullest. They made no mention of the fund
to buy private lands or the matter of hunting. Superintendent Cole politely requested copies of the
letter to forward to his superiors. Victor Hayek, of the MAS, responded "cordially," promising to
send them and thanking Cole for attending the forum in April. It is uncertain whether the NPS
would have accepted such a solution, because the House Committee on Public Lands killed H.R.
4703 in early August. Charles Stokes gloated in *Desert Views*, the Joshua Tree village's newspaper,
that it died because of its "demerits." This accompanied his four-page article blasting the NPS and
the bill, echoing many of his statements and letters over the previous year. Gone was the plan to
cut out mineralized areas. Gone, too, was the appropriation to buy inholdings. The miners still did
not have open access to mine, but they had defeated a reviled compromise. And, a month earlier,
the NPS learned that Henry Kaiser and his company had bought all rights to the Eagle Mountain
iron ore deposits within the monument. This would become a much-greater threat to the agency's
mission than all of the gold prospectors put together.[41]

Never Give Up

Congressman Harry Sheppard, showing the irrepressibility of a politician, immediately began planning to reintroduce his legislation after consulting with the NPS and his constituents. He urged the
agency to study again the mining situation and the boundaries to see if any adjustments might be
made to improve his next bill. James Cole returned to his maps and aerial photos and, in January
1947, conducted another field investigation with biologist Lowell Sumner and regional land officer
Raymond Hoyt [no relation to Minerva]. A month later, Hoyt submitted their report, proposing
several adjustments from the boundaries in the previous Sheppard bill. One new change was a
proposal to eliminate three tiers of sections from the monument's western end at Morongo Canyon.
The existing boundary ran in and out of the canyon, and some of the land was listed as a Native
American reservation. Initially, Cole wanted to add the rest of the canyon to the monument, but
Hoyt disagreed, citing too many private holdings. The team also recommended keeping the Gold
Park Mining district in the Pinto Mountains, because there were only three moribund claims in the
area and bighorn sheep used it for winter habitat. Other recommendations included adding the
eastern portion of the Coxcomb Mountains and extending the southeastern boundary to include
more of the Pinto Basin. Ironically, the failure of H.R. 4703 prompted NPS officials to try and
retain more of the original monument than they had been willing to settle for a year earlier. Conrad
Wirth, however, as Chief of Lands for the NPSS, disagreed. He readily accepted the exclusion of

the western sections, but balked at the other changes. He suggested to Sheppard that he make the acceptable change, modify the language a bit, and submit a new bill to alter Joshua Tree's boundaries. He also encouraged him to repeat the proposed appropriation for $215,000 for land acquisition.[42]

On March 26, 1947, Sheppard introduced H.R. 2795 with two changes from his previous bill: the elimination of fifteen sections of land at Morongo Canyon and the addition of four sections in the western part of the Eagle Mountains previously excluded from the original monument because of sales of railroad land in the area. The latter would provide additional range for bighorn sheep. Interior Secretary Julius Krug submitted a short letter to the Committee on Public Lands, repeating all of the justifications for the boundary changes and land-acquisition funds. He added that the monument could not be developed for public use until these problems were solved. New Superintendent Frank R. Givens suggested that, this time, the NPS should not broadcast its desire for support in the hopes that, by being quiet, the miners and their allies might not notice. This seemed to work for a while, but then the congressional committee announced its plan to hold a public hearing on the bill. After that, the agency lost no time in contacting its traditional allies and asking them to appear at the hearing. NPS officials were more optimistic about this hearing, which would be held by legislators instead of an organization that had opposed the bill from the start.[43]

Shortly after submitting his recommendations for the latest boundary bill, Cole transferred to a less-stressful position as regional biologist at the NPS's regional office in Omaha, Nebraska, but he did not escape the latest round of JTNM boundary disputes. As the date for the hearing approached, Cole agreed to defend, once again, the boundaries he had recommended. Meanwhile, environmental organizations prepared to participate more actively in the debate. Herbert Maier encouraged Givens to secure as many speakers as possible to support the bill, especially members of local Chambers of Commerce. Maier also warned that Charles Stokes undoubtedly would level "ill-founded" charges against the agency's personnel and that he should be answered "graciously and straightforwardly."[44]

The hearing took place on October 1, 1947, and it began with a series of protests against a land exchange that would secure acreage in Joshua Tree National Monument by exchanging it for government land to the north of the monument. A group of would-be homesteaders wanted the same land for small, five-acre tracts. Present was Congressman John Phillips in whose district part of the national monument lay after a recent adjustment to congressional boundaries. He defended Sheppard's bill in general but opposed a provision granting the Secretary of the Interior the right to set prices for private inholdings in any NPS unit. The next speaker was Stokes who, between his presentation and answers to questions from the committee, took up a large amount of the available time. Once again, he accused Cole and other personnel of designing the bill for political reasons and personal profit. As he continued to berate the NPS, California Congressman Clair Engle asked him what specifically he wanted with regard to the future of the monument. Stokes answered:

I would use the Park Service's threats in that case. They repeatedly threatened—and I have the official record taken by a State reporter—that, "if we don't get the land, we will abolish the Monument." I say, if that is all you will do, okay. Does that answer you?[45]

The rest of the hearing showed that the brief cordiality offered in the exchange between Victor Hayek and James Cole was long gone. Each side held to its position. Lloyd Mason Smith, the director of the Palm Springs Desert Museum, fired back:

The whole matter, as it appears to our Museum, is not merely the saving in the wild state of a few acres of land, but it is a policy [that] is being jeopardized. Should the dictates of a few selfish short-sighted men deprive our future generations of their natural heritage? It has happened too often in the past. If it happens here, what's to stop other groups from taking slices out of Yosemite and Yellowstone as well? If the minerals mentioned were vitally needed in the National Defense, or the land urgently needed for settlement, that would be something quite different. But are these miners and land-seekers interested in abolishing the Monument purely because of a patriotic nationalistic motivation? I rather think not.[46]

During the course of the hearing, another minor boundary adjustment became a focus of Stokes and other inholders in their efforts to discredit the NPS. Agency planners had decided to remove three parcels of private land south of Twentynine Palms to simplify administration. Two of the parcels lay along the western edge of the main road into the monument immediately south of the Oasis of Mara. By deleting these two parcels, the NPS could avoid responsibility for nearly two miles of road maintenance. A third parcel owned by a man named Beech consisted of an apron of land north of the mountains and immediately northwest of the other two. Cole believed that moving the boundary back to the mountains would establish a more-obvious boundary. Stokes seized upon the fact that Joshua Tree Ranger Hesmel Earenfight owned the parcel north of Beech and accused him of benefitting financially from the boundary adjustment. Cole answered that Earenfight owned that land before there was a monument, that he had been in the army in Europe when the decision was made to exclude Beech's property, and that it was uncertain whether the value of the ranger's land would go up or down after having the monument boundary move away from the edge of his property. Cole also denied new assertions by Stokes and several of his allies that he had intimidated them and told them he "would have them out of [the monument] one day or know why."[47]

Despite the spirited defense of H.R. 2795 by environmentalists, local Chambers of Commerce, and the NPS, it, too, died in committee. In February 1949, a frustrated Representative Harry Sheppard told *The Desert Trail* that he would not introduce the bill again. This left the task to Representative

John Phillips, who introduced H.R. 4116 on April 8, 1949. The NPS had studied again the boundary situation, including a new field survey by biologist Lowell Sumner. The new bill would add the eastern slope of the Coxcomb Mountains to give more range to bighorn sheep and delete six sections of land along the western entrance road from Joshua Tree village. Two of the sections contained subdivisions, and park planners believed they would be impossible to acquire. The bill still included an appropriation of $215,000 for land acquisition and a stipulation that the President could proclaim further boundary revisions. Once again, it was referred to the Committee on Public Lands.[48]

By this time, many in the House of Representatives were familiar with the efforts to amend Joshua Tree's boundaries. H.R. 4116 still contained sections that some members of Congress opposed, and the outlook for its passage again looked dim. This time, however, Phillips and the NPS were ready. Director Drury advised Phillips to drop the provisions for presidential power to amend the boundaries in the future and the appropriation of funds for land acquisition. After his first bill faltered in the first session of the 81st Congress, Phillips reintroduced a revised bill, H.R. 7934, without those sections, in the second session on March 30, 1950. It also included a provision that answered a major concern of miners by explicitly stating that the land removed from the monument would immediately be open to mining exploration and claims. Now, it just boiled down to boundary changes. The bill proposed a deletion of 289,500 acres, including the mountains around the Pinto Basin, fifteen sections of land at Morongo Canyon, six sections near the western entrance road, and three parcels near Twentynine Palms. The areas to be added brought the southwestern boundary to the MWD's aqueduct and added sections in the western Eagle Mountains and the eastern slope of the Coxcomb Mountains (Map 3.3). The additions meant that the monument would suffer a net loss of nearly 267,000 acres.[49]

With the unpopular portions removed and growing support from environmental groups, H.R. 7934 seemed poised, finally, to address the monument's problems with mining. The House of Representatives passed the bill on June 20, 1950. It then went to the Senate, where members of its Committee on Interior and Insular Affairs saw it for the first time. After some debate, the Senate committee added another section that ordered the NPS, U.S. Geological Survey (USGS), and U.S. Bureau of Mines (BOM) to restudy the mineral resources of the land that would remain in the monument. The NPS unsuccessfully tried to convince the senators that enough study had already been done. As the bill went to a joint House–Senate committee to hammer out the differences, it ordered the agency to report the results of the new study by February 1, 1951. Members of the lower house agreed to the Senate amendment, and the bill passed on September 25, 1950. As Public Law 81-837, it removed more than one-third of the monument's land, including the Iron Chief Mine, the Dale Mining District, most mountains east of Range 9 East, and several troubling areas of private land along the northern boundary. It also deleted nearly all of the more than 5,000 claims

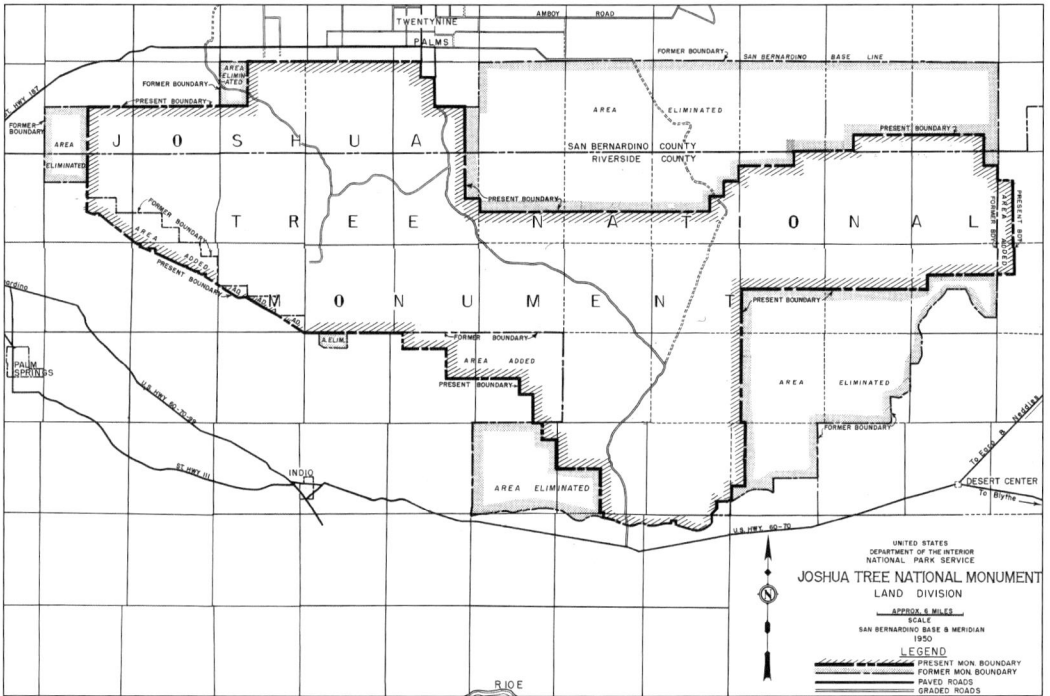

MAP 3.3. This 1950 National Park Service map shows the boundary changes effected by the U. S. Congress that year. Three large areas of the Pinto, Eagle, and Cottonwood Mountains returned to the Bureau of Land Management in a futile effort to placate miners. The monument also lost three small areas in the western segment to "simplify" management. Legislators added two small areas of land by extending the boundary in the southwest to the Colorado River Aqueduct and taking in the eastern flank of the Coxcomb Mountains. In all, the monument lost nearly 267,000 acres.

that existed in the eastern part of the original monument. A later land survey determined that the revised monument contained 558,550 acres.[50]

Angry after their defeat, members of the Western Mining Council bitterly complained, in late November 1950, that the NPS was stalling on the three-agency mineral study due to be submitted to Congress in two months. Agency officials hurriedly formed a study team with the other agencies and surveyed the remaining monument over the following month. One week before the February 1, 1951, deadline, Assistant Secretary of the Interior Dale Doty submitted to the President his report based on the required study. Doty stated that the gold mines still in the monument were both small and inactive. He wrote that, by contrast, "there is clear proof that what now remains under the reduced Monument boundaries contains a variety and wealth of physical, geological, and archaeological features, as well as exceptional desert flora, and scenery, and interesting and rare wildlife, such as cannot be equalled [sic] in any of our national monuments within the United States."[51] Doty reminded the President that these findings corroborated those by the GLO and the NPS prior to the passage of the act and that any claims within the monument that existed prior to 1936 retained their rights to operate.

The Miners' Last Effort

After the boundary change and completion of the resurvey required by Public Law 81-837, NPS officials hoped that miners would be satisfied (Map 3.4), but their hopes proved premature. Several newspapers reporting on the boundary change implied that the entire monument was open to mining. This led to dozens of inquiries at the monument's office about available land, including many from uninformed people who innocently wanted land for recreational homes, airstrips, and other purposes. In addition, Superintendent Givens informed Tomlinson that some unscrupulous individuals would sell a claim in the monument for $100 cash with the remainder of the purchase price to be paid from the proceeds of the mine. They would then offer to assess the mine, declare it worthless, and reacquire it after the disappointed new owner abandoned it. The seller would then repeat the entire process with a new would-be miner. Meanwhile, the traditional foes of the monument acting through another association, the Riverside County Chamber of Mines, turned to the California State Senate to see if it could open the monument to mining. Givens characterized their effort:

> This recent action by the miners is merely another step in a nibbling process to do away with
> the monument. A few individuals are antagonistic to the monument for personal reasons
> but the agitation is due to the necessity for an organization to agitate to justify its existence.
> That they represent a non-existent public and a non-existent demand is evidenced by the

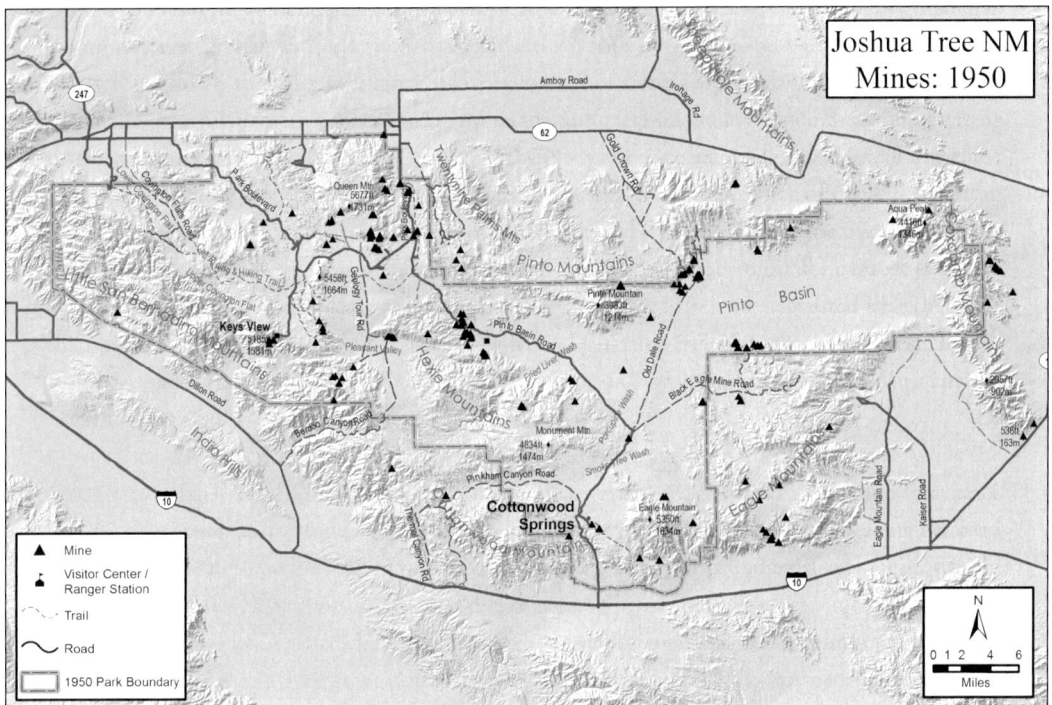

Joshua Tree NM
Mines: 1950

247

Amboy Road

Ironage Rd

62

Eagle Hole Mountains

Goat Crown Rd

Coxcomb Mountains

Queen Mtn
5677ft
1731m

Aqua Peak
4411ft
1346m

Park Boulevard

Coxcomb Little Road

Geology & Hiking Trail

Twentynine Palms Mts

Pinto Mountains

Pinto Basin

Boy Scout Trail

5458ft
1664m

Geology Tour Rd

Pinto Mountain
3983ft
1214m

Pleasant Valley

Keys View
4583ft
1381m

Pinto Basin Road

Old Dale Road

Squaw Tank Wash

Dillon Road

Pushawalla Wash

536ft
163m

Berdoo Canyon Road

Black Eagle Mine Road

The San Bernardino Mountains

Hexie Mountains

Eagle Mountains

Monument Mtn
4834ft
1474m

Smoke Tree Wash

2975ft
907m

Indio Hills

10

Pinkham Canyon Road

Kaiser Road

Cottonwood
Springs

Eagle Mountain
5350ft
1634m

Eagle Mountain Road

10

Thermal Canyon Rd

Cottonwood Mountains

▲ Mine

⛺ Visitor Center /
Ranger Station

- - - Trail

〜 Road

☐ 1950 Park Boundary

N

0 1 2   4   6
Miles

MAP 3.4. The 1950 boundary change excluded some of the major mines from Joshua
Tree National Monument, especially in the Old Dale area and Eagle Mountains.
The most significant exclusion was the Eagle Mountain Mine, where huge iron-ore
deposits led to an enormous operation, with hundreds of employees and a company
town. Elsewhere in the mountains surrounding the Pinto Basin, miners ignored the
new opportunity to file claims. Data source: Joshua Tree National Park GIS files.
Delta Cartography.

almost total absence of any new activity after the "highly mineralized" areas were deleted and opened to mining.[52]

One of the most compelling arguments used by miners was the need for minerals for the nation's defense. With World War II a recent memory and the Korean conflict underway, the mining associations reiterated their argument that America's security depended on free access to strategic resources throughout the desert. The onset of the Nuclear Era focused attention on new types of resources, especially uranium. On May 6, 1952, *The Indio News* reported on a meeting of the Western Mining Council, at which amateur mineralogist Ray Hetherington asserted he had found uranium and other "rare earth" materials within Joshua Tree National Monument. He added that the USGS planned to conduct an aerial survey to confirm the presence of these resources. This revelation tremendously excited those who criticized the monument and the federal government. Howard D. Clark, the secretary of the mining organization, commented that "the remaining part of the monument is not non-mineral by a mere act of Congress."[53] He added that Congressman Phillips had promised to introduce a bill to open the monument if there was proof that strategic metals existed there. Charles Stokes reiterated his accusations of malfeasance and duplicity by the NPS. William F. ("Bill") Keys (Fig. 5.2), ignoring the fact that the Kaiser Corporation was actively working its Eagle Mountain Mine, blamed the NPS for holding up iron mining by refusing to build roads in that area. He also declared that mines were attractions for tourists and that the agency's argument that mining destroyed Joshua trees was baseless propaganda. County supervisor Homer Varner complained that the agency refused to build the road from Thousand Palms to Twentynine Palms. After everyone expressed their frustration to a sympathetic audience, the group drafted a letter opposing government "land grabs" in the West.[54]

Hetherington's mention of a USGS study startled monument officials, and Assistant Director Ronald F. Lee requested more information from the science agency. Dr. John C. Reed reported that an airborne scintillometer study, in May 1952, showed some "interesting anomalies" within the monument, but they were not significant enough to justify an immediate ground check. He promised to notify the NPS if his agency planned further investigation. At the same time, Joshua Tree officials coped with an upsurge in illegal mining in the monument. In one case, Alford Maxwell, of Los Angeles, requested permission to use a monument road to work a mine he hoped was in the land eliminated by the 1950 boundary revision. It turned out his claim lay within the monument. In another case, K. B. Tillman, of Desert Hot Springs, had staked two claims many years before on land owned by the SPRR. The NPS had purchased that land, and it explained to Tillman that his claims were invalid originally and invalid at the present time and that his letter to President Dwight D. Eisenhower would not secure any right to mine.[55]

In August 1953, Maurice Nordstrom, of the Riverside County Chamber of Mines, launched a new campaign to open Joshua Tree National Monument to mining. In a letter to Secretary of the Interior Douglas McKay and copied to President Eisenhower, Nordstrom described the 1950 act as one that benefitted only the Kaiser Steel Company and the NPS itself, the latter by straightening a few boundaries for easier administration. He admitted that Congressman Phillips told him that his colleagues would not pass a bill to enable mining in the monument. Nordstrom blamed this on NPS's opposition. Then, he got to the heart of his argument:

> Prior to 1936 the area embraced within the Joshua Tree Monument was prospected and mined principally for gold. There was no prospecting for uranium, cobalt and the many other strategic metals for which a national demand has been created in the last fifteen years. Permission to prospect that area for the many essential minerals needed by this country, many of which must now be imported from foreign sources [that] could easily be cut off in the event of an emergency, is vitally important and cannot be brushed aside by a statement that this restricted region must be kept intact for the benefit of botanists, entomologists, etc. As an attraction for tourists the Monument is a failure. It is devoid of beautiful scenery and of any comfort for the tourist, an area most of them are glad to get out—never to return. Why then, should the government continue to operate the monument as an expense to the American Taxpayer? [56]

This time, Nordstrom and the miners he represented meant to gain access to the monument or do away with it entirely.

As the latest mining threat escalated, environmental organizations took greater interest. The National Parks Association, a local group from Banning called the Trailfinders, and local chapters of the Sierra Club and Audubon Society asked the NPS to notify them of any developments affecting the monument. A new organization formed in 1954 with important implications for future conservation action in the American Southwest. Randall Henderson, publisher of *Desert Magazine* since 1937, Edmund Jaeger, and some 100 others formed the Desert Protective Council specifically to combat the designs of the mining faction at Joshua Tree. The organization would later grow to become a major force in promoting environmental causes throughout all the deserts of the United States.[57]

Assistant Secretary of the Interior Orme Lewis explained the same legal and economic points in a rebuttal of Nordstrom's arguments, which he copied to Congressman Phillips and Senator Thomas Kuchel. The miners then decided to approach San Bernardino County's Board of Supervisors. Their complaints led the supervisors to schedule a hearing on the issue for July 19, 1954. To counter the miners' efforts, Joe Momyer and several others from the Sierra Club's local chapter met with the supervisors and with the miners themselves. They listened to the arguments of the miners but then defended the monument and urged the supervisors to pass a resolution supporting it. Although the meeting was amicable, the two sides' opinions remained fixed. As the hearing approached, the NPS decided to attend and offer information if asked but not make a formal presentation. Environmentalists and other monument allies would argue to save the monument.[58]

The hearing opened at 2:00 p.m. at the San Bernardino County Health Building. Maurice Nordstrom spoke first and acknowledged that the miners needed official approval by San Bernardino to match that which they already had from Riverside County. He reviewed the history of mining in the area, explained that just one of the mining organizations had more than 600 members who could have attended, reiterated their desire to have the same opportunities that were available in Death Valley, and then introduced several other representatives of mining organizations. His allies took different approaches in bolstering the mining position. A Mr. Peters, of the Western Mining Council, ridiculed conservationists, denied that mining negatively affected bighorn sheep, stressed the economic importance of mining to the county, and dismissed claims that mining brought substandard roads and shacks into the area. He added that he personally had built 110 roads, and none were substandard. Tom Quinn, from the same organization, wondered why Kaiser could mine in the monument and not the average man. Apparently, he was unaware that the iron mine was no longer in the monument. Les Spell, of Twentynine Palms, focused on the strategic values of the resources and concluded, "I would rather give our boys material for fighting than a hayload full of flowers."[59]

Joe Momyer, of the Sierra Club, led the speakers who opposed additional mining, including geologist and conservationist John P. Buwalda, Edmund Jaeger, and several other scientists and teachers. They answered Nordstrom's 600 local miners by stating that they represented 8,000 Sierra Club members, 2,000 Boy Scouts, 3,000 women in twenty-six clubs that supported national parks, and a woman who trained teachers, each of whom would have 1,500 elementary school students in her career. In addition, upon Momyer's request, Superintendent Samuel King presented detailed statistics on visitation from 1941 through June 1954. The figure for 1953 was 172,423 persons in 48,168 cars. He explained that the NPS had counters at the entrances and multiplied the number of cars by 3.5 to get the number of persons. This caused Nordstrom to comment that he visited the monument two or three times a month, and every time he was counted as 3.5 persons. Later, he would use this logic to dispute NPS's attendance figures, which he claimed were inflated to bolster the agency's position. The anti-mining group then offered the standard arguments about the recreational, educational, and economic benefits of the unit in its protected state. Charles Stokes then offered the novel contention that tourists rather than miners caused most of the damage in the monument. By this time, however, the miners must have known they had failed. Immediately after Stokes, the supervisors voted unanimously to oppose eliminating the monument or opening it to new mining claims.[60]

This blow to the miners' campaign still did not stop them. They next approached the California State Senate, where they succeeded. In early 1955, the state senators passed Resolution No. 5, which urged the president and Congress "to permit, with proper provision to prevent damage to the scenic desert growth, prospecting and mining within the Joshua Tree National Monument."[61] NPS and interior officials pondered this latest step, and, after some delay, Assistant Secretary of the Interior Lewis responded that the state senate had no legal authority to change policy that was part of the Antiquities Act. Lewis did offer one consolation to the miners, however. The department had given permission to the Atomic Energy Commission (AEC) to investigate the monument for "fissionable material." Environmental groups were unhappy with this news. Harry C. James, of the Desert Protective Council, warned the regional director that he would have to allocate a much-larger staff of rangers to Joshua Tree in order to cope with "a regular fever of prospecting." Numerous conservation and outdoor-recreation groups and individuals embarked on a letter-writing campaign to the President, Congress, and NPS, decrying the idea of mining and even the survey to investigate its possibilities. It soon became clear that the public attitude was decidedly evolving toward protection rather than exploitation.[62]

During the next year, mining enthusiasts explored within the monument and filed claims that monument officials subsequently found and negated. Correspondence for and against opening the monument to new claims continued to flow, and editorials argued both sides. The AEC did not inform the NPS about any radioactive materials, which agency officials took to mean that none of economic quality existed. The last organized attempt by miners came with a letter from the secretary of the Riverside County Chamber of Mines to Senator Thomas Kuchel in July 1956. Helen Bixel cited the NPS's recently publicized *Mission 66* plan for Joshua Tree, including its provision to acquire the remaining private lands.[63] She challenged all the NPS-supplied data and studies indicating a lack of significant mineral resources, and she appealed to Senator Kuchel for help in opening the monument to mining for strategic minerals that, she stated, occurred in proximity to iron ore. Kuchel dutifully forwarded the letter to the NPS, with a request that the officials answer the charges. By now, the agency had a form letter to respond, which cited all the laws, studies, and hearings that had emerged during the previous two decades. Acting Director E. T. Scoyen also added a new justification for ignoring the miners' insistence. Two years earlier, Congress had passed Public Law 83-703, the "Atomic Energy Act of 1954," which included a stipulation that exploration and operations on lands in national parks, monuments, and wildlife areas were prohibited unless "the President by Executive

Order declares that the requirements of the common defense and security make such action necessary." This, it seemed, was an insurmountable impediment to the mining organizations.[64]

Problems with mining in Joshua Tree continued, of course, but the organized campaign to change the monument's policy was over. Many miners continued to ask for permission to mine, and illegal prospecting occurred occasionally, but these efforts were scattered and sporadic. Dealing with mining became a law-enforcement issue and a bureaucratic process of determining the validity of remaining pre-1936 claims. The threat of mining had cost the monument more than one-third of its acreage and untold hours of staff time. The long battle brought deep animosity to the agency from some neighbors and also a growing group of allies. Geographic and demographic patterns emerged as well. Officials in San Bernardino County were friendlier to the monument than those in Riverside County. Twentynine Palms was more supportive than the village of Joshua Tree. Old timers were divided on the relative merits of the monument, while the most-vicious criticism came from miners and developers in and near Los Angeles.

This type of debate occurs whenever a new national park or monument is proposed, and thus it underlies the larger history of the NPS. Yellowstone National Park was established in 1872 before any use by white settlers began. Since that time, there has always been a constituency, usually nearby, that prefers traditional uses and little regulation to NPS control. President Bill (William J.) Clinton used the Antiquities Act of 1906 to proclaim national monuments that remain under control of the U.S. Forest Service or the BLM, which allow more consumptive uses. Presidents George W. Bush and Barack Obama continued to placate some opponents by using this approach. Meanwhile, in 2016 efforts to create national parks in Idaho, Maine, and elsewhere continue to suffer virulent opposition, often from participants in shrinking extractive industries.

FIG. 4.1. Once President Franklin D. Roosevelt proclaimed Joshua Tree National Monument in 1936, National Park Service leaders knew they faced a huge challenge in land acquisition. Not only did the Southern Pacific Railroad Company control more than 200,000 acres, but homesteaders and miners held thousands of other properties in grants and mining claims. This photo shows the home place of Mickey Thornton in the New Dale Mining District. Thornton's identity and occupation are unknown. Photograph by George A. Grant, September 30, 1941. Harpers Ferry Center, Grant Collection JOTR #339, National Park Service.

CHAPTER FOUR

Land Acquisition 1936–1956

THE ISSUE that most worried Roger Toll and other National Park Service (NPS) officials during the campaign to establish Joshua Tree National Monument (JTNM) was the amount of non-federal land within it. All the NPS and General Land Office (GLO) inspections confirmed this troubling reality. In 1941, almost five years after its establishment, Chief of Planning Thomas Vint, the agency's lead landscape architect, flatly stated, "One look at a map showing the private lands in the area is frightening."[1] Indeed, during that period, the NPS had not acquired a single acre of surveyed non-federal land, nor would it do so for another seven years. In addition, thousands of mineral claims meant that even tracts of undisputed federal land were potentially blocked from recreational development and access for visitors (Plate 22). The land situation hindered every other aspect of planning and developing the young monument. During Joshua Tree's first twenty years, the NPS worked out ways to acquire valuable property through purchase, exchange, condemnation, and invalidation of mining claims.

After their inspection in March 1937, Regional Engineer Frank Kittredge and Regional Landscape Architect Ernest Davidson summarized the status of land ownership within the new JTNM. They reported that the Southern Pacific Railroad Company (SPRR) owned 187 sections and held rights to an uncertain number of others within its twenty-mile indemnity strip. Private individuals or groups owned thirty-four sections, the State of California held thirty-five sections of school lands, and there was no information on another sixty-two sections (Fig. 4.1). They also recommended "that no developments whatever be undertaken in the Monument until such time as the private holdings, or at least the key property be acquired by the Government" and commented that the only positive in the land-acquisition situation was that some locals offered to help the NPS purchase land through which its proposed north-south road from Twentynine Palms to Indio would pass.[2] Thirteen months later, Superintendent Merriam and NPS naturalist James Cole added:

> The most difficult and important problem confronting the administration and development of Joshua Tree National Monument hinges upon the private land situation. There is little that can be, or should be done, in developing the area until the private land holdings are diminished or abolished . . . Certainly, the monument cannot be successfully administered when every other section is privately owned.[3]

In September 1939, Merriam and Cole accompanied landscape architect R. L. McKown on another inspection as the monument began its fourth year of existence. McKown elaborated on why the
NPS needed to delay development until it could acquire enough land to assure the monument's survival:

> There are three factors to be kept in mind which will develop as soon as any work is started
> in the monument. (1) Land values will increase, resulting in a greater cost to the Government
> to acquire private holdings; (2) Landscape values will be destroyed which are important
> to the monument. If work is started on the roads, private land which heretofore may have
> been inaccessible may have connecting roads brushed out by private owners, whereas if the
> Government acquires these lands no additional roads may be necessary; (3) If work is once
> started local pressure to continue the work is sure to develop.[4]

In addition to delaying development, NPS officials decided to maintain secrecy about any planning
for the future. Thomas Vint worried that any leaks to the local public from the numerous inspection reports would "aggravate the already serious problem of land acquisition."[5]

Acquiring Railroad Lands

The non-federal land in Joshua Tree consisted of two types: surveyed and unsurveyed. Most of the
privately owned parcels had been surveyed by the GLO, in some cases decades earlier. This was
the case for the western half of the monument, where the most important scenic resources were.
The eastern part of the monument held most of the unsurveyed land. GLO research showed that
the SPRR held the rights to more than 100,000 acres of unsurveyed land as part of its indemnity
option. Because this vast acreage remained largely unthreatened by intrusion, NPS land specialists
focused on securing the surveyed land to forestall subdivision or other development "contrary to
park purposes" (Map D).[6]

Despite this logical preference, the first transfer of land to JTNM unexpectedly came from
SPRR's unsurveyed indemnity strip. The U.S. Congress worked out a deal with the railroads that became part of the Transportation Act of 1940. Prior to this act, the federal government did not pay for
its employees and materials to ride the trains of railroad companies that had received extensive land
grants to build their lines. Those companies now sought to change that by returning unclaimed lands,
so they could begin charging the government for transport as they did everyone else. The Transportation Act legislated that deal, and the SPRR relinquished its unclaimed lands in the indemnity strip
that slashed diagonally across the monument. In one bold stroke, the NPS suddenly gained 105,240
acres, which reduced the railroad's remaining holdings to approximately 135,000 acres.[7]

The NPS fruitlessly negotiated for surveyed land for almost twelve years after the monument's proclamation. When the agency finally secured some surveyed land in 1948, it came as a result of highly convoluted negotiations involving the railroad, a private company seeking a location for filming movies, and a number of real-estate speculators. The Southern Pacific Land Company, a subsidiary of the SPRR, remained the primary target during these frustrating years. The company steadily refused to exchange its land for other federal desert land. Its executives believed they already held the highest-quality land in the desert and that selling it was the only reasonable option that would satisfy their stockholders. They offered to sell all their remaining land in the monument to the government for ninety-three cents per acre, but regional officials mournfully replied that the federal government had no money for outright land purchases.

In April 1938, at the request of the NPS, GLO inspector Samuel E. Guthrey returned to the monument with two assistants and spent three weeks gaining an overview of its land and water resources, with specific attention to the railroad's land. Their report took the form of an appraisal, first describing the geography and resources of the region and its history of ownership and human use, and then calculating the potential worth for agriculture, mining, and grazing of each of the SPRR's sections of land. Although Guthrey mistakenly surveyed the entire area formerly proposed by Minerva Hoyt, he carefully analyzed each piece of the railroad's property. He reported that (1) the area was largely barren, with only two sites feasible for camping, Quail Springs and Cotton-wood Springs; (2) all the significant mineral resources lay east of Range 8 East and all the scenic areas west of it; and (3) the railroad had recently sold 18,000 acres of its best land in the monument for slightly more than $1.37 per acre. In spite of that sale, he concluded that the NPS should pay $24,286 for the estimated 242,860 acres of land "reputed to be in railroad ownership." This amounted to barely ten cents per acre. Needless to say, the SPRR was not interested.[8]

Despite SPRR's offer to sell its land under the appraised value, the NPS saw no real option other than a land exchange. Congress continued to refuse allocations for direct purchase of private lands in the national park system. The federal government, however, still controlled more than 9,000,000 acres of public domain in California. Section 8 of the Taylor Grazing Act enabled federal land agencies to exchange those lands outside grazing districts for lands it desired in its "reservations or withdrawals." Frustrated NPS officials hoped they could find land somewhere that the railroad would accept in trade. James Cole worried that the sale of railroad land to private individuals would destroy any prospect of protecting the monument's most scenic and popular resources. He commented that the only positive in the situation was that most buyers had been unable to develop their purchases because of the scarcity of water.[9]

By January 1941, a desperate NPS asked the SPRR to hold off selling its land until such time as the U.S. Congress might relent and provide money to acquire its monument inholdings.

Company land commissioner D. G. Christen, although sympathetic, offered little hope. The SPRR still owned much of the land in the Lost Horse Valley and other critical parts of the monument. When World War II started a few months later, the NPS found itself with a skeleton staff and even less money to spend. An offer by the railroad in 1942 to sell its acreage in Joshua Tree to the agency remained well out of reach. Meanwhile, threats of private purchase and development increased. In May 1945, Superintendent James E. Cole (Fig. 3.2) reported that developer James F. Whitehorn, who already owned land inside the monument near the western entrance, was interested in buying land around Hidden Valley and other key parts of the monument. He also suspected that Minerva Hamilton Hoyt (Fig. 2.1) had put Whitehorn up to it. While it is true that Hoyt was deeply frustrated with the endless delays in developing the monument for public use, it seems highly unlikely that she would suggest or even condone private acquisition of its land for development. Regional Director Owen Tomlinson did not offer comment on Cole's speculation but did write to Whitehorn about his proposal to build a hotel and other resort facilities in the monument. He issued the agency's regular warning about scarce water resources and then informed the developer that the NPS did not want any lodging facilities in Joshua Tree, as the surrounding communities were quite capable of handling any visitors. Finally, he suggested that Whitehorn come and see the land and the minimal water resources for himself before buying anything from the railroad.[10]

Meanwhile, Land Commissioner Christen, of the SPRR, offered again to sell 4,846 acres around the monument's main road and Pinto Wye to the NPS without success. He reiterated that the company would not exchange land with the government and, furthermore, it would proceed to sell the land to anyone who would pay. Christen's letter alarmed agency officials. NPS Director Newton Drury wrote:

> If officials of the Southern Pacific are successful in disposing of their holdings within Joshua Tree to private individuals, as indicated in previous correspondence and by Mr. Christen, there is little hope for the national monument. It is hard for us to reconcile ourselves to their attitude, particularly since any large company such as Southern Pacific is somewhat of a public trust, and in this case derives considerable revenue from rail travel to western parks and monuments. It would seem that the least they could do would be to reserve their lands for the United States until such time as they can be purchased or exchanged.[11]

Drury decided to appeal to those who had helped establish the monument nine years earlier, hoping to use the Minerva Hoyt connection again. At his urging, Joshua Green, a former Mississippian and confidant of Hoyt, wrote letters to Congressman William Whittington, of Mississippi, and President Harry Truman, urging them to honor both Hoyt and former President Franklin Roosevelt by finding money to buy the railroad's lands in JTNM. Green even went so far as to suggest to the President that the monument could be renamed "The Franklin D. Roosevelt Joshua Tree National

Monument." On July 9, 1945, Drury sent a dense, three-page, single-spaced letter to Whittington, explaining all the details of the monument's land problems, particularly the threatened sale of the railroad's Lost Horse Valley lands to developers who wanted to subdivide the area into ranch estates of twenty to forty acres. He reiterated Green's hope that Congress would find a way to provide "legislative relief" before the monument was "irreparably damaged." At the same time, the SPRR sold some of its acreage to James Whitehorn, further threatening the future of Joshua Tree National Monument.[12]

While the NPS struggled to prevent private development from destroying the heart of the monument, the potential change in the boundary, aimed at placating the miners, became part of the land-acquisition equation. At first, some office leaders in Washington, D.C., hoped that part of the railroad land might lie within the area to be returned to the public domain, but Regional Director Tomlinson soon discovered that relatively little of the railroad's land would be removed by the pending legislation. NPS officials then speculated on whether they could tempt the SPRR to exchange Lost Horse Valley land for some of the mineralized land to be eliminated from the monument. Finally, they decided that the best approach would be to attach a rider to any bill involving change in the boundary that would provide $215,000 for the purchase of all the remaining railroad land in the monument. Presumably, they hoped Congress would see it as recompense for losing a third of the unit's land. As explained earlier, however, when Congressman Sheppard's H.R. 4703 bill went to the Committee on Public Lands, that provision caused his colleagues to kill it.[13]

As 1945 drew to a close, Superintendent Cole complained that the SPRR's officials "should be embarrassed" at what their subsidiary land company was doing. Then, on December 17, he received a phone call from developer Dick Curtis, who blithely informed him that he planned to purchase 3,447 acres of Lost Horse Valley land from the railroad. Cole immediately informed Tomlinson that, if this purchase occurred, the NPS would control a mere twenty-six percent of the Lost Horse Valley and lose part of the road connecting it to Keys View. He concluded, "If all these lands are not acquired by the Government, it is the opinion of this office that the Park Service has lost Joshua Tree National Monument and might better delete the entire area from the National Park system."[14]

Initially, Cole believed that Curtis wanted to establish a dude ranch in the valley, but it turned out he actually represented a company that planned to build a permanent set for filming western movies, plus accommodations for 200 people. It seems that the San Fernando Valley was no longer acceptable for making these films because of frequent air traffic and the boring familiarity that audiences now had with that location. In 1940, filmmakers had shot "Buck Benny Rides Again" in the monument, and it seemed a perfect place to acquire for future films (Fig. B). Curtis and the company he represented envisioned a full-scale western town to be called "Pioneertown." It needed a dramatic backdrop and plenty of space for chase scenes. Company executives had investigated the Alabama Hills near Owens Valley but considered that area too far from Hollywood. Pioneertown, Inc., had plenty of money, and, this time, it looked like the monument was doomed.[15]

NPS Director Drury immediately launched a campaign with a choice: Either raise money for land acquisition or divert the attention of Pioneertown, Inc., to another location. He again appealed to Joshua Green, but the Mississippi native could not find any serious donors. Then, Drury contacted the Garden Society of America, pleading for assistance in averting the purchase. This led to a complicated process that allowed the NPS to acquire much of the railroad's land in the heart of the monument. Mrs. Robert Wright, of the Garden Society, contacted several leading members of the organization for help. One of them was Alma Chickering, the wife of the lead attorney for the SPRR. Allen L. Chickering, a member of both the Sierra Club and the Save-the-Redwoods League, was already well-known for his conservation work. He was a botanist of sufficient merit to have a species of hybrid sage named after him, and, later, he became a pillar of the California Historical Society. He was not on the SPRR's Board of Directors, but his influence was substantial. In late February, monument officials received the welcome news that he had convinced the board not to sell its Lost Horse Valley land to Dick Curtis and his company. Instead, the SPRR sold 12,000 acres of land northwest of the town of Yucca Valley. Like its property in the monument, the railroad only owned alternate sections there and this created an opportunity for the NPS.[16]

A few months earlier, the Kaiser Corporation asked for more land to expand production at its Eagle Mountain Mine. The NPS decided to carry out what it called a tripartite exchange. In this case, Kaiser would buy railroad land in the Lost Horse Valley and then trade it with the NPS for the land it needed at the mine site. The deal fell through, but the tripartite arrangement remained a good idea, because the federal government still owned the alternate sections northwest of the park that now interested Dick Curtis and his partners. Negotiations proceeded and, by April 1946, both the SPRR and Curtis supported the idea. The railroad offered even more land, and Pioneertown, Inc., was a willing buyer. The deal would be a win for all parties. The railroad would sell its land and not be stuck with even more desert acreage it did not want. Curtis's group would have a huge block of contiguous territory to host western film makers. Finally, the federal government would get thousands of acres of inholdings in the monument by exchange with Curtis.[17]

By April 1946, it seemed that a solution to the railroad's inholdings was at hand. Indeed, an optimistic NPS began courting other private individuals and local governments for similar deals. Early in 1947, the City of Los Angeles offered to purchase 24,000 acres of railroad land in Joshua Tree and trade them for equivalent acreage in the Owens Valley and Mono County. Four decades earlier, the city had purchased much of the land in the distant mountain valley and built a highly controversial aqueduct from the Owens River to the city. It depleted much of the water that local farmers in that region needed, and they reacted with outrage and violence, repeatedly blowing up portions of the aqueduct and threatening Los Angeles officials. With its insatiable demand for water unfulfilled by both the existing Owens Valley Aqueduct and the Colorado River Aqueduct that passed just south of Joshua Tree, the city sought more land and water rights in Mono County north of its previous purchases.

Some NPS officials were wary of such an exchange. Frank Kittredge, Superintendent of Yosemite National Park, warned that "any exchange which would involve the turning over to the City of Los Angeles of public lands in the Mono Basin is a hornet's nest and the answer should be definitely— no." In addition to a sense of fair play and a reticence to get in the middle of a bitter controversy, Kittredge also did not want to "jeopardize any future relationships [with Mono County citizens] in case there should be a desire for rounding out the boundaries of Yosemite National Park or Devil [sic] Postpile National Monument."[18]

At the same time, a developer named Seth Brady made an extraordinary request for a tripartite exchange. Like most speculators, he bristled with optimism and ambition. He announced his intention to buy up to 60,000 acres of railroad land in the monument, which he would exchange for a similar amount of public domain just west of the Colorado River. Brady told Superintendent Cole he had made arrangements to buy the alternate railroad sections already and wanted to gain complete control of the land for grazing purposes. Unfortunately, the Bureau of Reclamation (BOR) had withdrawn much of the land to build facilities for controlling "flowage and seepage" from the Colorado River. The GLO and its successor, the Bureau of Land Management (BLM), generally cooperated with the NPS, but the BOR absolutely would not alter its classification or its plans. Negotiations wore on for nearly two years, with Brady first suggesting that the flood-control facilities would not interfere with his grazing scheme and then offering to take land further west, near the Chocolate Mountains. By February 1948, however, a BLM investigator found that Brady had not paid any money to the SPRR and, in fact, had no connection to it at all. It seems that a Mr. L. S. Estle had bought the railroad's lands and Brady had taken an option for that property two years earlier but had paid nothing. It also turned out that a grazing lease was held by yet another individual. When contacted, Estle promised to file a written protest against any attempt by Brady to secure adjacent public land. NPS land specialist Bernard Manbey dismissed Brady as a "typical Los Angeles promoter." Thus ended what seemed, for a while, to be an outstanding opportunity to rid the monument of railroad inholdings.[19]

One side effect of the Brady fiasco was that it further dissuaded the NPS from making an exchange with Los Angeles. Hopeful agency land officials thought there would be insufficient land left after the Curtis and Brady exchanges, plus other recent tripartite applications, to satisfy the needs of Los Angeles. But, suddenly, Brady and Los Angeles were both out of the picture. The Curtis exchange became even more important. The major step remaining for this tripartite exchange was to execute all the procedures and forms with the BLM. Initially, the land agency asked the NPS to exchange acreage that was part of President Franklin Roosevelt's withdrawal of land in 1933, but park officials refused. Then, another problem arose: The BLM had classified most of the land that Pioneertown, Inc., wanted as open to small-tract claims. At the urging of the NPS, the BLM had forestalled these claims, but pressure grew, as war veterans demanded that the bureau follow its own land classification.[20]

Twelve years after the establishment of Joshua Tree National Monument, the NPS had not acquired any land other than that given up by the SPRR under the Transportation Act of 1940. The most-hopeful initiative was the Curtis exchange, made possible by the SPRR's willingness to hold the lands from any other sale until this exchange could be executed. In 1948, Joshua Tree contained nearly a quarter of all the non-federal land in the entire national park system. The war was over, and quiet promises to help from Congress and the Truman administration seemed to be wishful thinking. Then, suddenly, Charles A. Richey, the NPS's Acting Chief of Lands, sent a letter on August 11, 1947, to Regional Director Tomlinson, authorizing him to purchase $10,000 worth of land from the railroad in order to "show our good faith as a result of their cooperativeness in withholding them from sale." Richey reminded Tomlinson that the land to be purchased should not include any parcels that were part of the evolving Curtis exchange.[21]

Joshua Tree officials hurriedly identified the sections of land they wanted, but the BLM's investigators appraised them at $25,554. Amazingly, SPRR's officials agreed to sell them for only $10,324. Later, it became known that Allen Chickering had convinced the SPRR's board to accept the lesser amount. On April 15, 1948, the NPS bought 12,826 acres from the railroad company. The SPRR, pleased that the government finally had done something, relented a little on its refusal to exchange land directly with the agency. The company did have some specific pieces of land through which its tracks ran that would facilitate its operations. One eighty-acre parcel lay along its tracks near the northeastern shore of the Salton Sea. Its value was sufficient that the government was able to trade for 2,240 acres of land in the monument. Later, in December 1949, another exchange took place, netting 640 acres of land in the monument for 7.36 acres near Yuma, Arizona, where the company wanted to develop a switching yard.[22]

Word of the pending Curtis exchange brought other groups and individuals who wanted to work out similar tripartite arrangements with the NPS and SPRR. In June 1948, Superintendent Frank Givens identified six others in the works in addition to the one with Curtis. The BLM, however, had to delay completion of the Curtis exchange in order to reappraise the land. People who had filed small-tract claims on the government's land that the movie company was supposed to receive had filed a legal challenge. By this time, Curtis and his associates were beyond impatient and relinquished parts of several sections of land they desired to placate the small-tract applicants. Meanwhile, others continued to file on exchange lands, threatening the entire deal. Finally, on October 20, 1948, BLM officials rejected the remaining small claims and approved the exchange. The NPS received 18,234 acres primarily in and around the Lost Horse Valley. Pioneertown, Inc., consolidated its holdings around the western town it had already begun to construct. Forty-five small-claim applicants from Los Angeles challenged the decision, but the Secretary of the Interior upheld his bureau's decisions. The tripartite exchange had finally worked. During the next nine months, the NPS completed three more exchanges with Joseph Trottier, Carl Allen, and the City of Needles, adding another 7,500 acres of railroad land to the monument. And, a little to the north, Pioneertown began hosting television shows and movies with Roy Rogers, Gene Autry, and the Cisco Kid.[23]

The change in the boundary in 1950 gave the NPS greater incentive to acquire railroad lands within the monument. Nobody in the agency was happy about losing a third of the unit's territory, and, perhaps, senior officials in Washington, D.C., felt a little guilty. A new urgency seemed to grip park officials, and this first appeared in the form of another allocation for the outright purchase of railroad land in the western part of the monument. Regional lands specialist Bernard Manbey negotiated a purchase that took place on June 6, 1951. The NPS received 11,819 acres of land for $10,785. Once again, the SPRR sold the land for well under the appraised price of $13,685.[24]

Meanwhile, NPS officials completed several more tripartite exchanges for railroad lands, including one with Emil Ritter for more 14,506 acres on August 13, 1951. The Desert Trail reported that, during the previous three years, the monument had secured 53,110 acres of railroad land by exchange. That land, added to the big purchases in 1948 and 1951, meant the Park Service obtained nearly 78,000 acres of railroad land in just three years. Then, in June 1952, the SPRR announced that it would not undertake any more tripartite exchanges. Fortunately for the NPS, the SPRR's board agreed to honor the exchanges already underway. Between March 1952 and August 1956, the government completed six more tripartite exchanges, adding another 20,658 acres of former railroad land to the monument.[25] A side effect of all these exchanges was a strained relationship between the NPS and the BLM. Marion Clawson, former director of the latter agency, later wrote:

> The Joshua Tree National Monument in southern California included within its boundaries a considerable acreage of land, originally public domain that had been included in a land grant to the Southern Pacific Railroad. Eventually, a number of exchanges with the railroad were made so that the company obtained public domain outside the Monument. This case was complicated by the fact that many individuals, some of whom were World War II veterans, had applied for the land that went to the railroad in exchange, and they protested their loss vociferously. The Bureau had to permit the claimants to file for other public lands, a solution that placated but did not really please, those involved. In such exchanges, the Bureau of Land Management bears the headaches and the expenses, while the real benefits accrue to the National Park Service.[26]

State Exchanges

Six weeks before the proclamation that established JTNM, Congress passed a bill that transferred more than 300,000 acres to the California state parks department, enabling it to expand what is today Anza-Borrego Desert State Park.[27] Had the order of legislation been reversed, the NPS might have been able to exchange the state lands in Joshua Tree for some of the acreage that Congress gave to the state. After being rebuffed in its efforts to donate state lands without mineral rights to the federal government, the California State Lands Commission (CSLC) had reevaluated its position. On March 24, 1937, the Acting Secretary of the Interior wrote to California's Senator William McAdoo, suggesting that he get the state to repeal its law, withholding mineral rights from land donated to the federal government.[28] Instead, the state enacted a new law ordering its lands commission to exchange property with the federal government only on an equal acreage or value basis. Henceforth, the NPS would have to work out either direct exchanges with the state or try for tripartite agreements with parties interested in acquiring federal lands outside the monument, as they had with the SPRR. Both the CSLC and the NPS hoped to complete a deal for all the state's school lands in the monument. The state commission asked for acreage north of the All-American Canal, but that land was unavailable, due to a withdrawal by the BOR that the Secretary of the Interior refused to revoke. This seemed to quash any immediate opportunity for a direct exchange. At a meeting in December 1941, a frustrated state officer, A. P. Ireland, suggested that the NPS had been "asleep at the switch," because other federal agencies, including the U.S. Forest Service (USFS), had been using this method to clear their reserves. A few days later, World War II halted all efforts to acquire land for the monument.[29]

When the war ended, Superintendent Cole raised the issue again. He warned that, while the state was unlikely to sell its land in the monument to private citizens, hunting could take place on its sections. In addition, one of the state's sections was just inside the boundary along the road from Twentynine Palms, which the NPS considered as a site for the monument's headquarters. The coming change in the boundary would eliminate some of the state's holdings but not those in the most-desirable part of the monument.[30] In 1947, Regional Director Tomlinson proposed using lands that the U.S. military no longer needed to exchange with the state for its property in Joshua Tree and Death Valley National Monuments. The CSLC enthusiastically agreed, and both agencies focused on the Barstow Anti-Aircraft Reserve, also known as Camp Irwin, which the U.S. Army might declassify and return to the public domain. The CSLC soon identified enough plots it wanted in the base to eliminate the state's holdings in both national monuments. On December 5, 1947, the U.S. Army declared Camp Irwin surplus, and expectations rose. The NPS even went so far as to ask the state to acquire tax-deeded, private lands in the monument to exchange for former military land. The state was unenthusiastic about that option but quite pleased about shedding the school lands in the monuments. Then, the bottom fell out. Although army officials had declared the base surplus, they had not officially transferred the land back to the BLM. By September, they reconsidered their decision, causing Herbert Maier, of the NPS's regional office in San Francisco, to complain to the director that this was the first time in twelve years the agency and the CSLC had been able to agree, and it now appeared to be unraveling. And, indeed, the army did reverse its decision and eventually developed the National Training Center at Fort Irwin. Another opportunity for land acquisition in Joshua Tree came to naught.[31]

Another possibility appeared while the ill-fated exchange of military land was under consideration. Retired U.S. Army Colonel Robert A. Ellsworth approached the CSLC, seeking a tripartite exchange for about 10,000 acres. He had purchased from the railroad its alternate sections immediately west of the Salton Sea, with the intent of developing a large tourist resort. To proceed, he needed the intervening sections that were still in federal control and sought to have the federal government trade the land by the Salton Sea with the state for some of its holdings in Joshua Tree. He then would buy them from the state, giving him ownership of most of what is today Salton City. Once again, complications immediately appeared. The state already owned some of the land near the Salton Sea, but it was reserved for the expansion of Anza State Park. In addition, the BOR had withdrawn some sections to cope with overflow from the Salton Sea and for an irrigation canal to benefit the Imperial Irrigation District. State Lands Commissioner Ireland managed to convince the state parks agency to relinquish its withdrawal. His office was as anxious as the NPS to complete successfully an exchange of Joshua Tree inholdings. On March 26, 1948, Ireland applied for 9,624.47 acres of federal land to be exchanged for 9,600 acres of unsurveyed school lands in JTNM.[32]

Unfortunately for Colonel Ellsworth, the NPS, CSLC, and BOR remained obstinate. As time passed, Colonel Ellsworth increased the amount of land he wanted by another 4,481.67 acres, which pleased the CSLC and the NPS but did nothing to encourage cooperation from the BOR. Wesley Nelson, of the water agency, informed the BLM that six of the sections Colonel Ellsworth wanted were unavailable, due to their importance for reclamation purposes. Furthermore, the Atomic Energy Commission (AEC) withdrew some of the same land for a test base. Colonel Ellsworth responded by agreeing to drop four of the sections, but he maintained that two of them, currently containing the northern edge of Salton City, were the heart of his development plan. He added that the Coachella [actually Imperial] Irrigation District officials had informed him that their canal would not go to the sections he wanted. He accused the BOR's field inspector of making an error in his report. In February 1949, NPS Associate Regional Director Maier wrote to Director Drury, bemoaning the twelve long years of failed efforts to complete an exchange with the state, the unexpected reversal of the Camp Irwin deal, and the impasse that threatened to collapse the land exchange at Salton Sea. He urged the director to appeal to the AEC and the BOR to release their withdrawals, so this relatively small exchange could break the gridlock. Six weeks later, the BOR flatly refused.[33]

At that point, the situation rapidly deteriorated. In August 1949, Colonel Ellsworth urged the Secretary of the Interior to overrule the BOR. A month later, BOR officials again refused to change their decision. In October, the NPS appealed to the CSLC to get Ellsworth to drop his requirement for the two controversial sections. He refused. In November, the NPS informed

Ellsworth that it could do nothing more about the situation. By December, Maier contacted the state office about a completely separate part of the Salton Sea's shoreline that might be available for a direct interagency exchange. Finally, on June 15, 1950, after much more effort and correspondence, L. T. Hoffman, of the BLM, bluntly informed Ellsworth that the withdrawals would not be revoked, that his agency was, therefore, no longer involved, and that there was no reason to have another meeting about the subject.[34]

After receiving that letter, Colonel Ellsworth realized that, to salvage any portion of his development plan, he would need to drop his applications for the sections withdrawn by the BOR and the AEC. In late June, he told Superintendent Givens that he would trade for government land in San Diego County. But, on July 7, he met with BLM and NPS officials and verbally agreed to amend his original application and remove the sections he could not acquire. In fact, he had new plans to take any available land around the Salton Sea, up to 100,000 acres if possible. He submitted a list of the desired lands, and all parties agreed it would have to go to the BOR to see if any more sections were under water withdrawal. Ellsworth agreed to make these new lands a separate application and to proceed with the original one, minus the BOR and AEC sections. As H.R. 7934, the Phillips boundary revision bill, appeared likely to pass, Herbert Maier warned that the state could only make available for exchange those sections that would remain in the monument after the boundary changed. The CSLC dutifully amended the application for exchange, and another year of tedious paperwork followed. Finally, on July 3, 1951, the NPS acquired 5,496 acres of surveyed state land in the western part of JTNM almost fifteen years after the monument was proclaimed.[35]

As in the case of the Curtis-SPRR-NPS exchange, the success of this tripartite deal finally seemed to break the logjam and allow the NPS and CSLC to negotiate direct exchanges. The state, like the railroad, held two types of land: identified sections and indemnity lands. In January 1952, Regional Director Lawrence Merriam reported that the CSLC still held 25,455 acres, approximately half of it indemnity lands. Bernard Manbey urged the state agency to identify the indemnity sections it wanted in order to clarify Joshua Tree's land status. This led to a direct exchange, in February 1955, that secured 1,280 acres for the monument. Negotiations commenced for far more state property, and the land-acquisition picture looked truly promising for the first time in nearly two decades.[36]

Tax Deeded Private Lands

Land owned by private citizens composed the third group of properties the NPS needed to acquire. The Security Land Corporation had sold numerous tracts in the Pinto Basin, but development of these properties failed because of a dearth of water. Former SPRR land in the western part of the monument had better hydrologic prospects, and parcels were scattered through the most scenic areas as well as along the main road from Twentynine Palms to Cottonwood Spring. Even if the NPS decided to risk increasing land values by paving the road, it could not do so without permission from the landowners of parcels through which it passed. This was one reason why the agency refused to improve the roads in the monument, despite constant urgings from local citizens. Another reason was that the NPS used the promise of paved roads and vastly increased tourism to try to convince Riverside County to donate to JTNM many of the tax-delinquent parcels it held.

Of all the complicated land-acquisition problems that the NPS faced in JTNM, the so-called tax-deeded lands were the last to be solved (Map C). The Security Land Corporation had defaulted on the taxes on much of its land in the Pinto Basin. The buyers of more than 1,000 parcels of its land then did the same. The lack of water sank the appraised value below the amount of taxes due. Many small owners asked the NPS to buy their land, but the agency had railroad and state lands as higher priorities. In addition, the federal government might have to pay the back taxes, if it acquired such property. In December 1936, A. W. Burney, of the NPS, contacted the auditor of Riverside County, asking for information about the tax-deeded lands within the monument. Deputy Auditor H. H. Hoffman responded that the federal government could probably clear the back taxes for $12,000. Most of the land had been delinquent since 1931, some of it even longer. He also noted that the bulk of the lands within the national monument would be deeded to the state in another six months and that a moratorium on tax sales would be in place until January 1938.[37]

In 1941, the issue of tax-deeded lands arose again when NPS officials learned that California's Revenue and Taxation Code provided that non-productive land that was tax delinquent would be classified as "of recreational value only." This meant that it could return to the county, which could then donate it to or exchange it with the federal government. Legally, the state could not donate it directly to the monument. NPS lands specialist Bernard Manbey speculated on whether the state could hold the land and let his agency develop it, and NPS officials knew the state would be much more cooperative than Riverside County. This hopeful line of inquiry halted with the onset of World War II.[38]

After the war, the NPS's attention returned to the problem of tax-deeded private land. In August 1946, Manbey and agency attorney Sidney McClellan met with representatives of the California Office of the Controller. They agreed that JTNM would become the test case for dealing with similar problems in other national park units and federal areas. Uncertainty about title and whether the original owners could reclaim the lands by paying their back taxes complicated the procedure. State Controller C. F. Proctor concluded that the best solution would be to have the county's Board of Supervisors buy back the land from the state, giving clear title and cutting off the redemption right of any former owner. The cost to the county would be a nominal $1.00 per deed. After this procedure, the negotiations between the NPS and the county could proceed.[39]

Three days later, one of Proctor's agents wrote to inform the NPS that, in reviewing their newly legislated duties, they found a regulation that allowed the state to donate land directly to the federal government for military "or other public purposes." He asked if the national monument qualified as a public purpose. This looked much more promising than dealing with the county, but it was the first of a series of disappointments to bedevil acquisition of tax-deeded lands. Apparently, the state ceded jurisdiction to the federal government in California's national parks. It did not do so in national monuments. Hence, the NPS could not accept the Joshua Tree land from the state without a cession of jurisdiction. This seemed to eliminate an easy solution to the problem. The state could declare the land for recreational purposes, but the NPS would still have to go through Riverside County.[40]

In February 1947, NPS Director Drury quizzed Acting Regional Director Maier about progress and was informed that Superintendent Cole was too busy with the negotiations regarding railroad land to deal with this problem. A recent election had installed new people on the Riverside County Board of Supervisors, and Cole argued that he would have to start negotiations all over again. By the time Maier replied, however, Frank Givens had replaced James Cole as superintendent and restarted the negotiations. What he found was disheartening. County officials and citizens were highly antagonistic toward the monument. He reported:

> Not only are they swayed by the miners, hunters and other groups, but they feel that San Bernardino County has reaped all the benefits of the Monument which is mainly in Riverside County. Some of their grievances are real—others are imaginary.[41]

Givens met with several county officials and confirmed that they fully supported miners who were trying to open the monument to new claims. Givens explained the benefits that Riverside County would enjoy if it donated the tax deeded lands: (1) the NPS would oil the main road, sixty-five miles of which lay within Riverside County; (2) visitors would be encouraged to take a loop through the monument, entering at Twentynine Palms and exiting by Cottonwood Spring, whereupon they would continue their vacations in the Coachella Valley; (3) the NPS would probably build a utility area, a ranger station, a campground, and park residences in the southern part of the monument; (4) the NPS would extend the southern boundary of the unit to the Metropolitan Water District's (MWD) aqueduct, as proposed in the boundary change bill; and (5) the NPS would establish a separate monument or extend Joshua Tree's boundary south to include land near Chiriaco Summit for a unit honoring General George Patton. Givens also pointed out that the Sheppard's boundary-revision bill would delete five townships around Kaiser's iron mine, allowing it to expand and hire more workers. The superintendent reported that the county officials were less combative after hearing this pitch but still wanted to wait to see the outcome of the bill. For a short time, it looked hopeful, but three months later, Givens dolefully reported that the county supervisors summarily rejected the idea of a donation.[42]

In May 1948, the NPS tried another approach, asking the CSLC to buy the tax-deeded land from the State Office of the Controller, as mentioned earlier. The CSLC would be reticent to sell the land to private individuals or companies, but, hopefully, it would exchange those lands for federal property along with the state's school sections it already held. Initially, A. P. Ireland was agreeable, but soon problems arose. In some cases, the title to the tax-deeded lands would not be fully vested in the state for a period of at least five years. Then, it appeared that Riverside County might insist that the CSLC should choose only federal land in that county to exchange with the NPS. That threat did not materialize, so JTNP's officials identified 963 parcels of land totaling 8,411 acres that they hoped to secure from the state. In December 1949, however, Ireland informed the NPS that state legislators would have to pass a law to allow this complicated exchange. He sorrowfully concluded that "it is doubtful that the Commission would wish to foster such legislation."[43]

Ireland's letter forced federal officials to negotiate again with the Riverside County Board of Supervisors. In response, NPS leaders set aside $12,000, the same amount the county had proposed in 1937. Unfortunately, the 1950 boundary change had added 11,000 more private acres, many of them tax delinquent, to the monument between the old southwestern border and the new one at the MWD's aqueduct. In addition, more than thirteen years had passed, which meant that both land costs and tax burdens had risen. In early 1951, Bernard Manbey again contacted C. F. Proctor to ask his advice. Proctor outlined several approaches that could work, but he strongly recommended that the NPS simply condemn all the tax-deeded land in the monument in a single action. This would avoid a public auction by the county, which would force the NPS to bid against all other parties. Through the summer, Superintendent Givens and his staff investigated the various property records and discussed their proposed condemnation with county officials.[44]

Initially, county supervisors seemed receptive to the idea of a friendly condemnation. The tax-deeded land was a burden on local taxpayers, and several believed Superintendent Givens when he listed the long-term advantages to the county that full development of the monument would bring. The NPS had enemies, however, who found some supervisors receptive to their ideas. Three types of opponents wanted to scuttle any deal that added land to the monument. First, miners remained unsatisfied with the boundary change and pressed even harder to have the monument opened to new mining claims. Led by the Western Mining Council, they tried to block any and all efforts to support JTNM. Second, proponents of a road connecting Indio to Twentynine Palms through the Little San Bernardino Mountains were angered by the NPS's tepid response to their idea. Third, many local business and political groups did not want the federal government to control any more land in the county. They argued that the federal government already held forty-seven percent of the land in California, from which counties could not derive any taxes. This attitude presaged an argument that became a hallmark of the "sagebrush rebellion" several decades later.[45]

In August 1951, Givens tried again to get county supervisors to donate 7,588 acres of tax-deeded land in the Pinto Basin. He explained that the NPS sought a smaller amount of acreage, because much of the rest was either not tax delinquent or required a period of five years before it could be so classified. On October 8, the supervisors again refused. Many of the NPS's critics were present at the board meeting. Colonel Nordstrum, of the Riverside County Chamber of Mines, thanked the board for not allowing an increase in the monument's territory. Indio resident Ole Nordland wrote to the supervisors, wondering why the only roads improved in the monument led from Twentynine Palms to the Lost Horse Valley in San Bernardino County. This seemed to resonate with several board members, despite Givens's explanation that the NPS could not improve roads across the private land so prevalent in Riverside County.[46]

After this rebuff, agency officials speculated on whether the county would be willing to exchange land with the monument or, failing that, accept a tripartite exchange, if another buyer could be found. In an effort to simplify the procedure, they decided to separate the Pinto Basin lands from those in the Hexie Mountains region, where Joseph Wachowski held an option on more than 10,000 acres. One NPS ally on the board was its chairman, Irwin Hayden. He began meeting quietly with Givens during the spring of 1952. He reported that the board's vote against the donation had been closer than it might appear, and the NPS should condemn the land in order to "take the heat off" the supervisors. He also intimated that the action should come as a "surprise" to the county, thus heading off any political outfall from such an action.[47]

By 1953, the NPS stopped looking for alternate solutions and prepared to file for condemnation. A few months earlier, regional officials reversed themselves and told Givens to include the Hexie Mountains area in the condemnation, because the mining lobby had no legal rights in such a judicial procedure. That would bring the total land in the suit to 17,083 acres. Chief of Lands Conrad Wirth notified the regional director that the NPS had $10,000 from land-acquisition funds available for Joshua Tree. In June 1953, new superintendent Samuel A. King learned that the Wachowski lands and those of the Coachella Irrigation District were not tax-deeded. NPS land officials amended the condemnation application to 10,921 acres. Then, King reported that the county valued each acre at twenty dollars but would accept fifty percent of its worth, equal to approximately $12,434. In October 1953, after a hasty adjustment to the new funding requirement, NPS Solicitor Clarence Davis formally requested that Attorney General Herbert Brownell, Jr. initiate proceedings for condemnation.[48]

Immediately, another problem arose when U.S. Department of Justice lawyers ordered the NPS to track down and notify the former owners, an expensive process fraught with peril, because some owners could still pay the back taxes and reclaim their land. Riverside County officials

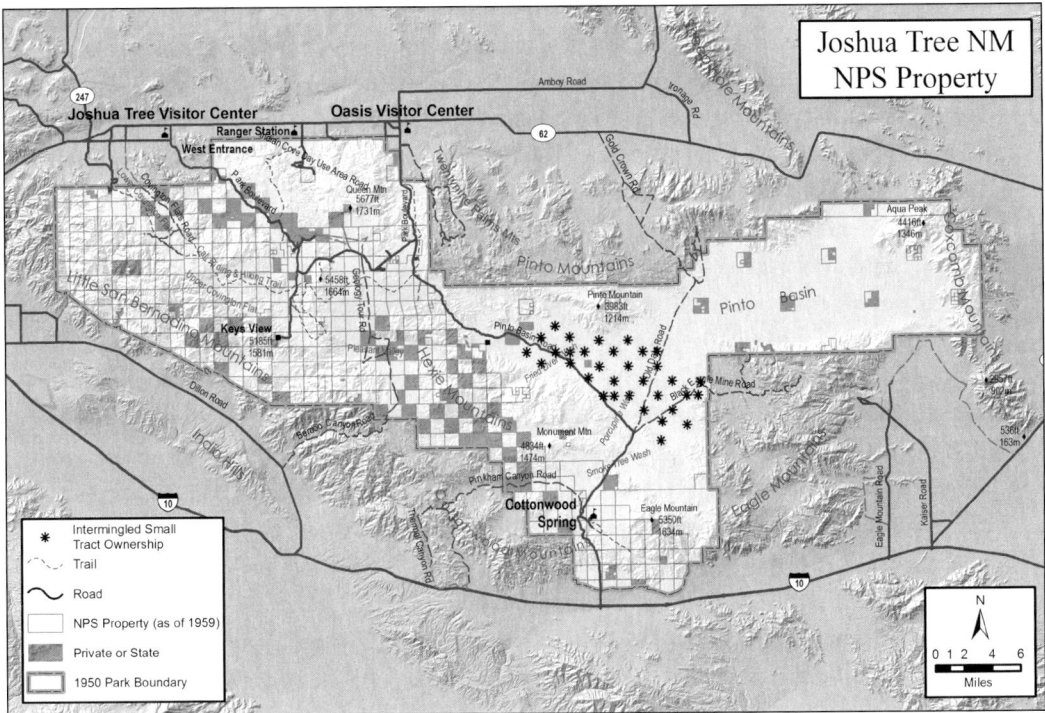

Joshua Tree NM
NPS Property

Amboy Road

247
Joshua Tree Visitor Center   Oasis Visitor Center
Ranger Station
West Entrance
62

Pinto Mountains

Aqua Peak
4416ft
1346m

Pinto Basin

Pinto Mountain
3983ft
1214m

Keys View
5185ft
1581m

Hexie Mountains

Little San Bernardino Mountains

Dillon Road

Monument Mtn
4834ft
1474m

Cottonwood
Spring

Eagle Mountain
5350ft
1634m

Eagle Mountains

Kaiser Road

10

10

Legend:
* Intermingled Small Tract Ownership
Trail
Road
NPS Property (as of 1959)
Private or State
1950 Park Boundary

N
0 1 2   4   6
Miles

MAP 4.1. Non-federal lands in Joshua Tree National Monument led many National Park Service officials to despair during the early days of the monument. Between 1936 and the end of the 1950s, the agency acquired more than 200,000 acres through a congressional deal with the Southern Pacific Railroad Company as well as land swaps, donations, and the occasional appropriated purchase. Nevertheless, thousands of private and state-owned acres remained in the primary visitor area, the Hexie and Eagle Mountains, and in the failed Security Land Corporation subdivision in the Pinto Basin. Data source: Joshua Tree National Park GIS files. Delta Cartography.

answered that they had neither the personnel nor the money to undertake such a search. More than a year passed, while the NPS conducted title research and hired a former county clerk to locate the owners and notify them. Finally, on April 1, 1955, federal lawyers filed for condemnation. After a few final adjustments, the government claimed 1,013 parcels, totaling 10,838.50 acres. A month later, government lawyers amended the action to a "declaration of taking." This meant that the NPS would immediately control the land, preventing any sales or development while the case proceeded. Finally, on May 4, 1956, the court ruled in favor of the taking. Two years later, a ruling on an appeal revested a small amount of the land to its previous owners, but it was a fraction of the total action. The NPS had cleared a huge hurdle by an unpopular but necessary process. As in the cases of the tripartite exchanges with Curtis for SPRR's land and Ellsworth for state land, this condemnation and the funds from Washington, D.C., to complete it broke a deadlock and allowed JTNM to further its critical land-acquisition program (Maps 4.1 and D).[49]

Another type of private land existed in JTNM that proved troublesome to the NPS in later years. The Colorado River Aqueduct passed through the southeastern part of the unit and, after the legislative removal of territory in 1950, abutted the monument's southwestern boundary. The June 18, 1932, act that authorized the aqueduct across federal land included not only a substantial right-of-way for the canal itself, but also parcels of nearby land for work camps, borrow pits, and areas to hold spoils from digging the waterway. The MWD held dozens of parcels of land along the southern and eastern edges of the monument. Significantly, the act ordered that any parcels not needed for purposes of the aqueduct revert to the federal government. Superintendent Cole and his successors repeatedly tried to acquire these scattered non-federal tracts. Two factors influenced the progress. First, these areas were a very low priority, because incompatible development seemed highly unlikely, if not illegal. Second, the MWD remained loath to part with any land until its engineers were certain that it would no longer be needed. Some of the dozens of parcels of MWD's lands, ranging from a few acres to more than 200 acres, would later present the NPS with difficult management problems.[50]

Mining Claims: The Other Private Lands

Joshua Tree National Monument began its existence during the middle of the Great Depression. Many men who lost their jobs in that difficult era moved to the deserts to file gold-mining claims and try to eke out a living. In 1929, the government set the price of gold at less than $21.00 per ounce. In order to support mining, the fixed rate rose to $35.00 per ounce by 1935. Small operators worked many mines, but larger companies quickly moved in on promising claims. These businesses hired dozens of men, revived old stamp mills, and reclaimed old pits, while occasionally working the tailings from earlier operations. In 1941, the GLO estimated that the monument had nearly 8,800 claims.[51] The presidential proclamation that established Joshua Tree stipulated that existing claims filed properly under the Mining Act of 1872 would continue within the new reserve. GLO inspectors, however, undertook validity studies of the existing ones at the request of the NPS. Miners had to follow specific rules to maintain a mining claim, including continuous mining activity and an annual production of minerals amounting to at least $100. Claims could be lost if either of these conditions were unmet or if the land was being used for a non-mining purpose such as a recreational home site. If an individual patented a mining claim, the tract became private property and could not be challenged. To patent a claim, however, a miner needed to have the site properly surveyed and show evidence of sufficient ore to encourage a "prudent man" to invest at least $500 in improvements on the claim. The GLO typically did not examine claims on public-domain land until the owner applied for a patent. The vast majority of claims in Joshua Tree were unpatented, but conversion of the area to a national monument warranted closer inspection of these unproven operations. Because of the long lapse between the original mining boom and the Depression-era revival, many claims had been abandoned or forgotten, but no one bothered to cancel them, unless a new claimant filed on the same area. The NPS hoped that proper investigation would simply eliminate the vast majority of these de facto inholdings.[52]

Two problems complicated the voidance of mining claims. First, miners had frequently avoided tedious paperwork and trips to the county recorder's office by vaguely describing the locations of their claims. Then, if they located a deposit somewhere relatively nearby, they could move to it and argue that it was the original site. This was illegal but commonly practiced throughout the desert. It added to the confusion already created by multiple claims worked by the same individuals and the use of the same mine names by different parties. The second problem related to the legal proceedings necessary to invalidate a claim. For each claim, the GLO had to either contact the claimant or publish an official notice in an area newspaper. In the case of a few negative declarations, the cost of this procedure was small, but, here, the land office faced thousands of potential adverse decisions. It simply did not have the manpower to process all the claims nor the money to publish notices. Furthermore, if the land office "adversed" a claim, its owner could appeal the decision, which then required a hearing. All of these issues delayed the final cancellation of some mining claims, despite determined work by the inspectors.[53]

GLO inspectors led by Samuel Guthrey began examining mines and mining claims early in 1937. They quickly learned that a very big job lay ahead. In his multi-purpose investigation in March 1937, Guthrey reported that there were more than forty groups of mining claims being worked in 150 locations, employing 250 men and paying $40,000 per month in wages. Virtually all this activity was occurring in the eastern portion of the monument.[54] Vigorous work by the inspectors allowed a satisfied Superintendent Cole to announce, in his 1941 annual report, that the GLO had adversely reported 3,170 claims, and another 600 investigations were nearing completion. Notices had been sent to 2,170 claimants, and only nine had led to appeals. As the investigators continued, they were particularly successful in the western part of the monument, where they found only twenty-eight of 3,782 claims valid. In the much more active eastern region, they declared 405 claims valid out of 5,000. Records kept by the GLO and its successor, the BLM, show that most claims were adversely ruled after letters to the claimants went unanswered. Inspectors rejected others, because they were filed after the establishment of the monument. Progress stopped, however, with the advent of World War II. The federal government issued order L-208, which stopped all gold mining, and shortages of money and personnel canceled field examinations.[55]

Among the mining claims invalidated by the GLO were a number owned by William F. ("Bill") Keys. Over the years, Keys had claimed, bought, inherited, and otherwise possessed a variety of mines and millsites that he occasionally leased to others for different lengths of time. Most were in the western part of the monument and largely inactive. In April 1941, mineral investigators filed adverse reports on eight of them, including the Desert Queen, Lang, and Key millsites and the Mountain View, Pine Cove, Pine Springs, and Pleasant Valley lodes. A year later, the commissioner of the GLO declared Keys's Big Chief Millsite null and void. The latter was significant, because it included the Barker Dam and reservoir, a public water reserve that Keys fenced for his own use. The Desert Queen Mine #1 also received an adverse ruling, but a supplemental inspection reversed that decision. As for the rest, Keys immediately filed appeals. J. H. Favorite, the regional field examiner, later wrote, ". . . we found that Keys was claiming numerous mining claims that had been located under different names at different times, and we had considerable difficulty in working out with him the question of just what ground was covered by these different locations."[56]

Several factors delayed the hearing on the eight adversed claims, not the least of which was the arrest of Bill Keys on a murder charge. He secured a continuance of the case, citing the difficulty of defending his claims from jail, and the attention of the land office's case shifted to its many other appeals. It was not until years after his release from San Quentin that Keys himself brought attention to his dubious mineral rights. In August 1956, the NPS learned that Keys intended to patent several mines in the monument. By this time, he and his wife (Fig. 5.2) owned nearly 880 acres of land, a fact that caused the San Bernardino Welfare Department to question his right to collect public funds for "old age security." Subsequent investigation showed that most of the pre-1936 lodes that Keys claimed had been filed on land belonging to the SPRR. Hence, they were invalid from the beginning. Two of the veins extended into what had been public domain, however, and the commissioner declared those portions valid.[57]

While Keys battled to keep his many mining and millsite claims, GLO/BLM inspectors resumed investigations after the end of World War II. But, on November 16, 1945, the NPS told them to stop their evaluation of the eastern part of the monument, because Congressman Sheppard's H.R. 4703 might remove most of the remaining active mines. This was, perhaps, fortunate, since the land office had run into trouble processing the cases it had already decided. BLM regional administrator Marion Clawson complained to his director that his inspectors had reported adversely on 4,385 claims. The commissioner had declared 2,450 of them officially null and void. There remained 3,620 claims in the eastern part of Joshua Tree to be examined. The numbers of claims reported favorably remained the same as 1941: twenty-eight in the western portion and 405 in the eastern portion. The compelling number in Clawson's report was 1,050 cases held in the district's land office in Los Angeles, pending publication of notices. Clawson believed it would cost $30,000 to publish them and require two additional clerks to do the work. He told the NPS that it would have to pay for both. He did not receive a response; hence, the complaint to his boss. As long as the notices remained unpublished, the claims were still valid. The 1950 boundary change removed many of the unexamined claims, and, thereafter, the NPS grudgingly began paying to have the adversed ones in the shrunken monument finalized.[58]

After two decades of worry and desperate work, the NPS could look at the remaining land in the monument with some pride and satisfaction. The agency had secured thousands of acres of private, railroad, and school lands with procedures that gave promise of similar success in the future. Tedious and expensive work also eliminated thousands of mining claims. After excising most of the remaining mineralized areas in 1950 and defeating the last organized attempt to open the entire unit to new claims, JTNM officials could move forward with confidence that the monument would survive and, hopefully, become the important preserve and popular attraction that Minerva Hoyt predicted it would be.

FIG. 5.1. The Lost Horse Mine in 1967 before the headframe collapsed. From 1894 to 1931, the mine produced more than 10,000 ounces of gold and 16,000 ounces of silver. The mine has also suffered dangerous deterioration below the surface, and the park site remains unstable. Photograph by Donald Black. Joshua Tree National Park Photo Archives, Cat. 20575, Image 1370.

CHAPTER FIVE

Early Management of Joshua Tree National Monument

THREATS POSED BY MINING, the adjustment to the monument's boundary in 1950, and the tortuous land-acquisition process delayed but did not stop planning for Joshua Tree National Monument (JTNM). National Park Service (NPS) policy and experience with land management highlighted opportunities and limitations within the monument. The original inspections by Roger Toll and Harold Bryant were cursory at best. Even before the NPS opened its first office in Twenty-nine Palms, regional officials had to assess the situation on the ground and seek answers to many questions. What was the water situation, so critical to any development? What roads existed, and which ones should be improved for use by visitors? Which traditional land-use activities could continue, and which should be stopped in a new national park unit? Related to this was the need for basic research and resource management. What was the status of bighorn sheep and other fauna? How much damage had years of vandalism and theft done to the flora of the monument? How significant and widespread were the traces of Native American inhabitance? In addition, the agency had to plan and develop the area to be a proper unit of the national park system. Where should the NPS establish its permanent headquarters? Where should it put trails, campgrounds, and other infrastructure? Finally, what should rangers emphasize when interpreting the monument for the visiting public? After the opening of the business office on September 19, 1940, the pace of these activities increased, in spite of all the time consumed in battling miners and negotiating with landowners. After the boundary settlement in 1950, it dramatically accelerated just in time to absorb the service-wide building bonanza that accompanied the NPS's new *Mission 66* program.

The staff at Joshua Tree remained small during this time, starting with just James Cole and reaching only thirteen full- and part-time employees by 1954. During the war years, the monument had several acting superintendents, but seldom more than three other employees at one time. Harold S. Hildreth became the first ranger in January 1941 but lasted only six months. He had a family and could not support them in Twentynine Palms on a park ranger's salary. John W. Stratton transferred from Lassen Volcanic National Park, and Cole hired a local man, Hesmel Earenfight, to replace Hildreth, but both soon disappeared into the military. They returned after the war, and Earenfight stayed on for many years thereafter. Several maintenance employees also worked in the monument in between stints in the military. During Cole's military service, he was replaced by acting custodians Walter G. Attwell, Duane D. Jacobs, Walter Ketcham, and Frank R. Givens. On

March 4, 1947, Givens reassumed leadership of the monument, when Cole left for a position in the regional office. Samuel A. King replaced Givens in April 1953 and served until 1957. Meanwhile, a cavalcade of regional and national officials helped with evaluative inspections and planning.[1]

Securing Water in Joshua Tree

The key to development in JTNM, once land and boundaries were secure, was water. In 1936, the NPS had some experience with arid units, but few matched the paucity of water in Joshua Tree. No permanent streams flowed through the monument. The few settlers within its boundaries had no commercial agriculture, and the only irrigation supported a small subsistence orchard and vegetable garden owned by William F. ("Bill") Keys (Fig. 5.2). Available water came from three sources. The major aquifers lay relatively deep and resulted from precipitation millennia earlier. The springs that supported early cattle herds and mining operations stemmed from water that entered mountainous terrain, percolated through the rock and soil layers, and appeared at the surface at the base of the uplands. After irregular rain events, water also collected in natural or human-made rock depressions called "tanks" or flowed briefly in short, ephemeral streams. High evaporation rates, however, made these sources sporadic at best. NPS officials knew that any hope of drawing visitors to the monument lay in finding more water, securing the legal right to tap it, and constructing the infrastructure to deliver it. In addition, more water would be necessary to protect and increase the signature fauna of the unit, particularly the desert bighorn sheep.

Many of the early inspectors of the new unit gave pessimistic evaluations of the existing water sources. After his visit in March 1937, landscape architect Ernest Davidson wrote, ". . . owing to this extremely difficult water question, it may very likely be impossible to develop camp sites, or other sites, for over-night use within the boundaries, even were such a development desirable."[2] He added that the Lost Horse Mine shaft reached a depth of 500 feet without finding water (Fig. 5.1). A year later, James E. Cole carried out a more careful survey and listed twenty-two sources, including Cottonwood, Quail, and Stubbe Springs and Barker Dam. The remainder consisted of private wells and ephemeral tanks. He lamented that Twentynine Palms had plenty of groundwater, but it did not flow into the monument.[3]

Clearly, the NPS needed a specialized study by a competent hydrologist not only for long-term development planning, but for locating a headquarters facility. Regional Geologist J. Volney Lewis conducted the study in 1941, with special attention to possible headquarters sites. In his report, Lewis described the underlying water basins, the influence of faults, and the significant points where water occurred or where relatively shallow wells could be dug. He identified twenty-three springs, nine tanks, and seventeen wells inside the monument's boundaries (Map 5.1). More than 100 wells and

Joshua Tree NM Historical Water Sources

247
Joshua Tree Visitor Center
Oasis Visitor Center
Amboy Road
Ironage Rd
62
Gold Crown Rd.

Keys Ranch Wells
Barker Dam
Queen Valley Reservoir
Pine Spring
Lang Well
Black Rock Spring
Quail Springs
Twentynine Palms Hwy
Water Tanks
White Tank
Pinto Mountains
Aqua Peak 2416m 7436m
Little San Bernardino Mountains
Geology Tour Rd (4WD)
5458ft 1664m
Stubbe Spring
Lost Horse Spring
Hidden Tank
Stirrup Tank
Pinto Mountain 5398ft 1274m
Pinto Basin
Pinto Wells
Keys View 4530ft 1381m
Squaw Tank
Hansen's Well
Pleasant Valley
Pinto Basin Road
Old Dale Road
Placer Canyon Reservoir
Pinyon Well
Ruby Lee Well
Pinkham Well and Spring
Black Eagle Mine Road
5336ft 1626m
5350ft 1631m
Hexie Mountains
Monument Mtn 4834ft 1474m
Dillon Road
Indio Hills
Berdoo Canyon Road
Pinkham Canyon Road
Smoke Tree Well
Conejo Spring
Eagle Mountain 5350ft 1631m
Cottonwood Springs
Lost Palms Oasis
Eagle Mountains
Eagle Mountain Road
Kaiser Road
10
10

Legend:
▲ Water Source
Visitor Center / Ranger Station
Trail
Road
1950 Park Boundary

N
0 1 2 4 6
Miles

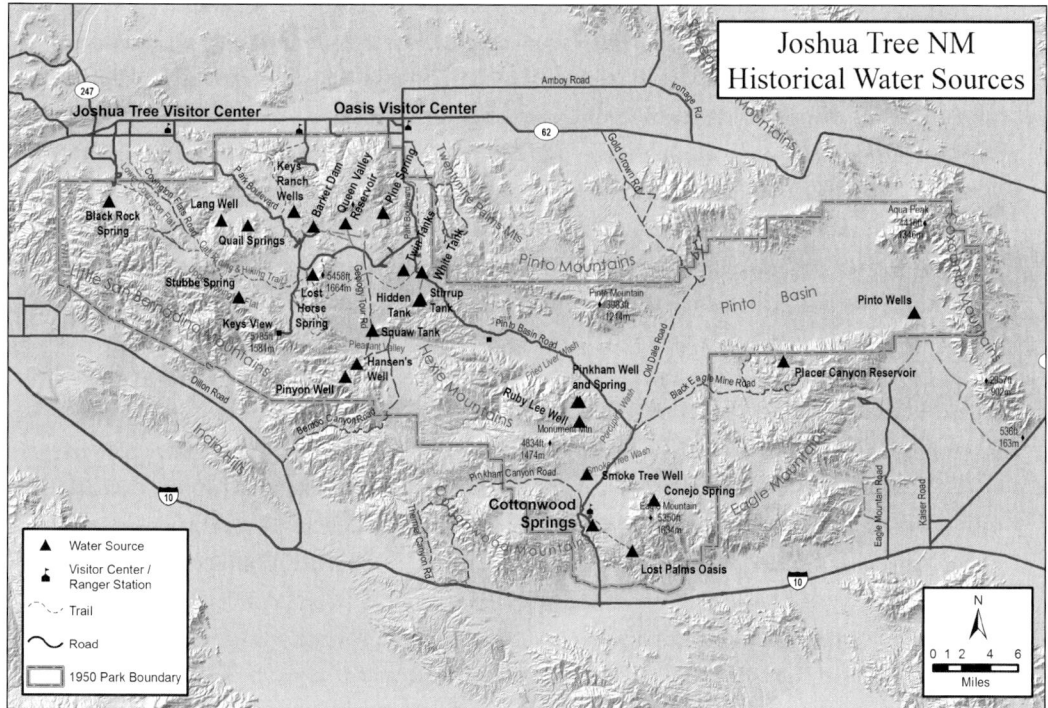

MAP 5.1. During the five decades prior to the establishment of Joshua Tree National Monument in 1936, settlers and miners developed most of the significant water sources in the area. The majority lay in the Mojave Desert portion, in the western part of the park unit. A geological study identified many ephemeral sources as well, but a subterranean flow of groundwater to the wells of external settlements and a slow decrease in annual precipitation meant that all but the Cottonwood Spring ran out of surface flow by 1983. Data source: Linda Greene, "Historic Resource Study: A History of Land Use in Joshua Tree National Monument" (1983), Denver Service Center, Joshua Tree National Park Library, 305. Delta Cartography.

the Oasis of Mara existed just outside the unit's boundaries, primarily in and around Twentynine Palms. Lewis evaluated seven potential sites for a headquarters office, and, although he did not make a specific recommendation, he clearly thought the Oasis of Mara was superior to the others. He recommended a more detailed study, including an evaluation of water quality by a sanitary engineer.[4]

World War II derailed any further investigation of water sources, but Superintendent Cole's return, in May 1944, renewed the search for water and the legal rights to use it. Chester Pinkham accompanied Cole on several trips into the southern part of the monument to find tanks and other sources that he remembered from his mining trips decades earlier. Cole suggested that wells be dug on government land and windmills be used to bring the water to the surface for the benefit of wildlife. Acting Director Hillory Tolson rejected that idea, claiming that such intrusive structures had no place in a national park unit. Although the NPS found additional tanks and drilled a few experimental wells, it became obvious that the future of the monument depended on accessing the known water sources. Unfortunately, the uncertainty of water rights doctrine in California, coupled with Joshua Tree's bizarre land-ownership patterns, confused NPS officials and resulted in still more lengthy legal procedures.[5]

The Confusing Case of California Water Rights

The rights to water in the western United States are very complicated. One significant characteristic of American water rights is that state law is generally preeminent, although there has been much tension and judiciary wrangling over federal rights since settlement of the West began. California is particularly difficult, because state law recognizes three separate systems for water rights: pueblo rights, riparian rights, and appropriative rights. Pueblo rights date from the Spanish and Mexican periods and do not apply in the Joshua Tree area. It is a type of appropriation where the water necessary for a town from a nearby source preempts that of an individual. It is based on the common good. Riparian rights derive from English common law and apply over most of the United States. In this system, a landowner may divert and use water running through or alongside his or her property. California adopted this system upon achieving statehood in 1850. The third system, however, sometimes called the "doctrine of prior appropriation," already existed in California prior to statehood. Gold seekers worked it out in the Sierra Nevada foothills, where inadequate water for mining demanded a different approach. In this case, the first person to divert water for a beneficial use has a prior right against all other users. This "first in time, first in right" system prioritized users but outlawed wasteful or unfair use. By using both the riparian and appropriative systems throughout most of the state, California assured that its lawyers would have plenty of work. Over the years, court cases and subsequent legislation sought to address and clarify the inconsistencies.[6]

One result was the creation of what became the California State Water Board in the Water Commission Act of 1913. Legally, those who wish to appropriate water must apply to the board, which then holds a hearing. A person can argue that he or she has priority or that another applicant is requesting an amount beyond what is considered "reasonable use." All prior appropriations established before 1914 remained unchallenged, but those subsequent to it fell under more scrutiny. In most cases, the federal government is just another claimant. The U.S. Supreme Court affirmed this arrangement in a 1935 case that emphasized the separation of federal land rights from state water rights. The U.S. Congress also reinforced this with the McCarran Amendment passed in 1952. One important caveat in this arrangement is that the federal government can overrule the state's water allocation, if it threatens downstream navigation. Significantly, the California Supreme Court ruled, in 1903, that the "reasonable use" criterion also applies to groundwater.[7]

Despite this apparent nod to state's rights, the federal government did secure priority rights for any reserve it established. In a 1908 U.S. Supreme Court decision, the federal government established an appropriation right to supply the Fort Belknap Indian Reservation in Montana with enough water for the residents to carry out irrigated agriculture. It did not affect prior appropriations but curbed excessive claims by subsequent applicants. Further court action extended the "reserved rights doctrine" to national parks, national forests, and national wildlife refuges. Thus, the NPS could argue that Joshua Tree's purposes of preservation and recreation entitled it to water on and under monument land that was not already appropriated in 1936. If prior claims existed, however, the agency would have to negotiate with the owners and, quite possibly, have to buy them out. This was particularly bothersome in cases where springs or wells within the monument had already been tapped to supply users outside the boundaries.[8]

Another type of federal water reservation, the public water reserve, also exists in arid portions of the American West. Grazing in the region relied entirely on the availability of water for free-range livestock. As long as it remained part of the commons, wealthier ranchers could file land claims on tracts of land that had springs or waterholes and then keep out competing cattlemen or sheepherders. This led to conflict and occasionally violence. The General Land Office (GLO) took note and, on March 29, 1912, began removing public lands with water sources from alienation in order to keep them open to homesteaders and small operations. The U.S. Geological Survey (USGS) recommended specific sites, and President William Howard Taft approved their withdrawal and chronological enumeration. Public Water Reserve 14 included the water impounded by Bill Keys at the Barker Dam (Plates 24 and 25). In 1926, President Calvin Coolidge simplified the process when he issued "Executive Order of April 17, 1926," setting aside what is called "Public Water Reserve No. 107." This sweeping order removed from "settlement, location, sale or entry" all springs and waterholes, as well as the surrounding land for a distance of one-quarter mile, on unappropriated and unreserved public land. In 1945, Superintendent Cole identified seven public water reserves in the monument, including Barker Dam, Quail, Stubbe, Cottonwood, and Lost Horse Springs, Stirrup Tanks, and two other unnamed sources.[9]

Later developments in water law have highlighted the difficulties inherent in operating under dual legal doctrines. One controversial situation involves water on federal land that has not been set aside as any type of reserve. The federal government has contested state primacy in controlling "non-reserved" water on the public domain in a number of controversial cases. The courts have tended to cite the "reasonable use" precedent to decide individual cases, meaning that both states and the federal government have won and lost. Yet, Congress enacted a "non-reserved" water right in the bill that upgraded Great Sand Dunes in Colorado from a monument to a park in 2000. The law enables the park to claim groundwater outside its immediate boundaries but within its hydrologic basin in order to preserve the ecological diversity in the unit. In some cases, the rise of environmentalism in American society has led to increasing federal success, particularly in the contest between consumptive and "instream" uses. The former refer to all the uses for human purposes that have been the traditional bases of appropriative claims. Beginning with environmental organizations' defense of Mono Lake against the removal of its tributary waters by the City of Los Angeles, however, courts have confirmed that biological health, recreation, and scenic qualities are also reasonable uses. For Joshua Tree National Park (JTNP), these changes in water law may enable the NPS to draw water from the public domain outside the unit, while protecting water that originates within it. One further amendment to Joshua Tree's water rights came in 1996, when the California Water Resources Control Board ruled that "all surface water on unappropriated land at the time of reservation [is] the minimum amount necessary to fulfill the primary purpose" of the park.[10]

Sources within the Monument

The problem of securing adequate water in Joshua Tree National Monument stemmed from more than just aridity. Three issues worried monument officials. First, several businesses tapped springs inside the monument to supply their activities outside its boundaries. Second, residents in the monument had claimed most known sources decades earlier. Finally, rapid settlement around the monument drew heavily on local aquifers that, in turn, increased the outflow of groundwater from the monument. The first two meant that complex and expensive solutions had to be found within the framework of California's water regulation system either by legal challenge or purchase. The latter meant that the fight evolved over a diminishing resource. During the first two decades of the monument, there was a desperate attempt to find and secure the rights to the few water sources and overcome vigorous resistance from those who owned or had developed them. Superintendent

James Cole and his successors faced yet another combative situation, as they sought to ensure the monument's survival.

Four important water sources in Joshua Tree posed complex and prolonged management problems: Lost Palms Spring, the Pinto Wells, the Lost Horse Wells, and the reservoir behind Barker Dam. Several neighboring businesses took water from the monument, a reality that particularly aggravated NPS planners. One irksome case in the southern part of the unit was a pipeline that drew water from Lost Palms Canyon and conveyed it to a roadside tourism development beside U.S. 60 (Interstate 10) south of the monument. Joseph Chiriaco owned a gas station-gift shop operation at Shaver Summit and a water right dating back to 1900 that he purchased in 1933. In July 1946, he told Superintendent Cole that he would like to enlarge his water-diversion system in order to expand his business. Cole immediately asked the regional director to initiate a study of Chiriaco's water rights to the oasis at Lost Palms Canyon. Chiriaco's predecessors had installed a pipeline that crossed more than five miles of government and Southern Pacific Railroad Company (SPRR) lands, and Cole suspected that this was a case of trespass.[11]

After a two-year delay, Chiriaco officially applied to expand the system and showed paperwork indicating he had rights to take more water. This would relieve him from having to buy water outside the monument and truck it to his site. New superintendent Frank Givens reiterated his predecessor's recommendation to investigate the businessman's water rights and legal permission to maintain a pipeline crossing through the government's and railroad's properties. Givens feared that any increase in water diversion from the oasis would kill the native palms. During a subsequent inspection and further legal research, questions arose concerning conflicting dates of both land acquisition and water appropriation. JTNM officials learned that Chiriaco did have an appropriative right to the water but speculated they could block his application to increase his diversion, based on the riparian rights that should accompany federal ownership of the land. The NPS could claim that maintaining the health of the palm oasis was a reasonable use. Trespass by Chiriaco's pipeline was another matter. Givens and other agency officials figured they could block enlargement of the pipeline on this basis, but they were unsure they could force Chiriaco to remove the existing one. In any event, other issues and duties distracted JTNM's staff, and Chiriaco decided to bide his time for another decade.[12]

A much larger and more important source of water known as the Pinto Wells existed further east, near a major, dry wash leading from the Pinto Basin to the Chuckwalla Valley. The Metropolitan Water District of Southern California (MWD) acquired the land and an appropriation to drill a well here in 1933 to supply one of its construction camps for the Colorado River Aqueduct. The federal law authorizing the aqueduct stipulated that the land and the water right would return to the government when the district no longer had any use for them. Yet, on January 1, 1947, the Los Angeles utility leased the well to the Kaiser Steel Corporation for twenty-five years. The utility

argued that its rights remained in force, because the old construction camp still hosted a maintenance crew. When Kaiser secured the lease, it applied to the NPS for permission to pipe a much
larger amount of water to its Eagle Mountain Mine for milling ore and supplying its growing work
camp. A Kaiser-sponsored study showed that the existing well could produce 5,000 gallons per
hour, much more than what the NPS would need in that remote corner of the monument. Congressman Sheppard's H.R. 4703 bill would remove the mine from the monument but not the well.
Associate Director Arthur Demaray saw no reason to disapprove a larger extraction from the well.
He reasoned that Congressman Sheppard also would have the land under the well removed from
the monument, if the agency blocked Kaiser's plans.[13]

After the revision to the unit's boundary in 1950, the mine lay outside the monument but still
drew most of its water from the Pinto Well. Then, late in December 1954, Superintendent Samuel
King discovered that Kaiser had quietly drilled a second well to a depth of 575 feet on monument
land. Kaiser executives blithely informed King that they needed more water for the town developing alongside the mine and would submit an application soon. The initial reactions from King and
his superiors were both concern and outrage. When King inspected the new well, now called Pinto
Well #2, Kaiser officials admitted they had made a mistake. They confessed that they thought the
boundary of the monument was one-half mile further north. They added that Pinto Well #1 (Fig.
6.2) was sufficient for the mine but that more water was needed for the "lawns, trees, shrubs, sanitation, and other domestic use" for 625 people living at the mine site. They asked for advice from the
superintendent on what they should do next.[14]

The NPS faced an uncomfortable dilemma. The well was a fait accompli, the region's miners still
sought to reopen the monument to new claims or eliminate it, Kaiser was the biggest employer in an
economically depressed area, and local legislators favored expansion of its operations. Superintendent
King recommended that the company be given a three-year special-use permit to use water from the
sixteen-inch well, renewable thereafter by further application. According to Kaiser's hydrologists, Pinto
#2 would produce 1,500 gallons per minute without affecting the water table, but Regional Director
Lawrence Merriam warned that the well sat at the bottom of the basin and could draw enough water to
ruin any opportunity for the NPS to drill on surrounding higher ground. Nevertheless, he speculated
that a revocable permit might be unavoidable. Regional Solicitor Jackson E. Price agreed and reasoned
that the NPS should approve the new application, because Kaiser could just drill more wells on the ten
acres it leased from the MWD for Pinto Well #1. Price thought the NPS could control how much water Kaiser took from its new well but would be powerless if the company drilled more wells on MWD's
land. He proposed that, if the NPS did issue a permit, it should prohibit use of any of the new water
for mining. The company could only use it to supply the town, where its workers lived.[15]

Ultimately, NPS officials decided to deny a permit. Instead, they forced Kaiser to cap Pinto Well #2 and brought a trespass charge against the company. They continued to negotiate with the company, but the two parties disagreed about several basic provisions. Kaiser asked for three times the per-capita water requirement generally allowed by the government. NPS negotiators remained leery of the impact the water withdrawal would have on wildlife in the Pinto Basin and any future development plans. They challenged Kaiser to obtain water from wells outside the monument, especially in the Chuckwalla Valley. Hydrologists reported that some of the monument's groundwater flowed into that valley but did not agree on whether drawing water from wells there might ultimately drain the Pinto Basin. Kaiser's representatives offered to drill horizontally from the new well to the old one and proposed a variety of tripartite and direct exchanges for land, mines, or whatever they thought the NPS might want. Kaiser wanted a permit for at least twenty years to justify the enormous investment it would make in further development of the mine and its town. The NPS refused to consider any more than five years and preferred two or three. Some agency officials worried about how the public would react to a huge allocation of water to Kaiser, while they rejected small applications such as Chiriaco's. In 1956, as the monument's second decade drew to a close, Pinto #2 remained capped. Kaiser started negotiating directly with senior NPS officials in Washington, D.C., and then surprised the agency by drilling a third well on its leased MWD property, very close to Pinto #1. Once again, JTNM's officials knew nothing about Pinto Well #3 until it began pumping. The company continued to negotiate for Pinto #2 water but demonstrated it would not be denied the resources necessary for its economic growth.[16]

The Chiriaco and Kaiser withdrawals bothered JTNM officials, but their greatest concerns lay in the western half of the monument. The Lost Horse Wells on the Ryan homestead formed one obvious source in the area most suitable for "visitor use." Ranchers Tom and Jepp Ryan used the water to support their grazing and mining operations. In 1941, Superintendent Cole suggested that one of the water rights still held by Jepp Ryan was invalid, because the land had been patented to the SPRR in 1912, when the area was first surveyed. Furthermore, Ryan had not patented the mill along with the mine. A three-mile pipeline carried water from the old mill site to the mine across both railroad and government lands. Cole found that Ryan had not sought permission from either landholder and technically was in trespass. The superintendent nevertheless cautioned against taking action to deprive Ryan of his water, because it would benefit the railroad and make acquisition of its land more difficult. Subsequently, the NPS dug its own wells on nearby government land, but Ryan's Lost Horse Well #1, on his patented homestead, remained the primary producer in the area.[17]

Two Visions: Water, Grazing, Park Policy, and Bill Keys

Barker Dam and the cattle that used its water proved to be the most-contentious issue for James Cole and several succeeding superintendents. When Bill Keys moved to the area, he identified all possible sources of subsistence and acquired them as they became available. By 1936, he ran one of the last herds of cattle in JTNM, held title to multiple mineral claims, millsites, and water sources, and threatened anyone who trespassed or challenged his perceived rights. Keys claimed nine separate water sources, including Barker Dam, Cow Camp Reservoir, and Split Rock Reservoir. Most had small dams to augment the pools of springwater or rainfall he used to supply his cattle and mill ore. Barker Dam was the most reliable source and one of the closest to his Desert Queen Ranch (Plates 31). Through a variety of traditional homestead entries, stock-raising entries, and acquisitions by relatives and friends, Keys and his wife, the former Frances Lawton, (Fig 5.2) procured enough land to block all but the northern and eastern sides of the reservoir, which were too rugged to allow access. Certain that he alone owned the water, Keys built a fence to deny its use by other cattlemen and, ultimately, by the monument that surrounded it. He then focused on increasing his herd to a size necessary to support himself and his family.[18]

James Cole later reported that JTNM supported grazing in only two areas. James Cram's operation included Cottonwood Spring, but it primarily used a large range area outside the monument. World War II and General George Patton's desert-tank training shut down that operation, when the U.S. Army took over most of the public domain he used. The other centered on the Lost Horse and Pleasant Valleys, which Keys used in summer and winter, respectively. C. O. Barker and Will Shay had used these valleys until 1923. Emmett Shay who, like his father, served as the sheriff of San Bernardino County, and James W. Stocker represented the type of big cattle business that had formerly monopolized the range and water holes. Cole suspected they had not purchased proper permits or established water rights for the original operation but simply moved into the area. They, too, wanted access to graze their livestock in the monument. Interestingly, Stocker was the under-sheriff of San Bernardino County. They used their prominent positions to the advantage of their cattle business. Bill Keys was the only man who still grazed cattle in the area they coveted. He had clashed previously with Barker and Shay and even wounded one of their employees. As a miner and homesteader, Keys represented an intrusion and a threat to big-time cattle operators, and a virulent enmity built up between them. Keys maintained throughout his life that most of his woes were caused by the Shay faction, including his later shootout with a neighbor and problems with the NPS, in general, and James Cole, in particular.[19]

The first sign of trouble in this grazing and water-rights feud came in October 1936, during Colonel Thomson's inspection. Keys mentioned that he expected 150 additional cattle to be delivered

FIG. 5.2. William F. ("Bill") and Frances Keys clashed with the National Park Service (NPS) over its attempt to curtail their mining and grazing businesses. Keys had achieved dubious fame earlier, when he was part of a scam perpetrated by the infamous conman "Death Valley Scotty" (Walter Scott). His reputation as a dangerous man came from rumors that he had killed a man near Death Valley and shot a member of the competing Barker and Shay cattle operation. Keys was sent to prison for killing neighbor Worth Bagley in 1943 but was later pardoned. Although Keys was a strident opponent of the NPS, he later became the major source of data about the park's history and the focus of is interpretation program. Photographer and date unknown. Joshua Tree National Park Photo Archives, General Collection.

in the next few days. An appalled Superintendent Thomson told Keys that grazing would not be permitted on government land in the monument. Keys later wrote that he immediately canceled his order for the cattle. Thomson also recommended to his superiors that grazing never be permitted in Joshua Tree. Director Arno Cammerer agreed but cautioned that Keys had every right to graze cattle on his own land, much of which he had obtained with stock-raising homestead grants. Meanwhile, Keys believed that cattleman H. W. Stacey convinced the new superintendent to deny him grazing rights on government land, so he could gain the range for his herd. His suspicion was reinforced when Stacey applied to the NPS for a grazing permit on land that Keys used. The old prospector then applied for a permit for the same land. Shortly thereafter, he entered a partnership with a Mr. Lawrence, who brought eighty head to the monument from the Pacific Coast. The two soon had a falling out, and Lawrence later removed his cattle after Cole informed him they could not stay, because he had no grazing rights. The NPS decided not to issue a permit to anyone.[20]

Real trouble began when James Cole arrived in September 1940 with instructions to develop the monument. As the last of the active cowboy–prospectors in JTNM, Keys represented a way of life already gone from most of the West. He was a jack-of-all-trades and a master of many. He was also extraordinarily independent, self-sufficient, and willing to defend his perceived rights, violently if necessary. He also proved amazingly opportunistic, as he turned much of the Lost Horse and Pleasant Valleys into a near-fiefdom. He clashed with the bureaucracy of the NPS on many issues, including mining claims, water rights, property rights, and grazing rights. He understood and used the legal procedures to acquire rights and titles but ignored the law if he thought he could.[21] Superintendent Cole expressed sympathy for Keys as an old-timer who should be treated well and, if possible, given leeway to continue his grazing, mining, and other economic pursuits. Cole, however, also had to enforce the law and NPS policy on a monument that was in grave danger of failing. When he contacted Keys about controlling his cattle and allowing government employees and visitors access to the public water reserve at Barker Dam, Cole met stiff resistance.[22]

Grazing is one of the more difficult issues a new park or monument faces. Secretary of the Interior Franklin Lane's 1918 letter to Director Stephen Mather, based on the latter's own ideas, specified that grazing could only take place in areas where visitors seldom traveled, and in cases where no harm would come to the natural resources. Widespread grazing in parks and monuments during World War I, however, caused unacceptable damage. In 1925, Secretary Hubert Work ordered that grazing should be phased out of the parks as soon as possible. During World War II, the NPS resisted grazing far more stringently and successfully, but it still took place in some units, including Joshua Tree. Grazing can persist in a park unit under several circumstances. First, a person can maintain a herd of animals on his or her own property within a park. Second and far more common, grazing permits issued before a unit is established can be maintained through the life of the permit or if lawmakers so order. During the two world wars, the government encouraged more meat production by opening some parks to temporary grazing. A third factor that helped those who wanted to run livestock in the parks is a reticence among NPS officials to suspend aggressively traditional activities by residents who lived in the area before the unit's establishment. Many campaigns to create parks, like the one for Joshua Tree, are controversial. The long-term damage to the agency's reputation, if it is high-handed, will complicate further management across the system. All three of these circumstances prevailed in Joshua Tree with Bill Keys and his cattle operation.[22]

Keys also refused to accept the NPS's contention that the reservoir at Barker Dam was a public water reserve. He argued that he personally had done so much hard work to augment its storage capacity and had used it for such a long time that it rightfully belonged to him. At the same time, every action the NPS took threatened the lifestyle Keys had built during the previous three decades. He saw his mining claims adversed until he had little left but Desert Queen #1. Most of the water rights and wells he claimed were found to be on public water reserves, on SPRR land, or, in one case, homesteaded by his most visible antagonist, Worth Bagley. He struggled throughout his life to patch together enough economic activities to subsist and raise a family. He even briefly worked on a road crew for the NPS before finding that work unrewarding. Grazing was the core of a diminishing opportunity to continue his livelihood. When the NPS ordered him to keep his cattle on his own land, he realized that this, too, faced closure. According to a later range study, the land Keys owned might support three or four cattle, hardly enough to carry on a business.[23]

During his first year as superintendent, Cole tried to convince Keys that he would have to allow others to use Barker Dam's water and confine his cattle to his own land. Then, after consulting with the regional director, Cole offered to work out a permit for Keys that would restrict his cattle to Pleasant Valley, an area that would not be frequented by visitors and, hence, would not overtly challenge the agency's directives. Cole maintained that he always treated Keys and his wife with courtesy, and their conversations were calm and forthright. Conversely, Keys harbored a growing dislike for Cole because of his interference with the prospector's property and livelihood. Despite superficial courtesy when they met, Keys fired letters to senior NPS officials, the governor of California, and the Secretary of the Interior, bitterly complaining about every aspect of JTNM's management. In July 1941, Keys and his wife wrote to Secretary Ickes and complained about the elimination of most of their mining claims, the destruction of vegetation and natural beauty that visitors and a movie company caused at the monument, and their belief that Minerva Hoyt and local realtors engineered the monument's proclamation for their own financial benefit. Keys added that the NPS had cut down "hundreds of truckloads of Joshuas and other yuccas and growth" in order to build an unnecessary road.[24]

On July 4, 1942, as the Barker Dam and grazing issues grew bitter, a fire started in Joshua Tree that further incensed Keys. Two weeks later, he sent a letter to Lawrence Merriam, of Yosemite National Park, and Regional Director Owen Tomlinson, and this time he focused specifically on Cole. He accused the superintendent of harassing him about his cattle and argued that grazing had prevented fires before the area became a monument. He reiterated that Cole had a road built that caused his workers to remove truckloads of plants and dump them down mineshafts. He insisted that he owned Barker Dam and its reservoir and accused Cole of deliberately and repeatedly tres-passing, in one instance driving across a field of grain. He added, ". . . if this keeps up my property will be as trampled down as some other places that he and his friends like to picnic at." Keys went on to complain about destruction caused by the Paramount Motion Picture Company and the fact that Cole did nothing to stop it, that the superintendent had used 200 tons of valuable ore from a mine dump to line his new road, that he told his men to take pipe and other equipment from a mine to use for some purpose, and that he was simply currying favor from Minerva Hoyt, who was busy selling railroad land. Keys also accused Cole of personal malfeasance:

> When the fire of July 4th started Mr. Coles [sic] was up at the view with a car full of women and coming back saw the fire soon after it started, but usually when he is wanted he is either nowhere to be found or sitting in his office at Twentynine Palms. All this area needs is enough cattle on the range and one good ranger ON THE JOB [emphasis in the original].[25]

In addition to the fire, what spurred Keys's angry letter was the intensifying conflict over the water behind Barker Dam. Cole and Hesmel Earenfight went to the Keys's home and, not finding William, spoke to Frances about using the water there to fight any future fires in the area. Apparently, she agreed, but, during the course of the conversation, the superintendent mentioned that the NPS had every right to cut the fence blocking access to it and the agency could put up a fence and deny use of the water to the Keys. Cole was technically and legally correct, but it was not a tactful approach to solving the problem. Frances Keys, it turned out, was the more volatile one of the couple, and the monument's officials drove away with her enraged voice ringing in their ears.[26]

By this time, officials at all levels of the NPS were well aware of Bill Keys and the difficult problems he posed at Joshua Tree. Nevertheless, Cole's immediate supervisors pressed him for a response to the charges in this most recent letter. On August 10, 1942, the superintendent submitted his eight-page, single-spaced answer to each point Keys had made. He began with a general assessment:

As you know, Mr. Keys or rather Mrs. Keys, who wrote this letter is my pet problem. I have always been very sympathetic with them and have withheld judgment and action against them for over two years, hoping all the time that in some manner we could work out these problems without adverse consequences to the Keys. Such an attitude, I realize now, was a mistake. These people do not understand kindness and assume such actions are a sign of weakness. Accordingly, they take advantage of every situation possible. They not only will not cooperate, but of late have become quite defiant. I am glad that they wrote this letter because it is evident now that this office henceforth has no alternative but to see that they obey all Park Service regulations regardless of the consequences. There is a small element of truth in practically all the statements and accusations the Keys made in their letter. But in almost every case they either omit part of the facts or twist the truth so that it appears very unfavorable. If we were dealing with respectable people some of their statements would be serious, but the Keys have a very poor record in this area.[27]

Cole then answered the specific charges. He admitted that his road crew cut between fifty and seventy-five truckloads of yuccas and other low vegetation after approval from the regional engineer, but he argued that this was a small amount for sixty-six miles of road. He added that all of the mine shafts claimed by Keys were timbered with Joshua trees and that the prospector still ignored regulations that forbid gathering firewood in the monument. He explained that he asked Keys to keep his cattle in Pleasant Valley as per regulations, but Keys would not do so, insisting that he receive a permit to graze hundreds of cattle in the Lost Horse Valley. The superintendent also investigated the common ranchers' claim that grazing suppressed fire and found it to be false, because the cattle did not actually eat the grass; they ate the brush. He admitted that he had crossed the Keys's grain field but explained that it had just been planted and was unrecognizable. He again described the situation at Barker Dam, a public water reserve near a mill that was probably illegal. He suggested that Minerva Hoyt should be warned about the Keys' accusation that she was personally profiting from the sale of SPRR's land. He categorically denied that he had sanctioned destruction by the movie company or that his men took pipe and equipment from mines in the area. Finally, he expressed outrage at the implication in the charge that he was with a "car full of women" when the recent fire started. In fact, it was his wife and two of her relatives, and his wife had dropped him off to start fighting the fire, while she drove to Twentynine Palms for assistance.[28]

Understandably, things went downhill from there. Within a week, Cole sent two terse and formal letters to Keys warning him that, by allowing his cattle to roam over the government's property and posting signs that those lands were official cattle-grazing areas, he was in violation of the monument's regulations. He threatened prosecution for both infractions. Keys answered the letters but did not address the specific charges. He stated he would take the matter up with Washington, D.C., "to see if the Bill of Rights is still in effect." Keys added, ". . . regarding a swimming hole for your friends at Twentynine Palms it seems to me that in all this 800,000 acres you could find a place to make them one without interfering with individuals living in the area." He then "notified" Cole to keep off his property, including his ranch and mining claims.[29]

At this point, Acting Regional Director Herbert Maier wrote to Cole about the escalating conflict. He asked the superintendent to soften his language in any further correspondence with Keys and warned that, "should the matter come to trial I think you know the kind of verdict a local jury might hand down in the case of an 'old timer' claiming that the government is trying to run him out." Maier cautioned against starting a court case during the war, when funds were so tight. He also ordered Cole to fulfill a regional office request from ten months earlier to prepare a grazing permit for Keys.[30] The superintendent sent back a proposed permit but let his feelings be known:

> It is with reluctance that we recommend any type of grazing permit for Mr. Keys. All our better judgment and intuition tells us that to do so will only prolong this problem and make administering the monument just that much more difficult. This belief is held because we know that Mr. Keys cannot be trusted to live up to his agreements and it will be necessary for this office to constantly check to be sure no violations occur.[31]

The permit specified that Keys could only have twenty cattle, the same number he had when the monument was proclaimed, he had to keep them in Pleasant Valley, and the permit would end in five years.

On October 23, 1942, Maier, Cole, and four other JTNM employees met in Twentynine Palms to discuss the Barker Dam-Keys grazing situation. They still awaited a final ruling from the GLO on both the dam and millsite but expected a favorable decision and speculated on whether to erect a fence that would block Keys from accessing the water. Thereafter, the discussion turned to where and how Keys should be arrested and tried after he violated the regulations. Then Maier, soon-to-be acting superintendent Duane Jacobs, and two others visited Keys at his home. Cole, who was preparing to leave for military service, did not attend. The NPS men tried to discuss the problem at Barker Dam and the grazing permit they had offered, but they had considerable trouble getting Keys to stop complaining about Cole. He did respond that the useful land in Pleasant Valley consisted of only 6,000 acres and that he needed more than 52,000 acres for the seventy-five head of livestock he claimed to own. The officials explained they could not allow cattle in the Lost Horse Valley either legally or from a visitor-use standpoint. Keys answered that he had to have that area to keep his cattle operation going. The conversation remained polite, but Maier later wrote:

> The impression carried away of Mr. Keys was that he is conscious of his nuisance value and, while probably desirous of selling his holdings to the government according to his own statement, believes he will obtain a higher price by laying great stress on his work over the past 32 years in homesteading and pioneering than if his property were to be appraised purely on land value.[32]

After leaving Keys, the group returned to Twentynine Palms, where Maier talked to Frank Bagley. The latter described Keys as a "dangerous individual" who had shot several men in the past and would not hesitate to shoot an NPS officer. Bagley added that Keys was calm and pleasant most of the time but was "capable of violent outbursts resulting from emotional instability." He further stated that Keys wanted to be the "Death Valley Scotty" of the area. After this interview, Maier recommended that the NPS ask the Federal Bureau of Investigation to review Keys's past. Maier then traveled to Death Valley to interview the famous conman. Scotty described Keys as a "tough customer" who should not be trusted.[33]

Keys continued his personal battle with the NPS by complaining to federal officials, on December 3, 1942, that the monument's employees were squandering gasoline and rubber tires by aimlessly driving around the monument in multiple vehicles during the wartime emergency. JTNM officials conducted research and reported all vehicle use during the previous few months and justified each trip. Maier sent the figures to the director, adding that two men from the Automobile Club of Southern California were checking maps for the army and that some of the 80,000 troops stationed nearby also traversed the monument. He suggested that Keys was, perhaps, confused and thought those vehicles belonged to the monument.[34]

On January 9, 1943, Acting Superintendent Jacobs documented a relatively amicable meeting he had with Keys earlier that day:

> Our general discussion of about an hour was along more reasonable lines than heretofore. Apparently our former rebuttals, if somewhat blunt, of his accusations against former Superintendent Cole have had their effect and he has "soft-pedalled"[sic] this line of talk, at least for the time being. It now appears that there is a better chance of working out a satisfactory grazing permit if favorable advice is received from the Director. Our stand on Barker Dam was reaffirmed, that is, as far as the Service is concerned the decision of the G.L.O. is final. While Keys is still touchy on this point it is evident that his former positive assertions are somewhat shaken, evidence that his protests have been answered unfavorably or ignored.[35]

At this point, Bill Keys was desperate. He claimed to have seventy-five cattle, but Jacobs thought he might actually have only forty-five or fifty. At sixty-three years old, his way of life was almost at an end, but Keys would go on fighting through every legal means. He appealed the adverse rulings on his mines and on his Big Chief Mill near Barker Dam. He stubbornly negotiated for a grazing permit that would allow up to 400 cattle in the monument. He continued to monopolize the reservoir behind Barker Dam and chafed at the loss of all his other water claims. Particularly galling was the fact that a well he had traditionally used lay on property now owned by his most bitter enemy, Worth Bagley (no relation to Frank). Keys believed that the Shay group had convinced the former Los Angeles lawman to buy SPRR land that included the well. That property also cut off the direct route Keys used to travel from his ranch to one of his mines. Jacobs, in the above memorandum for the files, wrote "an interesting and potentially explosive situation has developed from the bitter feeling between Keys and his closest neighbor, Mr. Worth Bagley, and has resulted in at least one instance of rifle shots being fired at Keys in warning by Bagley."[36]

On May 11, 1943, life suddenly changed for Bill Keys. He crossed Bagley's property to water his cattle and repair a pump. After discerning the cause of the problem with the pump, he began the drive back to his ranch by the same route. He soon encountered Bagley, who fired a pistol at him and then began angling for a better shot. Keys explained later that he returned to his vehicle, grabbed his rifle, and shot back, killing Bagley. After finishing a few mundane tasks, he drove to Twentynine Palms and surrendered to the constable. During the subsequent investigation, lawmen found that the killing had occurred just inside Riverside County and that any trial would be held there. Because there were no witnesses, the case depended on how much the authorities believed Keys when he claimed self-defense. Most people in the area knew the reputation of Keys but also knew that Worth Bagley was a dangerous and unstable person. It turned out that the Los Angeles County Sheriff's Department laid off Bagley, upon learning that his erratic behavior might be due to a brain tumor. Bagley's wife later admitted that he harbored a monomaniacal hatred for Keys and obsessed about killing him. The trial began on July 7, and the official charge was changed to manslaughter. Unfortunately for Keys, his lawyers were unable to introduce evidence of Bagley's mental problems. The jury found him guilty, and Judge George R. Freeman recommended that he serve nine years at San Quentin Prison. His lawyers appealed but to no avail. During the appeal, Frances Keys sold all of their cattle to pay lawyers' fees. Because of wartime exigencies and the advanced stage of the grazing permit offered to Keys, the NPS issued it instead to James Stocker, one of the prisoner's perennial enemies.[37]

Bill Keys spent more than five years in jail and prison. Frances had to move back to Los Angeles to get a job and care for their four children, while friends checked on the abandoned ranch. One friend of Keys did much more. Erle Stanley Gardner, a former lawyer and the author of the eighty-two Perry Mason novels (1933–1973), believed that Keys had been unfairly convicted and began legal inquiries and appeals that led to his release on October 25, 1948. Gardner continued his pursuit of exoneration, until Governor Goodwin Knight pardoned Keys on July 12, 1956.[38] In the meantime, Keys tried to put his life back together at his Desert Queen Ranch. He reapplied for grazing rights, which the NPS ignored. He added height to Barker Dam, although he had no right to do so. He tried to patent his mine claims, as described earlier, only to lose most of his long-delayed appeals against the 1941 adverse rulings. He even contemplated turning his property into a dude ranch or resort for a time. In 1961, more adverse rulings came from the Bureau of Land Management (BLM), formerly the GLO, eliminating several of his Desert Queen claims. Frances died in 1963, and Keys blamed the federal government for causing the worry and stress that killed her. A year later, he sold his property with the retained right to live the rest of his life at his home, as I discuss in Chapter 6. During his later years, he became much friendlier to the monument's staff and a source of important historical information. Bill Keys died in 1969 at the age of eighty-nine. He remained independent to the end and, ironically, became the primary interpretive figure for JTNP.[39]

Developing the Monument for Visitors

In order to develop the monument, NPS officials needed to evaluate its resources and design an overall plan. They found a landscape crisscrossed by a maze of narrow wagon trails and rutted automobile tracks, with active and abandoned mines, rudimentary dams, and some ranching infrastructure but relatively few homesteads. Some sites such as Indian Cove, Cottonwood Spring, and the Oasis of Mara showed traces of camping and picnicking stretching back many years. Although in better shape than Devil's Garden, the monument's vegetation showed the effects of cutting for mine timbers and firewood. Land ownership, scarce water, the threat of losing the eastern part of the monument, and the geographical distribution of the monument's tourist attractions shaped the NPS's planning. Early inspectors identified the Oasis of Mara, Indian Cove, Hidden Valley, Keys View, Split Rock, Lost Horse Valley, Fortynine Palms, and Cottonwood Spring as sites of special interest. They rated Covington Flat, Pleasant Valley, Cholla Cactus Garden, Lost Horse Mine, and the Lost Palms Oasis as secondary sites. Bill Keys owned much of the land surrounding his homestead, which precluded any development there. Had he sold his holdings immediately to the government, the NPS might have located the headquarters there.

The establishment of a headquarters complex, including an office, maintenance facility, park residences, and museum, was critical to the unit's development for visitors. Unfortunately, the monument's many problems prevented the agency from even assigning personnel to it during the first four years. James Cole began operations in an office rented in a county building in Twentynine Palms. NPS leaders hoped this would be a short-term solution and ordered inspectors and JTNM officials to place a high priority on finding a proper site for a permanent headquarters. Nevertheless, a combination of factors delayed a final solution to this important issue for nearly twenty years.

Initially, it appeared that finding a location for the headquarters might be uncharacteristically easy to solve. The raison d'etre for Twentynine Palms was the Oasis of Mara, the spring that had drawn both Native American and pioneer settlers to the area (Fig. 5.3). A development company called the Twentynine Palms Corporation (TPC) offered to donate the oasis to the NPS during the final stages of the campaign to establish the monument. After the proclamation, the corporation reiterated its offer to donate acreage. The corporation's board of directors had several motives for making this magnanimous offer. David Faries, of the board, explained that the oasis was biologically and historically significant and should be protected, but the company could not maintain it. Earlier, he had failed to get the City of Twentynine Palms to take it over as an urban park. Now, he saw the NPS as the logical custodians of this important resource, despite the fact that it was well north of the monument's boundary (Plate 35). Also, development of TCP's hotel and other property would benefit from proximity to a nationally protected park preserve. Indeed, realtors from Twentynine Palms enthusiastically backed the idea, even as they planned to subdivide the land surrounding the oasis tract.[40]

The NPS reacted favorably to the offer, but some of its officials expressed doubts that complicated the situation. During their March 1937 inspection, Frank Kittredge and Ernest Davidson told Faries that the company would have to donate a considerable amount of acreage to the government plus a right-of-way for a parkway connecting the tract to the monument. Davidson described other offers from Yucca Valley and the village of Joshua Tree but favored the oasis site, if the water quality proved acceptable. In July, David Faries traveled to Washington, D.C., and urged Chief of Planning Thomas Vint to accept the donation. Vint replied that a study would be needed before the agency could commit to accepting a donation. Merel Sager and P. T. Primm conducted that study in September and concluded that the oasis was the best site, although the company's offer of a 200-foot right-of-way for the parkway was inadequate.[41]

During the next two years, the NPS continued to negotiate with the corporation, while studying a variety of other options for its monument headquarters. Kittredge advised the director that the agency should hold out for a 700-foot right-of-way but accept one of 400. The corporation asked that the agency move the southern boundary of the tract north to avoid encroaching on a planned residential development. JTNM's officials wanted enough acreage to house a maintenance complex, two or more residences and other buildings, as well as the headquarters office. After an inspection in April 1938, Yosemite's Superintendent Lawrence Merriam and James Cole recommended building the facility inside the monument, where the agency could develop it the way it wanted and not be placed "at a disadvantage" by accepting a gift from a private company. They identified two possibilities:

FIG. 5.3. A 1952 air photo of the tree-lined Oasis of Mara showing the linear orientation along the Pinto Fault between the park's headquarters on the right and the Twentynine Palms Inn on the left. The fault allowed groundwater to reach the surface, enabling the palms and other vegetation to grow there. Recently, extensive urban use of the area's wells has caused the water table to fall, forcing the National Park Service to irrigate the grove. Photograph from the collection of early surveyor Bill Hatch that is maintained by Elizabeth Meyer, of Twentynine Palms, California.

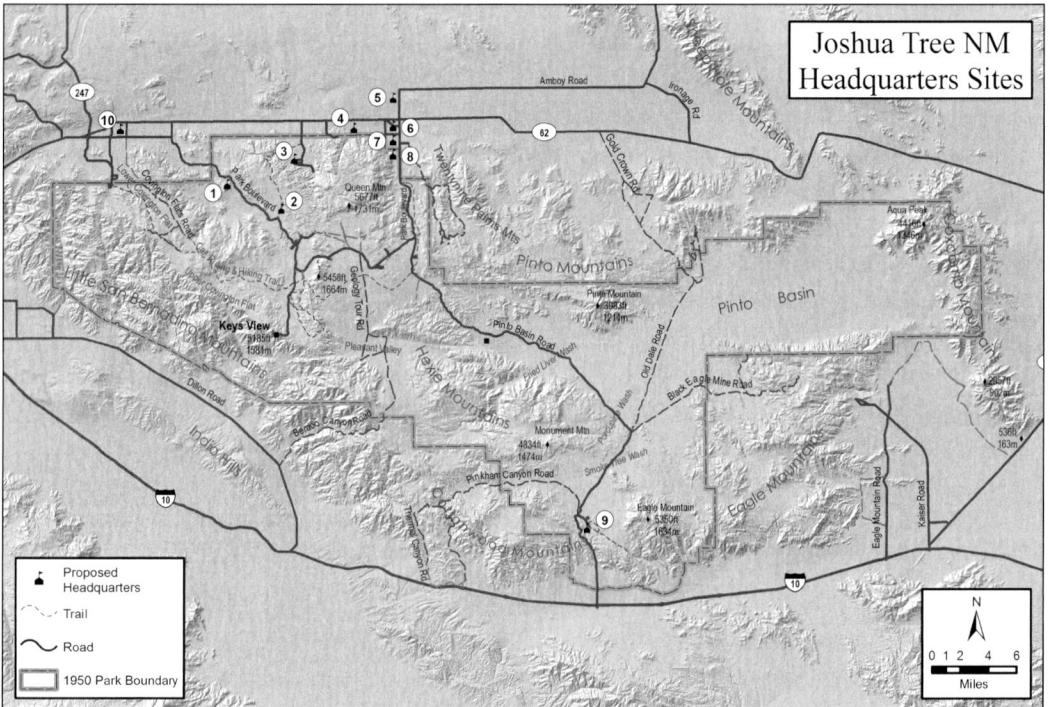

Map 5.3. The National Park Service (NPS) identified four serious options from ten different sites for its headquarters complex: The Oasis of Mara (6), the "monument" site (8), the northern end of the Lost Horse Valley at or abutting the Keys's homestead (2), and on the Chemehuevi Reservation (7). The land in the latter two proved impossible to acquire, and a land donation offer by the Twentynine Palms Inn made the Oasis the favorite, although it was outside the park's boundary. Other areas briefly considered were Quail Spring (1), Indian Cove (3), Bureau of Land Management's land north of Fortynine Palms (4), Twentynine Palms North (5), Cottonwood Spring (9), and Warren's Well in Yucca Valley (10). Data source: Research of NPS's plans and correspondence by the author. See notes 42 and 43 for this chapter. Delta Cartography.

the northern end of the Lost Horse Valley, where Bill Keys had his home, mines, and water sources, and immediately inside the monument's boundary south of Twentynine Palms. The latter, referred to as the "monument site," was already federal land and along the main road, but it would require the NPS to purchase water and power from the town.[42]

By summer 1940, NPS planners considered seven other potential sites in addition to the Oasis of Mara and the two described above. These included 160 acres of the Chemehuevi Indian Reservation southwest of the oasis, Indian Cove, Quail Spring, an unspecified tract in Twentynine Palms north of the oasis, a BLM site north of Fortynine Palms, Cottonwood Spring, and a site by Warren's Well in Yucca Valley (Map 5.2). Several of these involved donations of land to the monument by private owners, who saw lucrative opportunities for development on their land adjacent to the donated tract if the NPS located its headquarters there. After another survey by landscape architect Ernest Davidson, the agency narrowed the choices down to four favorites: the Oasis of Mara, the Chemehuevi Indian Reservation, the monument site, and the public domain area north of Fortynine Palms.

Superintendent Cole summarized the advantages and disadvantages of the four candidates in May 1941. The monument site would not be threatened by adjacent development, would avoid flood damage, and afford scenic views, but it would require expensive transmission of water and power and be some distance from amenities in the town. The public-domain site had water and access to power, but it was limited in size, not on either the Twentynine Palms Highway or the monument's entrance road, and included some state land. The Chemehuevi site had plenty of water and was close to the town for services and amenities, but it was susceptible to high winds, flooding, and adjacent private development. In addition, it was by no means clear that the NPS could acquire the land. The Bureau of Indian Affairs (BIA) initially refused to transfer the land to the NPS, despite the fact that no members of the tribe actually lived there. Finally, the Oasis of Mara site sat alongside the monument's entrance road, had easy access to municipal water, services, and amenities, and was itself an area of relatively luxuriant vegetation and many birds.[43]

On June 3, 1941, Chief Planner Thomas Vint chaired a meeting at the regional office in San Francisco to review plans for Joshua Tree and make a number of decisions, including where the headquarters should be placed and whether to accept the TPC's offer to donate the oasis. The group, including Ernest Davidson, lands specialist Bernard Manbey, and several others unanimously decided that the oasis site was the best choice. They also agreed that the donation had to include at least eighty acres and be free of any restrictions or conditions. If the corporation would not agree to these stipulations, the NPS would build at the monument site as its second choice.[44]

Four days later, H. G. Johansing and C. G. Fitzgerald, of the TPC, asked Superintendent Cole if the NPS still wanted the donation, because the company planned to build more structures and also donate acreage for a Catholic church at the northeastern end of the tract. Cole admitted that the NPS planned to accept the donation and would adjust the boundary of the tract it wanted to allow for the church. After learning this, Herbert Maier opined that park planners should help the diocese design the church, so that its architecture would be appropriate to the region and the monument. Two months later, Twentynine Palms realtor F. R. Whyers, representing the TPC, visited the NPS's office in Washington, D.C. He was in the capital to pursue his own agenda, which included getting a U.S. Army aviation training base established near the town. He assured Vint that he would try to get the TPC's board to approve an eighty-acre donation. He admitted that he owned land near the oasis and was anxious to develop it, once the government accepted the corporation's donation.[45]

On August 7, 1941, David Faries informed Maier that the corporation had approved the donation and that he wanted to meet with NPS officers to work out the details. For a while, it appeared that everything would transpire just as the NPS wanted, yet problems surfaced once detailed negotiations began. Regional officials had a plan ready for the complex that spread the headquarters office, a maintenance facility, and a number of park residences along the southern edge of the oasis tract. The corporation, however, had its own plans for that area and forced the NPS to adjust its southern boundary of the tract. This meant that the entire headquarters complex would need to be east of the oasis, on fewer acres, and very close to the future church. Thus, NPS planners retreated to their offices to design an entirely new development scheme.

Months passed, World War II began, and NPS planning and development halted. On January 17, 1942, David Faries visited the JTNM's office to complain about the lack of progress in finalizing the donation. Cole explained that accepting the area at that time would require that he or his only remaining employee would have to patrol and maintain the area. He argued that two men could not handle the delicate and deteriorating oasis tract as well as the 1,200-square-mile monument. Three weeks later, *The Pasadena Star-News* released a story about the imminent transfer of the oasis to the monument. After that optimistic report, both parties stepped back to reconsider the deal. The few NPS planners not yet drafted by the military worked on details of a master plan that included a headquarters at the oasis, while the corporation mulled over its own plans and the agency's request for a minimum of eighty acres.[46]

On January 14, 1943, Faries sent a new offer to NPS Director Newton Drury. The TPC offered a tract of the oasis of fifty-eight acres with five conditions: (1) the property would only be used as a public park and headquarters site, (2) it would not be used for camping, stabling horses, or to store maintenance equipment and supplies, (3) the NPS would immediately assume possession and maintenance of the area, (4) the NPS would build its office within five years or one year after the end of the war, whichever came first, and (5) the NPS would use adobe or similar materials appropriate to the desert region for the structure. On January 27, Acting Director Hillory Tolson responded that the NPS needed at least eighty acres, that a maintenance area was part of the complex it planned to put at the site, that it would not officially own and patrol the site until President Roosevelt issued an official proclamation adding it to the monument, and that construction of the complex awaited congressional appropriation, which was unlikely to come any time soon. Tolson thanked the corporation for the offer, "whether or not an agreement can be reached."[47]

As the war proceeded, no further planning for a headquarters site took place. In June 1943, the Oasis of Mara opportunity briefly reappeared when John Baker, Executive Secretary of the National Audubon Society, told Acting Superintendent Duane Jacobs that the conservation group might accept a donation of ten acres there for a bird reserve and museum. He wondered if the NPS might want to collaborate on the museum and later take it over permanently. The agency remained non-committal, and Director Drury ordered JTNM officials to continue renting office space in Twentynine Palms. More time passed, the war ended, and still the NPS did nothing to solve its headquarters problem. Finally, in May 1946, Culbert W. Faries, brother of the now-deceased David, asked Superintendent Cole if the agency remained interested in the oasis. Cole, after consultations with landscape architect Sanford Hill, informed the regional director that the disadvantages of the oasis site outweighed the advantages. He admitted that its convenience was hard to ignore but feared it would become an expensive burden on the agency, that private development would encroach on it while potentially drawing enough water to cut off the flow of the spring, and it would be difficult to protect from overuse by townsfolk.[48]

Another year passed, and the NPS decided to construct a maintenance and utility complex within the monument. In April 1947, Frank Givens recommended a site adjacent to the junction known as Pinto Wye, where roads diverged westward toward Lost Horse Valley and southeastward toward Cottonwood Spring. Many advantages—including complete ownership of the land by the government, close proximity to projects within the monument, and easy road access—overcame the need to import water and power. In addition, the area could be hidden from visitors, a feature that NPS landscape architects argued was necessary to avoid detracting from the scenery and ambience of the monument. The maintenance area would include sheds for large vehicles, two huge tanks for road oil, one or more borrow pits, and a variety of workshop and office structures. Significantly, elimination of the utility function from the headquarters area meant that fifty-eight acres would be a reasonable option for the remaining development.[49]

Still, the NPS did not act. Another year passed before Arthur Blake, of the Sierra Club, contacted Superintendent Givens with news that the TPC was still willing to donate the oasis and up to thirty acres around it, if the NPS would protect it. Shortly thereafter, the Pasadena Audubon

Society encouraged the agency to preserve the oasis as a bird sanctuary. Then, on June 4, 1948, the San Bernardino Board of Supervisors told Givens that it needed the space it rented to the NPS for its own office. The NPS would need to move within a year. In September, Acting Director Arthur Demaray ordered regional officials to reopen negotiations with the corporation. On October 4, Givens met Culbert Faries in Los Angeles to discuss aspects of planning and developing the tract, should the NPS accept a donation of twenty-five to thirty acres. Faries mentioned that the TPC's Board of Directors would insist that the government begin construction of its office within one year. Givens replied that immediate congressional funding was uncertain and, perhaps, the corporation would like to construct the building and amortize the cost through monthly rentals to the agency. Faries seemed agreeable and further suggested that the southern and western boundaries of the tract be curved in such a way that would allow the corporation's residential development but still give the monument almost sixty acres. Givens met with the TPC's board on October 13 and found that the directors insisted on only one condition: The NPS would not use water from the spring for purposes outside the oasis tract. Both parties agreed, pending approval by Director Drury, and they also decided to keep quiet about the deal until it was finalized.[50]

The TPC wanted to settle the contract before the end of 1948, but underestimated the complexities that dogged any decisions by the NPS. Regional Naturalist Dorr Yeager and Regional Counselor Sidney McClellan independently suggested that legal acquisition of the tract by proclamation under the Antiquities Act of 1906 would not work, because the area did not possess any "objects of historic or scientific interest." This meant that Congress would have to pass an act to accept the donation. Everyone in the NPS knew what sorts of pitfalls could come from that approach. Several weeks of debate followed, as NPS officials sought a way to receive TPC's donation without having to involve Congress. They consulted Edmund Jaeger and other experts, considered archaeological and historic evidence, and tried to gauge what level of significance would be needed to use the Antiquities Act. Regional Director Tomlinson finally appealed to Director Drury for advice, adding that he would take no further action concerning the donation until he received a response. Associate Director Demaray answered on November 22 and confirmed that the NPS would use the Antiquities Act to accept the donation. Senior officials reasoned that the act "contemplates that there may be reserved and included in the monument for purposes of administration, care, and management areas of land which do not contain such objects but are needed for administrative and management purposes."[51]

Despite this good news, 1949 began with several further complications. Tomlinson arranged for a surveyor to map the exact coordinates of the potential land donation. Engineer H. F. Cameron, Jr. completed the survey but offered a grimly pessimistic evaluation of the area. He described it as dirty and degraded and believed it would require considerable cost to clean and maintain, while townspeople would insist on using it as a public park. He proposed that the NPS accept ten or twelve acres for its headquarters buildings and forget about the rest. Nevertheless, regional officials told Givens to ask the TPC for a draft deed that included a certified resolution to donate the land and a statement by the California Secretary of State that the corporation was in good standing. Some of the detail in the agency's request confused TPC's officials, and, ultimately, the NPS prepared the final form for the deed. Then, TPC officers informed the NPS that they had drawn the boundary on the section line, which happened to be the middle of the monument's entrance road, now named Utah Trail. The NPS dropped the parkway idea and its fifty feet of roadway, so the county would maintain the entire road. By October 1949, Drury approved the final plat and final deed, only to have the TPC demand a final requirement. Board members insisted that the NPS add a clause specifying that the land would return to the corporation, if the NPS did not use it for a headquarters facility. They feared that, if the monument did not develop the land, it would return to the public domain and be available for small-tract homesteads. NPS officials agreed to add that condition. On January 10, 1950, more than fourteen years after TPC's first offer, the corporation officially deeded a 57.8-acre tract with the oasis to the NPS (Map 5.3; Fig. 5.3). The agency successfully used the Antiquities Act, but final processing and filing of the deed came too late to be included in the act that changed the monument's boundaries in 1950. Hence, the Oasis of Mara and the headquarters remained outside the legal boundary of the monument. On June 30, 1961, Congress passed Public Law 87-80, which added the exclave to the monument.[52]

Yosemite Superintendent Charles Thomson offered the first evaluation of the road situation in Joshua Tree and belied the problems that would later surface in designing a workable road plan:

> It would require a comparatively small expenditure for roads even if it were to be thoroughly opened up. Except in the northeast section, it is a road builder's dream. The great alluvial fans not only repose in almost absolutely constant gradients of two to four percent, for miles and miles; but they are composed of disintegrated granite, which only requires to be bladed into road sections and treated with oil.[53]

At the same time, GLO inspector Samuel Guthrey dismissed the road-network issue with a brief comment that the only road in the monument was a rough wagon trail from Twentynine Palms to Cottonwood Spring. Both missed the more obvious problem, choosing which roads to improve from among the plethora of unsuitable tracks across the desert. Regional Engineer Frank Kittredge and Regional Landscape Architect Ernest Davidson conducted the first serious appraisal of the roads in March 1937. They commented on the situation:

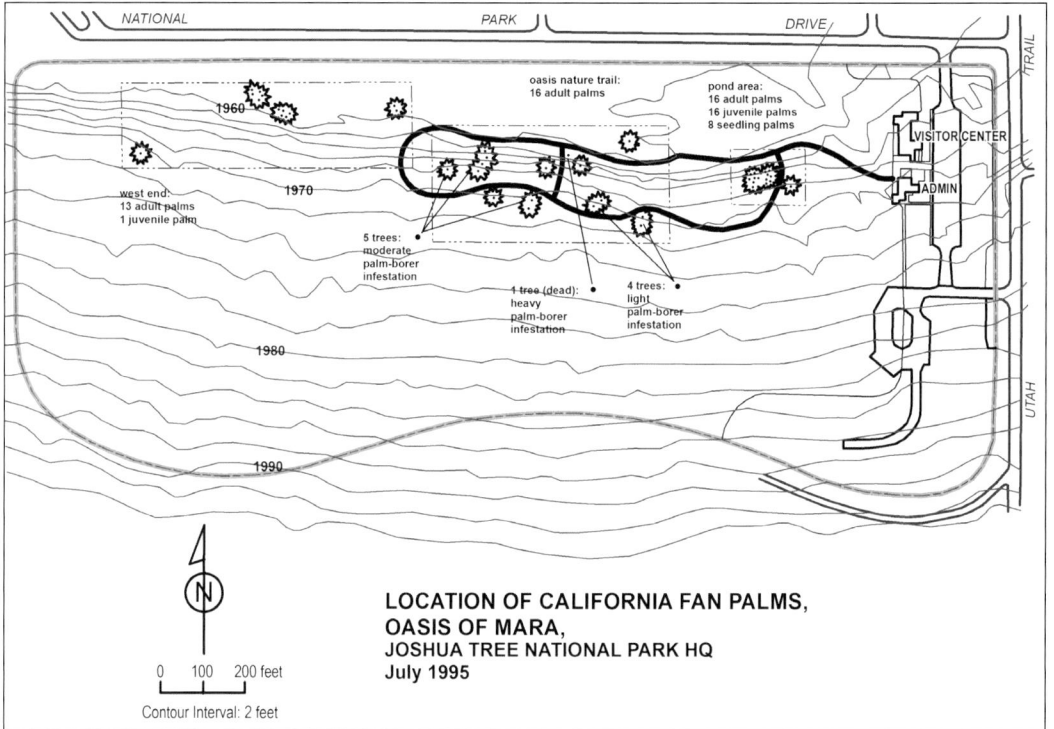

NATIONAL   PARK   DRIVE

TRAIL

oasis nature trail:
16 adult palms

pond area:
16 adult palms
16 juvenile palms
8 seedling palms

VISITOR CENTER

ADMIN

1960

1970

west end:
13 adult palms
1 juvenile palm

5 trees:
moderate
palm-borer
infestation

1 tree (dead):
heavy
palm-borer
infestation

4 trees:
light
palm-borer
infestation

1980

UTAH

1990

N

LOCATION OF CALIFORNIA FAN PALMS,
OASIS OF MARA,
JOSHUA TREE NATIONAL PARK HQ
July 1995

0   100   200 feet

Contour Interval: 2 feet

Map 5.3. A 1995 map of the 57.8-acre Oasis of Mara tract donated by the Twentynine Palms Corporation and the site of the headquarters complex of Joshua Tree National Park. The curved boundary at the southern edge allowed real-estate development to proceed, and the road on the eastern boundary at Utah Trail relieved the National Park Service of responsibility for the road. A well-signed interpretive trail now runs from the visitor center around the palms. Source: "Headquarters Landscape and Oasis of Mara Action Plan" (1996), Joshua Tree National Park Library, 23.

The Auto Club of Southern California has placed many directional and informational signs[;] however, there are so many auto trails crisscrossing through the area that there should be a general resigning by the Park Service. It would be almost impossible for a stranger at the present time to follow through to objectives without losing himself and having to retrace his way.[54]

They identified three northern entrance roads from Quail Springs, Twentynine Palms, and the Old Dale mines that coalesced to exit through a southern entrance at Cottonwood. They noted an abandoned route from Twentynine Palms to Indio through a washed-out canyon but believed that the cost of construction would preclude its development. Kittredge and Davidson described the roads as "little more than two ruts crossing the sand through the rocks" (Plates 1 and 2). Despite this condition, they preferred primitive roads for economic reasons but admitted that the public would probably demand improvements. They also accurately predicted that a fight would ensue over the north-south route through the monument.

A host of other recommendations followed during the next three years. Regional Planner Merel Sager agreed that the roads should remain primitive until a master plan was complete and suggested that any additional north-south road "should be discouraged." Superintendent Lawrence Merriam recommended that no roads be built in the eastern part of the monument until the boundary issue was settled. Regional Landscape Architect Sanford Hill noted that many in the NPS opposed having an entrance near Quail Spring but would have a hard time eliminating the existing road. He also suggested that the NPS improve an old track accessing the Lost Palms Oasis. Another regional landscape architect, R. L. McKown, identified a circular route from Twentynine Palms via the Lost Horse Valley and Quail Spring and back to CA 62 as the top priority for improvement, followed by a road to Keys View. He further suggested that the roads to Indian Cove and Covington Flat should be improved later, but the NPS should not develop any road from the south or one from Indian Cove to the Lost Horse Valley. Regional Engineer R. D. Waterhouse studied several canyon routes from Twentynine Palms to Indio and dismissed them all as too expensive to build and difficult to maintain. He added that neither of the counties claimed any roads within the monument, except a short one through its eastern edge.[55]

Two main issues surfaced during these early road inspections: identifying a planned system from among the myriad options and deciding if an improved road from the south should enter the monument and, if so, where. Ultimately, Superintendent Cole designed the initial road plan. He had accompanied most of the regional officials on their inspections and laboriously studied the options as part of his duties. Cole sought advice from engineer and Death Valley Superintendent Theodore Goodwin and then chose which of the myriad tracks would be graded to the quality necessary for travel by visitors. During his first nine months at Twentynine Palms, he used the mon-ument's tiny budget to grade a rough system of roads. In May 1941, Chief of Planning Thomas Vint inspected the network the young superintendent had selected and incorporated it into the monu-ment's 1941 master plan. The plan certified all of the 117.6 miles of roads Cole had graded as part of the official "National Park Road System." The network included the three northern entrance roads plus a spur into Indian Cove, the existing roads from Twentynine Palms and Old Dale that met on the edge of the Pinto Basin and continued through Cottonwood Spring to CA 60, and spur roads to Keys View, Pleasant Valley, Split Rock, and Stubbe Spring (Map 5.4). The plan also included unimproved roads to Lost Horse Mine and past Stubbe Spring to Covington Flat. Ultimately, the NPS did not improve the latter and turned the road to Pleasant Valley into the Geology Tour Road, which is still unpaved. Most of Cole's design exists today as paved roads or jeep trails in the park. Later realignment of some road segments does not detract from his accomplishment. Vint's master plan recommended that more than 200 miles of other "desert auto trails" be obliterated.[56]

James Cole and Thomas Vint quickly sorted out the primary road system, but the decision on a north-to-south road would take much longer and cause considerable controversy. Several rough wagon roads snaked through the Little San Bernardino Mountains to link Twentynine Palms with the Coachella Valley. Routes included Berdoo Canyon, Thermal Canyon, Pushawalla Canyon, and a westernmost one called the Blue Cut (Maps 5.4 and 5.5; Plate 7). The 1941 master plan showed only the low-elevation road through Cottonwood, and Vint strongly opposed any other route. Cole had inspected the various mountain routes and decided that, if the NPS had to develop one, it should be through Blue Cut. Although somewhat longer, it contained the shortest stretch of extremely rugged terrain.[57] Superintendent Goodwin explained the core issue:

> Agitation is continual in Riverside County for a road connecting Palm Springs with 29 Palms via Berdoo Canyon, Blue Cut[,] or some other of the canyons tributary to the head of the Salton Basin. The advisability of this road is largely a question of Service policy. It would undoubtedly bring in a large increase in visitors by completing a loop from Whitewater to 29 Palms to Palm Springs, but a road of reasonably high standard would involve heavy construction costs in reaching the summit of the Little San Bernardino Range from the Salton Basin and it is a question as to whether or not it would not serve as well to improve the existing Indio Road bringing traffic in via Pinto Basin, although this distance would be considerably greater.[58]

Unquestionably, the financial and political aspects of the situation figured prominently in this debate. Joshua Tree was deeply threatened by the mining lobby, potential developments of private land, and a probable change in the monument's boundary of unknown extent. It had a small staff,

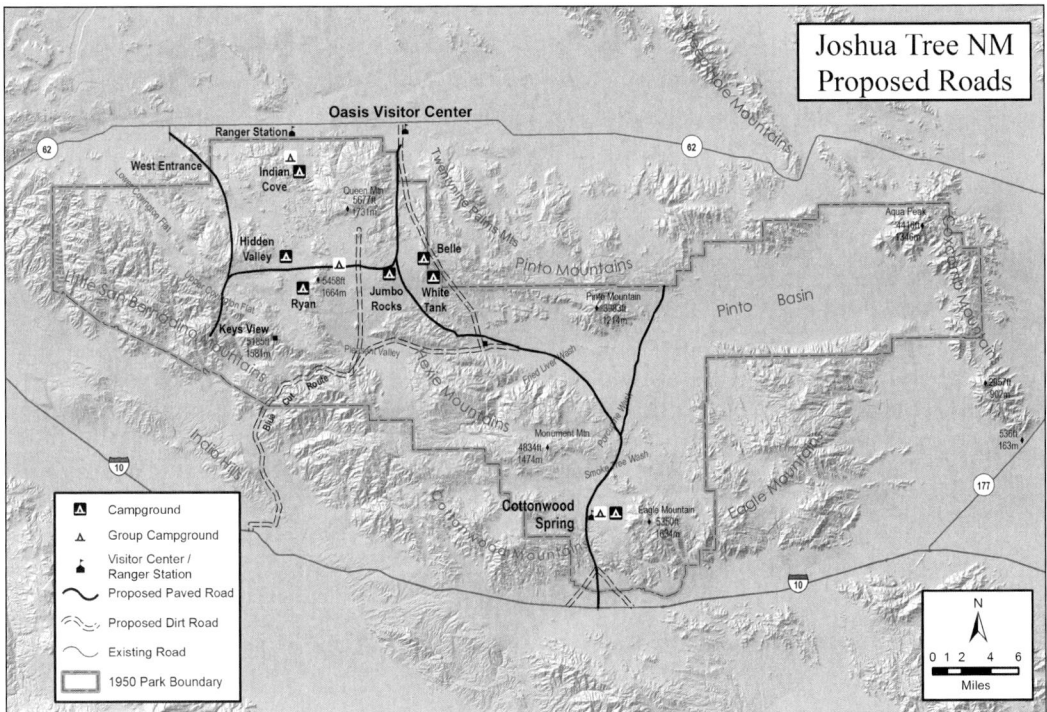

Joshua Tree NM
Proposed Roads

Oasis Visitor Center

Ranger Station

West Entrance

Indian Cove

Hidden Valley

Belle

Keys View

Ryan

Jumbo Rocks

White Tank

Pinto Mountains

Pinto Basin

Aqua Peak

Cottonwood Spring

Eagle Mountain

Legend
- Campground
- Group Campground
- Visitor Center / Ranger Station
- Proposed Paved Road
- Proposed Dirt Road
- Existing Road
- 1950 Park Boundary

N

0 2 4 6
Miles

MAP 5.4. The road and campground systems for Joshua Tree National Monument as planned by James E. Cole and Thomas Vint in 1941. Residents of Indio and other cities and towns in the Coachella Valley insisted on a difficult route further west to shorten their drives to Twentynine Palms and, ultimately, to Las Vegas. Their favorite option became known as the Blue Cut road, where an old wagon trail existed. The road from the eastern Pinto Mountains to Porcupine Wash remains unpaved today. Data source: National Park Service, "The Master Plan Joshua Tree National Monument California Preliminary Edition 1941," Joshua Tree National Park Map Archives. Delta Cartography.

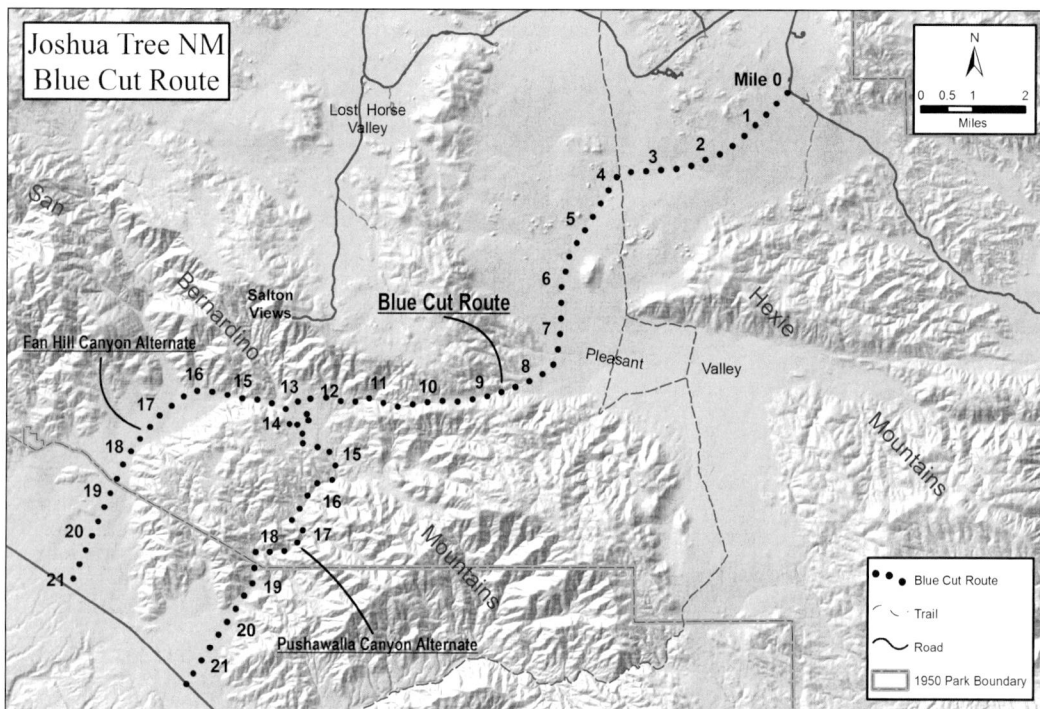

MAP 5.5 The "Blue Cut" route offered two main options, both through rough and rocky terrain that promised high costs for construction and maintenance. In addition to the high price, the National Park Service wanted to avoid opening the mountains to automobile tourism, when an adequate road already passed by the popular picnic area at Cottonwood Spring. Data source: E. E. Erhart, "Reconnaissance Report of Proposed Blue Cut Route in Joshua Tree National Monument Riverside and San Bernardino Counties California" (March n.d., 1955), Joshua Tree National Park Archives, Acc. 651, Cat. 19430, D30, Folder 038.

considering its size and a miniscule budget, and it desperately needed local support to survive all the threats. In 1941, however, JTNM was, unquestionably, a second-level unit of the national park system. First, it was desert and still suffered from the lingering stigma that the dominant American culture attached to such lands. Second, it was a monument and not a park. Third, the NPS had only begun establishing units based on representation of biological or historical resources a decade earlier. Most senior officials in the NPS began their careers when the criterion for establishing a park was unparalleled magnificence. The cost of building a road through the Blue Cut was small compared to those entailed in engineering feats such as the Going-to-the-Sun Road in Montana's Glacier National Park or Tioga Pass Road in Yosemite National Park, units often described as among the "crown jewels" of the nation. But, to many NPS leaders, Joshua Tree was no Glacier or Yosemite.[59]

NPS officials decided that the only north-to-south road should be the existing one through the Cottonwood Spring area, regardless of the appeals of Coachella Valley residents and their politicians. They did not anticipate, however, the lengths to which first Indio, then Riverside County, and finally the California State Legislature would go to demand a shorter and more scenic route. More than a decade passed between the 1941 master plan and the next shot in this war of wills. During that time, Joshua Tree's boundary changed but not enough to eliminate the road via Cottonwood Spring. This cemented the NPS's decision to make it the only north-to-south route. In 1952, the U.S. Marine Corps opened a base in Twentynine Palms that promised a surge in population north of the monument. Meanwhile, the more developed towns in the Coachella Valley built approach roads near the monument's boundary to encourage federal support for this route. In January 1954, the Riverside County Board of Supervisors and the Coachella Valley Advisory Planning Committee passed resolutions requesting that the NPS survey the Blue Cut route for the road.[60] Director Conrad Wirth bluntly responded:

> It is believed that such a road would not benefit the operation or administration of the Monument in any respect and that its construction, and subsequent maintenance and administration, would impose an unwarranted burden of cost upon the general public. It is believed, too, that such a road would be detrimental to the unusual natural values of the area, would be unfair to the general public to whom these values are to bring pleasure, and at variance to a responsibility with which the Service is charged, namely, to regulate the development and use of the areas it administers in such manner and by such means as will preserve and protect the scenic and other values of the areas for the enjoyment of present and future generations.[61]

In using some of the language from the NPS's own 1916 organic act, Wirth signaled the hardened opposition of the agency to this much-desired road. Six weeks later, the California State Assembly passed a resolution requesting its construction. This moved the controversy to another level, and the NPS soon realized that it faced yet another divisive issue. Allies, including conservationist Bertha Fuller, an old friend of Minerva Hoyt, and the Twentynine Palms Chamber of Commerce, opposed the Blue Cut Road, and soon letters to Congressman Harry Sheppard and other legislators brought the fight to national attention. By June 1954, the NPS ordered its highway engineer, H. S. Shilko, to survey the Blue Cut route and estimate the cost of building the road. He carefully analyzed two possible paths through the rugged canyon and estimated the costs of construction and maintenance. He then calculated the probable level of use and what entrance fee should be charged to visitors, if the agency tried to amortize the cost of construction. His figures reinforced the NPS's decision. Shilko claimed that either route would push the cost of the road to more than $1,500,000. He suggested that, perhaps, 6,300 vehicles, principally from Indio, would travel the road annually, necessitating an entrance fee of $12.80 per vehicle. He believed that no one would pay that much. Reduction of the entrance fee to a more reasonable $2.00 per vehicle would require 40,215 vehicles per year through the new entrance, a figure completely impossible to manage on such a slow and difficult road. Once again, the NPS refused to build the road.[62]

Coachella Valley boosters and their supporters remained unfazed. Throughout the summer of 1954, correspondence flew back and forth between members of the public who favored or opposed the Blue Cut route, federal officials, and legislators. Superintendent Samuel King asked the commander of the marine base to comment on the Blue Cut Road, and he received a welcome response that it would be inadequate for military use. Regional Director Lawrence Merriam, however, criticized King for implying that the military could traverse the monument at all. On July 30, the NPS requested a survey of the route by the federal Bureau of Public Roads. In March 1955, the bureau released its careful evaluation of the Blue Cut options as well as the rest of the road system in the monument. The conclusion again was stark. Lead engineer E. E. Erhart calculated the cost of the cheapest route via the Blue Cut at $1,642,000, compared to a modest $100,000 to improve significantly the monument's entire existing road system. With this nominally independent evaluation, the NPS justified its continued opposition to any route through the canyons of the Little San Bernardino Mountains.[63]

Coachella Valley denizens took this rebuff in stride, as its commercial and political leaders passed more resolutions in support of a shorter route to Twentynine Palms. This time, they focused on an old wagon road through Berdoo Canyon, hoping that, perhaps, this would not be as objectionable as the Blue Cut route. The NPS responded that this road was, if anything, worse than the Blue Cut, because it suffered periodic flooding. Soon, promoters raised Pushawalla Canyon again as a possibility. At the same time, most visitors and residents of San Bernardino County insisted that the NPS pave the monument's existing roads, especially the heavily used one from Twentynine Palms to Hidden Valley. In answer to an inquiry from California's U.S. Senator Thomas Kuchel, Director Wirth pointed out that the limited construction budget for JTNM should be used for that more-worthy purpose. After a pause, the Riverside County Board of Supervisors tried to revive the Blue Cut option in late 1957 by proposing that it be part of a route to connect its 260,000 people to Las Vegas, but a separate initiative to develop a freeway through the Morongo Basin diverted attention away from the twenty-year campaign for a road through the Little San Bernardino Mountains. By 1958, environmentalists actively opposed any route that opened a new mountain pass in the monument. Soon, Senator Kuchel wrote a well-publicized letter to the Indio City Council, flatly refusing to back any additional roads in Joshua Tree. Influential editor Randall Henderson wrote editorials in his popular *Desert Magazine*, condemning any new mountain road.[64]

In response, the road's proponents turned to California's other senator, William Knowland, and to local congressman Dalip Saund for support. The latter wrote to Director Wirth, requesting a public hearing on the matter to be held in or near the monument. On June 17, 1958, Assistant Director Eivind Scoyen held a hearing at JTNM, as requested. About sixty-five people attended, primarily from Riverside County and conservation organizations. Among the former were several prominent members of the Western Mining Council, who still sought to open the unit to unregulated mining. Scoyen pointedly announced that the hearing was to enable the public to present any "new" data on this old issue. Riverside County administrative official Robert T. Anderson first explained that, by 1980, the population of the Coachella Valley would outnumber that of Twentynine Palms at least eight to one. He then made a pitch for the Berdoo Canyon route, promising that the county would build a road up to the boundary to connect with the proposed monument road. He added that both the Berdoo Canyon and Pushawalla Canyon routes dated from decades earlier, that they should be considered public roads, and that, if the NPS had opened its first road to the monument from the south, it would now be the main entrance rather than the one at Twentynine Palms. Members of the Sierra Club and the Desert Protective Council countered that the monument's resources were more important to the American people than the convenience of a few towns in the Coachella Valley. Scoyen added that the overwhelming preponderance of correspondence on the issue opposed any new roads in the monument. After the hearing, in which nobody's mind changed, Scoyen and several JTNM officials drove south of the monument and approached the boundary near Berdoo Canyon. There, they found limited but unmistakable evidence of recent attempts to drive through the old passageway.[65]

Following the hearing, Indio, Palm Springs, and Riverside County passed new resolutions demanding further study and eventual construction of a road through one of the canyons into the monument. As late as April 3, 1959, *The Riverside Daily Press* reported that a new study would soon take place. Riverside County developed the road into Berdoo Canyon past the border of the monument onto land formerly owned by the Coachella Valley Water District. The NPS protested this incursion and erected signs clarifying that this was federal government land. At the same time, the agency significantly upgraded the road via Cottonwood Springs and broadcast its plans to build a visitor center and new campground for that area. Once again, NPS officials stonewalled and eventually outlasted its opponents. They owed much to officials in Twentynine Palms, who passed a resolution against the road that would terminate in their town, and to environmentalists, who succeeded in portraying the Coachella Valley people as selfish elites who would destroy a wild section of the monument to shorten their drive by thirty miles.[66]

JTNM planners elected to leave most of the roads and trails in the Pinto Basin unimproved. Only the road from Old Dale received occasional grading. Nevertheless, the NPS struggled to resist an expansion of illegal roads there during World War II. General George Patton decided to train American tank forces in California's desert, and he established one of the major bases, Camp Young, on land surrounding Joseph Chiriaco's roadside tourist center. The Desert Training Center officially opened on April 30, 1942. Later, the U. S. Army built a second camp just east of the Coxcomb Mountains. Political pressure to open the parks to military use began even before the United States entered the war. Congressman Estes Kefauver, of Tennessee, introduced a bill to turn over national parks and forests to the military, suspending the laws and policies of the public land agencies. Conservation organizations tentatively supported legitimate use of the forests but strongly opposed transfer of the national parklands. Although the parks escaped outright take-over by the military, local commanders requested permission to conduct training exercises in Pinto Basin. NPS regional officials took a political risk and refused. Nevertheless, it soon became apparent that tanks and other heavy vehicles used some of the monument's rough roads and occasionally conducted off-road maneuvers. Complaints to senior military officers met sympathetic words but little action to stop the incursions.

In February 1943, Regional Director Owen Tomlinson and several other NPS officials inspected the area and found that the army had graded a road across part of the Pinto Basin. What had been a pair of tire ruts now appeared as a twelve-foot-wide swath through the desert, with deep tank tracks ground into it. Occasional departures from the road for maneuvers exacerbated the damage. Two problems occurred with this blatant intrusion. First, military traffic had eliminated or severely damaged the vegetation and compacted the soil to a degree that made regeneration of plants uncertain. Second, the transformation of this rough track into a wide road invited further use by new military recruits and civilian miners. During the next several months, the NPS repeatedly asked the army to repair the damage it had done. Superintendent Jacobs met Colonel R. H. Elliott, who explained that he could not spare enough soldiers to rehabilitate the entire road but would order them to obliterate evidence of it just inside the monument's boundaries. Thereafter, military officers posted signs and even ran patrols near the monument's boundary to stop their troops from entering the monument.[67]

Staff and Visitor Facilities

In November 1950, the NPS began construction of its new headquarters complex at the Oasis of Mara, with walkways around the oasis. The office building, which included a visitor contact desk and a small museum display, was completed a little more than three years later (Plate 33). On April 3, 1954, a large crowd gathered for the dedication, during which Edmund Jaeger recalled the hard work of Minerva Hoyt, the immense effort underway to acquire private lands, and the woeful loss of one-third of the monument. He celebrated the original purpose of the unit, to protect its vegetation, and hoped that the lands taken away could be restored some day. A jubilant crowd of more than 500 applauded the botanist and the long-delayed achievement the NPS reached that day. Finally, JTNM had a permanent headquarters complex, where its rangers, planners, and resource managers could direct the development of a stable and increasingly popular unit. Two years later, the NPS added a small operations and maintenance building to help protect the monument's new management center.[68]

A lack of funding limited construction within the national monument itself. By the end of Joshua Tree's second decade, the maintenance operation at Pinto Wye consisted of a surplus Quonset hut, another small building, and some storage tanks. Other elements of the 1941 master plan such as housing for employees and a museum remained aspirations. The NPS had more success opening campgrounds. Once the change in the unit's boundary and acquisition of a headquarters area seemed certain, the agency opened seven campgrounds by the end of 1950 (Fig. E). Ryan Campground followed in 1954, anticipating the development of a long-distance equestrian trail. In choosing the areas for campgrounds, NPS planners sought appropriate terrain, enough space to expand in the future, and visual seclusion from the road. Later, officials would expand and better organize most of them. The dense network of existing trails and auto-tracks simplified development of recreational trails, but planners also designed interpretive nature trails at Cap Rock (Fig. 5.4), Indian Cove, the Cholla Cactus Garden, and the headquarters. By 1956, as NPS officials explored routes for a California Riding and Hiking Trail, the nucleus of infrastructure for visitors within the monument was in place for the anticipated boom in tourism.[69]

FIG. 5.4. The extraordinary complexity of boulder piles, as seen here at Cap Rock, plus the compelling skies and dark vistas have resulted in an increase in visitation to Joshua Tree National Park that far outstrips the rate of increase for the national park system as a whole. Photograph by the author (original in color), January 2014.

Natural Resource Evaluation and Management

Congress established Joshua Tree primarily to protect its vegetation and other natural resources. The monument's first superintendent, James E. Cole (Fig. 3.2), was a trained naturalist, but the small, underfunded staff at JTNM barely paid any attention to the vegetation and wildlife in the capacious unit. The heavy workload of defending against mining and acquiring private land limited the NPS's resource-management activity. In addition, George Wright, who formed the NPS's biology program and personally funded much of its work, died in an automobile accident in 1936. His death led to a decline in the natural-resource office and reinforced a lack of attention to the science of ecology by agency leaders, just as academic research in it dramatically increased. During the monument's first twenty years, local officials carried out rudimentary inspections and censuses, but four problems demanded greater attention: (1) the impact of the "boundary change" would affect all the flora and fauna, (2) the presence of an infestation of exotic mistletoe at the Oasis of Mara, (3) a human-caused burn at Fortynine Palms, which showed that managing fire would be necessary in the desert, and (4) the fate of desert bighorn sheep as the unit's water resources dwindled. Regional officials and visiting scholars conducted the bulk of this research, due to the small monument staff and the low priority given to JTNM by senior NPS officials.

The flurry of inspections that followed the monument's establishment focused primarily on planning infrastructure and surveying the private-land situation. The first to comment on the new monument's natural resources was Yosemite Superintendent Charles G. Thomson, who expressed surprise and admiration at the richness of vegetation in the western part of the monument. He strongly recommended that "university experts" in biology, geology, and archaeology be invited to "learn the story" of the new unit. In April 1938, Lawrence Merriam and James Cole found evidence of illegal hunting, concluded it had wiped out the deer in the area, and warned that it must be stopped to protect the few remaining bighorn sheep.[70] Regional Biologist Lowell Sumner was the first to undertake a specific inspection of natural resources. He visited Joshua Tree during January 1940 to assess its wildlife, as the threat of renewed mining intensified and a change in the unit's boundary seemed inevitable. Sumner was the only voice to propose retention of Pinto Basin, and he also favored extending the southern boundary to close off the canyon entrances and deter poaching. Sumner, however, was a realist about the impact of his scientific advice:

> As mentioned previously, the need of the bighorn for a spacious range would also be filled
> if the Pinto Basin were retained. We realize, however, that these considerations must be
> balanced against the fact that the area would not be very attractive recreationally and that

steps might have to be taken to definitely discourage tourists from traveling through it in the summer. The Wildlife Section is not making specific recommendations regarding boundary changes because it is realized that many considerations other than wildlife are involved.[71]

The significance of the forthcoming boundary change drew other NPS scientists to Joshua Tree during these critical prewar years. In late March 1941, field biologist Joseph S. Dixon visited the monument and considered the question of reintroducing antelope. He suggested that water would be the determining factor and that the NPS would need to drill deep wells to sustain a population of the animals. He added that illegal hunting in the Cottonwood Spring area needed immediate attention from the monument's staff.[72] In October 1941, Lowell Sumner returned as part of the official team developing specific recommendations for the boundary change. He again suggested that Pinto Basin should be retained and the southern boundary extended but repeated that other considerations might outweigh those of the wildlife. This time, he argued, in a letter to Chief Biologist Victor Cahalane, that scenic and recreational qualities should justify keeping the Pinto Basin:

> In answer to your request for data on Pinto Basin and possible boundary change, fauna would be reduced if the eastern part is cut out including bighorn and antelope, which would be a gamble in any event. The vegetation is much more interesting than an initial survey would show. From the standpoint of wildlife alone, it might not justify keeping the eastern part, but [with] the prospect of five-acre homesteads littering the basin we recommend maintaining the area as part of the monument.[73]

The fact that the boundary change in 1950 did not eliminate the floor of Pinto Basin reflects Lowell Sumner's modest but persistent voice in favor of wildlife.

Throughout the 1940s, attention to the vegetation, wildlife, air quality, and fire preparedness languished. Most of the attention to vegetation, the raison d'etre of the monument, focused on stopping the plunder and destruction of high-profile plants. Theft of cactus continued, because so few rangers patrolled the 825,000-acre unit, and miners continued illegally to take juniper and pine for firewood or stabilization of mineshafts. The assault on Joshua trees decreased, but periodic requests for their use in boxes and as surgical splints during World War II demanded continued vigilance. JTNM officials wanted much more research on the monument's namesake species but had little time to do any themselves, even as ranger Hesmel Earenfight, on his own initiative, began a simple, long-term study on a grove of Joshua trees near Hidden Valley. Earenfight was a trained engineer who had come to Twentynine Palms to escape asthma. He worked in JTNM from 1942 until 1965 and, during those years, measured the height of all the Joshua trees in the stand to chart growth through time. His study provided interesting data but little of scientific value, because he did not record precipitation, soil quality, or other environmental conditions. His work is still note-worthy, since so little else was being done to understand the unit's flora.[75]

When the NPS accepted title to the Oasis of Mara, an unexpected problem came with the palm grove. The drier, eastern part of the oasis upon which the NPS built its new headquarters had an extensive growth of mesquite (*Prosopis juliflora*) as well as the palms. A species of parasitic mistletoe (*Phoradendrum californicum*) infested many of the mesquite trees, and the dissemination of its seeds by a type of silky flycatcher (*Phainopepla nitens*), promised to affect the rest. All three species are native to the California deserts. The owners of the Twentynine Palms Inn and visitors to the oasis complained about the infestation and urged the JTNM's officials to eradicate the mistle-toe. Pathologist Willis Wagener, from the U.S. Department of Agriculture, studied the situation in September 1953 and reported that it could lead to the deaths of most of the older mesquite trees. He explained that the isolated location of the oasis, with respect to other groves of mesquite, resulted in a concentrated and heavy growth of mistletoe that destroyed branches and left disfigured trees. He showed surprising sensitivity to NPS policies, however, by warning that elimination of the native mistletoe would challenge the agency's core mission and lead to the virtual elimination of the silky flycatchers that subsist on the mistletoe's berries. Nevertheless, he recommended testing different chemical blends of herbicide to find one that could be applied during the short dormant season of the host mesquite and kill the mistletoe. During the next three years, the pathologist tried different varieties of herbicide, with poor results. The mistletoe proved more resistant to the herbicide than the host mesquite trees, and pruning the dead branches was too expensive. NPS officials continued to search for another solution to stop the disfiguration of the oasis's vegetation.[76]

Fire management at Joshua Tree was initially considered unnecessary. In his 1936 inspection, Charles G. Thomson dismissed fire as a concern, reflecting the common perception at the time that a desert has insufficient vegetation to burn. This complacency ended on July 4, 1942, when a man named Randolph burned debris on his inholding in Hidden Valley, only to have it escape and char 165 acres. During the fire, Peter Mahrt, a road foreman for the monument, climbed a tree to put out a burning branch, suffered smoke inhalation, and died. This isolated tragedy added gravitas to the issue of potential fire in the monument. Seven years later, two teenagers managed to set fire to the grove at Fortynine Palms Oasis (Fig. 5.5). Of the fifty-three large palms growing there, forty-four burned completely, except for their trunks, six suffered partial burning, and three remained un-harmed. Monument officials soon realized that low levels of moisture in the air, soil, and vegetation, plus occasional lightning storms and human foibles, disproved Thomson's optimistic evaluation.[77]

Fig. 5.5. Fortynine Palms Canyon was one of the most heavily visited palm groves in the national monument and a popular picnic spot for locals and visitors. Regrettably, in 1949, two teenagers started a fire that burned nearly all the mature California fan palms in the canyon. Some of the palms survived, and new growth has replenished the grove. Photographer and date unknown. Joshua Tree National Park Photo Archives, Cat. 20575, Image 702.

In 1941, Superintendent Cole began an annual census of wildlife that continued under his successors. In most years, the lists included badgers, bighorn sheep, bobcats, coyotes, eagles, two species of fox, jackrabbits, mountain lions, mule deer, and quail. The reports included estimated numbers of each species, but these were highly conjectural, because they were derived either from spot observations by rangers and visitors or the tracks and scat of larger mammals. In an early case of wildlife manipulation in Joshua Tree, the California Fish and Game Commission released exotic Chukar partridge at Lost Horse Well and Stubbe Spring in 1937. Most died out by 1944, but a few remain near Pinto Wye. The cessation of hunting over much of the monument led to fairly rapid increases in the populations of kit fox, Gambel's quail, and coyote, while numbers of mule deer exploded from 1941, when none were actually seen, to an improbable estimate of 300 three years later. Thereafter, estimates of the deer population declined, as census techniques improved, and numbers of bighorn sheep increased.[74]

When President Franklin D. Roosevelt established Joshua Tree National Monument, the NPS had little understanding of the complex interrelationships that shape a biological community. Instead, it sought to protect and, if necessary, reintroduce glamorous mammal species, including desert bighorn sheep and pronghorn antelope (*Antilocapra americana*). The latter once occupied much of California's desert country, but widespread hunting eliminated them from the monument's area decades earlier. Biologists such as Edmund Jaeger and early NPS inspectors thought they should be reintroduced to the newly preserved land. During his January 1940 inspection, Lowell Sumner studied the issue and concluded that too many of the water rights lay outside NPS control for the antelope to survive. A decade later, Sumner returned after Superintendent Givens suggested that the NPS had obtained enough water sources. The visit did not change Sumner's mind or recommendation. These conclusions by no means stopped the periodic calls for bringing back pronghorn antelope, but they quelled any competition for resource-management funding.[78]

The fate of the bighorn sheep was the only natural resource issue to receive serious attention during this time (Plate 26). Not only was it a significant factor in the revision of the monument's boundary, but it also shaped land acquisition, grazing policy, and interpretive planning for visitors. Despite these conditions, research on managing the species arose only after the NPS encountered problems at Lake Mead National Recreation Area in Arizona and Nevada and at nearby Death Valley National Monument. Unlike most national parks and monuments, Lake Mead allowed hunting. Bighorn sheep avoid people, but the huge reservoir allowed hunters in boats to approach areas they would not normally access. The NPS did not have full jurisdiction and found the fish and game departments of Arizona and Nevada unwilling to change their policies of allowing sixty sheep to be taken from the area annually. The Lake Mead staff briefly pondered artificially enhancing springs to draw the bighorn sheep away from the reservoir, but postponed the idea until research on the species could show that the animals would use them.[79]

At Death Valley, the problem stemmed from competition for forage and water by feral burros left over from the heyday of mining. The non-native burros reproduced at a vigorous rate and displaced native bighorns at a number of water holes. In May 1954, Lowell Sumner warned that the burros could eventually eliminate bighorn sheep in JTNM. One obvious solution would be direct culling of the burro herds by shooting. The public, however, associated burros with the history of mining and settlement in the desert. Like horses, they represented a link with the romantic past as well as potential pets. Sumner suggested a major research program that would test the feasibility of letting hunters capture "wild burros alive for subsequent disposal as circus animals, mountain pack animals, etc." At the end of his report, he suggested that Joshua Tree also should have a major study of bighorn sheep, even though no burros were present because of drought conditions that threatened the availability of water for the monument's smaller herd.[80]

On June 17, 1954, Dr. Helmut K. Buechner, of the State College of Washington (now Washington State University), contacted the NPS and requested information about bighorn sheep in the parks and monuments. Assistant Regional Director Herbert Maier responded with information about the problems at Death Valley and Joshua Tree, focusing on the suspected reasons for their decline in both monuments. After summarizing Death Valley's feral burro problem, Maier noted unexplained deaths among the bighorns in Joshua Tree and Superintendent Samuel King's speculation that a species of lung worm might be infecting them. Maier concluded with a comment that "the availability of funds and manpower necessarily will determine the rate of progress in the required investigations."[81] This proved fortuitous, because Dr. Buechner was engaged in a study of bighorn-sheep problems across the United States under the auspices of the Conservation Foundation, of the New York Zoological Society. He offered to help with the studies and to pay for certain expenses, including five hours of flying time to advance the censuses of bighorn sheep at both Joshua Tree and Death Valley.[82]

As it turned out, the bigger monument took the bulk of the money, but Joshua Tree received enough to fund a five-day survey of its bighorns by Sumner in September 1955. He surveyed eleven springs used by bighorn sheep and determined that only Stubbe Spring and Fortynine Palms Oasis proved reliable throughout the year. Four other springs provided water, except during summer. He conservatively estimated only fifty-five bighorn lived in JTNM after the loss of the mountains surrounding Pinto Basin in the 1950 boundary change. Sumner then discussed the mule deer that traveled singly or in smaller groups. He speculated about competition between the two species, but concluded that the NPS needed to protect both since they were both native. He recommended that the NPS rehabilitate several of the springs to conserve water, minimize public use at important sites such as Stubbe Spring and Cottonwood Spring, and carry out an intensive study of bighorn sheep during the dry season. Finally, he asked the NPS to allocate $500 for more research during fiscal years 1956 and 1957. Surprisingly, the NPS provided half the money Sumner requested, enabling the study of Joshua Tree's bighorn sheep to continue.[83]

By 1957, the plight of bighorn sheep across the national park system had drawn more attention from the federal government as well as academics and resource managers from the western states. It became a high-profile issue and led to multiple conferences and research studies. John D. Goodman, of the University of Redlands, brought students on field trips and conducted research in Joshua Tree during a span of three years. In March 1957, he reported that water was the determining factor in the numbers and distribution of bighorns and that tourist activity at Stubbe Spring was sufficiently disturbing to justify closing the area to the public. He could find no evidence of a lungworm infestation, however. Superintendent Elmer Fladmark agreed with Goodman's analysis and forwarded a copy to Lowell Sumner.[84]

At the same time, the drought in Joshua Tree threatened many species in addition to the bighorn sheep. Naturalist Donald Black recommended removing a large willow tree near Stubbe Spring to save water, but Regional Chief Naturalist Dorr G. Yeager overruled him, citing the tree's importance for smaller wildlife. Lowell Sumner then argued that Black's recommendation was based on data from California Fish and Game that showed removal of one willow tree could double or triple a spring's flow. He suggested that piping additional water to the spring might help, but, if it did not, " . . . we may have to weigh one willow against 20 bighorn." Ultimately, rangers removed the tree, but it did not stop the decline in the spring's flow.[85]

As the first two decades of JTNM passed, the natural resources of the monument still received limited attention, except for its signature animal species. Bighorn sheep had achieved star status, but that did not solve the problems that threatened their survival in the monument. The relative lack of aggressive natural-resource management at JTNM was not an isolated case. University-based scientists continued to advance ecology and wildlife management, while the NPS focused on other matters. Chief of Interpretation Ronald F. Lee highlighted the problem, as Director Conrad Wirth inaugurated his massive *Mission 66* development program:

> The biological resources in the national parks and monuments require a greater measure of attention than our present staff and facilities allow. These resources are subject to adverse forces resulting from increased visitation, construction of new area facilities, and the continuing pressure of intensive land-use on adjacent areas. The special role of the national parks and monuments, particularly the natural areas, to provide the public with opportunities to

see, enjoy, and learn about wild animals in their natural environments presents a challenge
we have only begun to meet.[86]

After two decades, natural resources at JTNM remained poorly understood and negligently managed. Soon, problems would arise that threatened the viability of the unit as a biotic preserve.

Cultural Resources

Cultural resources initially received little attention throughout the national park system, in spite of
the Antiquities Act. Two laws passed just before President Roosevelt proclaimed Joshua Tree National Monument, however, improved the preservation of archaeological and historical resources. The
first law enabled a reorganization in 1933 of the executive branch of the federal government. That
reorganization brought archaeological national monuments from the U.S. Forest Service and battle-
fields, memorials, and historic forts from the War Department into the national park system. These
joined specific historical units established at the urging of Horace Albright, NPS's second director.
The first two from that group were George Washington Birthplace National Monument and Colonial
National Monument (now a national historical park), both in Virginia and established in 1930. The
second law was the Historic Sites Act of 1935. It ordered the Secretary of the Interior, through the
NPS, to carry out a survey of the nation to record and, if feasible, preserve historic buildings, sites, and
objects. The law also ordered the agency to cooperate with state, local, and private organizations in
this effort. Finally, the act established an Advisory Board on National Parks, Historic Sites, Buildings,
and Monuments. This panel assumed a major role not only in deciding the fate of historic resources,
but also in reviewing new sites proposed for addition to the national park system.[87]

Despite these laws, archaeological and historical features at Joshua Tree received minimal attention during the hectic two decades after the unit's proclamation. The early inspections described
some of these resources but did not engender substantial research or preservation. Archaeologists
had brought attention to the cultural resources of the monument in publications such as a 1929
monograph by Julian Steward on petroglyphs that described those near Keys Ranch and a major
article on the Pinto Basin culture published by the Campbells in 1935.[88] The first mention of archaeological resources at Joshua Tree by the NPS came in a report of an April 1938 inspection by
Superintendent Merriam and James Cole. The latter wrote:

> E. W. C. Campbell and W. H. Campbell have done much work in the area and many arti-
> facts they collected are in the Southwest Museum in LA. Evidence of human habitations
> dated as 15,000 to 20,000 years old have been found in the Pinto Basin by the Campbells.[89]

Oddly, during his inspection a year later, C. Marshall Finnan reported that the Campbells told him that there was nothing of value in the monument, and it should never have been proclaimed. Perhaps they still smarted from Minerva Hoyt's sabotage of their efforts to create a state park in the area.[90]

In 1941, Joseph Dixon stumbled onto a rock shelter one-quarter of a mile from Cottonwood Spring, while assessing the wildlife of the young monument. He found numerous artifacts and pieces of broken pottery. He subsequently reported, "It is hoped that this material, which merits study by the anthropologists at the University of California, may shed important light on the culture of the Indian tribes which formerly inhabited this region." This led Superintendent Cole to request a full archaeological survey of the monument for both interpretation and development planning. Unfortunately, his request yielded nothing for another decade.[91]

Research and planning for cultural resources did receive some meager attention after the 1950 boundary change assured survival of the monument. Louis R. Laywood conducted a very brief survey of the Pinto Basin on his way to a more-extensive survey of Death Valley National Monument. He found numerous projectile points, which he gave to Superintendent Givens for the unit's museum collection. He insisted that a major survey of the basin should be undertaken immediately and suggested that artifact-rich caves with possible human remains could exist. Unfortunately, his suggestion garnered no further action by the NPS, although university scholars and private collectors took notice. Two years later, Superintendent Samuel King had to warn the wife of a worker at Kaiser's iron mine that her husband would not be allowed to remove relics on the surface, even if he promised to turn them over to the agency.[92]

Another problem that surfaced quickly and grew to be a major source of controversy was the way in which the monument's staff stored what artifacts it did have. The administration building at the Oasis of Mara had no room for additional employees, let alone storage and display of cultural relics. The answer, always meant to be temporary, was to place the materials as well as the library and archives in one of the garage bays in the adjacent maintenance facility. Most items wound up in cardboard boxes with no climate control. As the collection grew, it spread to a second bay in the garage (Fig. 5.6). In 1949, Regional Museum Curator Walter Rivers submitted a lengthy plan for a proper museum structure that would benefit interpretation and properly store fragile materials. At the time, NPS officials coveted the collection of materials donated by the Campbells to the Southwest Museum in Los Angeles. A brief inquiry about transferring it to JTNM brought an immediate and resounding no from the urban museum. In 1957, as the NPS pondered construction of the visitor center, Superintendent Elmer Fladmark submitted a wildly optimistic prospectus for a museum that raised the necessary square footage from 1,000 to 6,000.[93]

Compliance with historic preservation policy was straightforward during this period. The monument had little to protect. Former owners could still remove most of their mining equipment,

FIG. 5.6. One of the garage bays that held Native American artifacts from the Campbell Collection and other museum materials until 1993. Archaeologists, museum curators, and local Native Americans all decried conditions that saw some artifacts wrapped in plastic, with inadequate temperature control and less delicate remains such as mortars and pestles buried behind the buildings. Photographer and date unknown. Joshua Tree National Park Photo Archives, General Collection.

if their claims were nullified. The Ryan and Keys families still owned their homesteads. The only structure at the Oasis of Mara, a ramshackle adobe home, was torn down in 1947, three years before the property passed to the NPS. Unfortunately, many of the larger mine structures deteriorated, due to disuse and harsh climatic conditions. In any event, what funds were available for historic preservation went either to major parks such as Yosemite or to Death Valley, which had historic mining as one of its primary purposes. Cultural resource protection at JTNM remained a secondary program pursued only enough to allow minimal interpretation for visitors. It would take another set of federal laws and the nation's bicentennial in 1976 to move it into the spotlight.[94]

Visitors and Interpretation

During the monument's first full year of operation in 1941, 23,964 persons entered Joshua Tree. The majority came from adjacent communities. The following year, a similar number visited, in spite of World War II. For the next three years, however, wartime shortages drastically reduced tourism. After the war, visitation slowly increased, reaching 93,615 by 1950. Thereafter, improvements in roads, installation of campgrounds, and construction of the headquarters office at the Oasis of Mara increased tourism until, in 1956, monument officials recorded 312,889 visitors, a respectable number for a desert unit. Yet all was not well at the monument. Twentynine Palms had expected the NPS to develop the unit much more quickly. Business leaders chafed at the revenues from tourism they claimed were lost, due to the agency's dawdling development program. At the same time, the small JTNM staff faced problems with illegal entry, vandalism, wood-cutting, and even arson committed by neighbors and some visitors. James Cole and his successors hoped that, through education, they could convince visitors to follow the regulations and appreciate the resources contained in the young monument.[95]

Interpretation is the name given by the NPS for providing information and education to visitors. Interpretive rangers are the personnel most often met by visitors. Any function or object that provides information—including signs, guided walks, campfire programs, public relations, community outreach, and education programs for schools—are their responsibility. For many years at Joshua Tree, the interpretation division also conducted research and managed natural and cultural resources. Development of visitor programs at JTNM languished through most of the monument's first two decades. Shortly after James Cole became the monument's first employee, he asked Director Drury for a camera with which he could take slides of the vegetation. Acting National Park Service Chief Naturalist R. E. Rothrock responded that the NPS only had two cameras with close-up lenses, one for reproducing slides at NPS's headquarters in Washington, D.C., and another on loan in the Virgin Islands. In 1947, Superintendent Givens reported that the monument had no interpretation program other than talks to occasional groups of visitors. He added:

What the visitor does not now see or understand is more important than what he does see, i.e., the scientific aspects would be of greater interest to many visitors, if properly presented, than the scenic attractions. The flora, fauna and geology of the desert are far less known than in other types of areas.[96]

Givens outlined personnel and development needs to carry out properly the educational mission, including two ranger-naturalists, a program of campfire presentations, a museum and laboratory in Twentynine Palms, a smaller museum at Pinto Wye, and roadside exhibits at key scenic areas.

In 1951, tentative efforts to provide information began with the installation of viewfinders and signs at Keys View and development of an outline for a natural-history guide. Three years later, JTNM opened its headquarters office at the Oasis of Mara and signed an agreement with the Southwest National Monuments Association to sell books and other monument-related goods. Contact with visitors significantly increased but not to the extent monument officials had hoped. Many visitors still entered the unit by way of its west entrance and either departed the same way or through the Cottonwood Springs area. Elsewhere in the monument, officials erected signs and issued brochures that gave information about specific trails and features, while encouraging visitors to refrain from vandalism and inadvertent destruction. Yet these tangible objects suffered from mischief and theft. Vandals destroyed glass-covered exhibit signs at the Oasis of Mara Nature Trail, forcing the monument to issue printed brochures. Rangers addressed large groups of Boy Scouts, Marines, and recreational clubs, but there was no regular schedule of nature walks and campfire talks for the average visitor. Finally, as the monument celebrated its twentieth anniversary, Ranger Bruce Black prepared the first formal interpretation program. It signaled that the unit finally had matured enough to carry out one of the NPS's primary functions.[97]

Joshua Tree National Monument improbably survived its first twenty years of existence. It had staved off threats from mining interests, established a successful land-acquisition program, and developed a headquarters complex, new campgrounds, and road network. Yet it remained understaffed, underfunded, and often ignored by the upper echelons of the NPS. Visitation steadily increased, but those visitors found little guidance in understanding the science and history of the unit. Natural-resource management was haphazard and focused on a single species of wildlife. Programs for the study and preservation of cultural resources did not exist. Visitors, neighbors, and residents alike gave up their perceptions and traditional uses grudgingly. Survival of the monument owed a great deal to its first superintendent, James Cole. In the midst of vicious personal attacks, he made the decisions that established the patterns of development for the future and shaped the change in the monument's boundary that defeated the miners. He reached his lowest ebb when his superiors demanded explanations in response to the letters from Bill Keys. But, in the midst of it, Chief of Planning Thomas Vint wrote to the director:

> Superintendent Cole is doing a fine job. He knows the area, gets out and around it, explains the desert flora and fauna with ease and simplicity. He can roll a rock out of the road in the desert sun and peck at a typewriter by lamplight. He has what the National Park Service grew up on.[98]

The first twenty-years of JTNM brought almost continuous tension and considerable frustration. The very survival of the unit was an achievement. Regional and monument officials desperately hoped to build on that and enjoy greater success in the future.

PART III

PROTECTING A DESERT NATIONAL PARK

AFTER 1956, the National Park Service (NPS) at Joshua Tree National Monument (JTNM) faced continued threats and grudging support from its own leadership. At the same time, American culture had evolved, and with it came enhanced support for protection of the environment, including the desert. Environmental awareness increased, "saving the environment" became popular, and the nation underwent a stunning legal transformation. The NPS grew in scientific expertise, while adapting to legislation that mandated public input in most management decisions. The U.S. Congress converted JTNM to a national park in 1994, expanded its acreage to ninety-six percent of its original 1936 size, and designated the majority of its new land to wilderness. The staff became more professional, especially those engaged in the management of natural and cultural resources. Yet, at the same time, the NPS lost manpower amidst a downsizing of the executive branch of the federal government during President Ronald Reagan's presidency and an increasing discordance between the agency and many lawmakers.

Few people now call for elimination of Joshua Tree National Park (JTNP). But what of the attitude toward the desert areas around it? In Chapter Six, I cover the two decades after 1956 when the *Mission 66* program added to the monument's infrastructure and the Wilderness Act of 1964 modified the unit's recreational use. In Chapter Seven, I cover events from 1977 to 1996 and highlight the transformation of natural-resource management to a model program, the chaotic process of general management planning, and the extraordinary impact of the California Desert Protection Act of 1994. In Chapter Eight, I argue that the status of JTNP is assured, but extreme threats around it still endanger its resources. In a final epilogue, I ponder the role of the public's perception of JTNP, in particular, and of deserts, in general, as the park moves ever forward in the twenty-first century.

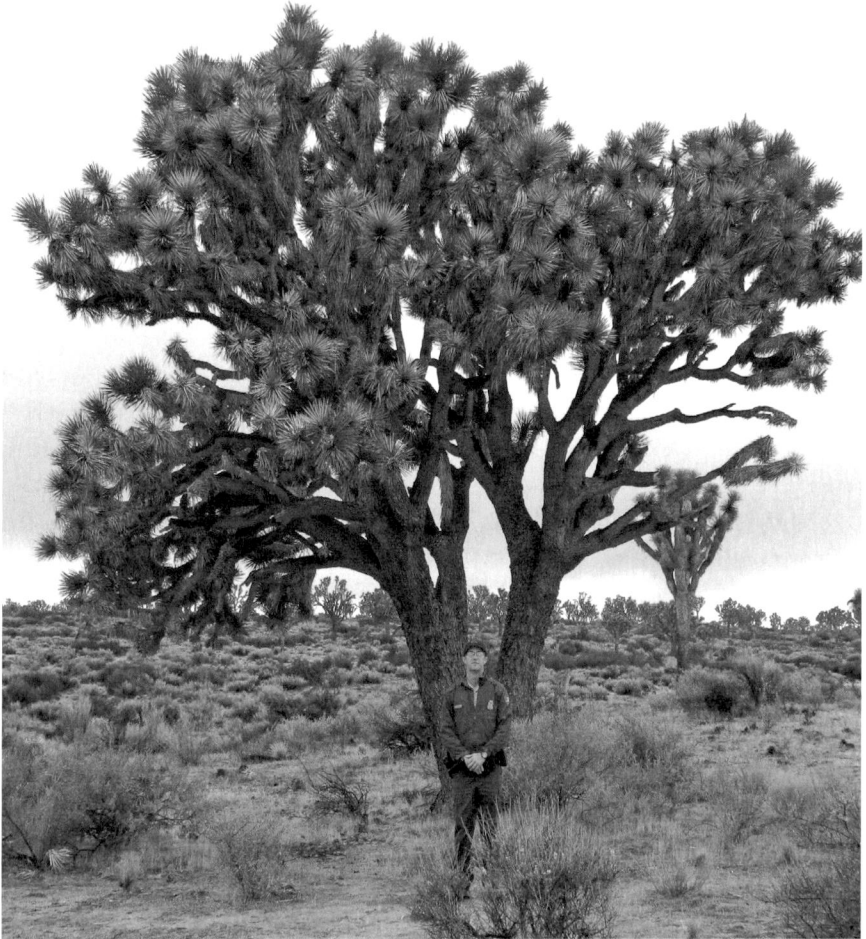

FIG. 6.1. Joshua Tree National Park Ranger Chad Riggin stands next to one of the largest Joshua trees in the relatively cool and better-watered Covington Flat area of the park. The vegetation here and in the wilderness areas nearby includes arboreal species such as the single-leaf pinyon (piñon) pine (*Pinus monophyllia*) and California juniper (*Juniperus californica*) as well as the park's namesake species (*Yucca brevifolia*). During the mid-1970s, hearings to establish portions of the park as official wilderness exposed conflicting goals between environmental activists and Superintendent Homer Rouse. The activists wanted the entire area included in the wilderness, despite the existence of a road, whereas Rouse wanted to develop the area and build a road to it from Hidden Valley. Neither got what they wanted. Unpaved Covington Road continues to supply ingress to the higher country, which is surrounded by wilderness. To Rouse's great frustration, his plan for development and an internal park road to the area died in contentious hearings. Today, one must still leave the park by either of the two northern entrances and then drive to Covington Road to explore the region. Photograph by the author (original in color), January 2013.

CHAPTER SIX

Joshua Tree Matures 1957–1976

DURING THE THIRD AND FOURTH DECADES of Joshua Tree's existence, the monument gained in popularity and a more secure status, while completing most of the development necessary for visitors' enjoyment and safety. At the same time, a revolution in environmental legislation rewrote the rules for planning and managing the national park system. Joshua Tree National Monument (JTNM) began the period with the system-wide *Mission 66* program that provided funding at a level Superintendent James Cole (Fig. 3.2) could only have imagined. It ended with the designation of the majority of the monument's land as legal wilderness. During that time, the National Park Service (NPS) at JTNM continued to acquire land, finalized the geographical framework of its infrastructure, benefitted from increased external research on its natural and cultural resources, and coped with a 133 percent rise in annual visitor numbers to 728,900. As threats to the monument's land, water, flora, and fauna continued, an increasingly powerful conservation movement provided both support and criticism in the struggle to combat those threats.

This was also a time when there was a major shift in American culture, as modern environmentalism began to spread among the broader public and led to legislation that transformed resource management throughout the nation. During the 1950s, scientists and environmental organizations had pressed the government to take more responsibility for protecting the air, water, and land resources of the nation. From 1963 through 1973, the U.S. Congress enacted four major laws that reshaped the way the NPS and every other federal land agency operates. Passage of the Clean Air Act in 1963, the Wilderness Act in 1964, the National Environmental Policy Act in 1969, and the Endangered Species Act in 1973 dramatically redesigned natural-resource management, while narrowing the options the NPS could select in its planning and administration. Though modified by succeeding congresses and tested in court many times, these laws strongly reinforced the NPS's mission, as defined in the 1916 Organic Act.

In 1955, Congress passed the Air Pollution Control Act, which declared that air pollution was a danger to the public's health but preserved primary responsibilities for controlling it to state and local governments. Congress then expanded that law when it passed the Clean Air Act of 1963, and it has amended the act repeatedly, notably in 1967, 1970, 1977, and 1990. The purpose of the new legislation was to protect, control, and enhance the nation's air quality by way of a federal program that would be coordinated with local, state, and tribal governments. Among its provisions, the act established a federal classification system of air-quality standards for different land-use areas in the U.S. Units of the national park system are designated Class I, which means they should have the highest level of air purity. This has proven to be a problem for Joshua Tree, located as it is down-wind of Los Angeles, but the law demands continued monitoring and a search for a solution to chronic pollution levels higher than appropriate for a national park.[2]

The Wilderness Act of 1964 allows Congress to give strict protection to tracts of federal land by forbidding motorized and mechanical vehicles and tools, construction of buildings or other structures, and any large-scale environmental alteration. The bill defines a wilderness in this way:

> an area of undeveloped Federal land retaining its primeval character and influence, without permanent improvements or human habitation, which is protected and managed so as to preserve its natural conditions and which (1) generally appears to have been affected primarily by the forces of nature, with the imprint of man's work substantially unnoticeable; (2) has outstanding opportunities for solitude or a primitive and unconfined type of recreation; (3) has at least five thousand acres of land or is of sufficient size to make practicable its preservation and use in an unimpaired condition; and (4) may also contain ecological, geological, or other features of scientific, educational, scenic, or historical value.[1]

The wilderness concept stemmed from a U.S. Forest Service (USFS) classification of "primitive areas" that resulted, in part, from a response to the establishment of the NPS in 1916 and its steadfast promotion by Stephen Mather as the only agency qualified to protect the nation's natural values. USFS veterans Aldo Leopold and Arthur Carhart, during the 1920s, and Bob Marshall, during the 1930s, developed the idea and Wilderness Society Director Howard Zahniser wrote the final bill. When it passed, it immediately created fifty-four wilderness areas on 9,100,000 acres of national forest land. During the late 1950s, the NPS opposed the idea, because it removed planning options for the agency on any land designated as legal wilderness. After its passage, however, the NPS had no choice but to evaluate its lands for designation. By early 2016, the national park system accounts for 44,000,000 of the nearly 110,000,000 acres of wilderness in the U.S. (Fig. 6.1). The 1964 act also created wilderness study areas that are managed like wilderness, until their suitability for the wilderness system is determined.[3]

On the last day of 1969, Congress passed the law that most impacted the way the NPS operates. The National Environmental Policy Act (NEPA) not only established the Environmental Protection Agency (EPA), but also set policy and planning procedures that powerfully challenged traditional land management. First, it ordered all federal agencies to carry out their duties with the minimum possible impact on the environment. Second, it forced the agencies to use interdisciplinary planning, list and evaluate the expected impacts of each action, and compare any action to a "no change" option. Finally, all planning and environmental-impact analysis had to involve the public. No longer could national park or forest managers contact a few "experts" of their own choosing and design master plans or management decisions behind closed doors. These rules enabled environmentalists and others to participate in all phases of resource management and to sue the government to stop plans, if they deemed the planning or environmental-review processes inadequate. The early master plans for JTNM were artifacts of the past. NEPA allowed anyone to participate and potentially challenge the monument's planning and administration.[4]

The fourth of these transformative acts was the Endangered Species Act. It requires federal agencies to ensure that their actions do not harm threatened and endangered species of plants and animals or result in loss of their habitat. The law tremendously increased the duties of the U.S. Fish and Wildlife Service by ordering it to maintain lists of species in danger of extinction or threatened by sustained losses in population or habitat. Significantly, the law can affect the activities of private individuals as well as federal employees. Once a species is listed as endangered, land managers must take extraordinary steps to protect it and its habitat. Joshua Tree has both faunal and floral endangered or threatened species that dramatically influence all land-use decisions. Every aspect of management at JTNM changed as these four laws and others stemming from enhanced American environmentalism took effect.[5]

The Program for Land Acquisition Improves

In May 1957, the NPS reported that the State of California and private land owners still held nearly 80,000 of the 557,934 acres in the monument, despite hard-won successes with the Southern Pacific Railroad Company (SPRR) and the state regarding land exchanges and condemnation of tax-deeded land. These non-federal lands remained a threat to the monument's future, due to their wide range and scattered distribution. Particularly troubling were the parcels that remained in the western half of the monument and along the main road. Yet JTNM's officials had reason to be optimistic. Congress and NPS leaders seemed to recognize the problem and allocated some annual funds for additional purchases and exchanges of land. After the NPS completed the last tripartite land exchange with Carl Allen, the SPRR announced that it might be willing to negotiate more exchanges. The California State Lands Commission (CSLC) also looked for more direct exchanges for some of the 24,000 acres it still held in the monument.[6]

During the next twenty years, the NPS reduced non-federal lands in JTNM by seventy-five percent to fewer than 20,000 acres (Map D). By the end of this period, the prospect of wilderness designation for much of the monument's acreage lent urgency to the process. The agency used every means at its disposal to acquire properties, including condemnation. Director Conrad Wirth's *Mission 66* program brought some funds for land acquisition during its early years. In 1960, President Dwight Eisenhower supported a proposal to allocate $1,500,000 for acquiring all the remaining private property in JTNM, but Congress refused to provide the funds.[7]

Passage of the Land and Water Conservation Fund Act (LWCFA) in 1964 proved more useful, for it provided much-needed funding for land acquisition in the national park system. A vigorous environmental movement began changing the nation's land policies during the activist era of the 1960s. Groups such as the Sierra Club, Wilderness Society, and myriad grass-roots organizations rejected the consumptive-use prescriptions of the USFS and Bureau of Land Management (BLM)as well as *Mission 66*'s initiatives to build more structures in the national parks. Environmentalists accused the government of misusing the last dwindling resources and wild regions of the nation. In addition, studies by the Outdoor Recreation Resources Review Commission documented a woeful lack of recreational opportunities for most Americans. The LWCFA created a fund to purchase land for recreational purposes. The money is drawn from admission charges to federal recreation areas, sales of surplus properties, and taxes on motorboat fuel. Congress directed that some of the money go to the national park system, some to other federal agencies, and some to match state expenditures for their park systems. Although later administrations diverted much of the money to other purposes, the immediate effect on the national park system was a surge in land acquisition.[8]

From 1957 to 1976, the NPS continued land exchanges and used money from these programs to acquire many of the remaining properties in a systematic fashion. It began auspiciously in 1957, when the CSLC exchanged 12,381 acres in the monument for parcels of federal land all over the state. Another round of exchanges with the state commission between 1961 and 1963 brought another 1,888 acres under federal control. At the same time, the SPRR again offered to exchange its property in the monument for land of equal value near Barstow. Unfortunately for the NPS, the deal for 13,000 acres in the monument failed, due to problems with the land the railroad wanted. In 1961, another opportunity to gain SPRR land appeared when the Kaiser Corporation offered to buy all the railroad's remaining property and exchange it for three townships adjacent to its Eagle Mountain Mine. Kaiser's mining engineers suspected that the iron-bearing seams extended into the monument, and, in any case, the company would welcome the use of the water from that area in the existing mine. The problem was that Kaiser needed fee-simple title to the land, which would require an act of Congress to change the monument's boundary. NPS officials carefully considered the offer before finally declining, on the basis that the monument had already lost enough land in 1950.[9]

In 1958, two important bilateral exchanges highlighted efforts by the NPS to control areas that had been sold by the railroad and were now threatened by development. First, the agency bought 451 acres plus a home in Lost Horse Valley from longtime foe Charles Stokes. Today, a ranger station sits on that property (Plate 32). A few months later, JTNM's officials worked out exchanges with Stanley Broxmeyer for important parcels in Lower Covington Flat, near the entrance road from Joshua Tree village. He traded 3,207 acres in the monument for 160 acres near Palm Springs. The latter were appraised at more than $1,000 per acre.[10]

The Broxmeyer exchange was significant, because it addressed a growing fear among JTNM's officials about residential development within the unit's boundaries, especially along the rapidly suburbanizing northwestern edge of the monument. One troubling threat to that part of JTNM came from George Willett, who applied to the San Bernardino County Board of Supervisors to subdivide his inholding near the road from Joshua Tree village. To his dismay, the supervisors rejected his plan, claiming that the area's location prevented it from conforming to the county's standards for a subdivision. He vowed to sell all the Joshua trees on his land, if he could not develop his property. On May 16, 1960, he gathered media and local officials to witness the cutting of a large Joshua tree on his property. Visitors stopped to see what would happen, and some argued with Willett, as he explained his reasons for the cutting. Superintendent William Supernaugh soon arrived and convinced him to delay cutting the tree until they could meet that evening. Willett wanted to trade his 1,080 acres in the monument for 19,000 acres in the Chuckwalla Valley, but he ultimately settled for fewer but more valuable acres along the Southern California coast. Another proposed subdivision by Desert Cove Properties near the western entrance road drew more than 600 letters of protest before the county supervisors rejected it on similar technicalities. These threats led the supervisors to pass a resolution, requesting the federal government to take immediate steps to eliminate inholdings. The resolution stated that the board expected other proposals for development and that "local subdivision and zoning ordinances cannot legally be so restrictive that they prevent the use of private land."[11]

After the failure of the Kaiser-SPRR-NPS deal and the flurry of exchanges with the CSLC, action with the big landholders subsided. For the remainder of the 1960s, NPS officials carried out a steady stream of purchases, exchanges, and takings from small landholders. A new source of support began in 1962, with the establishment of the Joshua Tree Natural History Association. The cooperating association immediately set up a fund for donations to help with land acquisition. At the same time, the Desert Protective Council took a more-aggressive approach, demanding that the NPS do more to defend against threats of development within the monument. Between September 1963 and August 1969, the NPS acquired dozens of parcels, totaling nearly 7,500 acres from twenty-nine different parties.[12]

One significant purchase in 1966 was the property of William F. ("Bill") Keys, which would become the premier site for interpreting the region's history (Plate 31). As his health began to fail, Keys knew he would need to sell his property for money to survive. He offered it to the NPS for

$25,000, with the stipulation that he could remain there for the rest of his life and be buried there beside his wife. Once again, funding problems meant the NPS did not have the money to act. Former racecar driver, sometime actor, and businessman Henry E. Tubman from Los Angeles bought all 879 acres in October 1964, with the exception of the family cemetery, and agreed to let Keys stay. Tubman planned either to exchange the property for federal land outside the monument or develop a dude ranch on it. He lined up financial backers for the dude ranch, but negotiating with the NPS, BLM, and Government Services Administration was so slow and complicated that his investors finally backed out. After an appraisal showed Tubman's land in Joshua Tree was worth $345,000, he exchanged it for surplus military land at the former Camp Elliott near San Diego on June 28, 1966. Bill Keys lived on the property exactly three more years before dying on June 28, 1969.[13]

During the late 1960s, Joshua Tree officials began to study the possibility of asking Congress to designate a large portion of the monument as wilderness. This meant that any development and any mechanized access or use would be prohibited by law. The Wilderness Act allowed for some exceptions, in cases of private lands within designated wilderness. This reality galvanized NPS officials to try to acquire private holdings in the areas they wanted to establish as wilderness. After years of delay stretching back to 1953, NPS officials rushed through a purchase of 7,411 acres from Joseph Wachowski in September 1969 and an exchange with the Coachella Valley Irrigation District for another 3,596 acres in January 1970.[14] NPS planners released their proposal for wilderness areas in JTNM in 1971 and held a hearing, as required by NEPA. Inadvertently, everyone forgot to invite representatives from the SPRR to comment. Eventually, the railroad's executives noticed the ongoing planning for wilderness, the fact that their company still owned considerable land in those areas, and the apparent snub at the hearing. In response to a draft environmental statement issued by the monument, SPRR land manager W. F. Herbert wrote to JTNM Superintendent Peter Parry on June 28, 1973:

> The Southern Pacific Land Company has been negotiating for the sale or exchange of its remaining property within the monument since April 1957...I am disturbed to find that we were not included in the list of interested parties consulted or coordinated with prior to the announcement of a public hearing on December 10, 1971. I believe it is also necessary that a comment be made somewhere in your Environmental Statement to the effect that no further Environmental Statements, Impact Reports or other such studies are necessary before granting reasonable road access across federal lands to owners of private land inside the monument.[15]

During the time between the wilderness hearing and Herbert's letter, NPS officials had purchased nearly seventy more small tracts of land, but this letter got their immediate attention.

Comfortable with the railroad's apparent willingness to withhold sales to private parties, they had largely ignored the biggest private landholder. Disgruntled SPRR land officials sold 544 acres of land within the monument's southwestern boundary to a company called the Oasis Valley Corporation. Superintendent Parry hastily apologized for the oversight and explained that the announcement had gone to *The Federal Register* and most regional newspapers. He asked if the company had any more plans to sell its acreage in the monument. Serious negotiations started immediately, and, on November 14 and 15, 1974, the NPS bought 12,458 acres from the SPRR. Three months later, a final purchase brought another 505 acres from the company.[16]

As planning and legislation for wilderness areas at Joshua Tree proceeded, NPS land officers concluded ever costlier purchases. Agency records show that, between September 1970 and passage of the Joshua Tree wilderness bill in late October 1976, the NPS bought more than 450 tracts of land, in addition to the SPRR's purchases. During 1975 alone, the NPS worked out a four-way exchange with Riverside County, The Nature Conservancy, and private land owners that allowed it to acquire one-third of that county's private acreage in the monument in seventy-five tracts for $787,677. Unfortunately, NPS leaders had to suspend further acquisitions that year, leaving twenty more tracts offered by owners in limbo. The high price of an April 1976 purchase of Jellystone Park, a commercial recreation facility on the northwestern corner of the monument, depleted the budget for further land acquisition. During the previous decade, the once-popular eighty-acre park suffered a decline in attendance, and its three corporate owners—Jellystone Campground, Ltd., Yucca Valley Recreational Association, Inc., and Hi-Desert Memorial Hospital, Inc.—searched for a way to recoup some of their investment. The NPS paid $457,500 for the land and structures in what is known today as Black Rock Canyon.[17]

JTNM planners suggested one further opportunity for acquiring land that senior officials promptly rejected. The update of the monument's *Mission 66* plan in 1964 included a proposal to change the unit's southern boundary. The 1950 adjustment had brought the southwestern boundary to the Metropolitan Water District of Southern California's (MWD) aqueduct (Fig. 1.2). The south-central boundary, however, from Pushawalla Canyon through the Cottonwood Mountains, still lay well north of the aqueduct. Nearly half of the 96,000 acres necessary to reach the aqueduct in that area had been in the original monument, but they were eliminated in 1950. Acting Regional Director Leo J. Diederich explained that all that land had been returned to the public domain, because more than half of it was privately owned:

> It is acknowledged that extension of the southern boundary would be desirable. This has always been recognized. However, as will be seen from the Master Plan, more than half of the proposed addition consists of privately-owned [sic] and State-owned lands arranged in a huge

checkerboard pattern. More than 10,000 acres of these lands are owned by the Southern Pacific Railroad Company, and we feel sure that the Company would object strenuously to having these lands included in the Monument again. Our relations with the Company are excellent at the present time and it would be most unwise to jeopardize these relations. The possibility of acquiring these lands, either by purchase or exchange, seems remote. This situation led to the elimination of Monument lands in this area now proposed for addition to the Monument. [18]

The NPS would have to wait another thirty years before Joshua Tree gained this important addition.

Validating Mines and Coping with their Legacy

While the land-acquisition program at JTNM advanced, the BLM continued to evaluate unpatented mining claims in Joshua Tree, in response to NPS requests. Early in 1963, the bureau declared a number of old claims, including twelve held by Bill Keys, null and void after their claimants lost appeals to the Secretary of the Interior. At the same time, the widow of Chester Pinkham relinquished another eleven lode claims and millsites without contest. These actions, plus acquisition of the Mastodon Lode Mine and Winona Placer Claim at Cottonwood Springs, further diminished the threat of mining during the 1960s, especially in the western half of the monument. In 1971, geologist Thomas Clements surveyed twenty-two sections of land in JTNM for potential mineral value. The request for this survey did not originate from the mining lobby seeking to reopen the monument to new claims but from real-estate appraiser Albert L. Johnson, who wanted information on any mineral deposits that might affect the price of the property and the validity of various claims. It is uncertain why he thought land in the monument might be saleable. Clements reported that all but one of the sections had no significant resources. The one exception on the northern flank of the Little San Bernardino Mountains had "titaniferous magnetite" in quantity, but Clements believed the difficulty of extracting the titanium rendered it uneconomical. In 1973, investigators conducted a validation study and found that miners were actively working only three claims in the entire monument.[19]

In 1976, Congress dealt a serious blow to mining as an economic activity in the national park system. For many years, environmentalists challenged the Mining Act of 1872 and failed miserably. The laws that stemmed from the California gold rush and still allow claims to be filed on most federal land have proven immune to the onslaught of increased environmental concern and concomitant legislation across the nation. Most national park units had always been off-limits to new claims, but those filed before Congress had created a park could continue. Mining existed in relatively few park units, mainly Death Valley, Joshua Tree, and Organ Pipe Cactus National Monuments, Whiskeytown-Shasta National Recreation Area, and several parks in Alaska, but the NPS considered it inappropriate in reserves dedicated to preserving ecological systems and scenery. The NPS finally scored a victory with the Mining in the National Parks Act of 1976, which requires mine owners to file work plans that include how they will mitigate damage at the mines and avoid impacting other areas when transporting ore over a park's roads. The costs of developing and filing the plan, rehabilitating damaged landscapes, and careful transport through parks simply made many mines too expensive to work. In short order, the few working mines in Joshua Tree ceased production. The NPS opportunistically pursued the moribund mines to further its goal of fee-simple ownership. By 1984, a brief survey found only twelve patented and nine unpatented mining claims in the monument, none of them active.[20]

Although mining was no longer a serious threat to the monument, its physical legacy still posed hazards for visitors. As early as 1949, Superintendent Frank Givens worried about the government's liability in cases of invalid mines:

> It appears that we might be liable if a visitor fell into the shaft located on a claim which had been invalidated. This is based on the assumption that an invalidated mining claim automatically becomes Monument land. However, it is believed that we cannot lay claim to structures on invalidated claims until the former claimants have been served notice to remove or demolish their improvements…In the Monument no assessment is required to hold a claim and we cannot correct a hazard that might exist even though the mine might be abandoned—or claimed to have been abandoned by a claimant who might become involved in a damage suit.[21]

Regional Director Owen Tomlinson responded that "the Service would owe a duty to the public if hazardous conditions were known to exist" on any unpatented claim. He ordered Givens to post warning signs, give claimants ninety days to remove their improvements, and cover any open shafts.[22]

Although the orders were clear, the magnitude of the task delayed their implementation. During the mid-1960s, Joshua Tree personnel finally began identifying and listing hazardous mines. In 1968, ranger John Wise reported thirty open mines or cisterns in the Lost Horse District alone. Five years later, maintenance supervisor Roy O. Curbow requested funds to close just ten of the eighty most-dangerous mineshafts near areas of heavy use by visitors. He estimated that costs would range from $300 to $8,000 per mine. Regional Director Howard Chapman denied the request. Rangers then covered some open shafts with simple chainlink fencing, only to have visitors cut or pry them open to explore the old mines. As the United States became ever more litigious, the NPS sought more permanent barriers. Yet two considerations influenced the steps the agency could take. First, officials wanted to keep the grates or other structures over mine openings as visibly unobtrusive as possible. Second, the cost of such barriers remained well beyond the operating budgets of most parks and monuments. Finally, in May 1978, Regional Director Stanley Albright approved the expenditure of $101,000 to close just ten of the mineshafts at Joshua Tree.[23]

Struggling with Diminishing Water

By the late 1950s, the supply of water in the monument showed a troubling pattern. Quail Spring went dry in 1957, to no one's surprise, given the amount of settlement nearby. Pine Spring also failed the same year. In 1961, Covington Well went dry for the second time. Finally, in 1968, Stubbe Spring ran out of water. The latter was particularly worrisome because of its implications for the monument's wildlife. Across the monument, further drops in groundwater aquifers and increasingly common shortfalls at visitor facilities spelled trouble for the NPS. In 1966, the agency purchased the Ryan property in the Lost Horse Valley, including the rights to Lost Horse Well #1. JTNM officials ranked this as their top priority for acquisition. After the land purchase, a regional office employee cleaned out and rehabilitated the well. Along with government-drilled wells nearby, it supplied a roadside facility known as the Ryan Water Station, which served six campgrounds with 265 campsites plus other visitors and staff. Yet even that source failed in 1974, ostensibly due to a minor earthquake that shifted the fault and blocked water from rising to the surface. A year later, JTNM officials temporarily closed the restrooms at Cottonwood, due to insufficient water. Both closures aggravated visitors and made travel in the monument more difficult.[24]

At the same time, the NPS sought to control or terminate water removals by Joseph Chiriaco and Kaiser's Eagle Mountain Mine. On June 19, 1957, Chiriaco renewed his application for a larger pipeline across both NPS's and BLM's property to his roadside business south of the monument. This action set off a complex correspondence that illustrated why these matters take so long to complete. NPS solicitors, regional office specialists, and JTNM Superintendent William Supernaugh wrote back and forth to get information and agree on a response. At the same time, they had to deal with BLM agents, Joseph Chiriaco, and his attorney. Each step required a series of questions, replies, and further debate. This time, Chiriaco also wanted to develop a reservoir near his property and, perhaps, acquire public-domain land immediately west of his facility, where he could drill a well. He gave JTNM officials conflicting information about his desire to donate, sell, or exchange his water right in the monument for that land. NPS officials again investigated his right and again concluded that it was cloudy, at best, but could probably be perfected on the basis of his long history of use. Ultimately, they recommended that the monument should issue a revocable permit and see if the BLM would issue one allowing the pipeline to cross its land. In the meantime, the name Shaver Summit was changed to Chiriaco Summit to honor the pioneer businessman.[25]

Months and then years elapsed. More problems surfaced, including a spatial conflict between Chiriaco's reservoir and the MWD's right-of-way. Finally, on July 1, 1966, Chiriaco received a twenty-year special permit to continue using the existing pipeline. By 1969, however, the permit gave him little solace. Precipitation declined during the rest of the decade, and the oasis at Lost Palms dried up for months at a time. The flow from the spring in nearby Munsen Canyon shrank to less than one gallon per hour. Both increased dramatically after rainfall, but Chiriaco increasingly depended on water he purchased from a utility-owned well outside the monument. The following year, an NPS appraiser evaluated the water right, including the pipeline, and concluded it was worth $1,500. More time passed. In 1974, JTNM officials offered to buy the water right, but Chiriaco refused. Then, in 1976, a new generation of agency solicitors decided to investigate whether his appropriative water right had lapsed, due to lack of use for more than five years. The old pipeline lay broken in places, jammed with debris in others, and had clearly been abandoned. Forty years after the monument's birth, it looked like there might be a chance to eliminate a legal intrusion that had already become pointless.[26]

Meanwhile, the Kaiser Corporation broadened its attempts to gain access to Pinto Well #2 on JTNM property, while simultaneously digging several new wells in the Chuckwalla Valley. In 1957, the company negotiated with NPS officials in Washington, D.C., and, for a brief time, it appeared the company might sidestep opposition by JTNM and the NPS's regional office. Senior agency officials learned that the Kaiser Corporation held title to sixty acres of land in the Chalmette Battlefield in what is today Jean Lafitte National Historical Park. An exchange of that land for the rights to water from Pinto Well #2 appealed to the agency's leaders. In this case, however, it was the complex structure of the corporation that doomed the agreement. The Kaiser Aluminum Company owned the land at Chalmette and contemplated industrial development there. Kaiser's Eagle Mountain Mine was controlled by a separate company under the umbrella corporation. Kaiser Aluminum refused to give up its land for the benefit of Kaiser Steel. The deserts of Joshua Tree narrowly escaped NPS's preference for another resource in another part of the country. Ironically, Kaiser Aluminum later donated some acreage at Chalmette, perhaps seeking to appear reasonable and supportive.[27]

Later in 1957, the Kaiser Corporation settled the trespass action but then faced NPS questions about the legality of drilling a new well on land belonging to the MWD. Monument and regional officials wondered how a single well on a temporary withdrawal to supply the construction crew of the aqueduct had turned into two wells, pouring water into a huge mine and town. Did Kaiser, as lessee, have the right to drill what became Pinto Well #3? Did the MWD have the right to allocate so much more water to a separate, unrelated operation? In the face of these questions, Kaiser continued to press for access to Pinto Well #2. Between 1957 and 1962, the NPS offered several

FIG. 6.2. Pinto Well #1 sits on land held by the Metropolitan Water District of Southern California. For decades, the Kaiser Corporation drew water from it for its Eagle Mountain Iron Mine community. The company also built two more wells, one of which lay on the park's land. The National Park Service capped the illegal well and refused all attempts by the company to reopen it. Now, the mine is closed, and the future of its enormous complex and that of Pinto Well #1 are in doubt. Photograph by the author (original in color), January 2013.

special-permit options, which the company would not accept. In December 1957, Kaiser turned down a two-year permit, arguing that the investment was too great to settle for such a short time. Company executives also turned down a modified permit, on the basis that the right of renewal was unspecified and the amount to be charged was too high. In December 1962, the NPS offered another two-year permit for a lower price, but Kaiser did not even respond.[28]

While these negotiations proceeded, Fred Kunkel, of the U.S. Geological Survey (USGS), completed a study of the water resources in the Pinto Basin. In his 1960 report, he estimated that the water table at Kaiser's Pinto Well #1 had declined about twelve feet in the previous three years (Fig. 6.2). He added that Pinto Well #3 also had declined to a similar level, despite the fact that no water had been taken directly from it. He concluded that the large amount of water available under the basin made this insignificant. Kunkel believed the aquifer was too deep to be used by native vegetation. He concluded, " . . . because the effect of pumping from the existing wells in Pinto Basin cannot upset the ecological balance within the Monument, because the quantity of stored water in Pinto Basin is very great, and because the natural subsurface ground-water outflow is relatively small, any attempt to limit pumping to an estimate of perennial yield will not allow full utilization of this important natural resource of stored water."[29] Three years later, another study by J. E. Weir, Jr. and J. S. Bader corroborated Kunkel's findings. Kaiser, meanwhile, drilled three wells in the Chuckwalla Valley, which, ironically, it did not use to capacity.[30]

After five quiet years, Kaiser again approached the NPS seeking access to Pinto Well #2. The company was engaged in long-term planning for its Eagle Mountain Mine and community and wanted to secure permission to use the well under emergency conditions. Plans called for increasing the population at the company town to more than 3,500 residents. Kaiser had tried to work out an arrangement with the MWD to tap the aqueduct and replace the supply to cities in Southern California with water from the state's Feather River Project. The state, however, insisted on a seventy-five-year contract, which Kaiser refused to accept. The company revived its request for a perennial agreement to use JTNM water in unusual circumstances when its existing wells proved inadequate.

In late June 1967, Kaiser and NPS officials met for two days in San Francisco and debated the request. Manuel Morris, of the NPS, posed several questions to Joseph M. Trihey, the lawyer for Kaiser, including, "Why did the company not wait until it had an emergency to make the request?" and "Why was it not using its Chuckwalla Valley wells to their capacity?" Trihey answered that the expensive development planned for the mine required absolute assurance of water before the company could commit funds and that users of groundwater south of the Chuckwalla Valley complained that Kaiser already was using too much of the aquifer. Morris answered that the NPS was not a public utility in the business of supplying water and that Kaiser's current pumping was lowering the water table at nearly one foot per year; but if the company could show it had exhausted all other possible sources and the water would only go to support the residents of the town, then the government might consider a two-year special permit, with a fee equal to that charged by the region's utilities. During the following year, the NPS formally offered these stipulations in writing and also reassured the company that it would not withhold water from the town's residents in a true emergency. In September 1968, Kaiser Steel replied that it could not definitively show it had exhausted all other water sources and, therefore, could not sign a permit under the government's conditions. Again, the issue subsided, and Pinto Well #2 remained unused.[31]

NPS officials wanted to control the amount of water that Kaiser took from JTNM, and this drove its solicitors to consider a lawsuit against the MWD, seeking revestment of the ten-acre property and water right to the federal government. The Los Angeles utility had granted another lease to Kaiser in 1963, this time for twenty-five years. On July 12, 1968, six NPS officials, including field solicitor W. J. Costello and Superintendent William Supernaugh, met at the MWD's headquarters with eleven of its senior officers and lawyers, including general manager H. J. Mills. The latter opened the meeting by asking, "Why did the NPS want to take away land from the water district?" A lengthy discussion ensued, which brought both information and emotion to the table. MWD officers reminded the park men that the MWD had acquired a number of land parcels under the 1932 congressional act that authorized the aqueduct for water diversion and allowed repair-crew staging in case of damage. They believed that the NPS's effort to reclaim the Pinto Wells tract would endanger MWD's rights on all the emergency parcels. There followed an intense debate about the propriety of allocating the water to Kaiser and the ebbing water table in Pinto Basin. Eventually, someone from the MWD accused the NPS of "governmental confiscation of privately owned water rights." The NPS representatives retaliated that this appeared to be a case of "exploitation of publicly owned assets by private concerns." Eventually, cooler heads prevailed, and everyone agreed that legal action should be a last resort. Nevertheless, the MWD followed the meeting with a letter, flatly refusing to relinquish its water holding. NPS solicitors briefly contemplated filing for condemnation but reasoned that their chance of success was relatively small. By late 1969, they decided to table the issue for a more-propitious time.[32]

After failing to work out deals with Kaiser and the MWD, the NPS let the situation regarding the three Pinto Wells subside again. As monument officials worked on their "wilderness proposal," however, the presence of wells, pipelines, and other infrastructure in the lonely Pinto Basin was obnoxious. Furthermore, miners from Eagle Mountain frequently used the parcel as a recreational site, which gave them easy access to the rest of the basin. The NPS wondered yet again whether it could challenge the MWD's "temporary" land claim and remove the "donut hole" of development from JTNM's least-humanized territory.

Filling Out the Infrastructure in Joshua Tree

During the twenty years from 1957 through 1976, the NPS initiated or completed construction of much of the infrastructure that visitors to the park see today. At the same time, agency officials pondered and then dropped an elaborate plan for additional structures. Harsh weather conditions, ever-increasing use by visitors, vandalism, and even arson led inspectors from the NPS's regional office in San Francisco to conclude that the monument was both understaffed and underfunded.

JTNM received minimal funds for development during its first two decades, but that support abruptly changed with the inauguration of *Mission 66*. At the end of World War II, the annual budget for the entire national park system was a mere $5,000,000. After the war, Congress focused on numerous international and domestic issues, while funding for the national park system inched up to a level similar to that of the pre-war years. During the same period, visitation in the parks shot up by more than 460 percent from its 1941 level. NPS Director Conrad Wirth reported that, between 1950 and 1955, visitation soared from 33,200,000 to 56,500,000, while the agency's budget only increased from $30,100,000 to $32,900,000. The virtual abandonment of maintenance during the war, followed by a decade of underfunding, had left facilities in all parks in dismal condition.[33] In a widely read 1953 article entitled "Let's Close the National Parks," nationally renowned author and historian Bernard DeVoto succinctly described the problem in one of his monthly "Easy Chair" columns in *Harper's Magazine*:

> Congress did not provide money to rehabilitate the parks at the end of the war, it has not provided the money to meet the enormously increased demand. So much of the priceless heritage which the Service must safeguard for the United States is beginning to go to hell.[34]

The deterioration of infrastructure in the parks consumed Director Wirth. He focused so much on establishing or improving facilities that many environmentalists later accused him of fostering overdevelopment and ignoring the protection of natural resources. He revealed his preoccupation with the physical improvements of the national park system in a *Reader's Digest* article:

> It is not possible to provide essential services. Visitor concentration points can't be kept in sanitary condition. Comfort stations can't be kept clean and serviced. Water, sewer and electrical systems are taxed to the utmost. Protective services to safeguard the public and preserve park values are far short of requirements. Physical facilities are deteriorating or are inadequate to meet public needs. Some of the camps are approaching rural slums. We actually get scared when we think of the bad health conditions.[35]

Mission 66 was Wirth's answer. The program was a master stroke of organization, promotion, and publicity worthy of the NPS's first director, Stephen Mather. Wirth presented it as a comprehensive renewal of America's valuable heritage, focusing primarily on infrastructure for visitors and staff. It would last a decade and end in 1966, the fiftieth anniversary of the NPS; thus, the title *Mission 66*. Wirth's preoccupation with material improvements for people and the national park system's wide distribution sold well to Congress. Ultimately, legislators allocated $1,000,000,000 for the program, while more than quadrupling the NPS's annual budget.

When *Mission 66* began at Joshua Tree, the monument had a headquarters building, an incomplete maintenance complex, eight campgrounds, four nature trails, and a basic pattern of roads. Except for the roads, most dated from the previous eight years. *Mission 66* planners identified a variety of options to round out JTNM's necessary infrastructure: a visitor building with exhibit space and several residences for rangers at the Oasis of Mara headquarters; additional maintenance structures at Pinto Wye; a relocated campground plus a ranger station and residences at Cottonwood Spring; improved facilities at other campgrounds and picnic areas, including amphitheaters and better comfort stations; ranger stations and residences at Lost Horse Valley and Indian Cove; and entrance stations at Pinto Wye, Joshua Tree Village, and Cottonwood Spring. They also planned to upgrade the road system in a significant way, by realigning the Pinto Wye and Cap Rock intersections, adding more miles of trail for hikers, and designing a lengthy equestrian trail with another campground specifically for horse riders. Planners also considered a "View-Overlook Building" at Keys View, an entrance station at Indian Cove, and a road connecting Covington Flat to the Lost Horse Valley but dropped those ideas, as sentiment for additional development waned.[36]

JTNM officials celebrated the completion of the headquarters office at the Oasis of Mara in 1954 as a turning point for the eighteen-year-old unit, even as it remained one component of a complex as yet unfinished (Plate 33). As early as 1941, plans called for multiple units of employee housing. In addition, the office building quickly proved too small for the staff and entirely inadequate for a museum and exhibit space. Furthermore, problems with the building surfaced within a few years. Sunshine and high temperatures warped some of the wood and destroyed paint on the building's exterior, while inside portions of the flooring cracked and shifted, probably due to creep along the Pinto Fault. A lovely reflecting pool gathered dust, leaves, and waste, while rambunctious children occasionally fell into it. Much needed to be done to finalize the complex and repair or adapt various details.[37]

One hallmark achievement of *Mission 66* across the U.S. was the establishment of visitor centers, buildings that housed visitor-contact desks, exhibit space, and offices for ranger-interpreters. In many cases, they also provided office space for resource-management specialists. The typical *Mission 66* visitor center eschewed rustic architecture and used modern materials and techniques to maximize space, efficiency, and utility. Cecil Doty, at the Western Office of Design and

Construction, was the premier agency architect during the modernizing *Mission 66* period, and he designed the visitor center at Joshua Tree. Landscape architecture historian Ethan Carr later described Doty's attention to cost limits and efficiency in his visitor centers: "Their flat roofs, stark geometric massing, and contemporary materials confirmed that the architect's transition to modernist design was complete."[38] Completed in 1963, Joshua Tree's visitor center proved an immediate success with visitors and nearly quadrupled the space available for staff offices and reception of visitors (Plate 34).

Throughout the *Mission 66* decade, Joshua Tree's plans included residences for rangers at the Oasis of Mara, yet they were never built. As late as January 1962, a *Mission 66* planning update showed seven residential structures for the area, including an apartment building. Yet a draft master plan issued in 1971 showed none. Several factors contributed to the change in plans. First, construction of housing at Cottonwood Spring and Indian Cove ameliorated the housing crisis, while improvement of the western entrance road allowed more employees to live in Joshua Tree village, where rental and house prices were lower than in Twentynine Palms. Second, flooding and poor drainage made the area immediately south of the oasis suspect. Finally, JTNM officials recognized that, even with a headquarters office, maintenance building, and visitor center already in place, they would likely need the space in the future for additional administrative structures.[39]

The NPS continued to adjust and improve the Oasis of Mara area, at least partially in response to criticism from residents of Twentynine Palms. Planners extended and realigned the path around the oasis, while blocking all entrances, except the one through the administrative complex. They built larger restrooms at the visitor center, converted the reflecting pool to a garden display, repaired the ugly deterioration of the main office's exterior, and also undertook extensive study of how to salvage the badly damaged oasis ecosystem in order to improve the most-accessible public showplace in the monument.[40]

Cottonwood Spring at the southern edge of JTNM presented another problem and opportunity. Local hydrology supported the oasis there and provided the unit's most-reliable source of water for visitors. Miners, hunters, picnickers, and squatters had operated there for decades. The campground, established in 1949, proved immensely popular, and that was the problem, for campers crowded the oasis and removed vegetation for campfires. JTNM officials realized that they would need to move and expand the campground. With *Mission 66* funds, they decided to build a ranger station and residence complex in order to protect the area and firmly establish the site as the only southern entrance to the unit. During 1959, planners from the NPS's Western Office of Design and Construction evaluated a variety of locations for both the new campground and the official structures and considered, but then dropped, the idea of building on the site of the recently invalidated Winona Mine. Instead, they selected an area one-half mile northwest of the oasis and close to the road for a combination ranger station/entrance facility, several residences for employees, and a campground that, eventually, would hold 150 sites. Between 1964 and 1965, the NPS built the ranger contact station, three residences, and a campground consisting of sixty-two sites, but the planned expansion of the campground never occurred. The oasis itself became a day-use area and trailhead.[41]

During the rest of *Mission 66*, the NPS added more-durable tables and comfort stations to campgrounds and picnic areas, upgraded and realigned some of the roads, and converted the Charles Stokes homestead into a ranger station and residence near the monument's primary visitor zone (Plate 32). For a while, JTNM officials debated whether to construct a building at Keys View to provide shelter and a rooftop platform for sightseers. Ultimately, they abandoned that idea, fearing it would create more congestion at the site. An early effort to improve recreational offerings for visitors was the development and dedication of a section of the California Riding and Hiking Trail that traverses the Pacific Coast ranges, loops over to the Pacific Coast Trail in the Sierra Nevada, and then proceeds southeast through the desert to the border with Mexico. It enters the monument near Black Rock Canyon and runs thirty-six miles through Covington Flat, Lost Horse Valley, and the White Tank area before exiting close to the entrance station at Twentynine Palms. Linked with Ryan Campground, it provides horseback riders with a variety of experiences of the monument's scenery, while keeping them well-removed from automobile traffic. Development began in July 1957. On May 30 and 31, 1958, Equestrian Trails Incorporated held its annual ride on the new trail and participated in its official dedication. The trail was the first project completed in JTNM to be funded entirely by the *Mission 66* program.[42]

Although Conrad Wirth's heralded program ended in 1966, increased funding enabled JTNM officials to build or plan more structures at areas popular with visitors. One site that needed immediate attention was Indian Cove. As an area easily accessed from Twentynine Palms, it suffered uncontrolled crowding and occasional vandalism. JTNM officials realigned some of the campgrounds and built a ranger station and residence in 1970 to help control the popular area. Meanwhile, heavy use of the Hidden Valley area led agency planners to consider building a complete visitor center near Cap Rock (Plate 20). Recent completion of the Oasis of Mara visitor center notwithstanding, many believed a new center amidst the primary tourist attractions was needed. During the next five years, plans for the facility expanded to include offices, a display area, restrooms, a visitor-contact desk, and a 200-seat auditorium. These ambitious ideas led NPS officials to begin research for a new master plan to accompany a wilderness study and plan for the backcountry. A planning team appointed by the regional director debated every aspect of the monument, including the road system, entirely new development areas, additional visitor centers, new trails, and even the location of the headquarters. It may seem unusual that, after so much effort and expense to construct roads, buildings, and other facilities during the previous sixteen years, the NPS would reevaluate the entire operation and infrastructural design of the monument. Yet nearly 643,000 visitors arrived in 1970, an increase of 106 percent over the number at the start of *Mission 66*. Popular areas such as Keys View and Cottonwood Springs as well as Indian Cove and Hidden Valley became increasingly overcrowded. With Southern California projected to nearly double its population by the late 1980s, the NPS believed that a total rethinking of the monument's facilities was appropriate, given the proximity of JTNM to so many millions of people.[43]

The planning team released its draft master plan and wilderness proposal on December 22, 1971. It contained nine ambitious proposals divided into two groups. The four "primary" proposals included development of the Wonderland of Rocks area as a major day-use zone, construction of a road linking Covington Flat to the main transport grid, closure and rehabilitation of seventy-one miles of old mining roads, and establishment of ten "primitive" areas, totaling 538,000 acres or ninety-six percent of the monument. Five "secondary" proposals consisted of relocating campgrounds from the day-use area around Hidden Valley, designing a vehicular nature trail through the Wonderland of Rocks, restoring several historic mining properties as visitor attractions, constructing the Cap Rock facility as a visitor center, and developing a ranger station, housing for employees, and a campground at Pinto Wells.[44] Although theoretically separate, the monument's wilderness proposal affected the goals of the master plan. As early as 1967, some NPS officials had expressed doubts about building the road to Covington Flat. During a hearing on wilderness, in February 1972, Larry Moss, representing the Sierra Club and several other organizations, argued that the existing rough dirt road should be closed and the tract added to the wilderness areas.[45]

As occurred at other units of the national park system at this time such as Sequoia National Park to the north and Cumberland Island National Seashore in Georgia, the public rejected almost all the concepts for further development. The reaction was severe enough that a chagrined NPS first separated the master plan from the effort to craft a wilderness proposal and then dropped it entirely. Although the ambitious idea for a Cap Rock Visitor Center was abandoned, due to the decline of the Ryan Water Station and cutbacks in funding, NPS officials did complete a few specific goals from the discarded plan. They converted the Wonderland of Rocks to a day-use area and enlarged, but did not relocate, several campgrounds. They also rehabilitated the Lost Horse Mine (Fig. 5.1), improved trails to it and to the Wall Street Mill (Plate 30) and Barker Dam (Plate 24), closed dozens of old mining roads, and converted the old wagon trail to Pleasant Valley into the Geology Tour Road. Meanwhile, acquisition of Jellystone led the NPS to modify its buildings, redesign its campground by eliminating sixty percent of the sites, and replace the swimming pool, mini-golf course, rodeo yard, and tennis, basketball, and shuffleboard courts of the commercial resort with several fire-control structures, a ranger station, picnic tables, and trailheads appropriate for the newly renamed Black Rock Canyon.[46]

One further development proposal arose among members of the public and surprised JTNM officials. During a visit to the monument by California Congressman Jerry Pettis, several locals mentioned the imminent closure of a national cemetery in San Bruno, California. They commented that Joshua Tree had a vast amount of unused acreage and that a new national cemetery could be established there. Superintendent William Supernaugh thought they were joking, but on January 10, 1967, *The San Bernardino Sun* reported that the American Legion Post in Yucca Valley would soon ask the congressman to sponsor a bill to establish a cemetery on 112,000 acres of the monument. Pettis introduced the bill on February 15 and welcomed support from the San Bernardino County Economic Development Commission. American Legion member Harold A. Bahr, originator of the idea, dismissed opposition from Superintendent Supernaugh and from Equestrian Trails Incorporated, which faced the closure of part of the young riding and hiking trail. He suggested that the latter should not object to giving up their "once-a-year" ride to support patriotism. NPS biologist James K. Baker responded with a lengthy editorial in *The Desert Trail*, highlighting the purposes of national parks, the importance of wilderness for future generations, and the need to prevent inappropriate "invasions." He admitted that the cemetery would not be like the many profit-seeking ventures whose promoters tried to set up in the parks, but it would violate park principles, including "(1) that the activity results in no impairment of significant natural or scenic values, (2) that it does not itself become a primary attraction, and (3) that it does not lessen the opportunity for others to enjoy a Park for the purposes for which the Park was established."[47]

By March, environmental organizations answered the idea with a flood of opposing letters and editorials. This, in turn, brought a letter demonstrating the misinformation that often attends these controversies. Los Angeles attorney George Nilsson wrote to House Interior Committee Chairman Wayne Aspinall, angrily criticizing the BLM for asserting that a military cemetery was incompatible with a park's purposes. Nilsson added, "I should think four townships should be enough to include all the Joshua Trees. Certainly 5,000 acres out of half a million would not be missed." Somewhere he lost the facts that the NPS ran the monument and the American Legion wanted 112,000 acres. Aspinall forwarded the letter to the NPS, and Deputy Director Harthon L. Bill responded that the agency already managed thirteen national cemeteries, and that, in 1962, the Bureau of the Budget studied the issue of new national cemeteries and concluded there should be no further expansion, except at Arlington National Cemetery. Soon, Congressman Pettis's bill died quietly.

Wilderness in Joshua Tree National Monument

Separation of wilderness planning from the ill-fated master plan allowed the NPS to proceed with a process its employees initially greeted with either indifference or outright opposition. NPS Director Conrad Wirth followed earlier traditions that favored parks as scenic creations for the ultimate benefit of current and future visitors. During its early days, the NPS justified automobile access for visitors as necessary to survive threats from the USFS, but, in the mid-1930s, conservationists began criticizing the agency for opening up primitive areas with grand road projects. Three decades later, environmental organizations sought to restrict the agency legally from building any more roads. That wilderness was coming to the parks was a certainty. As early as 1968, the NPS created a hypothetical "Arroyo National Park" in order to demonstrate to field employees what types of issues could affect planning for wilderness areas in their own units. In August 1970, an official request for lists of "important issues" arrived at each national park unit. Two months later, Congress designated the first two wilderness areas within the national park system at Petrified Forest National Park in Arizona and Craters of the Moon National Monument and Preserve in Idaho.[48]

Superintendent Supernaugh reported five issues that he thought would affect designation of a wilderness area in JTNM: inholdings, mining claims, Joseph Chiriaco's water right, the old road in Pushawalla Canyon, and a power line that crossed the southeastern part of the monument. During subsequent development of the wilderness proposal, this list would expand considerably. Planning for the proposal began immediately with wilderness specialists in the Washington, D.C., office taking the lead. In August 1971, senior officials met with Congressman Jerry Pettis, who surprised them with a host of complaints about management at JTNM, including inactivity on programs he and others supported, a lack of cooperation in law enforcement, and poor communication with his office. During the next two months, Superintendent Peter Parry and staff from JTNM and NPS's regional office hurried to address the legislator's concerns. In the meantime, planners released a "Wilderness Study" in August 1971 that proposed ten separate wilderness areas, totaling 325,200 acres, fifty-eight percent of the monument's total area. The planners took the spirit of the Wilderness Act literally and left out unimproved roads, areas in the Little San Bernardino Mountains and Pinto Basin with inholdings, a one-eighth-mile buffer inside the monument's entire boundary and around campgrounds, existing mines, and water installations, and a huge area around Covington Flat, where the master plan called for a new road and interpretive facilities.[49]

On February 2, 1972, NPS planners held a public hearing on the proposal in Twentynine Palms. John Henneberger, a wilderness coordinator from the Denver Service Center (DSC), presented an outline of the proposals to a crowd primarily composed of environmentalists and four-wheel-drive enthusiasts. A few locals and scientists rounded out the audience. Twenty-five individuals spoke, occasionally mixing in comments about the controversial master plan. First up were representatives of the National Parks and Conservation Association, Sierra Club, and Wilderness Society. All three organizations complimented the NPS for its effort but found glaring omissions in the plan. Edward Beveridge suggested that all private land should be included in wilderness as well as the Covington Flat area. Larry Moss, of the Sierra Club, offered nine specific suggestions to close roads, including the one to Covington, eliminate buffer zones, include additional lands near Indian Cove and Keys View, and bring the wilderness boundaries closer to the remaining roads. The net effect of these suggested changes would be eight larger wilderness areas, totaling 58,200 more acres, another ten percent of the monument.[50]

D. H. Stephens, President of the Twentynine Palms Chamber of Commerce, spoke next. He assured the audience that he believed in preserving the national parks and generally favored the NPS plan but then requested that part of the area be excluded so a state road could be built from Berdoo Canyon via Split Rock to the monument's headquarters. He added, " . . . now, before we get upset about this proposed route polluting the Monument with smog caused by automobiles, let's remember that by the time this route would be constructed, sometime around 1985, the automobile industry will have the auto pollution problem solved." This optimistic pronouncement caused Dr. Henry Weber, of the California Garden Clubs Federation, to accuse Stephens of reviving the Blue Cut Road controversy. The NPS's designs for development in the Covington area also drew much criticism. Dr. Sylvia Broadbent, an anthropologist from the University of California, Riverside, warned that the area should be closed for a minimum of ten years to allow for a full archaeological investigation. George Anderson went further by proposing that the entire monument be closed for a decade until scientists, social scientists, and even theologians could properly evaluate it. Many speakers decried the use by jeeps and other off-road vehicles even on old, unimproved roads.[51]

Of course, motor enthusiasts did not remain mute. Wendell Ford, stated that the problem was not law-abiding drivers but lackadaisical NPS law enforcement against irresponsible ones. Jack Edwards, from the California Association of Four-Wheel-Drive Clubs, argued that every citizen has a right to access the nation's parks. Jerry Wendt, from the same group, added that, without the roads, visitors could not access many areas during one day. Harold Huffman explained that he was a lifelong photographer of Joshua Tree's landscapes, and he needed vehicular access to all the existing roads. Ron Crandall, a high school teacher, opposed closure of the roads, because it would deny his students the opportunity to take field trips and do research in the monument. He explained that his groups would volunteer to pick up litter left by other drivers. These comments did not go unchallenged by advocates of wilderness. L. B. Graff, quoted a disabled professor Garrett Hardin, who stated, " . . . the beauty and value of wilderness is knowing that it is there." Don Black, speaking off the record as an individual rather than in his role as a JTNM naturalist, rebuffed Crandall, stating that the monument was not a learning reservoir for schools.[52]

After the hearing, NPS planners resumed work to create an official recommendation for wilderness. In June, they added portions of the Little San Bernardino Mountains, Covington Flat, and Stubbe Spring and released a draft proposing 350,800 acres. Two months later, they reissued the recommendation, after shrinking some of the buffers and classifying much of the privately owned portions of Pinto Basin and the Old Dale Mining District as "potential wilderness." The new proposal recommended 372,700 acres for wilderness and 66,800 acres for proposed wilderness. The additional parcels reduced the number of discrete wilderness areas to eight, as the Sierra Club had suggested. The NPS still resisted adding the Covington area.[53]

During the next two years, the NPS combined the wilderness proposal at Joshua Tree with those from nine other national park units located primarily in the Southwest. After President Richard Nixon endorsed the wilderness recommendation in November 1973, the House of Representatives held a hearing on March 25 and 26, 1974, at which NPS Director Ronald H. Walker explained that JTNM would adjust its recommendation, if it could buy a large amount of land from the SPRR. The agency completed that purchase on November 4, 1974. On May 21, 1975, Kansas Congressman Keith Sebelius introduced H.R. 7190, an omnibus wilderness bill that included the monument's August 1972 wilderness recommendation. The acquisition of 12,800 acres of SPRR land, however, enabled the NPS to combine them with intervening sections of government land and shift 33,100 acres from proposed wilderness to the bloc intended for immediate designation. That raised the total to 405,800 acres. The following November, the House committee held another hearing, at which Director Walker explained why the NPS believed the new additions should be included. Still unsatisfied, Ms. Raye-Page, of the Wilderness Society, recommended that Congress designate the 33,700 "potential" acres as full wilderness. Sierra Club member Lyle Gaston urged the committee to go beyond that and add 62,000 more acres.[54]

Pressure continued to come from environmental groups, forcing the NPS's wilderness studies chief to quiz Superintendent Rouse about the areas left out of the earlier bills. Rouse explained the reasons why each had been excluded but agreed that most could be added, because some inholdings and mining claims were no longer valid. He still opposed adding MWD's parcels, several roads that Riverside County claimed, Covington Flat, and the recently acquired Black Rock Canyon. In March 1976, Congressman Sebelius notified Director Gary Everhardt that his bill now included acreage available for wilderness after the railroad purchase. Three weeks later, Representative Shirley N. Pettis, who replaced her husband in Congress, co-sponsored an alternate omnibus bill that added even more land desired by the environmental organizations. Under H.R. 13160, JTNP would have 429,690 acres in seven wilderness areas and 37,550 acres of potential wilderness (Map H). Rouse reviewed the bill and wondered why Pettis ignored all the NPS's explanations for excluding areas. His greatest concern was the elimination of his idea to build an interpretive center at Covington Flat and develop an internal access road from Hidden Valley to it. The new bill would include 10,880 acres in and around the scenic forest as wilderness. Rouse bemoaned the fact that visitors still would need to exit the monument and drive fifteen miles outside its boundary to reach the area. He also regretted that the NPS would no longer have any planning options there. It bothered him that wilderness and potential wilderness composed almost eighty-five percent of the monument's land under the Pettis bill. His concerns had no effect. Omnibus bills often succeed, because they have something to offer to many legislative constituencies. H.R. 13160 was no exception. On October 20, 1976, President Lyndon Johnson signed Public Law 94-567, establishing wilderness areas in ten national parks and monuments, including Joshua Tree. Although the total of wilderness and proposed wilderness acreage in JTNM still fell short of what some environmental groups wanted, it was 142,040 acres more than the NPS had proposed in 1971.[55]

The Management of Natural Resources Evolves

The staff at JTNM understood that the monument legally existed to protect its botanical resources. The geological wonders and wildlife reinforced its status as nationally significant. But, at the time, management of natural resources lacked attention, scientific inquiry, and data not only in Joshua Tree, but across the entire national park system. Despite George Wright and Lowell Sumner, the naturalists' voices in park-management issues were often lost in the cacophony of engineers, landscape architects, and recreation-focused planners. Yet ecology and environmentalism grew to challenge the status quo during the 1960s and 1970s. Criticism of Director Wirth's preoccupation with infrastructure during *Mission 66* mounted, as researchers raised one issue of natural-resource mismanagement after another. In 1959, Dr. Stanley Cain, of the University of Michigan, told an audience at a conference on wilderness that the NPS had virtually no program of basic ecological research, and that meant that the agency's management of its resources was a failure. He concluded that " . . . the Service is missing a bet by not having an adequate natural history research program."[56]

Following the election of John F. Kennedy as the 35th President and his appointment of Stewart Udall as Secretary of the Interior, Cain served on an advisory board that, eventually, turned the situation around. Chaired by renowned ecologist A. Starker Leopold, the board met in 1963 to consider overgrazing by elk in Yellowstone National Park, and the scientists there seized the opportunity to go much further. They called for the NPS to adapt its management philosophy to one based on science, even if it meant sacrificing objects of popular scenery. They urged the NPS to maintain or recreate "a vignette of primitive America," meaning as the Europeans found it (later research would refute the concept of naturalness after millennia of Native American habitation). Among the specific recommendations were reintroduction of predators that had been eliminated by early park managers and the return of fire to appropriate ecosystems. Secretary Udall ordered the NPS to follow these proposals in all its units. That same year, another panel of experts, chaired by William J. Robbins, released a report on research in the national park system, starkly stating:

Research by the National Park Service has lacked continuity, coordination, and depth. It has been marked by expediency rather than by long-term considerations. It has in general lacked direction, has been fragmented between divisions and branches, has been applied piecemeal, has suffered because of a failure to recognize the distinctions between research and administrative decision-making, and has failed to insure the implementation of the results of research in operational management.[57]

In spite of these high-profile reports, many senior NPS officials stubbornly clung to the older policies they had used for decades. It would take several more critical reports and the replacement of those officials, as they retired, by scientifically trained employees to effect the necessary changes.

At JTNM, the messages of the "Leopold Report" and "Robbins Report" led to more scientific research but little change in administration. A natural-resource management plan in 1974 listed twenty-nine projects, all of them basic research proposals. The list included four on desert bighorn sheep, four on other fauna, two on palm oases, ten on other vegetation, three on geology, and one each on air quality, weather, water, soil, fire, and the overall impact of humans. An update in 1977 called for the development of specific plans for baseline data, fire management, and the Oasis of Mara area.

Bighorn sheep, however, continued to draw the most attention for research and management, as waning springs and human intrusion stressed the monument's flagship species. Different opinions on biology and policy contributed to conflict and inaction that further threatened the species. In August 1958, Chief Ranger Hesmel Earenfight recommended that the NPS copy a program initiated by Richard Weaver, of the California Fish and Game Commission, in the Coxcomb Mountains outside the monument's boundary. Weaver had constructed "an oversize guzzler" to provide water for the band of bighorns that frequented the area (Plate 23). In 1960, JTNM ranger Robert Palmer installed a similar device near Lost Palms Oasis, but it soon became clogged with debris and was then buried. A year later, Robert D. Powell stated, in his census report on bighorns, that forty or more natural water sources had gone dry and the NPS should replace them with artificial sources. Censuses during the next two years showed a continuing decline in the number of bighorn sheep.

Stubbe Spring remained the most-important source for the animals, and some blamed their dwindling population there on humans visiting the site. In 1964, however, independent researchers Ralph and Florence Welles argued that a lack of water was the culprit and noted that the bighorn sheep accommodated themselves quickly to the quiet hikers and readily approached them at the spring. Soon, the JTNM began bringing any dead sheep carcasses to the Public Health Service in Las Vegas for study. That office performed autopsies on bighorn sheep, as part of a program to assess the danger from nuclear testing in Nevada. Most of the sheep sent by the monument proved to be old and apparently had died from natural causes. Nevertheless, the "mystery" of decreasing numbers of sheep drew public attention and controversy.[58]

Superintendent William Supernaugh began his thirteen-year tenure at JTNM two months after Earenfight recommended adding guzzlers to the monument. Despite the device at Lost Palms Oasis, Supernaugh generally rejected the idea of artificial water sources. That policy soon drew anger and condemnation from the scientific community and his own staff of naturalists. Resource management ranger James K. Baker later wrote that Supernaugh would not budge from his opinion that the sheep could "take care of themselves." When the press reported Ralph Welles's criticism of Supernaugh's position, the superintendent tried to revoke NPS funding of his research on bighorn sheep. The regional office in San Francisco had a new biologist, none other than former superintendent James Cole, who ignored Supernaugh and renewed the contract with Welles in June 1965. Two years later, Supernaugh rejected another study by the Welles couple, claiming it was based on erroneous data from his own staff members, William Dengler and James Baker. A year later, Supernaugh's resistance to "artificial features in a national park" brought him into conflict with a group of wildlife experts, including eminent biologist A. Starker Leopold, Robert M. Linn, the director of the NPS's new Office of Natural Science Studies, and Lowell Sumner, the dean of NPS wildlife ecologists. A few weeks later, Regional Director John A. Rutter summarily ordered Supernaugh to take the $3,000 allocated and build a guzzler at Stubbe Spring.[59]

As this policy conflict unfolded, the superintendent defended himself against rising criticism. The California Department of Fish and Game tried to take control of all management of bighorn sheep in the monument only to be told bluntly that federal officials would ignore them. Supernaugh subsequently criticized another report by the Welles duo and warned the regional director that, "since the new officers of the Desert Protective Council are of the rabid conservationist type, it may be that your office, or the Director's office will be hearing from them."[60] In 1970, no rain fell on the catchment apron feeding the guzzler at Stubbe Spring, and it went dry. The superintendent delayed allowing his rangers to carry water to the guzzler, in the hope that a thunderstorm might accomplish the task naturally. Many birds died and rangers found a dead bighorn sheep nearby. Thereafter, Dr. Martin Prochnik, a science advisor to the Secretary of the Interior, demanded answers. Supernaugh humbly assured him that JTNM would do everything necessary to protect the bighorn sheep. The following summer, rangers built a 1.5-mile pipeline to the Stubbe Spring tank, erected two more guzzlers at historic but dry water sites, and programmed five more for the following fiscal year. At the same time, Charles G. Hansen, of the Office of Natural Science Studies, recommended the construction of twenty-one guzzlers or adits (horizontal tunnels at the bottom of a slope or wash) throughout the monument. Any thought of leaving the bighorn sheep to fend for themselves was finished.[61]

The one thing that became abundantly clear through all the attention and conflict was the need for much more research on bighorn sheep to understand their water and forage needs, patterns of movement, and tolerance of drought and disturbance. The resource-management plan of 1974 listed research projects on the species as four of its top five priorities. The document proposed eight installations for water. A year later, Dr. Charles Douglas, an NPS scientist based at the University of Nevada, Las Vegas, issued several reports that highlighted problems in the management of bighorns and the need to coordinate research on the species. He noted that rainfall had decreased from 4.5 inches per year to barely one inch during the previous two decades, and the flow of water at Stubbe Spring had dropped from 222 gallons per day in 1948 to zilch in 1968. Douglas recommended a program of trapping, marking, and placing radio collars on sheep in the monument and supported Superintendent Homer Rouse's decision to close the road to Fortynine Palms that summer to dissuade noisy visitors from driving off sheep at its oasis.[62]

Research on other fauna in the monument contributed some basic information but no specific recommendations for management. An animal census in 1961 noted that burros lived in the mountains just outside the monument, but none appeared within its borders. By 1976, the situation remained the same, although JTNM officials worried about their proximity. Wildlife biologists generated lists or brief reports on birds, ground squirrels, insects, mule deer, snakes, and tarantulas. Coyotes drew some attention, because they begged for food at the campgrounds. Armand Sansum, of the monument's maintenance staff, complained that employees at the Cottonwood Spring residences surreptitiously fed coyotes and badgers, leading to aggressive behavior by both species. Surprisingly, one of the culprits he tattled on was naturalist William Dengler. The inoffensive desert tortoise (Plate 27) also fell under official review, because people who adopted them as pets kept dropping them off in Joshua Tree, regardless of where they found them. In 1971, a desert tortoise club brought forty to the monument. Officials worried that the new additions might be a different subspecies, could carry diseases, and dumping them in bunches would disrupt the tortoise-forage balance in easily accessible areas.[63]

The vegetation of Joshua Tree fared about the same as the fauna, with grand goals for research, modest accomplishments, and a compelling focus on one management issue. The agenda set by the 1974 resource-management plan included basic studies on paleoecology, energy exchange, and plant succession plus specific proposals for the ecology of pinyon-juniper, Joshua tree, and creosote bush communities. After nearly forty years, JTNM officials wanted to understand better what had been the primary raison d'etre for the unit. Lynn Loetterle listed twenty-four rare and endangered plants in 1975, a number that would decrease in subsequent studies. Finally, in 1977, Patrick J. Leary, a graduate student at the University of Nevada, Las Vegas, completed a thesis entitled "Investigation of the Vegetational Communities of Joshua Tree National Monument, California." It

proved to be the most-comprehensive botanical study ever done at the unit and installed Leary as
an important consultant on floral issues at the monument.[64]

The fate of the fan palms at the Oasis of Mara continued to be the primary issue for the management of vegetation. Mistletoe-infested mesquite with deep taproots choked the palms and drew
water from the diminishing aquifer (Plate 37). A 1964 fire at the western end of the oasis, near the
Twentynine Palms Inn, forced JTNM officials to scramble for answers to four practical questions:
how to clear the mesquite, whether or not to use prescribed burns, how to restore water, and how
to treat periodic flooding. In 1966, William Dengler recommended increased manual removal of
mesquite, a time-consuming and expensive option already underway but sporadically. This also
required the application of chemicals to prevent recurrent growth by stump sprouting. One controversial solution was the deliberate use of fire in controlled burns. A "prescribed burn" was fast
and cheap and might be historically appropriate.[65] The ultimate question behind this approach was
later voiced by the regional plant ecologist:

> The Oasis of Mara, which was visited Wednesday morning along with Superintendent An-
> derson, is by far the most complex and sensitive piece of real estate that I have encountered
> while working with the government...To fully understand the problem, one must ask, what
> is natural? Since Indian and European man have inhabited the oasis for an estimated 10,000
> years, are man's influences on the current system natural? Or is that state, prior to man's
> intervention natural, a period so long ago that it is hard to comprehend? [66]

The influence of humans bedeviled decision-making regarding the oasis. When the NPS
developed the layout for the headquarters area, a low wall was built around it to emphasize its
separation from the surrounding town. Later, the NPS built a berm near the wall and a drainage
ditch to resist destructive flooding they perceived to be caused by urbanization. Subsequent studies, however, showed that palm oases traditionally experience occasional flooding by "sheet flow," a
shallow movement of water covering a large area. This kind of flood did not harm the palms and
carried away debris that added to the fuel load for fire. Although NPS experts blamed the decrease
in the water table on nearby urban wells, the decline in annual rainfall and competition from the
understory vegetation also contributed to the problem.

In 1972, the JTNM released a rough draft entitled "Management Plan for Oasis of Mara" that
included proposals to remove mesquite manually and to apply chemicals to the stumps. The highly
detailed proposal identified a step-by-step procedure for cutting and clearing understory vegetation and debris and for using a careful "burn-a-bush" technique on the mesquite. The proponents

of this laborious project predicted that it would take 172 "man-days" and cost $7,500. The NPS remained hesitant about implementing the proposal. Uncertainty about the history and ecology of the oasis and the glaring public spotlight focused on it made resource managers cautious. In August 1973, the USGS agreed to conduct a hydrological survey of the oasis to inform a final management plan. This required approval from regional archaeological experts, due to the area's cultural significance. Seven months later, regional official Jim Agee submitted data from his historical analysis of the oasis that seemed to show that mesquite was prominent during the Native American period, but it was subsequently cleared by Euro-Americans. Hence, he suggested, the famous picture of the palms standing virtually alone presented an unnatural scene (Plate 36). He warned against any use of prescribed burns until ecologists completed further research.[67]

A few other natural-resource topics received passing attention from 1957 to 1976. Management of fire away from the Oasis of Mara continued on a total-suppression basis, and no major fires occurred during the two decades. A survey of the unit in 1963 reported 208,500 acres susceptible to fire, 29,000 of them on non-federal land. The natural-resource management plan of 1974 proposed a study of fire ecology throughout the varied vegetation communities of the JTNM, citing the 1948 Randolph Fire to justify it. The monument's outline of planning requirements suggested that a fire-management plan be developed, but complacency and an agreement to allow the California Division of Forestry to suppress all fires gave it a low priority. JTNM officials also noticed that smog occasionally obscured the vista at Keys View. As early as 1956, the Public Health Service announced it would monitor air quality in eleven national park units. The closest one to JTNM was Grand Canyon National Park in Arizona. No true desert areas received monitors, despite the fact that JTNM's 1974 resource-management plan recommended a four-year study by university scientists to evaluate the effect of smog, particularly ozone, on vegetation in the monument.[68]

Keys Ranch and Other Cultural Resources

A heightened focus on historical and cultural resources accompanied the sweeping environmental legislation during this period. Two important laws significantly changed the rules for the NPS and other federal agencies: the National Historic Preservation Act of 1966 and President Richard Nixon's Executive Order 11593 in 1971. The first of these strengthened protection of historic and archaeological resources in four ways. First, it established the National Register of Historic Places (NRHP or National Register), a list of structures and sites nominated and approved for legal protection. Second, it created an Advisory Council on Historic Preservation to approve any nomination to the National Register and monitor plans that might affect them. Third, it authorized and funded state offices of historic preservation to monitor, in a similar fashion, sites within their boundaries. Fourth and, perhaps, most significant, section 106 of the act ordered the federal government to evaluate any action's impact on a federal historic property or site receiving federal preservation funds and minimize that impact. So-called "106 compliance" does not mean a structure on the National Register or listed as eligible for it cannot be affected or even removed; it does require consultation by the advisory council and the state historic preservation officer and then a careful recording of all details of design and construction. The NPS administers the national register program.[69]

Five years after the act, historic preservation advocates convinced President Richard Nixon to issue Executive Order 11593. This policy moved federal historic preservation to a proactive stance by ordering agencies to take stock of all buildings, structures, and sites under their control and assess their suitability for nomination to the National Register. Specifically, each agency, including each unit in the national park system, had to provide a list of eligible sites by July 1, 1973. At JTNM, this order shook the staff out of its historic-preservation lethargy and forced it to analyze the monument's cultural resources. Once officials began their survey, they had to follow the tight regulations embodied in the National Historic Preservation Act.[70]

The story of cultural resource preservation at Joshua Tree between 1957 and 1976 includes five separate but related elements: archaeology, museum storage, identification of sites for the National Register, the fate of the Lost Horse Mine, and the controversy surrounding the future of Keys Ranch. During the mid-1950s, the NPS finally addressed the requests for an archaeological survey made by James Cole and Louis Laywood. In November 1956, Superintendent Elmer Fladmark submitted an archaeological base map, derived from piecemeal private explorations and Laywood's survey, and requested funds for more work. At the time, Professor William J. Wallace, of the University of Southern California, was busy surveying the archaeology of Death Valley National Monument. A few months later, the agency's chief of interpretation, Ronald Lee, recommended that a small portion of the $2,500 set aside for the larger monument be used for a cursory inspection of JTNM. In November 1957, Wallace and several others spent three days looking over Squaw Tank, Deep Tank, and the Pinto Basin. Curiously, he dismissed the latter as "disappointing" but also recommended much more research.[71]

While NPS officials discussed a memorandum of agreement for Wallace to conduct a full survey of the monument, two former graduate students from the University of California, Berkeley, requested permission to identify sites for proper treatment by archaeologists at their alma mater. NPS officials told Francis and Patricia Johnston they would have to coordinate with William Wallace. During the next several years, the Johnstons identified a number of sites with petroglyphs or artifacts, which they dutifully reported to JTNM officials. Meanwhile, Wallace and his students excavated sites near Squaw Tank and at Sheep Pass (between Lost Horse Valley and Queen Valley).

Ultimately, Wallace surveyed approximately two and one-half percent of the monument, primarily in the western half, where the dangers of vandalism and theft were greater. Later in the decade, Joshua Tree contracted for two more site-specific surveys, with George Kritzman at Indian Cove and Dennis O'Neil at Barker Dam.[72]

By 1969, enough archaeological work had occurred at Joshua Tree to warrant an overview and a plan for further research. This resulted, in part, from the heralded acquisition of much of the material still in the possession of Elizabeth Campbell on July 15. Regional Archaeologist Leslie E. Wildesen began her research plan by formally acknowledging that Joshua Tree had been established to preserve biological elements from both the Mojave and Colorado Deserts. She followed with a statement of archaeological significance that enumerated three themes, the period of early man from 9000 to 2000 BCE found mostly in the Pinto Basin, the proto-historic period from 1000 CE to the mid-nineteenth century, and the contact period thereafter. Wildesen then suggested several research proposals, including a complete survey of the entire monument, a comparison of its findings to other desert areas in California, test excavations at Stirrup Tank and Conejo Well, and a detailed study of the road to Cholla Cactus Garden.[73]

Six years later, Thomas King, who later became the senior archaeologist for the Advisory Council on Historic Preservation, wrote an archaeological overview of JTNM, in which he summarized past research, criticized several elements in Wildesen's report, and offered his own recommendations in the form of four questions that needed answers: (1) What brings people to occupy deserts? (2) How do desert people conceptualize space? (3) What are the reasons for and the effects of small group size and mobility? and (4) What are the effects of "marginal" living? He concluded with yet another call for a systematic survey of the entire monument, starting with developed areas and roads. Superintendent Homer Rouse admired the expertise King brought to the study but posed a question that often follows research at national parks: Of what use is the study for managers? He found little that could be translated to an agency form to request funds for a specific project.[74]

Another aspect in the reports of both Wildesen and King concerned the storage and cataloguing of museum materials, especially the Campbell Collection. The collection included many very old artifacts as well as human remains from the early-man period. Placement of these materials in the maintenance garage bays outraged the archaeologists (Fig. 5.6). Superintendent Rouse bristled at the criticism and accused King of ignoring the new security system and plans to add a proper storage and display room to the visitor center. Nevertheless, every cultural resource inspection or plan decried the situation.

Decisions about the extensive array of materials at Keys Ranch heightened the criticism. In 1974, Donald J. Colville, acting as JTNM's superintendent, answered a demand from the NPS's

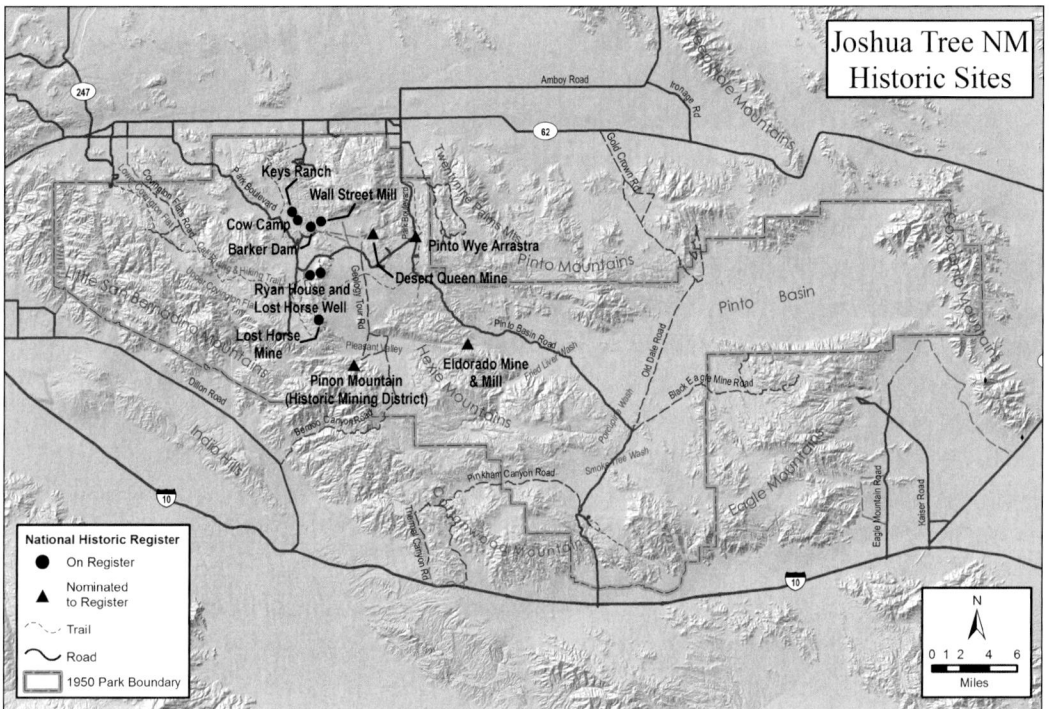

MAP 6.1. Joshua Tree National Monument sites nominated for the National Register of Historic Places by 1983. The Desert Queen Mine area was proposed as an historic district, but only the mine itself was added to the National Register. Data source: Linda Greene, "Historic Resource Study: A History of Land Use in Joshua Tree National Monument" (1983), Denver Service Center, Joshua Tree National Park Library, 471. Delta Cartography.

regional office to explain the location and condition of all cultural-resource items. Although the visitor center had twenty-four cabinets devoted to artifact and specimens, the bulk of the resources were stuffed into bays at the maintenance garage at headquarters plus part of the Quonset hut at Pinto Wye. Furthermore, the staff took the amazing step of burying a "truckload" of metates and other stone relics behind the garage's bays. In February 1975, a visiting preservation specialist suggested that JTNM buy a modular, climate-controlled structure called a "Bally building" for the Campbell Collection, but Superintendent Rouse insisted that modification of the garage bay would suffice.[75]

Historic Preservation

Establishment of the National Register for Historic Places and Executive Order 11593 forced the NPS to locate and nominate qualified historic features. The agency sent specialists from regional offices or other support centers to carry out most of the work. An inspection in 1969 by agency historian Benjamin Levy found the monument's staff enthusiastic about historic preservation, but he cautioned that Superintendent Supernaugh opposed listing some sites such as Ryan Ranch. Nevertheless, in February 1972, historian F. Ross Holland, from the DSC, proposed nine sites for listing, including (1) Keys Ranch, (2) the Ryan House, (3) Lost Horse Mine, (4) Cottonwood Oasis, (5) the Oasis of Mara, (6) Cow Camp, (7) Desert Queen Mine, (8) Wall Street Mill, and (9) Barker Dam (Map 6.1). During the next two years, JTNM and NPS's regional officials collected photographs and added more data on each site to the forms as requested by the Washington, D.C., office. Regional Historian Gordon Chappell submitted the final forms in June 1975. One of the requirements on each form is classification of the structure or site as national, regional, or local in significance. Chappell's forms identified all nine as local in significance, the lowest ranking. After submission of the forms, all nine became eligible for the National Register and, hence, legally protected by the National Historic Preservation Act. During the next seven months, the Advisory Council on Historic Preservation added six of the sites to the register but classified Lost Horse Mine, the Oasis of Mara, and Cottonwood Oasis only as eligible because of issues that might be solved in the future.[76]

The Lost Horse Mine and its mill presented JTNM with problems that often plague historic mines: subsidence, due to collapsed shafts and stopes beneath the surface, and disintegration of above-ground structures, due to weathering, wind, and gravity. During the early 1960s, the mine and mill still looked as if operations had ceased recently (Plate 28). The mine hoist still stood, the ten-stamp mill was intact, and equipment and debris littered the site. It offered a fine opportunity for interpretation, if it could be cleaned up and stabilized. Then, in 1964, Ranger Alsen Inman found nine sticks of dynamite at the 200-foot level with tracks of both adult and child visitors nearby. The dynamite appeared to be at least twenty-five years old. Inman reported that the mine's timbers seemed to be in fair condition, but the ladders were not. Three years later, another ranger, James Lynch, inspected the surface features and found more-serious problems. In particular, he noted that the prominent headframe might soon collapse. At the time, visitors could still drive to the mine. Lynch suggested that the road be closed and the entire mine fenced "to prevent someone from falling onto the sunken grate, breaking through the rotten floor or getting hit by the tower falling."[77] Benjamin Levy and other historians considered the mine a worthy site for interpretation of the mining era and, perhaps, the premier historic structure in the monument, but a storm knocked over the headframe in early 1970, diminishing their enthusiasm for the site as a prime attraction for visitors.[78]

The most controversial site for preservation and interpretation at JTNM was Keys Ranch (Plate 31). The decision to preserve it and its addition to the National Register made it the largest display of cultural artifacts within the monument. In 1973, JTNM officials chose Bill Keys's multi-faceted subsistence complex to be the monument's Bicentennial Celebration site. Officials in the NPS were, by no means, unified in this decision. During the years after the death of his wife, Frances, in 1963, Keys collected ever more castoff tools and equipment, including one entire junkyard, according to a later NPS report. After the old miner's demise, his heirs removed some artifacts and papers of personal value, but the bulk of the material belonging to the estate remained onsite. The NPS failed to provide funds to protect the ranch, but Warner Brothers Studio rescued it, with a $15,000 donation in 1970. A year earlier, the movie company had constructed a life-size replica of the Yuma Territorial Prison in the Pinto Basin and filmed "There Was a Crooked Man," starring Kirk Douglas, Henry Fonda, and Burgess Meredith. Warner Brothers made the donation to thank the NPS for allowing it to film in the monument. The NPS used that money to buy the mining equipment and other materials from Keys's heirs. With the purchase, Superintendent Supernaugh solemnly promised one of the Keys' daughters that the NPS would protect the ranch and interpret it for visitors.[79]

The NPS sent a team of historic-preservation officials to JTNM in July 1971 to inspect several of the potential register sites identified by Benjamin Levy. Team member Dave Clary described Keys Ranch: "If this were any place else, it would be declared a public nuisance and the guy would be made to clean it up; but since it's in a National Monument, we're going to preserve and interpret it." Team leader Glennie Murray added, ". . . any way you cut it, it's a mess—cleaned up there would be nothing to interpret."[80] They called the ranch house a "shack" and predicted its imminent collapse, but admitted that Bill Keys had been an exceptional stonemason, as evinced by a formidable chimney. In spite of this evaluation, the NPS headquarters in Washington, D.C., ordered that every unit in the national park system should develop a site to commemorate the nation's bicentennial. Since the ranch had the largest collection of historic structures in Joshua Tree, it was the only realistic option. In January 1975, as JTNM interpreters prepared the program for the bicentennial, another team of historical specialists, led by Gordon Chappell, visited the ranch to decide its long-term fate. They recommended that the buildings be removed or allowed to disintegrate. This supported the monument's own leaders, who proposed a policy of "benign neglect."[81]

As the Advisory Council on Historic Preservation pondered the ranch's nomination to the National Register, Superintendent Rouse asked for a study to determine its archaeological significance. Keith Anderson, of the NPS's Western Archaeological Center in Tucson, Arizona, recommended Patricia Hickman. Her 1976 report on the Desert Queen Ranch elevated Bill Keys to the status of a regional entrepreneur, competing with nearby towns, operating far-reaching financial links, and shaping the destiny of the desert country. She called for extensive future research to learn the full story of how Keys manipulated the environment and society to gain economic and social control. She also strongly recommended that the site's status be raised to the level of regional significance.[82]

Historians Gordon Chappell and Thomas Mulhern, of the NPS's regional office, vigorously disputed Hickman's conclusions, especially one that called for additional research in order to understand the Bill Keys story. What ensued was a debate between historians and anthropologists over the place of academic versus applied research to satisfy the management needs of the NPS. Chappell challenged the integrity of the materials at the ranch and the purpose of Hickman's report:

> We have Region-wide, historic structures which are falling apart for which we cannot obtain adequate funding merely for structural preservation. Now here we have a proposal for 'long term research' on a property of strictly local significance, research which in the end has no practical application to the Service, research which will lead to conclusions that are of questionable validity due to the lack of integrity of the resource being studied, which can only be funded by the Service at the cost of historic structures elsewhere in the Region, including some of regional significance whereas Keys' Ranch is strictly of local significance.[83]

Regional Research Archaeologist Anderson answered that Hickman's study was well done and exactly what NPS policy required:

> The determination that historical properties contain archaeological (anthropological) information does not require a mindless insistence on preservation of properties as sacred shrines. The value of these resources lies in the information to be gained by their study. In most cases this value can be maintained by leaving the properties alone. Where man or nature is unavoidably destroying them, their values can be preserved by professionally

adequate recovery of data. However, policy and law require that such decisions be made after clear and open discussion, not on the basis of snap judgments, and that they be founded on agreement by professionals and management, not on inflexible resistance by either side.[84]

Ultimately, Anderson's view prevailed. The NPS embarked on a program that included further research, compilation of a list of artifacts, and development of techniques for their preservation and presentation to the public. It is uncertain what impact the diversion of funds to Keys Ranch had on other historic-preservation programs in the region. Hickman also urged the NPS to halt public tours at the ranch, fearing they might displace or damage artifacts. No one at JTNM paid any attention to that idea.[85]

Visitors, Crime, and Interpretation

From 1957 through 1976, annual visitation to JTNM rose sporadically from 320,267 to 748,441. Wet years produced more flowers and drew more visitors than dry years. Interpretive activities increased in number and scope, although they were restricted primarily to weekends and holidays. JTNM officials developed more venues for contact with visitors and new programs to extend their outreach. Vandalism and other illegal activities continued to stress the need for more communication, but insufficient personnel, low funding, and inadequate space limited what the staff could accomplish. The Joshua Tree National Monument [now Park] Association, established in 1962, helped by providing funds for programs and employees to assume some visitor-contact duties. Completion of the visitor center the following year gave the association and the monument's interpreters somewhere to work and to meet the public.[86]

During the next decade, Joshua Tree's few interpretation employees started most of the traditional programs used at other units of the national park system. Rangers erected natural-history signs, provided brochures for four nature trails, conducted winter and spring walks on holidays and weekends, gave campfire talks to groups, spoke to school classes and other groups outside the monument, taught desert-survival programs for the Marines at the Twentynine Palms base, and manned the visitor center daily. When available, they also staffed the new Cottonwood Entrance Station and the Lost Horse Ranger Station. However, some popular activities like ranger-led auto tours had to be cancelled because of insufficient personnel.[87]

Like most units of the national park system, JTNM boasted a select number of popular attractions that drew almost every visitor to these sites, while large expanses such as the Pinto Basin remained little traveled. Most of the popular features clustered between the entrances at Twentynine Palms and Joshua Tree village. Overnight stays in that area's five campgrounds increased much faster than did overall visitation, boosting the numbers of cars and people at those select attractions. The draft master plan of 1971 was an attempt to solve the problem, with its proposed Cap Rock Visitor Center. An "Interpretive Prospectus" accompanied the ill-fated plan and described five themes for interpretation of JTNM: early Native American life, desert ecology, the history of regional mining and ranching, geology, and desert animals. Although the NPS dropped both the 1971 draft management plan and the concomitant interpretive prospectus, the latter gave direction to the interpretation program during the remainder of the decade.[88]

The incidence of non-compatible land uses by the monument's neighbors, including grazing, wood-collecting, and poaching, decreased during the monument's third and fourth decades. Unfortunately, vandalism and crime did not. In 1971, *The Los Angeles Herald-Examiner* carried a story, documenting multiple problems at the monument caused by overcrowding, widespread crime, and an insufficient number of law-enforcement personnel. The report specifically mentioned defacement of rocks, theft of native vegetation, and an attempt to establish a marijuana farm as recent issues. Five years later, JTNM officials reported substantial damage at Fortynine Palms Oasis stemming from periodic overcrowding and vandalism. The NPS blamed young Marines at the Twentynine Palms base for some of the trouble. Base commanders strictly enforced laws and regulations but could not stop ill-conceived activities by off-duty troops. A riot at Stoneman Meadow in Yosemite National Park on July 4, 1970, highlighted the growing need for NPS law enforcement to become more aligned with urban police work. At JTNM, theft, vandalism, and drug infractions demanded law enforcement by rangers with police training. The shift of personnel and funds to law enforcement ultimately drew from the interpretation program. Visitors to JTNM and other national parks and monuments keenly missed contacts with traditional rangers and the programs they presented. Congress anticipated the problem by passing the Volunteers in the Parks Act in 1970, which enabled national parks and monuments across the country to enroll and engage unpaid volunteers, who soon manned visitor centers and entrance stations, allowing the interpretation staff to focus on in-park programs and educational outreach.[89]

In 1973, one of the more-bizarre episodes in NPS's history of law enforcement occurred at JTNM. The coincident rise of the 1960s counter-culture movement and drug use, expressed volubly in rock music, led many people, including musicians, to seek places of retreat. With the enormous entertainment industry in nearby Los Angeles, it followed that some discovered the monument and its assortment of geological and botanical wonders. Musician Gram Parsons, a member of The Byrds and founder of the Flying Burrito Brothers, particularly enjoyed the Cap Rock and Wonderland of Rocks areas. He visited the monument with Chris Hillman, another former member of The Byrds, Keith Richards of the Rolling Stones, Michelle Phillips of the Mamas and the Papas, and others from the contemporary music scene. He reportedly said:

I spend a lot of time up at Joshua Tree in the desert, just looking at the San Andreas Fault. And I say to myself, "I wish I was a bird drifting up above it."[90]

Unfortunately, on September 19, while staying at the Joshua Tree Inn, he died from a drug overdose at the age of twenty-six. Two days later, maintenance employees at Joshua Tree noticed smoke in the air near Cap Rock. What they found burning was the body of Gram Parsons still inside his casket. For several days, news reports speculated on how his body had gotten from Los Angeles International Airport (LAX), where it was due to be flown to a cemetery in New Orleans, to JTNM, 100 miles to the east.

As it turned out, Philip Kaufman, the singer's road manager, and Michael Martin, a personal friend, had convinced authorities at LAX to release the body to them. They hurried to fulfill a wish made by Parsons a few weeks earlier. He had told Kaufman that he wanted to be cremated and have his ashes scattered at Cap Rock. Although a court fined Kaufman and Martin $300 each, many in the music world congratulated the singer's manager for honoring his friend's wish. Subsequently, the NPS downplayed the incident and refused to acknowledge it in the interpretation program. In recent years, former Chief of Interpretation Joseph Zarki and consultants reviewing the unit's history program have urged officials to add the story to its interpretation. The NPS continues to resist, although it has allowed occasional ad hoc concerts at Indian Cove to honor the unit's musical heritage. The concerts have raised public awareness of both the singer-songwriter and Joshua Tree National Park.[91]

A Bad Report Card

During the final weeks of the successful campaign to establish wilderness in the monument, the Western Regional Office sent a team of experts to perform a "management assessment" of the unit and its staff. The survey team, headed by Regional Chief of Operations Gustav W. Muehlenhaupt, tried to be diplomatic and offered effusive praise whenever possible, but, overall, its 1976 report was a damning document. The team offered seventy-three recommendations, sixty-four of them the sole responsibility of Superintendent Rouse. Team members did not blame Rouse for all the problems but identified budget and staffing shortfalls and the cumulative effect of many years of inadequate operations.

At the time, Joshua Tree National Monument had five divisions reporting to the superintendent: administration, maintenance, interpretation, protection, and lands. The worst situation concerned natural resources, which the protection division managed in addition to its responsibilities for law enforcement, visitor safety, search and rescue, and fire protection. The management team repeatedly stressed the need for a separate resource-management division with its own budget and attached letters in the appendices, further arguing for immediate action. Other problems included the lack of a master plan since the *Mission 66* update in 1964, serious deterioration of roads, poor signage on trails, inadequate staffing in the protection and interpretation divisions, and the absence of safety and orientation information at Joshua Tree village, where more than half the visitors entered the unit. JTNM had weathered intense opposition, enormous land-acquisition needs, a major loss of territory, and minimal attention from senior agency officials. It had survived for forty years, but those problems had taken their toll.[92]

FIG. 7.1. The Center for Arid Lands Restoration is one of several notable accomplishments in natural-resource management by Robert ("Bob") Moon. He took over as a one-man Resource Management Division at Joshua Tree National Monument in 1981 after a report from the National Park Service's regional office in San Francisco decried the lack of coherent ecological care being provided by the monument's law-enforcement-oriented Protection Division. In short order, Moon secured funds, hired other specialists in the management and care of natural and cultural resources, established the highly successful nursery to produce native plants for revegetation, and, ultimately, drew the boundaries for the expansion of the unit that took place in 1994. Photograph by the author (original in color), January 2014.

CHAPTER SEVEN

Joshua Tree Enhanced, 1977–1996

JOSHUA TREE NATIONAL MONUMENT (JTNM) began its fifth decade faced with multiple problems in addition to those identified in the 1976 management report. A 1978 Statement for Management identified suburban encroachment, danger from abandoned mines, disruption and crime by Marines stationed at a nearby base, deteriorating roads, increasing air pollution, and potential development on remaining private inholdings as major concerns. A year later, in response to a system-wide survey request by the House Subcommittee on National Parks and Insular Affairs, Superintendent Rick Anderson added trespass by off-road vehicles, vandalism, invasion of exotic plants, and noise from low-flying military jets as well as artillery at the Marine base. Five major problems needed research, reevaluation, and action: Control of the land and water sources remained insecure in many areas of the monument; a lack of overall vision and coordination hampered planning and development; natural resources faced growing threats without an organized staff to study, much less manage, them; cultural resources received little attention from an overworked and understaffed interpretation division; and, finally, as visitation dramatically soared, physical damage from crowding at popular attractions and vandalism increased. Unfortunately, adequate funding to correct these problems seemed unattainable.[1]

In spite of these problems, JTNM's staff accomplished much between 1977 and 1996 to correct deficiencies and put Joshua Tree on solid management footing. Initially in these efforts, they continued to receive grudging attention and periodic criticism from some officials in the regional office in San Francisco and national headquarters in Washington, D.C. Yet, by the 1990s, JTNM enjoyed leadership by particularly capable superintendents and key additions to staff who started new programs in the management of natural and cultural resources, which finally brought respect and more funding from regional officials. Changing perception of the desert by environmentalists and legislators also led to a campaign that upgraded the unit from a national monument to a national park and added land that brought the total acreage back to ninety-six percent of its original 1936 total. From a somewhat disgraced national monument in 1977 to a popular national park in 1996, Joshua Tree began to resemble the vision Minerva Hoyt had for her beloved desert.

The Long Campaign: Land Acquisition

After the establishment of the Joshua Tree Wilderness, agency land officials continued to pursue the remaining non-federal lands in the monument. A 1977 National Park Service (NPS) survey showed that the agency controlled all but 11,470 acres in the monument, more than 7,000 of them in low-risk ownership by the State of California. The highly critical management consultation report had virtually nothing to say about the land acquisition program.[2] Furthermore, the remaining years of status as a national monument began auspiciously with the purchase of forty-five tax-delinquent properties from a more cooperative Riverside County on October 20, 1977. Most of the parcels were located in the Pinto Basin and ranged from five to twenty acres in size.[3] Nevertheless, a follow-up inspection by the regional office found problems with monument-based realty specialist David C. Hemstreet's program. Review team leader William E. Weidenhamer found Hemstreet too rigid or timid in pursuing some possible purchases. Several property owners offered to sell their land but held firm to prices higher than Hemstreet believed the parcels were worth. In some cases, the difference was only five or ten percent higher than what the NPS offered. Weidenhamer reported that one owner offered sixty acres for $54,000, but, for three years, Hemstreet refused to go above $49,500:

> I thought we should have purchased it. I don't believe we are buying many 60-acre tracts at Joshua Tree nor do I think it would set a precedent. Even if it did, if we could buy the whole project for only 9 percent over our appraised amounts, it would be a good deal the way land is escalating in California.[4]

Superintendent Rick Anderson vigorously defended Hemstreet, claiming that the property was located in a subdivision within the monument's boundary and that he, rather than the land officer, should be blamed for the slow progress there. Nevertheless, three months later, the regional director transferred all further responsibilities for land acquisition in Joshua Tree to his office in San Francisco.[5]

During the next fifteen years, land acquisition in JTNM continued at a slow and sporadic pace. The major achievement of the period concerned the same subdivision where Hemstreet balked at paying more than the government price. In the late 1950s, a group of investors purchased a section of land they named "Whispering Pines" just inside the northern boundary of the monument and accessible from the unpaved road to Covington Flat. In 1960, they signed a legal agreement to distribute the cost of maintaining a mile of road from the Covington Flat Road to their development. In order to prevent trespass and protect their properties, they erected fences and a locked gate on their road as well. The agreement could only be rescinded by a vote of the owners of the majority of the acreage in the subdivision.

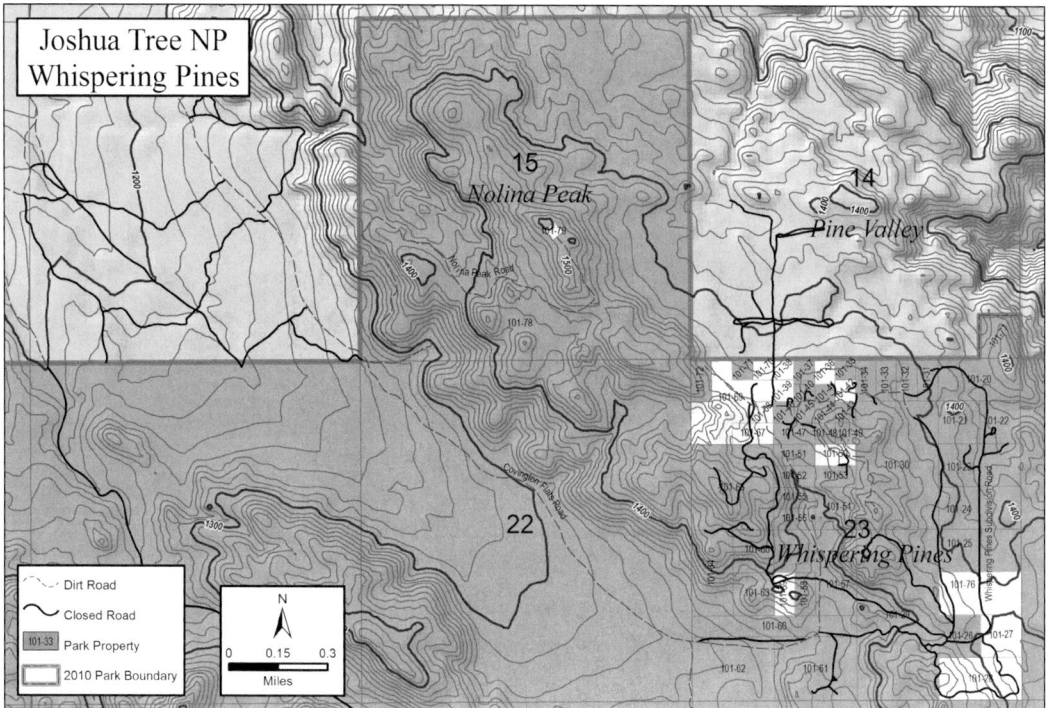

Map 7.1. The Whispering Pines development brought land purchasers and some home-building to Section 23 inside the northern boundary of Joshua Tree National Monument. The Pine Valley Association then purchased land in Section 14 outside the boundary, but access was blocked by rough terrain in adjacent Sections 11 and 13 and, first, to private and, then, National Park Service (NPS) ownership of Nolina Peak in Section 15. For decades, owners of the Pine Valley subdivision fruitlessly petitioned to cross over the monument's land from Covington Flat Road and Whispering Pines, which the NPS refused because of the precedent it would set. Eventually, the NPS bought out most owners in Whispering Pines, and the plan is now moribund. Data source: Pacific West Region (WRO) Land Resource Program Center. October 20, 2009. "Revised Joshua Tree National Park Land Status, Segment 104."

The NPS did not initially react to this intrusion into the monument as it did with those proposed for areas near the main road to Hidden Valley. Some of the owners in Whispering Pines built recreational homes, but problems arose by the late 1970s. Access to the Whispering Pines area proved more expensive than the owners had predicted. Heavy storms washed out not only the private road, but occasionally the Covington Flat Road. While the NPS struggled to grade and repair its road with limited funds, the subdivision's owners found their property inaccessible from time to time. Many of them, particularly the ones who had not yet built on their lots, decided that their best course was to sell to the NPS. Even those who had homes in the area were not averse to selling to the government, if they could retain rights to use the property after the sale.[6]

At the same time, another group calling itself the Pine Valley Association bought the section of land immediately north of Whispering Pines (Map 7.1). The Bureau of Land Management (BLM), known as the General Land Office prior to 1946, sold this land outside the monument to the association's members. Access to Pine Valley, however, was more difficult. The area lay to the east of Nolina Peak and also faced rugged terrain on the east and north. The only feasible routes for vehicle access to the area were over the private road from Whispering Pines or from a maintenance road to a radio tower on Nolina Peak and then through private property. The owners at Whispering Pines and a lawyer named Parker, who held the eastern flank of the mountain, steadfastly refused to allow access. For more than twenty years, the association sought a solution, appealing to both state and federal legislators for relief. One owner even graded an illegal road from government property in Whispering Pines, only to have the NPS force him to remove it and rehabilitate the route. For years, the group tried to convince the agency to allow an access road through the monument to their private land outside its boundary. NPS solicitors argued that allowing such access would set a bad precedent for the entire national park system and refused. Superintendent Anderson met with its representatives in October 1978 and encouraged them to execute an exchange with the BLM for accessible land closer to Joshua Tree village. Yet, eight years later, nothing had changed, perhaps due to the inferior scenic quality of the government's land.[7]

At Whispering Pines, the 1960 agreement held up NPS's acquisition of the tracts from willing sellers. The government could not acquire land with legal caveats such as the fencing and road maintenance fees. Hence, on April 25, 1979, the NPS executed a court-approved declaration of taking and acquired 475 acres of the subdivision. A number of the owners received retained rights agreements allowing them to stay for periods of eight to twenty-five years. Although registered as a condemnation, the action allowed the government, as the new majority owner, to dispense with the agreement's requirements, as the NPS acquired property from willing sellers. The plight of the Pine Valley owners remained a problem, even after JTNM expanded to include Nolina Peak immediately to the west. Elsewhere in the monument, the NPS purchased a scattered batch of properties, including a few from the Metropolitan Water District of Southern California (MWD), but these added fewer than 600 acres from private individuals and another 480 from an April 1980 exchange with the California State Lands Commission. Once again, a lack of funding stymied agreements between regional land officials and willing sellers. Under President Ronald Regan's administration and President George H. W. Bush's administration of the 1980s, the NPS could only purchase land from owners who could demonstrate a financial need to sell. Otherwise, the agency apologized to willing sellers and offered hope that more funds might appear in the future. As proponents of the California Desert Protection Act that would vastly expand Joshua Tree gathered support in early 1994, more than 10,000 acres of non-federal land still existed in the monument.[8]

Water Rights Again

Diminishing water resources continued to be a problem in Joshua Tree, despite the expiration of several historic water rights. At Black Rock Canyon, the NPS signed a water-conservation agreement with the Hi Desert Water District, which supplied the town of Yucca Valley. In the rest of JTNM, only the well near Cottonwood Campground provided a reliable source of water for visitors. The establishment of wilderness over most of the Pinto Basin highlighted a growing problem connected to Kaiser Steel's use of the MWD land around Pinto Well #1. Residents of the Eagle Mountain town used the property as a staging area for driving illegal off-road vehicles within the wilderness. The monument had too few rangers to patrol the huge roadless area and blamed employees of the mine for ignoring the law. The issue prompted NPS officials to reconsider the company's water rights as well as the validity of the MWD's inholding. Superintendent Rick Anderson raised the oft-asked question: Did the district have the legal right to sell water to Kaiser? He wanted closure on the Pinto Wells problem, and he wanted that doorway to illegal use by off-road vehicles absolutely eliminated. Demonstrating a remarkably resilient optimism, regional office solicitor John McMunn suggested that the water district might wish to donate the parcel to JTNM subject to a special-use permit guaranteeing water in the case of an emergency. Anderson dismissed that idea as unrealistic and focused on condemning or buying the land and water right. McMunn answered that the NPS would probably lose a condemnation case, but a purchase might work.[9]

A few weeks later, in January 1977, Kaiser Steel drew attention back to Pinto Well #2 on JTNM land. Senior Eagle Mountain Mine Supervisors Bob Dale and Dave Wicks explained to Superintendent Anderson that they expected operations to last at least another twenty-five years, and they still needed water to exploit additional ore resources that the company owned immediately outside the JTNM. Kaiser also held eleven claims inside the monument on the northern slope of the Eagle Mountains, but an appraisal in 1974 rated the chances of profit from them as nil.

JTNM officials nevertheless wanted those claims eliminated, and the company saw an opportunity. Eagle Mountain Mine manager John Englund offered to trade the 193 acres encompassed in the claims for permission to use Pinto Well #2 water. In 1971, the U.S. Congress had passed Public Law 91–383, establishing a policy whereby water and other resources within a national park unit could be secured by outside users under a set of strict conditions. The user had to prove (1) that the resource would be available to the general public, (2) that no other viable source existed, (3) that it was essential to his or her operation, and (4) that it would not lead to a future dependency or increased demand. Legislators extended the law in 1976, and it became a permanent part of NPS management. Unfortunately for Kaiser Steel, the law prevented JTNM from agreeing to the deal, because the company could not show that its use would benefit the general public and that it had no alternate sources of water.[10]

During the 1970s, Kaiser Steel tried and tried to get more water from JTNM, while keeping its own financial condition secret from the NPS. During that time, the company began to shift employees and their families away from Eagle Mountain to Desert Center, thirteen miles away. In order to support resettlement, the company increased its procurement of water from wells in the Chuckwalla Valley. But, at the same time, the international iron and steel business evolved in ways that hit the company hard. Demand for steel from its Fontana plant steadily dropped, due to competition from foreign countries. In 1981, Kaiser Steel announced that its operations at Fontana and Eagle Mountain would close. The company subsequently laid off its workers and closed down the town of Eagle Mountain. And there it was. Suddenly, the problem of the Pinto Wells appeared to be over. Still, Kaiser held on to its mining claims, water infrastructure, and access roads, while the MWD still refused to return its property and water right to the monument.[11]

Planning and Building a Better Monument

With so many problems with operations and resource protection before them, the staff at JTNM needed to generate a series of carefully wrought plans regarding transportation and development programs, natural and cultural resource programs, an interpretation prospectus, and studies of visitor use to address the monument's many shortcomings. The 1976 management consultation report had much to say about the infrastructure at JTNM. Although the investigators found most of the *Mission 66*–era buildings in good condition, their assessment of the roads was grim:

> The park has eighty-three miles of paved roads, of which seventy miles are deplorable. Thirteen miles of park road have been, or are in the process of being, reconstructed. The remaining seventy miles of road were never constructed but evolved over the years from graded roads to

the present state by a matrix of surface treatments and patches on top of patches. Generally road surfaces are rough with raveled edges in many sections.[12]

The inspection team recommended that the superintendent apply for regional funds to reconstruct the entire seventy miles of bad road. By 1978, JTNM had a plan to rehabilitate several roads but accomplished little. During the next six years, monument crews repaired specific problem spots on the recently recalculated eighty-four miles of paved roads, but only thirteen miles were adequate. The remainder averaged eighteen feet in width with soft, sandy shoulders and occasional sharp curves. Erosion breached sections whenever storms occurred. Funding remained scarce, and the project promised to be an expensive one.

A reprieve came in 1982, when Congress passed the "Surface Transportation Assistance Act," which provided money for upgrading roads in the national park system.[13] Two years later, the NPS completed a transportation study at Joshua Tree with help from the Federal Highway Administration (FHA). The transportation study team recommended that the NPS and FHA widen most of the roads to between twenty and twenty-six feet and add paved shoulders, apply three inches of asphalt to all the substandard areas, improve drainage, realign some sections to halt erosion and ease sharp curves, and add or expand parking areas. It recommended a program of steps through fiscal years 1985 to 1990 to accomplish all the work. Many of the components of the plan would be expensive, especially the control of erosion and damage from flash floods. The team also identified seventy-six miles of unimproved roads but offered no recommendations. A few years earlier, Riverside County had notified the NPS that it would no longer maintain the Gold Crown Road (Old Dale Road) in the monument or the Berdoo Canyon Road outside JTNM's boundary. NPS officials happily accepted this news and agreed to keep the former for four-wheel-drive vehicles only.[14]

Throughout the rest of the 1980s, work proceeded on the roads, though not at the pace hoped for in 1984. During that time, JTNM and Denver Service Center (DSC) officials continued to study traffic patterns, parking needs, automobile accident statistics, and other data. By 1989, they decided to redesign completely the transportation system through the Hidden and Lost Horse Valleys. Several problems were apparent along the route. Large recreational vehicles bogged down traffic as they tried to negotiate sharp turns, and more than thirty accidents per year endangered visitors and resources. In addition, congestion and other problems beset all of the intersections with spur roads to campgrounds or attractions such as Keys View and Barker Dam (Plates 10, 11, and 24). NPS planners proposed three options to redress the situation. One would further widen the existing east–west road, which would heavily affect the area's Joshua trees. A second would convert the existing road to one-way traffic and pave two dirt tracks to the north known as the Queen Valley and Barker Dam Roads to handle the vehicles going the other direction. This option

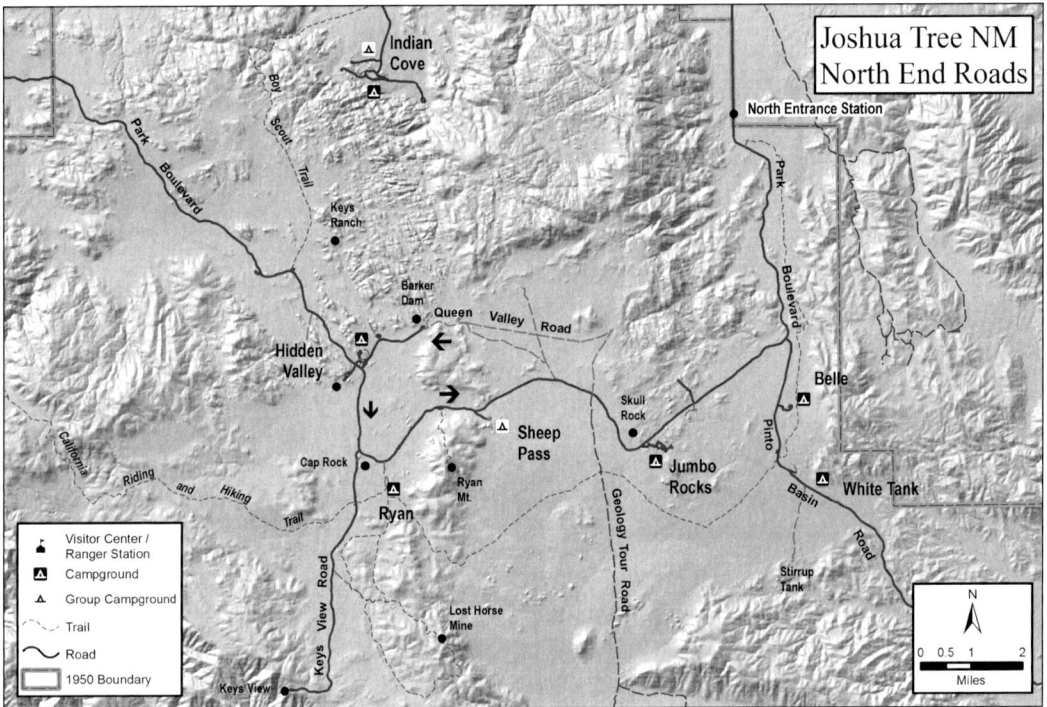

MAP 7.2. Heavy traffic and occasional accidents led National Park Service planners to consider paving the dirt tracks called the Barker Dam and Queen Valley Roads and converting the resulting loop into a one-way route. Ultimately, opposition from rock climbers, environmentalists, and others concerned about the need to remove scores of Joshua trees scuttled that proposal. Instead, road engineers paved the Barker Dam Road, maintained the two-direction flow, and limited large vehicles on some segments. Data source: "Environmental Assessment Reconstruction of Park Routes 12 and 13 and Associated Visitor Use Areas" (August 1991), Joshua Tree National Park Library. Delta Cartography.

soon became known as the Loop Road (Map 7.2). A third option was a combination of the first two, which kept more of the existing paved road designated for travel in both directions.[15]

During the next three years, the NPS conducted multiple onsite inspections and brought in a variety of consultants to assess potential damage to vegetation, desert tortoises, archaeological resources, and visitor safety in an intense effort to identify the best solution. Initially, the NPS preferred the one-way loop, even though this meant extra mileage and driving time for visitors who would want to access a site a short distance away but in the wrong road direction. The obvious benefit of this option was that none of the roads would have to be widened, which would save on maintenance, speed up traffic, and protect the Joshua trees. Both environmental groups and rock climbers opposed this. Local environmentalists preferred the Queen Valley and Barker Dam segments as quiet, slow, dirt roads with relatively little traffic. Rock climbers, who congregated at the nearby Wonderland of Rocks, feared congestion, parking problems, and threats to their activity, if the northern route became a major highway in JTNM.[16]

In August 1991, the DSC released an environmental assessment of the new preferred option for JTNM. This time, NPS planners offered to pave the northern roads but keep them narrow and one-way, while creating a mix of one-way and two-way segments for the rest of the loop. They also proposed to widen the road to Keys View and add a number of new parking lots. In November, JTNM officials held two public hearings on the plan, which met substantial opposition. At the same time, letters of opposition began appearing, some channeled through members of Congress. Eventually, the JTNM recorded 251 letters that corresponded with public statements at the two hearings. Seventy-five percent of the respondents opposed the preferred option primarily because it meant paving and realignment of the Queen Valley and Barker Dam Roads. Only five percent favored that option. Most people wanted more parking but opposed large, intrusive parking areas. To cope with large recreational vehicles, some suggested banning them from certain roads, including the one to Keys View. Almost everyone professed alarm at the idea of removing nearly 500 Joshua trees, which might be necessary under some options.[17]

After this reaction, JTNM planners initiated another round of inspections and studies to modify all the roads west of Pinto Wye. A consulting firm, Traffic Engineers, Inc., released a report in June 1992 that supplied important new information. First, traffic had increased over the previous year by almost ten percent. A solution would have to be found soon. Second, traffic on the northeastern part of the loop, Queen Valley Road, was one-sixth of that on Barker Dam Road on the northwestern part. It might not be necessary to pave all of it. Third, large vehicles made up a much smaller percent of the total traffic than originally estimated. This favored the idea of limiting vehicles on certain roads rather than widening the roadbeds. Fourth, the parking lots had reached capacity, and more would be needed. Finally and most telling, a one-way loop road would not improve the situation.

After digesting this information and pondering the public reaction, the NPS chose to pave the road to Barker Dam, keep the rest of the northern half of the loop unpaved, and reconstruct most of the other roads at the same width. JTNM workers also paved some of the rough parking lots. They still had to remove Joshua trees but replanted some of them in other locations.[18]

In the 1976 management report, a few aspects of the trail system in JTNM were criticized, but the tone was less severe and the recommendations less daunting. The inspectors merely suggested a few adjustments in the routes to combat erosion and improve signage, especially on the California Riding and Hiking Trail. Still, the public wanted more designated trails, and JTNM officials tried to comply. An organization called the Desert Trail Association, supported by the California Recreational Trails Committee, proposed an all-desert trail from Canada to Mexico that would pass through JTNM. Superintendent Anderson informed the group that he would approve the planned route across Pinto Basin, Smoke Tree Wash, and Pinkham Canyon, because it would be entirely cross-country. The association subsequently established segments of the long-distance trail in Oregon and northern Nevada, but the route through JTNM remained a vague plan through the rest of the period, leading to the boundary change in 1994. During this period, the NPS added one significant hiking route, called Lost Horse Trail. It covers a 4.5-mile loop from the site of the mine of the same name. The town of Desert Hot Springs proposed a combination hiking and horse-riding trail through the western edge of the monument and various other suggestions came from the Coachella Valley and the town of Yucca Valley, but the NPS postponed any further action until completion of a general management plan.[19]

From 1977 through 1996, the NPS added three significant structures to the aggregate of buildings in Joshua Tree as well as several offices and quarters at Black Rock Canyon, Cottonwood, and Pinto Wye. The agency finally built an entrance station on the road from Joshua Tree village, answering another criticism in the 1976 report. In 1985, it constructed a nursery for native plants at headquarters (Figs. 7.1 and 7.2) to supply vegetation for rehabilitating disturbed areas. Finally, after a widely publicized threat to remove JTNM's archaeological treasures, including the Campbell Collection, the monument built a museum storage building and library (Fig. 7.4), with up-to-date technology to preserve objects, documents, and appropriate literature in 1993.[20]

Bob Moon and the Rise of Resource Management

Completion of the Leopold and Robbins Reports thirteen years earlier and Secretary of the Interior Stewart Udall's subsequent order to manage the parks and monuments accordingly began the transition to more professionalism in both resource management and law enforcement throughout the national park system. High-profile parks such as Yosemite and Sequoia in California reorganized and hired resource specialists and on-site scientists fairly quickly, but other units lagged behind and

continued programs with law-enforcement rangers, some scientifically untrained, responsible for
natural resources. The 1980 "State of the Parks Report" to Congress reiterated the problems that
stemmed from the grudging implementation of scientific management, including insufficient funding
to hire trained professionals, inertia, intransigence among senior park or monument officials facing
changes to traditional procedures, and unwillingness among division chiefs to relinquish control of
programs and the funding they brought. All four affected JTNM. The 1976 management consultation team's report on resource management began with a flat statement:

> Of the many Natural Resource concerns at the Monument there are some that are critical.
> Man has impacted the natural environment here by competing for water, protecting the area
> from natural fire, introducing exotic species, and simply by being present which affects animal
> behavior and damages fragile native vegetation. Under these current unnatural circumstances
> which cannot be avoided, irreparable damage could occur in the next few years unless enough
> management effort is made.[21]

The inspectors then listed some of the most critical research needs, including provision of wildlife
guzzlers (Fig. 7.3), ecology and management of bighorn sheep, ecology of mule deer, the flow from
the springs and its relationship to vegetation, management of the fan palm oasis, fire management,
and the overall impact of humans.

In the document's appendix, Regional Resource Specialist Francis H. Jacot blamed senior NPS
officials steeped in a tradition of protecting a landscape rather than an ecosystem, and he suggested
the report did not go far enough. After pointing out five more shortcomings at JTNM, he summarized two elements of the problem:

> (1) Research and related efforts are proceeding at a commendable rate at [Joshua Tree National
> Monument], yet implementation and corrective actions at the park level are not receiving as
> great an emphasis as is warranted. To a degree I recognize the Superintendent does not have
> the wherewithal to do this and the basis for this situation rests above and beyond the park
> level; (2) Statements such as to "consider" seeking additional funds and placement of resource
> management above other park priorities and the funneling of existing park capabilities to
> management needs other than natural resources are examples which reflect a prevalent mental
> attitude which is far too widespread in the National Park Service. That is—changes continue
> to be needed which will unequivocally recognize the basic relationship of natural resources to
> natural parks by all levels of management. Only then can we attack the many problems which
> exist in practically every park within the System through more than active vocalization.[22]

Superintendent Rouse tried to defend himself and his staff, claiming that a number of specific problems resulted from delays caused by historic preservation laws and all the effort being poured into planning for the backcountry's management. At the time of the report, Donald J. Colville headed the Protection Division at JTNM, and Herbert D. Cornell served as a resource-management specialist. Robert ("Bob") Moon later stated that Colville reserved the resource-management task for the person he considered the least competent law enforcement ranger. Cornell had no scientific training and faced personal problems that eventually caused him to quit the NPS. Moon added that resource-management officials at the regional office in San Francisco regarded the staff at JTNM as incompetent and unworthy of significant support.[23]

Although JTNM had a resource management plan, ecologist Charles Douglas, of the University of Nevada, Las Vegas, and his students conducted virtually all research on natural resources. The NPS technically employed Douglas and based him at the university through a formal program in which it qualified as a "Cooperating Park Studies Unit." This program evolved from an agreement between one or more parks and a university to one that is now called a Cooperation Ecosystem Studies Unit (CESU) between several federal land-management agencies and universities to support research on many aspects of resource management. Douglas conducted or coordinated a number of important studies at JTNM, but he had other responsibilities, including a portfolio of projects at Death Valley National Monument. At the smaller monument, Cornell suffered from a lack of respect, training, and funds, as he tried to address recommendations by the outside scientists. Three problems hampered funding for resource management. First, according to ecologist Jerome "Jerry" Freilich, most funds for regional research never went past the "Sierra Curtain," by which he meant the glamorous Yosemite and Sequoia National Parks. Second, JTNM's poor reputation at the regional office meant low funding anyway. Third, Chief Ranger Colville diverted some of what money did come for resource management to other programs.[24]

Regional Director Howard Chapman soon appointed Rick Anderson to replace the departing Homer Rouse as JTNM's superintendent. He served fourteen years, which were marked by more criticism of JTNM's operations, but he did execute the transition to a full resource-management division reporting directly to the superintendent, as recommended in the management report. The change centered on the monument's first fully trained ecologist, Bob Moon. When Cornell resigned, Moon was working as a seasonal interpreter, but Anderson asked him to act as liaison to the BLM as it developed its plan for managing California's deserts. He promised Moon that he would create an official natural-resource position and encouraged him to apply. In February 1980, Moon accepted the offer for a part-time ecologist still under the control of the chief ranger. Colville initially refused to have a biologist on his staff, forcing Anderson to complete the hiring process. When the young biologist complained about the diversion of funds away from resource management, Anderson told Moon to report directly to him henceforth, but he left control of funding for resources with Colville. In early 1981, a new inspection from the regional office reported that the antagonistic situation between Colville and Moon prevented progress in resource management. Soon, Anderson received orders to create a proper resource-management division. Moon was given a major promotion and became a one-man division for resource management with his own budget.[25]

Under Bob Moon, both natural and cultural resource management improved rapidly. Regional officials recognized his ability and rewarded him with enhanced funding. After decades of meager funding, JTNM suddenly could get money for almost any natural-resource project. Moon hired permanent and seasonal employees, including the first position entirely devoted to cultural resource management. It was time to get to work on long-neglected programs. Ten issues dominated the natural resource agenda: (1) the need for more basic research and a monitoring program for all natural resources; (2) saving the palms at the Oasis of Mara; (3) a huge demand for native plants to rehabilitate old roads and inholdings; (4) a large-scale invasion of the monument by exotic grasses and brush; (5) worsening air quality; (6) increasingly large wildfires; (7) management of bighorn sheep and maintenance of the guzzlers; (8) protection of the desert tortoise, a newly listed threatened species; (9) coping with exotic animals; and (10) cooperation with other agencies and international programs for environmental protection. As the years passed, extraordinary external threats heightened the complexity and gravity of these programs.

The most obvious need was baseline information about the natural resources of the monument. After more than four decades, the staff had minimal data on all of the ten issues. As quickly as he could, Moon established contacts with university and other NPS scientists, sought research funds and grants for many of the issues identified in the 1974 resource-management plan, and hired trained scientists such as Jerry Freilich to fill permanent or seasonal positions in his expanding division. At the same time, ecologists and wildlife specialists across the country urged the agency to create an official inventory and monitoring (I&M) program at all the natural-resource parks to help gauge large-scale environmental change. In fiscal year 1992, the NPS initiated a programmatic I&M plan in approximately 250 parks, spanning ten major biomes. The expensive program required each unit's staff to prioritize its resources so that the limited funds could be distributed around the system according to greatest need. A revision of the natural resource management plan the following year listed thirty-two projects at JTNM to collect data and monitor resources. Top priorities included the desert tortoise, a basic vegetation map, endangered plants, bighorn sheep, and a geographic information system (GIS).[26]

Back to the Oasis

During the late 1970s, the NPS continued to wrangle with the two critical problems at the Oasis of Mara—an overabundance of infected and dying mesquite and a lack of adequate water for the palms—but new data and a few hard decisions helped. First, in 1977, graduate student Karen Frazier submitted a master's thesis entitled "An Ecological Study of the Fan Palm Oases of Joshua Tree National Monument," which provided welcome geographical, hydrological, and ecological data on the five palm oases: Mara, Fortynine Palms, Lost Palms, Munsen Palms, and Cottonwood Spring. At the same time, Regional Director Howard Chapman approved a revised proposal for the Oasis of Mara to remove mesquite manually over several years until conditions would allow for prescribed burns. JTNM employees laboriously removed two-thirds of the mesquite during the next three summers. In spring 1978, a maintenance crew converted a small wildlife drinker at the eastern end of the oasis into a concrete-lined pond. Finally, after a visit from regional resource management official Bruce Kilgore the following year, JTNM officials proposed a major redesign of the hydrologic system to include a 1,425-foot pipeline from the city's water line to the oasis, with smaller feeder lines to each cluster of palms. They also breached a few areas in the wall around the oasis and dug drainage ditches to circulate natural runoff to the palms. Archaeological studies determined where the digging necessary to install this system would not impact cultural resources.[27]

After Bob Moon's appointment, the program to develop a full management plan for the oasis accelerated. In winter 1982, the resource staff tried two small test burns to gauge the results on the vegetation. An arson fire followed a few months later, giving the scientists a larger area to collect data. Moon and fire-ecologist Sue Husari, from Pinnacles National Monument (now Park), submitted an "Oasis of Mara Action Plan" in the final days of 1983. The plan called for restoration of the oasis to its appearance in the 1920s, well after Euro-American influence began. In addition to more research, the plan proposed most of the actions contemplated during the previous decade, including additional manual removal of mesquite, application of herbicide to the stumps, prescribed burning to maintain an open understory, supplemental watering when the water table sank below the reach of palm roots, and removal of barriers to sheet flooding. It proposed to allow natural processes to take over after these restorative steps.[28]

During the next decade, JTNM officials installed the irrigation system, finished clearing mesquite from the vicinity of the surviving palms, planted native species grown in the monument's nursery, redesigned a paved trail to minimize social trails, and planted a demonstration garden between the visitor center and the maintenance facility. After 1986, JTNM executed several prescribed burns up to one acre in size, while a pair of sizeable earthquakes in 1992 further corrupted the natural flow of water and led to greater reliance on the pipeline to bring in city water. In 1996,

JTNM issued a second "Oasis of Mara Action Plan" that approved a scheduled application of irrigation, pruning of mesquite, reestablishment of native understory vegetation, and further human manipulation of the ecosystem necessary to maintain the 1920s tableau.[29]

Other Places, Other Plants

In 1980, the NPS compiled assessments of natural resources for its "State of the Parks" report. At JTNM, Bob Moon investigated damage to the vegetation communities in the monument and found those systems to be in "disrepair." Decades of mining, 200 miles of old roads, impacts by visitors, and invasive exotics disrupted the landscape, much of it in wilderness. Research showed that regeneration of desert plants and their colonization of disturbed areas was extremely slow. Moon and his staff searched the monument for native vegetation to transplant in the damaged zones but had little success. Most of the native transplants died within a year, due to compacted soil, which inhibited water absorption, and competition from invasive exotics. Plants grown from seed failed, because their roots developed too slowly to access water, while suffering browsing by rabbits and other herbivores. Moon checked commercial nurseries for more mature native plants but found few, due to a lack of public demand. Finally, he secured a $5,000 allocation from the regional office to set up a small nursery at JTNM's headquarters.[30]

After considerable trial and error, the JTNM staff worked out methods for raising more mature plants that could survive. One key advance came in the form of pots six inches in diameter and thirty inches deep that allowed the fledgling plants to develop deeper tap roots in a stable soil column. Experimentation with a variety of local plants led to adaptation of pot sizes to fit the requirements of sixty different species. During the springs of 1990 and 1991, the staff planted 1,509 nursery-grown plants along JTNM's roads. A year later, seventy-seven percent survived. By that time, the nursery had expanded to 12,500 square feet, including two greenhouses, and could grow 10,000 plants (Figs. 7.1 and 7.2). The success of this program soon caught the attention of other national parks and agencies. In 1992, the Bureau of Mines approached JTNM's newly named Center for Arid Lands Restoration, seeking help to revegetate abandoned mines and millsites. Eventually, Joshua Tree began supplying Lake Mead National Recreation Area, the Marine base in Twentynine Palms, and even the huge U.S. Army base at Fort Irwin. At JTNM, the addition of new wilderness lands and Superintendent Ernest Quintana's program to revegetate former inholdings and construction borrow pits made the nursery program a very high priority.[31]

Many of the proposals listed in the 1974 Resource Management Plan dealt with vegetation around the remainder of the monument, and all focused on basic research. One result was a reduction in the number of threatened species on the list from twenty-four to ten. Active management of the

FIG, 7.2. The Center for Arid Lands Restoration, as Bob Moon's nursery has become known, now supplies plants to revegetate road cuts, borrow pits, and other damaged lands in Joshua Tree National Park as well as the Twentynine Palms Marine Base, the U. S. Army's National Training Center at Fort Irwin, and Lake Mead National Recreation Area. The long pots allow desert plants to develop roots fully before replanting, which improves their chances of survival. Photograph by the author (original in color), January 2014.

plant communities remained an expensive future task. Yet the intense work at the Oasis of Mara highlighted a problem affecting not only the other oases, but most water sources in the monument. Three species of tamarisk (*Tamarix ramosissima*, *Tamarix chinensis*, and *Tamarix aphylla*), all invasive shrubs from Asia, had moved into JTNM and were outcompeting the native vegetation for water. The story is a familiar one. Gardeners and landscapers imported species of tamarisk to the United States for ornamental purposes as well as erosion prevention in arid regions. By 1960, the plants spread along major rivers of the Southwest to interior desert springs, streams, and washes. Today, it dominates many arid habitats and nearly every drainage system in the Southwest. Tamarisk does not exhibit weedy characteristics in its native habitat, but it is an aggressive invader in the U.S. Its tap roots can grow more than eight feet in one year, and the plants exude salt, which inhibits survival by nearby native species. JTNM rangers began removing tamarisk manually in 1975, but stump sprouting and efficient seed dispersal meant each effort was a temporary solution. A year later, officials started using herbicides to poison the stumps. Nevertheless, a survey in 1985 of the Cottonwood Spring area by George San Miguel found that cutting away eighty percent of the trees still left thousands of seeds on the ground. Sporadic removal and application of herbicides continued throughout the 1980s and, in 1992, became a steady annual program.[32]

By 1986, other exotic plants raised eradication of invasive species to seventh on the priority list of natural-resource projects. Another unwelcome invader was Russian thistle (*Salsola tragus*), widely known as tumbleweed throughout the West. This hearty plant spreads its seeds by rolling across the landscape with the wind. It rapidly colonizes any disturbed ground such as roadsides. Invasive grasses pose a more widespread threat because of the fuel they provide for fires. By the early 1990s, crimson fountain grass (*Pennisetum setaceum*), a popular ornamental in neighborhoods around Joshua Tree, red brome grass (*Bromus madritensis subsp. rubens*), and cheatgrass (*Bromus tectorum*) invaded much of the western part of JTNM. Unlike native bunchgrasses, they form dense ground coverage and fill the intershrub spaces that are typically devoid of native plants, making the surface much more prone to fire. All of these invasive species are aggressive competitors for water, and some are unpalatable to native fauna. They present a major problem for all land agencies in the Southwestern deserts and are the foci of vigorous interagency eradication efforts.[33]

Air Quality Fails Legal Standards

In 1978, Ranger Don Cornell completed a survey of visibility at JTNM, answering a request from the Environmental Protection Agency for a national assessment of Class I values. In his sketchy outline, he identified four sources of pollution: Los Angeles, agriculture in Coachella Valley, Kaiser's Eagle Mountain Mine, and a proposed fossil-fuel generating plant in Lucerne Valley, forty miles away. Cornell also added dust, smoke from fires, fog, and various activities by visitors to JTNM as visibility inhibitors. He surveyed ten areas and found seven suffered "undesirable visibility impairment," including Keys View. The following year, Regional Director Howard Chapman officially protested a proposal before the San Bernardino Board of Supervisors to lower the standard for nitrous oxide to benefit a chemical plant in Trona. Shortly thereafter, Bob Moon submitted a report that identified "integral vistas" in the monument and noted a steady decline in visibility during the previous three years. The increase in smog in JTNM was obvious, but its effect on vegetation remained uncertain.[34]

During the summer of 1983, state and NPS specialists recommended a system of air-quality monitors for JTNM and research on the effects of pollutants, especially ozone, on vegetation. In September, James Bennett, of the NPS's Air Quality Division (AQD) in Denver, contacted the Southern California Edison Company to see if it would cooperate in monitoring air quality in the monument. He drily commented that "there is some evidence that air quality at Joshua Tree National Monument may not be pristine." The following spring, the AQD proposed a study by Dr. Patrick J. Temple, of the University of California, Riverside, to bio-monitor areas in JTNM. At each site, Temple planned to collect foliage and soil samples over one summer to evaluate the effects of pollution. At the end of 1985, he submitted his report, which showed that levels of ozone occasionally reached potentially lethal levels and that squaw bush (*Rhus trilobata*) could be a useful indicator of ozone damage.[35]

A few months later, the AQD informed JTNM officials that a contractor would install an automated air-quality monitoring system at the Lost Horse Ranger Station. Apparently, the program suffered from inadequate supervision, because the agency installed a new monitoring system in July 1987 and warned that any data from before that time was "questionable." Every year thereafter, JTNM requested funds for monitoring and research on the biotic damage from air pollution. In 1991, it appeared that funding for the air-monitoring program at JTNM might end. Superintendent David Moore protested and argued that it should be upgraded to include particulate matter. The looming possibility of a giant landfill adjacent to the monument justified further expanding resources for monitoring and studying air quality. The 1993 addendum to the resource management plan requested $60,000 for monitoring for the next two years, plus another $4,500 to evaluate damage to the squaw bushes. Each year, the deterioration of visibility and measurable amount of biotic damage from pollution increased until 1994, when JTNM administrators routinely reported that the unit had the worst air quality in the entire national park system.[36]

Fire Becomes a Problem

The invasion of exotic grasses and deposition of nitrogen from air pollution in JTNM created a crisis in fire management during this twenty-year period. Native desert plants evolved in nitrogen-poor soils with low-density dispersal. Fires were traditionally small in area, usually less than one acre, and slow to spread. The invasive grasses came from areas with soils richer in nitrogen, and the deposition of nitrogen by air pollution helped them advance into the deserts of JTNM. The first sign of trouble came one year after the staff admitted that a fire-management plan should be developed, despite the fact that state foresters had responsibility for fire control. On Sunday, August 13, 1978, a park technician discovered a lightening-ignited fire burning five acres near Covington Spring. Fire officials from California Division of Forestry (CDF) arrived with a tanker truck within thirty minutes but could not access the fire because of rough terrain. After two hours, air tankers began dropping fire retardant on the blaze. Shortly thereafter, ground crews arrived, and their numbers swelled to more than 200 by the end of the day. At that point, the fire had consumed 900 acres. In the morning, state fire authorities diverted the air tankers to other fires but quickly returned them in the afternoon, when the fire broke through the retardant lines. That day, the fire grew to 2,000 acres. Later, a monument official wrote, "the now disproved myth that fires won't burn in the desert was still holding sway."[37]

As day three began, the fire spread to 3,300 acres and headed toward the Lost Horse Ranger Station and several inholdings with structures. That evening, bulldozers began clearing lines along the advancing front of the fire. Air tankers dropped more than 72,000 gallons of retardant, some of which contained colorful dyes. The fire lines held on the fourth day, but a few hot spots still burned. The fire boss declared the fire out on August 18 after five days. It had burned 6,142 acres of prime habitat for bighorn sheep in an area university biologists had declared one of the most important in the monument. The CDF used fifteen air tankers and six helicopters to drop more than 206,000 gallons of fire retardant. Ultimately, 617 people participated in the suppression effort. Much of the burned area had contained a pinyon pine-juniper woodland. The "Joshua Fire" brought immediate analysis and some recrimination. NPS botanist Thomas Gavin inspected the area five years after the fire and reported:

> At Quail Springs, I saw a 10-15-foot fire line that was constructed next to and parallel to a dirt road. . . . Retardant that has been dropped in the past and apparently did very little to stop the advance of fire, now stains much of the landscape around Lost Horse Ranger Station. No one will debate the loss of "wilderness area values" as a result of past suppression and therefore the need to minimize these losses through planning is critical.[38]

The NPS rejects the use of these visually offensive methods unless absolutely necessary. Fire-fighters, including those working for the CDF, focus on the quickest and safest means to suppress a wildfire. Bob Moon later told a reporter, "I'd rather have a few more acres burn than live with a (bulldozer) trail for 200 or 300 years."[39]

NPS's management guidelines stated that each park unit with vegetation must have a fire-management plan. At JTNM, the need was now obvious. Between 1979 and May 30, 1984, Joshua Tree experienced thirty-nine more lightning-caused fires, four of them more than 100 acres in size, plus nineteen smaller, human-caused blazes. Virtually all of them occurred in the scenic and well-vegetated western part of the monument. On May 31, 1984, a big fire broke out in Lost Horse Canyon and consumed 4,120 acres. Seven firefighters were injured, one seriously. By that time, fire management was a top priority. Moon hired Sue Husari in 1982 to help develop the necessary plan. In February of that year, she submitted a program for pre-suppression responsibilities, including acquisition and storage of fire-fighting materials, employee training in fire suppression, increased aerial reconnaissance after lightning storms, and a station to monitor humidity, wind, and other weather conditions. Although Husari later transferred to Pinnacles National Monument (now Park), she continued to participate in fire-management planning at JTNM. In December 1982, Su-perintendent Anderson forwarded four fire-management "objectives" to the regional director. They reflected the years of research on fire ecology and the expertise of Husari and Moon: (1) allow fire to burn where it has traditionally shaped wilderness ecosystems; (2) eliminate unacceptable environ-mental damage due to suppression efforts, especially in wilderness; (3) establish fire-management zones based on natural fire regimes, land tenure, and public safety; and (4) provide for rapid and aggressive suppression of all fires that do not meet planned objectives.[40]

Three months later, the regional office approved a program of "modified suppression" for nat-urally occurring fires at JTNM. Crews were to continue to suppress fires but use outcrops, washes, and existing roads to limit their spread rather than creating fire lines. They were also to keep the suppression efforts to the smallest area possible and constantly monitor weather conditions to deter-mine when they can let a fire burn itself out. In spite of these advances, it took another nine years for JTNM to produce a complete fire-management plan. During that period, Regional Forester Tom Gavin, fire ecologist Tom Nichols, and an inter-agency fire-management team visited to help design a plan that followed national policy but specifically addressed Joshua Tree's complex assemblage of sensitive resources. Between 1983 and 1992, prescribed-fire crews carried out sixteen burns, including one planned for 1,250 acres in 1987 that escaped to burn 1,615 acres. From 1985 to that year, the monument recorded fifty wildfires, including the escapee. The 1992 final plan, a revision of the management objectives set out a decade earlier, established a fire-management decision scheme and divided the monument into three zones. Zone One covered the main tourist area in Hidden and

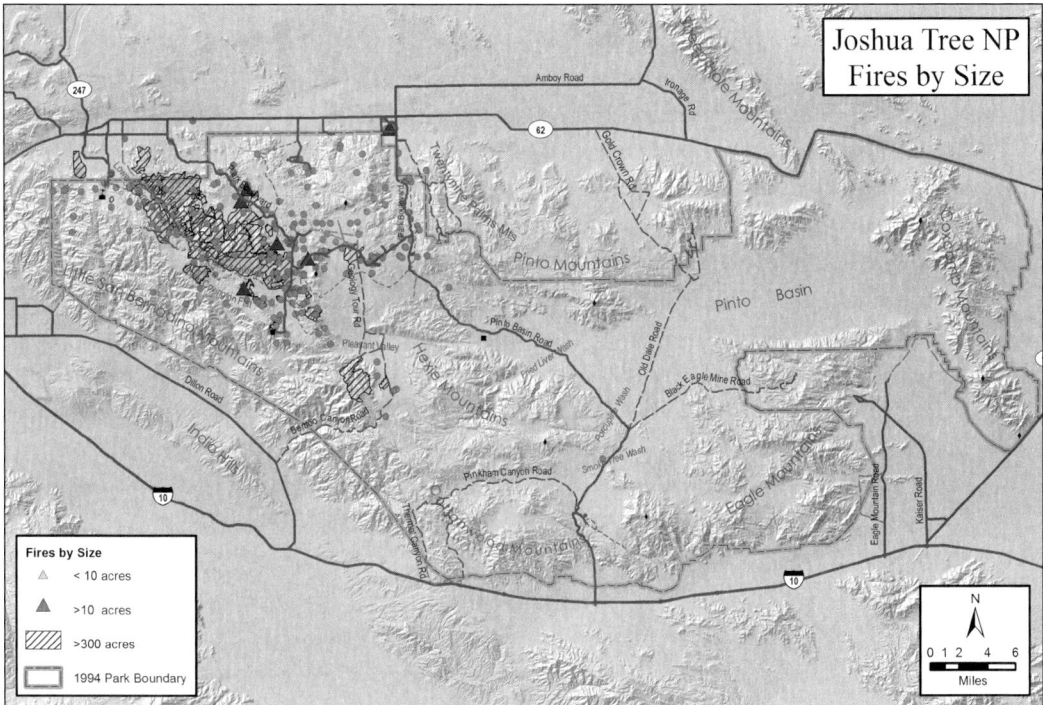

MAP 7.3. The fire history of Joshua Tree National Monument and Park. Predictably, nearly all fires occur in the more heavily vegetated Mojave Desert portion of the unit, especially in and around Covington Flat. Another notable fact is that fires have become larger and more frequent in recent years. This is due, in part, to the deposition of air pollutants that encourage the dense growth of exotic grasses and shrubs. Data source: Joshua Tree National Park GIS files. Delta Cartography.

Lost Horse Valleys plus campgrounds and historic structures where complete suppression was the policy. Zone Three lay near the boundary in the upper elevations above Covington Flat, the most fire-susceptible area, and targeted it for annual ten-acre prescribed burns but strict suppression of all wildfires. Zone Two covered the rest of the unit. There, NPS would continue to research fire behavior and impacts in order to develop a habitat-sensitive framework of responses, including suppression near visitor areas, key resources, and boundaries, and a let-burn policy with occasional prescribed fires under close supervision in the rest of the zone. The mandatory public hearing and other publicity drew no opposition, and the regional office, in its "Finding of No Significant Impact," approved the plan on October 26, 1992.[41]

In early spring 1995, the NPS's fire management officer for the desert region predicted a grim fire season in the upcoming summer. Seven years of drought followed by unusually high rainfall the previous year left a great buildup of fire fuel across the entire region. At JTNM, the trouble started on July 31, once again in the Covington area. This time it spread into adjacent BLM and San Bernardino County lands and ultimately reached 5,521 acres in size. Proximity to the JTNM boundary brought swift and extensive suppression efforts, including twenty-eight ground crews. Multiple air tankers and helicopters dropped nearly 300,000 gallons of water and retardant. By 6:00 p.m. on August 3, when the incident commander certified that the fire was controlled, it had already cost nearly $1,500,000. The only benefit to come from the Covington Fire was the opportunity to monitor the area's recovery and gain new data for future management (Map 7.3).[42]

The Pros and Cons of Bighorn Guzzlers

After the establishment of wilderness over most of JTNM, management of bighorn sheep became more complicated. Mounting but still insufficient scientific data suggested that guzzlers might not work after all, while maintaining them in the wilderness was difficult and time consuming. The hard-won program for guzzlers did not fit the legal word or spirit of the Wilderness Act of 1964, nor did it follow NPS policy that ordered minimum interference in natural processes. In late 1978, Charles Douglas recommended construction of four more guzzlers, including one barely a mile west of Stubbe Spring, but urged more research on the bighorns to determine how much water they actually need. Some studies indicated that a bighorn could go months without water, subsisting on moisture from barrel cacti and other vegetation. Other data suggested that water from guzzlers might inflate the population and deleteriously affect local forage. Periodic checkups on the existing guzzlers found that many soon stopped functioning, due to clogging debris, washouts, or leakage (Fig. 7.3). JTNM officials had used dynamite to blast out the adit in the Coxcomb Mountains. which severely cracked the surrounding rock and rendered it all but useless. Furthermore, bighorn sheep apparently ignored several of the guzzlers.[43]

FIG 7.3. Water is of utmost importance in a desert. Park biologists use a guzzler, consisting of a broad rock face or piece of sheet metal, to direct precipitation or piped water to a catchment tank or trough. Aiding desert bighorn sheep (*Ovis Canadensis nelsonii*) was the primary motive behind this unnatural management tool, but other animals benefited from the water or, in some cases, died upon falling into the troughs. Downhill from the metal sheet, two National Park Service employees conduct repairs. Photographer and date unknown but after 2000 (original in color). Joshua Tree National Park Natural Resource Division files.

Although other resource issues crowded the bighorn's place as the dominant animal subject, research and censuses intensified during the 1980s and early 1990s. Charles Douglas and other scientists tagged and collared sheep and conducted aerial and camera censuses, while pathologists examined any sheep carcasses found in the monument. Rangers monitored working guzzlers with cameras to see if sheep or any other animals used them. During the early 1990s, the Mine Reclamation Corporation, a subsidiary of Kaiser, provided thousands of dollars for research on the bighorns in an effort to placate the NPS, which opposed Kaiser's plan to turn the Eagle Mountain Mine into a landfill. Years of data collected by different scientists with different methods of measurement left unclear how the bighorns survived long, hot drought periods when the few remaining permanent and ephemeral seeps, springs, and guzzlers dried up. An inspection in June 1992 of artificial water structures in JTNM found the guzzler at Stubbe Spring in disrepair, the Pine City guzzler overgrown with vegetation, and the Coxcomb Adit holding minimal water.[44]

The California Desert Protection Act added more than 234,000 acres of land to the upgraded Joshua Tree National Park with three more guzzlers in wilderness or proposed wilderness areas. This coupled with finalization of a general management plan forced the NPS to revisit the question of placing or maintaining artificial features in designated wilderness. The 1994 act specified that the BLM could access guzzlers in its wilderness areas by vehicle but did not explicitly give the NPS equal permission. Investigation showed that the three new guzzlers were ineffective as water sources for bighorn sheep and most other animals. As the NPS began research for a management plan of the backcountry/wilderness, the days of artificially supplied water for bighorns appeared close to an end.[45]

Endangered and Exotic Fauna

Bighorn sheep dominated wildlife research and management until April 2, 1990. On that date, the U.S. Fish and Wildlife Service (USFWS) listed the Mojave Desert populations of the desert tortoise (*Gopherus agassizii*) as a threatened species (Plate 27). The tortoise immediately became the Joshua Tree animal with the strictest legal protection, something the desert bighorn sheep never enjoyed. The desert tortoise is a medium-sized terrestrial reptile that occurs in most of the Mojave and Colorado Deserts. Despite its wide range, wildlife experts noticed a decline in populations throughout the Southwest by the late 1970s. The BLM listed it as a species of concern in its 1980 plan for the California Desert Conservation Area. A variety of direct and indirect threats seemed to cause the fall in numbers. Direct threats included collisions with motorized vehicles, vandalism, illegal collecting, and disease, possibly contracted from pet tortoises released by their former owners. Loss of habitat from construction and agricultural development, recreational activities, atmospheric pollution, and invasion of exotic plants posed indirect threats. Although tortoises will eat exotic plants, they prefer native forbs that contain more nutrients than the invaders. Several native predators prey on tortoise eggs, hatchlings, and juveniles, including coyotes, kit foxes, badgers, skunks, and ravens. Fire can kill tortoises either by direct burning or indirect impacts such as loss of forage and shade plants, encouragement of low-value exotic plants, decreased soil stability, and increased erosion.[46]

John Barrow began serious research in the Pinto Basin in 1978 and estimated tortoise density at seventy-five to eighty per square mile. He concluded that the animal was endangered. In 1987, Alice Karl, a graduate student at the University of California, Davis, began a population study of the entire monument. She estimated that approximately 12,700 tortoises occupied some 250,000 acres of the unit. At that time, a substantial drought was underway, and it may have depressed the number. In 1990, Moon hired Jerry Freilich to carry out a long-term research and monitoring program. Soon, a controversy arose over the sampling methodology between Freilich and BLM scientist Kristen Berry. The latter had dominated the research on the desert tortoise for nearly twenty years. Her study of a one-square-mile plot led to the listing of the tortoise as a threatened species, and her survey method involved daily counts derived from walking through the plot over a lengthy period. Because this method cost so much, Freilich adopted a technique that used multiple volunteers to inspect four-kilometer-long (2.485 miles) lines, forming a box with teams to count the tortoises and measure their distances from the nearest line. Using many volunteers, even though they were not necessarily trained in wildlife biology, turned up considerably higher numbers than Berry had estimated. A bitter debate over the accuracy of the two survey methods ensued.[47]

In the meantime, the NPS adapted its management to match the requirements of the Endangered Species Act. On February 8, 1994, the USFWS classified 6,000,000 acres of Mojave Desert land as critical habitat for the tortoise, including a large area adjacent to the monument. JTNM then joined the interagency Desert Tortoise Management Oversight Group, founded in 1988, along with other desert national parks and monuments. The impact on desert tortoises became a prime issue in all forms of planning at JTNM, including land acquisition, the revegetation program, fire management, and all construction and road-repair projects. A major tortoise recovery plan issued by the USFWS and BLM identified fifteen human activities that were incompatible with preservation of the species. The NPS, in general, and JTNM, in particular, already banned fourteen of them. The only exception was "competitive organized events on designated roads," and speed-limit signs in JTNM took care of that.[48]

As scientific interest and targeted resource-management funds at JTNM grew, research studies identified other rare or endangered animal species that lived within or passed through its boundaries. A survey in 1994 by the staff ecologist listed three reptiles, thirteen birds, and seven mammals in decline. Four of the mammal species were bats, a group of animals that had received little attention at JTNM before 1992. That year, contract-biologist Pat Brown received funds for a two-year study of bats in the mountains around Pinto Basin. The natural resource management plan of 1993 listed bat research on its project agenda for the first time, but, despite the fact that JTNM contained at least 2,000 abandoned mine shafts that it sought to close, no further research took place for the rest of the decade. Other rare animals in Joshua Tree included several predatory birds, the badger, and the Colorado Desert fringe-toed lizard (*Uma notata notata*).[49]

Animals are important resources in JTNM, requiring much attention and research. Unfortunately, exotic animals and misbehaving natives demanded much of the resource-management staff's time and effort. Coyotes continued to beg at campgrounds and wherever else people congregated. Lacing human food with nauseating lithium chloride failed to discourage them. The keen-sniffing relative of dogs simply ignored the bait. In 1987, Santa Monica Mountains National Recreation Area reported that one coyote had attacked some people. JTNM focused on educating visitors, while searching for ways to discourage the beggars. Nothing seemed to work. In 1997, a ranger finally shot one aggressive animal, an action not widely publicized. In 1982, Bob Moon warned that feeding by visitors plus a mild, wet winter resulted in a population of native ground squirrels at Black Rock Canyon that was ten times the hypothesized carrying capacity. He worried that the huge numbers and the rodents' familiarity with humans as a source of food could spread the bubonic plague they carried to visitors.[50]

Four exotic animals also required management's attention. For years, JTNM officials had worried about feral burros that inhabited areas surrounding the monument. Starting in 1980, rangers noticed small groups occasionally feeding inside the boundary, and, in 1982, at least one small herd moved in to stay. Concern for bighorn sheep galvanized resource managers to draw up a management plan for burros and take action. This brought JTNM face to face with an issue that bedeviled other parks in the western United States: Public sentiment and consequent legislation insisted on non-lethal methods to control horses and burros. The scientific and environmental communities solidly backed any solution that would keep out these prolific breeders. Most of the public rejected the most obvious solution: shoot them. In 1984, JTNM officials sent a proposal to the regional office to initiate live capture and removal of the burros. They received a reply cautioning them not to publicize any actions they might take. Finding and capturing the wily animals proved to be far more expensive and time consuming than resource managers hoped. Soon, they petitioned the regional director for funds to track them by plane or helicopter. In 1985, rangers captured five burros near a guzzler and sent them to the BLM's Adopt-a-Burro Program. Ironically, that program had redistributed hundreds of burros to pet enthusiasts, including some living next to Joshua Tree. Thereafter, "due to owner negligence or design," some had escaped into JTNM, primarily across the northwestern boundary near Joshua Tree village and Yucca Valley. In August 1994, JTNM adopted a "Burro Management Action Plan," in which several methods for capture were proposed; but if they proved impossible in individual cases, "direct reduction" (shooting) was an option. The list of conditions for adopting the latter method, however, assured that rangers would rarely use it.[51]

Among the hazardous animals in JTNM are recent invaders from the south. Brazil imported honey bees from Africa during the 1950s, hoping to breed a bee better adapted to the tropical climate. These African honey bees interbred with European bees and then spread north, until they officially reached the United States on October 19, 1990. Africanized bees are fiercely protective of their hive and much more aggressive than European bees. In August 1993, Jerry Freilich reported a large swarm of unfamiliar bees in Twentynine Palms and determined that, despite efforts by some communities to control them, their eradication probably would be impossible. From a resource-management viewpoint, their appearance did not change policy, because the European honey bee was also exotic to JTNM. On the other hand, they posed a threat to visitors and especially to rock climbers. Soon, frightening stories of climbers, who disturbed nests in the rock crevasses and suffered an immediate and painful attack, circulated on the Internet and in guide books. Most of the latter sought to comfort readers by explaining that the bees would only follow a fleeing person for half a mile.[52]

Two unexpected exotic animals appeared in JTNM that illustrated the difficulty of managing a national park unit amid rapid suburbanization. Several dams built by early settlers still held water, except during severe drought. Local neighbors and a few tourists felt that goldfish and domesticated ducks might enhance these ephemeral reservoirs, particularly the one behind Barker Dam. If enough water collected, it allowed the fish to reproduce and grow to considerable size. Ducks meanwhile learned how to avoid coyotes and bobcats and displaced native waterfowl. During the 1960s, a run of dry years lowered the water behind Barker Dam to a level where rangers could capture or shoot the ducks and poison the goldfish with a chemical called rotenone. By 1989, more precipitation and more illegal stocking of fish recreated the goldfish problem. During the first week of December, rangers pumped out much of the water and supervised visitors in capturing the fish, presumably to take home as pets. Thereafter, resource-management officials again poisoned the water and established a policy of waiting one week to see if predators remove any domestic ducks before taking action. When Barker Dam is dry, as it was in 2014 and 2015, these management programs are unnecessary, but easy access has allowed vandals to deface the dam itself.[53]

For most of its history, JTNM operated under a chain of NPS command with little input from state and other federal agencies in the desert, other than reciprocal reviews of proposed plans. Yet JTNM operated in a region, nation, and world focusing more and more on coordinated conservation. The chaos that attended the BLM's California Desert Conservation Plan of 1980 plus a campaign to increase protected areas in the desert required interagency management and recognition

of the monument's place in the world's ecosystem. Interagency cooperation initially focused on specific issues such as those addressed by the Desert Tortoise Management Oversight Group. By 1994,
it appeared likely that a major transfer of land from the BLM to the NPS would take place. Despite
considerable animosity, the two agencies began cooperating on resource-management issues. This
cooperation led to the establishment in 1994 of a major working group called the Desert Managers
Group (DMG), which also included the USFWS, California State Parks, and all four branches of
the U.S. Department of Defense. Subsequently, the U.S. Forest Service (USFS), U.S. Geological
Survey, Bureau of Indian Affairs, California State Lands Commission, California Department of
Fish and Wildlife, California Department of Transportation, and three counties joined. San Bernardino County is a member, but, as of July 2016, Riverside County is not. Working groups within the
organization tackle many of the resource issues that plague Joshua Tree on a regional basis. Major
projects include the desert tortoise, exotic weeds, climate change, illegal dumping, restoration of
habitat, and even land acquisition. Each agency retains individual authority over its territories but
benefits from vastly increased communication and expertise. Unfortunately, budget concerns and
different priorities among member agencies have hampered participation in this ground-breaking
effort at cooperation in resource management.[54]

Prior to these interagency projects, the international conservation community recognized the
importance of California's desert, including JTNM. Scientists and diplomats gathered at a United
Nations Educational, Scientific and Cultural Organization (UNESCO) conference in 1970 and
organized a "Man and the Biosphere" program to coordinate research and management of representative terrestrial and marine ecosystems of the world. Each biosphere reserve contains one or
more core areas of strict legal preservation, such as a national park, a buffer zone of compatible
land use, and a transition area of agriculture and other uses. Eventually, the system is meant to
include examples of all the world's biomes and spread the knowledge and practice of sustainable
use everywhere. An international committee reviews applications submitted by chapters in each
country to assure that the proposed areas meet historical, ecological, and land management criteria.
In 1975, the U.S. committee unilaterally accepted a proposal for the "Mojave and Colorado Deserts
Biosphere Reserve" to include four core areas: Death Valley National Monument, Joshua Tree
National Monument, Anza-Borrego Desert State Park, and the Santa Rosa Mountains Wildlife
Management Area. In 1983, an ad hoc group of scientists submitted the proposal to the international committee that approved its official designation the following year. Recognition of the
region's significance was pleasing but in no way influenced management at Joshua Tree. Although
the NPS has a sign noting its status, a rise in the public's antipathy to internationalism has muted
any other publicity.[55]

The Management of Cultural Resources Improves

Between 1977 and 1996, several new laws and better financial support helped archaeology and historic preservation advance at JTNM. Chief of Interpretation William ("Bill") Truesdell hired Rosalie Pepito as the museum's full-time curator to handle increasingly numerous and complex responsibilities. Later, she became the full-time cultural-resource specialist in the Resource Management Division. Archaeological work increased, while protection for its artifacts benefitted from Native American participation. The Campbell Collection narrowly escaped removal to a facility in Arizona. Several additional sites became eligible for the National Register of Historic Places (National Register). Both the Lost Horse Mine and Keys Ranch presented problems that took technology and extra funding to forestall. By 1996, JTNM had a cultural-resource plan, a small but professional staff, and more funding. Like the natural-resource program, cultural resources evolved from a minor component of the Interpretation Division to a significant program of a large national park.

One of the most important changes affecting archaeology in JTNM was a dramatic increase in participation by Native Americans living in the area. The archaeological remains and rock art of Native Americans in the monument fascinated many NPS officials, but, for much of the unit's existence, they ignored the descendants of the people who left those artifacts. No one in the NPS thought about their presence, unless it affected land acquisition or the proposed location of the headquarters. In 1957, U.S. Marine Corps Sergeant Leonard A. Webber, a member of the Shoshone Tribe from the Fort Hall Reservation in Oregon, briefly drew attention by insisting that he had the right to hunt in Joshua Tree. His claim stemmed from the federal government's 1868 treaty with his tribe, which stated that a member of the tribe can hunt on any "unclaimed land" in the country. Webber interpreted this clause to include national parks. The acting regional solicitor in Portland denied Webber's claim on various technical grounds, including the semantics of the 1868 treaty. During the early 1970s, Native Americans across the country demanded that human remains and other grave objects be returned, only to have the NPS warn its employees about potential "theft" by protest groups. In later years, the activism of the American Indian Movement and other civil rights groups plus legal challenges to the government's haphazard interpretation of its treaties led to laws and court rulings that afforded Native Americans a voice in their own affairs, including their cultural traditions.[56]

Two laws affect the way the NPS interacts with various tribes and protected archaeological resources associated with their ancestors. First, Congress passed the Archaeological Resources Protection Act in 1979, which included three provisions: (1) It gave teeth to the enforcement of the Antiquities Act of 1906 by establishing penalties for the removal or destruction of archaeological sites or artifacts; (2) it mandated a government permit and oversight process for archaeological research on federal property; and (3) it ordered federal agencies to cooperate with museums, groups, or individuals who possessed such artifacts. The purpose clearly was to benefit archaeological science, but its effect was initiation of dialogues with Native Americans who had long claimed that their graves and materials were under siege for profit. A second law, the Native American Graves Protection and Repatriation Act of 1990, specifically addressed those issues by ordering federal agencies and any museum or university that receives federal funding to return human remains and associated funerary items to the descendants of the tribe to which the deceased belonged. Across the nation, every archaeology collection had to contact local tribes and investigate the origins of any human remains. If the claim by a modern tribe proved valid, the remains were returned for reburial with appropriate ceremony.[57]

Passage of these two laws highlighted an increasing legal respect for the remaining Native American tribes and their religious and treaty rights. Amendments a year later to the National Historic Preservation Act in 1992 led the Advisory Council on Historic Preservation to order the NPS to consult with Native American and Native Hawaiian groups and compile a list of their important cultural sites eligible for the National Register. This meant those areas would have compliance protection from Section 106, and tribes could halt random development or destruction of their culturally significant places. The NPS saw the handwriting on the wall even before passage of the amended act and issuance of the advisory council policy. At JTNM, the condition of the Campbell Collection caused serious concern among the Cahuilla, Chemehuevi, Mojave, and Serrano tribes. Assisted by sympathetic anthropologists such as Lowell Bean, they were the first to oppose strongly a transfer of the collection to a safer storage facility out of state. Later, the Chemehuevi, with the support of the other local tribes, claimed the human remains in the collection and reinterred them with accompanying funerary objects.[58]

Progress in surveying the archaeology of JTNM continued to fall well short of what its practitioners wanted. Late in 1977, Superintendent Anderson submitted a draft of a cultural-resource management plan to the regional office. The plan's authors admitted that the monument had been remiss in following the dictates of Executive Order 11593 by not working on an archeological survey of the unit and recommended compilation of data from existing research and initiation of a field survey. Seventeen months later, regional official John H. Davis finally responded and described the plan as "incomplete," suggesting that JTNM continue to carry out surveys "as needed" prior to any road work or other project. In the interim, Anderson had requested funding to expand the archaeologically surveyed acreage of the monument from two percent to fifteen percent. Davis could only answer that he hoped Congress would allocate more money for cultural-resource programs across the national park system.[59]

By 1981, most of the money available for archaeology at JTNM was tied up in surveying the Oasis of Mara before its modification. Two years later, another cultural-resource plan reiterated the same need for a survey, citing JTNM's non-compliance with the NPS's own management policies. Between 1985 and 1989, specialists from the Western Archaeological and Conservation Center in Tucson, Arizona, conducted a number of surveys prior to realignments of the road system in the western part of JTNP. In 1987, Carol Martin, of the center, reported that more than 250 sites had been identified in the two percent of the monument already surveyed. She asked for $56,920 to do sample studies of 150 plots in order to develop a predictive model of where to look for other sites. Virtually all archaeological research conducted over the next several years, however, stemmed from rehabilitation of seventy-five miles of roads in JTNM. In October 1990, the chief ranger reported that 719 archaeological sites had been investigated, and a volunteer had documented the location of an additional 604. They occurred on five percent of the monument's land. He also noted that funds from the Archaeological Resources Protection Act made more work by contract specialists possible, which resulted in a rapid rise in citations for illegal damage by visitors at some sites, including displays of rock art. Some of those cited were rock climbers who defaced the ancient drawings by accident or design. Through the first half of the 1990s, archaeological surveys continued to accompany construction projects, but research on the environmental adaptations by Paleo-Indians and historic tribes, a focus pioneered by the Campbells, also helped clarify the unit's human history.[60]

The 1990 report by the chief ranger also noted that JTNM held more than 120,000 artifacts from archaeological sites and historical structures. By that time, the Campbell Collection had expanded to three bays in the old maintenance facility behind the headquarters. During the previous decade, complaints about storage of the collection had risen to a crescendo. In 1987, Thomas Mulhern, of the regional office, strongly recommended that all the cultural material at Joshua Tree be moved to the Western Archaeological and Conservation Center. With little hope of getting funds for an addition to the visitor center for storage, most of JTNM's staff agreed. Once word of the move leaked to the public, however, the NPS found itself in an unexpected controversy. Not only did the local tribes express outrage, but universities, museums, local towns, and many members of the public in Southern California also blasted the agency for planning to move the materials out of state. Soon, Congressman Jerry Lewis, of California, got involved and secured $187,000 from Congress to build a storage building behind the maintenance garage. The climate-controlled building opened in 1993 and is still crowded, but the Campbell's materials and other archaeological and historical artifacts are finally protected (Fig. 7.4). During this controversy, JTNM secured a position for a museum curator. Melanie Spoo filled that position in 1992 and still managed the facility in 2016.[61]

In 1977, the history program at JTNM also needed more baseline research and preservation, despite the addition of six sites to the National Register during the preceding twelve months. One

FIG. 7.4. The storage conditions for Joshua Tree's museum specimens, especially the Campbell Collection, almost forced the National Park Service to move the artifacts to a secure facility in Tuscon, Arizona. Intense opposition from local tribes, scholars, residents, and politicians resulted in sufficient funding from the U.S. Congress to build a state-of-the-art facility at the Oasis of Mara, so the valuable materials could be properly stored. Photograph by the author (original in color), January 2013.

conspicuous gap was a historic-resource study to identify and provide background information on extant structures, roads, and other artifacts from the years following the arrival of Euro-Americans. The purposes of such a study include identification of any sites worthy of evaluation for the National Register and provision of a general context for preservation and interpretation. Initially, Superintendant Anderson put the study fifteenth on its funding priority list, but, in 1981, the regional director ordered him to move it to the top of the list. NPS historian Linda Greene completed the study in 1983 and proposed four more sites for nomination to the National Register: the El Dorado Mine and Mill, Pinto Wye Arrastra, Eagle Cliff Mine, and Pinon Mountain Historic Mining District. It took another decade for final approval of eligibility for the four new sites, due to sporadic attention by the staff and recurrent editing of incomplete paperwork. In 1992, the DSC sent senior historian Harlan Unrau to evaluate the road system for the National Register. Ironically, he found none of the paved roads eligible because of the realignments undertaken during the previous decade. Unrau suggested that a few of the dirt tracks—including Old Dale Road, Covington Flat Road, and the Geology Tour Road—might be eligible, but no nominations followed.[62]

In addition to the National Register of Historic Places, each unit in the national park system maintains another "List of Classified Structures," which includes each individual building or constructed feature of importance. Hence, while Keys Ranch is a single site on the National Register, every building in it is a separate structure on the more detailed list, and each structure is classified for preservation, restoration, or documentation and removal. A list compiled in 1976 included thirty-four structures at Keys Ranch alone, including outhouses, storage sheds, walls, fences, and pieces of mining equipment. In spite of this substantial number, Superintendent Anderson submitted a list the following year of only twenty-two structures classified for preservation and one, the Ryan Ranch House, for restoration. The latter was dropped a year later after an arsonist's fire destroyed most of it. Since the NPS occasionally acquired private land with structures, Anderson ordered the buildings razed in order to return the areas to a natural environment. He also proposed that preservation meant protection from damage by humans, not normal deterioration from age and weather. This policy of "benign neglect" angered regional cultural resource official Thomas Mulhern, who wrote:

JOTR [Joshua Tree] is a very complicated area and one which we feel has not received all the attention it should have over the years. The move from a seasonal park to year round and the increasing visitation leaves the area with inadequate facilities and staffing. The California desert is the environmental and management challenge of the near future and JOTR is in the center.[63]

He followed this with several dozen comments on the need for specific cultural-resource needs. Shortly thereafter, experts from two national historic preservation programs, the Historic American Buildings Survey and Historic American Engineering Record, visited JTNM specifically to assess and record data on Keys Ranch, the Lost Horse Mine, and the Wall Street Mill. Attention from these national programs further stressed the significance of JTNM's historic structures.

Nevertheless, the three premier historical sites continued to draw most of the preservation attention and funds. In spite of the rehabilitation of Keys Ranch as the bicentennial project for JTNM, the complex still required numerous repairs. In February 1982, *The Desert Trail* urged the NPS to allow interest groups and volunteers from the local communities to help record, display, and interpret the site, but NPS leaders refused to turn over control of the site to the public. More serious trouble came at the Lost Horse Mine complex, which had already lost the headframe and other surface features (Fig. 5.1). In 1989, Mulhern reported the collapse of a stope that created a massive erosion trench twenty-six feet long, nine feet wide, and fifty feet deep. It extended toward the historic ten-stamp mill, the principal interpretive feature left at the site. Six years of worry and correspondence ensued before the NPS provided funds to solve the problem. In 1992, the Lost Horse complex became one of the first places to try out a remote camera system that sent images of the underground timbers supporting the mine and mill to inspectors on the surface. Most of the timbers appeared to be in fair condition, but, three years later, NPS engineers injected polyurethane foam under the mill to stabilize it in spite of concern that it might eliminate habitat for endangered bats. The site is still considered unsafe. The Wall Street Mill, one of the best preserved structures in the monument, initially drew attention, because the NPS considered restoring it to working condition for an interpretive display. As years of inaction passed, the structure suffered from theft, vandalism, and simple decay, until that plan was no longer feasible. Easily accessible in the primary area for visitors, it required much work just to save part of the building and the larger machine components.[64]

More than a Million: Visitors and Interpretation

During 1977, the year following America's bicentennial, 748,441 people visited JTNM. Visitation did not reach that level again until 1986. Thereafter, it increased rapidly, passing 1,000,000 in 1992 and reaching 1,239,982 in 1996. A huge population increase in the towns surrounding Joshua Tree, more troops stationed or training at the Marine base, a surge of interest in rock climbing, publicity from the rock group U2's *Joshua Tree* album released in 1987, and elevation of Joshua Tree to national park status in 1994 helped stimulate popularity. By 1991, the relative paucity of campsites and parking spaces led to reports by the press about overcrowding, danger to resources, and the assertion that Joshua Tree was another park unit being "loved to death." *The Riverside Press-Enterprise* reported that, during cooler seasons, some coastal residents drove to the monument on a Thursday, set up a camp-site for the weekend, and then drove back to work on Friday before returning for the weekend.[65]

In April 1991, Margaret Littlejohn, an NPS employee based at the University of Idaho, con-ducted a survey of visitors in JTNM. She found that foreign travelers made up thirteen percent of the total, while Californians accounted for seventy-six percent of American visitors. Of those, a slight majority were repeat visitors. Primarily, visitors sought out the major attractions in the western part of the unit, and only a bare majority stopped at the main visitor center, because most visitors entered and exited the monument at the western entrance. Interestingly, seventy-one per-cent watched rock climbing, and four-fifths claimed to enjoy it. This would have implications for both general management and planning for the backcountry. Generally, visitors were satisfied with the quality and cleanliness of the unit's roads, campgrounds, and other facilities, somewhat belying the alarmist news reports. According to the survey, the per-capita tourist expenditure was $31.00, which, if extrapolated to the 851,239 visitors that year, equaled $26,388,409 spent at the monument. This unsophisticated formula does not take into account the economic multiplier effect. By 1999, the NPS applied a proper statistical model that showed JTNM contributed nearly ten times that amount to the local communities.[66]

Prior to the establishment of wilderness areas in JTNM, the NPS developed a rudimentary draft plan for the backcountry's management. The 1975 document banned camping within 500 feet of a trail, limited hiking parties to ten persons, and restricted use by stock, except on the California Riding and Hiking Trail. It also proposed a registration system to monitor wilderness use. The NPS already used these rules and procedures at the more popular national parks in the Sierra Nevada. Two months after passage of the 1976 Joshua Tree Wilderness Act, Superintendent Rick Anderson ordered his staff to barricade access by off-road vehicles to any old roads within the wilderness. This first and most obvious step set a strict tone for management of the backcountry/wilderness at JTNM.[67]

A dozen years later, JTNM officials released another draft of their management plan for the backcountry and wilderness areas. That 1988 plan reflected lessons learned at the monument and elsewhere in the national park system. Although only 3,369 visitors camped in the backcountry during the previous year, that number was 300 percent higher than the 1975 total. Overall visi-tation to JTNM had increased by only twenty-five percent. Programs such as Outward Bound regularly used Joshua Tree as a site to train its people. Federal law and NPS policy still banned off-road vehicles in the designated wilderness, but offenders bypassed or climbed over barriers to drive cross-country or on old roads targeted for rehabilitation. It did not help that rangers spent, on average, only four days per month checking the backcountry. The draft plan summed up JTNM policies for use by visitors at that time. Hikers could travel anywhere but still had to camp 500 feet from a trail and could only stay four days at one site. Up to fifteen people could camp together although any group with six or more people had to find a site with no vegetation. Policy on rock climbing allowed manually installed bolts, but climbers were asked "to be ethical, considerate and restrained" in their use. It also urged rock climbers to use chalk that would blend in with the rock faces. Horses, mules, burros, and llamas could be used as riding stock or pack animals on non-wilderness trails and between them and appropriate campsites. The people who brought them were responsible for bringing in feed pellets and carrying out the animals' waste.[68]

Despite the rapid increase of visitors, the interpretation program continued to suffer from understaffing and inadequate funding, and, throughout this period, the Interpretation Division had only three permanent, full-time employees. JTNM's full-time and part-time seasonal employees varied in number from ten to fourteen, but the annual budget for the entire division dropped from more than $180,000 to $154,000 during the Reagan administration. At the same time, the pressing need for law-enforcement rangers to patrol and carry out search and rescue continued to sap funds and personnel. In 1988, the Interpretation Division budget had only climbed back to $164,089. During the 1990s, funding improved, but increasingly the interpreters had to look for outside funding from special-agency programs or private industry grants. In 1991, JTNM received $5,000 as part of a Columbus Quincentennial grant with the Death Valley and Lake Mead National Park units. Once again, JTNM used the money at Keys Ranch.[69]

The following year, Linda Finn, a planner from the NPS's interpretation center at Harpers Ferry, West Virginia, compiled a task directive for an interpretive prospectus for JTNM, a basic plan for the visitor and education programs. She noted that the monument was a difficult place to interpret:

> Not only were park facilities not designed for the current and projected future visitor load, but they are not optimally located for the circulation patterns. To further hinder efforts to provide a good park experience, staffing has not kept pace with demand. In some cases visitor contact facilities have been closed; amphitheater programs have dwindled in number.[70]

This high-level report, coupled with better funding under the William J. (Bill) Clinton administration, helped the Interpretation Division, but its employees relied more and more on external funding. In 1995, one year after becoming a national park, Joshua Tree received $15,000 from Canon USA to train volunteers to help with a survey of water sources and a census of bighorn sheep. The following year, the National Park Foundation awarded $24,160 to support the "Parks as Classrooms" project in Joshua Tree.[71]

As the spotlight on Joshua Tree grew brighter, requests for special activities and law-enforcement problems multiplied. Veteran superintendent David Moore replaced Rick Anderson in 1992 and

FIG. 7.5. The proximity of a major urban center in Los Angeles and a U.S. Marine base in nearby Twentynine Palms, ease of access, rock climbing, camping, and enjoyment of the open spaces and other natural attractions of Joshua Tree National Park bring up to 2,000,000 visitors per year. And with them come societal ills, adding greater demands on rangers and resources for law enforcement. The National Park Service (NPS) relies increasingly on educational outreach within and beyond the park's boundaries to bring awareness of the system to and support from the public. Here, an NPS ranger's patrol vehicle is highly visible in one of the appealing campgrounds in scenic Indian Cove. Photograph by the author (original in color), January 2013.

immediately had to tell the BLM that a motorcycle trip it approved would not be allowed to pass through JTNM and exit via Berdoo Canyon or Pinkham Canyon. The NPS planned to close both dirt roads. The BLM did not seem bothered that the proposed route would pass through one of its wilderness study areas. The following year an editorial with a cartoon appeared in *The Desert Trail*, blasting the NPS for banning so many activities and providing so little for recreationalists. Moore wrote a rebuttal, citing the number of visitors, the unit's obvious popularity, and the reasons why national parks exist. He quoted the NPS's 1916 Organic Act and took a swipe at the newspaper's editors for printing such a piece when they should know better. When Ernest Quintana took over as superintendent in 1994 (Fig. 8.4), he routinely rejected requests for large-scale wedding ceremonies, loudspeaker-broadcast church meetings, and rifle-shooting in the Coxcomb Mountains.[72]

As the area around JTNM grew into a distant eastern exurb of metropolitan Los Angeles, the duties of the Protection Division increased exponentially. Search and rescue required large efforts, drawing in other employees, law enforcement from adjacent communities, and many volunteers. Remarkably, only two or three rangers patrolled the huge area most of the time (Fig. 7.5). Young male visitors often drove too fast, drank alcohol and smoked marijuana, and loudly celebrated in the campgrounds, requiring tiresome warnings from rangers. Many visitors were Marines from the nearby base at Twentynine Palms blowing off steam. JTNM had an excellent relationship with the base commanders, who never refused requests for help, but, throughout the years, a steady percentage of the Marines engaged in antisocial or criminal activities. As the number of troops increased, so did the number of troublemakers. Vandalism defaced historic structures, rock art, and exposed boulders in the heavily visited areas.

More serious crimes also occurred. One of the more bizarre episodes happened in July 1987. A man named Leslie Marr camped illegally near Phantom Ranch in Grand Canyon National Park and received a citation from a ranger. At this, he turned abusive and then violent, leading to his arrest. Marr subsequently skipped the hearing for his offense and phoned a bomb threat to the Grand Canyon's headquarters. On July 12, two California Highway Patrol officers tried to stop Marr for a traffic violation, but he sped away. The officers chased him to JTNM's headquarters, where he crashed through a retaining wall. The officers took cover and pulled their weapons when they heard a shotgun or rifle being loaded. Then, to their amazement, Marr lit a flare and apparently fired several shots that caused a fire to erupt and engulf him. An investigation showed that he had loaded his vehicle with ammunition, propane, gasoline, and matches and planned to use it as a car bomb at the Grand Canyon. Officially, his death was ruled a suicide. Although JTNM rangers were not involved, the episode demonstrated how futile is the effort to separate a national park from society's ills.[73]

Enforcement of drug laws was the most consistent and potentially serious law-enforcement problem at JTNM. Rangers enforce laws against the use of marijuana if it is blatant, but the real problem comes from stronger drugs, especially methamphetamine. In 1987, Chief Ranger D. Paul Henry suggested that half of the Marines at the nearby base had driven or hiked into JTNM to use or sell drugs. At the same time, the Morongo Basin became a landing area for drug smuggling from Mexico by aircraft. During the previous year, authorities had raided twenty-two labs in the area. Joshua Tree offered hundreds of square miles of rarely patrolled land and access for vehicles at sixteen locations. With only seven full-time rangers at the time, Henry worried that this pernicious criminal activity might spread into JTNM. His concern proved prophetic. In May 1991, *The Desert Trail* reported that JTNM had the highest number of drug arrests in the entire national park system. The rangers worked with local police, military police, and the Drug Enforcement Agency to combat the problem.[74]

Other crimes occurred that recalled those that plagued JTNM during its first few years. In October 1996, one hapless poacher had the misfortune of taking a reptile from the park under the watchful eyes of personnel from five federal and state agencies meeting to discuss surveillance operations aimed at stopping that very crime. After years of protection, all national parks and monuments in the deserts of the American Southwest reported a steep rise in poaching of reptiles and amphibians during this time. One other unusual crime from this period occurred in JTNM and has never been solved. On January 28, 1994, someone dug up the grave of Johnny Lang at Keys View and stole his skull and other bones. Bill Keys and others had buried the old miner in 1926, and, for sixty-eight years, he rested in peace. NPS rangers and many others wondered why anyone would commit such a ghoulish crime, but no trace of the missing skull has ever been found. The irreverence of this act along with vandalism, anti-social behavior, and serious crime have become unfortunate byproducts of higher visitation and the weakened role of rangers as interpreters, as they try to communicate the longstanding purpose of the national parks.[75]

The California Desert Protection Act

One impact of the modern environmental movement that evolved during the 1960s and 1970s was a new appreciation for the desert among California's population. Yet, despite the establishment of wilderness areas in both Death Valley and Joshua Tree National Monuments, the NPS remained unenthusiastic about its arid land units. Senior agency officials in Washington, D.C., stubbornly resisted adding another unit in the eastern Mojave Desert and routinely opposed expansion of the two existing national monuments or promotion of them to national park status. Instead, environmental organizations, including the Sierra Club and the Desert Protection Society, convinced Senator Alan Cranston, of California, and his successor, Dianne Feinstein, to carry out one of the most significant preservation campaigns in American history. With the California Desert Protection Act of 1994,

Congress preserved the second-largest amount of land in U.S. history, after the Alaska National Interest Lands Conservation Act of 1980, spearheaded by President Jimmy Carter. The law established Joshua Tree and Death Valley as national parks and added land to both, created the Mojave National Preserve, and converted sixty-nine of the BLM's wilderness study areas to official wilderness, among other provisions. The story of the campaign and its narrow passage by Congress is well told in other venues, but the specific part that Joshua Tree and its staff played is not well known.[76]

By the mid-1960s, California's desert had its supporters among environmentalists and regional residents, but most Americans and even most Californians still regarded it as a difficult and unfriendly place at best and a wasteland at worst. Hence, they allowed or ignored almost any use of the space and resources of the desert. One of the more popular annual events in the Mojave Desert was a motorcycle race from Barstow, California, to Las Vegas, Nevada. Hundreds of riders fanned out over a wide swath of land, roaring over and through any landscape or biotic feature they encountered. As the race grew in fame, the number of machines multiplied and the damage exponentially increased. This began to change in June 1967, when the BLM appointed J. Russell Penny as its state director for California. He was appalled by pictures of the race's area and appealed to the BLM's headquarters in Washington, D.C., for money to study the impacts of the race and how it should be mitigated. He set up an administrative committee to address the issue and, in January 1970, released a report stating that the California Desert would soon be an environmental disaster. Penny's concern and his committee's reports drew the attention of environmental organizations such as the Sierra Club as well as federal lawmakers. The latter proposed bills demanding a sensible California desert plan and a detailed mission statement for the BLM.[77] At that time, the BLM operated under nearly 200 years of land laws aimed primarily at dispensing federal land to the public. Meanwhile, environmentalists led by Peter and Joyce Burk began calling for a Mojave National Park to transfer management of much of California's portion of the Mojave to the NPS. In 1975, the BLM banned the Barstow-to-Las Vegas race because of its environmental damage. This met furious opposition from enthusiasts of off-road vehicles, many of whom could not understand why the government blocked their activities in such a barren and unsettled place.[78]

In 1976, Congress passed the Federal Land Policy and Management Act (FLPMA), which became the organic act for the BLM. It repealed nearly all previous land laws, except for the Mining Act of 1872, ordered the bureau to manage its lands rather than simply distribute them, and included an earlier bill introduced by Congressman Jerry L. Pettis, of California, to establish a California Desert Conservation Area encompassing 25,000,000 acres, one-fourth of the state. The law required the BLM to prepare a comprehensive plan for the new conservation area and study 5,700,000 acres of its desert land to identify areas suitable for designation as wilderness.[79] In December 1980, after intensive study and work, the BLM issued its California Desert Plan. It included a proposal for an Eastern Mojave National Scenic Area in the region where the race formerly took place, but it only recommended 2,100,000 acres as suitable for BLM wilderness. Both environmentalists and off-road vehicle organizations attacked the plan for diametrically opposed reasons. The former found the plan weak and well short of the desert's need for protection. The latter rejected the government's intrusion into the freedom of the desert, its principal attraction for many. Shortly thereafter, Secretary of the Interior James Watt stated his opposition to the California Desert Plan and to environmental regulation in general. Soon, the BLM reopened the Barstow-to-Las Vegas race, while Watt called for elimination of many of the proposed wilderness study areas.[80]

The Sierra Club, Wilderness Society, and other environmental organizations reacted to these setbacks by forming the California Desert Protection League (CDPL), with its mission to seek a bill that would create Mojave National Park, expand and upgrade Joshua Tree and Death Valley National Monuments, and rescue the many wilderness study areas identified by the BLM before Watt could get them eliminated. Led by Jim Dodson, Judy Anderson, Peter and Joyce Burk, and Elden Hughes, the group met with Senator Alan Cranston in December 1984 and urged him to submit a bill that they would develop. Anderson, Hughes, and others then consulted other environmentalists, scientists, and NPS personnel to map boundaries for the proposed parks and wilderness areas and to design a draft bill. At a meeting in February 1985, the CDPL confirmed that the bill should include upgrades in status for Joshua Tree and Death Valley to highlight existing desert resources and to justify adding more lands to improve their environmental management. A year later, on February 6, 1986, Senator Cranston introduced S.2061, as drafted by the environmental coalition. Far and away the most controversial portion of the bill was the proposal for a 1,500,000-acre Mojave National Park. Although less incendiary, the proposals to upgrade Joshua Tree and Death Valley to national parks also met swift opposition from the Reagan Administration, the BLM, and many who lived, mined, or recreated in areas proposed for addition to the monuments.[81]

In his book on the California Desert Protection Act, *California Desert Miracle*, activist and author Frank Wheat uses many pages to explain the ups and downs of the campaign, the intense conflicts over Mojave National Preserve, and the expansion and conversion of Death Valley National Park. The Joshua Tree National Park (JTNP) story is almost an afterthought. Yet it, too, generated conflict not only between those who favored or opposed the bill, but within the NPS itself. Congressman Jerry Lewis, whose district included much of San Bernardino County, strongly opposed NPS's control of any more of the desert. In an effort to undermine any campaign by environmentalists, he announced his intention to introduce a bill in 1984 to reclassify Joshua Tree and Death Valley as national parks but with no additional land. Joshua Tree Superintendent Rick Anderson publicly supported the idea, which drew the immediate and apparently unexpected wrath of Regional Director Howard Chapman. He arrived at the JTNM's headquarters and summoned Anderson, Bob

Moon and several others to a mandatory meeting. Later, Moon described the meeting as a severe dressing down of the monument's staff. Chapman explained the traditional differences between a national park and monument and why Joshua Tree did not deserve park status. The NPS had long avoided publicly ranking its units, but, internally, everyone knew that the acclaimed "crown jewels" of the national park system did not include desert areas. Indeed, Chapman berated Anderson and his staff for even thinking that a "kitty-litter park" could qualify for such status. Years later, he encountered Moon and apologized for that statement. Ironically, as the campaign unfolded, Chapman came to support strongly the California Desert Protection Act, and it cost him his job.[82]

As the CDPL planned its draft bill, Elden Hughes, of the Sierra Club, visited Joshua Tree in 1985 to learn what changes in JTNM's boundary the staff thought appropriate for the future park. He and Bob Moon spread out a map of the original 1936 monument and, relying on Moon's intimate knowledge of the area's physical and biotic resources and the ownership of the surrounding land, chose four areas to add. They sought to complete biological ranges, especially for bighorn sheep, improve management by incorporating external access points used by poachers and off-road vehicles, and reacquire land lost in 1950. The four additions totaled more than 246,000 acres and consisted primarily of federal land, with scattered state and private inholdings and various mining claims of unknown validity. Most of them were federal lands in the mountainous zones excised by the 1950 boundary change (Maps 7.4 and 7.5). The smallest parcel lay in the Pinto Mountains north of the monument and near the entrance road from Twentynine Palms. It consisted of approximately 7,500, acres, of which 600 belonged to the California State Lands Commission. An assessment in 1987 by the regional office estimated that it included 160 mining claims. The NPS later admitted that the area had no particular outstanding resources but merely facilitated management by having the boundary follow mountainous topography rather than invisible section lines of the federal land-division system.[83]

The second proposed addition included the remainder of the scenic Coxcomb Mountains on the eastern flank of JTNM. Every wildlife specialist from Lowell Sumner to Bob Moon recognized that having only the western half of these mountains limited the water available to bighorn sheep and exposed them to hunting and other threats in their natural range. The addition of 82,550 acres to the portion of the Coxcombs already in JTNM also offered to hikers the best opportunity for a true wilderness experience. Furthermore, the NPS had already proposed an eighteen-square-mile portion of the addition as a national natural landmark. The area included 2,240 acres of private land, 2,720 acres of state land, and 107 mining claims. The MWD's aqueduct tunneled under a corner of the addition, but none of these intrusions detracted from the extraordinary wilderness character of the mountains. The Coxcomb addition would automatically become wilderness in the proposal by Moon and Hughes.

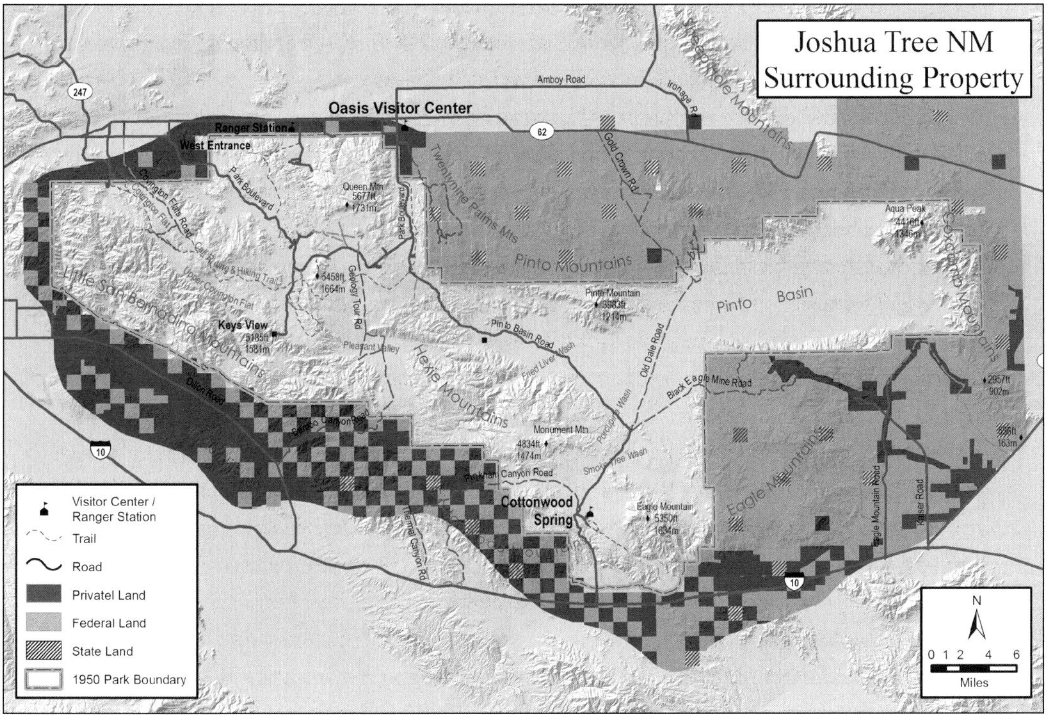

Joshua Tree NM
Surrounding Property

Amboy Road
Ironage Rd
Oasis Visitor Center
Ranger Station
West Entrance
62
Queen Mtn
5677ft
1731m
Park Boulevard
Twentynine Palms Mts
Gold Crown Rd.
Aqua Peak
4418ft
1346m
Little San Bernardino Mountains
Geology Tour Rd.
5458ft
1664m
Pinto Mountains
Keys View
5185ft
1581m
Pinto Mountain
3983ft
1214m
Pinto Basin
2957ft
902m
Quail Mtn
Pleasant Valley
Pinto Basin Road
Old Dale Road
Pinto Wash
Hexie Mountains
Geology Tour Rd.
Old Dale Road
Black Eagle Mine Road
5396ft
1634m
Eagle Mountains
Eagle Mountain Road
Kaiser Road
Monument Mtn
4834ft
1474m
Cottonwood Canyon Road
Smoke Tree Wash
Cottonwood Spring
Eagle Mountain
5350ft
1634m
10
Cottonwood Canyon Rd.
10

Visitor Center /
Ranger Station
Trail
Road
Privatel Land
Federal Land
State Land
1950 Park Boundary

N
0 1 2   4   6
Miles

MAP 7.4. Elden Hughes, of the Sierra Club, and Robert ("Bob") Moon pondered land
ownership around the 1950-era Joshua Tree National Monument to determine possible
additions for a California Desert Protection bill. Despite thirty-five years of openness to
new claims, most of the areas in the Pinto, Coxcomb, and Eagle Mountains had seen little
activity and remained in federal control. One huge exception was the Eagle Mountain
Iron Mine complex, with its town and transportation links southeast of the monument.
The Cottonwood Mountains area also had many privately owned parcels of former
railroad land. Data source: Denver Service Center, May 1994, Map 156/20.017A.
Delta Cartography.

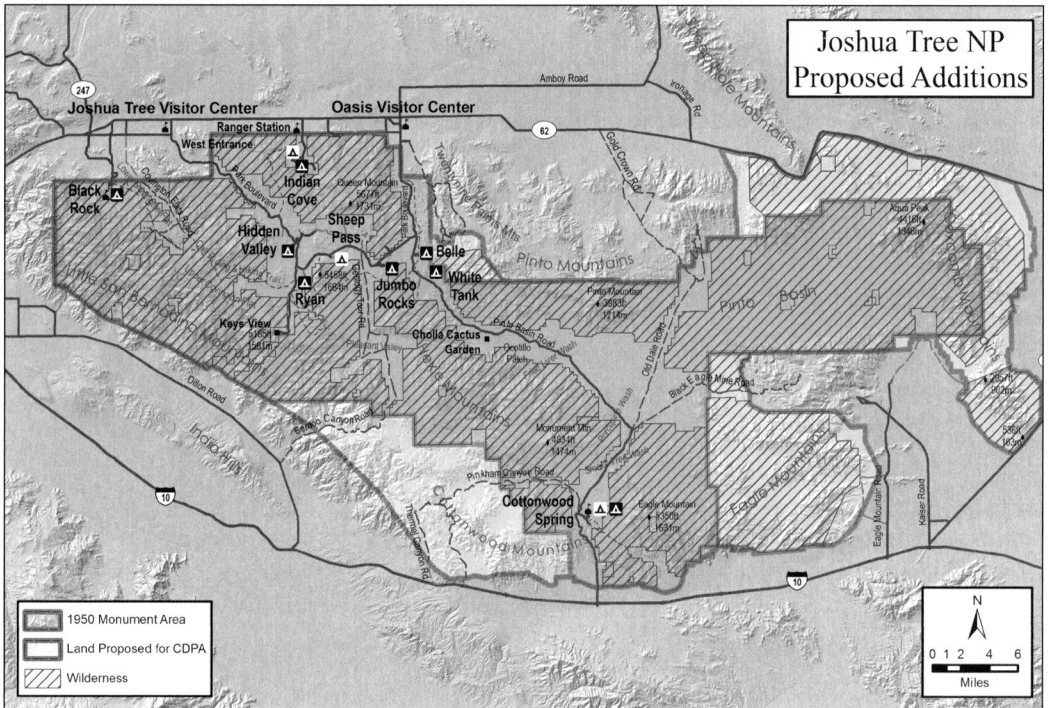

MAP 7.5. The California Desert Protection Act narrowly passed in 1994. It added four areas to a newly named Joshua Tree National Park. The smallest lay not far from the park's main road in the western Pinto Mountains. Two large parcels included much of the mountain land surrounding the Pinto Basin that had been lost in 1950, except for a tongue of land on which the Kaiser Corporation held for its iron mine. Finally, the U.S. Congress added a large swath of the Cottonwood Mountains, in spite of all the private lands. Except for the latter parcel, most newly added land immediately became designated as wilderness. Data source: Joshua Tree National Park GIS files. Delta Cartography.

The third segment to be added lay in the Eagle Mountains south of the existing monument. A substantial portion of those mountains was already in the unit, but a larger portion had been removed in 1950. The 80,400-acre parcel included most of the remainder of that range, except for a broad cherry-stem of private and public domain land under and around Kaiser's Eagle Mountain Mine. The proposed Eagle Mountain addition had 2,560 acres of private land, 3,200 acres of state land, and 475 unpatented mines and millsites. Most of the mining claims occurred near Kaiser's giant operation. The area was visible to hikers inside JTNM and drivers on Interstate 10 to the south of it. Section-line boundaries were unclear and led to off-road vehicle use and recreational mining on JTNM land. Adoption of topographic boundaries promised to ease these problems and improve management of the resident bighorn sheep.

The final proposal for addition consisted of the southern slopes of the Cottonwood and Little San Bernardino Mountains. This 76,000-acre tract promised to be the most difficult to acquire and manage, for it included 36,000 acres of railroad and other private lands in a checkerboard pattern that had been dropped from the original 1936 proclamation of the monument. On the plus side, only twelve mining claims existed, despite the ample evidence of earlier prospecting. Adding such a complex land-ownership problem to JTNM demanded a strong set of benefits to outweigh the disadvantages. This proposed addition revealed a fundamental motive that shaped the Joshua Tree section of the California Desert Protection Act (CDPA) as well as later actions of the NPS in JTNP. The area includes the access points for Thermal, Fargo, Berdoo, and Pinkham Canyons leading into the unit. JTNM's tiny staff could not control illegal use by off-road vehicles and vandalism. Poaching of wildlife and the prospect of major subdivisions on the existing southern boundary also worried the unit's managers. The area had visible scars from these activities that could be seen from Keys View. The threat of incompatible development led the NPS to seek buffers around JTNM in order to protect not only biotic resources, but also the night sky and quietude of the wilderness. The NPS sought this land simply to prevent other uses. Later, as the renewable energy boom swamped the California deserts with solar and wind farms, this motive would spawn aggressive attempts to add more land to JTNP.[84]

The BLM joined many locals, legislators, and Reagan Administration officials in vigorously opposing nearly every aspect of the Cranston bill. The bureau took seriously its new responsibility to manage its lands permanently and strongly promoted the multiple-use management prescription it shared with the USFS. The prospect of losing nearly 3,000,000 acres to the NPS appalled the BLM's California Director Ed Hastey and Gerald Hillier, its desert district director. They saw it as a blatant repudiation of their management philosophy, which it was. After all their work on the 1980 desert plan and the subsequent amendments forced by Secretary Watt and his allies, BLM leaders did not want to sacrifice any land, in spite of the fact that one of their own earlier reports described much of the eastern Mojave as worthy of national park status. Ed Hastey toured the state, convincing local politicians that their areas were better served by his agency. Inyo County became the first to pass a resolution opposing the bill. Soon, San Bernardino and other counties followed. Even the Twentynine Palms Chamber of Commerce, a traditional ally of JTNM, opposed the bill. Meanwhile, the Washington, D.C., office of the NPS ordered Regional Director Howard Chapman to have his staff study the proposal encompassed in Cranston's bill. In January 1987, Chapman approved a report that supported all purposes of the bill. This was more than new Secretary of the Interior Donald Hodel was prepared to accept, and he ordered NPS Director William Penn Mott to reject the report. Shortly thereafter, Howard Chapman retired under a cloud of antagonism from the secretary's office.[85]

After Hodel rejected the report, the NPS agreed to work with the BLM to reach some type of compromise. The acting director wrote a memorandum stating that the NPS was prepared to scale back the lands it wanted to 1,162,080 for Death Valley and 156,500 for Joshua Tree. At the same time, off-road vehicle organizations, hunters, and mining groups sensed victory and intensified their well-funded legal and publicity campaigns against any transfer that would "lock Californians out of their public lands." The BLM studied the new NPS proposals but then, as the "lead agency" in this planning effort, unilaterally issued an environmental impact statement entitled "The Monuments" in April 1989. It spelled out the bureau's preferred option to transfer a total of 108,574 acres to the NPS, almost entirely around Death Valley. The only addition to JTNM would be a 4,480-acre fragment of the Eagle Mountains proposal that held a small portion of the Pinto Basin. That land had been proposed in a failed 1983 bill to transfer BLM land adjacent to national parks and monuments to the NPS. As ordered by the Reagan and George H. W. Bush administrations, there was no mention of a Mojave National Park. Gerald Hillier and his staff curtly dismissed the remaining segments proposed for Joshua Tree, calling them "alternatives considered but rejected from detailed consideration." According to the report, the Pinto Mountains parcel had too many mines, which meant there must be enough minerals to offer future mining opportunities, the rest of the Eagle Mountains parcel should remain a wilderness area under BLM management, and the Cottonwood Mountains area contained too many private lands. BLM planners added that its Palm Springs Office could better manage the Coxcomb Mountains from the east. Elsewhere in the report, Hillier's planners justified their dismissal of an addition of land in the Funeral Mountains to Death Valley, because it would split management of a herd of bighorn sheep. They conveniently ignored the NPS's rationale that it needed the eastern flank of the Coxcombs to avoid a similar split in the bighorns' management.[86]

Reaction from environmentalists was swift and scathing. Upon viewing a draft of the environmental impact report, Elden Hughes told *The San Bernardino Sun* that "to say this document has fully addressed the situation is like erecting a pup tent in downtown Los Angeles and saying we have fully addressed the homeless situation."[87] The NPS might have reacted in the same way, except that political forces intervened. First, the Reagan and Bush administrations deeply opposed the bill introduced by Cranston, which had broad support from Democrats. Successive secretaries of the interior ordered the NPS to support officially a countering bill introduced by Congressman Jerry Lewis to enact the changes suggested by the BLM. Bob Moon later described the frustration local NPS officials felt, as the BLM repeatedly ignored their opinions and data. In addition to top-level opposition, Joshua Tree and Death Valley faced unexpected criticism from their own regional director, Stanley Albright. In later interviews, both Moon and former superintendent David Moore reported that Albright and the BLM's Ed Hastey were old friends and former classmates. Albright was sympathetic to his friend's plight, as environmental organizations pilloried the bureau over its management of desert lands.[88]

Senator Cranston's original bill never made it out of the U.S. Senate's interior committee, but he continued to fight for the desert's protection. Joined by Congressman Mel Levine, he reintroduced the same basic bill in 1987 and 1989 only to have them meet similar fates. Each time, however, the bills picked up more co-sponsors. In 1991, Congressmen Levine, George Miller, and Rick Lehman introduced H.R. 2929. It reflected efforts to placate some opponents by reducing the amount of wilderness and changing the designation of the Mojave unit to national monument which would allow hunting. Congressman Lewis submitted his BLM-sanctioned bill, and the two political parties quickly lined up behind their preferred versions. Senator Cranston, in his final days in government, aligned with his Democratic colleagues, while California's other senator, Republican John Seymour, vowed to do all he could to defeat the larger bill. Democrats who dominated the lower house defeated the Lewis bill and passed H.R. 2929. Seymour's opposition killed it in the Senate. Then, in the federal election of 1992, the Democrats gained the White House under President William J. (Bill) Clinton and both U.S. Senate seats in California, as Dianne Feinstein defeated Seymour and Barbara Boxer replaced Cranston.[89]

On January 21, 1993, Feinstein introduced S.21 to establish Mojave National Park, vastly expand Death Valley, convert seventy-four of the BLM's wilderness study units to designated wilderness, upgrade the two monuments to park status, and add approximately 234,000 acres to JTNM. During the ensuing twenty-one months that negotiations continued, vitriol flew back and forth between environmental groups and "wise-use" advocates, and various other stipulations became part of the growing bill, some of them completely unrelated to California's deserts. Congress held hearings, both chambers submitted reports, and slowly the complicated bill evolved into an act that barely garnered enough support in both the House of Representatives and Senate. On October 31, 1994, President Clinton signed the bill, enacting a law that protects 9,400,000 acres of desert habitat. A petulant Congressman Lewis tried to limit the NPS's budget at Mojave National Preserve to $1.00 the following year, but he harbored no apparent ill will toward the two enlarged and upgraded national monuments. Joshua Tree became a national park of nearly 790,000 acres, with the addition of all four of the parcels Bob Moon and Elden Hughes had proposed. Complex issues with delimiting the boundaries, acquiring private land, and adapting the new areas to the park's purposes lay ahead, but Joshua Tree had passed a huge threshold in its long struggle to be recognized as a major unit of the national park system.[90]

The General Management Plan

Planning was always a difficult issue for Joshua Tree. The variety and severity of threats plus under-staffing and contention between senior NPS officials and JTNP managers dragged out every planning procedure. Over and over, the regional office rejected plans outright or sent them back for extensive modification. One important document that Joshua Tree needed was a general management plan (GMP) that laid out goals for policy and development for all aspects of the unit during the ensuing ten to fifteen years. The last document of that type for JTNM was a *Mission 66* update written in 1964. A GMP would incorporate existing knowledge and coordinate or modify more specific plans. The public would have considerable input, as mandated by the National Environmental Policy Act, and it would become a legal policy document ranked fourth in importance behind presidential and congressional acts that established and amended the unit, the 1916 Organic Act of the NPS, and the NPS's system-wide management policies.

Throughout the late 1970s and most of the 1980s, the NPS thought about, discussed, and debated the need for a GMP at JTNM without accomplishing much. In 1977, Superintendent Anderson submitted an outline of planning requirements, listing issues and goals with the simple comment, "I certainly hope we are on the right track."[91] In 1980, he sent another package of information to the planners at DSC, who would actually develop the plan. On September 15, 1989, nearly a decade later and after a series of delays and other planning projects, the DSC finally issued a task directive for a GMP/development concept plan with an environmental assessment for JTNM. The directive named Mary Magee as team leader and predicted two years to complete the plan. After inspection trips, her team met with JTNM officials in December to review its progress. During the few months of work, the budget for phase one of the plan dropped from $50,000 to nil and then crawled back to $12,000, certainly a troubling sign. The planning team pondered a wide variety of topics, including even the introduction of private concessions into JTNM. Prominent issues for debate and decision included JTNM's carrying capacity for visitors, the impact of rock climbing,

Native American input into planning and management, ongoing problems with roads and parking lots, and inadequate space for offices and housing.[92]

Despite this promising work, four major problems bogged down general management planning at Joshua Tree: (1) repeated personnel changes on the planning team, with consequent delays; (2) interruptions in funding; (3) public debate over the proper use of the backcountry; and (4) the need to incorporate new lands added to the unit by the CDPA. In October 1990, the DSC issued a second task directive modified slightly to account for the previous year's information. A year later, it issued another one after Don Tiernan became team captain for the project. In March 1992, the DSC released a fourth iteration. Each of these was essentially a brand new start.[93] On January 27, 1992, Superintendent David Moore complained about the low priority given to JTNM by DSC officials:

> I have cooled off considerably since last week in regards to the progress of the General Management Plan for Joshua Tree National Monument. It seems that each time we try to get this plan on track and set some timetables for completion of tasks, another roadblock seems to come out of the Denver Service Center ... I thought that after the comments made concerning GMP needs by the Operations Evaluation team in October 1991, Joshua Tree National Monument would receive some special consideration. We also felt there would be some stable goals toward accomplishing the GMP in the next two years. Now I am informed ... since Joshua Tree is 10th priority for a GMP in the Western Region, and 16th overall by the Denver team, that members of our team are pulled to satisfy goals of other higher priority GMPs.[94]

Plodding progress continued. In April 1993, Moore wrote another angry letter about the DSC team. The cost of the plan had ballooned to $427,000, and he had just received a call indicating that the team's leader would be changed yet again. Moore had used JTNM funds to send staff members from the monument and specialists from the regional office to Denver in an effort to get the planners moving. He wrote to the regional director expressing outrage at the miserable progress they had made, particularly given the amount of money already spent:

> Each time the park has been requested to do our share or meet our deadlines, we have 100% met these objectives. The team from Denver switched members often, and when they sent new people to JOTR, we gave them a park overview and tried to bring them up to speed. ... You have heard me complain, and I have discussed our problems with other members of your staff, and they report that this is not an unusual case.[95]

Moore attached the latest agenda issued by the Denver team that predicted completion of the plan in another fifteen months.

In July 1994, the planning team and its new captain, Elaine Riddout, finally released a draft GMP with an environmental assessment for public review. It included three alternatives: the NPS's preferred option, a minimum requirements option, and no action. The public had seen earlier concept-drafts, attended hearings, and reacted according to their ideas and preferences. The regional office and other specialists had reviewed the draft repeatedly through its formation and offered many comments and suggestions. This draft incorporated compromises and new information gathered during the long planning process. Shortly after the latest round of public input began, the CDPA passed, expanding Joshua Tree's size and making it a national park. The NPS quickly revised the draft to include a record of public input and a strategy for managing the new lands. Rock climbing and other uses of the recently enlarged wilderness areas created enough heated debate to initiate work on a completely separate plan for the backcountry. The final GMP, without the backcountry portion, appeared in May 1995. Four months later, Regional Director Stanley Albright issued a record of decision officially adopting the plan. Thirty-one years had passed since the last master plan, fifteen since the NPS began collecting data, and six since the first task directive.[96]

From 1977 to 1996, there was improvement in every aspect of Joshua Tree's management as a national monument and park. As the new millennium approached, JTNP staff continued to improve the unit's planning, resource management, and services for visitors. Yet old problems and new threats within the park demanded ever more money, more personnel, and greater attention. At the same time, JTNP officials faced grave threats from external development, threats that again challenged the very purposes of the unit.

CHAPTER EIGHT

New Threats to the New National Park

AFTER PASSAGE OF THE California Desert Protection Act (CDPA) in 1994, the staff at Joshua Tree National Park (JTNP) has faced new lands, new responsibilities, and growing threats. Since that time, Joshua Tree has evolved in four distinct ways. First, the sources of funding, including operational base budgets, National Park Service's (NPS) allocations for projects, external grants, and recreational fees charged to the park's visitors have all increased, improving operations. In addition, several land trusts have acquired many of the inholdings, both old and new, and donated them to the park. Second, the NPS made significant and long-overdue advances in natural resource management in response to internal and external criticism and resulting legislative and policy changes. JTNP and other units in the national park system finally seem to have elevated science to the primacy the Leopold Report called for decades earlier. In pursuing a model developed by businesses, however, NPS leaders demand ever more accountability in terms of reporting, compliance, and documentation as well as foundation reports, management projections, and mission statements. This has caused the work load to expand faster than the incremental increase in the park's personnel. Third, tourists have increased in number, and their profile has altered. These changes require enhanced protection of resources, improved public communication, and more law enforcement, while increasing the economic impact of the park on surrounding communities. Finally, internal and external threats have placed JTNP in the greatest danger it has seen since the change in the monument's boundary in 1950. Park officials have adopted radical new ways to combat them, in some cases jeopardizing their careers. As the park celebrated its eightieth anniversary in 2016, it has become a lonely island of preservation facing seemingly unsolvable threats such as adjacent incompatible land use, worsening air pollution, and climate change. The future of JTNP hinges on the ability of a small staff and its allies in the public to resist these myriad threats.

Land Acquisition: New Needs and New Tools

The staff at JTNP realized the magnitude of the CDPA when it reviewed the park's land status in 1996 (Map D). Prior to the act, decades of effort had reduced non-federal acreage to less than two percent of the 561,000-acre monument, two-thirds of it in low-risk state holdings. The CDPA brought the amount of non-federal acreage to 57,281 acres, more than seven percent of the much larger park, with most of it located in proposed wilderness areas. The amount of non-federal land in the park could have been even larger if the NPS had not acted quickly following passage of the act. The Metropolitan Water District of Southern California (MWD), sensing its imminent passage, applied to the Bureau of Land Management (BLM) in 1993 to gain control of 2,200 acres of land near the Coxcomb Mountains. Half of the land subsequently became part of the park. The BLM rejected the application for that reason, but the utility appealed in March 1995. At the time, surveyors were still determining the final boundaries dictated by the CDPA. According to former Assistant Superintendent Frank Buono, the MWD convinced the BLM's boundary surveyors to exclude the area it wanted, hoping to have that boundary accepted as the legal document required by the act. In fact, the MWD had already built aqueduct-related facilities nearby. The BLM's preliminary map, as influenced by the MWD, incorrectly showed those facilities within the park portion, justifying a boundary that gave the water district land that was supposed to be in the park. Buono urged the BLM to redraw that portion of the map according to the CDPA and submit it before the preliminary version became official. Eventually, the two interior agencies adjusted the final boundary map to correct the mistake. Although the MWD later quitclaimed three parcels containing 106 acres to the park in 1997, it remains a major landholder in the park. In 2009, the MWD still held sixty-six parcels of land, totaling 2,560 acres, within the eastern and southern boundaries of the park.[1]

Fortunately for the NPS, three programs allowed vigorous acquisition of many new inholdings. First, the CDPA provided substantial congressional funds for land acquisition in the three park units and the new BLM wilderness areas. Second, Section 707 of the act ordered the NPS and BLM to prepare lists of land in the parks and wilderness areas held by the California State Lands Commission (CSLC) and public domain land in California that could be exchanged for it. JTNP dutifully prioritized thirty-seven parcels, totaling more than 15,080 acres, on April 12, 1995. Super-intendent Ernest Quintana (Fig. 8.4) listed wilderness sections in the Pinto Basin as most desirable, followed by those in the Coxcomb Mountains and Eagle Mountains. More than two years of intense negotiations followed, as the CSLC slowly identified the federal holdings it wanted and the Depart-ment of the Interior integrated JTNP's land requests with those from Death Valley National Park, Mojave National Preserve, and the BLM's many new wilderness areas. On December 23, 1997, Joshua Tree received title to 12,914 acres. Although the exchange did not eliminate all the state land from the park, it was the biggest land acquisition in almost forty years.[2]

Finally, three land trusts organized to donate funds to the NPS for land acquisition or to buy inholdings and donate them to the park. These programs have been so successful that recent superintendents of JTNP have tried to reclaim some of the land in San Bernardino County lost in 1950. The first to help was the Wildlands Conservancy (WC), founded in California in 1995. The organization purchases land to add to parks and wilderness areas, donates money for a park's educational and administrative purposes, and manages its own system of reserves. The conservancy primarily focused on negotiating with Catellus, the successor to the Southern Pacific Railroad Lands Company, for its vast holdings in and around Mojave National Preserve, but Catellus also held land in the Eagle and Cottonwood Mountains that were added to Joshua Tree. On October 29, 1999, the WC donated 14,239 acres of alternate sections to the park. Then, on June 18, 2002, it gave another 5,440 acres to the park in the same areas. Across both of the Southern California deserts, the conservancy purchased and donated more than 560,000 acres, the largest donation of land for conservation in U. S. history.[3]

The National Park Foundation (NPF) was the second organization to add land to JTNP. The U.S. Congress established the foundation in 1967 to "encourage private gifts of real and personal property or any income therefrom or other interest therein for the benefit of, or in connection with, the National Park Service, its activities, or its services, and thereby to further the conservation of natural, scenic, historic, scientific, educational, inspirational, or recreational resources for future generations of Americans." From September 2006 through December 2007, the NPF bought twenty-five parcels of land, totaling 1,784 acres, from eighteen willing sellers. Although many of the parcels lay in the Thermal and Berdoo Canyons, the foundation also acquired a few long-held parcels in the Pinto Basin.[4]

One notable characteristic of these land-trust programs is that they are content to let each other step up to a particular issue or area, while they focus their efforts elsewhere. The WC donated land to JTNP from 1999 to 2002. Then, the NPF stepped in from 2006 through 2007. At that point, a new group, the Mojave Desert Land Trust (MDLT) began aggressively to pursue inholdings in the three desert national park units. Established in Twentynine Palms in 2005, it has been the primary source of land acquisition for JTNP from April 2009 through 2015. The mission of the MDLT is to acquire land, protect it, and, when feasible, donate it to the national parks. By March 2013, it had acquired 532 parcels within the three parks, totaling more than 23,000 acres. Once again, most of the 4,400 acres donated to JTNP lay in the recently added area west of Cottonwood Spring.[5]

The MDLT also helped acquire land in Whispering Pines. The subdivision is no longer a major problem, although one private owner still has a structure in the area. A fire destroyed several houses and trailers, and the NPS condemned and removed another house for health and safety reasons. Their owners have sold to the trust or are not interested in rebuilding. The owner of the only remaining structure seems untroubled by the NPS's lack of maintenance on the road into the subdivision. Meanwhile, the residents of Pine Valley outside the park continue to search for a way to access their holdings. In 2000, they mounted a challenge to restore what they claimed was once a public road linking their property to the Covington Flat Road in the park. They tried to use Revised Statute 2477, which Congress passed in 1866 to encourage the settlement of the West by developing highways. The statute granted to counties and states a right-of-way across federal land when a highway was built. Building a road could mean as little as repeated use of a route or filling in the odd pothole along the way. Although the Federal Land Policy and Management Act of 1976 repealed the statute, it allowed "existing rights" to continue. Later, opponents of wilderness and preserved lands convinced some counties and states to claim the right to reopen roads they once "maintained," despite later laws that precluded vehicular access. Unfortunately for the people in Pine Valley who had ignored local regulations and codes to build their structures, San Bernardino County refuted their R.S. 2477 claim, leaving them once again at the mercy of NPS's regulations. In 2016, they were no closer to gaining legal access to their property.[6]

Rapid development along CA 62 from Yucca Valley to Twentynine Palms led JTNP officials to seek more land north of the park. One threat was the type of subdivision exemplified by Pine Valley. Another stemmed from energy companies that purchased small tracts of private land around scattered parcels of BLM property. When a company achieved enough territory, it would seek a permit to use the BLM land and develop a solar or wind facility spanning the entire area. Many of these plans included wind towers or other obtrusive structures within the park's viewshed. In contrast to its furious opposition to the CDPA, the BLM is willing to part with the many small, oddly shaped bits of property between the park and the Marine base at Twentynine Palms. In a conversation with JTNP Superintendent Curt Sauer, BLM California Desert Associate District Manager Jack Hamby offered to help transfer all these holdings to the park. Managing and patrolling these myriad little parcels was very difficult and expensive. Sauer politely refused this superficially magnanimous offer.[7]

Instead, the NPS focused on acquiring larger tracts adjacent to the park. Susan Luckie Reilly, a descendent of one of the founders of Twentynine Palms and a former employee at JTNP, offered to donate thirty-five acres of land east of Indian Cove. Although it involved a boundary adjustment, a 1996 amendment to the Land and Water Conservation Act allows the NPS to accept donated lands without an act of Congress, if the acreage does not exceed two percent of the existing unit. Simultaneously, JTNP acquired BLM acreage abutting the Reilly tract to increase the total addition to sixty acres. On August 28, 2003, JTNP published notice in the *Federal Register* of boundary changes, incorporating the Reilly donation, the BLM transfer, and a ten-acre parcel in Pine Valley purchased and donated by the Wildlands Conservancy.[8]

Joshua Tree National Park also seeks land outside its northwestern boundary to help establish wildlife corridors to the Marine base. In November 2000, a coalition of scientists, land managers, and environmental organizations met to plan a system of wildlife corridors in Southern California, linking both areas protected by the government and owned by private citizens. These corridors enable fauna to migrate safely and avoid isolation that can bring inbreeding and susceptibility to disease. One group called South Coast Wildlands formed to identify links from the southern Sierra Nevada to Baja California. In December 2008, the group produced a report that identified eight major links

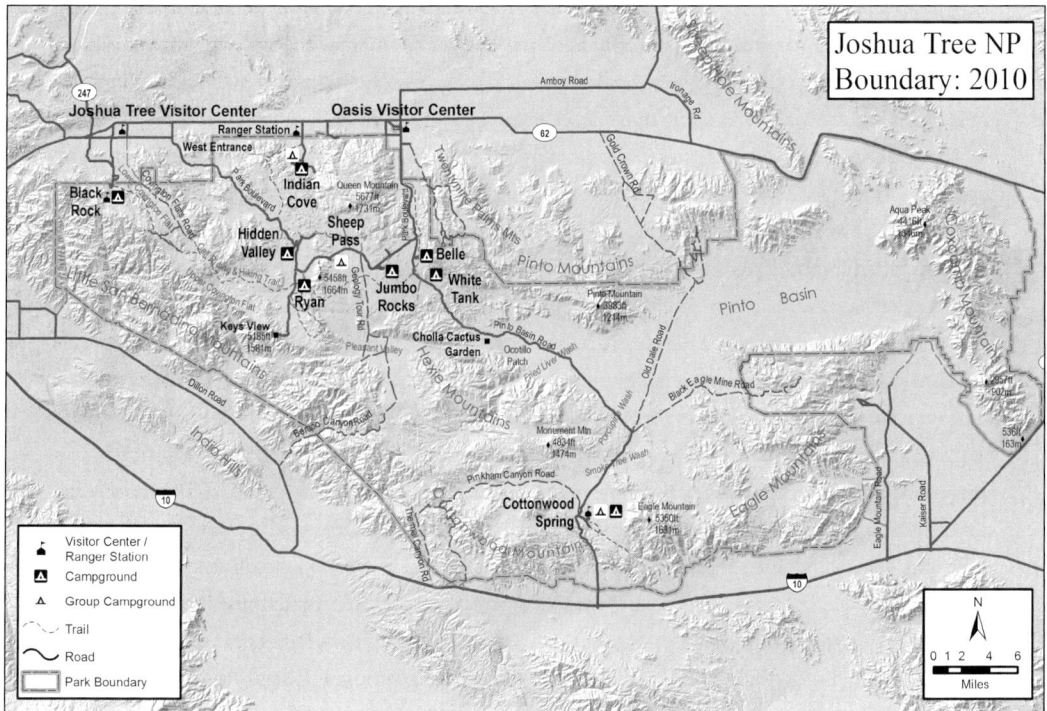

MAP 8.1. The boundaries of Joshua Tree National Park after 2009. Two modest additions adjacent to the original northern boundary consisted of Nolina Peak east of the Covington Flat Road, which could serve as part of a wildlife corridor to the Marine base at Twentynine Palms, and a few small parcels east of Indian Cove. A more ambitious proposal to make CA 62 the northern boundary met stiff opposition. Now, the National Park Service is eyeing the lobe of private land in the Eagle Mountains, where the Kaiser Corporation's defunct mine lies. Data source: National Park Service, "Digital Lands Files" (2013); available from the Western Regional Office Land Office. Delta Cartography.

for animals between the park and military base. Although the Marines use the latter for military exercises, their activities affect a small percentage of the land, and the absolute closure to the public makes it a de facto wildlife reserve. The MDLT strongly supports the goals outlined in the report and purchased Nolina Peak just west of the Pine Valley subdivision on October 3, 2008. It is part of a planned wildlife corridor to the base as well as an extension of uplands used by bighorn sheep and a viewpoint for visitors who access it from the road to Covington Flat. At the same time, the U.S. Navy used funds from a program called the "Readiness Environmental Protection Initiative" to acquire land southward from the base for flight paths that also serve as wildlife corridors (Map 8.1).[9]

In recent years, JTNP has also sought legislative action to add adjacent BLM land north of its boundary. In December 2009, U.S. Senator Dianne Feinstein, of California, introduced S.2921, a complex bill to create two new national monuments and new wilderness areas on BLM land and to transfer other parcels to the NPS. The Joshua Tree portion of the bill proposed adding four BLM parcels, totaling 2,879 acres, more than two percent of the park's acreage and, hence, requiring congressional action. Neither this bill nor its reintroduction as S.138 in 2011 passed. In the meantime, the NPS sought to acquire 114,660 acres in the Pinto Mountains east of Twentynine Palms and south of CA 62, land that was removed from the original monument in 1950. Initially called "the Saddle" by park officials, the "Old Dale Historic District" includes the 24,374-acre Pinto Mountains Wilderness Area in its southwestern portion. Local residents and off-road vehicle enthusiasts use the rest of the area for mining and vehicular recreation. In May 2012, the NPS released an economic analysis of the proposed transfer that predicted it would bring a minimum of 42,000 more visitors, $5,300,000 more money spent locally by those visitors, and at least 101 new jobs. It optimistically suggested that 314,000 new visitors, more than $40,000,000 in new revenue, and 650 jobs might result. In spite of these numbers, the reaction of the public in the local area was noisily negative. Very little private land exists in the "Saddle," but many mining claims are scattered in and around the former Dale Mining District. Late in 2013, JTNP's staff tabled the proposal, although addition of the BLM wilderness area may be sought in the future.[10]

Mining Ends in Joshua Tree . . . Or Does It?

During the 1980s, active mining in Joshua Tree National Monument (JTNM) ceased. Twelve patented claims, eleven of which belonged to the Kaiser Corporation, and nine unpatented claims existed. In 1987, the BLM eliminated the unpatented claims. The CDPA brought sixty-eight unpatented mines and one millsite into the park, but most of the claims have proven invalid. Art Parker held forty-six claims but lost them by failing to pay annual fees. Byron Walls held fifteen claims in Music Valley and filed one operation plan but quitclaimed all his mines when it appeared that a validity exam would declare one null and void. Four other claim-holders also failed to pay the annual fees. That left just Stephen Dwyer, who held three claims in the Eagle Mountains. Before the CDPA passed, Dwyer applied to the BLM to reopen an underground operation for andradite garnets at his Storm Jade #1 claim next to the Eagle Mountain Wilderness Study Area. He concurrently applied to develop a quarry and storage area within the potential wilderness. Even as BLM officials rejected the application for the quarry because of the agency's legal obligation to manage the surface land as wilderness, they approved the underground mine in April 1992. When that land became part of JTNP, Dwyer filed a plan of operations with the NPS, which initiated a validity examination conducted by American Geological Services and an NPS geologist. They concluded that the price of garnet was too low for a "prudent person" to carry out mining and expect to make a profit.[11]

Stephen Dwyer appealed to Congressman Sonny Bono, of California, for help and challenged the existing regulations. He did not pay the annual $100 fees from 1995 through 1997 and argued that he had conducted assessment work that excused him from paying. The NPS responded that the assessment work he conducted was itself illegal without approval from JTNP's superintendent. Dwyer met with two park officials and asked for a number of copies of files they insisted they had sent. He claimed that they sent only a few pages. He asked for a map of the area showing the new park boundary, to which they replied that none existed at that time. On February 5, 1997, Assistant Superintendent Frank Buono called Dwyer to discuss the increasingly tense situation. Buono later wrote that the miner accused the NPS of committing felonies by denying his civil rights. He also insisted that the NPS was enforcing imaginary laws, that his claims were outside the park, and that NPS regulations did not apply to him. Buono responded that each of those statements was wrong. Dwyer was shouting by this point and announced that JTNP officials were making a big mistake and would pay for it personally. During the same month, validity inspectors declared his other two claims null and void. He immediately launched appeals.[12]

By May 1997, Dwyer calmed down enough to submit a new plan for mining at Storm Jade #1 to the park. One month later, Superintendent Quintana informed him that it lacked necessary information on the scale of operations, compliance with state and local regulations, the types of vehicles and equipment he planned to use, an exact description of his proposed mining procedures, the anticipated impacts to resources, and the plan for how hazardous substances and tailings would be contained and reclaimed.[13] This infuriated Dwyer, who again complained to congressmen and editorialized in *The Desert Sun*:

> As a longtime resident and Earth Scientist, I can assure your readers that the park policies are what has [sic] led to the serious degradation of the park, not funding. Park policies have created this Wasteland National Park.[14]

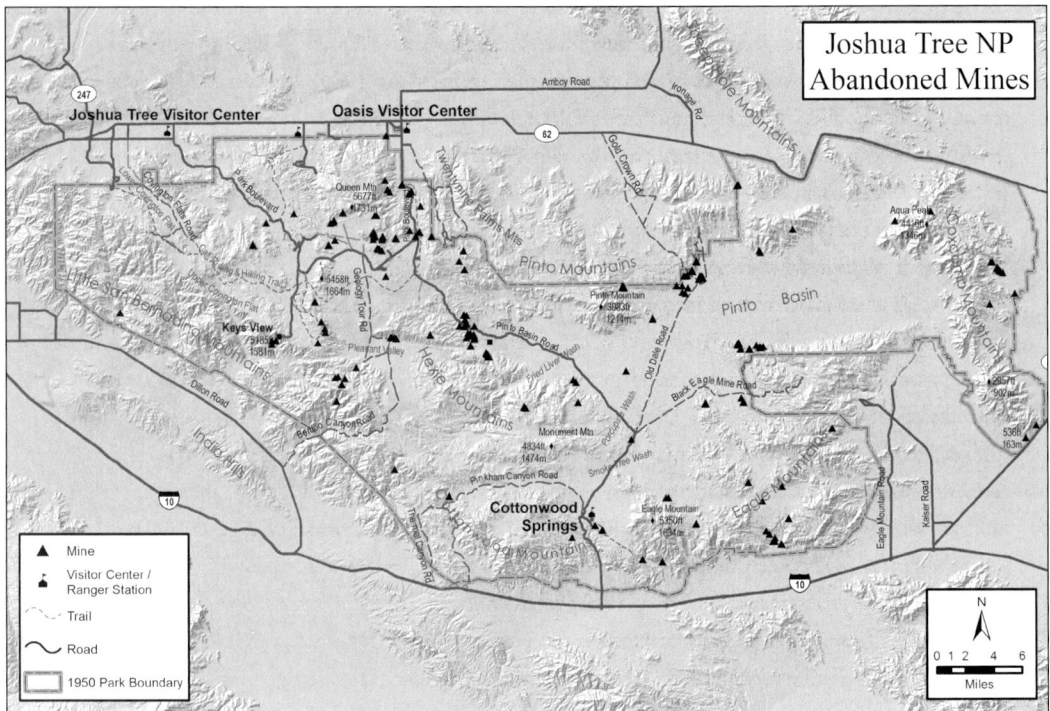

MAP 8.2. The land that makes up Joshua Tree National Park once had more than 8,000 mining claims. Dozens of them led to a significant mining infrastructure, including multiple pits, airshafts, wooden buildings, and water lines. The mineshafts and stopes, with their aging wooden supports, provide intriguing but dangerous lures to curious visitors. Decaying equipment, including dynamite, has also been found in some mines. The National Park Service is trying to block ingress to these dangerous tunnels, while still allowing resident bats to pass in and out. Data source: Joshua Tree National Park Natural Resource Division files. Delta Cartography.

Park officials continued to communicate with Dwyer in an effort to defuse the angry conflict. The disgruntled miner submitted another proposed plan of operations on May 1, 1998, which again failed to meet all requirement of the Mining in the National Parks Act. This time, the NPS gave much more information on why various conditions were not met as well as suggestions on how to correct the plan. Meanwhile, Dwyer lost his appeals for Storm Jade #4 and Little Storm Jade Mine. Two other parties submitted proposed plans of operation the following year with one success. Superintendent Quintana approved a proposal to access mines outside the park from a road within it submitted by the First Class Miners Club, of Twentynine Palms. In 2002, JTNP launched another legal challenge to Dwyer's last claim, arguing that it had insufficient minerals to justify a prudent person's operation. Six years later, Dwyer exhausted his last appeal, and mining in JTNP ended. He had appealed every contrary ruling from the initial quarry proposal through the 2008 adverse opinion on Storm Jade Mine #1, no doubt at considerable cost. Within the park, conformity with the tight regulations of the Mining in the National Parks Act and detailed plans required for an operation truly spelled an end to laissez-faire mining so long associated with the desert. Patented claims still exist in JTNP, but none are financially feasible under NPS regulations.[15]

The apparent end of mining at JTNM did not solve the problems it caused. Park officials faced four basic issues. First, the mines had to be safe for visitors. This meant covering the open shafts, removing or stabilizing structures, and eliminating dangerous equipment and explosives. Second, they had to determine if those structures were eligible for listing on the National Register of Historic Places (National Register). If so, the options for removal or cleanup were limited. Third, some mining operations had used cyanide or mercury to process ore, leaving toxic waste at the millsites. Finally, some mines harbored native species of bats, so filling the opening with polyurethane was not an option. All four problems dramatically raised the cost of treatment.

During the 1980s, park rangers studied the many mines in the monument to identify which needed approval from the historic preservation officials and which posed the greatest danger to visitors (Map 8.2). As the NPS began to prepare a management plan for the backcountry, David Shaver, Chief of the NPS's Energy, Mining, and Minerals Division, warned that topographic maps alone showed some 140 shafts and tunnels in JTNP. Those were a fraction of the total. He urged the staff to establish a systematic program for identifying threatening sites and prioritizing their remediation. This would legally establish that the NPS was addressing the problem and deflect lawsuits by injured parties, as it had in a BLM case. Superintendent Rick Anderson ordered physical scientist Mark Heuston to devote one day per week to develop the program. Heuston, however, informed the regional director that, with more than 2,000 "shafts, inclines, adits[,] and prospector test holes," the job would not be completed within two months as requested.[16] Instead, during the next two decades, Heuston and others collected data on the abandoned mines and closed some openings with polyurethane foam plugs or gates. New technology helped solve some problems. At the Lost Horse Mine, an historic site on the National Register, subsidence threatened its stamp mill. JTNP became the test site for a Borehole Video System that allowed park officials to scan the tunnels and shafts and determine exactly how to stabilize the mine. That success ignited a debate about whether they could use the machine in a designated wilderness area. Many officials argued that the temporary disruption of wilderness regulations could be excused, if the purpose was to rehabilitate an existing human intrusion.[17]

Beginning in the late 1990s, JTNP rangers carefully investigated the history of claims and determined that they actually represented about 300 mines. Of those, 120 had large or hazardous openings. In 1999, JTNP announced an ambitious five-year program to close the dangerous openings, but the process still continues in 2016. Some of the mine sites are substantial enough to require environmental assessments before treatment. Historic preservation officials will only approve a plan to fill a shaft with polyurethane, if the hardened foam will be covered with soil and the area's natural appearance restored. In 2001, the NPS signed an agreement with Bat Conservation International, Inc., to allow their members to inspect sites proposed for filling. If they find bats, the NPS must use grates that allow passage by the animals, while preventing access by humans. In 2003, Tetra Tech EM, Inc., collected samples from fourteen historic millsites to test for hazardous chemicals and metals. Twelve of the sites contained at least one substance higher than the Environmental Protection Agency's level for safety. The company recommended further testing and eventual removal of the hazardous tailings. Between 2001 and 2009, JTNP officials closed a few mine openings each year as funds allowed. Then, Congress passed the American Recovery and Reinvestment Act of 2009 to assist recovery from a national economic and employment crisis known as the Great Recession. It provided funds for environmental projects, including rehabilitation of abandoned mines. The unexpected boost in funding allowed JTNP to close forty openings at twenty-two mines in 2010. Work continues to improve visitor safety, while turning the park's mining past into a museum display.[18]

In a postscript to the story of mining, the hunt for strategic rare-earth minerals has renewed attempts to gain access to JTNP. A new generation of miners seeks the strategic materials, again arguing that the defense of the nation is at stake. The BLM and the Interior Board of Land Appeals have rejected recent claims within the park's boundary, based on the law against new filings that dates from 1936. The NPS maintains that it cannot approve mining claims because of that law and that prospective miners must get Congress either to change the law or change the park's boundary to exclude the mineral areas.[19]

Water, the Perennial Problem

Water resources at Joshua Tree continued to worry park officials, as years of drought became more common. A study of water quality in 1998 identified 266 "aquatic ecosystems" in JTNP, including ninety-five wells, eighty-six tanks, and eighty-five springs. Only 110 tanks and springs were natural. Many were dry part of each year or for years at a time. Control of its water resources remained critical to all the park's purposes. In the CDPA, Congress specified that all previously unappropriated water in the parks and wilderness areas belonged to the federal government, and no future claims would be allowed. The California Water Resources Control Board restated its legal jurisdiction and agreed with the federal law stating, "no persons hold any appropriative rights under California state law to use water from any source within Joshua Tree National Park." Still, both decrees did not affect rights established prior to the issuance of those documents. Hence, the heirs of Joseph Chiriaco, the MWD, and the Kaiser Corporation continue to hold rights within JTNP. Superintendent Quintana challenged the Chiriaco water claims at Lost Palms and Munsen Canyons on the legal basis that the rights had not been continually used. Although Margit Chiriaco-Rusche admitted that the roadside complex had not used water for some years, she worried that a serious drought might necessitate repairs to the pipelines and future use. Park records are unclear about the status of the old water right that continues to be moribund.[20]

Even before MWD officials built the Colorado River Aqueduct (Fig 1.2) during the 1930s, they envisioned using the desert's valleys for underground water storage. The Hayfield Valley, just south of JTNP, seemed a likely prospect. The utility proposed to pump water from the aqueduct into the dwindling aquifer during wet years and retrieve it during dry years. During the 1990s, MWD hydrologists studied nine basins to test the feasibility of the idea and dismissed six of them, including the Pinto Basin, for various physical and legal reasons, but they deemed Hayfield, Cadiz, and Chuckwalla Valleys as feasible, along with the heavily populated Coachella Valley. Development of the project in the Chuckwalla Valley worries the NPS, because recent studies show that groundwater from the park's Pinto Basin aquifer flows into its aquifer. In dry years, the potential exists for withdrawal of water from Chuckwalla Valley to affect the water table in the park.[21]

More Money for Infrastructure

Throughout the 1990s and into the new century, JTNP continued to repair and rehabilitate its roads and trails with a few notable changes. A comprehensive survey in 1999 by ranger and park historian Jeff Ohlfs found eighteen open, paved roads, totaling 82.51 miles; fifty-three open, unpaved roads, totaling 150.56 miles; twenty-six service or restricted roads, running 33.97 miles; and 170 closed roads or jeep trails that once covered 411.1 miles in the park. Many of the latter had already undergone rehabilitation and revegetation. The open, unpaved roads included 37.7 miles along nine routes added in the boundary change of 1994 and classified by the NPS as suitable only for "street-legal," four-wheel-drive vehicles. None of the new roads pass through wilderness areas or lands in private ownership. At the same time, JTNP closed more than sixty miles of similar dirt roads that did not fit the criteria.[22]

In June 1998, President William F. (Bill) Clinton signed the Intermodal Surface Transportation Efficiency Act that brought $6,000,000 to JTNP for road work. The park spent most of the money overhauling the road to Keys View and the parking and viewing areas at its end. The most popular viewpoint in the park suffered from serious overuse. Both off-pavement parking and social trails around the viewpoint compacted soil and damaged vegetation. Beginning in 2005, the NPS widened the road to twenty-four feet, the standard chosen for all paved public roads, and reorganized and expanded parking at the viewpoint. Park crews also resurfaced other paved roads to prolong their service and decrease the cost of maintenance. A notable addition to the reconstructed roads was a series of "tortoise trots," which are cuts in the curbs to provide an easy exit for the animals from the road. Park crews put these roughly every 100 feet along roads in Lost Horse, Queen, and Hidden Valleys and to Keys View.[23]

The park has also added new trails named Bigfoot, Bajada All Access, Fault, and Fan Canyon View plus a number of new structures to JTNP. Indeed, the building boom from 1996 through 2007 surpassed that of the *Mission 66* decade. During those twelve years, JTNP added three campground amphitheaters, all new comfort stations, four trailer pads or trailers, an entrance station at the park's west entrance, and seven major buildings. The Joshua Tree National Park Association purchased the first of these buildings for a new visitor center in Joshua Tree village in 2006. The NPS currently rents the space from the association, but it will pass to the NPS when payments on the property are complete. This arrangement has placed a financial strain on the association, but has allowed JTNP to avoid the need for government funds, while solving the problem of communicating with visitors who come through the most popular entrance.[24]

Several areas of JTNP received new structures, as the NPS finally addressed long overdue needs identified in the general management plan (GMP). Between 1998 and 2002, the NPS added a fire station and a dorm for firefighters and other seasonal employees at Black Rock Canyon. The increased fire danger in the nearby Covington Flat area made the location appropriate, despite its distance from the park's main road network. At Pinto Wye, site of the earliest government structure in the unit, the NPS added a new maintenance office building. The headquarters area at the Oasis of Mara used funds provided by the Federal Lands Recreational Enhancement Act to add three large buildings for the Protection, Maintenance, and Natural Resource Management Divisions between 2005 and 2007. Two years later, the Center for Arid Lands Restoration added a new greenhouse. The most ambitious plan came as a result of a 1992 earthquake, and subsequent discovery of fault shears under the Oasis of Mara Visitor Center. More than a decade of research culminated in the design of a plan to build a new visitor center west of the Catholic Church on property the government would have to acquire. The City of Twentynine Palms supported the concept, but members of several tribes historically associated with the oasis opposed any additional construction. As the compliance processes dragged on, the complexity and cost of acquiring land and building a much larger visitor center soon became infeasible. For the time being, the JTNP's administration has opted to retrofit and strengthen the current visitor center.[25]

Wilderness and the Backcountry

The CDPA designated 131,780 acres of the new lands in the park as wilderness, bringing the official total at that time to 561,470 acres. In 1997, JTNP found and corrected some errors in the 1976 survey of wilderness boundaries and converted 3,502 acres from potential wilderness to full wilderness. After these changes, JTNP managed a total of 557,802 acres of designated wilderness and 27,238 acres of potential wilderness, a total of 585,040 acres, according to the stipulations of the Wilderness Act of 1964. Most of the potential wilderness areas included private inholdings in the eastern and south-central parts of the park. Both NPS employees and environmental groups did not pause long before urging legislators to convert more of the potential wilderness to fully designated wilderness. On May 21, 2002, U.S. Senator Barbara Boxer, of California, introduced S.2535, the California Wild Heritage Act. This massive statewide effort included a proposal to convert six parcels of land in JTNP, totaling 36,672 acres, to wilderness. The majority of this acreage was located in the portion of the Cottonwood Mountains added in 1994. The bill failed to pass, as did several subsequent attempts during the next three years. In 2006, a new bill entitled the Northern California Coastal Wild Heritage Wilderness Act, sponsored by Senators Boxer and Dianne Feinstein as well as Congressman Mike Thompson, of California, did pass. It established seven new wilderness areas and expanded four more, all in the northern part of the state. Joshua Tree was unaffected.[26]

Despite these setbacks, California legislators repeatedly reintroduced wilderness bills affecting Southern California, which steadily gathered supporters. Eventually, Representative Rush Holt, of New Jersey, introduced H.R.146, the Omnibus Public Land Management Act of 2009, on January 6, 2009, which included a proposal for additional wilderness in JTNP. This bill passed easily, and President Barack Obama signed it on March 30. It was the largest land-conservation law since 1994 and affected multiple states. Section 1851 added 36,700 acres of wilderness and 43,300 acres of potential wilderness to JTNP. The additions incorporated the areas long sponsored by Senators Feinstein and Boxer as well as several other small parcels. As of July 2016, JTNP contains 591,618 acres of wilderness and 36,700 acres of potential wilderness, totaling seventy-nine percent of the park (Map E).[27]

Following completion of the GMP, the NPS turned its attention to developing a management plan for the backcountry. Earlier management plans prescribed general rules for camping, hiking, rock climbing, stock use, and commercial operations in the backcountry but did not differentiate zones for these activities. Increased use and pressure from recreational groups, especially rock climbers, plus the need to address the new land added by the CDPA required a more thoughtful and nuanced approach. The planning team led by Tom Gavin divided the area into two zones— wilderness, including potential wilderness, and what it called the "backcountry transition area." The latter could absorb far more human use and impact, despite continuing to be a part of what previously had been categorized as the "natural zone." Some of the land added in 1994 included dirt roads in Berdoo, Pinkham, and Thermal Canyons and elsewhere. Planners classified areas near roads or the MWD's aqueduct infrastructure as part of the transition zone. They proposed that the remainder be managed as wilderness. During the planning process, the NPS held several public meetings and issued a draft plan in November 1997. The park then hosted three public workshops, and the public submitted 1,122 written comments, which were dominated by concern over three contentious issues. More than 900 of the comments focused on rock climbing, another 100-plus on wildlife guzzlers in designated wilderness, and fifty-eight on equestrian use of the backcountry's trails. After analyzing the public response, the NPS adjusted the draft plan, issued a final plan in November 1999, and officially adopted it on January 4, 2000. Each of the three issues forced a deviation from the original draft plan.[28]

Rock Climbing

Rock climbing is a difficult issue for the management of visitors, because the NPS has always identified the activity as proper in its parks and monuments (Plate 19). "Bouldering" and rock climbing became popular in the United States after World War II, and climbers began appearing at JTNM during the 1950s. By the following decade, they recognized the monument as a worthy alternative to Yosemite National Park. By 1970, a guide to climbing routes in JTNM drew national and even international attention, although it only identified eighty routes, most of them in Hidden Valley. Up to this time, climbers usually drove pitons or "bolts" into the rock faces and connected ropes to them for safety. During the 1970s, a new generation of climbers preferred so-called "clean climbs," because they were more challenging and less intrusive on the environment. Nevertheless, bolting continued, especially by less-experienced participants. During the early 1980s, most climbers pursued routes originating in Hidden Valley Campground, and some came into conflict with campers at promising sites who were not there for rock climbing. This conflict is what drew NPS's attention to what would become its most controversial planning and management issue. By 1991, climbing was the reason more than a third of the visitors came to Joshua Tree, and most of the rest were spectators who enjoyed watching. Climbers spread throughout the monument, finding new areas to scale, while the fame of Joshua Tree continued to increase.[29]

The frequency of camper–climber conflicts became serious enough to cause Rick Anderson to enact rules in the superintendent's compendium in 1983, making it a misdemeanor to initiate a climb in a campsite without the registered camper's permission. Anderson also banned the use of motorized drills to place bolts. Nevertheless, during 1989 the staff still received multiple letters of complaint about rock climbers, claiming an unwritten right to occupy someone else's campsite all day. Accusations that climbers used battery-powered drills in the wilderness, where all motorized implements are banned, also increased. These problems at JTNM as well as at Yosemite, Grand Teton, and other national parks, led NPS leaders in Washington, D.C., in July 1991 to order that all units with recreational rock climbing develop specific plans for monitoring and managing the activity. Word quickly spread among the rock climbers, and they formed several advocacy groups to fight against any reduction of their privileges. Two organizations became active in Joshua Tree's planning. The American Alpine Club Access Committee, later simply known as "The Access Fund," not only brought pressure against potential curbs on climbing, but offered to pay for a new walk-in campground to relieve congestion at the established ones. JTNM waffled on accepting this donation for a campground near Sheep Pass until the offer lapsed. At the same time, a local, non-profit group calling itself the "Friends of Joshua Tree" (the monument) formed in Joshua Tree (the village) specifically to oppose any restrictions.[30]

JTNM officials immediately began working on a draft plan and conducted research to assess the impact of bolting in the monument. By October 1992, rangers ascertained that more than 4,000 climbing routes existed throughout JTNM, with at least 475 routes and 1,383 bolts in the wilderness area. By that time, the staff had already produced five drafts of a climbing plan and received comments from the various organizations claiming to have a stake in the outcome. Climbers' groups opposed restrictions; environmental groups demanded them. In January 1993, Superintendent David Moore met with his staff to decide on a final plan. The only unanimous decision among the employees was that all forms of bolting should be banned in wilderness areas. In February, Randy Vogel, a renowned climber, publisher of the most popular guide to climbing in Joshua Tree, and a leader of the Access Fund, threatened to take JTNM to court, if the superintendent enacted the bolting-in-wilderness ban. Vogel and other climbers claimed that JTNM officials had betrayed them after their cooperation in the planning effort.[31]

Moore signed the final draft of the Climbing Management Plan anyway on February 19, 1993. Vogel and fellow Access Fund member Paul Minault protested that Moore did not have the legal right to establish such a policy. Regional Director Stan Albright assured them that Moore had every right, according to the U.S. Code of Federal Regulations. Meanwhile, Solicitor Wendy Dinner, from NPS's regional office in San Francisco, warned Moore to be ready for a lawsuit. It was at this point the NPS removed backcountry/wilderness planning from the GMP process in order to simplify the latter. The Access Fund also brought pressure on the National Parks and Conservation Association (NPCA) for supporting the climbing plan by threatening to have a commercial company, Hi Tech Boots, remove its advertising from the association's magazine.[32]

JTNM officials took three steps after issuing the Climbing Management Plan. First, they placed a moratorium on bolting in the wilderness until further research could demonstrate its environmental and social impacts. Second, they initiated contracts for research with outside experts. The widespread occurrence of this conflict in parks and other protected areas drew a great deal of national public attention and proved a minor bonanza in funding for scientists. Finally, at a meeting held on February 25, 1994, they formed an advisory committee on rock climbing that included representatives of four climbing organizations as well as independent climbers and the Desert Protective Council. Oddly, despite receiving invitations, the Sierra Club, Wilderness Society, and NPCA did not send representatives. The Climbing Management Plan and these three actions became core components of the backcountry/wilderness planning effort that followed.[33]

During the next several years, researchers provided the NPS with biological and sociological data on the impacts of rock climbing. Colorado State University took the lead in these studies, despite its distance from Joshua Tree. In September 1995, graduate student Richard Camp completed a master's thesis on the impact of climbing on vegetation and bird diversity in the park. Unsurprisingly, he found that rock climbing was deleterious to cliff-side vegetation and bird-nesting. Basically, more climbing brought more damage. Of greater significance, Camp found that certain species of plants and birds were affected more than others. In addition, popular routes tended to collect litter at the cliff bases. A year later, George E. Wallace and Kesia Trench completed a study of rock climbers by using a NPS planning and management framework known as "Visitor Experience and Resource Protection" or VERP. They made four basic recommendations for the NPS to follow: (1) develop a zoning strategy that provides different degrees of climbing restriction and resource protection even in designated wilderness, a spatial division and gradation of protection used elsewhere in the national park system, particularly with conflict between hikers and horseback riders in the backcountry; (2) establish a permit system that would control the numbers of climbers at each route and allow replacement bolts to be used outside wilderness; (3) communicate more effectively with rock climbers through the advisory committee and incorporation of rock climbing into the

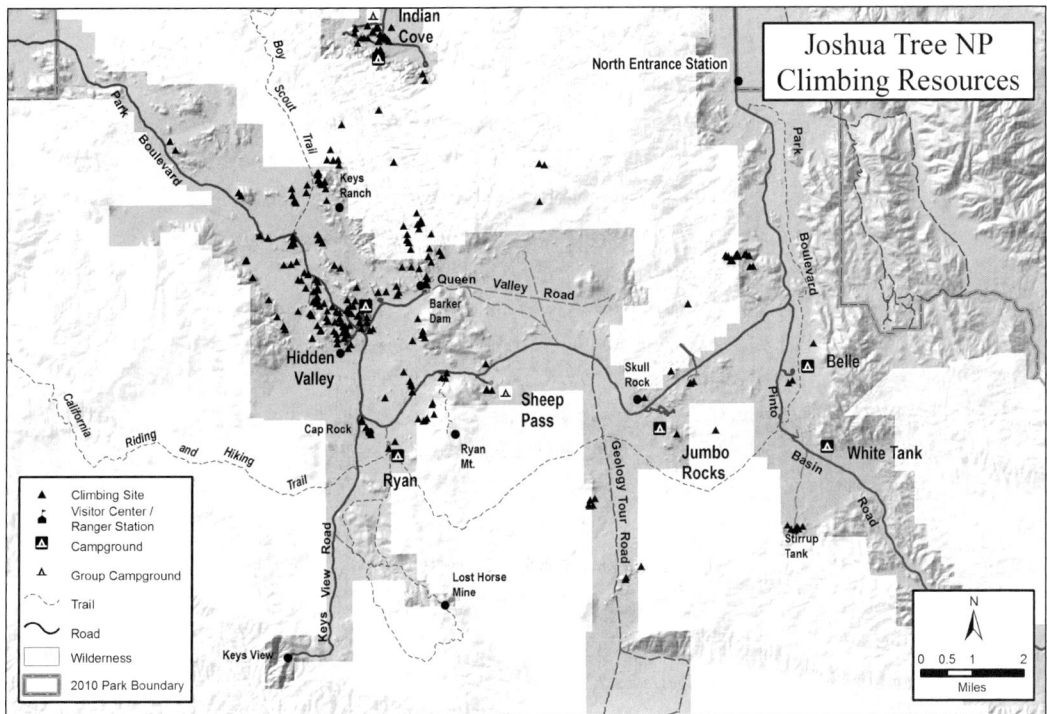

Legend:
- ▲ Climbing Site
- ⛢ Visitor Center / Ranger Station
- ⛺ Campground
- ⛺ Group Campground
- ┈┈ Trail
- ∿ Road
- ▢ Wilderness
- ▢ 2010 Park Boundary

MAP 8.3. Major rock-climbing areas in Joshua Tree's transition zone and wilderness. Although rock climbing occurs over much of the park's territory, Hidden Valley, where roads come close to the desirable terrain, remains the most-popular location. Fewer than two percent of climbers throughout the park access routes in the designated wilderness. This is due, in part, to the need to carry climbing gear and hike to reach more-remote areas and, in part, to more restrictions on the use of climbing bolts in legal wilderness. Data source: Joshua Tree National Park GIS files. Delta Cartography.

interpretive message of the park; and (4) monitor climbing areas to take protective measures where damage occurs.[34]

As planning continued for the management of the backcountry and wilderness, the issue of using bolts in JTNP, especially in the wilderness portion, became a heated national debate. By the late 1990s, Joshua Tree drew a quarter of a million climbers each year to try out more than 8,000 routes (Map 8.3). The park was one of the most-popular climbing destinations in the world, and it became the testing ground for policies for the NPS and other federal land-management agencies. Superintendent Ernest Quintana favored a ban on bolting in the wilderness and a permit system for new bolts in the rest of the park. Climbing groups, led by the Access Fund, vociferously protested what they saw as overregulation of one of the last expressions of "adventurous freedom" in the nation. They also decried the peril faced by climbers forced to operate without bolts as safety equipment. Some even carried out demonstrations in the park that taxed the small ranger force. They angrily rejected draft plans released in October 1996 and November 1997. A decision by the U.S. Forest Service to ban bolting in all its many wilderness areas further inflamed the debate.[35]

This controversy demonstrates one of the fundamental philosophical and administrative conundrums of the NPS. Even before the Organic Act of 1916, which mandated both preservation of resources for future generations and public recreation, park managers walked a fine line between the two. Throughout its subsequent years, the NPS has edged closer to resource protection in the face of greater use than anyone could have predicted in the early years of the national park system. The key constituency in the triangle of current park users, administrators, and future generations is the latter. The NPS legally must take into account the cumulative effects of past and current activities to prevent damage to a park's resources that will render them unavailable to future generations. On the other hand, parks are created in the political arena, so massive public opposition to restrictive policies can have political consequences.

At JTNP, the clamor of climbing groups and their sheer numbers forced a reevaluation of the draft management plan for the backcountry. On July 7, 1998, Superintendent Quintana met with representatives of the Access Fund, the Friends of Joshua Tree, the Wilderness Society, and the NPCA. The group hammered out a compromise, in which the NPS would (1) create a climbing committee to function as a subcommittee of the Joshua Tree National Park Advisory Commission (established by the CDPA for a ten-year period); (2) formalize a process to inventory social trails, designate the minimum number of trails needed to access climbing areas, and place physical barriers and signs to protect sensitive resources; (3) evaluate any restoration, protection, or additional management actions that may be needed; (4) allow but monitor replacement of existing bolts throughout the park; (5) ban motorized drills in wilderness areas; (6) allow climbers who have received prior approval from the superintendent to place new bolts there manually, as long as they do not exceed the number existing in 1998; and (7) permit use of a motorized drills and placement of new bolts outside the wilderness. Constant communication between the advisory committee climbing organizations and the NPS plus monitoring of sites would ensure temporary or permanent closures of damaged areas. In January 2000, the NPS released its record of decision, approving the final backcountry/wilderness plan and environmental impact statement with this set of policies.[36]

Rock climbing remained a serious issue at JTNP, in spite of this compromise. The California/ Nevada Regional Conservation Desert Committee of the Sierra Club and other environmental groups opposed the final plan after hearing that climber groups refused to meet with the NPS if Sierra Club members attended, but to no avail. In 2002, JTNP, with the cooperation of the Access Fund, hired Eric Murdock to conduct a new study of rock climbing in the park. Two years later, he submitted a report in which he analyzed the spatial patterns of climbing and various impacts it had. He found that fewer than two percent of the climbers operated in the wilderness area. Principal determinants in climbing choice were location and the quality and difficulty of a route. Presence of bolts did not seem significant in preference for climbing routes. Murdock also pointed out that the problem of social trails to the bases of climbing routes had worsened. His conclusion echoed that of the studies done a decade earlier. In 2009, further research determined that more than ninety percent of climbers operated within 2,700 meters (1.2 miles) of a paved road. The park's Climbing Committee addresses the social trails and protection of vertical vegetation, while periodic "Climbers Coffees" at Hidden Valley Campground during the peak climbing season, and the establishment of a "climbing ranger" position have further improved communication. Moreover, in 2013, with guidance from an updated Director's Order 41 on stewardship of the wilderness, input from the Climbing Committee, and new data from a thorough environmental review, Superintendent Mark Butler authorized JTNP's first installation of a fixed bolt in designated wilderness. He stated that he approved the installation, because it would have a net ecological benefit on the park's resources and provide enhanced climber safety.[37]

Bighorn Sheep and Guzzlers

After dominating the resource-management agenda for fifty-five years, bighorn sheep began to slip down Joshua Tree's project priority list in the 1990s. Between 1990 and 1994, only cursory census activity occurred, but not everyone ignored JTNP's most-glamorous species. From 1995 to 1996, the NPF and Canon USA funded a two-year study of bighorns that focused on finding better census techniques, identifying disturbed areas for revegetation, and eradicating invasive tamarisk. During the same period, the Mine Reclamation Corporation funded a study of seasonal movement of bighorn sheep and the effect that a loss of water drawn by its proposed landfill might have, and

Darren Divine and Charles Douglas concluded that the company should install one or more temporary water sources to direct the bighorn sheep away from Eagle Mountain landfill area. They also
proposed that, after completion of the construction phase, the sheep should be monitored to see if
new, permanent guzzlers might be needed.[38]

Meanwhile, the NPS debated whether it should maintain guzzlers in the wilderness at all. At
various times, up to eight water installations existed in the wilderness or proposed wilderness portions of JTNP (Fig. 7.3). The 1997 Draft Backcountry and Wilderness Management Plan focused
on three of them: the Coxcomb and Russi's Rocks guzzlers in the new Coxcomb Mountains land
addition and the Pushawalla guzzler near the old road through that canyon. During the mandatory
public review, the Society for the Conservation of Bighorn Sheep and many individuals protested the
decision to close vehicular access to the guzzlers, claiming that difficulty in maintaining them, coupled with disturbance from increased numbers of visitors, spelled doom for the park's herds. The
NPS offered to bring water to the sheep on foot, if a major drought occurred. The agency's favored
alternative proposed further monitoring of the guzzlers for three years to determine their use by
the bighorns. In 1999, JTNP decided to continue that program and extended it to four guzzlers
and the Coxcomb Adit. Studies of bighorn sheep and NPS's debate over the propriety of guzzlers
in the wilderness continued in the new century, spurred by evidence that several species of the
park's fauna, including bighorn sheep, had drowned in them when they were full. A study in 2004
commissioned by the National Aeronautics and Space Administration added fuel to the debate by
predicting that climate change could eliminate bighorn sheep over much of their remaining range,
including JTNP. In 2016, the NPS still conducted or sanctioned studies of the bighorn sheep and
sporadically maintained a few guzzlers equipped with remote cameras to record their use.

The issue remains controversial at all desert parks, because some wildlife biologists believe
they are not necessary and lead to deaths by drowning of other species. Other scientists and interest groups dedicated to saving the bighorns dispute these ideas. The NPS awaits completion of a
"water management plan" at nearby Mojave National Preserve, where the bighorn-guzzler issue has
led to lawsuits. Thereafter, JTNP will initiate its own similar planning process, which, based on the
park's history, is sure to bring acute attention and conflict.[39]

Horses and Other Stock Animals

Planning for stock use in the backcountry by JTNP staff led to debate about five specific issues: (1)
development of a trail system to coordinate access by hikers and equestrians; (2) coping with the
needs of horses, particularly on overnight trips; (3) group size; (4) the impact of horses on the endangered desert tortoise; and (5) the use of llamas and other non-traditional pack stock. Like other

parks with large backcountry areas, as Joshua Tree's popularity increased, so did conflict between hikers and horseback riders. In addition, bicycling adherents, although legally banned in wilderness, want to access trails in the backcountry transition area. This user conflict plus pressure to develop a regional trail system surrounding and including the park forced JTNP officials to assess all of its trails and organize them by user group and level of maintenance. Cross-country hiking is permitted throughout the park, but horse riding must follow designated routes.

The Final Backcountry Management Plan provided for 253 miles of equestrian trails and corridors that traversed canyon bottoms and dry washes. The two most heavily used routes are the California Riding and Hiking Trail and the Boy Scout Trail, which runs from Indian Cove southward past the Wonderland of Rocks. It also allowed equestrian access to corridors running along canyon bottoms, including Long and Pushawalla Canyons. Park officials later eliminated routes that do not follow designated trails. The plan also suggested portions of five trails, totaling slightly more than twenty-seven miles for off-road bicycling, including, ironically, part of the California Riding and Hiking Trail. JTNP, however, never developed the bicycle trails. In 2012, Superintendent Butler asked Chief Ranger Jeff Ohlfs to initiate a "Bicycle Management Directive" that clarified their use on the park's roads and trails. Today, JTNP is increasingly linking its trails with those of Yucca Valley and several communities south of the park in order to integrate the park's system with the regional trail plans developed by local counties and other land agencies.[40]

Even as the NPS has listed horseback riding as a proper activity in Joshua Tree since its origin, early in the planning process for management of the backcountry and wilderness equestrians feared they would be excluded from Joshua Tree altogether because of complaints by hikers, animal-rights advocates, and some environmental organizations. Thus, on June 17, 1994, JTNP hosted a meeting between staff members and horseback riding enthusiasts to address their concerns. The participants formed a "Horse Users Advisory Group" to facilitate park-user group communications similar to the one established for rock climbers. During the ensuing five years, the group brought several issues to the attention of JTNP's personnel. One issue that threatened equestrian use was the fate of the desert tortoise. Horseback riders, fearing that environmental groups would claim that horses trample tortoises and their burrows, vehemently argued that horses look where they step and avoid anything like another animal. Nonetheless, they agreed in principle to travel single file to minimize the impact on trails or roadsides.[41]

The Horse Users Advisory Group also sought improvements in opportunities for equestrian recreation and in established rules that protect the park's resources. Improved opportunities for overnight camping by horseback riders depended on two campgrounds: Black Rock Canyon, the most popular departure point for riders, and Ryan Campground, which had fallen into disuse and disrepair. At the urging of the advisory group, the JTNP staff conducted cleanups and repairs of both. Riders also sought more access points to bring their horse trailers and additional artificial water sources, because carrying water for the horses was not feasible, but JTNP officials rejected these options as inconsistent with the park's purposes and also refused to allow a horseback riding concession to set up in the park, because so many areas in neighboring communities could host them. The matter of group size also arose, and NPS planners surveyed other units plus some of the nation's national forests. They found no consistency with group sizes ranging from five to twenty-five in various areas and situations. Ultimately, JTNP officials adopted a flexible limit between twelve and twenty-five, depending on characteristics of the planned ride.[42]

One final issue was the use of llamas and other non-equine animals as pack stock in the back-country. Horse enthusiasts argued that llamas should be denied access to the park, because they are not a native or "traditional" animal in American history, they "spook" the horses when they meet on the trail, presenting a danger to them and their riders, and they would pass diseases to horses and bighorn sheep. For a while, Superintendent Quintana wavered on this policy, as letters from llama enthusiasts praised the animal's quiet and gentle nature. He ultimately followed the lead of Canyonlands National Park and banned all pack animals, except horses and mules.[43]

Natural Resources in the New Century

During the last two decades, significant changes in NPS's natural-resource policy have occurred. In a report released in 1987, the General Accounting Office found the agency had not implemented the changes in management recommended in the State of the Parks report seven years earlier. In 1992, three more events focused attention on the continuing relegation of scientific research on the national park system's natural resources to secondary status in decision-making. First, the National Academy of Sciences issued yet another report that called for an "explicit legislative mandate for a research mission of the National Park Service." The organization's committee recommended separate funding and reporting autonomy for the science program, the appointment of a chief scientist for the NPS, cooperation with external researchers, and an external science advisory board to provide continuing independent oversight. Second, the NPS released its own report called the "Vail Agenda," in which the ideas of a legislative mandate for science research and use of the "best available science" for management were endorsed. President Clinton, then recently elected, supported these recommendations.[44]

The third event of 1992 was the formation of the National Biological Survey by Secretary of the Interior Bruce Babbitt. Unfortunately, the transfer of most NPS scientists to the new agency that advises all branches of the Department of the Interior removed most of the people necessary to implement the recommendations. With their new responsibilities, former park scientists had less time to devote to fixing the NPS's research agenda. This setback, as well as the findings of the two

1992 committees, occurred while NPS historian Richard West Sellars was researching his comprehensive review of natural-resource management during the 120 years since Yellowstone became the
first national park in 1872. The release in 1997 of his book, *Preserving Nature in the National Parks*,
brought attention from both the public and Congress to the NPS's record of managing for the
appearance of resources rather than the science-based protection of natural processes. The following year, Congress passed the National Parks Omnibus Management Act, which mandated that the
Secretary of the Interior assure that the NPS manage its charges with the "highest quality science
and information." It also ordered the agency to apply science to all management decisions, expand
interagency and university coordination of research, and implement an Inventory and Monitoring
Program (I&M) in order to establish baseline data and carry out oversight of resource conditions.
The NPS finally had a legal obligation to do what scientists from George Wright to Lowell Sumner
and Bob Moon had long recommended.[45]

The dramatic improvement of the NPS's scientific research mission, backed by periodic special
funding from Congress, spread to JTNP and improved the programs of natural-resource management begun under Bob Moon. By January 2014, the park employed highly trained specialists
in wildlife, botanical, and geological sciences, more than a dozen other permanent or seasonal
personnel, and up to sixteen Student Conservation Association interns. These numbers did not
include members of the cultural-resource management staff. Both fundamental research and direct
management benefitted from funding attained through competitive grants and special NPS allocations. Advances in research plus inventory and monitoring of the park's ecosystems brought a better
understanding of resource-management needs and procedures. In 1996, Superintendent Quintana
submitted an application for natural-resource funds to support twenty-four specific programs.
Wildlife included bighorn sheep, desert tortoise, deer, burros, bats, mountain lions, invertebrates,
and migratory birds. Botanical programs included threatened and endangered plants, exotic vegetation, mosses and lichens, the creosote bush community, research on historic biota, and creation of a
basic vegetation map for the park. Expansion of air-quality monitoring, assessment of the effects of
pollution, better management of water resources, development of a geographic information system,
a review of the natural history collection, and research on the forbidding specter of global warming
completed the list.[46]

The recent history of JTNP has brought more information and a deeper understanding of the
resources and also the recognition that the larger staff and budget are still inadequate to cope with
rising threats. Many of these threats originate outside Joshua Tree's boundaries, including development plans for a pump-storage project at the site of the former Eagle Mountain Mine and a rash of
solar and wind projects north, south, and east of the park. Three groups of interrelated problems
exist, and atmospheric conditions exacerbate them all: (1) the fate of the park's wildlife impacted

by drought and extraordinary development schemes that will tip the ecological balance in the Eagle Mountain area; (2) invasive plants aided by nitrogen deposition and air pollution, which contribute to larger and more frequent fires; and (3) the impact of climate change that may alter every aspect of the park's resource profile.

In recent years, the park's staff has devoted much more time to researching smaller and less picturesque fauna, but six key animals still draw most of the attention and funding: bighorn sheep, desert tortoises, ravens, bats, coyotes, and feral burros. As discussed earlier, bighorn sheep continue to be the public's favorite, and any action that affects them is open to riveted attention and potential criticism. Nevertheless, the desert tortoise has become the linchpin of environmentalists' challenges as JTNP's primary threatened species. The susceptibility of the desert tortoise (Plate 27) to ravens (Fig. 8.2) that prey upon its young became a major factor in the fight against a plan to install a giant landfill at the Eagle Mountain Mine. Hikers' disturbance of other nesting native birds has periodically led the NPS to close several areas along the northern edge of the park. Bat populations are declining in spite of measures taken to ensure their access to abandoned mines. Disease may be the cause, but scientists do not fully understand chiropteran biology. Coyotes that beg in and around campgrounds continue to present a nuisance and potential danger to visitors. Rangers have had to shoot particularly aggressive individuals in order to maintain visitors' safety. Wildlife experts and rangers constantly monitor feral burros that live around the park and cross into it periodically. Should any group decide to stay, rangers will forcibly remove them.

As a postscript to the wildlife story, in June 1996, JTNP resource manager Pat McClenahan proposed a new study of the feasibility of returning pronghorn antelope to the park. Funding requests, data collection, and public comment followed during the next two years. Then, in May 1998, Harley Shaw, of the Juniper Institute, Inc., submitted a report that found the area unsuitable for the species. That seemed to curtail the excitement and scientific study for a while. In March 2010, however, *The Riverside Press–Enterprise* reported on a study underway to reintroduce pronghorn antelope to Mojave National Preserve. If the NPS reintroduces the animal there, it is likely that this resilient yet forlorn hope will resurface at Joshua Tree.[47]

In spite of long-range plans to increase the monitoring of air quality in JTNP, the park still has only three stations—at Black Rock, Cottonwood, and near its eastern boundary. Data from them and other standard weather stations in and around the park show two patterns. First, years of drought are becoming more common, which impacts all the biotic resources of the park. A study in 1999 by Harold DeLisle found that populations of amphibians had declined, due to the drier conditions. Later research suggested that the desert tortoise might also be negatively affected. The second pattern is a general stability in the amount of particulate pollution but continued problems with the level of ozone. A news report in 2011 stated that JTNP had exceeded the federal health standard on fifty-three days the preceding year. Nitrogen deposition has stabilized but at a level that continues to foster invasion by exotic grasses. Their density is increasing throughout the park but especially in the Covington Flat area, which, in 1999, led to the worst fire in Joshua Tree's history. Four lightning fires started on May 27 and, during the next eight days, burned 13,899 acres in the Covington and Quail Mountain areas. Joshua Tree lost a significant amount of its densest vegetation only to have the foreign grasses speedily colonize the newly opened ground. The Juniper Fire plus a number of other major fires in national parks brought a rare appraisal of NPS's fire management by its sister agency, the U.S. Fish and Wildlife Service (USFWS). It also initiated an intense effort to develop a new fire-management plan for JTNP, which included considerable input from fire specialists elsewhere in the national park system. Completed in 2005, it orders total suppression as the park's fundamental policy.[48]

The most-insidious and uncontrollable threat to Joshua Tree affects the entire world. Despite pockets of denial, the evidence is overwhelming that Earth's atmosphere and oceans are warming. While scientists amass data and try to predict the future, land and resource managers must face the impacts. JTNP exists because of its diverse array of vegetation, including its namesake species. The most popular portion of the park is the higher-elevation Mojave Desert, where Joshua trees, pinyon pines, junipers, and other species intolerant of higher annual temperatures grow (Plate 17; Figs. 3.3 and 6.1). Park records already show a temperature increase of more than one degree Fahrenheit since 1936. A predicted increase of at least three degrees by 2050 will bring four types of changes to the park. First, the range of Joshua trees will shrink, although dire predictions by the media of its complete disappearance from the area may be premature. Two research studies suggested different outcomes for the park, although there was agreement that the species would contract its range substantially over the entire Southwest. In 2011, Kenneth Cole and others at the U.S. Geological Survey (USGS) published evidence that a previous warming period 12,000 years ago coincided with the extinction of the Shasta ground sloths that consumed Joshua trees and spread the seeds in their scat. Subsequently, packrats and other rodents have served as the primary means of dispersing seeds for the species. The fact that their range is so small compared to that of the sloth means that in the present rapid warming, the seeds may not be dispersed to newly habitable areas quickly enough to survive over a large region. Another study by biologists Cameron Barrows and Michelle Murphy, of the University of California, Riverside, posits that the Joshua trees will survive in the park, but the distribution will contract and markedly change.[49]

A second outcome of dramatic warming may be decreased rainfall and increased drought conditions. Throughout the history of Joshua Tree, water resources have declined. Warmer temperatures may result in fewer rain events and greater evaporation. A further decline in water availability may result as well as damage from flooding during more severe convection storms. This will affect all the plant species and animals in the park. A third impact will be a greater invasion of exotic plants, especially weeds, which choke out native species and usurp the water. Finally, the continued proliferation of those exotics and other fire-tolerant annuals will increase biomass, leading to greater frequency and size of fires. The upshot of these changes will be a park in which the ecotone between the Mojave and Colorado Deserts shifts and blurs. Joshua trees and other higher-elevation species may shrink to a pattern of isolated pockets known as disjunct distribution. Such a situation hampers cross-fertilization and renders populations more susceptible to disease and pests. Loss of JTNP's signature species may be challenged by the public and force the NPS to deviate from its own mission by artificially maintaining Joshua trees where they cannot survive on their own. The answers to climate change lay in policy and lifestyle changes far beyond the control of a small federal agency trying to manage three percent of the nation's land.[50]

Cultural Resources

Cultural resource management continues to demand extensive data collection, more informed management, and better funding. The "Natural and Cultural Resources Management Plan 1999" stated:

> The park is rich in archaeological, historic, and ethnographic resources. Until we know and understand what we have, these resources will continue to be degraded to the point of total loss.[51]

Fortunately, the program benefitted from greater professionalism in the staff and research by NPS and university specialists. The start of the Recreation Fee Demonstration Project in 1997 helped provide additional funds for cultural-resource management received from the entrance charges paid by visitors to the park. From 1998 through 2000, JTNP brought in $3,852,807, eighty percent of which it kept for use in the park. The 1999 plan identified forty-nine goals for the park's cultural resources in four basic categories. Twelve projects focused on archaeology, including a deeper analysis of existing literature and artifacts, continued exploration for new sites throughout the park, assessments of specific areas such as Keys Ranch, and the inventory, monitoring, and restoration of sites already identified. Another category of goals sought to understand better past and present Native American culture. Two proposed projects concerned rock art, which, in recent years, had grown in public interest and, hence, endangerment. Cultural-resource officials also proposed three ethnographic projects reflecting belated recognition of the important heritage of tribes whose descendants increasingly affect the park's management. A third group of fifteen projects focused on historic research and management. The plan proposed fundamental research, stabilization of structures, and identification and completion of nominations to the National Register of Historic

Places, including cultural landscapes. Finally, seventeen projects focused on the museum and archives recently installed in the new state-of-the-art facility.[52]

Increased funding, especially from grants and programmed allocations from the NPS, has enabled archaeological surveys aimed at a deeper understanding of Paleo-Indian environmental adaptations, the type of research the Campbells pioneered, rather than just clearances for road construction. In 2002, the park released a report on archaeology in the wilderness area and the backcountry that identified twenty-four sites but concluded that "hundreds of other known, but unrecorded, sites" existed and would require much more money to protect. In spite of this, the popular areas for visitors continued to draw most attention. Major work took place along the roads in the western part of the park as well as in the Keys Ranch and Oasis of Mara areas. The status of the park's prehistoric rock art received a substantial boost with the release in 2006 of a "traditional use" study by Douglas Deur that relied heavily on ethnographic contributions from the Cahuilla, Serrano, Chemehueve, and Mojave tribes. While research on the Native Americans continues to focus on ethnobotany and ethnozoology, improved consultation with local tribes proved important when park workers found human remains near a popular hiking trail. Superintendent Curt Sauer contacted ten identified tribal groups. Several claimed the skeletal remains as ancestral and carried out a formal ceremony, with the re-internment of the remains at the site on November 5, 2006.[53]

Maintenance of historic structures continues to focus primarily on the three major historic attractions: Keys Ranch, the Wall Street Mill, and the Lost Horse Mine (Plates 30 and 31; Fig. 5.1). Keys Ranch, in particular, came under increased scrutiny after an investigation in 1999 found that mice, rats, ground squirrels, and bats had damaged several structures. This came at the same time as a decision to increase the number of public tours conducted at the estate. In 2005, the NPS approved a "Keys Ranch Comprehensive Plan" that included fourteen categories of recommendations, including coordination and implementation of structural rehabilitation, inventory of all objects at the site, reintroduction of the historic orchard and other landscape features, a better fire-management plan, and enhanced interpretation. Meanwhile, an inspection in February 2000 by Michael Scott, from the regional office in San Francisco, concluded that stabilization of the stamp mill and cookhouse at the Lost Horse Mine, Wall Street Mill, and several minor structures at other mine and mill sites would be necessary. After a fire occurred in the area, the NPS used lime to stabilize the Ryan Ranch Bunkhouse. It has significantly changed the original appearance of the structure.[54]

Efforts to complete the official "list of classified structures" (LCS) and nominate worthy sites to the National Register led to the inspection of other former mines and mills in Joshua Tree. By early 2014, the LCS included 140 buildings, mines, wells, and other structures primarily from the mining era. JTNP officials requested an evaluation by the regional office of four sites—Samuelson's Well #2, Crown Prince Mine, Pine City Mine, and Silver Bell Mine—to determine their eligibility for the National Register. Ralph B. Giles, Jr., completed the evaluation and concluded none were sufficiently significant. Two years later, another evaluation of eligibility found the park's headquarters building and visitor center at the Oasis of Mara equally unqualified. Three other sites received attention, and their status is still uncertain. The Oasis of Mara, the Cottonwood Oasis, and the Hayfield Rock Art District are apparently eligible but not yet listed on the National Register. All three qualify because of their prehistoric resources, unlike the rejected structures from the Euro-American era.[55]

Joshua Tree is participating in a relatively young program in historical-resource protection by identifying and managing cultural landscapes. Although landscape architecture has existed for centuries, it traditionally emphasized the deliberate creation of landscapes for those who could afford them. The concept of the cultural landscape, as used in historic preservation and the national park system, stems from the discipline of geography. Many American scholars cite geographer Carl O. Sauer's influential 1925 article, "The Morphology of the Landscape," as the definitive origin of the concept, but German geographer Otto Schluter actually developed both the concept and the term earlier.[56] The NPS defines a cultural landscape in this way:

> a reflection of human adaptation and use of natural resources and is often expressed in the way land is organized and divided, patterns of settlement, land use, systems of circulation, and the types of structures that are built. The character of a cultural landscape is defined both by physical materials, such as roads, buildings, walls, and vegetation, and by use reflecting cultural values and traditions.[57]

Cultural landscapes are significant and complex entities for two reasons. First, each is an accumulation of all the past activities in that place. Subsequent use has erased many impacts of previous human action, but some, although physically gone, shaped spatial patterns of organization and circulation that followed. These spatial patterns are not well-represented by the National Register. As with individual structures, an agency or organization that decides to preserve or restore a past landscape must choose what era to represent. Second, many cultural landscapes are both ecologically dynamic and still in use by people, meaning they may evolve. The NPS must also decide whether to interrupt natural processes and human use to maintain or reintroduce modification representing a particular period.

Inventories of cultural landscapes began at JTNP at Keys Ranch during the 1990s. Since that time, the NPS has identified and planned preservation for three other landscapes—Northern Piñon Historic Mining District, Hexie Mountains Historic Mining District, and Lost Horse Historic Mining District. The NPS is committed to preserving their visual appearance, including abandoned equipment and structures, roads and trails, and even tailings. Identification of a cultural landscape means a great deal to a park's historic preservation program, because most of the individual structures do not qualify for the National Register, but an entire landscape may be eligible. This is why the use of buried polyurethane foam to close mine shafts is preferable from a landscape point of view. Still, this presents a classic conundrum for the NPS, as it must balance historic landscape preservation, safety of visitors, and protection of endangered bats at each place.[58]

Completion of the new museum and archives building provided proper storage not only for the Campbell Collection, but also the park records, photos, library, and other material objects (Fig. 7.4). Yet only one person organizes, catalogs, stores, and preserves the full array of resources contained in the building. The museum's objects are in excellent condition, especially the archaeological artifacts, but the same cannot be said for the library and archival materials. In 2005, the regional office sent a team to evaluate the facility and develop a plan for the museum's management. The team made five recommendations: (1) develop the protocols for orderly growth and management of the archives, library, and museum; (2) improve information management tools and procedures; (3) develop partnerships with other park staff; (4) develop storage and study areas at work sites in the park; and (5) create a position for a journeyman museum curator. One major problem remains: Many employees neither create written records nor send anything to the archives. This is a service-wide problem, as identified by the NPS's history office in Harpers Ferry, West Virginia. Hence, writing a comprehensive administrative history of any national park is difficult at best.

The current archives at JTNP however, are well-organized and protected through the late 1990s. Everything after that resides in various personal files around the park or in boxes and shelves of unprocessed material. The library is small, but maintaining its organization depends on a few volunteers. Many books and reports disappear into various work files and are returned late, if ever. The photo archives are scattered within the museum's storage area or in the office of the curator. That single employee must cope with acquisition, proper storage, protocol for research access, and the requests of both employees and others for use or provenance of everything. She is the only one who knows where all the various items or data are located. The museum's management team suggested the five goals for the museum/archives collection. It is difficult to imagine how the lone worker can find time to develop them.[59]

Visitation and Interpretation

Between 1997 and 2015, visitation for the entire national park system rose nearly twelve percent to 307,247,252. Some of the years were lower, others much higher, especially the last two. During the same period, visitation to Joshua Tree also fluctuated but grew overall at sixty-five percent (see

Appendix B). The higher total reflects the increased population living around the park, more troops at the Marine base, and more interest in rock climbing.[60] In 2001, the park served as a test case for a socio-economic atlas to map population and social characteristics of the surrounding region. The authors predicted that the region consisting of San Bernardino County southward in California plus adjacent counties in Arizona and Nevada would increase its population by 35.7 percent by 2020. Riverside County ranked highest in predicted growth rate among the California counties. A follow-up visitor survey, conducted in 2006, showed that, while family groups as a percentage of total visitation rose by more than ten percent over the figure from the 1991 study, the portion of visitors from other countries declined from thirteen to eight percent. The latter was surprising, given the fame of JTNP among rock climbers around the world. It seemed unlikely that visitation to Joshua Tree could match this regional population growth rate, but, in fact, the total number of visitors to the park increased by forty-six percent just from 2013 to 2015, reaching 2,025,756 in 2015, with expectations it will be even higher in the National Park Service's centennial year of 2016. Despite this surge and the record number of visitors for the entire national park system in 2015, many senior NPS officials worry that the young, computer-literate generation of the future does not have the same interest in and support for the parks that earlier generations had. Still, JTNP's percentage rise in attendance continues to outstrip that of the system as a whole.[61]

Historically, the NPS has used economic studies to predict what a proposed park may bring to an area. Recently, studies also have focused on what economic impact existing parks have for their communities. Although the reasons for national parks are philosophical and cultural rather than economic, the reality in the American political scene is that they will garner more congressional and public support if they bring hard cash to their surrounding regions. A number of models exist for computing direct economic spending by visitors and park employees as well as the multiplier effect of those dollars in lodging, food, and other hospitality businesses and wages spent by their workers. Hence, it is somewhat difficult to compare figures from studies done by different researchers. Nevertheless, JTNP's economic impact is considerable. A study in 2004 of multiple units in the national park system, including Joshua Tree, found that visitors spent $49,300,000 at JTNP in 2004 and added $36,600,000 in value to the region. The same study estimated that the ratio of economic benefit from the park's visitors plus the services required by the park outweighed the cost, computed by estimating other potential land uses, by 7.5 to one. In a study specifically on Joshua Tree in 2010, the NPS found that visitors that year spent more than $60,000,000 and added $42,900,000 in value. In addition, this money supported some 800 jobs.[62]

As exurbia and new development close in on the western half of the park, JTNP rangers face more rescues, searches, and crime, both petty and serious (Fig. 7.5). They evacuate injured rock climbers and mount large-scale hunts for lost children and adults. The window of time to find a missing person during the summer months is a short one. Assaults, theft, and drug crimes continue. More common are traffic infractions, poaching, and willful vandalism. In 2009, rangers arrested a man for throwing more than 3,000 golf balls around the park as a tribute to dead golfers. More serious was a prank of applying graffiti to Barker Dam and other sites in order to send photos of it on the Internet. It proves that the same low mindset that burned Joshua trees in 1930 to send signals has flourished with new technology. In 2013, the park closed trails to Rattlesnake Canyon and Barker Dam to try and stop the vandalism.[63]

Increasing visitation, overcrowding at popular sites, and crime demand more education and interpretation from officials at JTNP. Added to this is the need to inform students and the general public about the resources, opportunities, and meaning of national parks. Time and again, public support has turned back efforts by politicians and businesses to dilute the mission of the NPS. Coincident with the NPS's soul-searching about science and natural-resource management came a reappraisal of the agency's role in education. In 2001, the NPS Advisory Board described the national park system as an unparalleled educational institution for understanding biological and historical processes and the "interconnection of all living things and forces that shape the earth." It recommended that education should be a primary mission of the NPS. The agency responded in its 2006 "Management Policies" by elevating interpretation to a research-based educational mission that does not shy away from controversial topics. In 2009, the National Parks Conservation Association urged Congress to "affirm in legislation that education is central to the success of the National Park Service mission, and that the Service has a fundamental role to play in American education over the next century."[64]

Joshua Tree's interpretation program stresses education by every means possible. Not only do the permanent and seasonal rangers lead walks and give presentations, but an increasing part of their workload is visiting schools or hosting classes in the park. Each year, they average 650 programs to more than 18,000 students within a 100-mile radius of the park. To further this program, they pursue multiple grants from both government sources and private foundations to carry out face-to-face dialogue and on-line communications via the Internet. Popular programs that involve the public in new ways have also become de rigueur. In 2008, JTNP started an artist-in-residence program that draws support from school districts, museums, and the media.[65]

Occasionally, the NPS asks consulting scholars to review the stories they tell. Three members of the Organization of American Historians traveled to JTNP in June 2008 to review the park's program for history and its presentation to the public. They recommended more research on neglected topics, more integration of existing knowledge into a larger context, and more training for the park's employees. One gap they highlighted in JTNP's interpretation program was the Gram Parsons episode and the popular culture connection that stemmed from it. In 2011, for its seventy-fifth anniversary, JTNP hosted a concert in Indian Cove that, in part, commemorated the life and legacy of the influential rock star. The importance of the entire interpretation program cannot be overemphasized. Although law enforcement has drawn much of the park's funds and staff positions, the job of communicating the purpose and benefit of the national parks remains a critical priority in the face of apathy, ignorance, and mounting threats from outside the park's boundaries.[66]

External Threats

Joshua Tree personnel face many threats to the resources within the park brought by underfunding and impacts by visitors. The longstanding perception of the park as an area of sand and stone in an inhospitable wasteland that is held by some NPS officials and many in the public does not help. Enhanced scientific management and supportive environmentalists counter many threats. Yet the park still may fall prey to the increasing intrusion of incompatible land uses surrounding the park. The more some people discredit the desert, the more it attracts others. Mining for gold and iron shaped the place in earlier decades. Now, the hunt for residential and resort tracts, space for the effluence of urban development, and the nation's insatiable demand for energy draw an ever tighter noose around Joshua Tree. Traditional qualities such as native flora and fauna, open recreational space, inspirational scenery, and historic places are affected by activities on the borders of a park. At even greater risk are air quality, dark skies at night, solitude, and the emotive quality of wilderness. As JTNP goes forward, its fate will be shaped by everything around it.

Construction of housing, golf courses, and other facilities abutting the park's boundary is introducing light and noise pollution, adding litter, disrupting natural runoff, and spreading intense recreational pressure, including illegal off-highway vehicles, into the park on both the northern and southern boundaries. These "edge effects" have always been a problem on the northwestern boundary. By 2006, Superintendent Curt Sauer began working with Twentynine Palms, Joshua Tree village, and Yucca Valley to coordinate their planning with the needs of the park. The three settlements willingly work with the NPS, but home construction continues on the very edge of the park wherever transportation access is available. The Twentynine Palms Band of the Mission Indians recently opened a large casino on their reservation, where the NPS once considered building its headquarters complex. The Tortoise Rock Casino has developed extensive infrastructure and drawn considerable crowds to the very boundary of the park.[67]

On the southern boundary, between Interstate 10 and JTNP, open land has attracted a variety of subdivision schemes that promise to expand the heavy footprint of excessive water consumption right up to the park. Areas of ingress such as Berdoo, Thermal, and Pushawalla Canyons and the

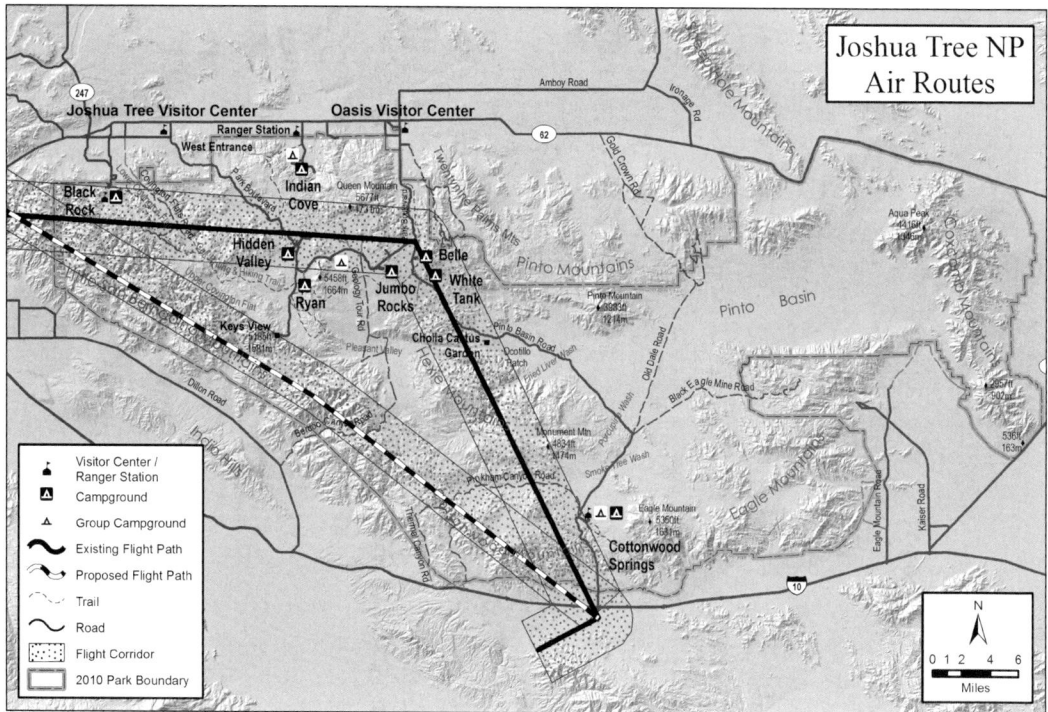

Joshua Tree NP Air Routes

247
Joshua Tree Visitor Center   Oasis Visitor Center
              Ranger Station   Amboy Road   Pinto Mountains
          West Entrance   62

Black Rock
567 ft
177 m

Indian Cove
Queen Mountain
5677 ft
1766 m

Hidden Valley
                Belle
          White Tank
Ryan   Pinto Mountains
5456 ft
1664 m
Jumbo Rocks
Keys View
5181 ft
1661 m   Cholla Cactus Garden   Pinto Mountain
                                              5456 ft
                                              1214 m   Pinto Basin

Pleasant Valley

Montgomery Mtn
4634 ft
1414 m

Eagle Mountain
5350 ft
1661 m   Eagle Mountains

Cottonwood Springs

10

Legend:
- Visitor Center / Ranger Station
- Campground
- Group Campground
- Existing Flight Path
- Proposed Flight Path
- Trail
- Road
- Flight Corridor
- 2010 Park Boundary

N

0 1 2 4 6
Miles

MAP 8.4. For years, visitors complained about low-flying U.S. Navy jets that streaked over all but one of Joshua Tree National Park's nine campgrounds on route VR-1257. Finally, in 2000, with the help of environmental organizations, park managers convinced the military to realign the route to follow the Little San Bernardino Mountains and avoid all the campgrounds, except Cottonwood Springs. Data source: Robert B. Pirie, Jr. to Dr. Dickson J. Hingson, February 10, 1997, Joshua Tree National Park Archives, Acc. 822, Cat. 30022, Box "EA of VR-1257," Folder 1c. Delta Cartography.

multiple parcels on the edge of the park held by the MWD likely will see more vehicle intrusion. In 2002, developer Richard Oliphant proposed an 8,800-acre project to be called Joshua Hills north of the town of Palm Desert. The new community would have abutted Joshua Tree and used land that many wanted for the recently established Coachella Valley Preserve. The plan for the huge project called for twelve golf courses, several retail centers, a world trade center, and at least 7,000 homes. Local opposition eventually killed the project, and The Nature Conservancy purchased the land for the preserve.

In 2016, another project, called Paradise Valley, appeared to be moving ahead on both sides of I–10 just west of the road leading to the park's entrance at Cottonwood Spring. GLC Enterprises, L.L.C., proposed the project in 1999 and has aggressively sought support from every park superintendent. The initial plan called for an area of 6,555 acres, a portion of which would be on land to be acquired from the BLM. The bureau refused to trade that land to the company, so the project is now expected to cover 1,800 acres, with several golf courses and 8,000 homes. Like Oliphant before it, GLC Enterprises promises it will emphasize open space, wildlife corridors, and ecological responsibility. The community will feature schools, businesses, and medical facilities. Lying east of the Palm Springs to Coachella City agglomeration, it is certain to draw further sprawl over the intervening land. If it proves to be a successful investment, real-estate developers are sure to push for more construction along Dillon Road north and west of the current Coachella Valley metropolitan zone. That will bring more people and their lights, noise, and vehicular toys to the southern edge of the park.[68]

Noise and light pollution disturb animals and also disrupt the "visitor experience." Another source of noise pollution with a much-longer history comes from aircraft passing overhead. Military jets are particularly obnoxious, because they often fly faster than the speed of sound and some pilots fly lower than they should. When land managers complain, some military commanders ignore them or ask for identification of the specific jets breaking the rules, a task almost impossible with the speed and maneuvers of the offending pilots. Officers at the Twentynine Palms Marine Base generally have cooperated, but the U.S. Navy chose a vector for planes from other bases that passed directly over eight of the park's nine campgrounds (Map 8.4).[69]

The CDPA addressed military overflights, but the act did not change the pattern over Joshua Tree. As complaints from campers and hikers increased, park superintendents began trying to negotiate with officials at Lemoore Naval Air Station as early as the mid-1970s. In 1986, Superintendent Anderson complained that, for the last ten years, Lemoore's officials ignored the problem. Regional Director Howard Chapman sent James Hiatt to Joshua Tree to monitor the situation, but he only stayed for two days and then reported that the problem was not serious. After passage of the CDPA, the Sierra Club agitated to have the flight path over Joshua Tree changed. Negotiations between the Navy and the NPS resulted in a new route that passes over the Little

San Bernardino Mountains south of the original route. It now only comes close to the Cottonwood Campground. The Navy adopted the new route in 2000 and complaints over low supersonic flights have decreased, though not disappeared.[70]

Plans for the Eagle Mountain Mine

The encroachment of suburbia and commerce around the edges of Joshua Tree worries park officials for all the reasons cited above. The threat of industrialization and the world's largest solid-waste dump, however, galvanized park officials and their allies to fight the biggest external threat ever posed for JTNP. The Eagle Mountain Mine, on land removed from the monument in 1950, became the site of a protracted battle that went to the U.S. Supreme Court in 2013 and entailed related land issues still not settled in 2016. Lying barely a mile south of the park's current boundary, it is a stark example of the dissonance of national parks with the common public perception of deserts as "sacrifice zones."

Mining for iron began on a small scale during the late-nineteenth century in the Eagle Mountains. In 1943, the U.S. Bureau of Mines estimated that vast resources, possibly more than 3,000,000 tons, existed at the site. The need for steel to build ships in World War II led Kaiser Industries to launch a Southern California subsidiary to take advantage of the ready market. The company acquired and expanded a steel mill in Fontana in 1942 and purchased the Iron Chief Mine from the SPRR two years later. Kaiser paid $1,000,000 for the mine and 2,746 acres of patented land inside JTNM. In January 1947, Kaiser Steel, Inc. requested a special-use permit for the monument's land adjacent to the mine. The NPS granted the permit, because it expected the land to be removed by boundary legislation. Kaiser built a railroad extension to the mine and began operations in 1948. Two years later, the boundary change removed all but 191 acres of Kaiser's land from the monument. In 1952, Congress passed Private Law 82-790, patenting an additional 465 acres to the company and belatedly giving it a railroad right-of-way across other BLM territory. Nonetheless, the law stipulated that, if the mine and milling did not operate continuously for a period of seven years, the land would revert to the United States.[71]

Throughout the next three decades, Kaiser Steel developed four interconnected pits, took millions of tons of iron ore from the site, and employed hundreds of workers. The company exported both iron ore and steel, much of it to Japan. Then, two newspaper reports in 1967 indicated that changes were coming. On January 25, *The Riverside Daily Enterprise* reported that many of the workers and other residents of Eagle Mountain, the company-owned town beside the mine, would move to a new development near the town of Desert Center. On the same day, *The Los Angeles Times* reported a temporary shutdown of the mine, due to decreased demand for its ore. Competition from foreign mines and mills heralded a decline that depressed the entire U.S. steel industry. In 1975, a desperate Kaiser Steel furloughed 1,200 workers, and many never worked for the company again. *The Los Angeles Times* reported in March 1981 that the company had suffered losses for eighteen consecutive fiscal quarters. Finally, news came the following November that Kaiser would end its operations at the Eagle Mountain Mine and Fontana steel mill. Two years later, *The Los Angeles Times* reported the poignant departure of the last students of the school in Eagle Mountain along with the rest of the 200 remaining residents.[72]

Kaiser Steel faced a decision about what to do with the massive mine and the scores of empty buildings in the abandoned town (Fig. 8.1). The company declared bankruptcy and formed the Mine Reclamation Corporation (MRC) to find a use for its holdings. In 1986, a partial solution came when Kaiser leased part of the town to a company called the Management and Training Corporation for a private, 200-man jail for low-risk offenders and parole violators. Three years later, the facility expanded to hold 500 prisoners. Nevertheless, the pittance that Kaiser earned from the facility did little to solve the main issues of using the mine and bailing out the bankrupt retirement system for its former employees. But then the company found an answer that seemed brilliant. By 1987, Los Angeles and other cities in Southern California produced more than 72,000 tons of waste per day. Four local landfills had closed since 1980, and the rest were nearing capacity. Only one new landfill had opened during that time. Rapid increases in both population growth and per-capita garbage production demanded a radical solution. Furthermore, the immense sprawl of suburbs and heavily congested roads meant viable solutions would have to be found at a distant site. What better place to put all that garbage than a giant hole in the ground far removed from population centers? Even better, a railroad line to the site already existed, and a single train could move waste that would take 450 garbage trucks to carry.[73]

In 1988, the MRC announced its plan for the Eagle Mountain Landfill and began seeking permits from Riverside County. JTNP received an official notice of the project from the Riverside County Planning Department on August 7, 1989, and a slightly amended one eight days later. The massive development would take place only three-quarters of a mile from the monument's southeastern boundary.[74] MRC, in its overview of the project, explained the need for such a large landfill, the advantages of the location, and the ways it would improve the environmental quality of Southern California. The landfill would accept 16,000 tons of waste per day for 100 years. The pits were underlain by solid rock, in an area with barely three inches of rain per year that was "several miles from any resident population." In addition, past mining had left tailings that could be used to line the pit and cover the garbage. Trains with closed railroad cars would carry the trash to the landfill, eliminating worries about windblown litter and offensive odors along the rail line. By vastly reducing both the garbage and the trucks in the region's major cities, the project would improve

FIG. 8.1. An aerial view in 2012 of the Eagle Mountain Mine less than two miles from Joshua Tree National Park. Proposals to convert the massive complex to the world's largest landfill or a pair of reservoirs that function as an energy-producing pump storage project threaten the park's resources with air pollution, deterioration of views and the night sky, eutrophication, and a radical ecological transformation. These and other development schemes have led the National Park Service to consider trying to add the land to the park. Photograph by Bruce Gordon (original in color) for EcoFlight and used by permission.

urban air quality and hence the health of the residents. The key to all of this was the removal of trash from the presence of the people who created it. The desert, with its harsh summer climate and low-population density, seemed to offer the perfect solution.[75]

As MRC developed its plan, several details became clear. First, it needed more land around the mine for treatment facilities and additional landfill space. Second, it needed a Federal Land Policy and Management Act right-of-way for the trash-hauling railroad to supersede the reversion clause established in Private Law 82-790. Up to that point, Kaiser avoided losing the land by periodically digging in the old pits. Third, it needed to redesign its road to accept 4,000 tons of trash per day brought by truck from Riverside County. That waste material, added to the rail deliveries, brought the total amount to be accepted at the landfill to 20,000 tons per day. One of the interesting aspects of the plan was that the trash would initially be deposited in the side canyons around the mine, some of which consisted of undisturbed government land. The pits would not be filled until decades after the operation began.[76]

The huge project required two separate approvals by two unrelated agencies. First, the BLM had to approve the land trade and new rights-of-way for the landfill's rail and road routes. The company sought 3,481 acres surrounding the mine in exchange for ten parcels of Kaiser land, totaling 2,846 acres, along the revised railroad right-of-way (Map G1). The latter would become substitute habitat for the desert tortoises displaced by the landfill. One parcel was already designated as critical habitat for the desert tortoise, three were within the Chuckwalla Bench Area of Critical Environmental Concern, but the remaining six had no recognized ecological value. The BLM would have to complete an environmental impact statement (EIS) to carry out these actions. Second, Riverside County had to approve the landfill itself, which required an environmental impact report (EIR) to satisfy the California Environmental Quality Act (CEQA). That 1970 law is the state equivalent of the National Environmental Policy Act (NEPA) and also requires a public review. In addition, it extends to any private development that requires approval by a state agency. Fortunately for MRC, a single document could serve as both the EIS and the EIR. It had to satisfy concerned citizens and agencies that the land exchange and the project itself would not significantly harm air, water, and biological resources.[77]

In May 1989, Kaiser sent its first project overview to Joshua Tree. On September 1, Superintendent Anderson and Robert Moon attended a scoping meeting on the plan in Riverside and submitted written comments eleven days later. Their concerns fell into four categories. First, the wilderness area of the Pinto Basin and surrounding territory made it a Class I air-quality zone. The landfill would bring more of the coastal cities' air pollution as well as the stink of the waste to the monument. Second was the impact on wildlife. Since closure of the mine, bighorn sheep had returned to pathways through the area and to water sources that would be affected by the dump. Two years

FIG. 8.2. The common raven (*Corvus corax*) is one of the most widely dispersed birds in the world, ranging over much of the northern hemisphere. It is also one of the most intelligent and adapts well to human activity. Throughout the Mojave and Colorado Deserts, ravens prey upon the threatened desert tortoise by snapping up the young before their shells harden. This raven at the Cholla Cactus Garden is keen to take a tortoise hatchling or anything edible dropped by the park's visitors. Photograph by the author (original in color), January 2014.

earlier, the Environmental Protection Agency (EPA) published a report with the conclusion that all landfills leak. Of greater concern from a legal standpoint was the impact that ravens drawn to the landfill (Fig. 8.2) would have on the endangered desert tortoise (Plate 27). The wily birds regularly prey upon young tortoises, which have relatively soft shells. A much larger raven population could ravage the protected tortoise habitat in the Pinto Basin. Other predators, including kit foxes and coyotes, would also gather around the landfill, seeking easy meals. A third category of problems included the airborne litter, noise, and light pollution from the landfill spilling into the Pinto Basin, the area of the monument that offered the most isolated wilderness experience. Finally, they challenged Kaiser's vague plan to monitor and mitigate any potential threats. With vehicle access illegal, how would they monitor the adjacent 92,000-acre wilderness parcel on foot?[78]

Anderson explained all these issues to *The Riverside Press-Enterprise* in an interview published on December 7, 1989, but he concluded with an odd statement:

> We don't want to be the bad guys here. We are not trying to prevent the project. We lived with the mine. But we want it to be as good an operation as it can get, so we don't have any problems.[79]

At the time, senior NPS officials were still hesitant about whether Joshua Tree was worthy of national park status, as proposed in the California desert protection bills. Furthermore, the NPS was part of a department that had a chain of command not always in complete agreement with the agency's preservation philosophy. Without backing from the George H. W. Bush administration, the NPS had to defer to the BLM.

Public response to the landfill scheme varied locally and regionally. For cities in Southern California, it offered many benefits with no obvious downsides. Many residents saw it as a way to remove a big problem from the middle of where people lived. For locals in Riverside County, there were a number of positive aspects to the plan. It would bring to the county up to six dollars per ton of trash in fees plus create jobs. Former employees of the mine faced a pension crisis due to the bankruptcy of Kaiser Steel. Notice of the landfill project had already raised Kaiser's stock prices by more than 600 percent and promised to rescue its retirement system. Most environmentalists opposed the plan, as did many people who lived near the site. Communities in Coachella Valley were split. The project would benefit local towns by trucking their waste to the site, but some feared that increased rail and truck traffic and potential train wrecks would prove unacceptable. The people who lived closest to the site worried about its impact on groundwater, especially in the Chuckwalla Basin, and two people, in particular, despaired enough to challenge the legality of the entire project. Donna and Larry Charpied lived and farmed jojoba three miles from the mine site (Fig. 8.3). Their operation and their quiet desert lifestyle would be completely disrupted if the massive landfill

FIG. 8.3. Donna and Larry Charpied established a farm to grow jojoba plants (*Simmondsia chinensis*) north of Desert Center and close to the Eagle Mountain Iron Mine. They raise the endemic plant species to extract its oil, which is used in hair and skin lotions. When the Kaiser Corporation sought to turn the mine into the world's largest solid-waste dump, they led a resilient campaign through state and federal courts to defeat it. In 2009, the Joshua Tree National Park Association presented the Charpieds with its annual Minerva Hoyt Desert Conservation Award, for their steadfast leadership in the twenty-year fight against the landfill. Photographer and date unknown. Photograph courtesy of Donna and Larry Charpied.

became a reality. After finding that lawyers' fees were prohibitive, Donna Charpied decided to learn the legal procedures necessary to halt the project on her own. They would become the legal and public faces of the opposition and the ultimate reason the landfill project failed.[80]

The first sign of trouble for MRC came when it began circulating a preliminary plan and EIR to various agencies that would be affected. The September 1990 draft included an "Ambient Air Quality Monitoring Plan," which the Air Quality Division of the NPS rejected. Agency scientists claimed that the landfill would increase ozone in a Class I area already suffering from serious pollution. After Riverside County and the BLM released their draft report to the public in July 1991, NPS scientists told *The Fresno Bee* that "dust and other particulate emissions from the project would contribute to the increase in desert haze which has been documented by the Park Service over the years."[81] In September, JTNP submitted its concerns in writing and requested that the final statement address them. Yet nothing seemed to change as the review process went forward. On April 13, 1992, Superintendent Moore wrote to Russell Kaldenberg of the BLM:

> Throughout the comment period, we have reiterated our concern that the draft EIS [DEIS] did not adequately address the project's proximity to a National Monument, International Biosphere Reserve[,] and Class I airshed. Given our commitment to preserving all animal and plant species for future generations, the DEIS's focus on specific threatened or endangered species does not adequately address our concerns.[82]

Moore reiterated that air-quality specialists at the Denver Service Center (DSC) found the air-quality models used for the document to be flawed. He again stressed the biological effects that adding an overabundance of nutrients to a nutrient-poor environment would have on the desert food web. Nevertheless, on June 3, 1992, Riverside County and the BLM issued their final EIS/EIR with only cosmetic changes. This would become a pattern in the ensuing years. The NPS supplied comments, usually backed with scientific data, only to have the BLM dismiss them as insignificant or ignore them entirely. This matched the BLM's response to NPS comments about the California desert protection bills under review at the same time.[83]

Just before the release of the final environmental impact document, a new organization entered the controversy. The Eagle Mountain Energy Company (EMEC) proposed an entirely different use for the abandoned mine pits. The enormous growth of Southern California's cities already taxed the power grid supplied by hydroelectric plants on the Colorado River and rivers in Northern California as well as nuclear and other types of generating stations. The area had enough electricity most of the time, but, during daylight and early evening hours and especially in summer, heightened demand threatened brownouts. The new company saw an opportunity to make the old mine into a battery of sorts for those high-use times. It would establish two reservoirs in upper and lower pits and turbines on the connecting pipeline. During the night, when the demand for electricity was low, the company would pump water from the low pit to the high one. During times of high demand, it would release the water back to the lower pit, passing through turbines to supply a surge of electricity to the power grid. On May 29, 1992, EMEC received a preliminary permit from the Federal Energy Regulatory Commission (FERC) to plan its official application for the project (Map G2). Both the NPS and MRC took note, and neither was happy about it. JTNP officials opposed the idea, because it threatened to lower water in the Chuckwalla Basin aquifer and then in the Pinto Basin aquifer. Like the landfill, it also threatened to alter the entire ecosystem by enriching it artificially. The extra surface water might increase numbers of herbivores and overtax the forage, while more numerous predators would reduce the population of the threatened desert tortoise. Proponents of the landfill saw it as direct competition for the same land. Although the two companies tried to negotiate, they wound up opposing each other in all the subsequent lawsuits and hearings.[84]

Although the NPS, from its Washington, D.C., office, remained quiet about the controversy brewing at its distant desert unit and ordered the regional office to do the same, the staff at Joshua Tree went public with its concerns. Opponents of the landfill held a rally in Riverside on June 16, 1992, and the monument sent ecologist Jerry Freilich. In uniform, he told the crowd and the media why JTNM did not want the landfill to take place. The following day, an article with a large picture of Freilich appeared in *The Riverside Press–Enterprise*. This prompted an angry response from Patricia "Corky" Larson and others on the Riverside County Board of Supervisors who supported the project. In addition, the Washington, D.C., office reprimanded JTNM's leaders for taking such a public stance on the issue. The rally brought out other allies in the fight against the project, including environmental organizations such as Greenpeace and the Sierra Club as well as California Assemblyman Steve Clute, who questioned whether the land exchange gave the government fair value or was even legal.[85]

After release of the final landfill EIS/EIR, officials at all levels of the NPS pondered the implications of the project. It lay entirely outside the legal boundary of the monument, so there were no easy legal methods to stop it. If Riverside County and the BLM approved it, the landfill would happen. The NPS had to make sure it influenced the project to make it as benign as possible for JTNM. Hence, in August 1992, monument officials met with MRC leaders to discuss a memorandum of understanding that would enable a group of scientists to monitor the impacts of the landfill and propose solutions to any problems that might occur. The program would be entirely supported by funds from the landfill, as would other research and land acquisition operations in Joshua Tree. This became the favorite option for the NPS leaders in Washington, D.C., even though their local and regional staffs still staunchly opposed the landfill. Superintendent Moore decided to delay signing a memorandum of understanding until the BLM issued a final decision on the land exchange.[86]

As summer turned to fall, the battle over the Eagle Mountain mine grew heated. The EPA reported that cracks in the bedrock underlying the mine meant it might be impossible to monitor contamination of groundwater. The BLM continued to ignore NPS's warnings about the inadequacies of the project's EIS. On October 6, 1992, after ten hearings, the Riverside County Board of Supervisors approved the project by a vote of three to two. Donna Charpied, already a leader of the opponents, yelled "shame on you" after the vote. The Riverside Press–Enterprise reported that supporters of the project "grinned broadly and offered back-slapping handshakes," while Richard A. Daniels, President of MRC, called the approval "a victory for the environment." The vote was not a surprise, because the positions of the five supervisors were well known by that time. Indeed, the Charpieds had prepared for this eventuality.[87]

In March 1993, Kaiser and MRC filed requests with FERC to oppose EMEC's application for a license to carry out its energy project. The following October, the BLM issued its "Record of Decision," approving the land exchange and new rights-of way for the landfill. Everything seemed to be falling into place for Kaiser and MRC. On December 2, however, the easy ride ended for the company. The Charpieds filed suit in Riverside County Superior Court, claiming that the environmental review did not address many significant impacts the project would have. A day later, the NPCA along with the Eagle Mountain Landfill Opposition Coalition and Steven Clute filed a similar suit in the same court. The day after that, EMEC filed a third suit. To top it off, a group of local citizens, including the Citizens for the Chuckwalla Valley led by the Charpieds, Steven Clute, and EMEC, challenged the land-exchange decision with the Department of the Interior's Board of Land Appeals. The energy company believed it had the upper hand, because FERC officials claimed that, under the Federal Power Act, their authority trumped that of the BLM. Regardless of the interagency debate, in January 1994 the Interior Board concluded that the land exchange warranted another look, so it issued a stay on the BLM's decision. At the same time, Riverside County ordered an inspection tour of the mine by state toxic-waste officials to determine whether Kaiser had dumped hazardous materials. This dealt a blow to the publicity campaign that Kaiser and MRC were running on local media.[88]

Because Riverside County was one of the parties being sued, the trial took place in the Superior Court of San Diego, California, with Judge Judith McConnell presiding. The hearing took three days in late June 1994. In Judge McConnell's ruling on the cases on July 26, she found the EIS/

EIR deficient, because it did not address the impact the growth of the town of Eagle Mountain would have on air and water quality or the effect of the landfill on the competing energy project. She also found that the document inadequately addressed seismic threats to the lining of the pits, the impact of ravens on the desert tortoise, and the effects of windblown litter, dust, and biological changes on JTNM. *The Desert Sun* reported that the landfill would not be supported at that time anyway, because a change in the membership of the Riverside County Board of Supervisors placed those against the project in the majority. Kay Hazen, a representative of MRC, told reporters that this would only delay the project, not stop it. Judge McConnell, however, also ordered the company and Riverside County to pay all court costs for both sides, another blow in a pattern of financial attrition that weakened the project.[89]

During the rest of 1994, the various parties in the conflict maneuvered to reintroduce or finally bury the landfill plan. One of the primary financial backers for the project, Browning-Ferris Industries, pulled out, further stressing the economic status of MRC. In spite of this, the company and Kaiser announced in September that they would appeal Judge McConnell's decision. In October, passage of the CDPA added lands east and west of the old iron mine to Joshua Tree. In the final stages of that bruising legislative battle, the bill's proponents made sure to add a statement that the expansion of Joshua Tree would not affect the debate about the landfill in any way. A bill that would pass by a single vote could not afford to become involved in what was becoming a national conservation issue. In November, the Riverside County supervisors decided not to appeal the court ruling and voided five of the permits it had issued for the project. As an election approached, however, several new candidates promised to revive it.[90]

The setbacks for the landfill offered encouragement to the EMEC. Yet it, too, faced challenges from the NPS. On April 29, 1994, the company applied to FERC for a license to develop its hydroelectric generation project. The NPS criticized the proposal, forcing the company to issue an amended version in May. A month later, agency officials submitted a response, arguing that the modified document still did not answer concerns about the environmental change the two reservoirs would bring, their effect on the ecology and wildlife of the region, the long-term diversion of water from local aquifers, and the cumulative consequences of both this project and the landfill, should both be approved. Although this reaction caused EMEC officials such as President Arthur Lowe to pause, the troubles besetting the landfill renewed their enthusiasm. In December, Superintendent Quintana (Fig. 8.4) requested an analysis by the Water Resources Branch of the NPS of the probable loss of water from the Pinto Basin Aquifer, if the hydroelectric project went ahead. That office reported that loss of groundwater in the Chuckwalla Valley Aquifer would not significantly affect the one in Pinto Basin.[91]

FIG. 8.4. Ernest Quintana began his National Park Service (NPS) career as a seasonal employee of Joshua Tree National Monument. In 1993, he became Superintendent of Joshua Tree and strenuously opposed the Eagle Mountain Landfill project. His public stance disturbed NPS officials in Washington, D.C., who finally ordered him to accept their compromise. Undaunted, he still opposed the project and received the Stephen Tyng Mather Award for his stance from the National Parks Conservation Association. Photographer and date unknown. Courtesy of Ernest Quintana.

If the opponents of the landfill proposal at Eagle Mountain felt relieved by Judge McConnell's ruling, 1995 brought a rude awakening. Kaiser rescued MRC from its financial troubles by purchasing seventy percent of the company. In January, the BLM signaled its support for the landfill by informing FERC that it opposed giving the newly renamed Eagle Crest Energy Company any more than forty-seven acres, the maximum available, if the land exchange with Kaiser/MRC succeeded. In April, Kaiser proposed a new plan for the landfill, while the BLM appealed the stay on its land exchange. Kaiser also paid for a study showing that Eagle Crest would take too much water and, therefore, its project should be cancelled. On May 6, the Riverside County Planning Department, backed by new members on the Board of Supervisors, released a "notice of preparation" for a new EIS/EIR.[92]

The BLM agreed to cosponsor the new study and asked JTNP to join it. Superintendent Quintana initially refused and reiterated his strong opposition to the project, but the regional and national offices of the two agencies took a different point of view. The senior officials believed that the best way they could protect JTNP was to influence the study from within. They also had less faith in the project's opponents and sought to get the best deal they could out of the situation. Coincident with this disagreement was a return to negotiations for a memorandum of agreement that would bring funds for monitoring the park's resources and additional research. Quintana discussed the options with Pat McClenahan, Chief of Resources Management, and other members of JTNP's staff and solicited opinions from around the national park system before relenting. On June 20, he notified the BLM that the NPS would cooperate. Nine days later, he sent a detailed, twelve-page description of environmental issues that worried JTNP personnel. Couched in courteous terms was the implicit warning that the list had better be taken seriously.[93]

Kaiser/MRC hired engineering consultant CH2M Hill and proceeded with the environmental review process throughout the rest of 1995. In the meantime, several attempts to derail projects at the old mine failed. Eagle Crest explained that it accepted the NPS as an intervener in its license application but opposed input from the National Biological Survey, the new agency under the USGS that included some scientists who once worked for the NPS. Many of them led the academic debate on the impact of the water project on the desert tortoise and other regional fauna. The company slowly continued its application process amid uncertainty about the competing landfill.

At the same time, JTNP officials challenged the legality of the land exchange between the BLM and Kaiser/MRC on the grounds that the CDPA required the federal land agency to prioritize acquisition of private land in national parks and wilderness areas rather than supply a company with several thousand acres for commercial development. The challenge failed, however, as did a campaign by the Charpieds to block renewal of the Eagle Mountain prison permit. Closing the prison initially appeared possible, because it had problems with the purity of its water system, and Superintendent Quintana had testified that light pollution from it threatened the wilderness experience in Joshua Tree. One interesting development was a unanimous vote by the Imperial County Board of Supervisors, in September 1995, approving a plan to develop an equally large Mesquite Landfill well south of the park. The existence of a substitute for the Eagle Mountain Landfill, while also decried by environmentalists, offered more ammunition for opponents of the Riverside County project.[94]

As Riverside County and the BLM developed the environmental review, it became apparent that they still ignored many questions and suggestions from JTNP officials. Several meetings between the NPS, BLM, Riverside County and CH2M Hill as well as public hearings did not persuade Quintana to sign the memorandum of agreement. In fact, his continued public criticism of the project brought angry inquiries from Congressman Jerry Lewis, who did not understand why a local NPS official continued his vocal opposition, while his superiors seemed satisfied with the monitoring and financial support being offered by the company. He accused the superintendent of trying to establish a "buffer zone" around JTNP that was contrary to the stipulations of the CDPA. Quintana began to hear periodic questions and occasional rebukes over his antagonism, but he remained undaunted.[95] Despite the danger to his career, he wrote:

> The citing [sic] of a major landfill within one mile of Joshua Tree National Park will be viewed as an uncontrolled experiment. This garbage dump project proposes to implement the best in technology and safeguards[;] however, we don't know, nor will we know for many years, what the outcome of that experiment will be. Should anything be discovered wrong, there is no way to stop the experiment. . . . A desert is, by definition, a place with few nutrients, little water, long distances between resources, short time windows for breeding and above-ground foraging, and low densities of plant and animal life. It seems likely, from a scientific standpoint, that placing 20,000 tons of trash per day in a place whose natural ecology is characterized by sparsity [sic] would have far-reaching effects. Many of these effects will fall into the category of being subtle, long-term, and hard to detect.[96]

In December, CH2M Hill summarized the many concerns over the project in a "draft significant criteria" report. By now, the list had expanded to include thirteen issues: quantity and quality of groundwater, public health and safety, the impact of increased traffic and transportation, air quality, adjacent land use, surface drainage and flooding, biological resources, the inducement to further growth and development brought by the project, geologic threats (including seismic activity), impact on visual and recreational experiences, intrusions against the purity and enjoyment of wilderness, competition for utilities and services, effects on cultural resources, impact on local paleontology, and energy consumption. JTNP criticized everything in the document, except road and rail transport and the effects on mineral, cultural, and paleontological resources. As 1996 began, the NPS's regional office publicly supported JTNP's position.[97]

In early February 1996, Kaiser/MRC submitted the new draft EIS/EIR to the NPS and asked for comments to be returned within three weeks. The document contained more than 600 pages of information, some of it highly technical, plus two volumes of previous comments by outside reviewers and the company's responses to them. Field Solicitor Ralph Mihan answered that, as a cooperating agency under NEPA regulations, the NPS was not going to be rushed into a hasty and incomplete review. Even the agency's Washington, D.C., office rejected this corporate attempt to circumvent standard procedures and demanded an extension until March. On the fourteenth of that month, JTNP sent its comments to the BLM. Once again, the NPS challenged the Kaiser/ MRC's assessment of impacts on air quality and water resources, the intrusion of night light, noise, and windblown litter in the wilderness, the threats to the desert tortoise and bighorn sheep, and the company's plan to mitigate them. A research study by Jerry Freilich, validated by desert ecologists James McMahon and William Schlesinger, showed that the long-term, cumulative impact of nutrient enrichment in the area would be substantial and its effect immeasurable until it was too late. The NPS used the term "eutrophication" to describe this process. Kaiser/MRC, Riverside County, and the BLM dismissed the NPS's comments and maintained, in a new publicity campaign, that they more than adequately addressed any ecological problems associated with the landfill.[98]

Meanwhile, all the non-government organizations and people who opposed the project were busy as well. Donna and Larry Charpied filed a freedom of information request with the NPS that turned up an e-mail from Kaiser/MRC lobbyist Anne Wexler to NPS Director Roger Kennedy. She argued that the final decision on the landfill was a state and local concern and that the NPS would benefit from the still-unsigned memorandum of agreement with the company. The Charpieds saw this as a conflict of interest, because Wexler and Kennedy both served on the Board of Directors of the National Park Foundation (NPF). After a two-week delay, the NPS's Office of Public Affairs responded that Wexler had spoken to Director Kennedy several times about the landfill, that, although he was Secretary Ex Officio of the foundation on which she served, he was not directly involved in any of NPS's actions with respect to the project. This accusation of malfeasance by the director gained little credence, but it convinced the Charpieds to view the NPS, outside of JTNP, as a foe rather than an ally.[99]

In July, when Riverside County and the BLM released the massive draft of the environmental document to the public, an order from the NPS came down the chain of command. Thereafter, the official position of the agency would come from the headquarters in Washington, D.C., and Superintendent Quintana would no longer represent the NPS in matters concerning Eagle Mountain. Michael Soukup, the associate director for NPS's natural resources, would serve as the agency's authority and contact. Soon, a new draft memorandum of understanding appeared. Officials from JTNP and the regional office continued to criticize it and the draft EIS/EIR. Nevertheless, on December 9, 1996, Acting Deputy Director Denis Galvin signed the agreement with Kaiser/MRC. The company promised to pay for a research center based in the Eagle Mountain town, provide $175,000 in advance payments, establish a trust to contribute ten percent of its funds to the NPF for its unrestricted use, and carry out multiple measures for monitoring and mitigation at costs of up to $900,000 per year. One month later, Riverside County and the BLM released their final environmental document. Superintendent Quintana told the press that he and his staff still opposed the landfill. In the meantime, Eagle Crest informed the FERC that its application for a license to build the hydroelectric complex remained active.[100]

The shift of authority for the NPS to its distant headquarters weakened the influence of Quintana and the local authorities, but once again the Charpieds and several environmental organizations took action. In January 1997, the Charpieds tried to challenge the agreement legally, while the NPCA bitterly criticized Galvin's decision to sign it. The conservation organization annually listed JTNP as the most-imperiled unit in the national park system in its popular magazine, *National Parks*. Former NPS Director William Whalen, after agreeing to review the agreement and the monitoring plan, approved both, further distancing the hierarchy in Washington, D.C., from the stance of its people in California. In September 1997, the Riverside Board of Supervisors approved the environmental study by a vote of four to one, and the BLM officially approved the land exchange. Both agencies claimed that the plan to monitor and mitigate harmful effects from the landfill was sufficient to allow the project.[101]

On October 15, the NPCA presented the Stephen Tyng Mather Award to Superintendent Quintana. As Executive Vice President Carol Aten presented the association's highest award, she described Quintana's selfless dedication to protecting his park's resources for future generations at the risk to his own career. This no doubt embarrassed some of his NPS bosses. At the same time, the association filed another suit in San Diego Superior Court, charging that the latest environmental-impact document still inadequately addressed the threats the landfill would bring to JTNP and the surrounding desert. The Charpieds filed a similar suit with the court and appealed the land exchange with the Department of the Interior's Board of Land Appeals.[102]

Once again, Judge Judith McConnell heard the two cases on December 31, and she issued her decision on February 17, 1998. To the dismay and frustration of Riverside County and Kaiser/MRC, she agreed with the plaintiffs that the huge environmental review still left too many issues inadequately researched and, hence, unresolved. McConnell allowed that the new document satisfied doubts about the impact of growth at Eagle Mountain town and the effects of seismic events on the landfill's liner. She also agreed that the land exchange had been sufficiently addressed. She rejected, however, the new document's claims that the project would have little impact on JTNP and on the desert tortoise. The decision was a grievous blow to Kaiser/MRC, after it spent millions of dollars on the environmental investigation, lobbying, and public relations. Company executives and Riverside County supervisors pondered what course to take for two months before announcing, in April, that they would take the case to the State Court of Appeals.[103]

On May 7, 1999, the landfill project's roller-coaster ride twisted again, when the appeals court overturned Judge McConnell's decision. The panel of judges rejected the contention that JTNP would be harmed, citing the disagreement between local NPS officials and their Washington, D.C., leaders, who signed the memorandum of understanding with Kaiser/MRC. If the senior officials in the NPS believed the mitigation efforts would suffice, the judges reasoned, then why listen to the local doubters? The court also disagreed with McConnell's reasoning on the tortoise and found that the provision of alternate habitat, especially along the railroad right-of-way in the Chuckwalla Bench Area of Critical Environmental Concern, would sufficiently compensate for the loss of the area surrounding the mine. A jubilant Kay Hazen, of the MRC, told reporters that the NPS as a whole formally approved the landfill and that Superintendent Quintana's concerns were merely his personal opinion. In response, Regional Director John J. Reynolds immediately wrote to tell her that she was seriously mistaken, but the public relations damage was done. Opponents of the landfill petitioned the California Supreme Court to review the reversal, but, in July, the high court refused to hear the challenge. Thus ended litigation at the state level.[104]

On the following October 13, after the review board rejected the latest appeal, the BLM again approved the land exchange and new rights-of-way for the road and railroad. The Charpieds immediately protested the project to state water and air pollution authorities but to no avail. By November, the focus returned to the memorandum of understanding between the NPS and Kaiser/MRC. A revised agreement promised an immediate contribution by Kaiser to the NPF of $75,000 plus ten cents per ton of trash to be used for JTNP in the future. Denis Galvin signed the new memorandum on July 10, 2000. The future looked grim for the landfill's opponents, but they had not exhausted every means at their disposal. During December 1999, the Charpieds and the Desert Protection Society filed suit in federal court, challenging the project's compliance with NEPA. At the same time, the NPCA filed a federal suit against the land exchange. Legal obstacles once again stymied any action on the massive project. This time, both suits included the NPS among the defendants.[105]

After more than eleven years, MRC had exhausted much of its capital, and even Kaiser grew weary of the incessant delays and political hurdles. Then, in August 2000, the Los Angeles Sanitation Department, a consortium of seventy-eight cities and the county, jumped into the fray. It initiated purchase of the Kaiser/MRC project for $41,000,000. Kaiser announced that the proceeds would benefit the retirees of its bankrupt steel subsidiary. Completion of the sale hinged on successful conclusions to the federal lawsuits. *The Riverside Press-Enterprise*, essentially neutral up to that time, complained:

> So here's LA, the fabled Imperial City that drank the Owens River and bought the Ontario Airport, that prefers to put its prisoners and its trash on somebody else's real estate, that gulps down great droughts of everyone's transportation dollars for its overpriced subways. Yes, meet the neighbors. And then remind us again how it is in the Inland area's long-term interests to help LA shrug off these natural constraints to growth.[106]

Superintendent Quintana questioned whether MRC had the right to sell to LA Sanitation, according to the stipulations of the agreement it signed with the NPS, which also held up completion of the sale.

For a while, events slowed, as both sides prepared for the federal trials to come. In September 2002, the Center for Biological Diversity, a conservation group, announced it would sue the project's proponents over violations to the Endangered Species Act regarding the desert tortoise. In November 2003, the Charpieds began a public campaign to return the entire Eagle Mountain area to JTNP. They based their "Give it Back" campaign on Private Law 82-790 of 1952 and maintained that Kaiser/MRC had not continued regular mining at the site and, therefore, should forfeit all of its land. They suggested that the entire 29,775 acres of land between the Coxcomb and Eagle Mountains be returned to JTNP and that the town should become a national historic landmark. Meanwhile, several other actions transpired. First, Superintendent Quintana left JTNP in 2003 to become the director of the Midwest regional office in Omaha. Apparently, his unflagging, almost rebellious, protection of Joshua Tree did not hurt his career. Curt Sauer replaced him and continued the park's steady opposition to the landfill. Second, problems at the prison in Eagle Mountain forced its closure after a fatal riot in 2003. Third, Eagle Crest, which had watched the unfolding drama over the Kaiser/MRC project with interest, received a new preliminary permit to develop a license application for its hydroelectric facility.[107]

After opponents of the landfill filed the federal lawsuits, Kaiser/MRC warned its investors that further troubles might ensue. Their concern stemmed mostly from the Los Angeles Sanitation District's purchase of the competing Mesquite Landfill project in Imperial County. Then, on September 20, 2005, Judge Robert J. Timlin dealt a crushing blow to the project. He ruled that, under Federal Land Policy and Management Act regulations, Kaiser/MRC and the BLM failed not only to assess eutrophication adequately and its impact on bighorn sheep, but also to consider the landfill as the highest and best use of the land. He overturned the land exchange, calling the BLM's Record of Decision "arbitrary, capricious, an abuse of discretion and not in accordance with the law." The Mesquite Landfill had a projected opening date of 2010 and would accept up to 20,000 tons of trash per day. By then, the massive urban area of Los Angeles would produce 40,000 tons of garbage per day. Still, Eagle Mountain's backers could salvage the project, if they could get past Timlin's ruling.[108]

In spite of this near-fatal blow to the landfill project, the next several years brought more threats in the Eagle Mountain area. First, the Houston-based Cornell Companies, which operated seventy-nine correctional facilities in seventeen states, applied to reopen the Eagle Mountain facility. The Charpieds filed protests, and, after a well-publicized inspection of the moribund jail, Riverside County decided not to issue a new permit. The Charpieds also opposed military training at the mine site but lost that appeal. After quietly maneuvering in the background, Eagle Crest filed a final license application on June 22, 2009. In January 2010, FERC issued a "Ready for Environmental Analysis Notice," opening another controversial round of criticism from locals and park officials and responses from the company.[109]

Kaiser/MRC and the BLM appealed Judge Timlin's decision to the Ninth Circuit Court of Appeals in January 2007. Judges Harry Pregerson, Richard A. Paez, and Stephen S. Trott reviewed the case and, on November 10, 2009, issued a two-to-one ruling, with Judge Trott dissenting. They reiterated Timlin's opinion that the BLM failed to consider the landfill use as the "highest and best" use of the exchange lands, did not consider a full range of alternatives in the EIS, and inadequately analyzed the effects of eutrophication on JTNP. The following month, Kaiser/MRC, the BLM, and a new entry, the Kaiser Voluntary Employee Benefit Association, filed for an *en banc* hearing that would involve all the judges of the Ninth Circuit Court, instead of just three. The retiree association also sought congressional help with an emotional plea that 4,000 of its 7,000 members had died during the twenty years the project had been delayed. Unfortunately for them, no member of Congress could influence the court. After the *en banc* appeal failed and the BLM finally gave up, Kaiser/MRC had one option left: an appeal to the U.S. Supreme Court. The NPS, USFWS, and a chastened BLM adopted opposing positions. On March 28, 2011, the Supreme Court refused to hear the case, which meant the Ninth Circuit's decision was final. In the meantime, the agreement signed by Kaiser/MRC and the NPS lapsed, because the company did not start its project within the ten-year window of time stipulated in it. The following November, MRC filed for Chapter Eleven bankruptcy.[110]

In spite of this amazing sequence of rejections, some of the more than fifty investors in MRC would not surrender. Chief among them were Kaiser and the Los Angeles Sanitation District. During the next two years, the companies and Riverside County periodically discussed restarting the entire project. Then, incoming President Barack Obama signaled his opposition to a legislative solution, and more than 100,000 people signed a petition to Secretary of the Interior Ken Salazar, demanding protection for JTNP. Eventually, the Los Angeles agency adopted a new plan called

"RENEW LA," in which it hopes to reclaim ninety percent of the region's municipal solid waste by 2025. Much of the rest will go to the Mesquite Landfill. On May 22, 2013, the district announced it would cease negotiations for the Eagle Mountain project.[111]

In January 2009, the Joshua Tree National Park Association presented Larry and Donna Charpied with its annual Minerva Hoyt Desert Conservation Award, for their twenty years of leadership in the fight against the landfill. The U.S. Supreme Court decision two years later meant they won. Kaiser still controlled the original mine and town but faced a challenge based on the Surface Mining and Reclamation Act of 1977, which requires reclamation of large surface mines within a limited amount of time. On May 26, 2011, the California Department of Conservation's Office of Mine Reclamation issued a fifteen-day notice to Riverside County, the lead agency for this surface-mining operation, to address matters of non-compliance with the law. The notice required Riverside County to notify Kaiser/MRC that the Eagle Mountain Mine was abandoned and reclamation was to begin and be completed, in accordance with an approved plan. This, in turn, raised the legal issue of whether this action triggered the conditions for the reversion of the land to the government under Private Law 82-790.[112]

These legal actions gave impetus to the ongoing "Give It Back" campaign, but it still faced a serious obstacle. In January 2012, FERC approved Eagle Crest's "Final Environmental Impact Statement for the Hydropower License." During nearly two years of reviewing earlier drafts, the NPS and its allies identified threats such as subsidence under the reservoirs, depletion of groundwater, eutrophication, negative impacts on biological resources and air quality, noise pollution, and deleterious effects from the transmission line. Eagle Crest dismissed all of them as overstated and insignificant. The federal commission decided solely on the basis of the low cost of this 1,300-megawatt project, as compared to generating equivalent energy elsewhere. A year later the company bought much of the acreage from Kaiser. On July 15, 2013, the California State Water Resources Control Board approved the project, clearing another major hurdle for Eagle Crest. Some JTNP officials fear they may be unable to halt this project. The introduction of artificial lakes into the desert may become a test of the scientific predictions of catastrophic ecological consequences.[113]

Initially, the NPS did not pursue the "Give It Back" campaign with the zeal of the Charpieds and others, because it would bring massively disturbed land, hazardous substances, and hundreds of structures into JTNP, necessitating a huge increase in both budget and personnel. Some members of the park's staff personally opposed adding the former mine site to a park that, in 2014, still had nearly 15,000 acres of inholdings. They maintained that the park was so short of funds and manpower that it could barely manage the property it already had. One member still insists that taking a part of a park unit away, allowing it to be environmentally trashed, and then taking it back establishes a bad precedent for the entire national park system. He suggests that this would make it easier for companies to secure a park's lands to exploit and return at will.[114]

Late in 2013, NPCA filed suit to overturn the land exchange that the BLM still had not reversed, despite the demise of the landfill project. The environmental group wants to prevent any industrialization around the defunct mine. In the spring of 2016, the NPS issued an "Eagle Mountain Boundary Study" aimed at bringing the former BLM land into the park. As part of the process, hearings will gauge the public's reaction to three scenarios. Option 1 would return some 22,500 acres of BLM land to the park but not affect any private land. Option 2 would give the park 24,800 acres, including some private acreage but not the area needed by Eagle Crest. Finally, Option 3 would bring 28,000 acres into the park, including the land now owned by the energy company. All three options exclude MWD land and promise that private land will only be acquired from willing sellers. What impact this might have on the pumped-storage project is unstated. As of July 2016, Eagle Crest awaited the BLM's approval of a right-of-way for its 500 kilovolt "generation interconnect line" and a water pipeline. One certainty is that addition of the mine to JTNP will bring its inclusion on the National Register of Historic Places.[115]

Energy Developments

Although attention has necessarily focused on threats from the Eagle Mountain Mine, another type of external development threatens to affect both natural resources and visitors' experiences in JTNP. The intense search for clean and renewable energy has increased exploitation of deserts in California and the nation dramatically. Wind turbines, thermal power plants, and solar receptors all have decades of history in the U.S. and in the deserts of California, but political decisions have brought the hunt to an entirely new level. The federal government, especially under President Barack Obama, and the State of California have elevated the renewable-energy program far beyond anything contemplated in the past (Fig. 8.5).

Two actions triggered the hunt for pollution-free power. The first was an executive order, issued on November 17, 2008, by California Governor Arnold Schwarzenegger that challenged state utilities to generate one-third of the state's electricity from renewable sources by 2020. The second was the federal American Recovery and Reinvestment Act of 2009, which provided benefits for renewable-energy projects begun before the end of 2010. On October 9, 2009, Secretary of the Interior Ken Salazar and Governor Schwarzenegger signed a memorandum of understanding to support fast-track approval of renewable-energy projects. One year later, they approved the Ivanpah Solar Electric Generating System just north of Mojave National Preserve. The facility, developed

FIG. 8.5. Joshua Tree National Park ironically faces solar power as a two-edged sword. The numerous planned energy projects around the park, some of them large-scale, can threaten intrusion into scenic views, disruption of the movement and activity of wildlife, and possible development of other commercial functions nearby. Yet the National Park Service espouses the use of solar-generated power as a responsible alternative to dwindling fossil fuels. Here, the Center for Arid Land Restoration has installed panels to generate power for the propagation of desert plants, management of the irrigation system, and other allied structural uses. Photograph by the author (original in color), December 2014.

by BrightSource Energy, Inc., based in Oakland, California, soon became the largest solar-power facility in the world. It generates power by using the sun's rays to heat water, which creates steam to turn its turbines. The demand for water in this desert environment led to questions from scientists and environmental groups.[116]

To address the concern over the environmental impact of these huge projects, a consortium of federal and state government agencies agreed, in May 2010, to develop a Desert Renewable Energy Conservation Plan (DRECP). The four principal agencies are the California Energy Commission, California Fish and Game, BLM, and USFWS. The purpose of DRECP is to designate areas deemed "low conflict" as open for development, while protecting wildlife areas and corridors. As planning moved ahead, the CSLC and the BLM signed an agreement, in May 2012, to foster the exchange of their lands and allow for the consolidation of properties for solar and wind-power development. Since then, utilities and private companies have submitted numerous applications for power plants, and the state and federal governments have approved some. DRECP released its draft plan in September 2014, citing six alternatives for public review. The BLM and the other agencies held eleven public meetings and received more than 16,000 comments. Reaction to the initial draft was mixed. Several counties and multiple communities found fault with specific portions of the plan peculiar to their areas. In response, the agencies modified land-area designations, provided more details on management of conservation lands, and clarified the environmental analysis. In late 2015, the governments released an amended plan for public review.

The most ambitious projects will take place on 10,000,000 acres of BLM land within the 22,500,000-acre DRECP region. Of the various areas the BLM manages, the largest component is the Riverside East Solar Energy Zone, which stretches from near Blythe, near the California/Arizona border, to within seven-tenths of a mile of JTNP. In the amended plan, although 43,439 of the zone's 202,896 total acres were eliminated to reduce impacts on the park, some tracts close to the park's eastern boundary remain available for development.

During this planning period, several projects in the Riverside East Solar Energy Zone California have received fast-track approval. One facility, the Desert Sunlight/First Solar Project, is complete. The 4,410-acre photovoltaic plant lies 1.4 miles from the park's boundary and adjacent to the jojoba farm of Larry and Donna Charpied. Noise and lights from its construction have disturbed their quiet lifestyle. Nearby, EDF Renewable Energy has received approval for a 1,208-acre solar facility called the Desert Harvest Solar Project. Ten miles from JTNP's southeastern boundary, BrightSource Energy, Inc., initiated a proposal called the Palen Solar Power Project. Although its 2,790-acre footprint was smaller than that of Desert Sunlight/First Solar, it would have consisted of two towers at least 750 feet in height. This type of structure generates power by directing sunlight from heliostat mirrors to receivers. Any bird or bat flying between these elements will die instantly.

In addition, the facility would have generated a bright light visible from the park and for miles in every direction, and ten Native American tribes identified the site as a traditional cultural property. Although the California Energy Commission approved the project, a committee of the commission disapproved an amendment requested by BrightSource in December 2013. Later, Abengoa Solar, a Spanish company, purchased the project and announced it would abandon the towers for another type of solar plant, but certification for the project by the commission expired on December 15, 2015. In early 2016, the company announced it would seek to develop a more-standard photovoltaic operation at the same site.[118]

While the Riverside East Solar Energy Zone draws most of the attention from JTNP officials, it is not the only area with applications for solar projects. A truly enormous area known as the Iron Mountain Solar Energy Zone was proposed for a 106,522-acre site ten miles northeast of JTNP. Had it been approved, it would have required transmission lines through the southeastern part of the park. Many national environmental groups opposed this zone, due to its proximity to five wilderness areas plus an historic airfield and camp used by General George Patton for training maneuvers during World War II. In addition, a variety of proposals for small-acreage parcels north of Joshua Tree are also under consideration. In some cases, these facilities are proposed for mixed private and public land that would be visible from the park.

Solar power is not the only kind of clean energy being sought in the Mojave and Colorado Deserts. Other proposals would place so-called "wind farms" very close to JTNP's boundary. These giant wind propellers, visible over long distances, can destroy birdlife. One area that was considered in early 2014 lies adjacent to the park's boundary close to the Eagle Mountain Mine and the Desert Sunlight/First Solar Project (Map F). Opposition by environmental, Native American, and wildlife preservation groups have forced some projects to be abandoned or modified, but the federal and state governments remain committed to achieving a minimum production of 20,000 megawatts in the two California deserts.

The Park Service faced and withstood gold miners during the monument's first two decades of existence. Joshua Tree now faces better-organized and government-supported miners of energy. In the middle of it all sits the Pinto Basin, with its broad flat surface and generous deep aquifer. Will park leaders resist future attempts to use JTNP's open land for the benefit of people who live elsewhere?[119]

Working at Joshua Tree National Park

The years following Joshua Tree's promotion to national park status in 1994 have been marked by more popularity, a higher profile worldwide, improved scientific management of resources, and more respect from senior NPS officials. Yet the threats posed by intensifying use, criminal behavior, external threats, and global warming present greater challenges for the future. On October 1, 2013, many of the functions of the U.S. government ceased, as the two political parties in Congress wrangled over budgetary and health-care issues. The shutdown lasted sixteen days. All national parks and monuments closed, and the NPS's 750,000 Websites became unavailable. During that time, some conservative states used their own funds to reopen certain popular parks in order to avoid the wrath of the general public. For the second time in twenty years, the American public grew very angry over their parks closing. National parks and monuments remain extraordinarily popular, especially as the nation and the world celebrates the centennial of the NPS in 2016 with record-breaking attendance. Predictably, soon after Congress reopened, a conservative lawmaker introduced a bill to take the national parks away from the federal government and turn them over to states or private companies. As the U.S. relentlessly looks for ways to cut taxes, this is a favorite solution of those who seek to minimize the federal budget and government workforce.

By 2015, the staff at JTNP coped with the results of another solution: freezing the budget and shrinking the workforce by attrition, while increasing the tasks that burden the remaining workers. This, of course, is the new work environment of twenty-first-century America. System-wide, the backlog of maintenance of the national parks is now four times the annual budget for the NPS. In every park and monument, the workload increases, as employees retire and some are not replaced. The level of stress that park employees face everywhere is daunting, while greater use of consulting firms dilutes the traditional experience that guided NPS management for a century. More time is spent by staff seeking grants for basic park programs. Higher visitation demands more contact time with visitors. The plethora of threats, short term or continuous, divert rangers and resource managers from their regular duties. Demands by the public and by politicians must be handled as quickly as possible, even if they are unreasonable. Park employees are pulled away to serve on planning teams and training missions that used to be handled by larger regional and national offices. After the government shutdown in 2013, the workload became even heavier. Joshua Tree, like most units of the national park system, now relies heavily on volunteers to handle day-to-day tasks that rangers used to do. Protection of the nearly 800,000-acre park, located in a fragile environment and facing grave threats, is an enormous job. The park's allies in the public and its cadre of volunteers will need to step up to these challenges to assure it will be protected "unimpaired" for future generations.

FIG. E.1. Two resources dominate the profile of Joshua Tree National Park: the compelling monzogranite rock piles that climbers so love and the seemingly malformed Joshua trees that attracted attention to the region in the first place. Here, young Joshua trees struggle to survive on the thin, rocky soil amid an evolving desert climate. Their distinctive presence in the park is now threatened, but the land itself will long provide a nationally significant recreational resource. Photograph by the author (original in color), December 2014.

Eighty Years Old and Growing in Popularity

ON AUGUST 10, 2011, Joshua Tree National Park (JTNP) celebrated its seventy-fifth anniversary as a unit of the national park system. Superintendent Mark Butler addressed a large crowd of the park's supporters, local dignitaries, and curious visitors. He thanked the chambers of commerce of Twentynine Palms, Yucca Valley, and Joshua Tree village, the National Parks Conservation Society, the Joshua Tree National Park Association, the Mojave Desert Land Trust, and several media and publishing groups for their support. He described the park and its importance:

> The park's open spaces, unique vistas, deep skies and wilderness values provide increasingly rare opportunities for personal challenge, health and well being, artistic expression, personal reflection and a connection to the vastness of the larger world. . . . In a land characterized by extremes—heat, dryness and intensity of light—the desert holds an astonishing array of life. California's deserts are recognized as a biodiversity hotspot, a place where the inventiveness, creativity and unbowed determination of life to exist never ceases to amaze.[1]

He cited the park's educational benefits and highlighted the challenges that the National Park Service (NPS) faced in the future. The message was a clear appeal to citizens both local and distant: to help the agency protect JTNP and all other units in the national park system.

One and a half years later, Superintendent Butler addressed another crowd gathered to commemorate the person most responsible for the existence of the national monument and park: Minerva Hamilton Hoyt (Fig. 2.1). On March 27, 2013, on the 147th anniversary of her birthday, JTNP celebrated the naming of a 5,405-foot peak in the park as Mount Minerva Hoyt. A twenty-year campaign had finally succeeded in getting the U.S. Board of Geographic Names to designate the previously unnamed mountain after Joshua Tree's first benefactor. The ensuing events included an actress playing Minerva Hoyt and a number of speeches relating the history of the campaign to create the original monument and Hoyt's central role in it. The occasion included the awarding of the annual Minerva Hoyt California Desert Conservation Award by the park's cooperating association to commemorate people who excelled in protecting desert lands.[2]

Both of these occasions showed how far Joshua Tree had come since 1936. When Minerva Hoyt first proposed a national park for the southern Mojave and northern Colorado Deserts, the reaction of the NPS was tepid at best. Roger Toll (Fig. 2.2), then Superintendent of Yellowstone National Park and an advisor to the NPS on additions to the growing national park system, pointed out many problems, including extensive private property and mining claims, the superfluity of another protected desert area after the establishment of Death Valley National Monument in 1933, and his personal belief that the area had few nationally significant natural or cultural resources. Then, when Joshua Tree became a national monument in 1936, it faced four major problems to solve: (1) acquisition of the property in the monument; (2) a lack of knowledge about the resources and how to manage them; (3) a host of internal and external threats; and (4) a general lack of respect for the desert and the unit by both the NPS and the general public. During its first fifteen years, it often appeared that the monument would completely fail, and, in 1950, it took a dramatic setback by losing a third of its land. Yet it has survived and is now one of the most-popular national parks in the entire system.

The original 1936 boundary of the monument reflected a difficult compromise forced by the existence of copious non-federal lands within the 1,100,000-acre area proposed by Minerva Hoyt and withdrawn from the public domain by President Franklin Roosevelt. More than 300,000 acres had to be excluded. In 1950, the monument lost another 267,000 acres in a forlorn attempt to placate miners. Despite these adjustments, the monument still faced a massive problem of land acquisition with little money available from the U.S. Congress. The history of land acquisition in Joshua Tree shows how the NPS has eliminated inholdings in order to improve management. It moved from highly complicated tripartite exchanges to friendly condemnations, to outright purchases and donations by non-government land trusts. Programs and laws such as *Mission 66*, the Land and Water Conservation Fund Act, and the California Desert Protection Act helped. But the key was slow and unrelenting progress, one parcel at a time, during the eight decades of the unit's existence. Developers came and went, and the NPS used every ally and civil law to outlast them. And still, in 2016, thousands of acres of inholdings exist within the park. The story continues.

The most-common land use prior to 1936 was mining for precious metals. Later, the massive Eagle Mountain Iron Mine brought large-scale development to the edge of the monument (Fig. 8.1). More than 8,000 claims had to be evaluated by the NPS's overworked sister agency, the General Land Office/Bureau of Land Management. It is likely that much of the land lost in 1950 will never be reacquired by JTNP. The one seemingly unassailable land law from the nineteenth century is the Mining Act of 1872. But two 1976 laws eased the burden. The Federal Land Policy and Management Act strengthened the rules requiring claimants to prove that a "prudent" person can make a profit in order to hold an unpatented claim. The Mining in the National Parks Act forced miners in Joshua Tree to undertake expensive environmental protection and remediation in securing and transporting ore. For virtually all of them, this has proven too complicated to pursue. Claims exist in the park but not active mining.

During the early days of Joshua Tree, there were numerous inspections and much debate over the resources and potential development of the unit. Critical to both was the input of Superintendent James E. Cole (Fig. 3.2) during the 1940s. The park that exists today is as much his legacy as that of all the superintendents who followed. He developed the plans for roads and camping, determined which lands to be excised or added in 1950, and coped with much of the abuse and personal challenges from existing residents and real-estate developers. Despite those achievements, Joshua Tree remained understaffed and underfunded for decades. Regional office and university experts such as Lowell Sumner and Charles Douglas helped, but no well-trained scientists actually worked at the monument until the 1980s. An embarrassing assessment of the unit in 1976 added to the evidence that natural-resource management still suffered neglect across the entire national park system, finally spurring the NPS to get serious. At Joshua Tree, the appointment of Bob Moon, Jerry Freilich, and Rosalie Pepito changed that dire situation. In 2016, inventory and monitoring funds, a geographic information system, vigorous research studies, and volunteer workers help promote the park's resource protection program. The resource management staff is still undersized, but it is competent, and the favorable reputation of the unit is widespread.

Joshua Tree National Park has faced numerous threats throughout its history. Poaching, wood cutting, overgrazing by cattle, and the prospect of wide-open mining faced the early monument. Sales of the Southern Pacific Railroad Company's land, developers, a steady decline in the availability of water, and concomitant worries about desert bighorn sheep troubled the monument's staff for decades. Recently, invasion of exotic grasses, increased occurrence and size of fire, serious air pollution, the impact of climate change, and the tightening grip of adjacent development mean the challenge of protecting the park is greater than ever in 2016 and beyond. A staff under increasing financial constraints, workloads, and stress must cope, but the task is daunting. The surrounding communities, especially Twentynine Palms, and advocates such as the Mojave Desert Land Trust, Joshua Tree National Park Association, Donna and Larry Charpied, and hundreds of park volunteers have helped. The uncomfortable reality faced by the NPS is that Joshua Tree and other national parks and monuments are not islands. In protecting natural and cultural resources, combating irresponsible or criminal behavior, and keeping the public educated and safe, the agency faces the positives and negatives of society as a whole.

Thus, as Joshua Tree celebrated its eightieth anniversary on August 10, 2016, and the NPS its centennial anniversary on August 25, 2016, we return to the concept of American perceptions of the desert. The Native Americans found the region habitable and life sustaining. The early explorers, both Spanish and American, disagreed. Only mineral wealth and a certain lawlessness brought Americans to the future parkland. Both miners and ranchers fundamentally could not understand that the arid expanse could be used for multiple purposes by many people. Hearkening back to the biblical prophets who retreated to the "wilderness" for reflection and avoidance of society's pressure, a few influential people turned to the desert for relaxation, exploration, and the search for knowledge. John C. Van Dyke, Edmund C. Jaeger, and Minerva Hamilton Hoyt saw the fragility of the desert and inspirational opportunities for people who could accept and even treasure its character (Fig. E.1). Patients with respiratory problems, auto-tourists from metropolitan Los Angeles, and small-tract land owners and homesteaders soon followed. The mystique of the desert continues to capture people, from rock climbers to rock music stars.

So what about the general public and NPS's attitudes towards the desert? Despite the increasing popularity of and growing numbers of visitors to JTNP, a negative impression persists among some. The NPS itself has not been immune. While few, if any, in the agency question the value of Yosemite, opinions about Joshua Tree have never been completely positive, harkening back to Roger Toll's declaration in 1934 that the area was unworthy of inclusion in the national park system. When an adjustment in the monument's boundary seemed inevitable, all NPS investigators except for Lowell Sumner dismissed the Pinto Basin as just another featureless desert valley with no recreational value. Although sophisticated natural-resource management lagged across much of the national park system even during the 1970s, Joshua Tree suffered an unusual amount of disdain from regional officials prior to the arrival of Robert ("Bob") Moon. Disrespect for the unit's leadership, relegation of its general-management planning program to secondary status, and the sneering reference to it as a "kitty-litter park" revealed uncertainty about the value of a desert park. Likewise, untutored or inexperienced members of the public still call the desert a wasteland. Thus, even in 2016, JTNP officials face questions such as, "Why not put the giant energy schemes out there?" There's nothing else of value there. As long as this ignorance and attitude prevail, Joshua Tree will never receive the full respect and support that the Sierra Nevada parks, for example, command.

Final Thoughts

Pondering the future of Joshua Tree National Park raises a mixture of hopes and worries. The park is extremely popular with visitors and enjoys considerable local and organizational support. Yet grievous threats surround and pervade it. Joshua Tree has survived more challenges than most national park units during its first eighty years. Will the public deem and use the desert as a dump or as a retreat? Time will tell what future generations will value and discover when they visit California's rugged and stark but sublime and beautiful deserts.

Perhaps it is fitting to conclude the first full history of Joshua Tree National Park by returning to the attributes—the park's fundamental resources and values—that underlie future management strategies for its care. In NPS's Website for JTNP, these are listed as "significance statements," of which there are eight, presented in the following order:

1. JTNP preserves a world-renowned, undisturbed population of Joshua trees, an integral part of the Mojave Desert ecosystem.
2. Outstanding examples of Mojave and Colorado Desert landscapes that converge at JTNP create a biologically rich system of plant and animal life characterized by iconic Joshua tree woodlands, native palm oases, and vast expanses of creosote scrub that are uniquely adapted to desert conditions. The park also contributes significantly to the connectivity of large protected areas across the California desert.
3. JTNP provides accessible and diverse opportunities in a remote desert wildland to a large and burgeoning urban population.
4. JTNP preserves a rich array of prehistoric, historic, and contemporary resources that demonstrate the integral connection between deserts, land use, and human cultures.
5. JTNP lies along one of the world's most-active earthquake faults: the San Andreas Fault. Geologic processes, including tectonic activity, have played, and will continue to play, a major role in shaping the mountains, valleys, and basins of the park.
6. JTNP offers unparalleled opportunities for research on arid-land ecosystems and processes, adaptation of and to desert life, sustainability, and indications of climate change. The proximity of the park to urban regions in Southern California and Nevada enhances the value of the park for scientific research and education.
7. Huge, eroded monzogranite boulder formations are world-renowned natural features that provide unique aesthetic, educational, and recreational opportunities for visitors to JTNP.
8. Geologic, climatic, and ecological processes create scenic landscapes unique to deserts and fundamental to the character of JTNP.[3]

The landscape always reflects the attitudes, behavior, and values of those who care for it. As Joshua Tree National Park enters its ninth decade as a unit of the national park system, the challenge remains as to how best to preserve this unique desert landscape that has withstood so much over the course of its natural and human history.

LIST OF SUPERINTENDENTS

Note: James E. Cole was the first official to come to Joshua Tree National Monument (JTNM). Prior to 1940, superintendents of Yosemite National Park monitored Joshua Tree, as described in Chapter 3. Also, every time a superintendent leaves a park, even if for a day, someone becomes an acting superintendent. Thus, they are not listed here, because the real superintendent remains in charge. Only when a superintendent of a unit retires is an official Acting Superintendent appointed in the interim. The following is the updated list from the National Park Service (NPS) as of August 25, 2016, NPS's centennial anniversary.

James E. Cole	9/19/40–10/30/42
Duane D. Jacobs	12/9/42–3/26/44
Frank R. Givens*	3/27/44–6/1/44
James E. Cole	5/6/44–3/1/47
Frank R. Givens	3/2/47–4/11/53
Samuel A. King	4/12/53–1/20/57
Elmer N. Fladmark	2/24/57–8/1/58
William R. Supernaugh	10/5/58–3/20/71
Peter L. Parry	4/18/71–7/7/73
Homer L. Rouse	7/8/73–8/14/76
Frederick T. Anderson	8/16/76–11/30/90
David Moore	6/30/91–12/2/93
Ernest Quintana	3/20/93–7/12/03
Curt Sauer	11/16/03–9/30/10
Mark Butler	1/30/11 3/1/14
David Smith	9/21/14–present

* Acting Superintendent

VISITATION TO JOSHUA TREE, 1941 TO 2015

Note: Officially, there are no records for visitation from 1936–1940.

1941	31,285	1966	408,600	1991	1,145,458
1942	23,691	1967	416,500	1992	1,220,539
1943	17,414	1968	489,400	1993	1,252,401
1944	7,640	1969	550,300	1994	1,184,871
1945	18,275	1970	643,000	1995	1,235,702
1946	36,605	1971	576,000	1996	1,095,046
1947	57,801	1972	602,752	1997	1,226,273
1948	59,157	1973	589,600	1998	1,410,312
1949	66,991	1974	509,900	1999	1,316,340
1950	79,129	1975	552,200	2000	1,233,935
1951	93,615	1976	728,900	2001	1,280,917
1952	141,416	1977	745,600	2002	1,178,376
1953	172,423	1978	602,453	2003	1,283,346
1954	260,700	1979	590,543	2004	1,243,659
1955	280,600	1980	545,357	2005	1,375,111
1956	312,900	1981	612,966	2006	1,256,421
1957	320,300	1982	673,201	2007	1,298,979
1958	365,300	1983	671,426	2008	1,392,446
1959	299,600	1984	663,798	2009	1,304,471
1960	320,100	1985	641,172	2010	1,434,976
1961	301,500	1986	783,224	2011	1,396,237
1962	331,500	1987	830,085	2012	1,396,117
1963	346,300	1988	955,246	2013	1,383,340
1964	343,400	1989	990,214	2014	1,589,904
1965	336,000	1990	1,022,396	2015	2,025,756

LIST OF ACRONYMS

AEC	Atomic Energy Commission
AQD	Air Quality Division (of the National Park Service)
BIA	Bureau of Indian Affairs
BLM	Bureau of Land Management (known as the GLO before 1946)
BOR	Bureau of Reclamation
BOM	Bureau of Mines
CDF	California Division of Forestry
CDPA	California Desert Quality Act
CDPL	California Desert Protection League
CDSL	California Division of State Lands
CSLC	California State Lands Commission
CEQA	California Environmental Quality Act
CESU	Cooperating Ecosystem Studies Unit
CSLC	California State Lands Commission
CSP	California State Parks
DMG	Desert Managers Group
DRECP	Desert Renewable Energy Conservation Plan
DSC	Denver Service Center
EIR	Environmental Impact Report
EIS	Environmental Impact Statement
EMEC	Eagle Mountain Energy Company
EPA	U.S. Environmental Protection Agency
FERC	Federal Energy Regulatory Commission
FHA	Federal Highway Administration
FLPMA	Federal Land Policy and Management Act
GIS	Geographic Information System
GLO	General Land Office (known as the BLM beginning in 1946)
GMP	General Management Plan
IDCL	International Desert Conservation League

I&M	Inventory and Monitoring Program
JTNM	Joshua Tree National Monument
JTNP	Joshua Tree National Park
LAACC	Los Angeles Area Chamber of Commerce
LAX	Los Angeles International Airport
LCS	List of Classified Structures
LWCFA	Land and Water Conservation Fund Act
MAS	Mining Association of the Southwest
MCSC	Mining Congress of Southern California
MDLT	Mojave Desert Land Trust
MRC	Mine Reclamation Corporation
MWD	Metropolitan Water District of Southern California
NEPA	National Environmental Policy Act
NPCA	National Parks [and] Conservation Association
NPF	National Park Foundation
NPS	National Park Service
SPRR	Southern Pacific Railroad Company
TPC	Twentynine Palms Corporation
UNESCO	United Nations Educational, Scientific, and Cultural Organization
USDA	U.S. Department of Agriculture
USDI	U.S. Department of the Interior
USFS	U.S. Forest Service
USFWS	U.S. Fish and Wildlife Service
USGS	U.S. Geological Survey
WC	Wildlands Conservancy

NOTES

General Notes: All statistics, such as visitation and acreage of the park and its wilderness areas, are accurate as of July 4, 2016. Whenever possible, the author refers to specific Indian tribes; otherwise, he complies with the National Park Service's guidelines in the general use of "Native Americans" for unknown and unspecified "native peoples." Likewise, the author uses terminology of the National Park Service such as "boundary change," "visitor use," and "wilderness proposal," even as he otherwise refrains from using nouns as adjectives throughout the text.

Acronyms Used in the Notes:

Acc.	Accession number
BLM	Bureau of Land Management (known as the GLO prior to 1946)
Cat.	Catalog number
DOI	U.S. Department of the Interior
DRECP	Desert Renewable Energy Conservation Plan
DSC	Denver Service Center (of the National Park Service)
GLO	General Land Office (known as the BLM beginning in 1946)
JTNM	Joshua Tree National Monument
JTNP	Joshua Tree National Park
LG	National Archives Regional Branch, Laguna Niguel, California (moved to Riverside)
NARA	National Archives and Records Center, Suitland, Maryland
n.d.	no date (or date unknown)
RG79	Record Group 79, National Park Service Records, National Archives (NARA)
SB	National Archives Regional Branch, San Bruno, California
WASO	Washington, D.C., office (NPS headquarters)
WRO	Western Regional Office (San Francisco, California)

Epigraph

John C. Van Dyke, *The Desert: Further Studies in Natural Appearances* (Baltimore, MD: The Johns Hopkins University Press, in association with the Center for American Places, 1999; originally published in a hardcover edition in 1901 by Charles Scribner's Sons, New York City), 59.

Introduction

1. Yi-Fu Tuan, "Desert and Ice: Ambivalent Aesthetics in Landscape," in S. Kemal and I. Gaskell, eds., *Landscape, Natural Beauty and the Arts.* (Cambridge, UK: University of Cambridge Press, 1993), 146–47; and Patricia Nelson Limerick, *Desert Passages: Encounters with the American Deserts* (Albuquerque: University of New Mexico Press, 1985), 167–70. 2. Limerick, ibid., 167.

3. Ibid., 166–74; and Diana Davis, "Wasteland: The Deep History of Defining Desert Wastes," a paper delivered at the annual conference of the American Society for Environmental History in San Francisco on March 13, 2014.

4. R. S. Williamson, "Report of Explorations and Surveys, to ascertain the most practicable and economical route for a railroad from the Mississippi River to the Pacific Ocean, made under the direction of the Secretary of War, in 1853–4," Vol. 5, Part 1, 38, available at http://quod.lib.umich.edu/m/moa/AFK4383.0005.001/74?rgn=full+text;view=image.

5. Perrin Selcer, "Men Against the Desert: Arid Lands Research and the Growth of Development, 1948–1964," a paper delivered at the annual conference of the American Society for Environmental History in San Francisco on March 13, 2014.

6. Limerick, *Desert Passages*, 167–68; Charles C. Reith and Bruce M. Thomson, eds., *Deserts as Dumps? The Disposal of Hazardous Materials in Arid Ecosystems* (Albuquerque: University of New Mexico Press, 1992), 5–6.

7. John C. Van Dyke, *The Desert: Further Studies in Natural Appearances* (New York, NY: Charles Scribner's Sons, 1901); Edna Brush Perkins, *The White Heart of the Mojave: An Adventure with the Out-of-Doors of the Desert* (New York, NY: Boni and Liveright, 1922); and George Wharton James, *The Wonders of the Colorado Desert* (Boston, MA: Little, Brown, and Company, 1906). Van Dyke's book and Perkins's book were reissued in new paperback editions as part of the *American Land Classics* series (Charles E. Little, series editor and George F. Thompson, series director) published by the Johns Hopkins University Press (in association with the Center for American Places), respectively, in 1999 and 2001.

8. Lary M. Dilsaver, "National Significance: Representation of the West in the National Park System," in Gary Hausladen, ed., *Western Places, American Myths* (Reno: University of Nevada Press, 2003), 111–32.

9. The television commercial for a Chevy Silverado that I refer to was seen by me on September 4, 2013.

Chapter One

1. D. D. Trent and Richard W. Hazlett, *Joshua Tree National Park Geology*. (Twentynine Palms, CA: Joshua Tree National Park Association, 2002), 10–23; Camille A. Holmgren and Julio L. Betancourt, "A Long-Term Vegetation History of the Mojave–Colorado Desert Ecotone at Joshua Tree National Park" (February 18, 2008), JTNP Library, 3–5; and Don Dupras "Self-Guided Geologic Tour in Joshua Tree National Monument," *California Geology*, Vol. 44, No. 9 (September 1990): 203–12.

2. Trent and Hazlett, *Joshua Tree Geology*, 29–37; and Robert P. Sharp *Geology Field Guide to Southern California* (Dubuque, IA: W. C. Brown Publishers, 1972), 11–16.

3. Trent and Hazlett, *Joshua Tree Geology*, 24–29; Dupras, *Geology Field Guide*, 206–07; and Margaret R. Eggers and D. D. Trent, "Overview of the Landscape and Geology of Joshua Tree National Park," in Margaret R. Eggers, ed., *Mining History and Geology of Joshua Tree National Park*. (San Diego, CA: San Diego Association of Geologists, 2004), 9–27.

4. Edmund C. Jaeger, *The California Deserts*, 4th Edition (Palo Alto, CA: Stanford University Press, 1965), 34–41; Trent and Hazlett, *Joshua Tree Geology*, 7–9; and Harold F. De Lisle, "Precipitation History for Joshua Tree National Park" (2000), JTNP Archives, Acc. 752, Cat. 25175, Folder 100.

5. Holmgren and Betancourt, "A Long-Term Vegetation History," 3.

6. Ibid., 1.

7. Jaeger, *The California Deserts*, 122–83; Patrick J. Leary, "Investigation of the Vegetational Communities of Joshua Tree National Monument, California," Master's thesis (Las Vegas: University of Nevada, June 1977), 1 and 399–403; and Holmgren and Betancourt, "A Long-Term Vegetation History," 3–5.

8. Leary, "Investigation of the Vegetational Communities," 399–403; and JTNP, "Plant Communities," available at http://www.nps.gov/jotr/naturescience/plant_communities.htm.

9. Jane Rodgers, "Joshua Trees," available at http://www.nps.gov/jotr/naturescience/jtrees.htm.

10. Harold DeLisle, "Creosote Bush," available at http://www.nps.gov/jotr/naturescience/creosote.htm.

11. JTNP, "Fan Palm Oases," available at http://www.nps.gov/jotr/naturescience/oases.htm.

12. JTNP, "Animals," available at http://www.nps.gov/jotr/naturescience/animals.htm.

13. JTNP, "Pinto Culture," available at http://www.nps.gov/jotr/historyculture/pintoculture.htm; Lary Dilsaver, William Wyckoff, and William L. Preston. "Fifteen Events That Have Shaped California's Human Landscape," *The California Geographer*, Vol. 40 (2000): 2–4; Michael A. Glassow, ed., "Channel Islands National Park Archaeological Overview and Assessment" NPS, Channel Islands National Park (December 2010), 2.1–2.10; and Elizabeth W. Campbell and William H. Campbell, *Southwest Museum Papers Number 9: The Pinto Basin Site* (Highland Park, CA: Southwest Museum of Los Angeles, 1935), 1–53.

14. Native Languages.org, "Native Languages of the Americas—California," http://www.native-languages.org/california. htm; Charlotte Hunter, "Indians," http://www.nps.gov/jotr/historyculture/indians.htm; and Douglas Deur, "The Rock Art of Joshua Tree National Park" (2006), NPS, WRO, JTNP Library, 12–23.

15. Duer, "The Rock Art," 12–23.

16 Ibid.; and Lowell Bean and Sylvia Vane, "The Native American Ethnography and Ethnohistory of Joshua Tree National Park: An Overview," (August 22, 2002), Cultural Systems Research, Inc., JTNP Library, 1–5 and 18–29.

17. Duer, "The Rock Art," 12–23; and Bean and Vane, "The Native American Ethnography," 6–237.

18. Duer, "The Rock Art," 21–23; Hunter, "Indians"; and Bean and Vane, "The Native American Ethnography," 11–14, 20–21, 31, and 37–38.

19. Bean and Vane, "The Native American Ethnography," 13–14, 20–21, 31, and 37–38.

20. Government Printing Office, "Executive Orders Relating to Indian Reservations from July 1, 1912 to July 1, 1922" (1922), Vol. 2, JTNP Library, Box "Ephemera," Folder "Interpretive Information Native Americans"; and Linda W. Greene, "Historic Resource Study: A History of Land Use in Joshua Tree National Monument" (1983), DSC, JTNP Library, 35–52.

21. Greene, "Historic Resource Study," 4–6; Warren A. Beck and Ynez D. Haase, *Historical Atlas of California* (Norman: University of Oklahoma Press, 1974), 15; John Francis Bannon, *The Spanish Borderlands Frontier 1513–1821* (Albuquerque: University of New Mexico Press, 1974), 151–66; and Center for Advanced Technology in Education, University of Oregon, "An Interactive Study Environment on Spanish Exploration and Colonization of 'Alta California' 1774–1776" (1999), a collection of diaries, letters and maps of the De Anza expedition, available at http://anza.uoregon.edu.

22. Greene, "Historic Resource Study," 4–6; and Bannon, *The Spanish Borderlands Frontier*, 221–28.

23. K. Jack Bauer, *The Mexican War 1846–1848* (Lincoln: University of Nebraska Press, 1974), 23–24; and T. H. Watkins, *California: An Illustrated History* (Tracy, CA: American West Publishing Company, 1983), 35–46.

24. Neal Harlow, *California Conquered: The Annexation of a Mexican Province 1846–1850* (Berkeley: University of California Press, 1982), 303–37; and Tom Gray, "Teaching with Documents: The Treaty of Guadalupe Hidalgo," NARA, available at http://www.archives.gov/education/lessons/guadalupe-hidalgo/.

25. Greene, "Historic Resource Study," 63–85.

26. Ibid.; and Samuel A. King, "A History of Joshua Tree National Monument" (1954), JTNP Library, 23–24.

27. F. Ross Holland, Jr., "Nomination of Cow Camp for the National Register of Historic Places" (December 1971), JTNP Archives, Acc. 651, Cat. 19430, H32, Folder 078.

28. Greene, "Historic Resource Study," 25–29 and 91; and D. D. Trent, "Geology and History of Mines of Joshua Tree National Park," in Margaret R. Eggers, ed., *Mining History and Geology of Joshua Tree National Park.* (San Diego, CA: San Diego Association of Geologists, 2004), 29–47.

29. Greene, "Historic Resource Study," 91–306; and Margaret R. Eggers and D. D. Trent, "Historic Mining Equipment and Processes Within Joshua Tree National Park," in Margaret R. Eggers, ed., *Mining History and Geology of Joshua Tree National Park* (San Diego, CA: San Diego Association of Geologists, 2004), 49–64.

30. Eggers and Trent, "Historic Mining Equipment," 49–64; and Otis E. Young, Jr., *Western Mining: An Informal Account of Precious-metals Prospecting, Placering, Lode Mining, and Milling on the American Frontier from Spanish Times to 1893* (Norman: University of Oklahoma Press, 1970), 178–233 and 283–84.

31. Rodman Paul and Elliott West, *Mining Frontiers of the Far West 1848–1880* (Albuquerque: University of New Mexico Press, 2001), 161–75; and D. D. Trent, "Geology and History of Mines," 30.

32. Greene, "Historic Resource Study," 255–61; and Trent, "Geology and History of Mines," 38.

33. Greene, "Historic Resource Study," 202–11; Trent, "Geology and History of Mines," 31 34; and NPS, "Cultural Landscapes Inventory Northern Piñon Mining District Joshua Tree National Park" (2009), JTNP Library, 14–17.

34. Greene, "Historic Resource Study," 154–59; and Larry M. Vredenburgh, Gary L. Shumway, and Russell D. Hartill, "Desert Fever: An Overview of Mining History of the California Desert Conservation Area: Eagle Mountain," available at http://vredenburgh.org/desert_fever/pages/riverside_county_04.htm.

35. IT Corporation, "Preliminary Assessments for the National Park Service Joshua Tree National Park" (July 2001), JTNP Library, Box "Uncatalogued materials."

36. Public Law 37–64. During the nineteenth century, one important function of the federal government was transferring its land to private ownership. The General Land Office (GLO) used a grid system designed by Thomas Jefferson and others in the Northwest Ordinance of 1787 to facilitate land disposal. The "Rectangular Land Division System" or "Township and Range" uses lines of latitude and longitude to start a grid that delineates thirty-six-square-mile segments called townships. These townships are divided into one-square-mile units called sections, each of which contains 640 acres of land. Early in American history, the government decided that 160 acres was a proper amount to sell or grant to prospective agricultural settlers.

37. U.S. Congress, "The Pacific Railroad Act of 1862," 12 Stat. 489; and James E. Vance, *The North American Railroad: Its Origin, Evolution, and Geography* (Baltimore, MD: The Johns Hopkins University Press, in association with the Center for American Places, 1995), 168–73. For more information on the Pacific Railroad Act of 1862 and the Southern Pacific Railroad Company, see Richard Orsi, *Sunset Limited: The Southern Pacific Railroad and the Development of the American West* (Berkeley: University of California Press, 2007).

38. John C. Van Dyke, *The Desert: Further Studies in Natural Appearances* (New York, NY: Charles Scribner's Sons, 1901).

39. "How Fabulous Coachella Valley Blossomed from Desert Wasteland," *The Los Angeles Times* (July 26, 1959); and Palm Springs Bureau of Tourism "Palm Springs History," available at http://www.visitpalmsprings.com/page/palm-springs-history/8180.

40. The Planning Center/DC&E, "Yucca Valley Community Profile," 9, available at http://www.yucca-valley.org/news/gpflipbook/files/inc/45517864.pdf.

41. Frank Bagley interviewed by Sue Moore, Twentynine Palms (October 28, 1968), transcript in JTNP Archives, Acc. 651, Cat. 19430, H1815, Folder 027A; City of Twentynine Palms "History of Twentynine Palms, California," http://www.ci.twentynine-palms.ca.us/History_of_29_Palms_California.77.0.html; and Vickie Waite, Al Gartner, and Paul F. Smith, *Images of America: Twentynine Palms* (Charleston, SC: Arcadia Publishing, 2007), 13–66.

42. "Pinto Basin Riverside County California" (n.d.), JTNP Archives, Acc. 00774, Cat. 27729, Box "Whatley and Flynn Land Tract," Folder 003.

43. Roy Harrod to Lake County Development Syndicate, Inc. (n.d.), ibid.; and "Speculate! This is Your Chance at California Real Estate Profits" (n.d.), ibid.

44. The records do not indicate which court. S. Moninger to W. H. Whatley (March 2, 1932), ibid.; R. E. Allen to Contract Purchasers of Pinto Basin Lands from the Security Land Corporation (April 25, 1932), ibid.; and *Pinto Basin Mutual Water Company v. Security Land Corporation* (July 25, 1932), California Superior Court No. 332,581, ibid.

45. The Metropolitan Water District, "The Metropolitan Water District of Southern California History and First Annual Report Commemorative Edition," http://www.mwdh2o.com/mwdh2o/pages/about/AR/AR1928.html; The Metropolitan Water District, "The District at a Glance," www.mwdh2o/pages/news/at_a_glance/mwd.pdf; and "Act of June 18, 1932" (47 Stat. 324).

Chapter Two

1. Presidential Proclamation 2193 (August 10, 1936), 50 Stat. 1760.
2. Conner Sorenson, "Apostle of the Cacti: The Society Matron as Environmental Activist," *Southern California Quarterly*, Vol. 58, No. 3 (Fall 1976): 407–29 and 411.
3. Ibid., 410–12.
4. George Wharton James, *The Wonders of the Colorado Desert* (Boston, MA: Little, Brown, and Company, 1918), 477.
5. "Reward Offered for Slayer of Giant of Desert," *South Pasadena Foothill Review* (June 27, 1930).
6. Ibid.
7. "Desert Parks Proposed" *The Los Angeles Times* (March 16, 1930); and Sorenson, "Apostle of the Cacti," 418. Early news reports listed the plural "Deserts" in the organization's title, but its own letterhead carried the singular form "Desert."
8. N. L. Britton, "The International Deserts Conservation League" (August 1, 1930), JTNP Archives, Acc. 805, Cat. 27730, Box "Desert Plant National Park," Folder 002.
9. *South Pasadena Foothill Review*, "Reward Offered."

10. Joint Parks Committee to William Spry (July 25, 1927), NARA, RG79, Entry 10, Box 2258, Part 1, "March 1933–February 1934." This letter and many others are summarized in Frank Givens, "Briefed Data on Joshua Tree National Monument—7/25/34 to 9/28/36," an unpublished chronology of correspondence (with some letters included) leading to the establishment of the monument (n.d.), JTNP Archives, Acc. 651, Cat. 19430, Folder 004, 1.

11. Sorenson, "Apostle of the Cacti," note 6.

12. The most detailed expression of the policies Mather and his lieutenants favored can be found in a speech by Superintendent John R. White of Sequoia National Park titled "Atmosphere in the National Parks." See Lary Dilsaver, *America's National Park System: The Critical Documents*, 2nd Edition (Lanham, MD: Rowman and Littlefield Publishers, 2016), 123–30.

13. W. H. Anderson to Harold Ickes (March 30, 1934), in Frank Givens, "Briefed Data," (n.d.): 4d.

14. H. C. Bryant to C. K. Edmunds (August 27, 1934), NARA, RG79. Entry 10, Box 2259, Part 3.

15. For information on the progressive movement and conservation, see Samuel P. Hays, *Conservation and the Gospel of Efficiency: The Progressive Conservation Movement, 1890–1920* (Pittsburgh, PA: University of Pittsburgh Press, 1999); and Roderick Nash, *Wilderness and the American Mind*, 4th Edition (New Haven, CT: Yale University Press, 2001).

16. Alfred Runte, *National Parks: The American Experience*, 4th Edition (Lanham, MD: Taylor Trade Publishing, 2010).

17. Rebecca Conrad, "The National Conference on State Parks: Reflections on Organizational Genealogy," *The George Wright Forum*, Vol. 14, No. 4 (1997): 28–43.

18. Camp Fire Club of America, "National Park Standards" (1929), NPS Archives, Harpers Ferry, WV, General Collection, Box K5410, "Policy and Philosophy to 1947," republished in *The National Parks Bulletin*, Vol. 14, No. 66 (December 1938): 5–7.

19. Lary Dilsaver, "Not of National Significance: Failed National Park Proposals in California," *California History*, Vol. 85, No. 2 (March 2008): 4–23 and 66–68; NPS, "Proposed Areas Resumes," NPS Archives, Harpers Ferry, L58, "Proposed additions to the national park system," Box 1, August 29, 1947; and Presidential Proclamation 2028 (February 11, 1933), 47 Stat. 2554.

20. Joseph Engbeck, Jr., *State Parks of California from 1864 to the Present* (Portland, OR: Graphic Arts Center Publishing Company, 1980), 17–33 and 50–55.

21. Frederick Law Olmsted, "Report of State Park Survey of California" (Sacramento: California State Printing Office, 1929), 3–13.

22. Ibid., 3–5 and 69.

23. Ibid., 51–52.

24. Ibid., 3–5.

25. Ronald Foresta, *America's National Parks and Their Keepers* (Washington, DC: Resources for the Future, 1984), 30–43; Roger Toll, "Report on the Proposed Desert Plant National Park," submitted to Director Arno Cammerer (April 7, 1934). This large package of materials included maps, photographs, descriptions of the area, supporting data, and expert opinions on the resources, as well as Toll's evaluation of the proposed area's significance, feasibility, and suitability. A list of desert species appears on page 27. JTNP Archives, Acc. 752, Cat. 25175, Folder 13; Presidential Proclamation 2032 (March 1, 1933), 47 Stat. 2557; and Presidential Proclamation 2232 (April 13, 1937), 50 Stat. 1827

26. Rimo Bacigalupi to Roger Toll (April 3, 1934), JTNP Archives, Acc. 805, Cat. 27730, Box "Desert Plant National Park," Folder 002.

27. Ibid.; and Walter Taylor to Roger Toll (August 22, 1932), NARA, RG79, Appendix 16, Entry 63 "Records of Roger Toll," Box 3, Folder "Joshua Trees."

28. Dietmar Schneider-Hector, "Roger W. Toll Chief Investigator of Proposed National Parks and Monuments: Setting the Standards for America's National Park System," *Journal of the West*, Vol. 42, No. 1 (Winter 2003): 82–90; and NPS, "Roger Wolcott Toll 1883–1936," available at http://www.nps.gov/history/history/online_books/sontag/toll.htm.

29. Olmsted, "Report of State Park Survey," 69; and Newton Drury to Roger Toll (January 31, 1933), NARA, RG79, Appendix 16, Entry 63, "Records of Roger Toll," Box 3, Folder "Joshua Trees."

30. Philip Munz to W. B. McDougall (September 30, 1932), ibid.; and Philip Munz, *A California Flora*, 2nd Edition (Berkeley, CA: University of California Press, 1963).

31. Newton Drury to W. B. McDougall (October 7, 1932), NARA, RG79, Appendix 16, Entry 63, "Records of Roger Toll," Folder "Joshua Trees."

32. W. L. Jepson to Dr. McDougall (July 18, 1932), ibid.; Thomas Vint to Roger Toll (February 4, 1933), ibid.; and Mary Beale, "The Road to Cima," *Madroño*, Vol. 2 (1931): 42–44.

33. Clinton G. Abbott to Newton Drury (January 13, 1932), JTNP Library, Binder "Early Plans for Joshua Tree National Monument," Manuscript "Desert Plants National Monument," 15.

34. Olmsted, "Report of State Park Survey," 69; and Minerva Hoyt to Arno Cammerer (July 18, 1933), NARA RG79, Entry 10, Box 2258, Part 1 "General Desert Plant, 1927–34."

35. Charles Vorhies to Harold Bryant (April 9, 1935), NARA, RG 79, Entry 10, Box 2259, Part 3; and Harold Bryant to Charles Vorhies (April 18, 1935), ibid.

36. Sorenson, "Apostle of the Cacti," 417.

37. California Assembly Bill 1292 introduced by Mr. Phillips (January 26, 1933), JTNP Archives, Acc. 805, Cat. 27730, Box "Desert Plant National Park," Folder 002; and Horace Albright to Mrs. Sherman Hoyt (June 1, 1933), NARA, RG 79, Entry 10, Box 2258, Part 1.

38. Sorenson, "Apostle of the Cacti," 419–20.

39. Public Law 72–425; John Phillips to Harold Ickes (July 18, 1933), NARA, RG 79, Entry 10, Box 2258, Part 1; California State Parks, "Planning Milestones," (Sacramento: California State Parks, 2004), 16, 47, and 85; and Diana Lindsay *Anza-Borrego A to Z: People, Places, and Things* (San Diego: Sunbelt Publication, 2001), 35–36.

40. Roger Toll (May 3, 1933), "Proposed Joshua Tree National Monument in California, Arizona or Nevada," Report to Horace Albright, NARA, RG 79, Appendix 16, Entry 63, Roger Toll Papers, Box 3, Folder "Joshua Trees."

41. Roger Toll to NPS Director (April 17, 1933), JTNP Archives, Acc. 805, Cat. 27730, Box "Desert Plant National Park," Folder 001.

42. Sorenson, "Apostle of the Cacti," 419–20; James Rolph, Jr., to the President (June 2, 1933), NARA, RG 79, Entry 10, Box 2258, Pt.1, Folder "General Desert Plant, 1927–34."

43. Minerva Hoyt to Conrad Wirth (July 8, 1933), NARA, RG 79, Entry 10, Box 2258, Part 1, Folder "General Desert Plant, 1927–34"; Minerva Hoyt to A. E. Dunaray [sic] (July 10, 1933), ibid.; Minerva Hoyt to Arno Cammerer (July 18, 1933), ibid; and Harold Ickes to Mrs. Hoyt (July 25, 1933), ibid.

44. Fred W. Johnson to NPS Director (July 28, 1933), ibid.

45. Executive Order 6361 (October 25, 1933); Minerva Hoyt to A. B. Cammerer (July 18, 1933), NARA, RG79, Entry 10. Box 2258, Part 1, "General Desert Plant 1927–34"; and A.E. Demaray to Mrs. A. Sherman Hoyt (June 27, 1933), ibid.

46. Frank Givens, "Briefed Data," 2; A. Schleicher to Harold Ickes (December 14, 1933), NARA, RG79, Entry 10, Box 2258, Part 1 "General Desert Plant 1927–34."

47. William Simpson to Harold Ickes (November 20, 1933), JTNP Archives, Acc. 805, Cat. 27730, Box "Desert Plant National Park," Folder 002.

48. Harold Ickes to William Simpson (December 13, 1933), NARA, RG79, Entry 10, Box 2258, Part 1 "General Desert Plant 1927–34."

49. James Rolfe to Franklin Roosevelt (March 1, 1934), NARA, RG79, Entry 10, Box 2258, Part 2, Folder 2; and Arno Cammerer to Mrs. R. H. McCoy (March 15, 1934), ibid.

50. Joshua Green to Par Harrison (June 2, 1934), ibid; Pat Harrison to Arno Cammerer (June 12, 1934), ibid; and Mrs. Edwin S. Fuller to Arnold [sic] Cammerer (June 5, 1934), ibid.

51. Benjamin Fenton to Arno Cammerer (June 16, 1934), ibid; and Arno Cammerer to Benjamin Fenton (June 20, 1934), ibid.

52. Frank Givens, "Briefed Data," 5–6.

53. Rachel Vordermark to Harold Ickes (September 15, 1935), NARA, RG79, Entry 10, Box 2258, Part 4; Harold Ickes to Arno Cammerer (March 26, 1936), ibid; A. E. Demaray to the Secretary (March 27, 1936), ibid; Harold Ickes to A. E. Demaray (March 31, 1936), ibid; Arno Cammerer to Harold Ickes (April 1, 1936), ibid; and Minerva Hoyt to Harold Ickes (May 4, 1936), ibid.

54. Hiram Johnson to Harold Ickes (March 10, 1934), NARA RG79, Entry 10, Box 2258, Part 2. This followed a letter from lawyer Flint MacKay to Johnson (March 7, 1934), urging him to intercede (ibid.); Roger Toll to the Director

(February 23, 1934), NARA RG79, Entry 10, Box 2258, Part 1, File "General Desert Plant 1927–34"; and Roger Toll to Director NPS (May 29, 1930), NARA, RG79, Entry 20, Roger Toll Papers, Box 13, Folder "Proposed National Parks."
55. To this day, field investigation teams are staffed with experienced National Park Service specialists to reduce subjectivity as much as possible. Years later, however, when ordered to evaluate a potential national seashore, one field team member asked for further explanation of the concept. His supervisor responded, "I'll know it when I see it."
56. Camp Fire Club of America, "National Park Standards" (1929), editorial note accompanying republication of the preceding in the *National Park Bulletin*, 5; NPS, "Criteria for Parklands," (Washington, DC: Planning Files, NPS Office of Planning, 1971); NPS, "Criteria for Parklands" (2007), http://www.nps.gov/legacy/criteria.html; William Everhart to the author (December 12, 1994); and NPS, "Proposed Areas Resumes" (August 29, 1947), NPS Archives, Harpers Ferry WV, L58, "Proposed additions to the national park system," Box 1.
57. Roger Toll, "Report on the Proposed Desert Plant National Park," 40–43.
58. Mrs. Campbell's letter to NPS archaeologist Jesse Nusbaum (March 30, 1934), is quoted in the latter's letter to the director of the National Park Service (February 23, 1955), WRO, Joshua Tree files, Folder "Joshua Tree National Monument 1968–1973."
59. Roger Toll, "Report on the Proposed Desert Plant National Park," 1.
60. Ibid., 35–36.
61. Roger Toll to the Director with attached correspondence and data from the Metropolitan Water District (April 16, 1934), JTNP Archives, Acc. 805, Cat. 27730, Box "Desert Plant National Park," Folder 1; and Conrad Wirth review of the proposed Desert Plant National Monument returned with approval from Arno Cammerer (June 7, 1934), NARA, RG79, Entry 10, Box 2259, Part 3.
62. Donald Alexander to Mr. Wirth with attached draft (June 15, 1934), NARA, RG79, Entry 10, Box 2258, Part 2, Folder 2; and Arno Cammerer to Mrs. A. Sherman Hoyt (July 2, 1934), NARA, RG79, Entry 10, Box 2259, Part 3; Public Law 59–209.
63. Roger Toll to Forrest Shreve (April 10, 1934), NARA RG79, Entry 10, Box 2258, Part 2, Folder 2; and Forrest Shreve to Roger Toll (April 19, 1934), ibid.
64. J. H. Hoeppel, et al., to Harold Ickes (June 5, 1934), JTNP Archives, Acc. 651, Cat. 19340, Folder 001; and H. I. Harriman to Mrs. A. Sherman Hoyt (June 6, 1934), NARA, RG79, Entry 10, Box 2259, Part 3.
65. Frederick A. Speik to H. C. Bryant (August 8, 1934), NARA, RG79, Entry 10, Box 2259, Part 3; and "Letter Suggested By Dr. P. A. Munz" (n.d.), ibid.
66. Minerva Hoyt to Harold Bryant (July 31, 1934), ibid; and NPS, "Dr. Harold C. Bryant." http://www.nps.gov/history/history/online_books/sontag/bryant.htm.
67. "Desert Park Aims Told," *The Pasadena Star-News* (August 11, 1934).
68. H. C. Bryant to Mrs. A. Sherman Hoyt (October 9, 1934), NARA, RG79, Entry 10, Box 2259, Part 3.
69. Estella Carr to NPS (September 13, 1934), ibid.; Jenny White to the President (September 17, 1934), ibid.; Faith E. Smith to Director, NPS (April 1, 1935), ibid.; Gordon Stewart to Department of the Interior (February 20, 1934), NARA RG79, Entry 10, Box 2258, Part 1, "General Desert Plant, 1927–34"; and Arno Cammerer to Jennie White (November 14, 1934), NARA RG79, Entry 10, Box 2259, Part 3.
70. C. A. Pinkham to W. C. Mendenhall (August 21, 1934) attached to a letter from W. C. Mendenhall to Arno Cammerer (September 5, 1934), ibid.; and Arno Cammerer to Chester A. Pinkham (September 11, 1934), ibid.
71. Chester Pinkham to Arno Cammerer (September 28, 1934), ibid.; H. C. Bryant to Mrs. A. Sherman Hoyt (October 9, 1934), ibid.; Chester Pinkham to Arno Cammerer (November 20, 1934), ibid.
72. Chester Pinkham to Arno Cammerer (November 20, 1934), ibid.; and Minerva Hoyt to H. C. Bryant (November 1, 1934), ibid.
73. Edmund Jaeger and Philip Munz, "Memorandum on Proposed Desert National Monument," (n.d.), Loye Miller to Harold Bryant (January 21, 1935), and Philip Munz to Harold Bryant (March 6, 1935), all in Frank Givens, "Briefed Data," 8–10.
74. Minerva Hoyt to H. C. Bryant (November 17, 1934), NARA, RG79, Entry 10, Box 2259, Part 3; W. P. Whitsett to Mrs. A. Sherman Hoyt (August 21, 1934), ibid; and James H. Howard to W. C. Mendenhall (October 25, 1934), ibid.
75. J. Lee Brown to Mr. Wirth (February 8, 1935), ibid.

76. H. C. Bryant to the Director (February 12, 1935), ibid.

77. A. E. Demaray to the Secretary (February 8, 1935), NARA, RG79, Entry 10, Box 2259, Part 3.

78. Ibid.; and Paul Shoup to Henry Harriman (April 1, 1935), NARA, RG79, Entry 10, Box 2259, Part 3.

79. Public Law 73-482; Executive Order 6910 (November 26, 1934); "Public Land Lists Clear," *The Los Angeles Times* (July 1, 1935); and Arno Cammerer to C. F. Impey (April 13, 1935), NARA, RG79, Entry 10, Box 2259, Part 3.

80. C. F. Impey to Arno Cammerer (May 31, 1935), NARA, RG79. Entry 10, Box 2259, Part 3; Arno Cammerer to C. F. Impey (June 12, 1935), ibid.; Arno Cammerer to Minerva Hoyt (June 21, 1935), ibid.; Minerva Hoyt to Arno Cammerer (July 19, 1935), ibid.; and Arno Cammerer to Harold Bryant (July 19, 1935), ibid. The punctuation in the quote is supplied by this author to a verbatim transcript of the original telegram.

81. Harold Bryant to the Director (August 15, 1935), NARA, RG79, Entry 10, Box 2258, Part 4.

82. Harold Bryant to Minerva Hoyt (October 18, 1935), ibid.

83. Edmund A. Schofield, "A Life Redeemed: Susan Delano McKelvey and the Arnold Arboretum," Arnold Arboretum, Harvard University (2011), http://arnoldia.arboretum.harvard.edu/pdf/articles/726.pdf; Philip Munz to Mrs. McKelvey (December 17, 1935), JTNP Library, Box "History/Legislation"; Susan Delano McKelvey to Frederic A. Delano (December 14, 1935), NARA RG79, Entry 10, Box 2258, Part 4; Susan Delano McKelvey to Henry W. de Forest (December 14, 1935), SB, RG79, Central Decimal Files, Box 303, Folder 605-01; H. W. de Forest to Susan Delano McKelvey (March 20, 1936), ibid.; and A. E. Demaray to Frank Kittredge (July 15, 1936), SB, RG79, ibid.

84. Arno Cammerer to Commissioner, GLO (January 10, 1936), NARA, RG79, Entry 10, Box 2258, Part 4; Fred W. Johnson to Arno Cammerer (February 3, 1936), SB, RG 79, Central Decimal Files, Box 303, Folder 605-01; A. E. Demaray to C. F. Impey (February 26, 1936), SB, RG 79, Central Decimal Files, Box 303, Folder 605-01; C. F. Impey to A. E. Demaray (March 31, 1936), SB, RG 79, Central Decimal Files, Box 303, Folder 605-01; and Conrad Wirth to the Director (January 13, 1936), NARA, RG79, Entry 10, Box 2258, Part 4.

85. Everett Dick, *The Lure of the Land* (Lincoln: University of Nebraska Press, 1970), 120; Paul W. Gates, *History of Public Land Law Development* (Washington, DC: Public Land Law Review Commission and Zenger Publishing Company, 1968), 285–91 and 301–04; California Lands Commission, "School Lands" (2011), http://www.slc.ca.gov/About_The_CSLC/School_Lands.html.

86. Harold Bryant to the Director (August 15, 1935), NARA, RG79, Entry 10, Box 2258, Part 4; and Frank Givens, "Briefed Data," 11–13A.

87. Arno Cammerer to Carl Sturzenacker (August 14, 1935), in Frank Givens, "Briefed Data," 13A.

88. Carl B. Stenaker to Arno Cammerer (September 4, 1935), ibid., 13e. It is uncertain why the later letter shows the name Stenaker, but Carl Sturzenacker was the state lands chief according to Paul Sabin, *Crude Politics: The California Oil Market, 1900–1940* (Berkeley: University of California Press, 2005), 98; Public Law 74-838; and A. E. Demaray to Frank Kittredge (July 15, 1936), SB, RG79, Central Decimal Files, Box 303, Folder 605-01.

89. Arno Cammerer to the Secretary (April 23, 1936), ibid.; and Kim Stringfellow, *Jackrabbit Homestead: Tracing the Small Tract Act in the Southern California Landscape, 1938–2008* (Chicago, IL: Center for American Places at Columbia College Chicago, 2009), 12–31.

90. Public Law 72-188; L. V. Branch to Director NPS (May 17, 1935), NARA, RG79, Entry 10, Box 2259, Part 3; A. E. Demaray to Commissioner GLO (May 18, 1935), ibid.; and P. T. Primm to Lawrence C. Merriam (May 18, 1935), ibid.

91. F. B. Weymouth to P. T. Primm (July 15, 1935), NARA, RG79, Entry 10, Box 2258, Part 4; and W. B. McDougall, "The Southern California Aqueduct Construction in its Relation to the Wild Life in the Proposed Desert National Monument" (August 5, 1935), ibid.

92. Fred Johnson to Arno Cammerer (April 30, 1935), JTNP Archives, Acc. 651, Cat. 19430, Folder 004; Telephone call transcript J. Lee Brown to Conrad Wirth (May 6, 1935), NARA, RG79, Entry 10, Box 2259, Part 3; A. E. Demaray to Commissioner General Land Office (May 10, 1935), NARA, RG79, Entry 10, Box 2259, Part 3; J. Lee Brown to Mr. Wirth (February 18, 1935), NARA, RG79, Entry 10, Box 2259, Part 3; and M. I. Wilson to the Secretary of the Interior (July 20, 1935), NARA, RG79, Entry 10, Box 2259, Part 3.

93. John Phillips to Harold Ickes (February 14, 1934), NARA, RG 79, Entry 10, Box 2258, Part 1; Cammerer is quoted in A. E. Demaray to Harold Bryant (September 27, 1935), NARA, RG 79, Entry 10, Box 2258, Part 4; Faith

E. Smith to Director, National Park Service (April 1, 1935), NARA, RG79, Entry 10, Box 2259, Part 3; M. O. Hert to National Park Service (December 5, 1935), NARA, RG 79, Entry 10, Box 2258, Part 4; and H. W. Stacey to the President (May 26, 1936), NARA, RG79, Entry 10, Box 2259, Part 3.

94. Minerva Hoyt to Arno Cammerer (January 30, 1935), NARA, RG79, Entry 10, Box 2259, Part 3.

95. Paul B. Witmer to Special Agent in Charge, GLO (September 18, 1935), NARA, RG 79, Entry 10, Box 2258, Part 4; J. H. Favorite to Louis R. Glavis (September 24, 1935), ibid.; and William F. Keys to Secretary of the Interior (March 12, 1936), ibid.

96. Arno Cammerer to Minerva Hoyt (February 5, 1936), in Frank Givens, "Briefed Data," 15.

97. Minerva Hoyt to Senator William G. McAdoo (February 10, 1936), NARA, RG79, Entry 10, Box 2258, Part 4.

98. Harold Bryant to the Director (February 17, 1936), SB, RG79, Central Decimal files, Box 303, Folder 605-01.

99. William McAdoo to Arthur Demaray (February 19, 1936), NARA, RG79, Entry 10, Box 2258, Part 4; Harold Bryant to Minerva Hoyt (February 20, 1936), ibid.; and Harold Bryant to Conrad Wirth (March 12, 1936), ibid.

100. Arno Cammerer to the Secretary (April 23, 1936), ibid.

101. Fred W. Johnson to Arno Cammerer (June 2, 1936), ibid.

102. Public Law 59-209; J. Lee Brown to the Files (June 5, 1936), NARA, RG79, Entry 10, Box 2258, Part 4.

103. Arno Cammerer to Secretary Ickes (July 23, 1936), ibid.; and G. A. Moskey to Acting Director (August 7, 1936), NARA, RG79, Entry 10, Box 2258, Part 2.

104. Presidential Proclamation 2193.

Chapter Three

1. The records in the Joshua Tree National Park (JTNP) Archives and San Bruno Branch of the National Archives (SB) contain these reports. There may have been other inspections for which there are no records. The provenance of each inspection is provided as they are cited below.

2. C. G. Thomas to the Director (November 8, 1936), JTNP Archives, Linda Greene files, "Report to the Director, NPS."

3. "Colonel C. G. Thomson, Yosemite Park Superintendent, Dies Suddenly in the Valley," *Mariposa Gazette* (April 8, 1937).

4. Art Kidwell, "Remembering James E. Cole: First Superintendent of Joshua Tree National Monument (1940)," *The Sun Runner* (September 1998): 16–17.

5. Presidential Proclamation 2028 (February 11, 1933); Public Law 73-49; and Death Valley National Park, "Mining in Death Valley" (2012), available at http://www.nps.gov/deva/naturescience/mining-in-death-valley.htm.

6. "Miners May Seek Change in Joshua Tree Monument Act," *The Los Angeles Times* (December 28, 1936).

7. FJR to Mrs. Sherman Hoyt (February 13, 1937), JTNP Archives, Acc. 651, Cat. 19430, L3023, Folder 104. The copy of this letter in the above files does not show the signature of the author, only the initials.

8. Superintendent JTNM to the Director, NPS (February 24, 1937), ibid.

9. S. E. Guthrey to Director of Investigations, DOI (May 6, 1937), JTNP Archives, Acc. 651, Cat 19430, L1417, Folder 024.

10. Ernest A. Davidson, "Landscape Features as Related to Development Program Joshua Tree National Monument" (April 19, 1937), JTNP Archives, Acc. 805, Cat. 27730, Box "Desert Plant National Park," Folder 003; and Frank Kittredge, "Report on Inspection Joshua Tree National Monument" (April 27, 1937), ibid.

11. 75th Congress, 1st Session, H.R. 7558, "A bill to extend the mining laws of the United States to the Joshua Tree National Monument in California" (June 17, 1937); and Arno Cammerer to Harry R. Sheppard (July 19, 1937), SB, RG79, Central Decimal Files, Box 297, Folder "C. G. Thomson."

12. Harry R. Sheppard to A. B. Cammerer (July 26, 1937), NARA, RG79, Entry 10, Box 2259, Part 5; Frank A Kittredge to Files (August 13, 1937), ibid.; and Arno B. Cammerer to Ben H. Thompson (August 20, 1937), ibid.

13. Merel Sager to the Director with accompanying report (September 16, 1937), NARA, RG79, Entry 10, Box 2261, Folder "General Reports 1936–41."

14. "Plan Launched to Realign Park Area," *The Los Angeles Times* (September 26, 1938); G. A. Moskey to Regional Director (March 21, 1939), NARA, RG79, Entry 10, Box 2260, Part 7; and Linda Green, "Historic Resource Study: A History of Land Use in Joshua Tree National Monument" (1983), DSC, JTNP, Library 397.

15. "Report on Joshua Tree National Monument by Inspector P. T. Primm and Junior Park Naturalist James E. Cole" (December 27, 1938), JTNP Archives, Acc. 752, Cat. 25125, Folder 4; Victor H. Cahalane to Mr. Wirth (February 23, 1939), JTNP Archives, Acc. 651, Cat. 19430, N14, Folder 007; and Frank R. Kittredge to the Director (April 11, 1939), JTNP Archives, Acc. 651, Cat. 19430, L14, Folder 020.

16. Linda Green, "Historic Resource Report," 397.

17. Lawrence Merriam to the Director (May 26, 1939), JTNP archives, Acc. 651, Cat. 19430, L1417, Folder 20; H. C. Bryant to Regional Director (March 14, 1940), ibid.; C. Leo Hitchcock to Arno B. Cammerer (June 5, 1939), ibid.; C. Marshall Finnan, "Report of Inspection of Joshua Tree National Monument" (1939) JTNP Archives, Acc. 651, Cat. 19430, H2623, Folder 065; H. Maier (July 21, 1941), "Notes on Joshua Tree National Monument Boundary Adjustment Meeting," JTNP Archives, Acc. 651, Cat. 19430, L1417, Folder 20; and Jerome A. Greene, "Historic Resource Study: Organ Pipe Cactus National Monument Arizona" (1977), DSC, 66–69.

18. O. A. Tomlinson to Messrs. Maier, Sumner, Lewis, Davidson, Superintendent Cole (July 17, 1941), JTNP archives, Acc. 651, Cat. 19430, L1417, Folder 20; Superintendent, JTNM to Regional Director (September 7, 1941), ibid.; and Herbert Maier to Major Tomlinson (September 30, 1941), SB, RG79, Central Decimal Files, Box 301, Folder 602.

19. Lowell Sumner, "Report of the Regional Biologist on the Joshua Tree National Monument Boundary Study" (October 6, 1941), JTNP Archives, Acc. 651, Cat. 19430, L1417, Folder 20; Ernest Davidson to Chairman Maier (September nd, 1941), SB, RG79, Central Decimal Files, Box 301, Folder 602; Guy L. Flemming to Regional Director Tomlinson (September 30, 1941), ibid.; and Superintendent to Regional Director (October 14, 1941), JTNP Archives, Acc. 651, Cat. 19430, L1417, Folder 20.

20. Herbert Maier to the Regional Director (October 13, 1941), SB, RG79, Central Decimal Files, Box 301, Folder 602.

21. Ibid.

22. G. E. Lavezzola to the Regional Director (November 19, 1941), JTNP Archives, Acc. 651, Cat. 19430, L1417, Folder 20; Superintendent, JTNM to the Regional Director (November 7, 1941), JTNP Archives, Acc. 651, Cat. 19430, N1621, Folder 27; and University of Nevada Oral History Program, "Mining and World War II" (2012), http://oralhistory.unr.edu/WWIIMine.html.

23. James E. Cole, "Joshua Tree National Monument Proposed Monument Boundary Revision" (September 27, 1944), JTNP Archives, Acc. 651, Cat. 19430, L1417, Folder 20.

24. James Cole to the Regional Director (January 11, 1945), ibid.; O. A. Tomlinson to Custodian, JTNM (January 19, 1945), ibid.; James Cole to the Regional Director (February 16, 1945), ibid.; and Herbert Maier to the Director (March 22, 1945), ibid.

25. James Cole to the Regional Director (October 24, 1945), ibid.; 79th Congress, 1st Session, H.R. 4703, "A bill to reduce and revise the boundaries of Joshua Tree National Monument in the State of California, and for other purposes" (November 15, 1945).

26. Charles L. Stokes to J. A. Krug (March 25, 1946), JTNP Archives, Acc. 651, Cat. 19430, L1417, Folder 19; James Cole to the Director (April 3, 1946), NARA, RG79, Entry 10, Box 2260, Folder 120-01; and Secretary of the Interior to Charles Stokes (April 19, 1946), NARA, RG79, Entry 10, Box 2260, Folder 120-01.

27. Secretary of the Interior to Charles Stokes (April 19, 1946), NARA, RG79, Entry 10, Box 2260, Folder 120-01.

28. Director Drury to the Regional Director (March 11, 1946), JTNP Archives, Acc. 651, Cat. 19430, L1417, Folder 20; and "Death Takes Desert Life Protector," *The Pasadena Star News* (December 17, 1945).

29. James Cole to Victor Hayek (April 5, 1946), JTNP Archives, Acc. 651, Cat. 19430, L1417, Folder 20.

30. Hillory Tolson to the Regional Director (April 12, 1946), ibid.

31. Herbert Maier to the Regional Director (April 24, 1946), JTNP Archives, Acc. 651, Cat. 19430, L1417, Folder 19; and "Southern California Regional Mining Conference" (April 17, 1946), California State Chamber of Commerce, Transcript in JTNP Archives, Acc. 651, Cat. 19430, L3023, Folder 161, 4–20. See, also, Kim Stringfellow, *Jackrabbit Homestead: Tracing the Small Tract Act in the Southern California Landscape, 1938–2008* (Chicago, IL: Center for American Places at Columbia College Chicago, 2009).

32. "Southern California Regional Mining Conference," 20–25 and 28–29. For more information on opposition to federal government management of land in the United States, see McGreggor R. Cawley and R. McGreggor Cawley,

Federal Land, Western Anger: The Sagebrush Rebellion and Environmental Politics (Lawrence: University Press of Kansas, 1993). For an international perspective, see David Harmon and Allen D. Putney, eds., *The Full Value of Parks: From Economics to the Intangible* (Lanham, MD: Rowman and Littlefield, 2003).

33. "Southern California Regional Mining Conference," 53.

34. Ibid., 55–57 and 60–61.

35. Ibid., 61–62.

35. Ibid., 62–63.

37. Ibid., 69–71.

38. Ibid., 72.

39. Ibid.; Herbert Maier to the Regional Director (April 24, 1946).

40. A. E. Demaray to the Director (May 17, 1946), NARA, RG79, Entry 10, Box 2260, Folder 120-01; 79th Congress, 1st Session, "Excerpt from hearing before House Public Lands Committee, May 22, 1946. H. R. 4703," ibid.

41. Victor J. Hayek to Committee on Public Lands (June 10, 1946), JTNP Archives, Acc. 651, Cat. 19430, L1417, Folder 019; Victor J. Hayek to James E. Cole (June 17, 1946), ibid; "Facts About the Sheppard Bill," *Desert Views* (August 24, 1946); and A. E. Demaray to Henry J. Kaiser (July 18, 1946). JTNP Archives, Acc. 651, Cat. 19430, L1417, Folder 019.

42. Raymond E. Hoyt to the Regional Director (February 27, 1947), JTNP Archives, Acc. 651, Cat. 19430, L1417, Folder 029; and Frank R. Givens to the Regional Director (March 17, 1947), JTNP Archives, Acc. 651, Cat. 19430, L1417, Folder 019.

43. 80th Congress, 1st Session, H. R. 2795, "A bill to reduce and revise the boundaries of Joshua Tree National Monument in the State of California, and for other purposes" (March 26, 1947); J. A. Krug to Richard J. Welch (May 8, 1947), JTNP Archives, Acc. 651, Cat. 19430, L1417, Folder 029; and Frank R. Givens to the Regional Director (June 24, 1947), JTNP Archives, Acc. 651, Cat. 19430, L1417, Folder 019.

44. H. L. Crowley to the Director (September 4, 1947), JTNP Archives, Acc. 651, Cat. 19430, L1417, Folder 019; and Herbert Maier to Custodian, Joshua Tree (September 19, 1947), ibid.

45. 80th Congress, 1st Session, "Hearing Before the Sub-Committee on Public Lands House of Representatives," San Bernardino, California (October 1, 1947), JTNP Archives, Acc. 651, Cat. 19430, A5415, Folder 610.01, 49.

46. Ibid., 56.

47. James E. Cole to the Regional Director (November 4, 1947), JTNP Archives, Acc. 651, Cat. 19430, L1417, Folder 019; and Frank R. Givens to the Regional Director (November 6, 1947), ibid.

48. "Sheppard Not to Refile Monument Bill," *The Desert Trail* (February 16, 1949); 81st Congress, 1st Session, H. R. 4116, "A bill to reduce and revise the boundaries of Joshua Tree National Monument in the State of California, and for other purposes" (April 8, 1949); and O. A. Tomlinson to the Director (May 11, 1949), JTNP Archives, Acc. 651, Cat. 19430, L1417, Folder 016.

49. 81st Congress, 2nd Session, H. R. 7934, "A bill to reduce and revise the boundaries of Joshua Tree National Monument in the State of California, and for other purposes" (March 30, 1950); and Conrad Wirth to the Regional Director (April 20, 1950), NARA, RG79, Entry 10, Box 2260, Folder "H. R. 7934."

50; Public Law 81-837; Dale E. Doty to Frederick J. Lawton (September 22, 1950), JTNP Archives, Acc. 651, Cat. 19430, L1417, Folder 016; Lawrence C. Merriam to Richard M. Leonard (April 9, 1952), JTNP Archives, Acc. 651, Cat. 19430, L3023, Folder 104; and Frank R. Givens to the Regional Director (May 9, 1951), JTNP Archives, Acc. 651, Cat. 19430, L1417, Folder 016.

51. C. L. Hinkleman to Clinton D. McKinnon (November 29, 1950), JTNP Archives, Acc. 651, Cat. 19430, L1417, Folder 016; and Dale E. Doty to the President (January 24, 1951), I.G, RG49, Bureau of Land Management Investigations, Box 38, Folder 1817800; and Edward M. MacKevett and Edward J. Matson "Mineral Survey Within the Revised Boundaries of Joshua Tree National Monument" (December 1950), SB, RG79, Central Files 1953-62, Acc. 79-92-001, Box 1, "L3023 JOTR Joint Survey of mineral and National Monument Values."

52. Frank R. Givens to the Regional Director (February 8, 1951), JTNP Archives, Acc. 651, Cat. 19430, L3023, Folder 104.

53. "Uranium Ore Found in Monument—Miners Urge Opening Area for Prospecting," *Indio News* (May 6, 1952).

54. Ibid.

55. Ronald F. Lee to Dr. John C. Reed (June 6, 1952), JTNP Archives, Acc. 651, Cat. 19430, L3023, Folder 104; John C. Reed to Ronald F. Lee (July 1, 1952), ibid.; Ronald F. Lee to Alford Maxwell (August 26, 1952), ibid.; and Herbert Maier to K. B. Tillman (May 6, 1952), ibid.

56. M. O. Nordstrom to Douglas McKay (August 27, 1953), JTNP Archives, Acc. 651, Cat. 19430, L1417, Folder 016.

57. Samuel A. King to the Regional Director (October 5, 1953), JTNP Archives, Acc. 651, Cat. 19430, L3023, Folder 104; The Trailfinders, "A Report of the Summer Meeting of June 8, 1952" (August 15, 1952), JTNP Archives, Acc. 651, Cat. 19430, L1417, Folder 016; and Desert Protective Council, "Around the Campfire 1954..." http://protectdeserts.org/index.php/about/history/.

58. Orme Lewis to Colonel Nordstrom (October 14, 1953), JTNP Archives, Acc. 651, Cat. 19430, L3023, Folder 151; Joe R. Momyer to Sam King (June 28, 1954), JTNP Archives, Acc. 651, Cat. 19430, H1415, Folder 002; and Samuel A. King to the Regional Director (June 30, 1954), JTNP Archives, Acc. 651, Cat. 19430, H1415, Folder 002.

59. "Summary of Hearing on Proposal that Joshua Tree National Monument Be Opened to Mining and Heard before Board of Supervisors of San Bernardino County at County Health Building, San Bernardino, Calif. at 2:00 P.M. July 19, 1954," JTNP Archives, Acc. 651, Cat. 19430, H1415, Folder 002.

60. Ibid.

61. James Roosevelt to the Secretary of the Interior (February 3, 1955), ibid.

62. Orme Lewis to Mr. Roosevelt (March 22, 1955), ibid.; Harry C. James to Lawrence C. Merriam (May 9, 1955), ibid.; and Ben H. Thompson to John Goodman (June 8, 1955), ibid.

63. *Mission 66* was a program developed by Director Conrad Wirth to renew America's national park system comprehensively by focusing primarily on infrastructure for visitors and staff. It would last a decade and end in 1966, the fiftieth anniversary of the NPS.

64. Helen B. Bixel to Thomas Kuchel (July 24, 1956), JTNP Archives, Acc. 651, Cat. 19430, L3023, Folder 151; E. T. Scoyen to Thomas Kuchel (September 14, 1956), ibid.; and Public Law 83-703.

Chapter Four

1. Thomas Vint, "Notes on Joshua Tree National Monument Trip May 9–12, 1941, accompanied by Superintendent Cole, Messrs. Davidson and Lange," (July 26, 1941), NARA, RG79, Entry 10, Box 2261, Folder "Reports, Joshua Tree Investigative."

2. Each section of land in the Township and Range Land Division System contains 640 acres or one square mile. Each township contains thirty-six sections. See Ernest A. Davidson, "Landscape Features as Related to Development Program Joshua Tree National Monument" (April 19, 1937), JTNP Archives, Acc. 00805, Cat. 27730, Box "Desert Plant National Park," Folder 003; and Frank Kittredge, "Report on Inspection Joshua Tree National Monument" (April 27, 1937), ibid.

3. James E. Cole, "Report on the Field Inspection Trip of Superintendent Lawrence C. Merriam and Junior Park Naturalist James E. Cole of Joshua Tree National Monument April 14 and 15, 1938" (1938), NARA, RG 79, Entry 10, Box 2261, Folder "Reports, General, 1937–41."

4. R. L. McKown, "Report on Joshua Tree National Monument" (November 1, 1939), JTNP Archives, Acc. 452, Cat. 25175, Folder 5.

5. Thomas Vint to Mr. Cammerer (June 13, 1940), NARA, RG79, Entry 10, Box 2260, Part 7.

6. The apparent discrepancy between the 72,000 acres of indemnity lands reported by the Southern Pacific Railroad Company in Chapter Two and the total of more than 100,000 reported here by the GLO may have come about due to an adjustment of the railroad's distribution of unselected indemnity acreage resulting from land alienation outside the monument's boundaries.

7. Herbert Maier to the Files (January 23, 1941), JTNP Archives, Acc. 651, Cat. 19430, N14, Folder 007; Public Law 73-482; Richard J. Orsi, *Sunset Limited: The Southern Pacific Railroad and the Development of the American West 1850–1930* (Berkeley: University of California Press, 2005), 128–29; and Superintendent, JTNP to Director, NPS (August 15, 1941), JTNP Archives, Acc.651, Cat. 19430, L1417, Folder 20.

8. S. E. Guthrey, C. C. Smith, J. J. Brosnan to B. B. Smith (June 24, 1938), JOTR Arch., L1417, Acc. 651, Cat. 19430, Folder "General Land Office Reports 1940–41."

9. Public Law 73-482; P. T. Primm and James E. Cole, "Report on Joshua Tree National Monument" (1938), JTNP Archives, Acc. 651, Cat. 19430, L1417, Folder 20.

10. D. G. Christen to Conrad Wirth (June 4, 1945), NARA, RG79, Entry 10, Appendix 2, Box 2266, Folder "610 Southern Pacific Lands"; James Cole to Regional Director (May 8, 1945), ibid; and O. A. Tomlinson to James F. Whitehorn (May 12, 1945), ibid.

11. Christen to Wirth (June 4, 1945), JTNP Archives, Acc. 651, Cat. 19430, L1417, Folder 20; and Newton Drury to the Regional Director (July 5, 1945), ibid.

12. Newton Drury to Will Whittington (July 9, 1945), NARA, RG79, Entry 10, Appendix 2, Box 2266, Folder "610 Southern Pacific Lands"; Joshua Green to Will M. Whittington (June 15, 1945), ibid.; Joshua Green to Harry S. Truman (June 15, 1945), ibid.; and H. L. Earenfight to the Files (May 6, 1946), ibid.

13. Herbert Maier to Custodian, JTNM (July 23, 1945), ibid.; and Regional Director Tomlinson to the Director, NPS (October 10, 1945), ibid.

14. James E. Cole to the Regional Director (July 27, 1945), ibid.; and James E. Cole to the Regional Director (December 17, 1945), ibid.

15. O. A. Tomlinson to Allen L. Chickering (December 29, 1945), ibid.

16. Mrs. Robert C. Wright to Mrs. Harry T. Peters (February 20, 1946), ibid.; Walter A. Starr, "Allen L. Chickering," *California Historical Society Quarterly*, Vol. 37, No. 1 (March 1958): 86–88; and Herbert Maier to the Custodian, Joshua Tree (March 27, 1946), NARA, RG79, Entry 10, Appendix 2, Box 2266, Folder "610 Southern Pacific Lands."

17. Herbert Maier to the Custodian, Joshua Tree (August 6, 1945) NARA, RG79, Entry 10, Appendix 2, Box 2266, Folder "610 Southern Pacific Lands."

18. Los Angeles Department of Water and Power, "The Story of the Los Angeles Aqueduct" (2012), http://wsoweb. ladwp.com/Aqueduct/historyoflaa/. For complete versions of the conflict, see William L. Kahrl, *Water and Power: The Conflict over Los Angeles Water Supply in the Owens Valley* (Berkeley: University of California Press, 1983); Norris Hundley, Jr., *The Great Thirst: Californians and Water: A History* (Berkeley; University of California Press, 2001), 139–71; and Frank Kittredge to the Regional Director (February 12, 1947), SB, RG79, Central Decimal Files, Box 302, Folder 605-01 "City of Los Angeles."

19. James E. Cole to the Regional Director (April 22, 1946), NARA, RG79, Entry 10, Appendix 2, Box 2266, Folder "610 Southern Pacific Lands"; James E. Cole to the Regional Director (February 24, 1947), ibid.; Herbert Maier to the Regional Director (April 24, 1946), SB, RG79, Central Decimal Files, Box 302, Folder 605-01 "Dick Curtis"; Newton Drury to the Commissioner, Bureau of Reclamation (May 26, 1947), SB, RG79, Central Decimal Files, Box 302, Folder 605-01 "Seth Brady"; and B. F. Manbey to Regional Director (February 4, 1948), SB, RG79, Central Decimal Files, Box 302, Folder 605-01 "Seth Brady."

20. O. A. Tomlinson to the Director, NPS (May 2, 1946), JTNP Archives, Acc. 651, Cat. 19430, L14, Folder 008.

21. Charles A. Richey to the Regional Director (August 11, 1947), SB, RG79, Central Decimal Files, Box 304, Folder "Exchange of Southern Pacific Lands."

22. Edgar I. Rowland to O. A. Tomlinson (February 3, 1948), ibid., Jackson E. Price and Conrad L. Wirth to the Director, NPS (March 9, 1948), NARA, RG79, Entry 10, Appendix 2, Box 2266, Folder "610 Southern Pacific Lands"; Roscoe E. Bell to Annetta Nesbit (May 9, 1949), SB, RG79, Central Decimal Files, Box 304, Folder 605.1; Roscoe E. Bell, "Southern Pacific Railway Company: Section 8, Private Exchange" (September 27, 1949), Bureau of Land Management Decision, SB, RG79, Central Decimal Files, Box 304, Folder 605.1.

23. Frank Givens to the Regional Director (June 17, 1948), JTNP Archives, Acc. 651, Cat. 19430, L14, Folder 009; Conrad Wirth to the Director, NPS (April 9, 1947), ibid.; Mastin G. White "Appeal from the Bureau of Land Management, Los Angeles 067465 et al" (December 13, 1948), ibid., Folder 008. Specific data on NPS land acquisition by date and parcel comes from NPS, "Digital Lands Files" (2009), available at the WRO in San Francisco.

24. B. F. Manbey to the Director, NPS (July 12, 1951), SB, RG79, Central Decimal Files, Box 404, Folder 605.1.

25. "Monument Acquires More Private Land," *The Desert Trail* (March 27, 1952); Charles A. Richey to the Regional Director (June 24, 1952), SB, RG79, Central Decimal Files, Box 304, Folder 605.1 "Southern Pacific"; and NPS, "Digital Lands Files" (2009).

26. Marion Clawson, *The Bureau of Land Management.* (New York, NY: Praeger Publishers, 1971), 178–79.

27. Public Law 74-838 (June 29, 1936).

28. Charles West to William McAdoo (March 24, 1937), JTNP Archives, Acc. 651, Cat. 19430, L14, Folder 007.

29. Frank Kittredge to the Director (June 2, 1938), SB, RG79, Central Decimal Files, Box 303, Folder 605-01, "School Lands Part I"; E. K. Burlew to Carl B. Sturzenacker (August 4, 1938), ibid.; and James E. Cole to the Regional Director (December 11, 1945), JTNP Archives, Acc. 651, Cat. 19430, L14, Folder 007.

30. James E. Cole to the Regional Director (December 11, 1945).

31. J. D. Coffman to Regional Director (September 11, 1947), SB, RG79, Central Decimal Files, Box 303, Folder 605-01; Thomas C. Havell to Director NPS (March 12, 1948), JTNP Archives, Acc. 651, Cat. 19430, L14, Folder 007; O. A. Tomlinson to Director, NPS (May 27, 1948), JTNP Archives, Acc. 651, Cat. 19430, L14, Folder 007; and Herbert Maier to Director, NPS (September 22, 1948), NARA, RG79, Entry 10, Appendix 2, Box 2267, Folder 610.1 "Joshua Tree (Purchase of Land).

32. O. A. Tomlinson to Director, NPS (March 18, 1948), JTNP Archives, Acc. 651, Cat. 19430, L14, Folder 007; A. P. Ireland to BLM (March 26, 1948), ibid.; A. P. Ireland to BLM (July 15, 1948), ibid.; and Wesley Nelson to Marion Clawson (October 7, 1948), SB, RG79, Central Decimal Files, Box 303, Folder 605-01 "School Lands." For a contemporary view of the Salton Sea, see Kim Stringfellow, *Greetings from the Salton Sea: Folly and Intervention in the Southern California Landscape, 1905–2005* (Santa Fe, NM, and Harrisonburg, VA: Center for American Places, 2005).

33. A. P. Ireland to BLM (July 15, 1948), JTNP Archives, Acc. 651, Cat. 19430, L14, Folder 007; Herbert Maier to Director, NPS (February 2, 1949), ibid.; and Herbert Maier to Director, NPS (March 29, 1949), ibid.

34. R. A. Ellsworth to A. P. Ireland (August 6, 1949), ibid.; A. E. Demaray to R. A. Ellsworth (September 20, 1949), ibid.; Herbert Maier to A. P. Ireland (October 14, 1949), ibid.; Herbert Maier to R. A. Ellsworth (November 17, 1949), ibid.; Herbert Maier to A. P. Ireland (December 8, 1949) ibid.; and L. T. Hoffman to R. A. Ellsworth (June 15, 1950), ibid.

35. Frank Givens to the Regional Director (June 23, 1950), JTNP Archives, Acc. 651, Cat. 19430, L14, Folder 007; Herbert Maier to Director, NPS (July 10, 1950), ibid.; B. F. Manbey to A. P. Ireland (January 18, 1952), ibid.; and A. P. Ireland to B. F. Manbey (January 25, 1952), ibid.

36. Lawrence Merriam to the Director, NPS (January 29, 1952), ibid.

37. R. T. Hicks to A. W. Burney (January 7, 1937), SB, RG79, Central Decimal Files, Box 307, Folder 610.

38. B. F. Manbey to the Regional Director (December 22, 1941), ibid.

39. Sidney McClellan to the Regional Director (August 21, 1946), JTNP Archives, Acc. 651, Cat. 19430, L14, Folder 007.

40. Thomas H. Kuchel to O. A. Tomlinson (August 22, 1946), ibid.; and Herbert Maier to C. F. Proctor (August 28, 1946), ibid.

41. Newton B. Drury to the Regional Director (February 3, 1947), JTNP Archives, Acc. 651, Cat. 19430, L14, Folder 009A; Herbert Maier to the Director, NPS (March 12, 1947), ibid.; and Frank R. Givens to the Regional Director (April 17, 1947), SB, RG79, Central Decimal Files, Box 307, Folder 610.

42. Frank R. Givens to the Regional Director (April 17, 1947), SB, RG79, Central Decimal Files, Box 307, Folder 610; and Herbert Maier to the Director, NPS (December 9, 1949), JTNP Archives, Acc. 651, Cat. 19430, L14, Folder 007.

43. Frank R. Givens to the Regional Director (August 11, 1949), JTNP Archives, Acc. 651, Cat. 19430, L14, Folder 007; and Herbert Maier to the Director, NPS (December 9, 1949), ibid.

44. B. F. Manbey to Superintendent (October 18, 1950), SB, RG79, Central Decimal Files, Box 307, Folder 610; and Sanford Hill to the Director, NPS (May 3, 1951), ibid.

45. "Mining Council Inquires into Land Donation," *Joshua Monument Desert Journal* (August 31, 1951); Frank R. Givens to Regional Director (October 10, 1951), JTNP Archives, Acc. 651, Cat. 19430, L14, Folder 007; and "Riverside Refuses Park Request for Tax-Deeded Land," *Joshua Monument Desert Journal* (October 12, 1951). For information on the sagebrush rebellion, see McGreggor R. Cawley and R. McGreggor Cawley, *Federal Lands, Western Anger: The Sagebrush Rebellion and Environmental Politics* (Lawrence: University Press of Kansas, 1993).

46. "Riverside Refuses Park Request for Tax-Deeded Land," *Joshua Monument Desert Journal* (October 12, 1951).

47. B. F. Manbey to C. F. Proctor (March 4, 1952), JTNP Archives, Acc. 651, Cat. 19430, L14, Folder 007; Frank R. Givens to Regional Director (April 29, 1952), ibid.; Sanford Hill to the Superintendent (May 2, 1952), ibid.; Frank R. Givens to the Regional Director (May 8, 1952), ibid.; Frank R. Givens to the Regional Director (July 11, 1952), ibid.; and Herbert Maier to Superintendent (June 9, 1953), ibid.

48. Raymond E. Hoyt to the Superintendent (July 30, 1952), ibid.; Herbert Maier to Superintendent (June 9, 1953), ibid.; Conrad Wirth to the Regional Director (February 12, 1953), SB, RG79, Central Decimal Files, Box 307, Folder 610; Samuel A. King to the Regional Director (June 19, 1953), JTNP Archives, Acc. 651, Cat. 19430, L14, Folder 007; and Clarence A. Davis to the Attorney General (October 2, 1953), JTNP Archives, Acc. 651, Cat. 19430, L14, Folder 007.

49. Herbert Maier to the Superintendent (October 20, 1953), JTNP Archives, Acc. 651, Cat. 19430, L14, Folder 007; Samuel A. King to the Regional Director (October 28, 1953), ibid.; V. M. Hyde to Samuel A. King (November 16, 1953), ibid; J. Reuel Armstrong to the Attorney General (April 16, 1956), WRO, JTNP Land Files, Folder "Tax Deeded Lands"; and "United States of America vs. 10,838.50 Acres of Land, More or Less, in the County of Riverside, California, et al." (August 15, 1958), WRO, JTNP Land Files, Folder "Tax Deeded Lands".

50. James Cole to the Regional Director (January 25, 1945), JTNP Archives, Acc. 651, Cat. 19430, L3031, Folder 230; "Act of June 18, 1932" (47 Stat. 324); and The Metropolitan Water District, "The District at a Glance," available at www.mwdh2o/pages/news/at_a_glance/mwd.pdf.

51. Timothy Babalis, "Draft Historical Context: The Pinyon Historic Mining District" (n.d.), unpublished manuscript supplied by the author May 13, 2010, 8–14; Linda Greene, "Historic Resource Study: A History of Land Use in Joshua Tree National Monument" (1983), DSC, JTNP Library, 393–99; Jessica L. K. Smith, "A Land of Plenty: Depression-Era Mining and Landscape Capital in the Mojave Desert, California," Ph.D. dissertation (Reno: University of Nevada, 2006), 1–27, 66–105, and 169–94.

52. Marion Clawson and Burnell Held, *The Federal Lands: Their Use and Management* (Baltimore, MD: The Johns Hopkins University Press, 1957), 226–28.

53. Babalis, 14; and Marion Clawson to the Director, BLM (December 16, 1947), NARA-Riverside, RG49, "BLM Investigations," Box 38, Folder 1817800.

54. Greene, "Historic Resource Study," 395.

55. James E. Cole (June 30, 1941), "Superintendent's Annual Report," NARA, RG79, Entry 10, Box 2261, Folder "Joshua Tree Superintendent's Annual Reports."

56. Superintendent James Cole later wrote that Keys had approximately 500 mining claims, all but twelve of which the GLO adversed by 1942. See James E. Cole, "Report of Pertinent Factors Relative to Grazing in Joshua Tree National Monument" (August 22, 1942), JTNP Library, Box "History/Trivia"; J. H. Favorite to James E. Cole (May 1, 1945), JTNP Archives, Acc. 651, Cat. 19430, L3023, Folder 095; Hillory A. Tolson to the Commissioner, GLO (October 23, 1945), JTNP Archives, Acc. 651, Cat. 19430, L3023, Folder 107; and Fred W. Johnson to the Director, NPS (August 28, 1941), WRO, Land Files, JTNP, Folder L1425 "Keys Unpatented Mining Claims."

57. Albert L. Johnson to the Regional Director (June 23, 1943), JTNP Archives, Acc. 651, Cat. 19430, H3015, Folder 005; Fred T. Johnston to Mr. R. R. Best (September 7, 1956), JTNP Archives, Acc. 651, Cat. 19430, H3015, Folder 006; George H. Wheatley to Superintendent, JTNM (October 10, 1957), JTNP Archives, Acc. 651, Cat. 19430, H3015, Folder 006; and U. S. Bureau of Land Management (November 3, 1961), "United States of America, "Hearing, Contestant v. Wm. F. Keys, F. M. Keys, Contestees," Contest No. 6897, JTNP Archives, Acc. 651, Cat. 19430, L3023, Folder 095.

58. Marion Clawson to the Director, BLM (December 16, 1947); Marion Clawson to the Director, BLM (February 13, 1948), NARA-Riverside, RG49, "BLM Investigations," Box 38, Folder 1817800.

Chapter Five

1. Samuel King, "A History of Joshua Tree National Monument" (1954), unpublished report, JTNP Library.

2. Ernest A. Davidson, "Landscape Features as Related to Development Program Joshua Tree National Monument" (1937), JTNP Archives, Acc. 805, Cat. 27730, Box "Desert Plant National Park," Folder 003.

3. James E. Cole, "Report on Field Inspection Trip of Superintendent Lawrence C. Merriam and Junior Park Naturalist James E. Cole of Joshua Tree National Monument, April 14 and 15, 1938" (1938), NARA, RG79, Entry 10, Box 2261, Folder "Reports, General, 1937–41."

4. J. Volney Lewis, "Ground Water Resources of the Joshua Tree National Monument California" (1942), WRO, JTNP Library.

5. Chester A. Pinkham to James E. Cole (July 20, 1945), JTNP Archives, Acc. 651, Cat. 19430, H1417, Folder 005; and Hillory A. Tolson to the Regional Director (December 22, 1944), SB, RG79, Central Decimal files, Box 297, Folder 208.

6. Norris Hundley, Jr., *The Great Thirst: California and Water: A History* (Berkeley: University of California Press, 2001), 51–60, 69–75, and 85–87.

7. Roderick E. Walston, "Western Water Law," *Natural Resources and Environment*, Vol. 1, No. 4 (Winter 1986): 48–52; and California State Water Resources Control Board, "History of the Water Boards" (2012), http://www.swrcb.ca.gov/about_us/water_boards_structure/history_water_rights.shtml.

8. James Cefalo, "Return of the Federal Non-Reserved Water Right," *University of Denver Water Law Review*, Vol. 10, No. 1 (Fall 2006): 45–71.

9. Benjamin H. Hibbard, *A History of the Public Land Policies* (New York, NY: Macmillan, 1924), 509; James Muhn, *Public Water Reserves: The Metamorphosis of Public Land Policy* (Provo: University of Utah Press, 2001), 67–150; and Linda Greene, "Historic Resource Study: A History of Land Use in Joshua Tree National Monument" (1983), DSC, JTNP Library, 347–49.

10. Norris Hundley, Jr., *The Great Thirst*, 360–64; Roderick E. Walston, "Western Water Law," 48–52; James Cefalo, "Return of the Federal Non-Reserved Water Right," 67–70; and NPS, "Land Protection Plan for Joshua Tree National Park" (1996), JTNP Library.

11. James E. Cole to the Regional Director (July 3, 1946), JTNP Archives, Acc. 651, Cat. 19430, L54, Folder 245.

12. Frank R. Givens to the Regional Director (August 9, 1948), JTNP Archives, Acc. 651, Cat. 19430, L3027, Folder 222; O. A. Tomlinson to the Custodian, JTNM (August 12, 1948), JTNP Library, Box "NARA Archives and Other Archives"; Frank R. Givens to the Regional Director (September 22, 1948), JTNP Library, Box "NARA Archives and Other Archives"; and Conrad Wirth to the Regional Director (November 9, 1948), JTNP Library, Box "NARA Archives and Other Archives".

13. James E. Cole to the Regional Director (November 7, 1946), JTNP Archives, Acc. 651, Cat. 19430, L1417, Folder 019; Julian Hinds to O. A. Tomlinson (October 28, 1947), JTNP Archives, Acc. 651, Cat. 19430, L54, Folder 244; and A. E. Demaray to the Regional Director (January 8, 1948), JTNP Archives, Acc. 651, Cat. 19430, L30, Folder 085A.

14. Samuel A. King to the Regional Director (December 10, 1954), JTNP Archives, Acc. 651, Cat. 19430, L1425, Folder 031; and George McMeans to E. S. King (December 27, 1954), ibid.

15. Samuel A. King to the Regional Director (December 29, 1954), ibid; Lawrence C. Merriam to the Director (January 6, 1955), JTNP Archives, Acc. 651, Cat. 19430, L1425, Folder 032; and Jackson E. Price to the Regional Director (January 25, 1955), JTNP Archives, Acc. 651, Cat. 19430, L1425, Folder 032.

16. Samuel A. King to the Regional Director (January 27, 1956), JTNP Archives, Acc. 651, Cat. 19430, L1425, Folder 032; and Lawrence C. Merriam to Donald E. Lee (December 20, 1957), JTNP Archives, Acc. 651, Cat. 19430, L1425, Folder 034.

17. Superintendent, JTNM to the Regional Director (February 7, 1941), JTNP Archives, Acc. 651, Cat. 19430, L54, Folder 247.

18. Greene, "Historic Resource Study," 433–40.

19. Ibid.; and James E. Cole, "Report of Pertinent Factors Relative to Grazing in Joshua Tree National Monument" (August 22, 1942), JTNP Library, History/Trivia box.

20. James E. Cole, "Report of Pertinent Factors"; Kerwin L. Klein, "The William Keys Ranch: Settlement on the Twentieth-Century California Desert," *Southern California Quarterly*, Vol. 73, No. 4 (Winter 1991): 355–84; and William F. Keys to Mr. Merriam (September 7, 1937), JTNP Archives, Acc. 651, Cat. 19430, H3015, Folder 026.

21. Greene, "Historic Resource Study," 433–40; Klein, "The William Keys Ranch"; and Art Kidwell, *Ambush: The Story of Bill Keys* (Twentynine Palms, CA: Desert Moon Press, 1979), 7–12.

22. James E. Cole, "Report of Pertinent Factors."

23. Ibid.; Greene, "Historic Resource Study," 439–440; Newton B. Drury to John Phillips (January 6, 1943), JTNP Archives, Acc. 651, Cat. 19430, A5615, Folder 038.

24. Cole, Report of Pertinent Factors"; and Frances M. Keys and William F. Keys to Harold Ickes (July 30, 1941), JTNP Archives, Acc. 651, Cat. 19430, H3015, Folder 005.

25. William Keys to Mr. Merriam and Major O. A. Tomlinson (July 18, 1942), JTNP Archives, Acc. 651, Cat. 19430, H3015, Folder 005.

26. Superintendent, JTNM to the Regional Director (August 10, 1942), ibid.

27. Ibid.

28. Ibid.

29. James E. Cole to William F. Keys (August 17, 1942), JTNP Archives, Acc. 651, Cat. 19430, H3015, Folder 005; James E. Cole to William F. Keys (August 18, 1942), ibid.; and William F. Keys to Mr. J. E. Cole (August 19, 1942), ibid.

30. Herbert Maier to James E. Cole (August 25, 1942), ibid.

31. Superintendent, JTNM to the Regional Director (August nd, 1942), ibid.

32. Herbert Maier to the Files (October 29, 1942), ibid.

33. Ibid.

34. William F. Keys to William Jeffers (December 3, 1942), JTNP Archives, Acc. 651, Cat. 19430, H3015, Folder 005; and Herbert Maier to the Director (January 29, 1943), ibid.

35. Duane Jacobs to the Files (January 9, 1943), ibid.

36. Ibid.; William F. Keys to the Regional Director (February 23, 1943), ibid.; and Mrs. Wm. F. Keys to United States Land Office (September 14, 1944), ibid.

37. Gordon Chappell, "Keys' Desert Queen Ranch Joshua Tree National Monument Preservation Study" (January 25, 1975), 1–14, ibid.; Kidwell, "Ambush," 3–144; and Klein, "The William Keys Ranch."

38. Kidwell, "Ambush," 147–80; and Klein, "The William Keys Ranch."

39. Chappell, "Keys' Desert Queen Ranch."

40. A. E. Demaray to Merel S. Sager (July 19, 1937), NARA, RG79, Entry 10, Box 2259, Part 5; Merel Sager to the Director (September 16, 1937), with accompanying inspection report, NARA, RG79, Entry 10, Box 2261, Folder "General Reports 1937–41"; Chief Engineer Kittredge and Regional Landscape Architect E. A. Davidson "Report on Inspection Joshua Tree National Monument" (April 27, 1937), JTNP Archives, Acc. 805, Cat.27730, Box "Desert Plant National Park," Folder 003.

41. Kittredge and Davidson (April 27, 1937); Ernest A. Davidson, "Landscape Features as Related to Development Program Joshua Tree National Monument" (April 19, 1937), JTNP Archives, Acc. 805, Cat.27730, Box "Desert Plant National Park," Folder 003; Merel S. Sager to the Files (February 15, 1938), JTNP, Acc. 651, Cat. 19430, L14, Folder 006; and Merel Sager to the Director (September 16, 1937), JTNP, Acc. 651, Cat. 19430, L14, Folder 006.

42. F. A. Kittredge to the Director (January 7, 1938), JTNP, Acc. 651, Cat. 19430, L14, Folder 006; and James E. Cole, "Report on Field Inspection Trip of Superintendent Lawrence C. Merriam and Junior Park Naturalist James E. Cole."

43. Ernest A. Davidson, "Report on Proposed Headquarters Sites Joshua Tree National Monument" (April 17, 1941), NARA, RG79, Entry 10, Box 2261, Folder "General Reports 1937–41"; James E. Cole to the Superintendent (November 1, 1939), JTNP, Acc. 651, Cat. 19430, L14, Folder 006; Frank Rogers to James Cole (September 23, 1940), JTNP, Acc. 651, Cat. 19430, L14, Folder 006; and James E. Cole to the Regional Director (May 16, 1941), JTNP, Acc. 651, Cat. 19430, L14, Folder 006.

44. B. F. Manbey to the Files (June 3, 1941), JTNP, Acc. 651, Cat. 19430, L14, Folder 006.

45. Superintendent, JTNM to the Regional Director (June 9, 1941), ibid.; Herbert Maier to the Superintendent, JTNM (June 19, 1941), ibid.; A. E. Demaray to the Regional Director (August 1, 1941), ibid.

46. David R. Faries to Herbert Maier (August 7, 1941), ibid.; Herbert Maier to Major Tomlinson, (August nd, 1941), NARA-SB, RG79, Central Decimal Files, Box 301, Folder 602; Superintendent, JTNM to the Regional Director (January 19, 1942), JTNP, Acc. 651, Cat. 19430, L14, Folder 006; and "29 Palms Gateway to Monument Proposed," *The Pasadena Star-News* (February 12, 1942).

47. David R. Faries to the Director (January 14, 1943), JTNP, Acc. 651, Cat. 19430, L14, Folder 006; and Hillory A. Tolson to David R. Faries (January 27, 1943), ibid.

48. Duane D. Jacobs to the Regional Director (June 8, 1943), ibid.; and James E. Cole to the Regional Director (May 3, 1946), ibid.

49. Frank R. Givens to the Regional Director (April 10, 1947), ibid.; and Herbert Maier to the Custodian, JTNM (January 22, 1948), ibid.

50. Frank R. Givens to Arthur H. Blake (April 26, 1948), ibid.; Carl King to Frank Givens (June 5, 1948), ibid.; Frank R. Givens to the Regional Director (June 8, 1948), ibid.; O. A. Tomlinson to the Director (August 12, 1948), ibid.; A. E. Demaray to the Regional Director (September 1, 1948), ibid.; Frank R. Givens to the Regional Director (October 1, 1948), ibid.; Culbert W. Faries to Mr. Givens (October 16, 1948), ibid.; and Herbert Maier to the Director (October 26, 1948), ibid.

51. Dorr G. Yeager to the Regional Director (November 9, 1948), ibid.; Sidney McClellan to the Regional Director (November 9, 1948), ibid.; O. A. Tomlinson to the Director (November 10, 1948), ibid.; Dorr Yeager to the Regional Director (November 19, 1948), ibid.; and A. E. Demaray to the Regional Director (November 22, 1948), ibid.

52. H. F. Cameron, Jr., to the Regional Engineer (January 5, 1949), ibid.; H. L. Crowley to the Superintendent, JTNM (February 18, 1949), ibid.; O. A. Tomlinson to the Director (March 8, 1949), ibid.; H. L. Crowley to H. F. Cameron, Jr. (May 16, 1949), ibid.; H. L. Crowley to the Director (October 31, 1949), ibid.; Hillory A. Tolson to the Regional Director (November 17, 1949), ibid.; J. Howard McGrath to Oscar L. Chapman (March 16, 1950), JTNP Archives, Acc. 651, Cat. 19430, L1417, Folder 27; Public Law 59-209; and Public Law 87-80.

53. C. G. Thomson to the Director (November 8, 1936), JTNP Archives, Linda Greene files, "Report to the Director, NPS."

54. S. E. Guthrey to Director of Investigations, DOI (May 8, 1937), JTNP Archives, Acc. 805, Cat. 27730, Box "Desert Plant National Park," Folder 001; and Frank Kittredge and Ernest Davidson, "Report on Inspection Joshua Tree National Monument" (April 27, 1937), JTNP Archives, Acc. 805, Cat. 27730, Box "Desert Plant National Park," Folder 003, 6–7.

55. Merel Sager to the Director with accompanying report (September 13, 1937), NARA, RG79, Entry 10, Box 2259, Part 5, 18–19; Lawrence Merriam to the Director (May 1, 1940), SB, RG79, Central Files, Box 297, Folder 207; Sanford Hill, "Report of Field Trip to Joshua Tree National Monument in company with Regional Engineer Crowley and Regional Architect De Long" (n.d.), SB, RG 79, Central Decimal Files, Box 297, Folder 207, 2; R. L. McKown, "Report on Joshua Tree National Monument" (November 1, 1939), JTNP Arch Acc. 452, Cat. 25175, Folder 5, 2–4; and R. D. Waterhouse, "Report on JTNM Trip covering October 20–26, 1940" (n.d.) SB, RG 79, Central Decimal Files, Box 297, Folder 207, 1–2.

56. T. R. Goodwin to the Regional Director with attached "Report on Joshua Tree National Monument" (March 18, 1941), SB, RG 79, Central Decimal Files, Box 297, Folder 207, 1–4; Thomas Vint, "Notes on Joshua Tree National Monument Trip May 9–12, 1941, accompanied by Superintendent Cole, Messrs. Davidson and Lange" (July 26, 1941), NARA, RG 79, Entry 10, Box 2261, Folder "Reports, Joshua Tree, Investigations" 2; and NPS, "Master Plan Joshua Tree National Monument" (1941) JTNP Library, digitally scanned version in Box "NARA Materials."

57. James E. Cole to the Regional Director (November 19, 1940), SB, RG79, Central Decimal Files, Box 300, Folder 600.

58. T. R. Goodwin, "Report on Joshua Tree National Monument," 1.

59. Major Stephen Long's dismissal of the Great Plains as the uninhabitable "Great American Desert" exemplified the northwestern European cultural response to dry lands. Although it is politically correct today to say all park systems units are equally valuable parts of a system, the modern drive to convert former national monuments to national parks belies it. See Hal Rothman, *Preserving Different Pasts: The American National Monuments.* (Urbana: University of Illinois Press, 1989).

60. Conrad Wirth to H. C. Begole (February 12, 1954), JTNP Archives, Acc. 651, Cat. 19430, D30, Folder 036.

61. Ibid.

62. California Assembly, "Assembly Joint Resolution No. 8—Relative to the construction of a road through Joshua Tree National Monument" (March 25, 1954), ibid.; Bertha Fuller to Representative Cecil King (June nd, 1954), ibid.; and H. S. Shilko "Proposed 'Blue Cut' Road for Joshua Tree National Monument Reconnaissance Survey" (July 2, 1954), JTNP Archives, Acc. 651, Cat. 19430, D30, Folder 038.

63. Lawrence C. Merriam to the Director (July 30, 1954), JTNP Archives, Acc. 651, Cat. 19430, D30, Folder 036; and E. E. Erhart, "Reconnaissance Report of Proposed Blue Cut Route in Joshua Tree National Monument Riverside and San Bernardino Counties California" (March n.d., 1955), JTNP Archives, Acc. 651, Cat. 19430, D30, Folder 038.

64. Samuel A. King to the Regional Director (April 22, 1956), JTNP Archives, Acc. 651, Cat. 19430, D30, Folder 036; Conrad Wirth to Senator Thomas H. Kuchel (July 24, 1956), ibid.; Robert T. Andersen to the Regional Director

(November 19, 1957), ibid.; "Officials Compare Freeway Expenses," *The Desert Trail* (November 27, 1957); "Kuchel Says No Hope for Blue Cut Highway," *The Daily Enterprise* (March 20, 1958); and Hillory Tolson to Randall Henderson (March 21, 1958), JTNP Archives, Acc. 651, Cat. 19430, D30, Folder 036.

65. Thomas E. Carpenter to the Regional Chief of Operations (July 7, 1958), JTNP Archives, Acc. 651, Cat. 19430, D30, Folder 035; and E. T. Scoyen to D. S. Saund (July 25, 1958), ibid.

66. City of Indio, "A Resolution of the City Council of the City of Indio, California, Requesting the National Parks [sic] Service to Provide an Entrance from the Coachella Valley to the Joshua Tree National Monument Through Blue Cut Canyon" (1958), Resolution No. 1015, JTNP Archives, Acc. 651, Cat. 19430, D30, Folder 036; "Blue Cut Road Study Due," *The Riverside Daily Press* (April 3, 1959); George F. Whitworth to the Regional Director (March 2, 1959), SB, RG79, Central Files 1954–61, Box 2, Folder "A4067 Areas 1954–61 H-L"; and Lawrence Merriam to the Superintendent, JTNM (March 4, 1959), SB, RG79, Central Files 1954–61, Box 2, Folder "A4067 Areas 1954–61 H–L."

67. 76th Congress, 3rd Session, H. R. 10632, "A bill to authorize the President temporarily to transfer jurisdiction over certain national-forest and national-park land to the War Department or the Navy Department" (October 8, 1940); Izaak Walton League, "Izaak Walton League Protests Military Use of National Parks" (November 26, 1940), JTNP Archives, Acc. 651, Cat. 19430, H1415, Folder 001; Ernest A. Davidson, "Notes and Pictures Relative to Proposed Army Maneuver Road at Joshua Tree National Monument" (February 25, 1943), JTNP Archives, Acc. 651, Cat. 19430, D30, Folder 048; and O. A. Tomlinson to Acting Superintendent Jacobs (May 21, 1943), NARA, RG79, Entry 10, Box 91, Folder 201.

68. Greene, "Historic Resource Study," 427.

69. NPS, "Master Plan Development Outline, Joshua Tree National Monument, California—General Development" (February 1957), JTNP Archives, Cat. 651, Acc. 19430, A6423, Folder 046.

70. Charles G. Thompson to the Director (November 8, 1936), JTNP Archives, Linda Greene Files, Folder "Report to Director, NPS 11/8/36"; and James E. Cole, "Report on Field Inspection Trip of Superintendent Lawrence C. Merriam and Junior Park Naturalist James E. Cole of Joshua Tree National Monument April 14 and 15, 1938" (1938), NARA, RG79, Entry 10, Box 2261, Folder "Reports, General, 1937–41."

71. E. Lowell Sumner, "Special Report on the JTNM with Reference to Antelope and Bighorn" (March 28, 1940), NARA, RG79, Entry 10, Box 2261, Folder "Reports, Joshua Tree, Investigative," 9–10.

72. Joseph S. Dixon, "Special Report on Wildlife Problems Joshua Tree National Monument California" (April 21, 1941), JTNP Archives, Acc. 00752, Cat. 25175, Folder 044.

73. E. Lowell Sumner, "Report of the Regional Biologist on the Joshua Tree National Monument Boundary Study" (October 6, 1941), JTNP Archives, Acc. 00752, Cat. 25175, Folder 031; and E. Lowell Sumner to Victor H. Cahalane (October 24, 1941), ibid.

74. "Annual Wildlife Report, Joshua Tree National Monument," 1941, 1944, 1946–51, 1953, 1955, and 1957, JTNP Archives, Acc. 852, Cat. 30023, Box 1, Folder 01.

75. Philip A. Munz to Mrs. McKelvey (May 8, 1942), JTNP Library, Box "Materials at NARA"; Superintendent JTNM to the Director (February 5, 1941), JTNP Archives, Acc. 651, Cat. 19430, N14, Folder 007; and Robert Moon, telephone interview by the author (March 25, 2013).

76. Burnett Sanford to Superintendent King (July 23, 1953), JTNP Archives, Acc. 651, Cat. 19430, N50, Folder 146; and Willis W. Wagener to Samuel A. King (May 2, 1956), ibid.

77. JTNM, "Fire History—Human Caused Fires—Joshua Tree National Monument" (1986), JTNP Archives, Acc. 651, Cat. 19430, Y14, Folder 001; Hesmel Earenfight interview with Susan Husari (January 8, 1982), transcript in JTNP Archives, Acc. 856, uncatalogued files, Folder "Fire Management Planning—Topside"; and "It's a Fact…," *The Desert Trail* (Progress Edition, September n.d., 1967).

78. Edmund B. Jaeger to Director, Biological Survey (September 20, 1939), JTNP Archives, Acc. 651, Cat. 19430, N14, Folder 004; Biologist [Lowell Sumner] to A. A. Nichol (March 25, 1940), ibid.; and Frank R. Givens to the regional Director (September 7, 1951), SB, RG79, Central Coded Files, Box 309, Folder 715-01.

79. Ronald F. Lee to the Regional Director (April 29, 1954), SB, RG79, Central Coded Files, N16, Box 30, Folder "N16 Vol.2 1-1-54 to 12-31-54."

80. Lowell Sumner to Assistant Regional Director Maier (May 14, 1954), SB, RG79, Central Coded Files, N16, Box 30, Folder "N16 Vol. 1 5-1-53 to 12-31-57."

81. Herbert Maier to Helmut K. Buechner (July 26, 1954), ibid.

82. Dorr G. Yeager to Lowell Sumner (October 7, 1954), SB, RG79, Central Coded Files, N16, Box 30, Folder "N16 Vol.2 1-1-54 to 12-31-54"; and Helmut K. Buechner to Dorr G. Yeager (November 9, 1954), ibid.

83. Lowell Sumner, "Joshua Tree National Monument Bighorn Range and Water Survey" (September 1955), JTNP Archives, Acc. 796, Cat. 26851, Folder 023; and Lowell Sumner to the Regional Director (April 26, 1956), SB, RG79, Central Coded Files, N16, Box 30, Folder "N16 Vol. 1 5-1-53 to 12-31-57."

84. John D. Goodman, "The Desert Bighorn Sheep of Joshua Tree National Monument" (nd [1957]), SB, RG79, Central Coded Files, N16, Box 30, Folder "N16 Vol. 1 5-1-53 to 12-31-57"; and Elmer N. Fladmark to John D. Goodman (March 13, 1957), ibid.

85. Dorr G. Yeager to Superintendent, JTNM (October 2, 1957), JTNP Archives, Acc. 651, Cat. 19430, N1621, Folder 029A; and Lowell Sumner to the Regional Director (October 8, 1957), ibid.

86. Ronald F. Lee to the Director (January 31, 1957), SB, RG79, Central Coded Files, N16, Box 30, Folder "N16 Vol. 3 1-1-55 to 12-31-57."

87. Public Law 72-428 passed on March 3, 1933 enabling President Roosevelt to issue Executive Orders 6166 on June 10 and 6228 on July 28 in the same year to accomplish the reorganization; and Public Law 74-292.

88. Julian Steward, "Petroglyphs of California and Adjoining States," *University of California Publications in Archaeology and Ethnology*, Vol. 24, No 2 (1929): 47–238; and Elizabeth W. C. Campbell and William H. Campbell, "The Pinto Basin Site: An Aboriginal Camping Ground in the California Desert," in *Southwest Museum Papers Number Nine: The Pinto Basin Site* (Highland Park, CA: Southwest Museum of Los Angeles, 1935), 9 and 21–31.

89. Cole, "Report on Field Inspection Trip."

90. C. Marshall Finnan, "Report on Inspection of Joshua Tree National Monument, California" (1939), JOTR Arch H2623, Fold 065.

91. Dixon, "Special Report on Wildlife Problems"; and Regional Director to Archaeologist Nusbaum (December 12, 1941), JTNP Archives, Acc. 651, Cat. 19430, H3015, Folder 090.

92. Louis R. Laywood, "Preliminary Appraisals of the Archaeological Resources of Death Valley and Joshua Tree National Monuments" (February 23, 1951), JTNP Archives, Acc. 752, Cat. 25175, Folder 040; and Samuel A. King to Mrs. Carl F. Janish (November 9, 1953), JTNP Archives, Acc. 651, Cat. 19430, H3015, Folder 089.

93. Walter Rivers, "Joshua Tree National Monument Museum Prospectus" (June 1949), JTNP Archives, Acc. 651, Cat. 19430, D6215, Folder 081; and JTNM, "Supplement to the Museum Prospectus Joshua Tree National Monument" (April 1957), ibid.

94. JTNM, "Old Adobe" (n.d.), JTNP Archives, Acc. 651, Cat. 19430, H1417, Folder 005.

95. JTNP, "Joshua Tree National Park Annual Visitation 1941–2009" (2009), JTNP Superintendent's Files.

96. James E. Cole to the Director (December 10, 1940), NARA, RG79, Entry 10, Box 2260, Part 7; R. E. Rothrock to Superintendent, JTNM (December 9, 1940), ibid.; and Frank R. Givens to the Regional Director (November 7, 1947), SB, RG79, Central decimal files, Box 300, Folder 600.

97. Art Kidwell and Jeff Ohlfs, "History of Joshua Tree National Monument" (1992), unpublished chronology available in the JTNP Library.

98. Thomas Vint, "Notes on JTNM Trip May 9–12, 1941, accompanied by Superintendent Cole, Messrs. Davidson and Lange" (July 26, 1941), NARA, RG 79, Entry 10, Box 2261, Folder "Reports, Joshua Tree, Investigations."

Chapter Six

1. Public Law 90-360; and Environmental Protection Agency, "Clean Air Act," available at http://www.epa.gov/air/caa.

2. Public Law 88-577.

3. Dennis M. Ross, *The Wilderness Movement and the National Forests* (College Station, TX: Intaglio Press, 1988); and The Wilderness Institute, "Wilderness Data Search" (2012), www.wilderness.net.

4. Public Law 91-190.

5. Public Law 93-205.

6. Jacques E. Crommelin to the Regional Director (January 6, 1956), JTNP Archives, Acc. 651, Cat. 19430, L1425, Folder 058; and B. F. Manbey to Richard Sporleder (April 18, 1957) JTNP Archives, Acc. 651, Cat. 19430, L7617, Folder 273.

7. "Eisenhower Asks Congress to Approve $1 1/2 Million to Purchase Private Land Within Joshua Tree National Monument," *The Desert Trail* (June 9, 1960).

8. Public Law 88-578; Jeffrey Zinn, "Land and Water Conservation Fund: Current Status and Issues" (2002), CRS Report for Congress, Order Code: 97-792 ENR.

9. NPS, "Digital Lands Files" (2009), available from the WRO Land Office; Manbey to Sporleder (April 18, 1957); Herbert Maier to the Director, NPS (September 2, 1960), WRO, Lands Files, Joshua Tree, Folder "L1425 Kaiser Steel"; and Conrad Wirth to T. M. Price (June 19, 1961), WRO, Lands Files, Joshua Tree, Folder "L1425 Kaiser Steel."

10. B. F. Manbey to the Regional Director (March 9, 1956), JTNP Archives, Acc. 651, Cat. 19430, A4027, Folder 033; and "Digital Lands Files."

11. Harold G. Fowler to Regional Chief of Operations (June 6, 1960), SB, RG79, Central Files 1954–61, Box 2, Folder "A5427 Folder 5 H to L"; "Acquisition of Private Lands in Monument Asked by Supervisors," *The Desert Trail* (January 31, 1962); "Exchange Monument Inholdings Resumes, Supernaugh States," *The Desert Trail* (June 13, 1962); Public Law 87-80; and Lawrence Merriam to the Director (January 9, 1962), NARA, RG79, Entry 11, Box 1741, Folder 1425.

12. "New Fund to Accept Donations for Buying Monument Inholdings," *The Desert Trail* (August 8, 1962); "Council Acts to Protect Joshua Tree Monument," *The Desert Trail* (March 14, 1962); and "Digital Lands Files."

13. "Colorful Old Miner Sells Famed Joshua Tree Ranch," *San Bernardino Daily Sun* (October 21, 1964); Henry E. Tubman to Senator George L. Murphy (April 13, 1965), JTNP Archives, Acc.822, Folder "Tubman Exchange"; Fred H. Johnson to Henry E. Tubman (April 8, 1966), JTNP Archives, Acc.822, Folder "Tubman Exchange"; "Henry E. Tubman," *The Hi-Desert Star* (October 9, 2004); and "Rites Set for Desert Bill, Prospector–Cowboy," *The Los Angeles Times* (July 2, 1969).

14. "Joshua Tree Monument Adds 11,713 Acres Private Land," *The Desert Trail* (nd 1970), JTNP Library, Clippings File; and "Digital Lands Files."

15. Public Law 91-190; W. F. Herbert to Peter Parry (June 28, 1973), JTNP Archives, Acc. 651, Cat. 19430, L7617, Folder 273.

16. Peter L. Parry to W. F. Herbert (July 3, 1973), JTNP Archives, Acc. 651, Cat. 19430, L7617, Folder 273; and "Digital Lands Files."

17. WRO, "Management Consultation Report Joshua Tree National Monument California" (January 1976), JTNP Archives, Acc. 651, Cat. 19430, A2623, Box 6, Folder 28A; JTNP, "National Park Service Buys Jellystone Park," NPS news release (April 6, 1976), WRO, Cultural Resources, Mulherne Files, Box 24, Folder "Clippings."

18. Leo J. Diederich, "Comments on Package Master Plan Joshua Tree N. M." (May 14, 1964), DSC, 156-MPNAR-Z1-339051.

19. Jens C. Jensen to James M. Siler (July 16, 1964), WRO, JTNP Files, Folder "Desert Queen Mine"; Thomas Clements, "Report on the Evaluation of the Mineral Interests in All or Part of 22 Sections in Joshua Tree National Monument, California" (September 14, 1971), JTNP Archives, Acc. 651, Cat. 19430, L3023, Folder 220A; and JTNM, "Statement for Management Joshua Tree National Monument California" (April 1982), JTNP Library, 15.

20. Public Law 94-429; and Draft of Letter from Regional Director, WRO to State Director, BLM (n.d. but after October 10, 1984), JTNP Archives, Acc. 651, Cat. 19430, L3023, Folder 109-1.

21. Frank R. Givens to the Regional Director (April 14, 1949), SB, RG79, Central Files, Box 297, Folder 208-43.

22. Owen Tomlinson to the Superintendent, JTNM (April 28, 1949), ibid.

23. John W. Wise to the Chief Ranger (July 19, 1967), JTNP Archives, Acc. 856, Box "Lands and Mining," Folder "Hazardous Mine Report 1973"; Roy O. Curbow, "Mine Shaft Safety Devices Proposal" (November 5, 1973), JTNP Archives, Acc. 651, Cat. 19430, D22, Folder 015; Homer L. Rouse to the Regional Director (August 22, 1975), JTNP Archives, Acc. 651, Cat. 19430, L3023, Folder 159; and Stanley Albright to the Superintendent, JTNM (May 3, 1978), JTNP Archives, Acc. 651.1, Cat. 28859, Box D22, Folder 017.

24. "Digital Lands Files"; Superintendent to the Regional Director (January 28, 1941), JTNP Archives, Acc. 651, Cat. 19430, L54, Folder 247; Art Kidwell and Jeff Ohlfs, "History of Joshua Tree National Monument," (1992), unpub-

lished chronology available in the JTNP Library; James K. Baker to Manuel Morris (April 25, 1968), JTNP Archives, Acc. 651, Cat. 19430, N3617, Folder 98; and William L. Werrell to the Regional Chief of Water Resources (June 27, 1975), JTNP Archives, Acc. 651, Cat. 19430, L54, Folder 260.

25. George B. Wheatley to the Regional Director (August 4, 1958), JTNP Archives, Acc. 651, Cat. 19430, L54, Folder 245; Herbert Maier to the Director (June 15, 1959), ibid.; Richard Buddeke to the Director (August 27, 1959), ibid.; Joseph L. Chiriaco, Inc., "Chiriaco Summit History" (2012), http://www.chiriacosummit.com/history.php.

26. Keith H. Corrigall to C. F. Woolpert (March 19, 1964), JTNP Archives, Acc. 651, Cat. 19430, L54, Folder 245; James M. Siler to Superintendent, JTNM (April 6, 1964), ibid.; Scott Stonum to the Superintendent, JTNP (July 12, 1995), Acc. 651.1/004, Cat. 28859, L54, Folder 098; Armand B. Sansum to the Superintendent, JTNM (September 8, 1969), JTNP Archives, Acc. 651, Cat. 19430, L54, Folder 245; Kenneth M. Kasper to Chief, Office of Land Acquisition and Water Resources, Western Service Center (October 8, 1970), JTNP Archives, Acc. 651, Cat. 19430, L54, Folder 245; Name Unclear, "Chiriaco Water Rights" (1974), WRO, Lands Files, JTNP, Folder "Chiriaco Water Rights," Docket No. AWR #3; and David C. Hemstreet to Superintendent, JTNM (June 7, 1976), WRO, Lands Files, JTNP, Folder "Chiriaco Water Rights," Docket No. AWR #3.

27. Lawrence C. Merriam to Donald E. Lee (December 20, 1957), JTNP Archives, Acc. 651, Cat. 19430, L1425, Folder 034.

28. Edward A. Hummel to the Regional Director (October 10, 1967), JTNP Archives, Acc. 651, Cat. 19430, L1425, Folder 033.

29. Fred Kunkel, "Summary of Hydraulic Conditions at Joshua Tree National Monument, Riverside County, Calif., 1956–59" (1960), U. S. Geological Survey, Ground Water Branch, Long Beach, California, JTNP Library, 17.

30. J. E. Weir, Jr., and J. S. Bader, "Ground Water and Related Geology of Joshua Tree National Monument, California" (1963), U. S. Geological Survey, Ground Water Branch, Long Beach, California, JTNP Library, 35–39.

31. Edward A. Hummel to the Regional Director (October 10, 1967), JTNP Archives, Acc. 651, Cat. 19430, L1425, Folder 033; C. F. Borden to Edward A. Hummel (September 3, 1968), ibid.; and Homer L. Rouse to the Regional Director (June 17, 1976), JTNP Archives, Acc. 651, Cat. 19430, L54, Folder 244.

32. John H. Davis to Field Solicitor, San Francisco Office with attached 1968 field report (July 14, 1976), JTNP Archives, Acc. 651, Cat. 19430, L54, Folder 259.

33. Conrad L. Wirth, *Parks, Politics, and the People* (Norman: University of Oklahoma Press, 1980), 234. For a full treatment of *Mission 66*, see Ethan Carr, *Mission 66: Modernism and the National Park Dilemma* (Amherst: University of Massachusetts Press, 2007), 54–66.

34. Bernard DeVoto, "Let's Close the National Parks," in Lary M. Dilsaver, *America's National Park System: The Critical Documents*, Revised Edition (Lanham, MD: Rowman and Littlefield, 2016), 163–69.

35. Wirth, *Parks, Politics, and the People*, 237–3.8

36. NPS, "Master Plan Development Outline, Joshua Tree National Monument, California—Buildings" (May 1957), JTNP Archives, Cat. 651, Acc. 19430, D3415, Box 16, Folder 055.

37. John B. Wosky to the Regional Director (June 28, 1960), SB, RG79, Central Files 1954–61, Box 2, Folder "A5427 Folder 5 H to L"; George F. Whitworth to the Regional Chief of Operations (May 20, 1959), SB, RG79, Central Files 1953–62, Box 2, Folder "A5427 #8 Various Areas"; and Harold G. Fowler to Regional Chief of Operations (June 6, 1960), SB, RG79, Central Files 1954–61, Box 2, Folder "A5427 Folder 5 H to L."

38. Carr, *Mission 66*, 140–41.

39. NPS, "Master Plan for the Preservation and Use of Joshua Tree National Monument, Volume III, General Park Information, Section H. Buildings Inventory" (January 1962), JTNP Archives, Cat. 651, Acc. 19430, A6423, Folder 043; and DOI, "Proposed Master Plan for Joshua Tree National Monument" (December 22, 1971), JTNP Archives, Cat. 651, Acc. 19430, D18, Folder 014E.

40. Peter L. Parry to the Regional Director (November 22, 1972), NPS-WRO, Planning Files, Joshua Tree National Park, Folder "Visitor Center Addition and Restroom Enlargement"; and Jerry A. Moore, "Individual Study Manual for the Twentynine Palms Oasis Environmental Study Area" (February 1972), JTNP Library.

41. George W. Norgard to the Regional Chief of Operations (March 30, 1959), SB, RG79, Central Files 1953–62, Box 2, Folder "A5427 #8 Various Areas"; Regional Chief of Operations to the Regional Director (February 21, 1961), SB, RG79, Central Files 1954–61, Box 2, Folder "A5427 Folder 5 H to L"; Greene, "Historic Resource Study," 422.

42. JTNP, Digital Maintenance Attributes Files—Buildings, Campgrounds, Roads, Trails. Maintenance Division (2013); "Monument Trail Planned," *The Desert Magazine*, Vol. 20, No. 7 (July 1957): 31; and NPS, "Program Dedication of the Riding and Hiking Trail Joshua Tree National Monument, May 31, 1958" (May 31, 1958), JTNP Archives, Cat. 651, Acc. 19430, A8215, Folder 057.

43. William R. Supernaugh to the Regional Director with attached discussion outline (September 30, 1966), JTNP Archives, Cat. 651, Acc. 19430, D18, Folder 014E; Henry Hinz to the Superintendent, JTNM (August 4, 1967), ibid.; William R. Supernaugh to the Regional Director (December 24, 1968), JTNP Archives, Hollinger Box, Loose file; JTNP, Digital Maintenance Files—Buildings (2013); and JTNM, "Listing of Major Questions to be Investigated by the Master Plan Team" (n.d.), JTNP Archives, Cat. 651, Acc. 19430, D18, Folder 014E.

44. DOI, "Draft Proposed Master Plan for Joshua Tree National Monument" (December 22, 1971), JTNP Archives, Cat. 651, Acc. 19430, D18, Folder 014E.

45. Ibid.; John A. Rutter to the Superintendent, JTNM with attached "Management Appraisal Report" (July 19, 1967), JTNP Archives, Cat. 651, Acc. 19430, A5633, Folder 039, 28; "Joshua Tree National Monument Wilderness Hearing, February 16, 1972," Transcript in JTNP Archives, Acc. 00812/004, Cat. 28768, General Management Plan Files, Folder 006; and Superintendent to the Regional Director (April 26, 1974), WRO, Planning Files, Joshua Tree National Park, Folder "Master Plan."

46. Homer L. Rouse to the Regional Director (April 26, 1974), WRO, Planning Files, Joshua Tree National Park File, Folder "Master Plan"; and Nicholas E. Weeks to the Regional Director (July 15, 1976), NPS, WRO, Planning Files, Joshua Tree National Park File, Folder "Black Rock Canyon Campground."

47. William R. Supernaugh to the Director (January 10, 1967), JTNP Archives, Cat. 651, Acc. 19430, L24, Folder 079; "Pettis Cemetery Bill Calls for County Site," *The Desert Trail* (February 22, 1967); "S. B. Economic Office Aids Legion Cemetery Site Plan," unidentified newspaper clipping in JTNP Archives, Cat. 651, Acc. 19430, L24, Folder 079; James K. Baker, "Joshua Tree National Monument—Its Significance to All of Us" (February n.d,. 1967), *The Desert Trail* clipping, JTNP Archives, Cat. 651, Acc. 19430, L24, Folder 079; George W. Nilsson to Wayne N. Aspinall (April 4, 1967), NARA RG79, Entry 11, Box 536, Folder A38; and Harthon L. Bill to Wayne N. Aspinall (May 1, 1967), NARA, RG79, Entry 11, Box 536, Folder A38.

48. Alfred Runte, *National Parks: The American Experience*, 3rd Edition (Lincoln: University of Nebraska Press, 1997), 240–42; David Louter, *Driven Wild: Cars, Roads, and Nature in Washington's National Parks* (Seattle: University of Washington Press, 2006), 121–25; Rosalie Edge, "Roads and More Roads in the National Parks and National Forests" (1936), in Lary M. Dilsaver, *America's National Park System*, 119–23; and Merle Stitt to Superintendents to Death Valley, Haleakala, et al. (September 20, 1970), JTNP Archives, Acc. 651, Cat. 19430, L48, Folder 241.

49. William R. Supernaugh to the Regional Director (October 2, 1970), JTNP Archives, Acc. 651, Cat. 19430, L48, Folder 241; Vince Hefti to the Deputy Director, Legislation (August 10, 1971), ibid.; and NPS, "Wilderness Study" (August 1971), JTNP Library.

50. JTNM, "Joshua Tree National Monument Wilderness Hearing" (February 16, 1972), Transcript in JTNP Archives, Acc. 812, Cat. 28768, Box 4, Folder 006. (Note: The identity of Edward Beverage is unknown.)

51. Ibid.

52. Ibid. (Note: The identity of Wendell Ford and L. B. Graff are unknown.)

53. Anon., "Notes on Wilderness Hearing 2-16-72" (February 16, 1972), JTNP Archives, Acc. 651, Cat. 19430, L48, Folder 240; NPS, "Wilderness Recommendation Joshua Tree National Monument California" (June 1972), JTNP Library; and NPS, "Wilderness Recommendation Joshua Tree National Monument California" (August 1972), JTNP Library.

54. Homer Rouse to JOTR Staff (December 6, 1973), JTNP Archives, Acc. 651, Cat. 19430, L48, Folder 242; Ronald H. Walker, "Statement before the Subcommittee on National Parks and Recreation, House Committee on Interior and Insular Affairs, on H. R. 13562..." (March 25, 1974), JTNP Archives, Acc. 651, Cat. 19430, L48, Folder 238; JTNM, "Statement of Important Issues Concerning Wilderness Recommendations for Joshua Tree National Monument" (October 7, 1975), WRO, Planning Files, Joshua Tree National Park File, Folder "Wilderness—Joshua Tree"; U. S. House of Representatives, H. R. 7190 "A bill to designate certain lands in Joshua Tree National Monument, Calif., as wilderness" (May 21, 1975); Howard H. Chapman to Superintendents, Chiricahua, Haleakala, Joshua Tree...with

attached statement (November 19, 1975), JTNP Archives, Acc. 651, Cat. 19430, L48, Folder 238; (Miss) Raye-Page, "Statement for the Wilderness Society on H. R. 7190" (November 10, 1975), JTNP Archives, Acc. 651, Cat. 19430, L48, Folder 238; and Lyle K. Gaston, "Joshua Tree National Monument Wilderness Proposal HR 7190" (November 10, 1975), JTNP Archives, Acc. 651, Cat. 19430, L48, Folder 238.

55. Homer L. Rouse to Jim Howe (March 9, 1976), WRO, Planning Files, Joshua Tree National Park File, Folder "Wilderness—Joshua Tree"; Keith G. Sebelius to Gary E. Everhardt (March 18, 1976), ibid.; U. S. House of Representatives, H. R. 7190 "A bill to designate certain lands within units of the national park system as wilderness; to revise the boundaries of certain of those units, and for other purposes" (April 9, 1976); Homer L. Rouse to the Regional Director (June 30, 1976), WRO, Planning Files, Joshua Tree National Park File, Folder "Wilderness—Joshua Tree"; and Public Law 94-567.

56. Quoted in Lowell Sumner, "Biological Research and Management in the National Park Service: A History," *The George Wright Forum*, Vol. 3, No. 4 (Autumn 1983): 18.

57. Both the Leopold Report and the Robbins Report are partially reprinted in Lary M. Dilsaver, *America's National Park System*, 237–62.

58. Hesmel L. Earenfight to the Regional Director (August 21, 1958), JTNP Archives, Acc. 651, Cat. 19430, N1621, Folder 029A; Jane Ashdown, "Joshua Tree Guzzlers Report and Inventory" (November 2002), JTNP Library, 6; Robert D. Powell, "Bighorn Sheep and Waterhole Report Joshua Tree National Monument" (1961), JTNP Archives, Acc. 796, Cat. 26863, Folder 028; and Ralph E. Welles and Florence B. Welles, "Second Interim Report Bighorn Research Joshua Tree National Monument" (March 15, 1964), JTNP Library, 6.

59. James K. Baker, "Recollections and Reminiscences: The JOTR 'Standoff'" (n.d.), JTNP Library, Unsorted documents box; William R. Supernaugh to the Regional Director (June 11, 1965), JTNP Archives, Acc. 651, Cat. 19430, N14, Folder 006; and James E. Cole to the Superintendent, JTNM (June 11, 1965), JTNP Archives, Acc. 651, Cat. 19430, N14, Folder 006.

60. Baker, "Recollections and Reminiscences"; "Stubbe Spring Notes" (1969), JTNP Archives, Acc. 651, Cat. 19430, N3043, Folder 094B; and William R. Supernaugh to the Regional Director (May 1, 1967), JTNP Archives, Acc. 651, Cat. 19430, N1621, Folder 029A.

61. Baker, "Recollections and Reminiscences"; Draft letter to Dr. Martin Prochnik, (nd [1971]), JTNP Archives, Acc. 651, Cat. 19430, D5039, Folder 071; and Charles G. Hansen to the Superintendent, JTNM (March 9, 1971), JTNP Archives, Acc. 651, Cat. 19430, N1427, Folder 014A.

62. JTNM, "Environmental Assessment Natural Resources Management Plan Joshua Tree National Monument" (October 1974), JTNP Library, 42–45 and 105–106; Charles L Douglas, "Coordination of Bighorn Research and Management in Joshua Tree National Monument" (June 1975), JTNP Archives, Acc. 852, Cat. 30023, Box 1, Folder 004, 2–3; Charles L. Douglas to Homer Rouse (September 5, 1975), JTNP Archives, Acc. 852, Cat. 30023, Box 1, Folder 004; and Charles L. Douglas "Bighorn Management" (July 12, 1976), JTNP Archives, Acc. 852, Cat. 30023, Folder 008.

63. Armand B. Sansum to Maintenance Supervisor, JTNM (July 30, 1971), JTNP Archives, Acc. 651, Cat. 19430, N1427, Folder 10; and Peter L. Parry to Clifford Matthews (June 16, 1971), JTNP Archives, Acc. 651, Cat. 19430, N14, Folder 007B.

64. JTNM, "Environmental Assessment Natural Resources Management Plan"; Lynn Loetterle to Resource Management Specialist, JTNM (September 11, 1975), JTNP Archives, Uncatalogued resource management files, Folder "N16-21 Endangered Species"; Patrick James Leary, "Investigation of the Vegetational Communities of Joshua Tree National Monument, California," Master's thesis (Las Vegas: University of Nevada, June 1977).

65. William Dengler to District Ranger Wilburn (September 19, 1966), JTNP Archives, Acc. 651, Cat. 19430, N2215, Folder 037.

66. Plant Ecologist, WRO to the Regional Director (January 24, 1983), WRO, Planning Files, Joshua Tree National Park File, Folder "Oasis of Mara Plant Reduction."

67. JTNM, "Oasis of Mara Action Plan for the Management of Natural Resources" (January 1984), ibid., 1–15; JTNM, "Management Plan for Oasis of Mara" (March 1, 1972), JTNP Archives, Acc. 651, Cat. 19430, N2215, Folder 037; and Jim Agee to Dr. Chuck Douglas (March 25, 1974), JTNP Archives, Acc. 651, Cat. 19430, N2215, Folder 037A.

68. John M. Mahoney, "Park Acreage Statistical Summary" (August 1, 1963), JTNP Archives, Acc. 651, Cat. 19430, Y26, Folder 052; JTNM, "Environmental Assessment Natural Resources Management Plan" (1974), JTNP Library, 77–80; JTNM, "Outline of Planning Requirements" (1977), JTNP Archives, Acc. 651, Cat. 19430, D18, Folder 013; and E. T. Scoyen to the Regional Directors, Regions One, Two, Three, Four and Five (August 15, 1956), NARA, RG79, Central Files 1953–62, Acc. 79-92-001, Box 1, Folder "L2435 Vol. 1 Region 4, 5-1-53 to 6-30-57."

69. See the text of both laws in Dilsaver, *America's National Park System*, 268–73 and 336–38; and Public Law 89-665.

70. Executive Order 11593 (May 13, 1971), 3 C.F.R. 154.

71. Ronald F. Lee to the Regional Director (April 25, 1957), WASO, Park History Office Files, Folder "Joshua Tree National Park"; and William J. Wallace to Dr. John Hussey (November 15, 1957), ibid.

72. Francis J. and Patricia H. Johnston to Elmer N. Fladmark (September 1, 1957), JTNP Archives, Acc. 651, Cat. 19430, H3015, Folder 089; Homer L. Earenfight to Francis J. and Patricia H. Johnston (September 5, 1957), ibid.; Russell K. Grater to Superintendent, JTNM (September 23, 1957), ibid.; William J. Wallace, "An Archaeological Reconnaissance in Joshua Tree National Monument," *Journal of the West*, Vol. 3, No. 1 (January 1964): 90–101; and Thomas F. King, "Fifty Years of Archaeology in the California Desert: An Archaeological Overview of Joshua Tree National Monument" (December 1975), NPS, Western Archaeological Center, 47–56.

73. Leslie E. Wildesen, "Archaeological Research Management Plan Joshua Tree National Monument" (August 1969), WRO. JTNP Archives, Acc. 651, Cat. 19430, H3015, Folder 084.

74. King, "Fifty Years of Archaeology," 47–77; and Homer L. Rouse to Keith Anderson (October 9, 1975), JTNP Archives, Acc. 651, Cat. 19430, H3015, Folder 087.

75. Rouse to Anderson (October 9, 1975); Donald J. Colville to the Regional Director (September 13, 1974), WRO, Mulhern Files, Box 26, Folder "JOTR Collections Management Plan"; and Betsy Hunter to Chief, Division of Museum Services (February 10, 1975), JTNP Archives, Acc. 651, Cat. 19430, H3015, Folder 013.

76. Benjamin Levy to the Chief Historian (February 5, 1969), WASO, Park History Files, Folder "Joshua Tree"; and F. Ross Holland to the Superintendent, JTNM (February 4, 1972), JTNP Archives, Acc. 651, Cat. 19430, H32, Folder 078. The individual National Register forms are found in several locations: Keys Ranch, Desert Queen Mine, and Wall Street Mill are in JTNP Archives, Acc. 651, Cat. 19430, H32, Folder 078; Lost Horse Mine, Oasis of Mara, and Cottonwood Oasis are in an uncatalogued Hollinger box in the JTNP Archives, Folder "National Register"; Barker Dam and Cow Camp are in WRO Cultural Resources Files in folders of the same names; and Ryan House is in JTNP Archives, Acc. 651, Cat. 19430, H3417, Folder 099.

77. Alsen E. Inman to Chief Ranger, JTNM (November 18, 1964), JTNP Archives, Acc. 651, Cat. 19430, H3015, Folder 071A; and James E. Lynch to the Chief Ranger, JTNM (June 13, 1967), ibid.

78. Robert V. Simmonds, "Historic Structures Report Lost Horse Mine Complex" (September 1970), JTNP Archives, Acc. 651, Cat. 19430, H30, Folder 069B.

79. Kerwin L. Klein, "The William Keys Ranch"; Benjamin Levy to the Chief Historian (February 5, 1969), WASO, Park History Files, Folder "Joshua Tree"; Director NPS to Mr. B. P. Mayer (September 24, 1971), JTNP Archives, Acc. 651, Cat. 19430, H3015, Folder 042A; and William Supernaugh to Mrs. Robert Garry (July 11, 1969), JTNP Archives, Acc. 651, Cat. 19430, H3015, Folder 007.

80. Glennie Murray to Staff Specialist, State and Private Liaison (July 29, 1971), WRO, Mulhern Files, Box 24, Folder "Joshua Tree NM Correspondence 1964–1974."

81. Gordon Chappell et al., "Keys' Desert Queen Ranch Joshua Tree National Monument Preservation Study," JTNP Archives, Acc. 651, Cat. 19430, H3015, Folder 035.

82. Patricia P. Hickman, "Country Nodes: An Anthropological Evaluation of William Keys' Desert Queen Ranch, Joshua Tree National Monument, California" (1976), JTNP Library.

83. Gordon S. Chappell to Acting Chief, Division of Cultural Resources Management, Western Region (November 19, 1976), WRO, Cultural Resources Files, JTNP, Folder "JOTR Hickman Studies."

84. Keith M. Anderson to Chief, Western Archaeological Center (February 25, 1977), ibid.; Arthur C. Allen to the Regional Director (May 19, 1976), WRO, Cultural Resources Files, JTNP, Folder "Keys Ranch Artifacts"; and Regional Historian, WRO to the Regional Director (August 5, 1976), WRO, Cultural Resources Files, JTNP, Folder "Keys Ranch Artifacts."

85. Patricia Hickman and Thomas King to Homer Rouse (July 10, 1975), JTNP Archives, Acc. 651, Cat. 19430, H3015, Folder 013.

86. "Annual Visits Joshua Tree National Monument," https://irma.nps.gov/Stats/Reports/ReportList; and "Joshua Tree National Park Association," http://www.joshua tree.org.

87. NPS, "Master Plan Development Outline Joshua Tree National Monument, California–Interpretation" (April 1957), JTNP Archives, Acc. 651, Cat. 19430, A6423, Folder 047; and JTNM, "Annual Interpretive Services Reports" (1964–1970), JTNP Archives, Acc. 651, Cat. 19430, K2621, Folder 013.

88. JTNM, "Interpretive Prospectus" (April 1972), WRO, Tom Mulhern Files, Box 24, Folder "Joshua Tree NM Correspondence 1964–1974."

89. "The Desert, How Long Will It Survive?" *The Los Angeles Herald-Examiner* (April 25, 1971); Seasonal Park Technicians (Interpretation) to Resource Management Specialist (April 22, 1976), JTNP Archives, Acc. 651, Cat. 19430, N22, Folder 032A; and Public Law 91-357.

90. "Parsons' Stolen Casket," *The San Francisco Chronicle* (July 2, 1991).

91. Ibid.; and Homer Rouse to the Regional Director, Incident Report (November 9, 1973), JTNP Archives, Miscellaneous Uncatalogued Files, Folder "Gram Parsons."

92. NPS, WRO, "Management Consultation Report Joshua Tree National Monument California" (January 1976), JTNP Archives, Acc. 651, Cat. 19430, A2623, Box 6, Folder 028A.

Chapter Seven

1. JTNM, "Statement for Management" (April 1978), JTNP Library; and Rick Anderson to the Regional Director (November 27, 1979), JTNP Archives, Acc. 651, Cat. 19430, L2621, Folder 081.

2. NPS, "Listing of Acreages" (1977), WRO, Lands Files, JTNP File, Folder "Gross Acreage of Joshua Tree Monument by County."

3. NPS, "Digital Lands Files" (2009), available from WRO.

4. Rick Anderson to the Regional Director with attached excerpt from "Overview Report" by William E. Weidenhamer (March 17, 1978), JTNP Archives, Acc. 651, Cat. 19430, L1425, Folder 063.

5. Ibid.

6. Sondra Humphries to Doris C. Rennick with attached 1960 "Declaration of Restrictions" (March 5, 2003), JTNM Land Files, Folder "Willing Sellers"; Joe Brown to the Regional Director (June 2, 1975), JTNP Archives, Acc. 651, Cat. 19430, L1425, Folder 075; Rick T. Anderson to Chiefs of Interpretation, Maintenance, Protection, et al. (February 14, 1978), JTNP Archives, Acc. 651, Cat. 19430, L1425, Folder 075; and Rick T. Anderson to Loran E. Perry (March 17, 1980), JTNP Archives, Acc. 651, Cat. 19430, L1425, Folder 045.

7. Rick T. Anderson to the Regional Director (August 10, 1978), JTNP Archives, Acc. 651, Cat. 19430, L1425, Folder 075; Rick T. Anderson to the Files (October 6, 1978), ibid.; Rick T. Anderson to the Regional Director (June 14, 1979), ibid.; and Rick T. Anderson to Assemblyman Bill Leonard (December 24, 1986), JTNP Archives, Acc. 651, Cat. 19430, L1425, Folder 054.

8. NPS, "Digital Lands Files"; and Edward R. Haberlin to Dixie Haldeman (December 31, 1986), JTNP Archives, Acc. 651, Cat. 19430, L1425, Folder 054.

9. John McMunn to the Regional Director (August 27, 1976), JTNP Archives, Acc. 651, Cat. 19430, L1425, Folder 033; and Rick Anderson to the Regional Director (November 15, 1976), NPS, WRO, Lands Files, Joshua Tree National Park File, Folder "Metropolitan Water District and Kaiser Steel."

10. Rick Anderson to the Files (January 14, 1977), JTNP Archives, Acc. 651, Cat. 19430, L1425, Folder 033; Charles T. Weiler, "Appraisal of Mineral Interests Inherent in the Kaiser Steel Corporation Properties in the Placer-Mystery Canyons Area Within the Joshua Tree National Monument Riverside, California" (January 1975), JTNP Archives, Acc. 856, Box "Lands and Mining," Folder "Kaiser Appraisal Report"; John Englund to the Regional Director (June 29, 1978), JTNP Archives, Acc. 651, Cat. 19430, L1425, Folder 063; NPS, "Director's Order 35A: Sale or Lease of Park Services, Resources, or Water in Support of Activities Outside the Boundaries of National Park Areas" (2004), http://

www.nps.gov/policy/DOrders/DOrder35A.html; and John McMunn to the Regional Director (October 6, 1978), JTNP Archives, Acc. 651, Cat. 19430, L1425, Folder 033.

11. "Kaiser to Furlough 1,200," *The Los Angeles Times* (June 27, 1975); "Arab is Buying Major Interest in Kaiser Steel for $57 Million," ibid., (March 24, 1981); "Kaiser to Close Fontana Steel Facility, Mine," ibid., (November 4, 1981).

12. NPS, WRO, "Management Consultation Report Joshua Tree National Monument California" (January 1976), JTNP Archives, Acc. 651, Cat. 19430, A2623, Box 6, Folder 028A. 24–25.

13. Public Law 97-424.

14. NPS and U. S. Federal Highway Administration. September 1984, "Transportation Study Road System Evaluation Joshua Tree National Monument," JTNP Library; Rick T. Anderson to A. E. Newcomb (March 22, 1982), JTNP Archives, Acc. 651, Cat. 19430, D30, Folder 030; and Rick T. Anderson to A. E. Newcomb (September 16, 1982), ibid.

15. Anne M. LaRosa to WRO Kilgore/Huddleston (August 11, 1989), Copy of a fax in WRO, Planning Files, Joshua Tree National Park File, Folder "General Management Planning Correspondence"; JTNM, "Environmental Assessment Reconstruction of Park Routes 12 and 13 and Associated Visitor Use Areas" (March 1990), JTNP Archives, Acc. 651, Cat. 19430, D30, Folder 043.

16. Donald V. Lee et al. to Whom It May Concern (July 23, 1991), JTNP Archives, Acc. 651, Cat. 19430, D30, Folder 046; and Greg Epperson to Stanley T. Albright (April 5, 1991), JTNP Archives, Acc. 651, Cat. 19430, D30, Folder 044.

17. JTNM, "Environmental Assessment Reconstruction of Park Routes 12 and 13 and Associated Visitor Use Areas" (August 1991), JTNP Library; "Seven mile loop road eyed for monument," *The Hi-Desert Star* (November 6, 1991); and JTNM, "Reconstruction of Park Routes 12, 13, and 112 Summary of Public Comments Received of [sic] the Environmental Assessment," JTNP Archives, Acc. 812, Cat. 28768, GMP/Backcountry/Wilderness Box 3, Folder 022.

18. Traffic Engineers, Inc., "Report of Traffic and Parking Data Joshua Tree National Monument" (June 1992), JTNP Archives, Acc. 651, Cat. 29958, D22, Folder 012.

19. WRO, "Management Consultation Report," 24–26; T. Scott Bryan to Superintendent, JTNM (May 24, 1982), JTNP Archives, Acc. 651, Cat. 19430, H1415, Folder 003; and Rick Anderson to T. Scott Bryan (June 3, 1982), JTNP Archives, Acc. 651, Cat. 19430, H1415, Folder 003; JTNP 2013, Digital Maintenance Attributes Files—Trails.

20. JTNP, Digital Maintenance Attributes Files—Buildings.

21. NPS Office of Science and Technology, "State of the Parks May 1980 A Report to Congress; WRO 1976, "Management Consultation Report" (1980), 16.

22. WRO, "Management Consultation Report," Appendix B.

23. Robert Moon, telephone interview with the author (March 25, 2013).

24. Ibid.; Jerry Freilich, telephone interview with the author (April 15, 2013).

25. Robert Moon (March 25, 2013).

26. Chief, Natural Resource Information Division to Superintendents, Natural Resource Park Units (July 30, 1996), JTNP Archives, Acc. 651, Cat. 28859, N16, Folder 007; David E. Moore to the Regional Director (October 28, 1993), JTNP Archives, Acc. 651, Cat. 28859, N16, Folder 005; David E. Moore to the Regional Director (October 1, 1993), JTNP Archives, Acc. 651, Cat. 28859, N16, Folder 003; and JTNM, "Resources Management Plan 1993 Revision" (1993), JTNP Library.

27. Karen S. Frazier, "An Ecological Study of the Fan Palm Oases of Joshua Tree National Monument," Master's Thesis (Las Vegas, University of Nevada, May 1977), JTNP Library; Howard H. Chapman to Superintendent, JTNM with attached environmental summary of proposed plant reduction at Oasis of Mara (April 25, 1977), JTNP Archives, Acc. 651, Cat. 19430, L7617, Folder 282; JTNM, "Oasis of Mara Action Plan for the Management of Natural Resources" (January 1984), JTNP Library, 1–57; and Bruce M. Kilgore to the Regional Director (March 6, 1979), WRO, Tom Mulhern Files, Box 24, Folder "Joshua Tree NM Correspondence 1976."

28. JTNP, "Headquarters Landscape and Oasis of Mara Action Plan" (1996), JTNP Library, 1–12.

29. Ibid., 1–12, Appendix II.

30. Robert Moon, "Evolution of the Center for Arid Lands Restoration" (n.d.), Huntington Library, San Marino, California. Frank Wheat Papers, Box 12, Folder 7.

31. Ibid; Mark Holden and Carol Miller, "New Arid Land Revegetation Techniques at Joshua Tree National Monument" (April 1995), in U. S. Forest Service, "Proceedings: Wildland Shrub and Arid Land Restoration Symposium," General

Technical Report INT-GTR-315; Ernest Quintana to Jennifer Haley (November 25, 1996), JTNP Archives, Acc. 651, Cat. 28859, N16, Folder 007.

32. Alice Turner to the Resource Management Division, JTNM (June 18, 1986), JTNP Archives, Uncatalogued Resource Management Files, Folder "N16-21 Endangered species"; JTNP, "NRCM Tamarisk Eradication in Joshua Tree National Park Phase II Implementation Plan" (n.d.), JTNP Resource Management Digital Files; and George L. San Miguel to Bob Moon (December 19, 1985), JTNP Archives, Acc. 796, Cat. 26909, N 1617, Folder 069.

33. JTNP, "Nonnative Species," http://www.nps.gov/jotr/naturescience/nonnativespecies.htm; JTNP, "JoshuaTree N. P. Exotic Plant Management Plan" (n.d.), Draft in the Resource Management Digital Files; and University of Georgia Center for Invasive Species and Ecosystem Health, "Invasive Plant Atlas of the United States," http://www.invasiveplantatlas.org/index.html.

34. Don Cornell, "Preliminary National Assessment of Class I Related Values: Visibility Report Joshua Tree National Monument" (August 28, 1978), JTNP Archives, Acc. 651, Cat. 19430, N3615, Folder 96D; Howard H. Chapman to James Mayfield (August 24, 1979), JTNP Archives, a loose report in unprocessed files Hollinger box; and Robert Moon, "Integral Vista Identification" (August 25, 1980), JTNP Archives, Acc. 651, Cat. 19430, N3615, Folder 96B.

35. James P. Bennett to Dr. Carl A. Fox (October 12, 1983), JTNP Archives, Acc. 651, Cat. 19430, N3615, Folder 96; Kenneth W. Stolte to the Regional Director (May 17, 1984), ibid.; and Patrick J. Temple, "Assessment of Impacts of Oxidant Air Pollution on Vegetation of Joshua Tree National Monument" (December 1985), JTNP Archives, Acc. 796, Cat. 26890, Folder 050.

36. JTNM, "Management Plan for Natural and Cultural Resources Joshua Tree National Monument October 1993 Revision" (October 1993), JTNP Library, 169–73; David E. Moore to John Christiano (August 7, 1991), JTNP Archives, Acc. 651, Cat. 19430, N3615, Folder 96; and JTNP, "Project Statement: Study of Air Quality Effects on *Rhus trilobata*" (1998), JTNP Archives, Acc. 651, Cat. 19430, N2217, Folder 019.

37. Howard Gross, "Air pollution in Joshua Tree National Park," *The Sun Runner* (Spring 2004): 30–31; and JTNM, "Joshua Fire (JOTR 78-01)" (1978), JTNP Archives, Acc. 651, Cat. 19430, Y1419, Folder 10.

38. Thomas M. Gavin to the Regional Director (January 24, 1983), JTNP Archives, a loose report in uncatalogued files.

39. "Monument fires pose problems," *The Desert Trail* (August 7, 1982).

40. JTNM, "Fire History" (n.d.), JTNP Archives, Acc. 651, Cat. 19430, Y14, Folder 001; Sue Husari to Bob Moon (February 23, 1982), JTNP Archives, Acc. 651, Cat. 19430, Y14, Folder 003; and Rick Anderson to the Regional Director (December 16, 1982), JTNP Archives, Acc. 651, Cat. 19430, Y14, Folder 003.

41. Bob Moon to the Superintendent, JTNM (March 8, 1983), JTNP Archives, Acc. 856, uncatalogued files, Folder "Fire"; Tom Nichols to the Regional Director (March 28, 1985), JTNP Archives, Acc. 651, Cat. 19430, Y1419, Folder 047; Pete Fielding to the Regional Director (July 31, 1986), JTNP Archives, Acc. 651, Cat. 19430, Y14, Folder 045; JTNM, "Fire Management Plan 1992 Revision" (1992), JTNP Library; and NPS, "Finding of No Significant Impact for Environmental Assessment Fire Management Plan Joshua Tree National Monument" (October 26, 1992), WRO. Planning Files, Joshua Tree National Park File, Folder "Fire Management."

42. Tom Patterson to Chief, Branch of Fire Management, WRO (March 17, 1995), JTNP Archives, Acc. 651, Cat. 19430, Y1419, Folder 017; Name unreadable, approved by Ernest Quintana and Pat Cooney, "Fire Narrative: Covington Agency: National Park Service" (August 5, 1995), JTNP Archives, Acc. 651, Cat. 19430, Y1419, Folder 015; and Pat Cooney, "Daily Incident Cost Summary" (August 4, 1995), JTNP Archives, Acc. 651, Cat. 19430, Y1419, Folder 014.

43. Jane Ashdown, "Joshua Tree Guzzlers Report and Inventory" (November 2002), JTNP Library, 1–10.

44. Ashdown, "Joshua Tree Guzzlers," 2–3; Charles L. Douglas and Leslie D. White, "Movements of Desert Bighorn Sheep in the Stubbe Spring Area, Joshua Tree National Monument" (November 1979), JTNP Archives, Acc. 852, Cat. 30023, Box 1, Folder 004; and Elena Robisch to Jerry Freilich et al. (June 29, 1992) JTNP Archives, Acc. 852, Cat. 30023, Box 1, Folder 011.

45. Public Law 103-433; and Ashdown, "Joshua Tree Guzzlers," 2–3.

46. U. S. Fish and Wildlife Service, "Desert Tortoise Recovery Plan" (June 1994), JTNP Library, 2–13; and William I. Boarman, "Desert Tortoise—*Gopherus agassizii*," available at http://www.blm.gov/ca/pdfs/cdd_pdfs/data.pdf.

47. JTNM, "Management Plan for Natural and Cultural Resources," (1993), 165–68; Jerry Freilich, telephone interview with the author (April 15, 2013); and Jerry Freilich to All Tortoise NRPP interested parties (May 11, 1995), JTNP Archives, unprocessed files in Hollinger box, Folder "Jerry Freilich, 1995 Professional Papers."

48. DOI, "Determination of Critical Habitat for the Mojave Population of the Desert Tortoise; Final Rule," *Federal Register*, Vol. 59, No. 26 (February 8, 1994), 5820–46; and JTNP, "Desert Tortoise" (n.d.), Briefing statement in JTNP Archives, Acc. 804, Cat. 28768, Box 4, Folder 003.

49. Ecologist, JTNP to T & E Coordinator (June 29, 1994), JTNP Archives, a loose report in uncatalogued resource management files; and JTNP "Joshua Tree National Park Natural and Cultural Resources Management Plan" (1999), JTNP Library, 301–05.

50. Don Cornell, "Research in Coyote Abatement Joshua Tree National Monument" (n.d.), JTNP, unprocessed resource management files, Folder "Coyote Management"; Kathy Billings to All Employees (April 13, 1994), ibid.; Ernest Quintana to Chief Ranger (September 29, 1997), JTNP Archives, Acc. 651, Cat. 28859, Folder 009; and Bob Moon to the Superintendent/Files (July 26, 1982), JTNP, Uncatalogued resource management files, Folder "Pest & Weed Control 1978–1985."

51. Laura Thompson to Bob Moon (October 25, 1984), JTNP. Uncatalogued resource management files, Folder "Burro Management"; and JTNM, "Burro Management Action Plan" (August 1994), ibid.

52. U. S. Government, *United States National Atlas* (2013), http://nationalatlas.gov/mld/afrbeep.html; Jerry Freilich to the Files (August 6, 1993), JTNP Archives, Acc. 651, Cat. 19430, N2219, Folder 064; and Bruce Grubbs, *Explore! Joshua Tree National Park: A Guide to Exploring the Great Outdoors* (Guilford, CN: Globe Pequot Publishers, 2006), 14.

53. JTNM, "Natural Resource Project Statement: RM-17, Non-Native Aquatic Wildlife Control" (1989), JTNP Archives, Uncatalogued resource management files, Folder "Barker Dam Management Files"; JTNM, "Monument to Give Away Goldfish" (November 30, 1989), ibid.

54. NPS, "Partnerships," http://www.nps.gov/partnerships/ca_dmg.htm; Desert Managers Group, "About Us," http://www.dmg.gov/about.php, and "Projects," http://www.dmg.gov/projects.php.

55. George Wright Society, "The UNESCO Man and the Biosphere Program: What's It All About?," http://www.georgewright.org/mab.html; Biosphere Reserve Ad Hoc Nomination Panel to United States Man and the Biosphere Directorate (November 28, 1983), JTNP Library. Today the wildlife area is part of the Santa Rosa and San Jacinto Mountains National Monument and the biosphere reserve also includes Boyd Deep Canyon Desert Research Center of the University of California, Riverside.

56. Sidney McClellan to Regional Solicitor, Sacramento (May 21, 1957), JTNP Archives, Acc. 651, Cat. 19430, L34, Folder 231; George D. Dysart to Leonard A. Webber (July 2, 1957), ibid.; Russell J. Hendrickson to the Regional Director, Southwest Region (March 16, 1971), JTNP Archives, Acc. 651, Cat. 19430, D6215, Folder 083; and Regional Director to Superintendents, Western Region et al. (January 26, 1973), JTNP Archives, Acc. 651, Cat. 19430, D6215, Folder 077.

57. Public Law 96-95; and Public Law 101-601.

58. Advisory Council on Historic Preservation, "Advisory Council on Historic Preservation Sets Policy for Native American, Native Hawaiian Consultation" (June 21, 1993), JTNP Archives, Acc. 812, Cat. 28768, GMP/Wilderness Box 2, Folder 030; and Rosie Pepito to Thomas Mulhern (August 24, 1988), WRO, Thomas Mulhern Files, Box 24, Folder "Joshua Tree NM, CA General File 1988";

59. Rick T. Anderson to the Regional Director with attached Draft Cultural Resources Management Plan (October 19, 1977), JTNP Archives, Acc. 651, Cat. 19430, H2215, Folder 093; John H. Davis to Superintendent JTNM (March 21, 1979), ibid.; and Rick Anderson to the Regional Director (March 20, 1979), JTNP Archives, Acc. 651, Cat. 19430, D18, Folder 013.

60. Carol A. Martin to the Superintendent, JTNM (September 15, 1987), JTNP Archives, Uncatalogued files in Hollinger Box, Folder "H92 Road Survey—Archaeolgical"; George A. Teague to Anthropologist, DSC (January 30, 1990), JTNP Archives, Acc. 651, Cat. 19430, H2215, Folder 053; and D. Paul Henry Memorandum (October 22, 1990), JTNP Archives, Acc. 651, Cat. 19430, H2215, Folder 085.

61. Thomas Mulhern to the Associate Regional Director, Resource Management (August 24, 1987), WRO, Thomas Mulhern Files, Box 26, Folder "JOTR-CR-RBI (RMP-UNLV)"; Rick Anderson to Honorable Jerry Lewis (February 22, 1989), JTNP Archives, Acc. 651, Cat. 19430, H1817, Folder 034; "City Moves to Keep Collection," *Desert Trail* (March 16, 1989); JTNM, "Congressional Add-on FY90 Appropriation" (January 14, 1991), Briefing Statement in JTNP Archives, Acc, 651, Cat. 28859, A8815, Folder 035.

62. Regional Director to the Superintendent, JTNM (July 29, 1981), WRO, Thomas Mulhern Files, Box 24, Folder "Joshua Tree NM 1984–1985"; Linda W. Greene, "Historic Resource Study: A History of Land Use in Joshua Tree National Monument" (1983), DSC, JTNP Library; Tom Mulhern to the Superintendent, JTNM (April 27, 1993), JTNP Archives, Uncatalogued Hollinger Box, Folder "National Register"; and Harlan D. Unrau to Manager, Westernteam, DSC (March 30, 1992), JTNP Archives, Acc. 856, uncatalogued files, Folder "Road Realignment National Register."

63. John H. Davis to the Superintendent, JTNM (April 13, 1976), JTNP Archives, Acc. 651, Cat. 19430, H3017, Folder 076; Rick T. Anderson to the Regional Director (June 30, 1977), JTNP Archives, Acc. 651, Cat. 28859, D22, Folder 017; and Tom Mulhern to Dan Olson (December 7, 1990), JTNP Archives, Acc. 651, Cat. 28859, D18, Box 3, Folder 001.

64. "Century old landmark—preservation needed?," *The Desert Trail* (February 25, 1982); Thomas D. Mulhern, Jr., to the Regional Director (April 7, 1989), WRO, Thomas Mulhern Files, Box 26, Folder "JOTR—Lost Horse"; Mark Heuston, "Trip Report: A remote video exploration of the Lost Horse Mine" (September 30, 1992), JTNP Archives, Acc. 856, Box "Lands and Mining," Folder "Trip Report Heuston, Mark"; "Lost Horse Mine strikes gold," *The Desert Trail* (September 25, 1996); and JTNP, "Lost Horse Mine," http://www.nps.gov/jotr/historyculture/lhmine/htm.

65. NPS, "Annual Visits Joshua Tree National Monument" (2014), https://irma.nps.gov/Stats/Reports/ReportList; and "Joshua Tree 'loved to death," *Riverside Press-Enterprise* (1991, full date not shown), JTNP Library, Clippings File.

66. Margaret Littlejohn, "Visitor Services Project Joshua Tree National Monument" (September 1991), JTNP Archives, Acc. 651, Cat. 28859, A8815, Folder 035; JTNP, "Joshua Tree National Park Generates Almost $240 Million For Local Economy" (April 8, 1999), JTNP Central Files, L14; and William Truesdell, interviewed by the author, JTNP Visitor Center (January 19, 2013).

67. JTNM, "Draft Backcountry Management Plan Joshua Tree National Monument" (1975), JTNP Archives, Acc. 812, Cat. 28768, Box 4, Folder 007.

68. JTNM, "Draft Backcountry Management Plan Joshua Tree National Monument" (September 1988), JTNP Archives, Acc. 812, Cat. 28768, Box 2, Folder 001.

69. JTNM, Annual reports of the Interpretation Division (January 28, 1981 and February 2, 1982), JTNP Archives, Acc. 651, Cat. 19430, K2621, Folder 014; Rick Anderson to the Regional Director (November 16, 1988), JTNP Archives, Acc. 651, Cat. 28859, K1815, Folder 003; and Curt Mossestad to the Regional Director (August 21, 1991), JTNP Archives, Acc. 856, unprocessed files, Folder "Parks as Classrooms, 1991."

70. David Moore to the Regional Director with attached "Interpretive Prospectus" (June 26, 1992), JTNP Archives, Acc. 651, Cat. 28859, D18, Folder 002.

71. JTNP, "Expedition into the Parks" (July 25, 1995), JTNP Archives, Acc. 651, Cat. 28859, K38, Folder 009; and Wilke E. Nelson and Patti Reilly to Ernest Quintana (June 26, 1996), JTNP Archives, Acc. 651, Cat. 28859, K18, Folder 002.

72. David E. Moore to John T. Ryfa (September 14, 1992), JTNP Archives, Acc. 651, Cat. 28859, A9029, Folder 037; and David E. Moore, "Editorial misses mark," *The Desert Trail* (June 17, 1993).

73. JTNM, "Twentynine Palms Marine Corps Air Ground Combat Center" (February 1990), WRO, JTNP Files, Folder "Briefing Statements Joshua Tree—1990"; and Michael P. Ghiglieri and Thomas M. Myers, *Over the Edge: Death in the Grand Canyon* (Flagstaff, AZ: Puma Press, 2001), 304–08.

74. D. Paul Henry to the Western Regional Office (June 9, 1988), WRO, Planning Files, Joshua Tree National Park File, Folder "General Management Plan Correspondence"; and "Drug arrests in JTNM highest in Park Service," *The Desert Trail* (May 9, 1991).

75. JTNP, "Man Charged in Poaching Incident" (October 8, 1996), Briefing Statement in JTNP Archives, Acc. 651, Cat. 28859, K38, Folder 009; and "Pioneer rancher's grave robbed," *The Hi-Desert Star* (January 30, 1994).

76. See, especially, Frank Wheat, *California Desert Miracle: The Fight for Desert Parks and Wilderness* (San Diego, CA: Sunbelt Publications, 1999).

77. Ibid., 1–23; Congressman Robert B. Mathias introduced H. R. 5289 (93rd Congress, 1st Session) on March 7, 1973, to establish a California Desert Conservation Area. On January 28, 1975, Congressman Jerry L. Pettis introduced H.R. 2271 (94th Congress, 1st Session) calling for the same conservation area with specifications for its management. Both congressmen had introduced earlier bills in 1971.

78. Wheat, *California Desert Miracle*, 21–22.

79. Ibid., xxiv; and Public Law 94-579.

80. BLM, "The California Desert Conservation Area Plan" (1980), BLM State Office, Sacramento, California; and Wheat, *California Desert Miracle*, xiv, 58–81.

81. Wheat, *California Desert Miracle*, 83–116; and 99th Congress, 1st Session, S. 2061, "The California Desert Protection Act of 1986 (February 6, 1986).

82. Wheat, *California Desert Miracle*; and Robert Moon, telephone interview (March 25, 2013).

83. Robert Moon, telephone interview with the author (March 25, 2013); WRO, "Resource Assessment for Features Proposed in the California Desert Protection Act" (January 1987), NPS, 3–4, JTNP Library.

84. WRO, "Resource Assessment," 4–8.

85. Wheat, *California Desert Miracle*, 119–210; "Monument enlargement eyed," *The Hi-Desert Star* (Yucca Valley, California) (November 3, 1991); and WRO, "Resource Assessment," 1–10.

86. Wheat, *California Desert Miracle*, 164–85; BLM, "The Monuments: Final Environmental Impact Statement" (April 1989), JTNP Archives, Acc. 651, Cat. 19430, L76, Folder 268A; and U. S. House of Representatives "Hearing on H. R. 1214, to provide for the transfer of administrative jurisdiction of certain public lands and for other purposes" (March 30, 1984), 98th Congress, 1st Session, 25–27.

87. Quoted in Wheat, *California Desert Miracle*, 184.

88. Moon (March 25, 2013); and David Moore, telephone interview with the author (March 30, 2013).

89. Wheat, *California Desert Miracle*, 288–300.

90. Public Law 103-433, "California Desert Protection Act of 1994" (October 31, 1994).

91. Rick T. Anderson to the Regional Director (May 5, 1977), WRO, Planning Files, Joshua Tree National Park File, Folder "Outline of Planning Requirements."

92. DSC, "Task Directive General Management Plan/Development Concept Plan Environmental Assessment Package No. 156 for Joshua Tree National Monument" (September 15, 1989), JTNP Archives, Acc. 812, Cat. 28768, GMP Files, Box 3, Folder 021; and Rick Anderson, "Close out Meeting with the GMP Team," (December 8, 1989), ibid., Folder 024.

93. All three of the subsequent task directives carried the same title as the first—"Task Directive General Management Plan/Development Concept Plan Environmental Assessment Package No. 156 for Joshua Tree National Monument." The provenances for them are as follows: September 1990, NPS, WRO Planning Files, JTNP, Folder "General Management Plan Correspondence"; October 1991, JTNP Archives, Acc. 651, Cat. 19430, D18, Folder 006; and March 1992, JTNP Archives, Acc. 651, Cat. 28859, D18, Box 4, Folder 002.

94. David Moore to the Regional Director (January 27, 1992), JTNP Archives, Acc. 812, Cat. 28768, GMP Files, Box 3, Folder 023.

95. David Moore to the Regional Director (April 2, 1993), ibid., Folder 021.

96. DSC and WRO, "General Management Plan Development Concept Plans Environmental Impact Statement Joshua Tree National Monument" (July 1994), JTNP Library; DSC and WRO, "Final General Management Plan Development Concept Plans Environmental Impact Statement Joshua Tree National Monument" (May 1995), ibid.; and NPS, "Record of Decision General Management Plan Development Concept Plans Environmental Impact Statement Joshua Tree National Monument" (September 7, 1995), JTNP Archives, Acc. 651, Cat. 28859, D18, Folder 006.

Chapter Eight

1. Frank Buono to Ernest Quintana (January 18, 1996), JTNP, Management Assistant Digital Files.

2. Ernest Quintana to Manager, California Desert District (BLM) (March 20, 1997), JTNP Archives, Acc. 651, Cat. 28859, L1425, Folder 065; Ernest Quintana to Heidi Porter (August 21, 1996), JTNP Archives, Acc. 651, Cat.

28859, L1417, Folder 008; Ernest Quintana to Chief, Land Resources Program Center, WRO (April 9, 2001), JTNP Archives, Acc. 651, Cat. 28859, L1425, Folder 042; and Karin Messaros, "Data-Tract no. 102-44 & 45" (June 4, 2010), Management Assistant Digital Files.

3. "The Wildlands Conservancy" (2013), http://www.wildlandsconservancy.org; Dana Rochat, telephone interview with the author (September 16, 2013); NPS, "Digital Lands Files" (2013), Available from the WRO Land Office; The Wildlands Conservancy, "Conservancy Makes Offer to Leverage Largest Conservation Acquisition in California History" (December 2, 1998), JTNP Archives, Acc. 651, Cat. 28859, L1425, Folder 064.

4. Public Law 90-209; and NPS, "Digital Lands Files."

5. Mojave Desert Land Trust, "Our History," http://www.mojavedesertlandtrust.org/history.php; and NPS, "Digital Lands Files."

6. Karin Messaros, interview with the author at JTNP (April 17, 2013); Revised Statute 2477 (43 CFR 1864.1-2 c (1); Ernest Quintana to Janet Scott (February 10, 2000), JTNP Archives, Land Files, Folder "Whispering Pines"; and BLM, "Revised Statute 2477 (R.S. 2477) California Desert District Background: February 13, 2003" (2003), http//www.blm.gov/ca/dir/pdfs/2003/ib/CAIB2003-023ATT2.pdf.

7. Karin Messaros interview (April 17, 2013).

8. Ernest Quintana to Sondra Humphries (February 5, 1998), JTNP Archives, Acc. 651, Cat. 28859, L1425, Folder 004; and NPS, "Joshua Tree National Park, CA: Boundary Revision To Include Adjacent Real Property," *The Federal Register*, Vol. 68, No. 167 (August 28, 2003): 51779.

9. Mojave Desert Land Trust, "Our History" (2013); Kristeen Penrod et al., "A Linkage Design for the Joshua Tree–Twentynine Palms Connection" (December 2008), available at http://www.scwildlands.org/reports/JT_TP_Connection.pdf; and JTNP, "Recent Acquisition of 'Nolina Peak' by the Mojave Desert Land Trust—Pending Boundary Change" (May 21, 2007), Management Assistant Digital Files.

10. 111th Congress, 1st Session, S. 2921, "California Desert Protection Act of 2010" (December 21, 2009); 112th Congress, 1st Session, S. 138, "California Desert Protection Act of 2011" (January 5, 2011); JTNP, "Justification for the NPS proposing to receive a transfer of administration of lands known as the 'Saddle'" (January 2012), JTNP Management Assistant Files, Folder LDSP-2008; and RPI Consulting and the National Parks Conservation Association, "Economic Effects of Saddle Transition on Joshua Tree National Park and the Morongo Basin" (May 2012), JTNP Management Assistant Files, unfiled report.

11. Robert D. Higgins to the Regional Director (February 3, 1987), JTNP Archives, Acc. 651, Cat. 19430, L3023, Folder 109-1; Russell Kaldenberg to Stephen Dwyer (April 24, 1992), JTNP Archives, Acc. 651, Cat. 28859, Folder 082; *United States v. Stephen Dwyer* (March 5, 2007), Contest No. CACA 43807, JTNP Archives "Storm Jade Files," Box 2, Folder "Record of Decision, USA v. Stephen Dwyer," 4–6.

12. Stephen M. Dwyer to Congressman Sonny Bono (December 8, 1996), JTNP Archives, Acc. 651, Cat. 28859, Folder 078; Frank Buono to the Files (February 5, 1997), JTNP, Physical Science Files, Folder "NPS File (1) Dwyer"; "Dwyer Mine Claims" (March 26, 1997), JTNP, Physical Science Files, Folder "NPS File (1) Dwyer"; Ernest Quintana to Stephen Dwyer (January 15, 1997), JTNP Archives, Acc. 651, Cat. 28859, L30, Folder 078.

13. Ernest Quintana to Stephen Dwyer (June 16, 1997), JTNP Archives, Acc. 651, Cat. 28859, L30, Folder 078.

14. Stephen Dwyer, "Joshua Tree policies bad," *The Desert Sun* (September 14, 1997).

15. Ernest Quintana to Stephen Dwyer (July 6, 1998), JTNP Archives, Acc. 651, Cat. 28859, Folder 084.1; Interior Board of Land Appeals to Stephen Dwyer (May 9, 1997), JTNP, Physical Science Files, Folder "NPS File (1) Dwyer"; Ernest Quintana to Michael Brady (November 9, 1999), JTNP, Physical Science Files, Folder "NPS File (1) Dwyer"; *United States v. Stephen Dwyer* (March 5, 2007), Contest No. CACA 43807, JTNP Archives "Storm Jade Files," Box 2, Folder "Record of Decision, *USA v. Stephen Dwyer*"; and *United States v. Stephen Dwyer* (July 3, 2008), Contest No. CACA 43807, JTNP Archives "Storm Jade Files," Box 2, Folder "Appeal *USA v. Stephen Dwyer* 3 July 2008."

16. David B. Shaver to the Regional Director (December 5, 1988), JTNM Archives, Acc. 812, Cat. 28768, Box 4, Folder 027; and Rick Anderson to the Regional Director (August 30, 1989), JTNP Archives, Acc. 651, Cat. 19430, L7617, Folder 272.

17. W. C. Ehler to Chief, Division of Abandoned Mine Lands (November 15, 1992), JTNP Archives, Acc. 856, Box "Lands and Mining," loose document.

18. Chris Holbeck, "Abandoned Mine Lands" (n.d.), JTNP, Physical Science Office, "Holbeck Files"; "Park Sees Bright Prospects for Ending Old Mine Shaft Perils," *The Los Angeles Times* (December 22, 1999); NPS, "General Agreement Between Department of the Interior National Park Service and Bat Conservation International, Inc" (April 23, 2001); Tetra Tech EM, Inc., "Park-wide Inspection of Inactive Historical Mills at Joshua Tree National Park Riverside and San Bernardino Counties, California" (May 2003), JTNP Library; JTNP, "Joshua Tree Will Close 22 Mines" (2009), http://www.nps.gov/jotr/parknews/recovery_mineclosures.htm; and Public Law 111-5.

19. Luke Sabala, telephone interview with the author (January 23, 2014).

20. G. Larson, S. E. Stonum, C. D. McIntire, and R. Herrmann, "Baseline Water Quality Survey—Joshua Tree National Park" (April 1998), JTNP Library; Ernest Quintana to Ralph Mihan (January 5, 2000), JTNP Archives, Acc. 651, Cat. 28859, L54, Folder 098; and Margit F. Chiriaco-Rusche to Ernest Quintana (November 9, 1999), JTNP Archives, Acc. 651, Cat. 28859, L54, Folder 098.

21. Black & Veatch and Woodward-Clyde, "Phase I Technical Feasibility Report for Offstream Storage on the Colorado River Aqueduct" (May 1998), JTNP Library; and Luke Sabala, interview with the author at JTNP (January 15, 2013).

22. M. Jeff Ohlfs, "Historical Listing of Open and Closed Roads and Jeep Trails of Joshua Tree National Park" (January 1999), JTNP Archives, Acc. 651, Cat. 28859, L3027, Folder 089; and JTNP, "Road System" (1995), Briefing Statement in JTNP Archives, Acc. 812, Cat. 28768, GMP Files, Box 4, Folder 003.

23. Public Law 102-240; and JTNP, "Environmental Assessment/ Assessment of Effect Keys View Road Reconstruction" (April 2005), JTNP Library.

24. JTNP, Digital Maintenance Attributes Files—Buildings, Trails (2013).

25. Ibid.; Public Law 108-447; Marcella Wells, "Front-end Evaluation Report for Joshua Tree National Park Oasis of Mara Visitor Center Project" (May 15, 2009), JTNP Library; JTNP, "The Oasis of Mara Cultural Center: A New Visitor Center for Joshua Tree National Park, A Fund Raising Prospectus" (n.d.), JTNP Library; Anderson Hallas Architects, "Value Analysis Study Joshua Tree National Park: Visitor Center Site Selection" (January 31, 2013), JTNP Library; Mark Butler to the Files (August 5, 2013), JTNP Superintendent's Files; and Mark Butler, interview with the author at JTNP (December 6, 2013).

26. JTNP, "Record of Decision: Backcountry and Wilderness Management Plan" (January 2000), JTNP Library, 35; and 107th Congress, 2nd Session, S. 2535, "California Wild Heritage Act of 2002," available at http://www.govtrack.us/congress/bills/107/s2535; and Public Law 109-362.

27. 111th Congress, 1st Session, H.R. 146, "The Omnibus Public Land Management Act of 2009," available at http://www.govtrack.us/congress/bills/111/hr/146/text; Public Law 111-11; and Superintendent David Smith, e-mail sent to the author, (July 5, 2016).

28. JTNP, "Joshua Tree National Park Backcountry/Wilderness Management Plan" (October 1996), JTNP Archives, Acc. 812, Cat. 28768, Box 2, Folder 003; JTNP, "Draft General Management Plan Amendment Supplemental Environmental Impact Statement Backcountry and Wilderness Management Plan" (November 1997), WRO, Planning Files, Joshua Tree National Park File, loose report; JTNP, "General Management Plan Amendment Supplemental Environmental Impact Statement Backcountry and Wilderness Management Plan" (October 1999), JOTR Library, 128–29; and William C. Walters to Chief, Administrative Services Division, NPS with attached Record of Decision (January 14, 2000), WRO, Planning Files, Joshua Tree National Park File, Folder "Backcountry Management Plan."

29. JoshuaTreeClimb.com, "Joshua Tree Climbing History 101," http://www.joshuatreeclimb.com/members/History/history101.htm.

30. The superintendent's compendium is a body of specific rules based on the Code of Federal Regulations and park policy that is published annually by each park's superintendent; Bob Moon to Brian Mattos (November 22, 1983), JTNP Archives, Acc. 651, cat. 19430, L3423, Folder 236; Bob Moon (October 1993), "Climbing Management Joshua Tree National Monument: A Brief History," JTNP Archives, Acc. 812, Cat. 28768, Box 3, Folder 018; Names Unreadable to Park Superintendent (April 1, 1989), handwritten message on a visitor comment form at Indian Cove protesting climbers invading their campsite from 7:00 a.m. through the entire day, JTNP Archives, Acc. 651, Cat. 19430, L3423, Folder 235; Brien F. Culhane to Jack Morehead (September 5, 1989), JTNP Archives, Acc. 812, Cat. 28768, Box 3, Folder 008; Randy K. Vogel to Rick Anderson (January 12, 1990), JTNP Archives, Acc. 651, Cat. 19430, D30, Folder 044; and Friends of Joshua Tree, Inc., "About," http://www.friends of josh.org/about/.

31. Moon, "Climbing Management Joshua Tree," 6; JTNM, "Joshua Tree National Monument Climbing Management Plan" (February 1993), JTNP Archives, Acc. 812, Cat. 28768, Box 3, Folder 005; Rich Roberts, "A Rocky Situation: Joshua Tree Superintendent and Climbers Are at Odds over Recent Ban on Bolts," *The Los Angeles Times* (1993, exact date not shown), JOTR Archives, Acc. 812, Cat. 28768, Box 3, Folder 010.

32. Moon, "Climbing Management: A Brief History."

33. Backcountry Ranger to the Superintendent, JTNP (April 6, 1994), JTNP Archives, Acc. 812, Cat. 28768, Box 3, Folder 003.

34. Richard Joseph Camp, "Impact of Rock Climbing on Bird and Plant Diversity in Joshua Tree National Park, California," Master of Science Thesis (Fort Collins: Colorado State University, 1995), iii–v; Richard J. Camp and Richard L. Knight, "Effects of Rock Climbing on Cliff Plant Communities at Joshua Tree National Park, California," *Conservation Biology*, Vol. 12, No. 6 (December 1998): 1302–06; George N. Wallace and Kesia Trench, "A Study of Rock Climbers in Joshua Tree National Park: Implications for the Visitor Experience and Resource Protection (VERP) Management Framework" (June 1996), JTNP Library.

35. JTNP, "Draft General Management Plan Amendment and Environmental Impact Statement, Backcountry and Wilderness Management Plan, Joshua Tree National Park" (March 18, 1997), WRO, Planning Files, Joshua Tree National Park File, Folder "Backcountry and Wilderness Management Plan"; Benjamin Marshall to Ernest Quintana (December 28, 1997), JTNP Archives, Acc. 812, Cat. 28768, Box 1, Folder 001; Sam Davidson (The Access Fund) to Ernest Quintana (February 26, 1998), JTNP Archives, Acc. 812, Cat. 28768, Box 4, Folder 004; and USDA Forest Service, "USDA Forest Service Bans Use of Fixed Anchors for Climbing in Wilderness" (June 1, 1998), News release in JTNP Archives, Acc. 651, Cat. 28768, K38, Folder 009.

36. "Groups compromise on bolting suggestion," *The Desert Trail* (July 2, 1998); and JTNP, "Record of Decision, Final General Management Plan Amendment and Environmental Impact Statement, Backcountry and Wilderness Management Plan, Joshua Tree National Park" (January 2000), JTNP Archives, Acc. 812, Cat. 28768, Box 1, Folder 014.

37. Joan Taylor to Ernest Quintana (July 28, 1998), JTNP Archives, Acc. 812, Cat. 28768, Box 1, Folder 002; Eric Murdoch, "Joshua Tree National Park Rock Climbing Wilderness Study: Final Report" (August 20, 2004), JTNP Library; Bernadette Regan, "Status of Joshua Tree National Park Climbing Management" (April 2009), JTNP Archives, Acc. 812, Cat. 28768, Box 3, Folder 023; and NPS, "Director's Order 41" (May 2013), JTNP Superintendent's files.

38. National Park Foundation/Canon USA, "Phase II Bighorn Sheep: Restoration and Conservation of Critical Habitat" (December 1996), JTNP Archives, Acc. 852, Cat. 30023, Box 1, Folder 007; and Darren D. Divine and Charles L. Douglas, "Bighorn Sheep Monitoring Program for the Eagle Mountain Landfill Project Phase One" (July 1996), JTNP Archives, Acc. 852, Cat. 30023, Box 1, Folder 017, 40–43.

39. NPS, "Draft Backcountry and Wilderness Management Plan" (November 1997), JTNP Library, 38–46; JTNP, "Joshua Tree National Park Natural and Cultural Resources Management Plan 1999" (1999), JTNP Library; "Bighorn Sheep Threatened by Climate Change," *Earth Observatory* (February 11, 2004), available at http://earthobservatory.nasa.gov/Newsroom/MediaAlerts/2004/2004021116504.html; and Andrea Compton, telephone interview with the author (May 20, 2013).

40. JTNP, "Backcountry and Wilderness Management Plan," 31–36 and 137–143; and JTNP, "Horseback Riding," http://www.nps.gov/jotr/planyourvisit/horseback-riding.htm.

41. Patricia Close, "The Way I See It: It's Time to Circle the Wagons," *Western Horsemen*, Vol. 59, No. 6 (June 1994), 22–24; Special Programs Ranger to the Superintendent, JTNP (July 24, 1994), JTNP Archives, Acc. 812, Cat. 28768, Box 3, Folder 002; and Jane de Helsby to Craig Faanes (June n.d., 1994), General form letter forwarded by de Helsby, JTNP Archives, Acc. 812, Cat. 28768, Box 3, Folder 002.

42. User Group Equestrian, "Proposal Back Country Management Plan (GMP for JTNM)" (July 25, 1994), JTNP Archives, Acc. 812, Cat. 28768, Box 3, Folder 002; and "Group Size Limits," JTNP Archives, Acc. 812, Cat. 28768, Box 3, Folder 009.

43. Dale J. Blahna and Kari S. Archibald, "Backcountry Llama Packing: What Do Other Wilderness Visitors Think?," *Yellowstone Science*, Vol. 5, No 3 (Summer 1997): 9–12; Shelly Abbott and Kori Abbott to Ernest Quintana (February 23, 1998), JTNP Archives, Acc. 812, Cat. 28768, Box 1, Folder 005; Walter D. Dabney to Files, Southeast Utah Group

(July n.d., 1997), JTNP Archives, Acc. 812, Cat. 28768, Box 1, Folder 005; Ernest Quintana to the Files (JTNP, September 5, 2002), JTNP Archives, Loose report in File "Manuscript Science Studies."

44. Relevant portions of the 1987 General Accounting Office report and the National Academy of Sciences report "Science and the National Parks" are found in Lary Dilsaver, *America's National Park System: The Critical Documents*, Revised Edition (Lanham, MD: Rowman and Littlefield, 2016), 375–78 and 393–98; Robert B. Keiter, *To Conserve Unimpaired: The Evolution of the National Park Idea* (Washington, DC: Island Press, 2013), 148–54.

45. Richard West Sellars, *Preserving Nature in the National Parks: A History* (New Haven, CT: Yale University Press, 1997); and Keiter, *To Conserve Unimpaired*, 152–54.

46. Ernest Quintana to Director, Pacific West Field Area (June 11, 1996), JTNP Archives, Acc. 651, Cat. 28859, N16, Folder 007.

47. Walter H. Sakai and Norman D. Hogg, "Animal Inventories in Joshua Tree National Park with Special Emphasis on Sensitive Species, Sensitive Areas and Lands Newly Added to the Park Under the Desert Protection Act" (August 2000), JTNP Library, 26–62; Ernest Quintana to All Employees (April 2, 1998), JTNP Archives, Acc. 651, Cat. 28859, N1621, Folder 014; Ernest Quintana to Chief Ranger, JTNP (September 29, 1997), JTNP Archives, Acc. 651, Cat. 28859, N1621, Folder 009; Michael Vamstad, interview with the author at JTNP (December 4, 2013); Harley G. Shaw to Dr. Henry E. McCutchen with attached report by The Juniper Institute (May 18, 1998), JTNP Archives, unprocessed Resource Management Files Box, Folder "Pronghorn Research"; and "Pronghorns, the second-fastest land animal in the world, could be re-introduced in the East Mojave," *The Riverside Press Enterprise* (March 19, 2010).

48. Luke Sabala, telephone interview (January 23, 2014); Harold F. DeLisle, "Declining Amphibian Populations in Joshua Tree National Park" (1999), JTNP Archives, unprocessed Resource Management Files Box, loose report; "Decline of desert tortoise in Joshua Tree linked to long droughts," *The Los Angeles Times* (December 13, 2013); NPS, "Assessment of Air Quality and Air Pollutant Impacts in Class 1 National Parks of California" (April 2001), JTNP Library, xxvi–xxvii; "Joshua Tree: Smog continues to plague national park," *The Riverside Press-Enterprise* (February 13, 2011); JTNP, NPS, "Juniper Fire Complex Burned Area Emergency Rehabilitation Plan" (June 7, 1999), JTNP Library; JTNP, "Joshua Tree National Park Fire Management Plan Environmental Assessment" (April 2005), JTNP Library.

49. JTNP, "Climate Change" (October 2012), JTNP Briefing statement, Superintendent's File; "Joshua Trees Losing Ground Fast," *KQED News* (2011), http://blogs.kqed.org/climatewatch/2011/03/24/joshua-trees-losing-ground-fast/?utm; Kenneth Cole, Lara Schmit, and Catherine Puckett, "Uncertain Future of Joshua Trees Projected with Climate Change" (March 24, 2011), http://www.usgs.gov/newsroom/article.asp?ID=2723; and Cameron W. Barrows and Michelle L. Murphy, "Modeled shifts in the distribution of vegetation resulting from climate change simulations within Joshua Tree National Park" (March 2011), Center for Conservation Biology, University of California, Riverside, 16–20.

50. JTNP, "Climate Change"; and Barrows and Murphy, "Modeled shifts in the distribution of vegetation," 16–20.

51. JTNP, "Joshua Tree National Park Natural and Cultural Resources Management Plan 1999," (1999), 13.

52. DOI and U. S. Department of Agriculture, "Recreation Fee Demonstration Program Interim Report to Congress" (April, 2002), Appendix 2.1; and JTNP, "Natural and Cultural Resources Management Plan," 53–207.

53. Jan Keswick, "Backcountry and Wilderness Archaeological Site Recording Project, Joshua Tree National Park, California" (June 2002), WRO, Thomas Mulhern Files, Box 26, Folder "JOTR Archaeology"; Carolyn Orbann, "Summary Archaeological Test Excavation Report for CA-SBR-746/H: Results of a Limited Phase II Project" (July 21, 2006), JTNP, Chief of Cultural Resources Files; Loy Neff and Ronald Beckwith, "Archaeological Testing at Thirteen Sites at Joshua Tree National Park, California" (2007), JTNP, Chief of Cultural Resources Files; Douglas Duer, "Joshua Tree National Park Traditional Use Study: The Rock Art of Joshua Tree National Park" (2006), NPS, WRO, JTNP Library; and JTNP, "Report on Final Disposition of Remains Wall Street Mill Trail, Joshua Tree National Park" (November 9, 2006), JTNP Archives, unprocessed files in Hollinger Box, Folder "Wall Street Remains."

54. Park IPM Coordinator to Division Chiefs, JTNP with attached Hoddenbach Consulting Inspection Report (October nd, 1999), JTNP Archives, Acc. 856, unprocessed files, Folder "IPM Inspection, 1999"; JTNP, "Finding of No Significant Impact Keys (Desert Queen) Ranch Comprehensive Plan Environmental Assessment" (January 22, 2005), JTNP Library; Michael Scott to Branch Chief of Cultural Resources with attached trip report (February 2000), JTNP Archives, Box "Miscellaneous uncatalogued files"; David Yubeta (February 27–28, 2007), "Joshua Tree

National Park Condition Assessment/Statement of Work Pinyon Wells/Henson Well Mill Site[/]Keys Ranch/Ryan Ranch," JTNP Archives, Uncatalogued Resource Management Files, loose report.

55. JTNP, "List of Classified Structures" (January 2013), JTNP Cultural Resources Digital Files; Ralph B. Giles, Jr., "Determination of Eligibility for Nomination to the National Register of Historic Places for Four Twentieth-Century Historic Sites Within Joshua Tree National Park" (August 1998), WRO, Thomas Mulhern Files, Box 24, Folder "Joshua Tree NM 1998"; Carey & Co., Inc. Architecture, "Determination of Eligibility Joshua Tree National Park Visitor Center, Twentynine Palms, California" (October 13, 2000), JTNP Archives, unprocessed files in Hollinger Box, Folder "Determination of Eligibility JTNP Visitor Center"; and Jan Keswick, interview with the author at JTNP Headquarters (January 12, 2013).

56. Carl O. Sauer, "The Morphology of Landscape," *University of California Publications in Geography*, Vol. 2, No. 2 (October 1925), 19–53; and Walter Roubitschek and Günther Schoenfelder, "Sein Wirken für die Geographie und die Leopoldina" ("Otto Schlüter (1872–1959): His work for the geography and the Leopoldina"), *Journal der Sächsischen Akademie der Wissenschaften* (*Journal of the Saxon Academy of Sciences*), Issue 5 (2010), available at http://denkstroeme. de/heft-5/s_227-232_roubitschek-schoenfelder.

57. NPS, "NPS-28: Cultural Resource Management Guideline" (1998), http://www.nps.gov/history/history/ online_books/nps28/28chap7.htm. The definitive book on the subject remains Arnold R. Alanen and Robert S. Melnick, eds., *Preserving Cultural Landscapes in America* (Baltimore, MD: The Johns Hopkins University Press, in association with the Center for American Places, 2000). See, also, Samuel N. Stokes, A. Elizabeth Watson, and Shelley S. Mastran, *Saving America's Countryside: A Guide to Rural Conservation*, Second Edition (Baltimore, MD: The Johns Hopkins University Press, in association with the National Trust for Historic Preservation and Center for American Places, 1997), especially 139–58.

58. NPS, "Keys Ranch Historic District Cultural Landscape Inventory" (2004), JTNP Library; NPS, "Hexie Mountains Historic Mining District Cultural Landscape Inventory" (2008), ibid.; NPS, "Northern Pinon Historic Mining District Cultural Landscape Inventory" (2011), ibid.; and NPS, "Lost Horse Historic Mining District Cultural Landscape Inventory" (2012), ibid.

59. NPS-PWR, "Joshua Tree National Park Museum Management Plan" (2005), JTNP Library.

60. NPS, "Annual Recreation Visitation by Park Type or Region (1979–Last Calendar Year)" (2015), https://irma. nps.gov/Stats/SSRSReports/National%20Reports/Annual%20Recreation%20Visitation%20Report%20by%20 Park%20Type%20or%20Region%20(1979%20-%20Last%20Calendar%20Year); and Jeff Ohlfs, telephone interview, March 18, 2016.

61. Jean E. McKendry, Kimberly L. Treadway, Gary E. Machlis, Robert B. Schlegel, and Adam J. Novak, "A Socioeconomic Atlas for Joshua Tree National Park and its Region" (2001), NPS Social Science Program, JTNP Library, 16–20; and Yen Le, Margaret A. Littlejohn, and Stephen J. Hollenhorst, "Joshua Tree National Park Visitor Study Spring 2004" (December 2004), University of Idaho Park Studies Units Visitor Services Project Report 152, JTNP Library.

62. Value added is the combination of the effect of spending by visitors on the two counties in which the park lies plus spending by employees of the park. The reason the spending total is higher is because much of the money goes out of the two counties to businesses based elsewhere. Daniel J. Stynes, "Impacts of Visitor Spending on the Local Economy: Joshua Tree National Park, 2004" (June 2006), JTNP Library; Philip S. Cook, ""Impacts of Visitor Spending on the Local Economy: Joshua Tree National Park, 2010" (April 2012), JTNP Library.

63. "Man litters national park with 3,000 golf balls," *The Desert Sun* (September 17, 2009); and "Historic Joshua Tree sites are blighted by urban ills," *The Los Angeles Times* (April 13, 2013).

64. Keiter, *To Conserve Unimpaired*, 154–56.

65. JTNP, "Education Program" (April 2012), JTNP, Superintendent's Digital Files; and JTNP, "Artist-in-Residence" (October 2012), ibid.

66. Cindy Ott, Laura Watt, and Raymond Rast, "Scholar's Reports by Cindy Ott, Laura Watt, and Raymond Rast of a visit to Joshua Tree National Park June 10–12, 2008" (2008), NPS–Organization of American Historians Report, JTNP Library.

67. Curt Sauer, "Potential Impacts to Park Resources & Multi-Jurisdictional Efforts to Facilitate Preservation of these Resources through Open Space Planning near Joshua Tree National Park" (February 2007), JTNP Superintendent's Files; Cord Media Company, "Twenty-Nine [sic] Palms Band of Mission Indians to Break Ground on New Casino" (2013), http://www.tortoiserockcasino.com/pdf/trcpress_012813.pdf; and Author observation (December 4, 2013).

68. California Intelligent Communities, "California Intelligent Communities Announces Development Plans for 9,000-acre Joshua Hills Community" (February 26, 2002), JTNP Archives, Uncatalogued materials; "Developer to unveil revised plan for 9,000-acre project," The Desert Sun (February 26, 2002); "$26-Million Deal Will Save 8,800 Acres of Fragile Desert," The Los Angeles Times (September 30, 2004); GLC Enterprises, LLC, "Paradise Valley Specific Plan" (April 3, 2012), JTNP Management Assistant Files; and "New town of 8,500 homes proposed east of Coachella," The Desert Sun (October 28, 2015), http://www.desertsun.com/story/money/real-estate/2015/10/28/paradise-valley-east-coachella-valley-joshua-tree/74755618/.

69. U.S. Navy and NPS, "Environmental Assessment for the Modification of VR-1257" (March 2000), JTNP Library.

70. Ibid.; Rick Anderson to the Regional Director (July 1, 1986), JTNP Archives, Acc. 651, Cat. 19430, Y14, Folder 045; Jim Haitt to Bob Binnewies (October 29, 1986), JTNP Archives, unprocessed files of Hollinger Box, Loose report; JTNP Briefing Statement for Secretary Bruce Babbitt (February 8, 1995), JTNP Archives, uncatalogued files for Eagle Mountain, Folder "Eagle Mountain Landfill"; and Robert B. Pirie, Jr., to Dr. Dickson J. Hingson (February 10, 1997), JTNP Archives, Acc. 822, Cat. 30022, Box "EA of VR-1257," Folder 1c.

71. U. S. Bureau of Mines, "Eagle Mountains Iron District" (1943), War Minerals Report 97, JTNP Archives, Acc. 797, Cat. 27731, Series 005, Box 7, Folder 019; "Kaiser Company Buys Iron Chief Mine in 29 Palms "Front Yard,'" The Desert Trail (February 25, 1944); O. A. Tomlinson to the Director (January 7, 1947), SB, RG 79, Central Decimal Files, Box 306, Folder 609-01; and Private Law 82-790, 66 Stat. A129.

72. "Plan told to build mine workers a town of their own," The Daily Enterprise (January 25, 1967); "Mine Workers Hang On and Hope," The Los Angeles Times (January 25, 1967); "Kaiser Mine to Furlough 1,200," Los Angeles Times (June 27, 1975); "Arab Is Buying Major Interest in Kaiser Steel for $57 Million," The Los Angeles Times (March 24, 1981); and "As Town Closes, Class Gets Tough Economics Lesson," The Los Angeles Times (May 29, 1983).

73. Riverside County, "Public Use Permit No. 585, Revised Permit No. 3 Expanded Statement of Project" (May 29, 1996), JTNP Archives, uncatalogued files for Eagle Mountain, Box 1, Folder "Prison"; and Mine Reclamation Corporation, "Eagle Mountain Project Overview" (May 1989), JTNP Archives, Acc. 651, Cat. 19430, L76, Folder 268.

74. Mine Reclamation Corporation, "Eagle Mountain Project Overview" (1989), JTNP Archives, Acc. 651, Cat. 19430, L76, Folder 268; and Rick Anderson to David Mares (September 12, 1989), ibid.

75. RECON Environmental Consultants, "Draft environmental impact statement, environmental impact report for the Eagle Mountain Landfill Project" (July 1991), JTNP Library.

76. Ibid.

77. BLM, "Eagle Mountain Land Exchange and Landfill" (March 12, 2004), briefing statement in JTNP Archives, Land Files, Folder "Eagle Mountain 2008"; and California Natural Resources Agency, "CEQA: California Environmental Quality Act" (2012), available at http://ceres.ca.gov/ceqa/docs/CEQA_Handbook_2012_wo.pdf.

78. Mine Reclamation Corporation, "Eagle Mountain Project Overview"; Anderson to Mares (September 12, 1989); and "EPA Says All Landfills Leak, Even Those Using Best Available Liners," Rachel's Hazardous Waste News #3, JTNP Archives, Acc. 812, Cat. 28768, Box 2, Folder 029.

79. "Trash landfill has wilderness guard worried," The Riverside Press Enterprise (December 7, 1989).

80. "Eagle Mountain plan to be debated," The Riverside Press Enterprise (November 11, 1991); "Kaiser Steel ties landfill to comeback," The Riverside Press Enterprise (n.d., 1991), JTNP Library, Clippings File; Paul F. Smith, "The Eagle Mountain Sting Operation—Part 4," The Sun Runner (November 2000): 22; Donna Charpied, interview with the author at Desert Center, California (January 24, 2013); and Ernest Quintana, telephone interview with the author (September 25, 2013).

81. "Park service fears proposed dump would worsen pollution in the desert," The Fresno Bee (July 18, 1991).

82. David E. Moore to Russell Kaldenberg (April 13, 1992), JTNP Archives, Acc. 651, Cat. 19430, L7617, Folder 286.
83. Ibid.
84. Eagle Mountain Energy Company, "Proposed Eagle Mountain Hydroelectric Project" (February 7, 1994), WRO Planning Files, Joshua Tree National Park File, Folder "Briefing Statements 1994."
85. Dr. Jerry Freilich, interview with the author at Olympic National Park headquarters (June 24, 2013); "Sierra Club, Greenpeace oppose regional landfill," *The Riverside Press-Enterprise* (June 17, 1992); David E. Moore to Patricia (Corky) Larson (July 6, 1992), JTNP Archives, Acc. 651, Cat. 19430, L7617, Folder 286; Steve Clute to Henri Bisson (December 4, 1992), JTNP Archives, uncatalogued files for Eagle Mountain, Box 1, Folder "Legal Stuff"; and "Legality of Eagle Mountain land deal questioned," *Riverside Press-Enterprise* (September 29, 1992).
86. NPS, "Draft Memorandum of Understanding Among National Park Service, Bureau of Land Management, U. S. Fish and Wildlife Service, the County of Riverside and Mine Reclamation Corporation" (June 30, 1993), JTNP Archives, Acc. 797, Cat, 27731, Series 1, Box 1; and JTNP, "Joshua Tree National Park—Mine Reclamation Meeting Proposed Agenda" (July 23, 1995), JTNP Archives, Uncatalogued Eagle Mountain Files, Box 1, Folder "Meetings/Trip Reports 1994–1999."
87. "Bedrock poses testing problem," *The Riverside Press-Enterprise* (October 3, 1992); and "Landfill wins county OK," *The Riverside Press-Enterprise* (October 7, 1992).
88. BLM, "Record of Decision Eagle Mountain Landfill Project Riverside County, California" (October 1993), JTNP Library; "Landfill Report 'Flawed,'" *The Desert Sun* (July 27, 1994); and Ernest Quintana to the Regional Director with attached background summary (May 9, 1994), JTNP Archives, Land Files, Folder "Eagle Mountain."
89. Superior Court of California, County of San Diego, "Statement of Decision—*NPCA et al. v. County of Riverside et al.* and *Laurence and Donna Charpied v. County of Riverside, et al.* Case No. 662907" (July 26, 1994), JTNP Archives, Acc. 651, Cat. 19430, L3023, Folder 193; and *The Desert Sun*, "Landfill Report 'Flawed.'"
90. "Kaiser joins MRC in appeal over landfill ruling," *The Desert Sun* (September 23, 1994); "County rescinds landfill permits," *The Desert Sun* (November 9, 1994); "County won't appeal ruling against landfill plan," *The Riverside Press-Enterprise* (November 2, 1994); U. S. House of Representatives Report 103-498, "California Desert Protection Act Legislative History" (October 9, 1994), JTNP Archives, Acc. 797, Cat. 27731, Series 1, Box 1; and "Candidates see merits of landfill," *The Desert Sun* (October 26, 1994).
91. Clem Palevich to Stanley Albright (May 11, 1994), WRO Planning Files, Joshua Tree National Park File, Folder "Eagle Mountain Pump Storage"; Patricia L. Neubacher to Michael Spencer (June 29, 1994), WRO Planning Files, Joshua Tree National Park File, Folder "General Environmental Compliance"; and Chief, Water Rights Branch to Superintendent, JTNP (December 2, 1994), JTNP Archives, Uncatalogued Eagle Mountain Files, Box 1, loose document.
92. Ed Hastey to Lois D. Cashell (January 6, 1995), JTNP Archives, Uncatalogued Eagle Mountain Files, Box 1, loose document; Mine Reclamation Corporation and Kaiser Eagle Mountain, Inc., "Eagle Mountain Landfill and Recycling Center Project Description" (April 14, 1995), JTNP Archives, Uncatalogued Eagle Mountain Files, Box 1, Folder "MRC/Eagle Mountain"; GeoSyntec Consultants, "Evaluation of Ground-Water Impacts Proposed Eagle Mountain Pumped-Storage Hydroelectric Project Chuckwalla Aquifer Riverside County, California" (March 1995), JTNP Archives, Uncatalogued Eagle Mountain Files, Box 1 loose report; Riverside County Planning Department, "Notice of Preparation for an Environmental Impact Report (EIR) for the Eagle Mountain Landfill and Recycling Center Riverside County, California" (May 6, 1995), JTNP Archives, Uncatalogued Eagle Mountain Files, Box 1, Folder "Correspondence."
93. Julia Dougan to Ernest Quintana (May 12, 1995), JTNP Archives, Uncatalogued Eagle Mountain Files, Box 1, Folder "NPS-BLM Correspondence"; Kathy Billings for Ernest Quintana to Julia Dougan (June 20, 1995), ibid.; and Ernest Quintana to Julia Dougan with attached "Issues Identification" (June 29, 1995), ibid.
94. CH2M Hill began in the 1930s when an Oregon State University engineering professor and three of his students formed Cornell, Howland, Hayes, and Merryfield which became known as CH2M. In 1971, the firm merged with Clair A. Hill and Associates to become CH2M Hill. See http://www.ch2m.com/corporate/about_us/history.asp; Office of the Solicitor to Ernie Quintana (May 10, 1995), Handwritten memo in JTNP Archives, Uncatalogued Eagle Mountain Files, Box 1, Folder "Superintendent Quintana Eagle Mountain"; Orlando H. Gonzales to Paul Clark (July 19, 1996), JTNP Archives, Uncatalogued Eagle Mountain Files, Box 1, Folder "Prison"; Ralph Raya to Gary Ollivier

(August 12, 1996), JTNP Archives, Uncatalogued Eagle Mountain Files, Box 1, Folder "Prison"; and "More landfill delays costly," *The Desert Sun* (September 8, 1995).

95. JTNP, "Eagle Mountain Landfill Scoping Meeting" (July 21, 1995), JTNP Archives, Uncatalogued Eagle Mountain Files, Box 1, Folder "Meetings/Trip Reports 1994–1999"; and Stanley Albright to Jerry Lewis (October 19, 1995), JTNP Archives, Uncatalogued Eagle Mountain Files, Box 1, Folder "Eagle Mountain Public Comments."

96. Ernest Quintana, Draft transcript of testimony about the landfill (n.d.), JTNP Archives, Acc. 797, Cat. 27731, Series 1, Box1, loose document.

97. Tom Peters to Joan Oxedine and Dave Mares (December 1, 1995), ibid., Folder "Eagle Mountain Landfill"; Ernest Quintana interview (September 25, 2013), JTNP Archives, Uncatalogued Eagle Mountain Files, Box 1, Folder "Meetings/Trip Reports 1994–1999."

98. Tom Peters to Ernest Quintana, et al. (February 2, 1996), WRO, Mulhern Files, Box 25, Folder "JOTR Eagle Mountain"; Ralph G. Mihan to Superintendent, JTNP (February 7, 1996), JTNP Archives, Uncatalogued Eagle Mountain Files, Box 1, Folder "NPS Internal Correspondence"; Frank Buono for Ernest Quintana to Henri Bisson (March 14, 1996), JTNP Archives, Acc. 812, Cat. 28768, GMP Files, Box 2, Folder 029; and National Parks and Conservation Association, "Briefing Sheet—Eagle Mountain impacts to Joshua Tree" (n.d.), JTNP Archives, Land Files, Folder "Eagle Crest Project."

99. Anne Wexler to Roger Kennedy (March 20, 1996), JTNP Archives, Uncatalogued Eagle Mountain Files, Box 1, Folder "Correspondence"; and David Barna to Donna Charpied (May 8, 1996), ibid.

100. Ernest Quintana interview (September 25, 2013); Michael Soukup to Ernest Quintana (August 2, 1996), JTNP Archives, Uncatalogued Eagle Mountain Files, Box 1, Folder "MOU with Mine Reclamation Corporation 1992–1999"; Stanley T. Albright to Julia Dougan with attached comments on the environmental impact report/statement (October 1, 1996), JTNP Archives, Acc. 797, Cat. 27731, Series 1, Box 1, loose document; NPS, "Agreement between the National Park Service and Mine Reclamation Corporation, Eagle Mountain Reclamation, Inc., Kaiser Eagle Mountain, Inc." (December 9, 1996), JTNP Archives, Uncatalogued Eagle Mountain Files, Box 1, Folder "MOU with Mine Reclamation Corporation 1992–1999"; "Agreement on landfill plan fails to silence critic," *The Riverside Press-Enterprise* (December 21, 1996); and Arthur W. Lowe to Fred Springer (September 6, 1996), JTNP Archives, Uncatalogued Eagle Mountain Files, Box 1, loose document.

101. Larry and Donna Charpied to Denis Galvin (January 6, 1997), JTNP Archives, Uncatalogued Eagle Mountain Files, Box 1, Folder "MOU with Mine Reclamation Corporation 1992–1999"; Brian Huse to Denis P. Galvin (January 8, 1997), JTNP Archives, Acc. 812, Cat. 28768, GMP Files, Box 4, Folder 0292; William J. Whalen, "An Analysis of the Agreement and Declaration of Covenants, Conditions and Restrictions between the Mine Reclamation Corporation/Kaiser Eagle Mountain and the National Park Service" (April 1997), JTNP Archives, Acc. 651, Cat. 28859, A44, Folder 020; "County gives Eagle Mountain landfill final OK," *The Riverside Press-Enterprise* (September 10, 1997); and BLM, "BLM Approves Eagle Mountain Land Exchange" (September 25, 1997), JTNP Archives, Uncatalogued Eagle Mountain Files, Box 1, Folder "Eagle Mountain Pumped Storage Project."

102. JTNP, "Joshua Tree Superintendent Ernie Quintana to Receive Stephen Tyng Mather Award" (October 15, 1997), JTNP Library, Clippings files.

103. "Judge blocks landfill," *The Desert Sun* (February 19, 1998); and "County will back Eagle Mountain effort," *The Desert Sun* (April 15, 1998).

104. California Court of Appeal, Fourth District, Division 1, "*National Parks and Conservation Association et al. v. County of Riverside and Kaiser Steel Resources, Inc., et al.* and *Lawrence Charpied et al. v. County of Riverside and Mine Reclamation Corporation et al.*" (May 7, 1999), No. D031056; and John J. Reynolds to Kay Hazen (May 18, 1999), JTNP Archives, Uncatalogued Eagle Mountain Files, Box 1, Folder "Internal Correspondence."

105. BLM, "BLM and Kaiser Complete Land Exchange in Riverside County" (October 13, 1999), JTNP Archives, Uncatalogued Eagle Mountain Files, Box 1, loose document; Mine Reclamation Corporation et al., "Amended and Restated Agreement Among the National Park Service and Mine Reclamation Corporation, Eagle Mountain Reclamation, Inc. [and] Kaiser Eagle Mountain, Inc." (January 2000), JTNP Archives, Land Files, Folder "Eagle Mountain Pre-2000"; and JTNP, "Eagle Mountain Landfill Project Status" (June 2011), Briefing statement in JTNP Superintendent's Digital Files.

106. As quoted in Paul F. Smith, "The Eagle Mountain Sting Operation—Part 9," *The Sun Runner* (April 2001): 20.

107. Mike Pool, "Eagle Mountain Land Exchange and Landfill" (March 12, 2004), BLM Briefing Statement, JTNP Archives, Land Files, Folder "Eagle Mountain 2008"; Margaret Adam to Amy Fesnock et al. (January 30, 2004), JTNP Archives, Uncatalogued Eagle Mountain Files, Box 1, Folder "Information provided by the Charpieds"; "Plan filed to reopen prison," *The Riverside Press-Enterprise* (September 15, 2006); and Arthur W. Lowe to Magalie R. Salas (March 10, 2006), JTNP Archives, Land Files, Folder "Eagle Mountain—Proposed Jails."

108. Kaiser Ventures, Inc., "Eagle Mountain Landfill Project" (n.d.), http://www.kaiserventures.com/p_waste. htm; United States District Court for the Central District of California–Eastern Division, *"Donna Charpied v. U.S. Department of the Interior and National Parks et al.* and *Conservation Association v. Bureau of Land Management et al."* (September 20, 2005), JTNP Archives, Land Files, Folder "Eagle Mountain 2005–2006"; JTNP, "Eagle Mountain Landfill" (October 21, 2005), JTNP Archives, Land files, Folder "Eagle Mountain—2007"; and "Group rallies to stop landfill," *The Desert Sun* (October 26, 2005).

109. "Report: Eagle Mountain ex-prison plans 'ill advised,'" *The Riverside Press-Enterprise* (August 25, 2007); and Donald H. Clarke to Kimberly Bose (April 23, 2010), JTNP Archives, Land Files, Folder "Eagle Crest Project."

110. U. S. Court of Appeals for the Ninth Circuit, *"National Parks and Conservation Association v. Bureau of Land Management; Department of the Interior and Kaiser Eagle Mountain, Inc.; Mine Reclamation Corporation—Case 05-56814"* (January n.d., 2007), JTNP Archives, Land Files, Folder "Eagle Mountain–2007"; U. S. Court of Appeals for the Ninth Circuit, *"National Parks and Conservation Association v. Bureau of Land Management; Department of the Interior and Kaiser Eagle Mountain, Inc.; Mine Reclamation Corporation—Case 05-56814"* (November 10, 2009), available at http://cdn.ca9.uscourts.gov/datastore/opinions/2009/11/10/05-56814.pdf; Robert V. Abbey to Wilma A. Lewis (January 19, 2010), JTNP Archives, Land Files, Folder "Eagle Mountain 2008"; and JTNP, "Eagle Mountain Landfill Project Status" (April 2011), Briefing statement in JTNP Management Assistant's Digital Files.

111. "Obama Administration Recognizes Joshua Tree National Park's Importance to the American People" (n.d. 2011), JTNP Management Assistant's Digital Files; Sanitation Districts of Los Angeles County, "Sanitation Districts of Los Angeles County Cease Negotiations for Eagle Mountain Landfill Project and Look to Expand Evaluation of Long Term Waste Management Strategies" (May 22, 2013), JTNP Superintendent's Digital Files.

112. Deanne Stillman, "Guardians of Joshua Tree" (January 7, 2009), *Plenty Magazine*, http://www.plentymag.com/features/2009/01/guardians_of_joshua_tree_print.php; Public Law 95-87; JTNP, "Eagle Mountain Landfill Project Status" (June, 2011), JTNP Superintendent's Digital Files.

113. Federal Energy Regulatory Commission, "Final Environmental Impact Statement for the Hydropower License" (January 2012), JTNP Superintendent's Files; *KCET*, "CA Signs Off On Controversial Project Next to Joshua Tree Nat' Park" (July 16, 2013), http://www.kcet.org/news/rewire/the-grid/hydroelectric-energy-joshua-tree-national-park-eagle-mountain.html.

114. Comments of Joshua Tree officials to the author during his research visits to the park in January and April 2013; and Mark Butler, interview with the author at JTNP (December 4, 2013).

115. Mark Butler, "Briefing Statement" (December 3, 2013), JTNP Superintendent's Files; NPS, "Joshua Tree National Park Boundary Study" (Summer 2015), ibid; and NPCA, "Joshua Tree National Park Eagle Mountain Boundary Study and Eagle Crest Talking Points" (Spring 2016), ibid.

116. Governor Arnold Schwarzenegger, "Executive Order S-14-08" (November 17, 2008), available at http://gov38.ca.gov/index.php?/executive-order/11072/; Public Law 111-5; Todd Woody, "In California's Mojave Desert, Solar-Thermal Projects Take Off," *Yale Environment 360* (October 27, 2010); California Energy Commission, "Ivanpah Solar Electric Generating System" (2014), http://www.energy.ca.gov/tour/ivanpah/; and "Paving a fast lane for desert solar," *The San Diego Union-Tribune* (January 1, 2013). An unforgettable visual account of Ivanpah can be found in Jamey Stillins, *The Evolution of Ivanpoh Solar* (Göttingen, Germany: Steidel, 2014).

117. DRECP, "Background" (2013), http://www.drecp.org/whatisdrecp/. The main website for DRECP has numerous documents that explain the organization, the plan and its alternatives.

118. Kevin Hendricks and Andrea Compton, "Renewable Energy Projects near Joshua Tree NP" (January 6, 2011), JTNP Management Assistant's files; Solar Energy Development Information Center, "Solar Energy Development

Programmatic EIS" (2012), http://solareis.anl.gov/sez/riverside_east/index.cfm; BLM, "Desert Sunlight Solar Farm" (2014), https://www.google.com/#q=desert+sunlight+solar+farm; BLM, "Desert Harvest Solar Farm" (2014), http://www.blm.gov/ca/st/en/fo/palmsprings/Solar_Projects/Desert_Harvest_Solar_Project.html; BrightSource Energy, Inc., "Palen" (2014), http://www.brightsourceenergy.com/palen#.UvK_rViYaM8; Renewable Energy World. Com, "California Energy Commission Splits on Blythe and Palen Solar Projects" (December 17, 2013), http://www. renewableenergyworld.com/rea/news/article/2013/12/california-energy-commission-splits -on-two-solar-projects; California Energy Commission, "Palen Solar Power Project" (December 15, 2015), http://www.energy.ca.gov/siting-cases/palen/; and Basin and Range Watch, "New Palen Solar PV Project Reactivated With Little Public Notice" (June 21, 2016), http://www.basinandrangewatch.org/Palen.html.

119. Hendricks and Compton, "Renewable Energy Projects near Joshua Tree NP."

Epilogue

1. Mark Butler, "75th Anniversary Presentation" (August 8, 2011), JTNP Superintendent's Files.

2. Mark Butler, "Mt Minerva Hoyt Dedication / Minerva Hoyt California Desert Conservation Award Ceremony" (March 27, 2013), ibid.

3. See http://www.nps.gov: "History and Culture: Joshua Tree National Park."

INDEX

Note: All maps, plates, and figures appear in *italics*.

ABOUT THE AUTHOR

Lary M. Dilsaver, a native Californian, is Professor Emeritus of Historical Geography at the University of South Alabama and a thirty-year volunteer researcher for the National Park Service. He has written more than forty articles and book chapters on national parks and historic landscapes, and he has authored or edited six books, including *Challenge of the Big Trees: The History of Sequoia and Kings Canyon National Parks, A Revised Edition*, with William C. Tweed (George F. Thompson Publishing, 2016), *America's National Park System: The Critical Documents* (Rowman and Littlefield, 1994; second edition, 2016), and *Cumberland Island National Seashore: A History of Conservation Conflict* (University of Virginia Press, in association with the Center for American Places, 2004).

ABOUT THE BOOK

Preserving the Desert: The History of Joshua Tree National Park was brought to publication in an edition of 1,300 softcover copies. The text was set in Adobe Jenson Pro, the paper is Huron Matte for the text and Huron Gloss for the gallery, respectively 70# and 80# weight, and the book was professionally printed and bound by Thomson-Shore in Michigan.

Publisher and Project Director: George F. Thompson
Editorial and Research Assistant: Mikki Soroczak
Manuscript Editors: Sherri Byrand and Purna Makaram
Book Design and Production: Ann Lowe and David Skolkin

Special Acknowledgments: The publisher extends grateful thanks to the Joshua Tree National Park Association, Joshua Tree National Park Association Fruge Fund, and, especially, Meg Foley, Executive Director, for their institutional and personal support of this project in every way.

Published 2016. First softcover edition.
Printed in the U.S.A. on acid-free paper.

George F. Thompson Publishing, L.L.C.
217 Oak Ridge Circle
Staunton, VA 24401-3511, U.S.A.
www.gftbooks.com

24 23 22 21 20 19 18 17 16   1 2 3 4 5

The Library of Congress Preassigned Control Number is 2016950021.

ISBN: 978–1–938086–46–5